Language
Network

Grammar • Writing • Communication

McDougal Littell
A HOUGHTON MIFFLIN COMPANY

Language Network

- Grammar, Usage, and Mechanics
- Essential Writing Skills
- Writing Workshops
- Communicating in the Information Age

McDougal Littell
A HOUGHTON MIFFLIN COMPANY

ISBN 0-395-96740-6

Acknowledgments begin on page 701.

6 7 8 9 – DCI – 05 04 03

Teacher Panels

The teacher panels helped guide the conceptual development of *Language Network*. They participated actively in shaping and reviewing prototype materials for the pupil edition, determining ancillary and technology components, and guiding the development of the scope and sequence for the program.

Cynda Andrews, Western Hills High School, Fort Worth School District, Fort Worth, Tex.

Gay Berardi, Evanston Township High School, Evanston School District, Evanston, Ill.

Nadine Carter-McDaniel, Townview Academic Center, Dallas School District, Dallas, Tex.

Sandra Dean, English Department Chairperson, Kerr High School, Alief School District, Houston, Tex.

Delia Diaz, English Department Chairperson, Rio Grande City High School, Rio Grande City School District, Rio Grande City, Tex.

Cynthia Galindo, Bel Air High School, Yselta School District, El Paso, Tex.

Ellen Geisler, English/Language Arts Department Chairperson, Mentor Senior High School, Mentor School District, Mentor, Ohio

Dr. Paulette Goll, English Department Chairperson, Lincoln West High School, Cleveland City School District, Cleveland, Ohio

Myron Greenfield, Davis High School, Houston School District, Houston, Tex.

Lorraine Hammack, Executive Teacher of the English Department, Beachwood High School, Beachwood City School District, Beachwood, Ohio

James Horan, Hinsdale Central High School, Hinsdale Township High School, Hinsdale, Ill.

Marguerite Joyce, English Department Chairperson, Woodridge High School, Woodridge Local School District, Peninsula, Ohio

Christi Lackey, North Side High School, Fort Worth School District, Fort Worth, Tex.

Jane McGough, Wichita Falls High School, Wichita Falls School District, Wichita Falls, Tex.

Dee Phillips, Hudson High School, Hudson Local School District, Hudson, Ohio

Dr. Bob Pierce, English Department Chairperson, Conroe High School, Conroe School District, Conroe, Tex.

Cyndi Rankin, John Jay High School, Northside School District, San Antonio, Tex.

Mary Ross, English Department Chairperson, Tascosa High School, Amarillo School District, Amarillo, Tex.

Robert Roth, Evanston Township High School, Evanston, Ill.

Carol Steiner, English Department Chairperson, Buchtel High School, Akron City School District, Akron, Ohio

Nancy Strauch, English Department Chairperson, Nordonia High School, Nordonia Hills City School District, MacEdonia, Ohio

Sheila Treat, Permian High School, Ector County School District, Odessa, Tex.

Ruth Vukovich, Hubbard High School, Hubbard Exempted Village School District, Hubbard, Ohio

Content Specialists

Dr. Mary Newton Bruder, former Professor of Linguistics at University of Pittsburgh (creator of the Grammar Hotline Web site), Pittsburgh, Penn.

Rebekah Caplan, High School and Middle Grades English/Language Arts Specialist, New Standards Project, Washington, D.C.

Dr. Sharon Sicinski Skeans, Assistant Professor, University of Houston-Clear Lake, Houston, Tex.

Richard Vinson, Retired Teacher, Provine High School, Jackson, Miss.

Technology Consultants

Dr. David Considine, Media Studies Coordinator, Appalachian State University, Boone, NC (author of *Visual Messages: Integrating Imagery into Instruction*)
Heidi Whitus, Teacher, Communication Arts High School, San Antonio, Tex.
Anne Clark, Riverside-Brookfield High School, Riverside, Ill.
Pat Jurgens, Riverside-Brookfield High School, Riverside, Ill.
Ralph Amelio, Former teacher, Willowbrook High School, Villa Park, Ill.
Cindy Lucia, Horace Greeley High School, New York, N.Y.
Aaron Barnhardt, Television writer for the *Kansas City Star* and columnist for *Electronic Media,* Kansas City, Mo.

ESL Consultants

Dr. Andrea B. Bermúdez, Professor of Studies in Language and Culture; Director, Research Center for Language and Culture; Chair, Foundations and Professional Studies, University of Houston-Clear Lake, Clear Lake, Tex.
Inara Bundza, ESL Director, Kelvyn Park High School, Chicago, Ill.
Danette Erickson Meyer, Consultant,Illinois Resource Center, Des Plaines, Ill.
John Hilliard, Consultant, Illinois Resource Center, Des Plaines, Ill.
John Kibler, Consultant, Illinois Resource Center, Des Plaines, Ill.
Barbara Kuhns, Camino Real Middle School, Las Cruces, N.M.

Teacher Reviewers

Nadine Carter-McDaniel, Townview Magnet Center, Dallas ISD, Dallas, TX
Frances Capuana, Director of ESL, Curtis High School, Staten Island, NY
Lucila A. Garza, ESL Consultant, Austin, Tex.
Dan Haggerty, Drama Department Chair, Lewis and Clark High School, Vancouver, Wash.
Betty Lou Ludwick, Wakefield Senior High School, Arlington, Va.
Linda Maxwell, MacArthur High School, Houston, Tex.
Linda Powell, Banning High School, Wilmington, Calif. (Los Angeles Unified School District)
Cindy Rogers, MacArthur High School, Houston, Tex.
Lynnette Russell, Lewis and Clark High School, Vancouver, Wash.
Joan Smathers, Language Arts Supervisor, Brevard School-Secondary Program, Viera, Fla.
Sharon Straub, English Department Chair, Joel Ferris High School, Spokane, Wash.
Mary Sylvester, Minneapolis North High School, Minneapolis, Minn.
Shirley Williams, English Department Chair, Longview High School, Longview, Tex.

Student Reviewers

Saba Abraham, Chelsea High School
Julie Allred, Southwest High School
Nabiha Azam, East Kentwood High School
Dana Baccino, Downington High School
Christianne Balsamo, Nottingham High School

Luke Bohline, Lakeville High School
Nathan Buechel, Providence Senior High School
Melissa Cummings, Highline High School
Megan Dawson, Southview Senior High School
Michelle DeBruce, Jurupa High School
Brian Deeds, Arvada West High School
Ranika Fizer, Jones High School
Ashleigh Goldberg, Parkdale High School
Jacqueline Grullon, Christopher Columbus High School
Dimmy Herard, Hialeah High School
Sean Horan, Round Rock High School
Bob Howard, Jr., Robert E. Lee High School
Rebecca Iden, Willowbrook High School
Agha's Igbinovia, Florin High School
Megan Jones, Dobson High School
Ed Kampelman, Parkway West High School
David Knapp, Delmar High School
Eva Lima, Westmoor High School
Ashley Miers, Ouachita High School
Raul Morffi, Shawnee Mission West High School
Sakenia Mosley, Sandalwood High School
Sergio Perez, Sunset High School
Jackie Peters, Westerville South High School
Kevin Robischaud, Waltham High School
Orlando Sanchez, West Mesa High School
Selene Sanchez, San Diego High School
Sharon Schaefer, East Aurora High School
Mica Semrick, Hoover High School
Julio Sequeira, Belmont High School
Camille Singleton, Cerritos High School
Solomon Stevenson, Ozen High School
Tim Villegas, Dos Pueblos High School
Shane Wagner, Waukesha West High School
Swenikqua Walker, San Bernardino High School
Douglas Weakly, Ray High School
Lauren Zoric, Norwin High School

Student Writers

Misha Dworsky, Walt Whitman High School
Renatta Gillespie, Cherry Creek High School
Lauren Hart, Towson High School
Elizabeth Kim, New Trier High School
Andrew Love, Alternative Community School
Candice Rhodes Mast, Turner Ashby High School
Adam Moses, Oak Park River Forest High School
Jason Nemo, Evanston Township High School
Erica Papernik, Niles North High School
Sophie Tyner, Evanston Township High School
Daman Valasquez, Monadnock High School
Sandra Williams, Nichols High School

Contents Overview

Grammar, Usage, and Mechanics

Essential Writing Skills

Writing Workshops

Communicating in the Information Age

Student Resources

Grammar, Usage, and Mechanics

3 Using Phrases

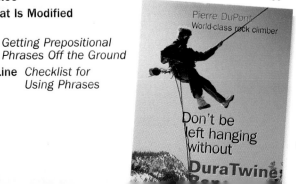

Pierre DuPont
World-class rock climber

Don't be
left hanging
without

DuraTwine

⑪ Punctuation 246

Student Help Desk

Punctuation at a Glance

Titles & Punctuation *Treating Titles with Care*

Punctuation with Quotation Marks *Inside or Outside?*

The Bottom Line *Checklist for Punctuation Marks*

Quick-Fix Editing Machine

Essential Writing Skills

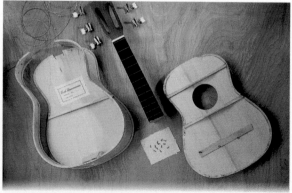

iNFORmaL   FORMaL

Writing Workshops

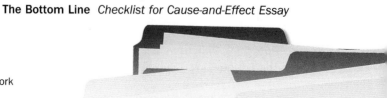

Communicating in the Information Age

Academic Skills

32 Preparing for Tests

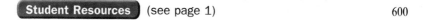

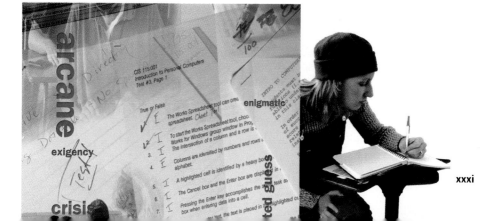

Special Features

Real World Grammar

Grammar in Literature

Power Words: Vocabulary for Precise Writing

Quick-Fix Editing Machine

Student Resources

Grammar, Usage, and Mechanics

A Closer Look

Open the back of an old-fashioned clock, and you'll uncover tiny gears, levers, and pins. You can watch them work together, performing their functions perfectly and predictably. Similarly, if you look closely at the parts of a sentence, you will see how they, too, work together to bring about meaning—even more amazing than the appearance of the right time on the face of the clock.

The Parts of Speech

A sorbish of bilm and churvy filbs krimmed beside a snarfy dorge.

Theme: Travel Stories

Now Guess This

What color were the filbs?

Can you answer this question? If you can, you have decoded a nonsense sentence solely on the basis of the forms and arrangement of its words. Clues like the ending -*ed* and the placement of a word after *a* can help you decide what kinds of words you are looking at. The categories of words—nouns, verbs, adjectives, adverbs—are called **parts of speech.**

Write Away: Decoder Game

Write the nonsense sentence shown above. One by one, cross out the nonsense words and write in real words that could replace them. Then try to label each word in the sentence with its part of speech. Save your work in your 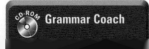 **Working Portfolio.**

Grammar Coach CD-ROM

Write the letter of the term that correctly identifies each underlined word.

Many <u>explorers</u> have been drawn to <u>Antarctica</u>, even though the
(1)   (2)
continent has the harshest environment in the world. <u>It</u> is dry, windy, and
(3)
extremely cold. Ninety-eight percent of its surface <u>is</u> a sheet of ice. In the
(4)
summer of 1911–1912, two groups of explorers actually <u>reached</u> the South
(5)
Pole. The English group, led by Robert Falcon Scott, picked their way

<u>carefully</u> across the <u>dangerous</u> ice with its deep crevasses. When they
(6)   (7)
finally reached the pole, however, they found that another team had been

there <u>before</u> them. The <u>Norwegian</u> group, led by Roald Amundsen, had
(8)   (9)
reached the pole one month before Scott, <u>and</u> they had left their flag to
(10)
mark the spot.

1. A. proper noun
   B. common noun
   C. action verb
   D. linking verb

2. A. proper noun
   B. common noun
   C. action verb
   D. linking verb

3. A. common noun
   B. preposition
   C. pronoun
   D. conjunction

4. A. pronoun
   B. conjunction
   C. action verb
   D. linking verb

5. A. common noun
   B. proper noun
   C. action verb
   D. linking verb

6. A. linking verb
   B. action verb
   C. adjective
   D. adverb

7. A. common noun
   B. action verb
   C. adjective
   D. adverb

8. A. preposition
   B. pronoun
   C. conjunction
   D. adverb

9. A. common noun
   B. linking verb
   C. proper adjective
   D. adverb

10. A. preposition
    B. conjunction
    C. pronoun
    D. adjective

Nouns

① Here's the Idea

▶ **A noun is a word that names a person, place, thing, or idea.**

Things: cameras, vehicle, cheetah

Persons: tourists, photographers, Chris

Ideas: surprise, suddenness, happiness

Places: Masai Mara Game Preserve, Kenya, lake, city

A **common noun** is a general name for a person, place, thing, or idea. Common nouns are usually not capitalized.

A **proper noun** is the name of a particular person, place, thing, or idea. A proper noun is always capitalized.

Common	river, mountain, pilot
Proper	Nile, Mt. Kenya, Charles Lindbergh

A **concrete noun** names an object that can be seen, heard, smelled, touched, or tasted.

An **abstract noun** names an idea, quality, or characteristic.

Concrete	shoe, car, perfume, thorn
Abstract	simplicity, beauty, truth, intention

A noun may be either **singular** or **plural** in form, depending on whether it names a single person, place, thing, or idea or more than one.

Singular	map, berry, deer, mouse
Plural	maps, berries, deer, mice

For more about spelling plural forms, see p. 651.

HOT TIP

Every noun is either common or proper, concrete or abstract, and singular or plural. For example, *desert* is common, concrete, and singular. *Great Lakes* is proper, concrete, and plural.

A **collective noun** refers to a group of people or things. Examples include *herd, family, crew, team,* and *staff.* Even when a collective noun is singular in form, it can be used to refer to a group either as a single unit or as a number of individuals.

The herd (unit) **runs away as we get close.**

The herd (individuals) **find hiding places in the brush.**

A **compound noun** is formed from two or more words. Some compound nouns are written as single words, some as hyphenated words, and some as separate words.

Compound Nouns	
One word	toothbrush, backpack, watermelon
Hyphenated word	self-knowledge, sister-in-law
Separate words	duffel bag, South Carolina, Taj Mahal

A **possessive noun** shows ownership or relationship. Possessive nouns are spelled with apostrophes.

Ownership   the tourist's passport
Relationship   the tourist's companion

❷ Why It Matters in Writing

The use of proper nouns in the description of a setting makes the setting seem more specific and real. How would the following passage differ if the writer had used common nouns, such as *plains* and *lake,* instead of the proper nouns she did use?

LITERARY MODEL

The Serengetti Plains spread from Lake Nyaraza, in Tanganyika, northward beyond the lower boundaries of Kenya Colony. They are the great sanctuary of the Masai . . . and they harbour more wild game than any similar territory in all of East Africa.

—Beryl Markham, *West with the Night*

❸ Practice and Apply

CONCEPT CHECK: Nouns

Write the nouns in each sentence, identifying each as common or proper and as singular or plural. Use a chart like the one below.

Example: Swahili is one of Kenya's major languages.

Noun	Common	Proper	Singular	Plural
Swahili		✓	✓	
Kenya's		✓	✓	
languages	✓			✓

Life on Safari

1. Life on safari offers a new perspective on humans and animals.
2. Many camps in Kenya's game parks are surrounded by fences.
3. Here the humans live inside the fences while the herds of elephants, giraffes, and gazelles wander freely.
4. Animals have the right of way on all roads.
5. At the Sarova Mara Camp in the Masai Mara Game Preserve, visitors are taught how to lock their tents.
6. The problem here is a troop of clever monkeys who unzip and raid the camp's unlocked tents.
7. At one lodge near the Samburu Game Preserve, a young boy patrols the dining area and chases away monkeys.
8. Endangered species, such as rhinos, are often moved to sanctuaries where they are protected.
9. Rhinos at the Lewa Downs Wildlife Conservancy roam 55,000 fenced acres.
10. Armed guards patrol on foot, in jeeps, and in airplanes to count and protect these rhinos.

➜ **For a SELF-CHECK and more practice, see the EXERCISE BANK, p. 600.**

CHALLENGE

Use the sentences above to do the following.
1. Find two possessive nouns.
2. Find two collective nouns.
3. Find two abstract nouns.
4. Find two compound nouns.

Personal Pronouns

LESSON 2

❶ Here's the Idea

▶ **A pronoun is a word used in place of a noun or another pronoun.** The word that a pronoun stands for is called its **antecedent.**

Malcolm **waved as he boarded the bus to the airport.**
🔺 ANTECEDENT   🔺 PRONOUN

An antecedent can consist of two or more words, and it may be in a sentence other than the one in which the pronoun occurs.

STANDS FOR

Malcolm and Hal **shared a** sandwich. **They munched on** it.

STANDS FOR

The forms of the personal pronouns are shown below.

Personal Pronouns	Singular	Plural
First person	I, me (my, mine)	we, us (our, ours)
Second person	you (your, yours)	you (your, yours)
Third person	he, him, she, her, it (his, her, hers, its)	they, them (their, theirs)

Like possessive nouns, **possessive pronouns** show ownership or relationship. In the chart above, possessive pronouns are in parentheses.

OWNERSHIP

Hal almost left his backpack **on the bus.**

Calvin and Hobbes by Bill Watterson

© 1986 Universal Press Syndicate

The Parts of Speech **9**

② Why It Matters in Writing

Pronouns help writers to achieve coherence. Notice how the personal pronouns in the following passage link the two sentences and link the second half of each sentence to the first half.

> **LITERARY MODEL**
>
> The next day the young sportsman hovered about the woods, and Sylvia kept **him** company, having lost **her** first fear of the friendly lad, who proved to be most kind and sympathetic. **He** told **her** many things about the birds and what **they** knew and where **they** lived and what **they** did with themselves.
>
> —Sarah Orne Jewett, "A White Heron"

③ Practice and Apply

CONCEPT CHECK: Personal Pronouns

Write each pronoun and identify its antecedent.

Journey to Scotland
1. Malcolm and his family flew to Scotland to see where their ancestors had come from.
2. They took a ferry to Lewis Island, where Malcolm's mother's grandmother had once lived with her family.
3. There they found her house, complete with its original furnishings.
4. "You must be my relatives, too," said Mrs. Morrison, opening the door to their knock.
5. "We are related to your great-aunt," said Malcolm.
6. "She was my great-grandmother," he added.
7. "I remember your grandmother," Mrs. Morrison said to Malcolm's mother. "She was younger than mine."
8. "In fact, you remind me of her," she added.
9. Mrs. Morrison showed the family the house and served them lunch.
10. They enjoyed the baked potato, but when she offered them haggis, only Malcolm ate it.

➡ For a SELF-CHECK and more practice, see the EXERCISE BANK, p. 600.

Other Kinds of Pronouns

❶ Here's the Idea

Some kinds of pronouns are used to perform special functions in sentences.

Reflexive and Intensive Pronouns

A **reflexive pronoun** "reflects," or represents, the subject of the sentence or clause in which it appears.

REFLECTS

Soo-ni **treats herself to a stroll through Chinese food markets.**

An **intensive pronoun** is used to emphasize a noun or pronoun that appears in the same sentence.

EMPHASIZES

The merchants **themselves enjoy sampling the goods.**

Reflexive and intensive pronouns are formed by adding -*self* or -*selves* to forms of the personal pronouns.

Reflexive and Intensive Pronouns			
	First Person	**Second Person**	**Third Person**
Singular	myself	yourself	himself, herself, itself
Plural	ourselves	yourselves	themselves

WATCH OUT

Reflexive pronouns should never be used alone. They must always have antecedents.

me

She buys souvenirs for herself and ~~myself~~.

Demonstrative Pronouns

Demonstrative pronouns point out specific persons, places, things, or ideas. They allow you to indicate whether the things you are referring to are relatively nearby (in time or space) or farther away. The demonstrative pronouns are *this, these, that,* and *those.*

The merchant tells Soo-ni, "My oranges are better than those in the other stall."

Indefinite Pronouns

Indefinite pronouns refer to persons, places, things, or ideas that are not specifically identified. Unlike other pronouns, they don't usually have antecedents.

Everyone in the market radiates energy.

Indefinite Pronouns	
Singular	another, anybody, anyone, anything, each, either, everybody, everyone, everything, much, neither, nobody, no one, nothing, one, somebody, someone, something
Plural	both, few, many, several
Singular or plural	all, any, more, most, none, some

Interrogative and Relative Pronouns

An **interrogative pronoun** introduces a question.

A **relative pronoun** introduces a noun clause or an adjective clause; it connects an adjective clause to the word or words it modifies.

Interrogative and Relative Pronouns	
Interrogative	who, whom, whose, which, what
Relative	who, whom, whose, which, that

Interrogative and relative pronouns look similar, but they function differently.

Who would believe the crowds and excitement?
    INTERROGATIVE PRONOUN

The merchants, who are eager for sales, shout to customers.
    RELATIVE PRONOUN

❷ Why It Matters in Writing

Notice how the writer of this sentence used relative pronouns to introduce clauses that add information in an economical way.

LITERARY MODEL

Maybe this man, who didn't believe in love, **CLAUSES** realized by the time his hair was white that in his heart was something which could be called love.

—Zhang Jie, "Love Must Not Be Forgotten"

❸ Practice and Apply

Write each pronoun and indicate what kind it is.

Tracking the Tibetan Ox

1. Travelers to Tibet are fortunate if they see wild yaks, because few of the large beasts remain today.
2. The furry animals, which may have 30-inch horns, weigh about a ton apiece.
3. Each of the animals can supply people with milk, fuel, wool, and transportation—or with meat.
4. Since the 1950s, most of the wild yaks on the Tibetan plateau have been killed for meat.
5. Hunters, who have used a new road to reach their prey, have reduced the herds to almost none.
6. The Chang Tang Reserve, which stretches across the plateau, provides protection for yaks today.
7. The Chang Tang Reserve itself covers 115,500 square miles, an area greater than that of Arizona.
8. Most of the yaks have deep black fur.
9. Occasionally, one appears whose coat is golden rather than black.
10. Travelers who have never seen a golden yak might ask themselves, What are we looking at?

➡ **For a SELF-CHECK and more practice, see the EXERCISE BANK, p. 601.**

Combine these groups of sentences, using relative pronouns.

Wildlife of India

1. Travelers in India rarely see wild animals nowadays. India used to be famous for its wild animals.
2. Forests once covered over 40 percent of the country. They were the homes of all the wildlife. The forests have been cut down.
3. Now wild animals are protected in only 3 percent of the country. Wild animals are increasingly endangered.
4. Some visitors want to see the wildlife. These people have to go to game preserves.
5. Animals are abundant in some game preserves. Game preserves are home to numerous species, including elephants.

PARTS OF SPEECH

LESSON 4 Verbs

❶ Here's the Idea

▶ **A verb expresses an action, a condition, or a state of being.**
The two main types of verbs are action verbs and linking verbs.
Both kinds can be accompanied by auxiliary verbs.

Action Verbs

An **action verb** expresses an action. The action may be physical
or mental.

> **My family and I drove 500 miles to Montana.** (PHYSICAL)

> **We wanted good weather for our vacation.** (MENTAL)

When an action verb can take a direct object (that is,
a word naming a person or thing that receives
the action), it is called a **transitive verb.**
When an action verb cannot take an
object, it is called an **intransitive verb.**

> **Mom locked Dad's wheelchair into place.**
> ⬆TRANSITIVE VERB   ⬆OBJECT

> **Uncle Lou snored loudly in the back of the van.**
> ⬆INTRANSITIVE VERB (NO OBJECT)

Linking Verbs

A **linking verb** links a word in the predicate to the subject.

> _LINKED_
> **We were happy to see the sign for Big Sky Country.**

> _LINKED_
> **The campsite appeared tiny beside the grand mountain.**

There are two groups of linking verbs: forms of _be_ and verbs that
express conditions.

Forms of *Be*

is, am, are, was, were, been, being

Verbs That Express Conditions

look, smell, feel, sound, taste,
grow, appear, become, seem, remain

Some verbs can be either action or linking verbs.

Dad tasted the fresh water. It tasted wonderful.
　　　ACTION　　　　　　　　　　LINKING

Uncle Lou smelled skunks. They smelled awful.
　　　　ACTION　　　　　　　　　　LINKING

If you can substitute a form of *be* for a verb, it is a linking verb.

Auxiliary Verbs and Verb Phrases

Auxiliary verbs, also called helping verbs, are combined with other verbs to form **verb phrases.** A verb phrase may be used to express a particular tense of a verb (that is, the time being referred to) or to indicate that an action is directed at the subject.

Small scraps of birch bark are crackling in the fire.
　　　　　　　　　AUXILIARY　　　　MAIN

Our muscles will be sore from chopping wood.
　　AUXILIARY　　MAIN

At last all the wood has been chopped.
　　　　　　AUXILIARY　　　　　MAIN

Auxiliary Verbs

be		have	do	can	should
am	were	has	does	could	may
is	being	had	did	will	might
are	been			would	must
was				shall	

Some of these verbs can also function as main verbs. For example, notice how *had* stands alone in the first sentence below and is a helping verb in the second sentence.

At the end of the evening, we had no more energy. (MAIN)

We had exhausted ourselves. (AUXILIARY)

❷ Why It Matters in Writing

Action verbs can be used to create strong images and metaphors. Notice how verbs in the following passage convey a picture of rain soaking into dry earth.

> The rain **began** with gusty showers.... And at first the dry earth **sucked** the moisture down and **blackened.** For two days the earth **drank** the rain, until the earth was full. Then puddles **formed** ....
>
> —John Steinbeck, "The Flood" from *The Grapes of Wrath*

❸ Practice and Apply

CONCEPT CHECK: Verbs

Write each verb or verb phrase and identify it as linking or action. Circle the auxiliary verbs.

Disabled Overcome Obstacles to Travel

1. Like everyone else, travelers with disabilities want fun vacations.
2. With a wide range of accessibility features available, travel seems easy.
3. Wheelchair travelers can choose rental cars with hand controls or transport in accessible taxis or vans.
4. Accessible tours are available for vacationers worldwide.
5. Cities such as Rome, with its hills and narrow cobblestone streets, appear manageable these days.
6. A tour to Nepal has featured a ride on an elephant's back through Royal Chitwan National Park.
7. Alaskan cruises expose people with mobility challenges to views of marine wildlife and scenic glaciers.
8. Various tour services provide communicators for deaf travelers and companions for the blind.
9. Skiers with disabilities can use special skis in a wide array of designs.
10. With careful arrangements, a traveler with special needs can experience adventure.

➡ **For a SELF-CHECK and more practice, see the EXERCISE BANK, p. 601.**

Adjectives

LESSON 5

1 Here's the Idea

▶ **An adjective limits the meaning of a noun or pronoun.** Words, like adjectives, that describe or give more specific information about the meanings of other words are said to **modify** those words.

We watched a terrific game on the outdoor field.

MODIFIES   MODIFIES

▲ ADJECTIVE   ▲ ADJECTIVE

An adjective answers the question *what kind, which one, how many,* or *how much.*

Adjectives

What Kind	Which One	How Many	How Much
fast ponies	**this** seat	**four** players	**no** time
green field	**that** goal	**most** fans	**more** noise
steamy afternoon	**these** friends	**both** teams	**enough** speed

Articles

The most common adjectives are the articles *a, an,* and *the.* *A* and *an* are **indefinite articles**. They are used to refer to unspecified members of groups of people, places, things, or ideas. Use *a* before words beginning with consonant sounds and *an* before words beginning with vowel sounds.

A fan yelled as we looked for an exit.

The is the **definite article,** used to refer to a specific person, place, thing, or idea.

The coach yelled as we left through the exit.

Proper Adjectives

Proper adjectives are formed from proper nouns. They are capitalized and often end in *n, an, ian, ese,* or *ish.*

Persian players originated the sport of polo.

British players popularized the game in India.

Proper Nouns	Shakespeare, Jamaica, Taiwan
Proper Adjectives	Shakespearean, Jamaican, Taiwanese

❷ Why It Matters in Writing

Writers use adjectives to express feelings and to add important descriptive details.

> **LITERARY MODEL**
>
> Have you ever seen
> anything
> in your life
> more **wonderful**
>
> than the way the sun,
> **every** evening,
> **relaxed** and **easy**,
> floats toward the horizon . . . ?
>
> —Mary Oliver, "The Sun"

❸ Practice and Apply

A. CONCEPT CHECK: Adjectives

Write each adjective in these sentences, along with the word it modifies.

Riding Swimming Horses
1. An enjoyable way to travel in a new country is on a horse.
2. We had a unique horseback ride in Jamaica.
3. In Jamaica, formerly a British colony, polo is popular among English immigrants.
4. To exercise polo ponies in the hot country, trainers let them swim in deep water.
5. In swimsuits, we rode polo ponies bareback in ocean waters.
6. My very competitive pony swam up between two other ponies.
7. I gripped only a green strap and held on for dear life.
8. The two adjacent horses smashed against my bare legs.
9. Unlike its reluctant rider, my pony wanted to win this water race.
10. The experience was both frightening and exhilarating.

➡ For a SELF-CHECK and more practice, see the EXERCISE BANK, p. 602.

B. REVISING: Adding Adjectives

Rewrite the following paragraph, adding adjectives and combining sentences to make it more interesting.

The Rough Sport of Polo

Today, polo is mostly played in England and the countries that were once British colonies. It is a sport for the rich. Only they can afford to maintain strings of ponies. At the same time, the sport is not for the faint-hearted. A match requires courage and daring. Ponies and players crash into each other. Players fall off their horses. That's why they wear helmets. Sometimes they accidentally hit each other with their mallets.

C. WRITING: Using Strong Adjectives

Choose one of the following postcard scenes and describe it fully, using sentences with strong adjectives. Try to be as exact as possible.

Adverbs

❶ Here's the Idea

▶ **An adverb modifies a verb, an adjective, or another adverb.**

MODIFIES

Mike scrambled quickly from the icy pond.
VERB

MODIFIES

He was extremely cold.
ADJECTIVE

MODIFIES

He had fallen into the pond quite accidentally.
ADVERB

An adverb answers the question *where, when, how,* or *to what extent.*

Adverbs	
Where	there, here, downstairs, northward
When	yesterday, soon, daily, never, again
How	slowly, happily, well, brightly
To what extent	almost, nearly, completely, somewhat

Many adverbs are formed by adding *-ly* to adjectives. Sometimes a slight change in spelling is necessary.

strong + *-ly* = **strongly**   honest + *-ly* = **honestly**

true + *-ly* = **truly**   happy + *-ly* = **happily**

Other Commonly Used Adverbs			
afterward	forth	near	still
already	hard	next	straight
also	instead	not	then
back	late	now	today
even	long	often	tomorrow
far	low	slow	too
fast	more	sometimes	yet

An **intensifier** is an adverb that defines the degree of an adjective or another adverb. Intensifiers always precede the adjectives or adverbs they modify.

EMPHASIZES

Fortunately, Mike was an extremely fast thinker.

↑ INTENSIFIER

Intensifiers

almost	more	only	really	too
extremely	most	quite	so	truly
just	nearly	rather	somewhat	very

❷ Why It Matters in Writing

Writers typically use adverbs to describe the ways things happen—slowly, for instance, or gradually or suddenly. Notice how the adverbs in the following passage not only describe the actions but convey information about the characters as well.

LITERARY MODEL

Gussie, in particular, fascinated me. He was spoiled, clever, casual; good-looking, with his mother's small clean features; gay and calculating. I saw that when I left and his mother gave me a sixpence. **Naturally** I refused it **politely,** but she thrust it into my trousers pocket, and Gussie dragged at her skirt, **noisily** demanding something for himself.

"If you give him a tanner, you ought to give me a tanner," he yelled.

"I'll tan you," she said **laughingly.**

—Frank O'Connor, "The Study of History"

❸ Practice and Apply

A. CONCEPT CHECK: Adverbs

Write each adverb in these sentences.

Fast, Fun, and Wet!
1. Quite often, when we travel anywhere, we go to water parks.
2. We have slid crazily down water slides at the Wisconsin Dells.
3. At the top of a slide, you sit carefully on a mat and nervously grip its edges.
4. Immediately, you start whizzing down, careening nearly uncontrollably from side to side.
5. When you finally reach the bottom, screaming happily, you splash suddenly into a pool of water.
6. You stand and want to repeat your ride again and again.
7. On top of a very tall water slide in Cincinnati, we waited anxiously while lightning crackled dangerously in the distance.
8. Luckily, we finally took our turn before the storm hit.
9. Once we even enjoyed an incredibly huge water park in Toronto, Canada.
10. Almost every big city has water parks, which are never empty during the summer.

➡ **For a SELF-CHECK and more practice, see the EXERCISE BANK, p. 602.**

For each adverb in sentences 1–5, identify the verb, verb phrase, adjective, or adverb it modifies.

B. WRITING: Using Adverbs to Describe Action

Write five sentences that describe the car race shown below, from the viewpoint of a driver. Use at least one adverb in each.

Prepositions

❶ Here's the Idea

▶ **A preposition shows the relationship between a noun or pronoun and another word in a sentence.**

Luis traveled **to** Guatemala **with** other teenagers.

Commonly Used Prepositions

about	before	down	of	throughout
above	behind	during	off	to
across	below	except	on	toward
after	beneath	for	onto	under
against	beside	from	out	underneath
along	between	in	outside	until
among	beyond	inside	over	up
around	but	into	past	upon
as	by	like	since	with
at	despite	near	through	within

Prepositions that consist of more than one word are called **compound prepositions.**

Because of his heavy pack, Luis had trouble hiking.

Commonly Used Compound Prepositions

according to	by means of	in place of	on account of
aside from	in addition to	in spite of	out of
because of	in front of	instead of	prior to

Prepositional Phrases

A **prepositional phrase** consists of a preposition, its object, and any modifiers of the object. The **object of a preposition** is the noun or pronoun that follows the preposition. Prepositional phrases are used as modifiers to express such characteristics as location, direction, duration, and time.

Beside a roaring river, Luis tripped and fell.
　↖PREPOSITION 　↖OBJECT

His ankle started to swell during the afternoon.

The shoe on his left foot no longer fit.

A sentence may contain more than one prepositional phrase. Each preposition has its own object.

The group traveled by boat to a health clinic.

A nurse at the clinic put a bandage around Luis's ankle.

Use a comma to set off a series of prepositional phrases that comes at the beginning of a sentence.

From time to time during the day, Luis complained.

 When a word that is commonly classified as a preposition is used without an object, it functions as an adverb. *Down* is used as an adverb in the first sentence below and as a preposition in the second.

Luis had trouble with his ankle after he fell down.

Luckily, no one else fell down the riverbank.

❷ Why It Matters in Writing

Because they help locate things in time and space, prepositional phrases are useful for describing a scene or giving precise directions. Notice how prepositional phrases help to make clear what is happening in the following passage.

LITERARY MODEL

We watched **on our screens** the footage captured **by his assistant's camera**, **in which** he was **up to his knees in muck**, a microphone **in his hand**, **in the midst of a bedlam of lost children, wounded survivors, corpses, and devastation**. The story came **to us in his calm voice**.

—Isabel Allende, "And of Clay Are We Created"

❸ Practice and Apply

A. CONCEPT CHECK: Prepositions

Write the prepositional phrases in these sentences. Circle the prepositions.

Teens Making a Difference

1. Some organizations plan trips for students, combining education, service, and adventure.
2. These trips offer young people special opportunities in other countries.
3. These teens visit small villages instead of tourist attractions.
4. They get to know the people in addition to the countryside.
5. Sometimes they work with local teenagers on projects.
6. One group built a campground in the wilderness.
7. In another location young people painted a school.
8. Before the trip, teens receive training and raise funds.
9. You can find information about educational and service-based travel on the Internet.
10. Search under the keywords *travel, educational,* and *youth.*

➜ **For a SELF-CHECK and more practice, see the EXERCISE BANK, p. 602.**

B. WRITING: Using Prepositions in Directions

Imagine that you and a friend are going to an informational meeting about educational and service trips for teens. You will meet at your family's apartment. Use the map below to prepare written directions for your friend to use in getting from school to your home. Underline the prepositions you use.

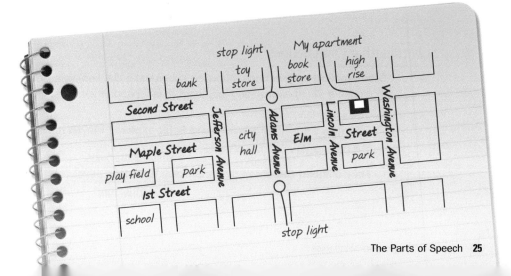

LESSON 8 Conjunctions

① Here's the Idea

▶ **A conjunction connects words or groups of words.** There are three kinds of conjunctions: coordinating, correlative, and subordinating. Conjunctive adverbs are adverbs that function somewhat like conjunctions.

Coordinating Conjunctions

Coordinating conjunctions connect words or groups of words of equal importance in a sentence.

> **Claudia and Peter visited the Yucatán Peninsula, but they stayed only a few days.**

Coordinating Conjunctions						
and	but	for	nor	or	so	yet

Correlative Conjunctions

Correlative conjunctions are word pairs that serve to join words or groups of words.

> **Neither Claudia nor Peter had been to Mexico before.**
> **They found it not only beautiful but also rich in history.**

Correlative Conjunctions		
both . . . and	whether . . . or	not only . . .
neither . . . nor	either . . . or	but also

Subordinating Conjunctions

Subordinating conjunctions introduce subordinate clauses—clauses that cannot stand alone—and join them to independent clauses.

SUBORDINATE CLAUSE
While they were there, Claudia and Peter explored Mayan ruins.
↑ CONJUNCTION

SUBORDINATE CLAUSE
They climbed the steep pyramids until their feet hurt.
↑ CONJUNCTION

Subordinating Conjunctions				
after	as though	if	so that	when
although	because	in order that	than	where
as	before	provided	unless	whereas
as if	even though	since	until	while

Conjunctive Adverbs

Conjunctive adverbs are used to express relationships between independent clauses.

CONJUNCTIVE ADVERB

The Mayans did not have telescopes; however, **they built and used astronomical observatories.**

Conjunctive Adverbs		
accordingly	furthermore	otherwise
also	hence	similarly
besides	however	still
consequently	instead	therefore
finally	nevertheless	thus

❷ Why It Matters in Writing

Writers use conjunctions to combine sentences in first drafts into smooth, more interesting sentences in later drafts. Notice how the second sentence below contains information that could have come from several sentences in an earlier draft.

LITERARY MODEL

On my first return visit to Texas, I stopped to hear a group of *mariachis* playing their instruments with proud gusto. I was surprised and probably embarrassed when my eyes filled with tears not only at the music, but at the sight of wonderful Mexican faces.

—Pat Mora, "The Border: A Glare of Truth"

❸ Practice and Apply

A. CONCEPT CHECK: Conjunctions

Write the conjunctions and conjunctive adverbs in the following sentences.

Opening a Mayan Pyramid

1. Many people visit Mexico or Central America to see the remains of the Mayan civilization.

2. The Mayan culture fascinates visitors because the Mayans achieved so much.

3. Mayans not only created a written language but also built many large pyramids.

4. In 1952, Mexican archaeologist Alberto Ruz climbed a 65-foot pyramid and made an important discovery.

5. While he was examining the inscriptions on top of the pyramid, he noticed a removable stone slab.

6. Beneath the slab, Ruz and his helpers found a stairway leading into the pyramid; however, it was filled with rubble.

7. They started to clear the stairway; still, it took them four field sessions to reach the bottom.

8. Not only did they find a chamber that contained human skeletons, but they also discovered another room.

9. When they entered that room, they found many objects made of jade.

10. Both the jade objects and the written inscriptions identified the chamber as the tomb of an important ruler.

➡️ **For a SELF-CHECK and more practice, see the EXERCISE BANK, p. 603.**

CHALLENGE Identify each of the words you listed as a coordinating conjunction, a correlative conjunction, a subordinating conjunction, or a conjunctive adverb.

B. WRITING: Using Conjunctions

Write conjunctions that can complete this passage.

Baja California

The Mexican peninsula called Baja California offers many kinds of recreation, including scuba diving **(1)** whale watching. In the Sea of Cortés, you might be lucky enough to see **(2)** blue whales **(3)** gray whales and sperm whales. Whale watchers also visit islands **(4)** they can observe many species of birds and land animals. They have their choice of going in motorboats **(5)** paddling in sea kayaks.

LESSON 9 Interjections

❶ Here's the Idea

▶ **An interjection is a word or phrase that expresses a feeling.** A strong interjection is followed by an exclamation point. A mild interjection is set off with commas.

> **Yikes! Have you ever seen such a tall building?**
>
> **Well, no, I guess I haven't.**

❷ Why It Matters in Writing

Interjections can add realism to your writing, particularly to dialogue.

> **STUDENT MODEL**
>
> The sleepy group got off the bus after riding all night. Dragging their suitcases, they rounded the corner into the sunlight.
>
> **"Wow!"** cried Rani, staring up at the skyscrapers.
>
> **"Whew!"** sighed Holly, sitting down on her suitcase. "This bag is too heavy."
>
> **"Uh-oh,** don't look now, but we have another block to go."

❸ Practice and Apply

CONCEPT CHECK: Interjections

Write the interjections in these sentences.

Chicago Snapshots
1. Here we are in Chicago, and wow, is it cold!
2. Hey, is it always this cold here in the winter?
3. Oh, no! You left your gloves in the hotel room?
4. Well, we can always get you another pair.
5. Brrr! Better hurry; it's about to snow.

Real World Grammar

Lab Report

Using precise language is especially important when you are writing about science, because others may need to duplicate your experiments in order to verify your results.

In the report below, one student, Eric, described an experiment he conducted. His lab partner, Courtney, wrote the questions after she tried to follow the notes the next day. Because Eric didn't describe his work precisely, Courtney had trouble repeating the experiment.

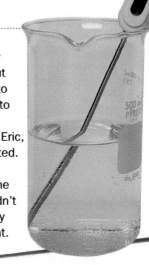

LAB REPORT

Purpose: To find the boiling point of a mixture of salt and water

Equipment:
lab stand with clamps
burner
one 1-liter container
one 500-milliliter container
thermometer that measures 0° to 200° Celsius
stopper
glass tube with a sharp bend

What kinds of containers?

This should be a 2-hole stopper, right?

Materials:
5 grams salt
200 milliliters water

Is tap water OK, or should I use distilled water?

Procedure:
Combine the salt and water in the large container. Stir the mixture with a glass rod until the salt dissolves. Put the container on the stand with its base about 5 centimeters above the burner. Insert the thermometer and the glass tube. Insert the stopper assembly. Heat the solution. Record the time and temperature every two minutes, as well as when the solution just begins to boil and when it begins to boil rapidly.

How should I attach the container?

Where does the thermometer go? Where is the stopper inserted?

Should I heat the solution slowly or quickly?

Use specific nouns and verbs	Use specific words to make your meaning clear. Instead of the general word *container,* use the name of the kind of container, such as *flask* or *beaker.*
Include necessary modifiers	Use modifiers to make the meanings of other words more specific. Instead of simply writing *water,* tell what kind of water by using a modifier such as *distilled* or *tap.*
Use prepositions for clarity	Choose prepositions, such as *into* and *through,* that tell precisely how the pieces are to be connected.

REVISED LAB REPORT

Purpose: To find the boiling point of a mixture of salt and water

Equipment:

lab stand with clamps

burner

one 1-liter **flask**

one 500-milliliter **beaker**

thermometer that measures
   0° to 200° Celsius

two-hole stopper

glass tube with a sharp bend

Materials:

5 grams salt   200 milliliters **distilled** water

Procedure: Combine the salt and water in the flask. Stir the mixture with a glass rod until the salt dissolves completely. **Clamp** the flask onto the stand, with its base about 5 centimeters above the burner. Insert the thermometer and the glass tube **through the holes in the stopper.** Insert the stopper assembly **into the neck of the flask.** Heat the solution **quickly.** Record the time and temperature every two minutes, as well as when the solution just begins to boil and when it begins to boil rapidly.

PRACTICE AND APPLY: Proofreading

Read the incomplete directions below. What else would you need to know before you could make biscuits? List your questions.

Ingredients:	Directions: Sift together flour, salt, and
1¼ cup sifted flour	powder. Add chunks of chilled butter.
½ salt	Once the butter is combined well, stir
powder	in the milk. Cut with a cutter dipped in
4–6 chilled butter	flour. Place on an ungreased baking
¾ milk	sheet. Bake 12 to 15 minutes.

Mixed Review

A. Nouns, Pronouns, Adjectives, Adverbs Read this passage from *The Great Railway Bazaar* by Paul Theroux. Then answer the questions below it.

(1) The hooting of the train woke me early the next morning for the sight of camels grazing among brown bushes and great herds of sheep bunched together on sandy hillsides. (2) The villages were few, but their design was extraordinary; they were walled and low and resembled the kind of sand castles you see parents making for their children at the seashore, with a bucket and spade. (3) They had tiny windows, crumbling ramparts, and inexact crenellations; impressive at a distance, up close they were visibly coming apart, the fortifications merely a feeble challenge to intruders.

1. What part of speech is *train* in sentence 1?
2. What part of speech is *me* in sentence 1?
3. What type of noun is *herds* in sentence 1?
4. What part of speech is *sandy* in sentence 1?
5. What type of pronoun is *their* in sentence 2?
6. What part of speech is *extraordinary* in sentence 2?
7. What type of noun is *children* in sentence 2?
8. What type of pronoun is *They* is sentence 3?
9. What part of speech is *visibly* in sentence 3?
10. What part of speech is *feeble* in sentence 3?

B. Verbs, Prepositions, Conjunctions, Interjections Read the following passage. Then identify each underlined word as an action verb, a linking verb, a preposition, a conjunction, or an interjection.

PROFESSIONAL MODEL

<u>Under</u> the lee of Child's Island they <u>stopped</u> at a
  (1)   (2)
sheltered beach, <u>since</u> Charley had promised the ladies a
        (3)
cup of tea at the first convenient spot. But when the men

<u>went</u> ashore for firewood, the wind <u>veered</u> and breakers
 (4)   (5)
began rolling <u>into</u> the bay. Captain <u>and</u> crew had to strip
        (6)   (7)
and shove the boat out <u>to</u> sea: "<u>Oh!</u> It was cold. And the
            (8)   (9)
sight of all hands naked <u>was</u> enough to make a cat laugh.
        (10)
We were red as lobsters and our teeth chattering."

—Bruce Chatwin, *In Patagonia*

Write the letter of the term that correctly identifies each underlined word.

During the 1200s, Marco Polo, an <u>Italian</u> traveler and trader, brought
(1)
Westerners some of <u>their</u> first substantial information about Chinese life
(2)
and customs. Marco and his father, Niccolò Polo, spent <u>several</u> years in the
(3)
court of the Chinese Mongol ruler Kublai Khan, returning to Venice in
1295. <u>Among</u> the Chinese <u>customs</u> described by Polo <u>were</u> the use of coal
(4)   (5)   (6)
as fuel, the use of paper money, and Kublai Khan's extensive postal
system. Polo dictated <u>a</u> book, *Description of the World.* <u>Because</u> printing
(7)   (8)
had not been invented in Europe (a form of printing was <u>already</u> in use in
(9)
China), the book was available only in handwritten copies. The book had a
widespread <u>effect</u> in Europe and helped to introduce a number of Chinese
(10)
innovations to the West.

1. A. proper adjective
   B. action verb
   C. proper noun
   D. common noun

2. A. demonstrative pronoun
   B. possessive pronoun
   C. proper noun
   D. common noun

3. A. adverb
   B. adjective
   C. preposition
   D. conjunction

4. A. conjunction
   B. interjection
   C. adverb
   D. preposition

5. A. verb
   B. adjective
   C. adverb
   D. noun

6. A. action verb
   B. conjunction
   C. linking verb
   D. preposition

7. A. adverb
   B. article
   C. preposition
   D. pronoun

8. A. subordinating conjunction
   B. correlative conjunction
   C. adjective
   D. preposition

9. A. preposition
   B. adverb
   C. adjective
   D. conjunction

10. A. conjunctive adverb
    B. preposition
    C. common noun
    D. adjective

PARTS OF SPEECH

Student Help Desk

Parts of Speech at a Glance

interjection		adverb	verb	adjective	adjective	noun	article	noun

Oops! You carelessly left your old but useful hat in the rain.

pronoun · · · · pronoun · conjunction · · · · preposition

Kinds of Nouns · Nouns to Remember

Every noun is either
- **common or proper**
- **concrete or abstract**
- **singular or plural**

Some nouns are
- **collective**
- **compound**

Joni and her family kept their memories in diaries and scrapbooks.

proper	common	common	common	common
concrete	concrete	abstract	concrete	concrete
singular	singular	plural	plural	plural
	collective			compound

Types of Verbs · Verbs to Revisit

Every verb is either a linking verb or an action verb.

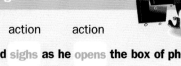

linking		action	action

Malik looks thoughtful and sighs as he opens the box of photographs.

intransitive · transitive

Every action verb is either transitive or intransitive.

Adverbs

STORY TEMPLATE

Once upon a time.

Suddenly.

Luckily.

Happily ever after.

© The New Yorker Collection 1998 Roz Chast

Types of Pronouns

personal   personal (possessive)

You have **your** own favorite memories.

interrogative   personal

What are **they?**

demonstrative   indefinite   relative   personal

Those are the **ones** **that** **you**

should give **yourself** time to ponder.

reflexive

The Bottom Line

Checklist for Parts of Speech

Have I . . .

_____ chosen precise nouns?

_____ used pronouns to avoid repeating nouns?

_____ selected specific verbs?

_____ added adjectives to identify nouns?

_____ used adverbs to describe actions?

_____ made good use of conjunctions to link ideas?

_____ used prepositions to clarify relationships?

_____ used interjections to show character in dialogue?

The Sentence and Its Parts

Humuhumunukunukuāpua'a

Theme: Amazing Facts

Amazing but True

The Hawaiian triggerfish is called *humuhumunukunukuāpua'a* in the Hawaiian language. Though the name seems long, it is actually very concise. *Humuhumu* means "to fit pieces together," and *nukunukuāpua'a* means "nose like a pig." Thus, one word takes the place of eight English words.

The English language has the largest vocabulary of any language, with 616,500 words and 400,000 technical terms. Amazingly, though, all of the possible sentences you can make with these words have only two basic parts: subjects and predicates. In fact, every day, as you think, talk, and write, you are forming hundreds of sentences with just these two components.

Write Away: Personal Best
In ten sentences, write ten amazing facts about your own life. Save the sentences in your 📁 **Working Portfolio.**

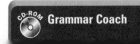

CD-ROM **Grammar Coach**

Choose the letter of the term that correctly identifies each numbered part of this passage.

In 1962, a brand-new baseball <u>team</u> made sports history. The New York
Mets <u>earned baseball's worst win-loss record</u>. Crusty manager Casey
Stengel <u>ranted and raved</u> at the young team. <u>During one particularly bad
game, he asked his players a rather sarcastic question.</u> "Can't anybody
here play this game?" There was only one <u>thing</u> worse than a Mets game,
according to Stengel. That was a Mets <u>double-header</u>. But Stengel did feel
<u>good</u> about the team's very first game. The officials canceled <u>it</u> because of
rain. Stengel's jokes won the hapless <u>team</u> many loyal fans.

  (1) ... (2) ... (3) ... (4) ... (5) ... (6) ... (7) ... (8) ... (9) ... (10)

1. A. simple subject
   B. complete subject
   C. simple predicate
   D. complete predicate

2. A. simple subject
   B. complete subject
   C. simple predicate
   D. complete predicate

3. A. compound subject
   B. compound verb
   C. complete subject
   D. complete predicate

4. A. declarative sentence
   B. imperative sentence
   C. interrogative sentence
   D. exclamatory sentence

5. A. declarative sentence
   B. imperative sentence
   C. interrogative sentence
   D. exclamatory sentence

6. A. compound subject
   B. compound verb
   C. simple subject
   D. predicate nominative

7. A. direct object
   B. indirect object
   C. predicate adjective
   D. predicate nominative

8. A. direct object
   B. indirect object
   C. predicate adjective
   D. predicate nominative

9. A. direct object
   B. indirect object
   C. predicate adjective
   D. predicate nominative

10. A. direct object
    B. indirect object
    C. predicate adjective
    D. predicate nominative

Simple Subjects and Predicates

❶ Here's the Idea

▶ **Every sentence has two basic parts: the subject and the predicate.**

The **subject** tells whom or what the sentence is about. The **predicate** tells what the subject is or does or what happens to the subject.

The world's tallest woman	stands almost eight feet tall!
SUBJECT	PREDICATE

The **simple subject** is the key word or words in the subject. The simple subject does not include modifiers, such as *The world's tallest* in the example above. To find the simple subject, ask who or what performs the action of the verb.

Sandy Allen wears size 22 sneakers.
Who wears size 22 sneakers? **Sandy Allen**

Stores do not carry her shoe size.
What do not carry her shoe size? **Stores**

The **simple predicate** is the verb or verb phrase that tells something about the subject. Modifiers are not part of the verb phrase, even if they interrupt the verb phrase.

People ask Allen about her height.
What do people do? ask

She does not mind their questions.
(Notice that the modifier *not* is excluded from the simple predicate.)

❷ Why It Matters in Writing

Both the subject and predicate are necessary for the meaning of the sentence to be clear. If the subject or predicate of a sentence is missing, the group of words is a **sentence fragment**. Sentence fragments do not express complete thoughts.

Allen gets her shoes from the National Basketball Association.

Without the subject, *Allen,* you wouldn't know whom the predicate refers to. Without the predicate, the only word left is *Allen.*

❸ Practice and Apply

Write the simple subject and simple predicate of each sentence.

Example: People have always enjoyed novelty acts.
Answer: People, have enjoyed

The Daring Young Flea on the Flying Trapeze
1. Maria Fernanda Cordoso runs an unusual small business.
2. She owns the Cordoso Flea Circus.
3. All the circus performers are fleas.
4. Samson lifts cotton-ball barbells high above his head.
5. Pierre crosses tinfoil swords with Pedro in a fierce duel.
6. Teeny floats through the air on a tiny trapeze.
7. Flamboyant fleas in colorful costumes dance to a Latin beat.
8. Harry Fleadini simply disappears.
9. The circus has been traveling all over the world.
10. People can hardly wait for the smallest show on earth.

➡ **For a SELF-CHECK and more practice, see the EXERCISE BANK, p. 604.**

Write *S* if a group of words is a complete sentence or *F* if it is a sentence fragment. For each fragment, tell whether the simple subject or simple predicate is missing.

Example: Animal behavior unpredictable.
Answer: F, missing simple predicate

The Curious Case of the Parental Parrot
1. A story about a peculiar pet was reported in England long ago.
2. At night, a pet parrot slept in a large outdoor birdhouse.
3. During the day, the bird in the woods.
4. One day, a pregnant cat climbed into the birdhouse.
5. Had a litter of kittens in the parrot's nest.
6. Then the new mother in the woods for food.
7. The parrot home early that day.
8. Must have been surprised by the uninvited kittens.
9. Was not at all frightened, however.
10. The motherly parrot adopted the kittens for her own.

Complete Subjects and Predicates

LESSON 2

❶ Here's the Idea

▶ The complete subject includes the simple subject and all the words that modify it. The complete predicate includes the verb and all the words that modify it.

Every generation	develops its own foolish fads.
COMPLETE SUBJECT	COMPLETE PREDICATE

Here's How Finding Complete Subjects and Predicates

Teens of the 1950s crammed into phone booths.

Complete subject Ask who or what is or does something.

Who crammed into phone booths? **Teens of the 1950s**

Complete predicate Ask what the subject is or does or what happens to the subject.

What did teens of the 1950s do? crammed into phone booths

Teens of the 1950s crammed into phone booths.
COMPLETE SUBJECT   COMPLETE PREDICATE

HOT TIP

Every word in a sentence is part of a complete subject or complete predicate.

❷ Why It Matters in Writing

When you add details to simple subjects and predicates, you help your readers more clearly picture what you mean.

STUDENT MODEL

DRAFT	*REVISION*
The couple won.	The weary young couple in the red outfits won a three-day dance marathon.

❸ Practice and Apply

A. CONCEPT CHECK: Complete Subjects and Predicates

Write each sentence and draw a line between the complete subject and complete predicate.

Example: Unusual contests / have drawn many participants over the years.

Rock Till You Drop?

1. Crazy tests of endurance swept the nation during the 1920s.
2. "Shipwreck" Kelly sat atop an Atlantic City flagpole for 49 days.
3. The stunt earned him the title "King of the Pole."
4. The Rocking Chair Derby was a more down-to-earth contest.
5. Contestants rocked back and forth for days.
6. Losers literally went off their rockers.
7. New York City's Noun and Verb Rodeo appealed to nonstop talkers.
8. Contestants breathlessly babbled for hours on end.
9. The toughest test of endurance was the Bunion Derby.
10. Andy Payne won the transcontinental footrace in a record 573 hours.

➡ For a SELF-CHECK and more practice, see the EXERCISE BANK, p. 604.

B. REVISING: Adding Details

On a separate sheet of paper, create complete subjects and predicates by adding details to the simple subjects and predicates below. Describe what's popular and newsworthy today.

Example: Teenagers are buying.
Answer: Today's teenagers are buying CD's and bell-bottom pants.

Newspapers	are reporting.
Television	is broadcasting.
Americans	are talking.
Radios	are playing.
People	are buying.

SENTENCE PARTS

Compound Sentence Parts

❶ Here's the Idea

▶ **A sentence can have more than one subject and verb.** A sentence part containing more than one of these elements is called a compound part.

A **compound subject** is made up of two or more simple subjects that share a verb. The subjects are joined by a conjunction, or connecting word, such as *and, or,* or *but.*

> **Alice and Leon** enjoy **a good adventure story.**
> **Daring feats and thrilling chases** are **exciting.**

A **compound verb** is made up of two or more verbs or verb phrases that are joined by a conjunction and have the same subject.

> **The adventure hero** endures **and** conquers.
> **The hero** conquers **and** captures **the villain.**

A **compound predicate** is made up of a compound verb and all the words that go with each verb.

> **Such stories** engage the audience **and** fire the imagination.

❷ Why It Matters in Writing

Correctly using compound subjects and predicates can help you avoid repetition and write more concisely.

> **STUDENT MODEL**
>
> *DRAFT*
>
> Charles Lindbergh was a real-life adventure hero. So was Amelia Earhart. Both pilots beat the odds. Both pilots successfully completed solo flights across the Atlantic Ocean.
>
> *REVISION*
>
> Charles Lindbergh and Amelia Earhart were real-life adventure heroes. Both pilots beat the odds and successfully completed solo flights across the Atlantic Ocean.

❸ Practice and Apply

A. CONCEPT CHECK: Compound Sentence Parts

Write each sentence below and underline the simple subject(s) once and the verb(s) twice.

Four Continents on Foot

1. Many people walk or jog around their neighborhoods.
2. Dave Kunst took this idea and ran with it about 20 million steps farther.
3. Kunst walked 14,450 miles around the earth and set a world record.
4. Kunst and his brother began their journey on June 20, 1970.
5. A mule hauled supplies and kept them company.
6. Comedy and tragedy struck along the way.
7. In Italy, a restaurant owner greeted the brothers and escorted the mule into his cafe for a free meal.
8. In Afghanistan, Kunst and his brother were shot by bandits.
9. Kunst's brother fought for his life but died.
10. Kunst recovered and completed his odyssey on October 5, 1974.

➡ For a SELF-CHECK and more practice, see the EXERCISE BANK, p. 605.

B. REVISING: Constructing Compounds

Combine each pair of sentences into a single sentence with a compound subject or predicate.

Example: My parents like Minnesota. I do too.
Answer: My parents and I like Minnesota.

Greetings from Minnesota!
1 Bemidji has great statues of Paul Bunyan and Babe the Blue Ox. Brainerd does too.
2 The Brainerd Paul Bunyan is 27 feet tall. It has hidden audio speakers. **3** It sits in an alcove. It "talks" to visitors.
4 The statue made me laugh. But it terrified my little brother.

USA 20

Julie Sanford
123 West Fourth Street
Chicago, IL
60660

SENTENCE PARTS

LESSON 4 # Kinds of Sentences

❶ Here's the Idea

▶ **A sentence can be used to make a statement, ask a question, give a command, or show feeling.**

Kinds of Sentences

Declarative London is a wonderful city.
This kind of sentence expresses a statement of fact, wish, intent, or feeling. It always ends with a period.

Interrogative Which attraction is the most popular?
This kind of sentence asks a question and ends with a question mark.

Imperative See for yourself! Read the guidebook.
This kind of sentence gives a command, request, or direction, and usually ends with a period. If the command or request is strong, it may end with an exclamation point.

Exclamatory You've got to see Madame Tussaud's wax museum!
This kind of sentence expresses strong feeling and always ends with an exclamation point.

 When an exclamatory sentence is preceded by another exclamation, either a period or an exclamation mark can be used at the end of the second sentence. **Example:** Wow! The wax figures there seem so real.

❷ Why It Matters in Writing

Using the four sentence types, you can vary the tone and mood of your writing. Read the four sentences below with expression. Notice how your tone of voice changes to convey the different meaning of each sentence.

> **You have never visited that museum.**
> **You have never visited that museum?**
> **Never visit that museum.**
> **You would love that museum!**

❸ Practice and Apply

A. CONCEPT CHECK: Kinds of Sentences

Identify the following sentences as declarative, imperative, interrogative, or exclamatory. Then rewrite sentences 6–10 according to the directions in parentheses.

Example: This exhibit gives me the creeps!
Answer: exclamatory

> **Waxing Poetic**
> **1.** What do the Dalai Lama, Billy Idol, John McEnroe, and Nelson Mandela have in common, in addition to their being famous?
> **2.** All of them have doubles in Madame Tussaud's wax museum.
> **3.** The wax models are very lifelike.
> **4.** Take an imaginary stroll through the Chamber of Horrors.
> **5.** Is that the notorious Jack the Ripper?
> **6.** He looks alive! (Change into a question.)
> **7.** Would you look over there? (Change into an imperative sentence.)
> **8.** Is that Marie Antoinette? (Change into a declarative sentence.)
> **9.** That guillotine looks very real! (Change into a declarative sentence.)
> **10.** Madame Tussaud narrowly escaped the guillotine during the French Revolution. (Change into an exclamation.)

➜ For a SELF-CHECK and more practice, see the EXERCISE BANK, p. 605.

B. WRITING: Using Sentence Variety

Writers of advertisements often use all four kinds of sentences to make their ads expressive and persuasive. Take a tip from the professionals and use all four kinds of sentences to write a tourism ad aimed at persuading vacationers to visit your town. Your ad may be serious or humorous.

🗂 **Working Portfolio** Take out the sentences you wrote for the **Write Away** on page 36. Revise the sentences so that all four kinds of sentences are represented.

Subjects in Unusual Positions

1 Here's the Idea

In most sentences, the subject is placed before the verb. In some sentences, however, the subject appears after the verb, while in others it is not stated at all.

Inverted Sentences

▶ **In an inverted sentence, the subject appears after the verb or between the words that make up the verb phrase.** An inverted sentence can be used for variety or emphasis. What effect does the inverted order have on the following sentences?

Usual Order: An 800-pound pumpkin grew in his garden.

Inverted: In his garden grew an 800-pound pumpkin.

Usual Order: The neighbors had never seen such a squash!

Inverted: Never had the neighbors seen such a squash!

Sentences Beginning with *Here* or *There*

▶ **When a sentence begins with *here* or *there*, the subject usually follows the verb.** *Here* and *there* are almost never the subject of a sentence.

The words *here* and *there* almost always function as adverbs of place or as expletives. **Adverbs of place** modify verbs by answering the question *where?* **Expletives** do not have meaning in and of themselves. These "subject delayers" introduce and draw attention to subjects.

Here is the World Pumpkin Confederation's official Web page.

Where is the Web page? The Web page is **here**.
Here is an adverb.

There are growers of giant vegetables all over the world.

There does not tell where. It is an expletive.

Questions

▶ **In most questions, the subject appears after the verb or between the words that make up the verb phrase.**

Subject After Verb:
   Was **the cabbage large?**

Subject Inside Verb Phrase:
   Did **you** see **it?**

In many questions that begin with *whom, what,* or *how many,* the subject falls between the parts of the verb.

   How many pounds did **the cabbage** weigh?

In some questions, however, the interrogative pronoun functions as the subject and comes before the verb.

   Who won **the contest?**

Imperative Sentences

▶ **The subject of an imperative sentence is always *you*.** Even when not directly stated, *you* is understood to be the subject.

   Request: **(You) Please eat your vegetables.**
   Command: **(You) Don't complain!**

❷ Why It Matters in Writing

You can vary the tone and emphasis of your sentences with inverted sentences and commands. This is especially useful in creating realistic dialogue and dialects, as in the following example.

> **LITERARY MODEL**
>
> "Quit that," said the woman. "Can't you see you're raising ashes?"
>
> "What harm is ashes?"
>
> "I'll show you what harm," she said, taking down a plate of cabbage and potato from the shelf over the fire. "There's your dinner destroyed with them."
>
> —Mary Lavin, "Brigid"

❸ Practice and Apply

A. CONCEPT CHECK: Subjects in Unusual Positions

Write the simple subject and simple predicate of each sentence below. Be sure to include all verbs that appear in verb phrases.

Example: Have you ever had a garden?
Answer: you, have had

> **Kings of the Cabbage Patch**
> **1.** Where can you get a good cabbage these days?
> **2.** Come to the annual cabbage competition in Palmer, Alaska.
> **3.** There is hot competition for the $4,000 first prize.
> **4.** Who grew the biggest cabbage?
> **5.** To Lesley Dinkel goes the title.
> **6.** Among his many triumphs was a 98-pound monster.
> **7.** Do the winners have advice for the rest of us gardeners?
> **8.** Here is their best advice.
> **9.** Protect your cabbages from moose.
> **10.** How can you argue with advice like that?

➡ **For a SELF-CHECK and more practice, see the EXERCISE BANK, p. 605.**

B. REVISING: Varying Sentence Structure

Change each sentence according to the directions in parentheses.

Example: Pumpkins are native to Central America. (Make into a question.)
Answer: Are pumpkins native to Central America?

> **Scary Spuds**
> **1.** You should read about the history of the jack-o'-lantern. (Change into an imperative sentence.)
> **2.** The jack-o'-lantern didn't originate in the United States. (Change into a question.)
> **3.** This Halloween tradition comes from Ireland. (Invert sentence order.)
> **4.** Long ago no pumpkins were available in Ireland. (Begin the sentence with *there.*)
> **5.** The first jack-o'-lanterns were made of potatoes and turnips! (Change into a question.)

LESSON 6 Subject Complements

❶ Here's the Idea

▶ **A complement is a word or a group of words that completes the meaning of a verb.** Complements include subject complements, direct objects, indirect objects, and objective complements.

A **subject complement** follows a linking verb and describes or renames the subject. There are two kinds of subject complements: predicate adjectives and predicate nominatives. Subject complements can also have their own modifiers, as in the second example below.

Predicate adjectives describe subjects by telling *which one, what kind, how much,* or *how many.*

During the 1930s, the jitterbug became popular.
SUBJECT   LINKING   PREDICATE
           VERB   ADJECTIVE

In comparison, today's dances seem very tame.
MODIFIER   PREDICATE ADJECTIVE

Predicate nominatives are nouns and pronouns that rename, identify, or define subjects.

The jitterbug is a dance variation.
SUBJECT   LINKING VERB   PREDICATE NOMINATIVE

Frank Manning was an inventive jitterbug dancer.
                PREDICATE NOMINATIVE

❷ Why It Matters in Writing

Subject complements, like the simple noun *man* in the model below, can themselves be modified to create a full description.

> **LITERARY MODEL**
>
> "Verenka's father was a very handsome, imposing, and well-preserved old **man**."
>
> —Leo Tolstoy, "After the Ball"

❸ Practice and Apply

Write each subject complement and identify it as a predicate adjective or a predicate nominative.

Example: Swing is big-band jazz.
Answer: jazz, predicate nominative

Swing and Slang
1. Swing music has become fashionable again.
2. One birthplace of swing was Harlem.
3. A famous swing dancer was George "Shorty" Snowden.
4. The jitterbug looks very difficult.
5. The dancers seem extraordinarily athletic.
6. Are you an alligator?
7. Alligators are fans of swing.
8. Don't be an ickie!
9. Ickies are hopelessly unhip.
10. They feel lost on the dance floor.

➡ For a SELF-CHECK and more practice, see the EXERCISE BANK, p. 606.

B. REVISING: Improving Subject Complements

Rewrite each sentence, replacing the vague or weak subject complement with a more precise one.

Example: After several dips and twirls, she felt weird.
Answer: After several dips and twirls, she felt dizzy.

Dangerous Dances?
1. Some dances are bad.
2. The Charleston may seem OK.
3. Still, its many kicks and twirls can become problems on a dance floor.
4. A kick in the shin is awful!
5. Bruises don't look nice.
6. The twist may be all right for strong, young dancers.
7. It is not a good thing for people with weak backs, however.
8. After a spin on the dance floor, their backs may feel lousy.
9. The jitterbug can also be bad.
10. Dancers must be physically well.

CHAPTER 2

Objects of Verbs

LESSON 7

❶ Here's the Idea

▶ Many action verbs require complements called direct objects and indirect objects to complete their meaning.

Direct and Indirect Objects

A **direct object** is a word or group of words that names the receiver of the action of an action verb. It answers the question *what* or *whom*. Consider the following sentence:

Many people save.

Notice that the sentence is missing information. You probably wonder what many people save.

Many people save **string.**
    ↑ DIRECT OBJECT

Other people keep **twist ties** from plastic bags.
    ↑ DIRECT OBJECT

An **indirect object** is a word or group of words that tells to what, to whom, or for whom an action is done. In a sentence containing both a direct and an indirect object, the indirect object almost always comes before the direct object. Verbs that often take indirect objects include *bring, give, hand, lend, make, offer, send, show, teach, tell,* and *write.*

Savers give **friends** **collecting advice.**
    ↑ INDIRECT OBJECT   ↑ DIRECT OBJECT

What do savers give? **advice** *Advice* is the direct object.
To whom do savers give advice? **friends** *Friends* is the indirect object.

Savers will proudly show **anyone** **their giant jars of pennies.**
    ↑ INDIRECT OBJECT   ↑ DIRECT OBJECT

For more about action verbs, see p. 14.

The words *to* and *for* never appear before the indirect object. *To* and *for* are prepositions when they are followed by a noun or pronoun. In such cases the noun or pronoun is an object of the preposition, not an object of the verb.

Objective Complements

An **objective complement** is a word or group of words that follows a direct object and renames or describes that object. Objective complements follow certain verbs and their synonyms: *appoint, call, choose, consider, elect, find, keep, make, name, think.* An objective complement may be a noun or an adjective.

Some people consider **themselves** savers.
DIRECT OBJECT   OBJECTIVE COMPLEMENT

What do some people consider themselves? **savers** *Savers* is a noun.

No one could ever call **the hobby** wasteful.
DIRECT OBJECT   OBJECTIVE COMPLEMENT

What could no one call it? **wasteful** *Wasteful* is an adjective.

Savers find trash a treasure.
Savers make tidy people crazy.

❷ Why It Matters in Writing

Objective complements convey information and add important details. They are especially useful when one is writing dialogue.

My mother took one step into my messy bedroom and joked, "I hereby rename you Pigpen!"

❸ Practice and Apply

A. CONCEPT CHECK: Objects of Verbs

Each sentence below has at least one object. Write each object and identify it as a direct object, an indirect object, or an objective complement. Identify each objective complement as a noun or an adjective.

Example: Hobbies bring people pleasure.
Answer: people, indirect object; pleasure, direct object

The Man Who Would Be String King
1. You must give Francis A. Johnson some credit.
2. This Minnesotan could teach the world patience.
3. He spent 41 years on a very special project.
4. During each of those years, he truly had a ball.
5. Slowly but surely, inch by inch, Johnson wound the world's largest ball of twine.

6. At 12 feet in diameter and 17,400 pounds, Johnson's sphere offered other string savers an irresistible challenge.

7. Super string saver Frank Stoeber brought Cawker City, Kansas, a measure of fame.

8. He made an enormous ball of twine Cawker City's biggest tourist attraction.

9. Some people might consider Texan J. C. Payne an odd guy.

10. His 6-ton, 13-foot-tall twine ball has made him famous.

➡ **For a SELF-CHECK and more practice, see the EXERCISE BANK, p. 606.**

B. REVISING: Creating Objects of Verbs

Rewrite each sentence below, replacing all the objects of the verbs to create ten different sentences. Add and change modifiers as needed.

Example: Do you save things? *Answer:* Do you save odd items?

1. Tell us your favorite pastimes.

2. Do your hobbies include sports?

3. Other people may think your hobby unusual.

4. But your hobby may make you happy.

5. How much time do you spend on your hobby?

6. Show us the results.

7. Could you turn your hobby into a career?

8. Many hobbyists teach other people their craft.

9. You might give beginners lessons.

10. You should consider your hobby fun.

C. WRITING: Creating Sentences with Complements

Using the information below, write five sentences about Lucy the Elephant. Include direct objects, indirect objects, and objective complements.

Lucy, the world's largest elephant

Located in Margate, New Jersey

Built in 1881 by James Lafferty, a real estate developer

Historic landmark

Stands six stories tall, weighs 90 tons

25,000 tourists visit each year

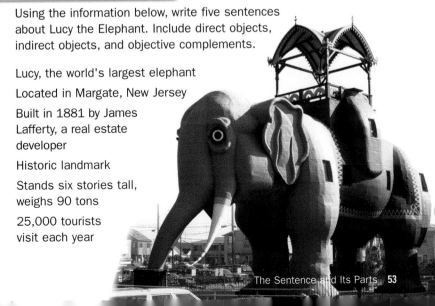

Sentence Diagramming

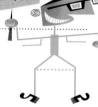

Mad Mapper

Here's the Idea

Diagramming is a way of visually representing the structure of a sentence. Drawing a diagram can help you see the relationships among the words in a sentence and better understand how the words work together to form a complete thought.

Watch me for diagramming tips!

Simple Subjects and Predicates

The simple subject and predicate are written on one line and separated by a vertical line that crosses the main line.

Spectators waited.

$$\text{Spectators} \mid \text{waited}$$

Compound Subjects and Verbs

For a compound subject or verb, split the main line. The conjunction goes on a broken line connecting the compound parts.

Spectators and contestants waited.

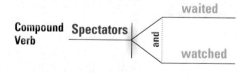

Compound Subject

Spectators
and
contestants
waited

Because there are two subjects, the left side of the main line is split into two parts.

Spectators waited and watched.

Compound Verb

Spectators
and
waited
watched

Because there are two verbs, the right side of the main line is split into two parts.

Spectators and contestants waited and watched.

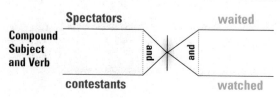

Compound Subject and Verb

Spectators
and
and
waited
contestants
watched

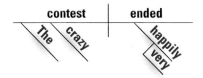

A. CONCEPT CHECK: Subjects and Verbs

Diagram these sentences using what you have learned.

1. Reporters chuckled.
2. Reporters chuckled and cheered.
3. Spectators and reporters stood and applauded.

Adjectives and Adverbs

Because adjectives and adverbs **modify,** or tell more about, other words in a sentence, they are written on slanted lines below the words they modify.

The crazy contest ended very happily.

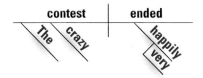

B. CONCEPT CHECK: Adjectives and Adverbs

Diagram these sentences using what you have learned.

1. The jolly judges grinned playfully.
2. A new champion finally was crowned.
3. The proud winner and her family smiled and bowed.

Subject Complements: Predicate Nominatives and Predicate Adjectives

Write a predicate nominative or a predicate adjective on the main line after the verb. Separate the subject complement from the verb with a slanted line that does not cross the main line.

May Gonzalez was the winner.   **She felt wonderful.**

May Gonzalez | was \ winner   She | felt \ wonderful
                      \ the

SENTENCE PARTS

Direct Objects

A direct object follows the verb on the main line.

The winner received a paper crown.

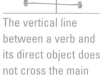

Sometimes a sentence has a compound direct object. Like other compound parts, compound direct objects go on parallel lines that branch from the main line.

The winner received a paper crown and a T-shirt.

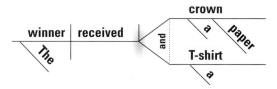

When you have a compound predicate with direct objects, split the line and show the compound parts on parallel lines.

She wore the crown and displayed the T-shirt.

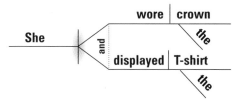

Indirect Objects

Write an indirect object below the verb, on a horizontal line connected to the verb with a slanted line.

The champion threw the crowd a kiss.

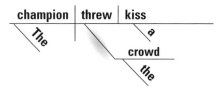

CHAPTER 2

Objective Complements

An objective complement follows a direct object on the main line. A slanted line that does not cross the main line separates the objective complement from the direct object.

The local newspaper called the contest delightful.

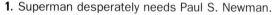

C. CONCEPT CHECK: Complements and Objects of the Verb

Diagram these sentences using what you've learned.

1. May Gonzalez was very happy.
2. The newspapers gave Gonzalez a great review.
3. Enthusiastic fans considered Gonzalez a terrific winner.

D. MIXED REVIEW: Diagramming

Diagram the following sentences.

1. Superman desperately needs Paul S. Newman.
2. Sylvester and Tweety Bird do too.
3. Many cartoon characters owe Newman their lives.
4. The reason is quite simple.
5. Newman is a prolific comic-book writer.
6. He has written 4,000 stories.
7. The imaginative writer does not draw comics.
8. He creates clever plots and writes snappy dialogue.
9. Newman considers himself lucky.
10. He enjoys his job and brings other people pleasure.

Looks like George has a subject and a predicament.

Real World Grammar

Contest Application

Whether you are applying for a summer job, competing for a special award, or entering a contest, you need to present yourself in the best possible light. Using proper sentence structure and good grammar skills will distinguish you from other applicants. Here's one student's e-mail application for a special award. She asked her English teacher to comment on her first draft.

Cyberstudent of the year

1st Prize Computer Workstation

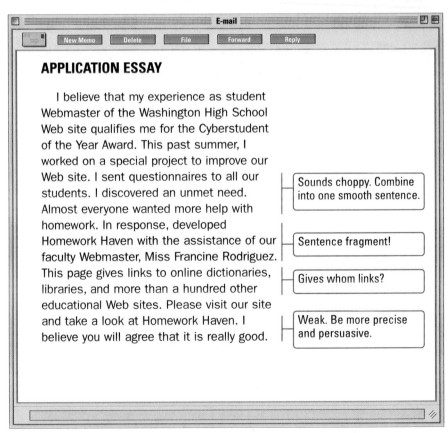

E-mail

| New Memo | Delete | File | Forward | Reply |

APPLICATION ESSAY

I believe that my experience as student Webmaster of the Washington High School Web site qualifies me for the Cyberstudent of the Year Award. This past summer, I worked on a special project to improve our Web site. I sent questionnaires to all our students. I discovered an unmet need. Almost everyone wanted more help with homework. In response, developed Homework Haven with the assistance of our faculty Webmaster, Miss Francine Rodriguez. This page gives links to online dictionaries, libraries, and more than a hundred other educational Web sites. Please visit our site and take a look at Homework Haven. I believe you will agree that it is really good.

Sounds choppy. Combine into one smooth sentence.

Sentence fragment!

Gives whom links?

Weak. Be more precise and persuasive.

CHAPTER 2

Using Grammar in Writing

Complete sentences	Communicate your ideas clearly by making sure every sentence has **both a subject and a predicate.**
Compound parts	Use **compound parts** to combine ideas and avoid repetition. Combining related ideas into one sentence makes your writing smoother and more concise.
Precise language	Use **clear, specific adjectives, pronouns, and nouns** as subject complements to express your ideas clearly and forcefully.

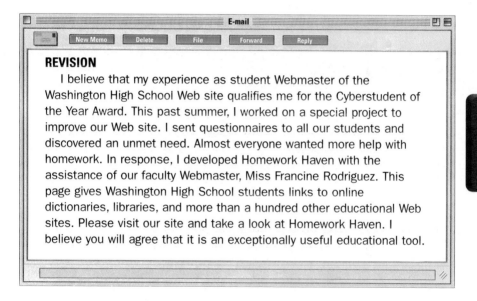

E-mail

New Memo | Delete | File | Forward | Reply

REVISION

I believe that my experience as student Webmaster of the Washington High School Web site qualifies me for the Cyberstudent of the Year Award. This past summer, I worked on a special project to improve our Web site. I sent questionnaires to all our students and discovered an unmet need. Almost everyone wanted more help with homework. In response, I developed Homework Haven with the assistance of our faculty Webmaster, Miss Francine Rodriguez. This page gives Washington High School students links to online dictionaries, libraries, and more than a hundred other educational Web sites. Please visit our site and take a look at Homework Haven. I believe you will agree that it is an exceptionally useful educational tool.

PRACTICE AND APPLY: Revising

Use the three writing tips above to revise the summer-job application below.

DRAFT

I believe I am a good candidate for a job as coaching assistant. In elementary school, I participated in the park district's summer sports program. I developed an avid interest in sports. Currently play center on the high school basketball team. In junior high, was a member of the baseball team. In addition, firsthand experience working with active children. As the oldest of five kids, I often baby-sit my little brothers and sister. I would love to put my knowledge and experience to work for the park district.

Mixed Review

A. Sentences and Sentence Parts Revise each of the following sentences based on the instructions in parentheses.

1. Goals are vital.
   (What kinds of goals? Add detail to the subject.)

2. Goals give purpose and direction.
   (Give to whom? Add an indirect object.)

3. You have set goals for yourself.
   (Change into a question.)

4. Did you set achievable goals?
   (Change into a command.)

5. Your goals should be challenging. But also practical.
   (Fix the fragment by combining the predicate adjectives.)

6. No use in setting unrealistic goals.
   (Fix the fragment by making it an inverted sentence beginning with *there.*)

7. Only discourage you.
   (Fix the fragment by completing the subject and predicate.)

8. It would be nice to make *The Guinness Book of World Records.*
   (Replace the weak predicate adjective with a more precise one.)

9. But not necessary.
   (Fix the fragment by adding a subject and verb.)

10. You should try to be the best you can be.
    (Change into an exclamatory statement.)

B. Subject Complements and Objects of Verbs Identify each underlined word as a direct object, an indirect object, a predicate nominative, a predicate adjective, or an objective complement.

> **PROFESSIONAL MODEL**
>
> **(1)** When Jean Bowman graduated from high school, she was truly a <u>senior</u>. **(2)** In fact, she was downright <u>old</u>. **(3)** At 87, Bowman became the world's oldest high school <u>graduate</u>. **(4)** Bowman quit <u>high school</u> in 1926 without earning her diploma. **(5)** She became a <u>homemaker</u>. **(6)** She also raised three <u>children</u>. **(7)** Bowman did not dare tell her <u>children</u> her secret. **(8)** She was afraid they would consider her <u>ignorant</u>. **(9)** Some 70 years after dropping out of high school, Bowman entered an adult education <u>program</u>. **(10)** Night school gave <u>Bowman</u> an opportunity to finish what she started so long ago.

Choose the letter of the description or term that correctly identifies each numbered part of the passage.

Music is not only an <u>art</u> but also a business. Many artists have earned
(1)

<u>millions</u> of dollars in the recording industry. <u>Elvis Presley and Aretha</u>
(2)   (3)

<u>Franklin</u> are the top male and female solo recording artists of all time.

Presley <u>had more than 170 hit singles and 80 top-selling albums.</u>
                        (4)

Franklin's magnificent voice has earned <u>her</u> 14 hit singles. <u>Can you guess</u>
                                       (5)   (6)

<u>which rock band has sold the greatest number of records?</u> This <u>honor</u> goes
                                                      (7)

to the Beatles. <u>The band has sold more than a billion discs and tapes!</u>
                                      (8)

Today, alternative rock and rap are <u>popular</u>. Will people consider these
                                          (9)

types of music <u>interesting</u> in the future?
                (10)

1. A. describes the subject
   B. completes the meaning of the action verb
   C. tells who receives the action
   D. describes the direct object

2. A. simple subject
   B. predicate adjective
   C. direct object
   D. indirect object

3. A. compound verb
   B. compound subject
   C. simple predicate
   D. simple subject

4. A. simple subject
   B. complete subject
   C. direct object
   D. complete predicate

5. A. direct object
   B. indirect object
   C. predicate nominative
   D. objective complement

6. A. interrogative sentence
   B. imperative sentence
   C. exclamatory sentence
   D. declarative sentence

7. A. predicate nominative
   B. predicate adjective
   C. direct object
   D. simple subject

8. A. interrogative sentence
   B. imperative sentence
   C. exclamatory sentence
   D. declarative sentence

9. A. predicate nominative
   B. predicate adjective
   C. direct object
   D. simple subject

10. A. predicate adjective
    B. direct object
    C. objective complement
    D. indirect object

SENTENCE PARTS

Student Help Desk

The Sentence at a Glance

A sentence has two parts: a subject and a predicate.

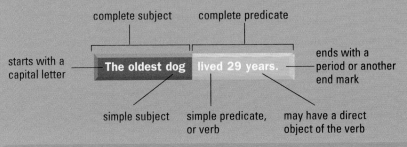

complete subject   complete predicate

starts with a capital letter — **The oldest dog** — lived 29 years. — ends with a period or another end mark

simple subject   simple predicate, or verb   may have a direct object of the verb

Subjects and Predicates   The Most Basic Sentence Parts

Sentence Parts	Example
Simple subject and predicate	The bear ran.
Compound subject and verb	The bear and her cubs ran and climbed.
Complete subject and predicate	The three cubs ran past our camp.

Objects of Verbs   Famous Identified Flying Objects

Type	Definition	Example
Direct object	A direct object receives the action of an action verb.	The visitors photographed the smallest **car.**
Indirect object	An indirect object tells to what, to whom, or for whom the action is done.	Joe gave **me** the book.
Objective complement	An objective complement follows a direct object and renames or describes that object.	Some people make Las Vegas their **home.**

Finding the Subject in a Sentence

Subject Contorts into Many Positions

1. In an inverted sentence, find the verb and ask yourself who or what did the action in the sentence.

Example: From the distance came the howl of a timber wolf. The verb is came. What came? Howl came. The subject is **howl**.

2. When a sentence begins with *there* or *here,* the subject usually follows the verb. To find the subject, reword the sentence with the subject at the beginning.

Example: Here is your passport.
Reworded: Your **passport** is here.

3. In most questions beginning with *where, when, why, how,* or *how much,* the subject falls between the parts of the verb phrase.

Example: Where will **you** go on vacation?

4. The subject of an imperative sentence is always *you,* even when the subject is not directly stated.

Example: **(You)** Look at these pictures.

The Bottom Line

Checklist for Editing Sentences

Have I . . .

____ made all sentence fragments into complete sentences, with both a subject and a predicate?

____ used compound subjects and verbs to combine sentences with similar ideas?

____ used the right kind of sentence for the intended tone and mood?

____ varied sentence structure so the writing is interesting?

____ used inverted sentences properly?

____ placed the indirect object before the direct object?

Using Phrases

Helicopter powered only by human flies!

Theme: Things With Wings

Human Flies?

Is there something wrong with this headline, or has genetic engineering finally caught up with Hollywood? Headlines are supposed to be condensed, but this one is mixed up—rather like the human fly himself.

One way to be more clear would be to write two sentences: *A helicopter flies. The helicopter is powered only by a human.* By using a phrase, however, you can make one sentence that uses fewer words and flows better: *Powered only by a human, a helicopter flies.* You can use phrases to improve your writing as long as—unlike the writer of the headline—you make clear what the phrase goes with.

Write Away: A Few of My Favorite Wings
What is your favorite thing with wings? A bird? A plane? A family pack from a chicken place? Answer this question in a paragraph and add it to your 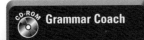 **Working Portfolio.**

Choose the letter of the term that correctly identifies each numbered item.

The longtime dream <u>of human flight</u> turned into reality in the early
(1)
1900s. According to Wilbur Wright, <u>one of the inventors of the first airplane,</u>
(2)
"Flight was generally looked upon as an impossibility, and scarcely anyone

believed it until he saw it <u>with his own eyes.</u>" The Wrights, <u>thinking</u> out of
(3)   (4)
the box, created their own machine <u>built</u> to fly people. Now almost everyone
(5)
can enjoy <u>jetting</u> from place to place.
(6)

For thousands of years, people could only imagine <u>soaring gracefully</u>
(7)
<u>through the air like birds</u>. To them, flying without the restraint <u>of gravity</u>
(8)
would have been <u>to know freedom</u>, but the possibility of <u>traveling more</u>
(9)   (10)
<u>than 30,000 feet above ground </u>was merely a pipe dream.

---

1. A. participial phrase
   B. prepositional phrase
   C. infinitive phrase
   D. appositive phrase

2. A. participial phrase
   B. prepositional phrase
   C. infinitive phrase
   D. appositive phrase

3. A. phrase modifying *it*
   B. phrase modifying *saw*
   C. phrase used as predicate
      nominative
   D. phrase used as direct object

4. A. present participle
   B. gerund
   C. infinitive
   D. past participle

5. A. present participle
   B. gerund
   C. infinitive
   D. past participle

6. A. present participle
   B. infinitive
   C. gerund
   D. past participle

7. A. phrase used as subject of
      sentence
   B. phrase used as object of
      preposition
   C. phrase used as direct object
   D. phrase used as predicate
      nominative

8. A. phrase modifying *to fly*
   B. phrase used as object of *without*
   C. phrase modifying *restraint*
   D. phrase used as subject

9. A. phrase used as subject
   B. phrase used as direct object
   C. phrase used as predicate
      nominative
   D. phrase used as object of
      preposition

10. A. gerund phrase used as subject
    B. gerund phrase used as direct
       object
    C. gerund phrase used as
       predicate nominative
    D. gerund phrase used as object of
       preposition

PHRASES

Prepositional Phrases

❶ Here's the Idea

A **phrase** is a group of related words that does not have a subject or a predicate. It functions as a single part of speech.

▶ **A prepositional phrase consists of a preposition, its object, and any modifiers of the object.**

"On the Wings of Morning" is a poem by the talented Maya Angelou.   PREPOSITIONAL PHRASE

Prepositional phrases are used to modify, or describe, a noun or pronoun.

> **LITERARY MODEL**
>
> Sounds like music and sounds like flying tents filled the sky, and those were pterodactyls soaring with cavernous gray wings, gigantic bats of delirium and night fever.
>
> PREPOSITIONAL PHRASES
>
> WORDS MODIFIED
>
> —Ray Bradbury, "A Sound of Thunder"

Notice that prepositional phrases can function either as adjectives or adverbs.

MODIFIES VERB   MODIFIES NOUN

The dragon flew to its secret lair inside the mountain.
              ADVERB PHRASE   ADJECTIVE PHRASE

Adjective Phrases

An **adjective prepositional phrase** is a prepositional phrase that modifies a noun or a pronoun. An adjective phrase usually tells *which one* or *what kind* about the word it modifies.

MODIFIES NOUN   MODIFIES PRONOUN

A bird in the hand is better than one in the bush.
      WHICH BIRD?   WHAT KIND?

 HOT TIP

While adjectives usually come just before the words they modify, adjective phrases usually come just after.

Adverb Phrases

An **adverb prepositional phrase** is a prepositional phrase that modifies a verb, an adjective, or an adverb. Like an adverb, an adverb phrase tells *how*, *when*, *where*, or *to what extent* about the word it modifies.

The tricky cuckoo lays its eggs in other birds' nests.

LAYS WHERE?

MODIFIES ADJECTIVE

Even cuckoo chicks are skillful at deception.

SKILLFUL HOW?

Soon after their emergence, they begin to imitate the other chicks. WHEN?

For a list of prepositions, see p. 89.

❷ Why It Matters in Writing

Using prepositional phrases is a good way to add specific details to your writing. Notice the kinds of details the author includes in the passage below.

> **LITERARY MODEL**
>
> Then one day they overheard the neighbors whispering: someone had come from Seoul with a permit from the governor-general's office to catch cranes as some kind of specimens. Then and there the two boys had dashed off to the field. That they would be found out and punished had no longer mattered; all they cared about was the fate of their crane.
>
> —Hwang Sunwŏn, "Cranes"

ADVERB PHRASES

ADJECTIVE PHRASES

PHRASES

❸ Practice and Apply

A. CONCEPT CHECK: Prepositional Phrases

Write each prepositional phrase and tell whether it is an adjective phrase or an adverb phrase. Then identify the word or words the prepositional phrase modifies.

Example: Birds are the only animals with feathers.
Answer: with feathers, adjective phrase, animals

> **The Bird Book of Records**
> **1.** The adult bee hummingbird belongs in any bird record book.
> **2.** Its length of approximately two inches makes it the earth's smallest bird.
> **3.** It and all other hummingbirds can hover like helicopters.
> **4.** They are also the only birds with backward flying ability.
> **5.** Another bird for the record books is the ostrich.
> **6.** At up to eight feet tall, the ostrich is the world's largest bird.
> **7.** The flightless ostrich is also a record holder for speed.
> **8.** Its 40-mph running speed makes it the fastest bird on land.
> **9.** A peregrine falcon's diving speed is over 200 mph.
> **10.** A peregrine falcon's air speed beats the ostrich's land speed by more than 160 mph.

➡ For a SELF-CHECK and more practice, see the EXERCISE BANK, p. 607.

B. WRITING: Adding Details

Rewrite each sentence by adding a prepositional phrase that begins with the preposition shown in parentheses.

Example: We had our hummingbird feeder hanging. (under)
Answer: We had our hummingbird feeder hanging under the deck.

1. So we could see it better, we moved the hummingbird feeder. (near)
2. The first hummingbird we saw hovered. (by)
3. The second hummingbird flitted quickly. (around)
4. Soon the two hummingbirds were drinking. (from)
5. We took lots of pictures. (of)

Appositives and Appositive Phrases

❶ Here's the Idea

▶ **An appositive is a noun or pronoun that identifies or renames another noun or pronoun.** An **appositive phrase** is made up of an appositive plus its modifiers.

APPOSITIVE

Leonardo da Vinci **, the great Renaissance painter,** was also an inventor.   APPOSITIVE PHRASE

Essential and Nonessential Appositives

An **essential** (or **restrictive**) **appositive** provides information that is needed to identify the preceding noun or pronoun.

The Italian artist **Leonardo da Vinci** drew a flying machine with flapping wings around 1500. (ESSENTIAL APPOSITIVE)

A **nonessential** (or **nonrestrictive**) **appositive** adds extra information about a noun or pronoun whose meaning is already clear. Eliminating the appositive does not change the basic meaning. Notice that nonessential appositives are set off with commas.

Leonardo da Vinci **, an Italian artist,** drew a flying machine with flapping wings around 1500. (NONESSENTIAL APPOSITIVE)

You as the writer determine whether the appositive is essential to the meaning of your sentence. If it is, do not use commas.

❷ Why It Matters in Writing

Appositives can draw attention to the qualities of a person, place, or thing that are important or relevant for your writing purpose.

PROFESSIONAL MODEL

In *It's a Wonderful Life*, one of the most popular movies ever made, a character named Clarence wants to get his wings. Clarence, an angel, must accomplish this goal by helping the character George Bailey realize what a wonderful life he has had.

NONESSENTIAL APPOSITIVES

ESSENTIAL APPOSITIVE

❸ Practice and Apply

A. CONCEPT CHECK: Appositives and Appositive Phrases

Rewrite each sentence, adding the appositive or appositive phrase shown in parentheses. Include commas if necessary.

> **The Wright Brothers Fly**
> 1. The Wright brothers owned a bicycle shop in Dayton, Ohio, in the late 1800s. (Wilbur and Orville)
> 2. Wilbur became interested in flying after reading a book about gliders. (the older brother)
> 3. The book was written by the German engineer. (Otto Lilienthal)
> 4. The Wright brothers then started building their own gliders in 1899. (engineless aircraft)
> 5. They tested their gliders on North Carolina's Outer Banks. (an area known for its steady winds)
> 6. In 1903 the brothers built their first biplane. (the *Flyer*)
> 7. On December 17, they flew the *Flyer*. (the world's first successful airplane)
> 8. This now renowned event was not officially recognized at the time. (the first airplane flight)
> 9. The aviator made his first official public flights while in France in 1908. (Wilbur Wright)
> 10. Today the *Flyer* is displayed at the National Air and Space Museum. (the Wrights' original airplane)

➡ **For a SELF-CHECK and more practice, see the EXERCISE BANK, p. 607.**

Write three sentences modeled after sentences 2, 3, and 4 above.

B. REVISING: Adding Information About Nouns

Combine each pair of sentences by incorporating the information in the second sentence as an appositive in the first sentence.

1. Old-time air shows featured stunts by performers such as Lincoln Beachey. Beachey was a famous daredevil pilot.
2. Today the world's largest air show is held in Oshkosh, Wisconsin. It is the Experimental Aircraft Association Annual International Fly-In Convention and Sport Exhibition.
3. For the yearly Fly-In, as many as 750,000 people visit Oshkosh. Oshkosh is a city of about 50,000.

Verbals: Participles

❶ Here's the Idea

A **verbal** is a verb form that acts as a noun, an adjective, or an adverb. Verbals may be participles, gerunds, or infinitives.

▶ **A participle is a verb form that functions as an adjective.** Like adjectives, participles modify nouns or pronouns.

MODIFIES   MODIFIES

Smiling, he ate another fried chicken wing.
     ⬆ PRONOUN   ⬆ NOUN

Participles may be **present participles** or **past participles**.

> **LITERARY MODEL**
>
> It [*Tyrannosaurus rex*] came on great oiled, resilient, striding legs.
>
> —Ray Bradbury, "A Sound of Thunder"
>
> PAST PARTICIPLE
> PRESENT PARTICIPLE
> WORD MODIFIED

A **participial phrase** consists of a participle plus its modifiers and complements. The whole phrase below modifies *he*.

MODIFIER ➘   ⬋ COMPLEMENT
Foolishly wasting time, he studied the broken creature.

To learn about the present and past participle forms of verbs, see p. 130.

❷ Why It Matters in Writing

By using modifiers made from action verbs, you can make your descriptions more lively and vivid.

> **LITERARY MODEL**
>
> And then, for some reason, Millicent thought of the heather birds. Swooping carefree over the moors, they would go singing and crying out across the great spaces of air . . . their wings flashing quick and purple in the bright sun.
>
> —Sylvia Plath, "Initiation"
>
> PARTICIPIAL PHRASES
> WORDS MODIFIED

❸ Practice and Apply

A. CONCEPT CHECK: Participles

Write the participial phrase in each sentence, and indicate whether it contains a present participle or a past participle.

Example: Most celebrated of all the insects, butterflies are admired by many people.
Answer: Most celebrated of all the insects, past participle

The Delicate Butterfly

1. Appreciated for their color and grace, butterflies are one of nature's glories.
2. Often bursting with color, their spectacular wings are covered with thousands of tiny scales.
3. In fact, these scales are the basis for their scientific name, *Lepidoptera*, meaning "scaly wings."
4. Visiting gardens, the butterflies flit among the flowers.
5. Driven by instinct, they use the flowers as meal stops.
6. Uncoiling their proboscises, they pierce the flowers.
7. Then, sucking through these straws, they feast on nectar.
8. Pollinating at the same time, the butterflies help the flowers.
9. Picking up pollen dust on their feet, they move from flower to flower.
10. On each, they wipe their feet and thus spread the pollen needed for reproduction.

➡ **For a SELF-CHECK and more practice, see the EXERCISE BANK, p. 608.**

CHALLENGE

In the above ten sentences, identify the noun or pronoun that each participial phrase modifies.

B. REVISING: Using Participial Phrases to Combine Sentences

Use participial phrases to combine each set of sentences and achieve a livelier tone.

Example: The western pygmy blue butterfly is one of the smallest butterflies. It has a three-eighths-inch wingspan.
Answer: Having only a three-eighths-inch wingspan, the western pygmy blue is one of the smallest butterflies.

1. The Queen Alexandra's birdwing is the largest butterfly. It has an 11-inch wingspan.
2. The twin-spotted sphinx displays large eyespots on bright wings. It uses them to ward off predators.
3. The Indian leaf butterfly has a perfect camouflage. It is shaped and colored like a leaf.

LESSON 4 **Verbals: Gerunds**

❶ Here's the Idea

▶ **A gerund is a verb form that ends in *-ing* and functions as a noun.** A **gerund phrase** consists of a gerund plus its modifiers and complements.

GERUND

Flying an airplane while tired can be dangerous.

GERUND PHRASE

Like nouns, gerunds and gerund phrases can act as subjects, complements (direct objects, indirect objects, or predicate nominatives), or objects of prepositions.

Gerund Phrases	
Function	**Example**
Subject	**Flying** got Icarus into trouble.
Direct object	Icarus tried **using wings made of wax.**
Indirect object	He wanted to give **flying like a bird** a chance.
Predicate nominative	His mistake was **straying too close to the sun.**
Object of preposition	The result of **doing so** was melted wings and a dip in the sea.

Don't confuse a gerund with a present participle. A gerund, as in the sentences above, can be replaced by the word *something*.

❷ Why It Matters in Writing

Gerunds and gerund phrases let you turn verbs into nouns so that you can talk about actions and activities as things. Using gerunds can improve the fluency of your sentences and make them more concise.

STUDENT MODEL

DRAFT

Some people write poetry. Pegasus—the mythical horse with wings—could be ridden. The two experiences have often been compared.

REVISION

Writing poetry has often been compared to **riding Pegasus**—the mythical horse with wings.

❸ Practice and Apply

A. CONCEPT CHECK: Gerunds

Write the gerund or gerund phrase that appears in each sentence. Then tell whether it is a subject, a direct object, an indirect object, a predicate nominative, or an object of a preposition.

Example: Singing is more than an expression of joy for birds.
Answer: singing, subject

Bird Songs
1. Birds sing as a means of communicating with others.
2. Honking during migration, for example, helps geese guide other flock members.
3. Screeching by one bird may alert others to a predator.
4. The response to this alarm call is often dashing for cover.
5. Males announce territory claims through robust singing.
6. With elaborate songs, they often try attracting females.
7. The male winter wren's specialty is crooning its courtship song.
8. The female winter wren, in turn, communicates with her young by warbling a quiet song.
9. Vocalizing isn't the only way birds can communicate.
10. The rat-a-tat drumming of bills on trees announces the presence of woodpeckers.

➡ **For a SELF-CHECK and more practice, see the EXERCISE BANK, p. 608.**

B. WRITING: Using Gerunds to Improve Sentence Fluency

Combine each pair of sentences below, turning the underlined words into a gerund phrase. Give the phrase the function indicated in parentheses.

Example: The young man wore wingtips. This made him feel older. (subject)
Answer: Wearing wingtips made the young man feel older.

1. The small boy released the fireflies. He enjoyed it. (direct object)
2. One of my favorite things to do in summer is this. I grill chicken on the beach. (predicate nominative)
3. I love to hang by the teeth from an airplane. You should give it a try. (indirect object)
4. Have you ever read Poe's "The Raven"? It is an awesome experience. (subject)
5. Patrice entertained her friends. She played her favorite CD from the band *Wings*. (object of preposition *by*)

Verbals: Infinitives

❶ Here's the Idea

▶ **An infinitive is a verb form, usually beginning with the word *to*, that can act as a noun, an adjective, or an adverb.** An **infinitive phrase** consists of an infinitive plus any modifiers and complements.

↱INFINITIVE

To find water striders, look in a freshwater pond.

INFINITIVE PHRASE

Infinitive Phrases	
Function	**Example**
Noun (Subject)	**To skate along the surface of the water** is easy for the water strider.
Noun (Direct object)	Water striders need **to find food in the water without sinking themselves.**
Noun (Predicate nominative)	The trick is **to use surface tension for support.**
Adjective	The water strider is an interesting insect **to watch on a calm summer day.**
Adverb	**To detect insects falling into the water near them,** water striders use sense organs on their legs.

❷ Why It Matters in Writing

By using infinitive phrases to combine sentences, you can sharpen the relationship between ideas.

STUDENT MODEL

DRAFT

Many moth species have evolved with an owl-face pattern on their wings. The pattern scares away birds.

REVISION

Many moth species have evolved with an owl-face pattern on their wings that serves **to scare away birds.**

❸ Practice and Apply

A. CONCEPT CHECK: Infinitives

Write each infinitive or infinitive phrase and indicate whether it acts as a noun, an adjective, or an adverb.

Example: Honeybees have the ability to make large quantities of honey and wax.

Answer: to make large quantities of honey and wax, adjective

Honeybees

1. A queen bee, some drones, and many worker bees are needed to form a honeybee colony.
2. The queen bee's main job is to lay eggs.
3. The drones, or male bees, exist only to mate.
4. The all-female worker bees have a lot more work to do.
5. They build the honeycomb as a place to raise young bees.
6. They also use it to store food, or honey.
7. To make their honey, bees combine their own enzymes with nectar from flowers.
8. Many animals, including bears, love to eat the honey.
9. They are eager to raid a hive.
10. To protect the hive, worker bees guard its entrance.

➡ **For a SELF-CHECK and more practice, see the EXERCISE BANK, p. 609.**

B. WRITING: Sharpening Ideas

Combine each pair of sentences below, changing one of them into an infinitive phrase.

Example: Dragonflies have evolved four large wings. The wings help them fly swiftly.

Answer: To help them fly swiftly, dragonflies have evolved four large wings.

1. Dragonflies can fly 50 to 60 miles per hour. They escape predators.
2. A dragonfly instinctively shapes its six legs like a basket. It captures insects in the basket.
3. A dragonfly nymph must molt, or shed its skin, 10 or more times. Through molting the nymph becomes an adult.

CHAPTER 3

A. Verbals Write each underlined portion of the passage below and identify the kind of verbal or verbal phrase it is.

LITERARY MODEL

As the clouds gathered outside, **(1)** <u>unnoticed</u>, the ringmaster cracked his whip, shouted his introduction, and pointed to the ceiling of the tent, where the **(2)** <u>Flying</u> Avalons were perched. They loved **(3)** <u>to drop gracefully from nowhere</u>, like two **(4)** <u>sparkling</u> birds, and blow kisses as they threw off their **(5)** <u>plumed</u> helmets and high-collared capes. . . . In the final vignette of their act, they actually would kiss in midair, pausing, **(6)** <u>almost hovering</u> as they swooped past one another. . . .

Anna was pregnant at the time, seven months and **(7)** <u>hardly showing</u>, her stomach muscles were that strong. It seems incredible that she would work high above the ground when any fall could be so dangerous, but the explanation—I know from **(8)** <u>watching her go blind</u>—is that my mother lives comfortably in extreme elements.

Harry launched himself and swung, once, twice, in huge **(9)** <u>calibrated</u> beats across space. He hung from his knees and on the third swing stretched wide his arms, held his hands out **(10)** <u>to receive his pregnant wife as she dove from her shining bar</u>.

—Louise Erdrich, "The Leap"

Specify the function of each underlined verbal or verbal phrase in its sentence in the passage above.

B. Rewrite Sentences, Using Verbals Combine each pair of sentences below, changing one of them into a verbal phrase.

1. Wasps are insects with wings. They are related to bees and ants.
2. Female wasps use their stingers for protection. With the stingers, they defend their nests against predators.
3. People often mistake yellow jackets for bees. This is a common error with sometimes painful results.

In your 📁 **Working Portfolio,** find the paragraph you wrote for the **Write Away** on page 64. Using verbal phrases, combine some of your sentences to eliminate unnecessary words.

Placement of Phrases

❶ Here's the Idea

When a phrase functions as a modifier in a sentence, you need to make clear what the phrase modifies in order to avoid confusing the reader.

A **misplaced modifier** is a word or phrase that is placed so far away from the word it modifies that the meaning of the sentence is unclear or incorrect.

Draft: The **ranger** explained how to find ducks **in her office.**
(WHY WERE THERE DUCKS IN HER OFFICE?)

Revision: In her office, the **ranger** explained how to find ducks.

A **dangling modifier** results when the word being modified is missing from the sentence.

Draft: **Coming home with the groceries,** our parrot said, "Hello!" (THE PARROT SHOPS?)

Revision: Coming home with the groceries, we heard our parrot say, "Hello!"

> **Here's How** Fixing a Misplaced or Dangling Modifier
>
> 1. Find the word the phrase modifies and move the phrase as close to that word as possible.
> 2. If the word the phrase should modify is missing from the sentence, add the word.

❷ Why It Matters in Writing

Misplaced and dangling modifiers result in writing that is confusing and sometimes unintentionally humorous.

STUDENT MODEL

DRAFT	REVISION
Peacocks are the favorite birds of many people, **with their colorful tails.** **Prancing around in search of a mate,** most observers are charmed.	**With their colorful tails, peacocks** are the favorite birds of many people. **Prancing around in search of a mate, peacocks** charm most observers.

❸ Practice and Apply

A. CONCEPT CHECK: Placement of Phrases

Rewrite each sentence below that has a misplaced or dangling modifier. If a sentence has neither, write *Correct*.

Example: Flying in a car-plane, the cornfields looked tiny.
Answer: Flying in a car-plane, my grandfather thought the cornfields looked tiny.

The Flying Car

1. Combining a car and an airplane into one vehicle for many inventors was a long-time dream.

2. Called "flying flivvers," Ford and other automobile manufacturers produced prototypes of flying cars.

3. These car-planes were a novelty for pilots including models with removable wings.

4. Using a flying car, trips could be made by air or the highway.

5. Long ago, one model, the Aerocar, was featured on a TV show.

6. Although produced from 1946 to 1967, the Aerocar company sold only five cars.

7. Less sturdy and less spacious than regular cars, comfortable ground transportation was not provided.

8. The car-planes had a problem with safety, handling worse than conventional airplanes.

9. Priced sky-high, flying cars were not only unsafe, but also expensive.

10. Flying cars never really caught on with the American public, making more sense in theory than in practice.

➡ **For a SELF-CHECK and more practice, see the EXERCISE BANK, p. 609.**

B. REVISING: Fixing Misplaced and Dangling Modifiers

Fix any dangling or misplaced modifiers in the following paragraph.

STUDENT MODEL

> In their heyday from the late 1930s to the early 1940s, people flew from Europe to the United States in "flying boats." The flying boats had large staterooms and served full-course meals offering many of the same luxuries as ocean liners.

PHRASES

Sentence Diagramming: Phrases

Mad Mapper

① Here's the Idea

Diagramming phrases can help you understand how phrases function in a sentence and enable you to use them more effectively in your writing.

Watch me for diagramming tips!

Prepositional Phrases

- Write the preposition on a slanted line below the word the prepositional phrase modifies.
- Write the object of the preposition on a horizontal line attached to the slanted line and parallel to the main line.
- Write words that modify the object of the preposition on slanted lines below the object.

Adjective Phrase

The nightingale sang a song of true love.

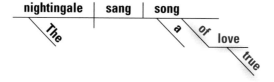

This adjective phrase modifies a noun used as a direct object. Adjective phrases can also modify pronouns.

Adverb Phrase

The eagle perched on a cliff by the sea.

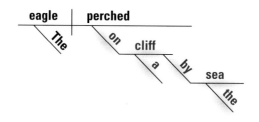

The first adverb phrase modifies a verb. The second phrase modifies the object in the first phrase.

A. CONCEPT CHECK: Prepositional Phrases

Diagram these sentences using what you have learned.

1. The farmer built the birdhouse of his dreams.
2. A falcon flew over my house.

Appositives and Appositive Phrases

Write the appositive in parentheses after the word it identifies or renames. Attach words that modify the appositive to it in the usual way.

The dipper, an aquatic bird of North America, can walk underwater.

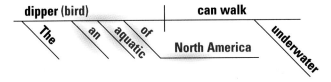

B. CONCEPT CHECK: Appositives and Appositive Phrases

Diagram these sentences using what you have learned.

1. The ostrich, a large bird from Africa, can run fast.
2. The kiwi, a bird from New Zealand, cannot fly.

Participial Phrases

- The participle curves over an angled line below the word it modifies.
- Diagram complements on the horizontal part of the angled line in the usual way.
- Write modifiers on slanted lines below the words they modify.

Suddenly leaving the flock, the goose disappeared.

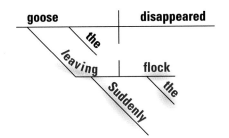

This is a present participial phrase. Past participial phrases are diagrammed in the same way. Notice how the participle is slightly curved.

Gerund Phrases

- The gerund curves over a line that looks like a step.
- With a vertical forked line, connect the step to the part of the diagram that corresponds to the role of the gerund phrase in the sentence.
- Diagram complements and modifiers in the usual way.

Flying a plane successfully usually requires experience.

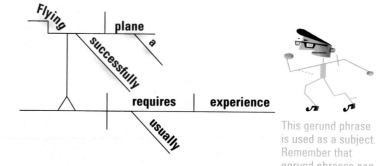

This gerund phrase is used as a subject. Remember that gerund phrases can be used in any way a noun can.

Infinitive Phrases

- Write the infinitive on an angled line, with the word *to* on the slanted part and the verb on the horizontal part.
- When the infinitive or infinitive phrase functions as a noun, use a vertical forked line to connect the infinitive to the part of the diagram that corresponds to its role in the sentence.
- When the phrase functions as a modifier, place the angled line below the word it modifies.

Infinitive Phrase as Noun

I want to see a spotted sandpiper soon.

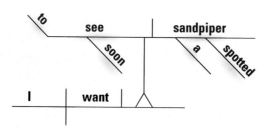

This infinitive phrase is a direct object. An infinitive phrase acting as a noun can also be a subject or a predicate nominative.

Infinitive Phrase as Modifier

It is time to launch my hang glider.

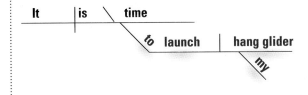

This infinitive phrase is an adjective modifying *time*. An infinitive phrase acting as a modifier can also be an adverb.

C. CONCEPT CHECK: Verbal Phrases

Diagram these sentences using what you have learned.

1. Camouflaged completely, the ptarmigan can hide easily.
2. Squawking loudly, the geese took off.
3. Hummingbirds enjoy drinking nectar from flowers.
4. We hope to see a yellow-shafted flicker today.
5. To find interesting things with wings is easy.

D. MIXED REVIEW: Diagramming

Diagram the following sentences. Look for all types of phrases.

1. The penguin, a flightless bird, can swim underwater.
2. Swimming swiftly requires strength.
3. Penguins breed in a rookery.
4. Incubated carefully, a penguin egg will hatch normally.
5. To see an emperor penguin someday would be a thrill.
6. Scientists have worked for years to understand penguins.
7. Penguins live in Chicago's Lincoln Park Zoo.
8. Swimming in cold water, they beat the summer heat.
9. People enjoy watching penguins through underwater windows.
10. Visitors come for miles to see birds in tuxedos.

Grammar in Literature

Enriching Description

Writers often use phrases to add descriptive details, streamline sentence structures, and improve sentence fluency. In the following excerpt, the author paints a picture of a young girl's impressions as she watches a white heron. What stands out in this passage is the use of phrases to develop a mood and reveal feelings.

A White Heron

—Sarah Orne Jewett

Springtime (1885), Lionel Percy Smythe. Private collection. Photo by Christopher Newall.

The child gives a long sigh a minute later when a company of <u>shouting catbirds</u> comes also to the tree, and <u>vexed by their fluttering and lawlessness</u>, the solemn heron goes away. She knows his secret now, the wild, light, slender bird that floats and wavers, and goes back <u>like an arrow</u> presently <u>to his home</u> <u>in the green world beneath</u>. Then Sylvia, <u>well satisfied</u>, makes her perilous way down again, <u>not daring to look far below the branch she stands on</u>, ready to cry sometimes because her fingers ache and her lamed feet slip. <u>Wondering over and over again what the stranger would say to her</u>, and what he would think when she told him how to find his way straight to the heron's nest.

> **Participial phrases** contrast the noisy catbirds with the solemn heron.

> **Prepositional phrases** express the beauty of the heron and his home.

> Well-developed **participial phrases** give specific indications of Sylvia's mixed emotions.

Using Phrases to Improve Description

Using phrases, writers can combine sentences to make their writing more fluid and concise. Each type of phrase can also help writers add specific kinds of detail.

Prepositional phrases	Use to express relationships of location, direction, time, or manner
Appositive phrases	Use to focus on the qualities of a person, place, or thing that are most important for your writing purpose
Participial phrases	Use to make your descriptions more lively and energetic by adding action words as modifiers
Gerund phrases	Use to talk about actions and activities as things
Infinitive phrases	Use to sharpen the relationship between ideas and make your writing more concise

PHRASES

PRACTICE AND APPLY: Combining Sentences

Combine each pair of sentences, turning the second one into the kind of phrase indicated in parentheses.

1. Herons preen the plumage of their prospective mates. They do this as part of their courtship ritual. (prepositional)
2. Herons feed in flocks when the food supply is limited. Herons are birds that usually prefer to be solitary. (appositive)
3. Herons learn where the good fishing spots are. They watch other fish-eaters from afar. (participial)
4. This is the normal behavior pattern for male and female herons. They build their nest as a joint project. (gerund)
5. Males and females also split responsibility for sitting on the eggs. This enables both of them to eat. (infinitive)

When you are done, compare your answers with a partner's.

Choose a draft from your 📁 **Working Portfolio** and revise it by combining sentences, using at least three kinds of phrases.

A. Phrases Read the selection. Then, for each underlined group of words, identify the kind of phrase it is and how it functions in its sentence.

PROFESSIONAL MODEL

(1) <u>Putting on a display to attract and impress a potential mate</u> is a common behavior pattern among the males of many bird species. (2) <u>Adding action to their natural gifts of brilliant plumage and melodious song</u>, they sometimes also strut, dance, and occasionally offer (3) <u>carefully selected</u> gifts of fruit, feathers, or flowers. But the bowerbird's strategy is (4) <u>to do something entirely different</u>. He is not interested in (5) <u>building a permanent nest</u>, but wants only (6) <u>to create a temporary "bower."</u>

"Come (7) <u>into my parlor</u>," the male bowerbird seems to beckon to females that stop (8) <u>to admire the mating courtyard he has constructed</u>. "Look at my beautiful creation, (9) <u>a perfect love nest</u>, and behold all the decorations I've gathered: bright feathers, colorful straws, bottle caps, leaves, and shells." He might add that, aside from humans, no other creature in the world rivals his willingness (10) <u>to go to so much trouble simply to please a mate</u>.

B. Misplaced and Dangling Modifiers Read the following paragraph for misplaced or dangling modifiers. Then, rewrite the paragraph to correct the errors.

Of the East Indies and southeastern Asia, the common name for the so-called flying lizard is flying dragon. Using outstretched folds of skin, the flying dragon does not actually fly but glides. Its "wings" fold close to its body when resting. The males attract females by displaying their colorful "wings" during the mating season.

Choose the letter of the term that correctly identifies each numbered part of this passage.

Sleeping with one eye open and one-half of the brain awake is an
(1)
unusual ability of birds. This phenomenon, unihemispheric slow-wave
(2)   (3)
sleep, allows a bird to watch for predators as it sleeps.
                     (4)
Recently, researchers at Indiana State University investigated this
                        (5)
phenomenon in the laboratory. They showed that birds are actually able to
             (6)
increase their unihemispheric sleeping time when there is a greater risk of
(7)
predators. By studying ducks, they learned that birds vulnerable to
            (8)
predators spend more than twice the amount of time dozing in
                                                     (9)
unihemispheric sleep than those not in danger. Birds using unihemispheric
                                                        (10)
sleep can literally "keep an eye out" for their enemies.

---

1. A. gerund phrase
   B. infinitive phrase
   C. appositive phrase
   D. participial phrase

2. A. participial phrase
   B. gerund phrase
   C. prepositional phrase
   D. infinitive phrase

3. A. infinitive phrase
   B. appositive phrase
   C. gerund phrase
   D. prepositional phrase

4. A. adjective prepositional phrase
   B. adverb prepositional phrase
   C. essential appositive phrase
   D. infinitive phrase

5. A. adjective prepositional phrase
   B. adverb infinitive phrase
   C. adverb prepositional phrase
   D. adjective infinitive phrase

6. A. adverb infinitive phrase
   B. adjective prepositional phrase
   C. adjective infinitive phrase
   D. adverb prepositional phrase

7. A. adjective infinitive phrase
   B. adjective prepositional phrase
   C. adverb infinitive phrase
   D. adverb prepositional phrase

8. A. gerund phrase acting as subject
   B. gerund phrase acting as predicate nominative
   C. gerund phrase acting as direct object
   D. gerund phrase acting as object of a preposition

9. A. participial phrase modifying *they*
   B. gerund phrase acting as object of a preposition
   C. participial phrase modifying *time*
   D. gerund phrase acting as direct object

10. A. gerund phrase
    B. appositive phrase
    C. past participial phrase
    D. present participial phrase

PHRASES

Student Help Desk

Phrases at a Glance

Kind of Phrase	Functions as	Example
Prepositional phrase	Adjective	The plane **on the left** is mine.
	Adverb	Ras flew **over the mountain.**
Appositive phrase	Noun	Mr. Foy, **the pilot,** is here.
Participial phrase	Adjective	Bats **wearing hats** look funny.
Gerund phrase	Noun	**Flying a helicopter** is exciting.
Infinitive phrase	Noun	Sue loves **to fly her ultralight.**
	Adjective	Crashing is something **to avoid.**
	Adverb	Ari flies **to relax.**

Clarifying What Is Modified — Up in the Air

Misplaced Modifiers

I was looking for the keys to the car **in the kitchen.**

(WHY IS THE CAR IN THE KITCHEN? THE WORD BEING MODIFIED IS *LOOKING*.)

I was looking **in the kitchen** for the keys to the car.

Dangling Modifiers

While talking on the telephone, my flying dragon ate my cereal.

(WHO WAS TALKING ON THE TELEPHONE? *I* WAS. THIS WORD IS NOT IN THE SENTENCE.)

While I was talking on the telephone,
my flying dragon ate my cereal.

Prepositions

about	as	down	off	toward
above	at	for	on	under
across	before	from	onto	underneath
after	behind	in	out	until
against	below	inside	over	up
along	beside	into	past	upon
among	between	near	through	with
around	by	of	to	without

Shoe by MacNelly — Dangling Participles

PHRASES

The Bottom Line

Checklist for Phrases

Have I . . .

____ used phrases to add details and to elaborate on my ideas?

____ used phrases to combine sentences and use fewer words?

____ used phrases to improve sentence fluency?

____ moved misplaced modifiers to make what they refer to clear?

____ added needed words to sentences with dangling modifiers?

Clauses and Sentence Structure

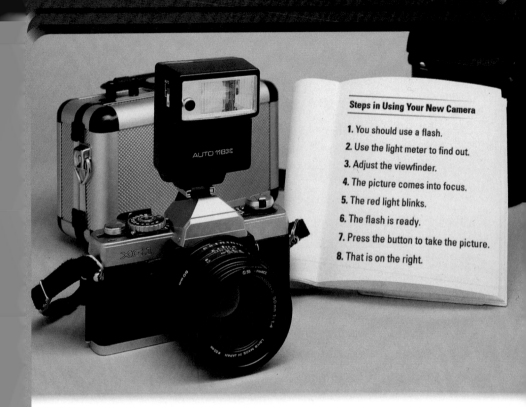

Steps in Using Your New Camera

1. You should use a flash.
2. Use the light meter to find out.
3. Adjust the viewfinder.
4. The picture comes into focus.
5. The red light blinks.
6. The flash is ready.
7. Press the button to take the picture.
8. That is on the right.

Theme: Inventions

What Am I Supposed to Do?

Have you ever tried to figure out how to do something from poorly written instructions? To improve the instructions in the illustration above, you could combine sentences to show the relationships between ideas: "Use the light meter to find out whether you should use the flash. Turn the lens until the picture comes into focus. When the red light blinks, the flash is ready. Press the button that is on the right to take the picture."

In this chapter, you will learn how to use clauses to construct sentences that show relationships between ideas clearly.

Write Away: How It Works

Write a paragraph explaining how one of your favorite inventions works. Put the explanation in your  **Working Portfolio.**

Grammar Coach

Choose the letter that correctly identifies each numbered part of this passage.

We take zippers for granted, but think about how much easier our lives
(1)
have become since zippers were invented slightly more than 100 years
(2)
ago. The first zipper was patented by Whitcomb L. Judson, an American
(3)
inventor, in 1893. Judson's zipper was called a clasp locker, and it had a

series of hooks and eyes that fastened together with a slider. Today's
(4)
zipper also has a slider, but it fastens together rows of snugly fitting teeth.
(5)
These rows remain fastened until the slider is pulled back, unlocking the
(6)
teeth. The toothed zipper that we use today was invented by Gideon
(7)
Sundback in 1913. The word *zipper* was not used until 1922, when a

company marketed galoshes that were called Zippers. They were given
(8)
that name because their sliding fasteners could close so quickly. Judson
(9)
and Sundback rarely get the credit they deserve for what they contributed
(10)
to modern life.

1. A. independent clause
   B. subordinate clause
   C. simple sentence
   D. compound sentence

2. A. independent clause
   B. subordinate clause
   C. simple sentence
   D. compound sentence

3. A. simple sentence
   B. compound sentence
   C. complex sentence
   D. compound-complex sentence

4. A. independent clause
   B. adjective clause
   C. adverb clause
   D. noun clause

5. A. simple sentence
   B. compound sentence
   C. complex sentence
   D. compound-complex sentence

6. A. independent clause
   B. adjective clause
   C. adverb clause
   D. noun clause

7. A. adjective clause
   B. adverb clause
   C. noun clause
   D. independent clause

8. A. essential adjective clause
   B. nonessential adjective clause
   C. noun clause
   D. independent clause

9. A. simple sentence
   B. compound sentence
   C. complex sentence
   D. compound-complex sentence

10. A. noun clause as subject
    B. noun clause as direct object
    C. noun clause as indirect object
    D. noun clause as object of a preposition

Kinds of Clauses

① Here's the Idea

▶ **A clause is a group of words that contains a subject and a verb.**

Professor Hardy is a brilliant inventor.
　　　　　↑ SUBJECT　↑ VERB

Independent Clauses

An **independent** (or **main**) **clause** expresses a complete thought and can stand alone as a sentence.

> **Professor Hardy is a brilliant inventor.**
> INDEPENDENT CLAUSE

Independent clauses can be connected by words like *and* and *but* to make sentences that express related ideas.

> **She is an inventor** and **her husband is a patent attorney.**
> INDEPENDENT CLAUSE　　　　　INDEPENDENT CLAUSE

Subordinate Clauses

A **subordinate** (or **dependent**) **clause** contains a subject and a verb but does not express a complete thought and cannot stand alone as a sentence. Subordinate clauses are introduced by such words as *because, that, when,* and *which* (see following pages).

> **Because she is imaginative**
> SUBORDINATE CLAUSE

By itself, a subordinate clause is a sentence fragment. For a complete thought to be expressed, a subordinate clause must be part of a sentence that contains an independent clause.

> **Because she is imaginative,** **her inventions are unusual.**
> SUBORDINATE CLAUSE　　　　　INDEPENDENT CLAUSE

> **She creates gadgets** **that no one has ever thought of before.**
> INDEPENDENT CLAUSE　　　　　SUBORDINATE CLAUSE

 Do not confuse a subordinate clause with a verbal phrase, which does not have a subject and a verb:

She creates gadgets, inventing mostly household tools.

For more on verbals, see pp. 71–76.

You can add important details to your writing through the use of subordinate clauses. In the cartoon below, Snoopy tries to improve on his usual beginning for a story—"It was a dark and stormy night"—by adding a subordinate clause. How well do you think he succeeds?

Peanuts by Charles Schulz

❷ Why It Matters in Writing

Recognizing independent and subordinate clauses will help you avoid one of the most common kinds of sentence fragments: a subordinate clause accidentally written as a sentence.

STUDENT MODEL

DRAFT

The synthetic fiber nylon generated great excitement. When it was introduced in 1939. Women soon came to prefer nylon stockings. Because they were much more durable than silk stockings.

FRAGMENTS

REVISION

When it was introduced in 1939, the synthetic fiber nylon generated great excitement. Women soon came to prefer nylon stockings because they were much more durable than silk stockings.

CLAUSES

❸ Practice and Apply

A. CONCEPT CHECK: Kinds of Clauses

Write the subordinate clause in each sentence below. If there is no subordinate clause, write *None*.

Good Car, Bad Car

1. Some useful inventions have caused serious problems.

2. A good example is the automobile, which became popular in the early 1900s.

3. The automobile is now one of our most important means of transportation, but it also causes much of our air pollution.

4. Some people who worry about our environment believe in restricting the use of cars.

5. They think that people should not be able to drive cars in certain places.

6. Others want to solve the problem by creating new inventions.

7. When we have better engines and fuels, they think, the problem will disappear.

8. Human beings, who are inventors by nature, will continue to create new inventions.

9. We should anticipate the effects that inventions can have.

10. If we do, perhaps future generations will not be endangered.

➡ **For a SELF-CHECK and more practice, see the EXERCISE BANK, p. 610.**

Write original sentences that imitate the clause structure of the first five sentences in exercise A.

B. REVISING: Eliminating Fragments

Rewrite the paragraph below, combining the fragments with complete sentences.

STUDENT MODEL

It's a Good Thing

   The emission control system is one invention. That has reduced air pollution from automobile exhausts. The system helps to eliminate harmful gases. Which can escape into the air and affect its quality. In many states, cars are inspected. If a car does not pass a series of tests that measure its emissions. It must be repaired and retested.

Adjective and Adverb Clauses

❶ Here's the Idea

Subordinate clauses can be adjective, adverb, or noun clauses.

Adjective Clauses

▶ **An adjective clause is a subordinate clause that is used as an adjective to modify a noun or a pronoun.**

MODIFIES NOUN

Willy Higinbotham is the scientist who invented the first computer game.
ADJECTIVE CLAUSE

MODIFIES PRONOUN

It was he who developed computer tennis.
ADJECTIVE CLAUSE

An adjective clause is introduced by a **relative pronoun** or by a **relative adverb.** These words are called relative because they relate adjective clauses to the words they modify.

Words Used to Introduce Adjective Clauses	
Relative pronouns	that, who, whom, whose, which
Relative adverbs	where, when, why

Have you seen the computer that Higinbotham used?

Have you seen the desk where Higinbotham sat?

Essential and Nonessential Adjective Clauses

An **essential** (or **restrictive**) adjective clause provides information that is necessary to identify the preceding noun or pronoun.

Tourists can visit the laboratory that employed Higinbotham.

A **nonessential** (or **nonrestrictive**) adjective clause adds additional information about a noun or pronoun whose meaning is already clear. Notice that nonessential clauses are set off with commas.

Brookhaven National Laboratory, which employed Higinbotham, is in Upton, New York.

That or *which*? Use *that* to introduce essential clauses. Use *which* to introduce nonessential clauses.

Adverb Clauses

> An adverb clause is a subordinate clause that modifies a verb, an adjective, or an adverb.

MODIFIES VERB

Charles Babbage paved the way for the computer **when he devised his "analytical engine."**

MODIFIES ADJECTIVE

Babbage's invention was important **because it proved machines' ability to perform mathematical operations.**

Computers can solve complicated math problems faster **than people can.**

MODIFIES ADVERB

Words Used to Introduce Adverb Clauses	
Subordinating conjunctions	when, because, than, where, after, before, although

For a more complete list of subordinating conjunctions, see p. 27.

❷ Why It Matters in Writing

Adjective and adverb clauses can supply details necessary to explain, support, and connect your ideas.

STUDENT MODEL

DRAFT

The first microwave ovens were too big for homes. These ovens weighed 750 pounds and stood five and a half feet tall. Moreover, they had to be attached to a source of water. These huge ovens cost more than most people could afford.

REVISION

When the first microwave ovens were introduced in 1953, they were too big for homes. These ovens weighed 750 pounds and stood five and a half feet tall. Moreover, they had to be attached to a source of water because they overheated very easily. These huge ovens, which cost $3,000, were too expensive for most people.

> Provides a specific time frame

> Explains why they needed water

> Supports the claim that the ovens were too expensive

❸ Practice and Apply

A. CONCEPT CHECK: Adjective and Adverb Clauses

Write the adjective or adverb clauses in the following sentences. After each clause, write the word or words that it modifies.

The Big Jump
1. Long before the Wright brothers flew the first airplane, the French inventor J. P. Blanchard was testing parachutes.
2. Sébastien Lenormand, who was a French physicist, made the first successful parachute jump from a tower in 1783.
3. With parachutes, early aviators could descend from balloons that stayed in the air.
4. Since the airplane was invented, parachutes have been used for emergency jumps from aircraft.
5. They can also deliver cargo, such as food and medicine, to places where land travel is difficult.
6. Parachutes work because air resistance slows them down.
7. They have large surfaces that trap a lot of air.
8. Because parachutists descend fairly rapidly, they sometimes injure themselves upon landing.
9. This is particularly true when jumpers land on rough ground.
10. Although parachuting is risky, many people love it.

➡ **For a SELF-CHECK and more practice, see the EXERCISE BANK, p. 610.**

B. REVISING: Adding Details

Combine each pair of sentences by changing one into an adjective or adverb clause. Use appropriate introductory words.

Example: Balloons are hard to steer. *Balloons do not have rudders.*
Answer: Balloons, which do not have rudders, are hard to steer.

Would You Like to Fly?
1. Jacques and Joseph Montgolfier invented the hot-air balloon. Jacques and Joseph were brothers.
2. The balloon was filled with hot air produced by burning wool and straw. The balloon was made of linen.
3. One of their balloons floated for more than five miles over the city of Paris. The balloon landed safely.
4. The airship developed from the hot-air balloon. The airship was kept aloft by hot air or gas.
5. The airship was easier to handle. The airship had propellers.

Noun Clauses

❶ Here's the Idea

▶ **A noun clause is a subordinate clause used as a noun.**

Like a noun, a noun clause can function in a sentence as a subject, a complement (direct object, indirect object, or predicate nominative), or an object of a preposition.

What you accomplish is up to you.
SUBJECT

You know **that you hold the key.**
DIRECT OBJECT

Give **whatever is most worthy** your best effort.
INDIRECT OBJECT

Then you will be **who you were meant to be.**
PREDICATE NOMINATIVE

Think about **how you can reach your goals.**
OBJECT OF A PREPOSITION

If you can substitute the word *someone* or *something* for a clause in a sentence, the clause is a noun clause.

A noun clause may be introduced by a **subordinating conjunction** or by a **pronoun.** A pronoun that introduces a noun clause does not have an antecedent in the sentence.

Words Used to Introduce Noun Clauses	
Subordinating conjunctions	that, how, when, where, whether, why
Pronouns	what, whatever, who, whom, whoever, whomever, which, whichever

That an inventor's life is hard is obvious.

What inventors must do to succeed is astounding.

The introductory word in a noun clause is sometimes omitted:

The owner's manual states (that) the time machine is guaranteed to work.

❷ Why It Matters in Writing

Noun clauses give you a way of referring to things that can't be named in one word but can be identified by what they're doing.

PROFESSIONAL MODEL

Whoever bought the professor's inventions soon — **SUBJECT**
regretted the mistake. The machines did whatever they — **DIRECT OBJECT**
felt like doing instead of what they were supposed to do. — **OBJECT OF PREPOSITION**

❸ Practice and Apply

A. CONCEPT CHECK: Noun Clauses

Write the noun clause in each sentence. Then indicate whether the clause functions as a subject, a direct object, an indirect object, a predicate nominative, or an object of a preposition.

Making a Spectacle

1. We do not know who invented the first eyeglasses, but glasses are mentioned in books written in the 1200s.
2. However, early spectacles probably offered whoever wore them little help.
3. In the 1700s, lenses were ground according to what was known about the science of light.
4. What kinds of lenses people need depends on the defects in their eyes.
5. A concave lens is what a nearsighted eye needs.
6. Whoever has a farsighted eye needs a convex lens.
7. Some people's lens needs depend on whether they are looking at close objects or distant ones.
8. This is why Ben Franklin invented the bifocal lens.
9. Bifocal lenses provide people with whichever kind of correction they need at a particular time.
10. Only an eye doctor can tell a person what kinds of lenses he or she needs.

➡ **For a SELF-CHECK and more practice, see the EXERCISE BANK, p. 611.**

CLAUSES

B. WRITING: Using Noun Clauses

Use each of the noun clauses below in a complete sentence to make a paragraph describing the theft of a hovercraft. Give the noun clause the function indicated in parentheses.

What I Need Is Help!

1. whoever took my hovercraft (subject)
2. what that person was thinking (direct object of *know*)
3. whoever saw what happened (indirect object of *give*)
4. which way the culprit went (direct object of *saw*)
5. where my hovercraft is now (object of preposition *to*)
6. what I would like to happen (predicate nominative)
7. that this is frustrating (subject)
8. how to get my hovercraft back (object of preposition *of*)
9. whoever finds it (direct object of *reward*)
10. how I plan to deal with the situation (predicate nominative)

C. WRITING: Explaining What It Does

Write a paragraph describing how someone might use the robotic underwater camera pictured at the right to explore the ocean floor or to investigate a sunken wreck. Use at least three noun clauses.

A robotic underwater camera designed and built as a part of a mechanical engineering class at the University of Florida.

Sentence Structure

LESSON 4

① Here's the Idea

A sentence's structure is determined by the number and kind of clauses it contains.

▶ **The structure of a sentence may be simple, compound, complex, or compound-complex.**

Simple Sentences

A **simple sentence** consists of one independent clause and no subordinate clauses.

> **Two friends** invented **the first trivia game.**

A simple sentence may have a compound subject or verb.

> **Chris Haney and Scott Abbott** created **and** marketed **it.**
>   COMPOUND SUBJECT   COMPOUND VERB

For more on compound sentence parts, see pp. 42–43.

Compound Sentences

In a **compound sentence** two or more independent clauses are joined together.

>   INDEPENDENT CLAUSE
> **Bette Nesmith typed on an electric typewriter,** and
> **she often made mistakes.**
>   INDEPENDENT CLAUSE

Independent clauses can be joined by a comma and a coordinating conjunction, a semicolon, or a semicolon with a conjunctive adverb and a comma.

> **She could have erased them, but that took a lot of time.**

> **Nesmith did not erase her errors; she covered them with a mixture of water and white paint.**

> **Nesmith was not happy with the name "paper correction fluid"; consequently, she gave the mixture a catchy brand name.**

For more on conjunctions and conjunctive adverbs, see pp. 26–27.

WATCH OUT

Avoid using commas to join independent clauses that should be separate sentences. For more on "comma splices," see page 120.

Clauses and Sentence Structure **101**

Complex Sentences

A **complex sentence** contains one independent clause and one or more subordinate clauses.

SUBORDINATE CLAUSE

If cockleburs had not clung to his jacket, | George de Mestral
might never have invented Velcro.   INDEPENDENT CLAUSE

INDEPENDENT CLAUSE

He was curious to know the reason | why they clung so tightly.
    SUBORDINATE CLAUSE

Compound-Complex Sentences

A **compound-complex sentence** contains two or more independent clauses and one or more subordinate clauses.

SUBORDINATE CLAUSE   INDEPENDENT CLAUSE

When de Mestral studied the burs, | he saw tiny hooks on their
surfaces becoming entangled in loops of fiber, | and | this
observation inspired him to invent the hook-and-loop fastener.
    INDEPENDENT CLAUSE

SUBORDINATE CLAUSE   INDEPENDENT CLAUSE

While another might have been annoyed, | he was intrigued, | and
he thought of a use | to which the phenomenon could be put.
INDEPENDENT CLAUSE   SUBORDINATE CLAUSE

❷ Why It Matters in Writing

By using compound sentences to connect main ideas and complex sentences to add subordinate ideas, you can express complicated thoughts clearly and achieve sentence variety.

STUDENT MODEL

Kurt Vonnegut's story "Harrison Bergeron" is about a futuristic society in which people are forced to be equal. In this society, no one is allowed to be bright, and no one is allowed to be talented. These qualities are forbidden because they threaten the equality policy of those who are in power. However, one person—Harrison Bergeron—demands that his uniqueness be acknowledged.

SUBORDINATE IDEAS

CONNECTED MAIN IDEAS

❸ Practice and Apply

Identify each sentence as simple, compound, complex, or compound-complex.

Bubble Gum
1. Some inventions are created by accident.
2. Walter E. Diemer worked for a chewing-gum company.
3. He was an accountant, but he wanted to improve the company's gum.
4. He did experiments because he wanted chewier gum.
5. He didn't succeed, but he did come up with something that became a successful product.
6. He produced a mixture that could be blown into bubbles.
7. This mixture was the first bubble gum.
8. Diemer had pink food coloring, which he added to the gum.
9. The gum was fun to chew, and the color made it attractive.
10. If Walter Diemer had not experimented, he would not have discovered bubble gum, and we might not have it today.

➡ **For a SELF-CHECK and more practice, see the EXERCISE BANK, p. 612.**

Combine sentences 6 and 7 into a compound-complex sentence.

CHALLENGE

B. REVISING: Achieving Sentence Variety

Rewrite this paragraph by following the directions below it.

Chewing Through the Ages
(1) Chewing gum has a long history. **(2)** The ancient Greeks chewed hardened sap. **(3)** It came from the mastic tree. **(4)** Over 1,000 years ago the Maya of Mexico chewed chicle. **(5)** Native Americans later taught European settlers to chew gum. **(6)** During the 1850s people chewed paraffin wax. **(7)** It wasn't as good as gum. **(8)** It crumbled or stuck to the teeth. **(9)** Modern chewing gum was originally made with sugar. **(10)** In the mid-1900s companies began making sugarless gum.

1. Combine sentences 2 and 3 to form a complex sentence.
2. Combine 4 and 5 to form a compound sentence.
3. Combine 6, 7, and 8 to form a compound-complex sentence.
4. Combine 9 and 10 to form a compound sentence.

In your 📁 **Working Portfolio,** find the paragraph you wrote for the **Write Away** on page 90. Use clauses to combine sentences and vary the sentence structure of your paragraph.

LESSON 5

Sentence Diagramming

Mad Mapper

Here's the Idea

Diagramming can help you understand sentence structures by showing how the clauses in sentences are related.

Watch me for diagramming tips!

Simple Sentences

Simple sentences are diagrammed on one horizontal line, with a vertical line separating subject and predicate. The horizontal line may be split on either side to show a compound subject or a compound verb.

Orville Wright and Wilbur Wright tossed a coin.

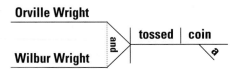

Remember that sentences with compound subjects and verbs are still simple sentences. To refresh your memory about diagramming simple sentences, see pages 54–57.

Compound Sentences

- Diagram the independent clauses on parallel horizontal lines.
- Connect the verbs in the two clauses by a broken line with a step.

Orville won and Wilbur lost.

The conjunction goes on the step.

A. CONCEPT CHECK: Compound Sentences

Diagram these sentences, using what you have learned.

1. Orville piloted the plane, and Wilbur stayed on the ground.
2. Orville flew first, but Wilbur flew longer.

Complex Sentences

Adjective and Adverb Clauses

- Diagram the subordinate clause on its own horizontal line below the main line, as if it were a sentence.
- Use a dotted line to connect the word introducing the clause to the word it modifies.

Adjective Clause Introduced by a Relative Pronoun

The brothers, who did not like school, never graduated.

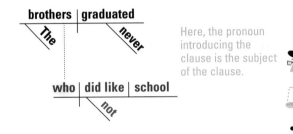

Here, the pronoun introducing the clause is the subject of the clause.

Adjective Clause Introduced by a Relative Adverb

The schools where they were enrolled frustrated them.

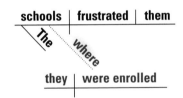

The adverb introducing the clause goes on the broken line.

Adverb Clause

After Orville started a printing business, they launched a newspaper.

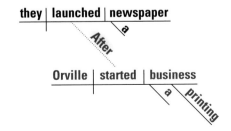

The conjunction goes on the dotted line, which connects the verbs in the two clauses.

Noun Clauses Diagram the subordinate clause on a separate line that is attached to the main line with a forked line. Place the forked line in the diagram according to the role of the noun clause in the sentence. Diagram the word introducing the noun clause according to its function in the clause.

Noun Clause Used as Subject

What they designed was a glider.

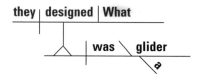

Here, the pronoun introducing the clause functions as a direct object in the clause.

Noun Clause Used as Direct Object

They patented whatever was successful.

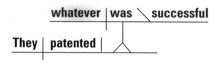

Here, the pronoun introducing the clause functions as the clause's subject.

B. CONCEPT CHECK: Complex Sentences

Diagram these sentences, using what you have learned.

1. Wilbur, who was the older brother, tested the glider.
2. People could not believe what they saw.

Compound-Complex Sentences

Diagram the independent clauses first. Attach each subordinate clause to the word it modifies.

They designed next a motorized airplane, and the plane, which was powered by gasoline, succeeded.

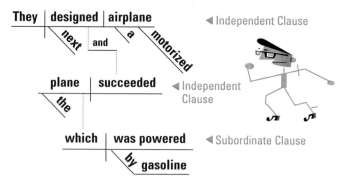

They conducted their first successful flight at Kitty Hawk, and residents are proud of what their town contributed to the history of flight.

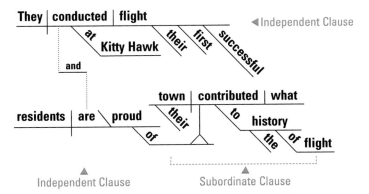

C. CONCEPT CHECK: Compound-Complex Sentences

Diagram these sentences, using what you have learned.

1. Orville flew a plane that crashed, and he was injured.
2. Orville, who was injured, recovered, but his passenger died.

D. MIXED REVIEW: Diagramming

Diagram the following sentences. Look for all types of clauses.

1. The brothers earned money but had problems.
2. Wilbur died and Orville worked alone.
3. Every airplane that flies uses their ideas.
4. After Orville retired, he won many awards.
5. Whoever flies can thank the Wrights.
6. After they invented the airplane, travel became easier and the world became smaller.
7. Their first plane is on view, and it impresses whoever sees it.

Frank and Ernest by Thaves

Grammar in Literature

Sentence Structure and Dramatic Writing

In writing the passage below, Ray Bradbury had a tough job. He wanted to describe a scene with no people but much human drama—a "smart" house whose owners have died in a nuclear holocaust. Using a variety of sentence structures, Bradbury created a mood of hysteria, desperation, and finally resignation.

There Will Come Soft Rains

Ray Bradbury

Yellow Vase (1990), Roy Lichtenstein. Copyright © 1990 Estate of Roy Lichtenstein/Gemini G.E.I.

At ten o'clock the house began to die.

The wind blew. A falling tree bough crashed through the kitchen window. Cleaning solvent, bottled, shattered over the stove. The room was ablaze in an instant!

> Short **simple sentences** list chance events leading to the disaster.

"Fire!" screamed a voice. The house lights flashed, water pumps shot water from the ceilings. But the solvent spread on the linoleum, licking, eating, under the kitchen door, while the voices took it up in chorus: "Fire, fire, fire!"

> A **complex sentence** shows the house reacting to the spread of the fire.

The house tried to save itself. Doors sprang tightly shut, but the windows were broken by the heat and the wind blew and sucked upon the fire.

> A **compound sentence** ties an action of the house to opposing actions of heat and wind.

The house gave ground as the fire in ten billion angry sparks moved with flaming ease from room to room and then up the stairs. While scurrying water rats squeaked from the walls, pistoled their water, and ran for more. And the wall sprays let down showers of mechanical rain.

> An **adverb clause** shows the power and speed of the fire.

But too late. Somewhere, sighing, a pump shrugged to a stop. The quenching rain ceased. The reserve water supply which had filled baths and washed dishes for many quiet days was gone.

> A return to short **simple sentences** slows the pace.

Revising to Vary Sentence Structure

Good writers do not plan their sentence structures in advance. As they compose and revise, they use structures that feel right for particular purposes—structures that have the right tones and rhythms. Every sentence structure is based on one of three ways of arranging clauses.

Letting an independent clause stand alone	Focuses attention on a single idea. In a series, can create a choppy rhythm.
Combining independent clauses	Connects ideas of equal importance. Can create a smooth and balanced flow.
Adding subordinate clauses	Adds a layer of supporting ideas. Can help create momentum and complexity.

PRACTICE AND APPLY: Revising Sentence Structure

The paragraph below consists entirely of simple sentences. To improve its clarity and style, try rewriting it, varying the sentence structures. Follow the directions below, or think of your own way of revising the paragraph.

(1) The principal flipped a switch. **(2)** The "smart" classroom began to operate. **(3)** The students looked around for the teacher. **(4)** The teacher was not there. **(5)** A friendly face appeared in a screen. **(6)** The screen was mounted on the wall. **(7)** The desks automatically gave the students an electric jolt. **(8)** They didn't pay attention. **(9)** Some students talked. **(10)** They were ejected from their seats into the hallway.

1. Combine sentences 1 and 2 to form a compound sentence.
2. Combine 3 and 4 to form a compound sentence.
3. Combine 5 and 6 by making sentence 6 an adjective clause.
4. Combine 7 and 8 by making 8 an adverb clause.
5. Combine 9 and 10 by making 9 a noun clause (using *whoever*).

After you have revised the paragraph, read both versions aloud with a partner and discuss how you think your changes have improved it.

Choose a draft from your 📁 **Working Portfolio** and revise it by combining sentences in at least three of the ways suggested above.

Mixed Review

Clauses and Sentence Structure Read the passage. Then write the answers to the questions that follow.

> **LITERARY MODEL**
>
> **(1)** For a refugee who had never seen a motorized vehicle or indoor plumbing until he was 9, this was an unimaginable honor. **(2)** When the Worcester paper ran a picture of me standing next to President Kennedy, my father rushed out to buy a new suit in order to be properly dressed to receive the congratulations of the Worcester Greeks. **(3)** He clipped out the photograph, had it laminated in plastic and carried it in his breast pocket for the rest of his life to show everyone he met. **(4)** I found the much-worn photo in his pocket on the day he died 20 years later.
>
> **(5)** In our isolated Greek village, my mother had bribed a cousin to teach her to read, for girls were not supposed to attend school beyond a certain age. **(6)** She had always dreamed of her children receiving an education. **(7)** She couldn't be there when I graduated from Boston University, but the person who came with my father and shared our joy was my former teacher, Marjorie Hurd. **(8)** We celebrated not only my bachelor's degree but also the scholarships that paid my way to Columbia's Graduate School of Journalism. **(9)** There, I met the woman who would eventually become my wife. **(10)** At our wedding and at the baptisms of our three children, Marjorie Hurd was always there, dancing alongside the Greeks.
>
> —Nicholas Gage, "The Teacher Who Changed My Life"

1. What kind of clause is the first subordinate clause in sentence 1?
2. What kind of clause is the second subordinate clause in sentence 1?
3. What words are modified by the clauses referred to in questions 1 and 2?
4. What kind of subordinate clause is in sentence 2?
5. What is the independent clause in sentence 2?
6. Is sentence 2 complex or compound-complex?
7. Is sentence 3 simple, compound, or complex?
8. What is the adjective clause with *that* left out in sentence 4?
9. Is sentence 5 simple, compound, or complex?
10. Is sentence 6 simple, compound, or complex?
11. Is sentence 7 compound, complex, or compound-complex?
12. Is sentence 8 simple, compound, or complex?
13. What is the subordinate clause in sentence 9?
14. Is sentence 10 simple, compound, or complex?
15. How many essential adjective clauses are there in the last four sentences?

Choose the letter that correctly identifies each numbered part of the passage.

Inventions differ from discoveries, although the two are closely related. A
(1)   (2)
discovery occurs when something in nature is first observed or recognized.
(3)
An invention is the creation of something that never existed before. For
(4)   (5)
example, humans discovered fire, but they invented the match to start a fire.
(5)
Before the 1900s whatever was invented was made mainly by people
(6)
who worked alone. Many were artisans or mechanics, and they had little
(7)   (8)
education. Today, most inventors are engineers and scientists who work for
(9)
large companies, and their inventions belong to the companies. We can
thank inventors for what they have done to improve our lives.
(10)

1. A. simple sentence
   B. independent clause
   C. subordinate clause
   D. compound sentence

2. A. simple sentence
   B. independent clause
   C. subordinate clause
   D. compound sentence

3. A. essential adjective clause
   B. nonessential adjective clause
   C. adverb clause
   D. noun clause

4. A. essential adjective clause
   B. nonessential adjective clause
   C. adverb clause
   D. noun clause

5. A. simple sentence
   B. compound sentence
   C. complex sentence
   D. compound-complex sentence

6. A. noun clause as subject
   B. noun clause as direct object
   C. noun clause as indirect object
   D. noun clause as object of a
      preposition

7. A. nonessential adjective clause
   B. essential adjective clause
   C. adverb clause
   D. noun clause

8. A. simple sentence
   B. compound sentence
   C. complex sentence
   D. compound-complex sentence

9. A. compound-complex sentence
      with two subordinate clauses
   B. complex sentence with two
      subordinate clauses
   C. compound sentence with two
      independent clauses
   D. compound-complex sentence
      with two independent clauses
      and a subordinate clause

10. A. noun clause as subject
    B. noun clause as direct object
    C. noun clause as indirect object
    D. noun clause as object of a
       preposition

CLAUSES

Student Help Desk

Sentence Structure at a Glance

A clause is a group of words that contains a subject and a verb. A clause may be either independent or subordinate. An independent clause may be a simple sentence, or it may be combined with one or more other clauses.

| independent clause | = simple sentence |

independent clause + independent clause = compound sentence

independent clause + subordinate clause = complex sentence

independent clause + independent clause

+ subordinate clause = compound-complex sentence

Punctuating Clauses   Hinges and Bolts

Use a Comma	Example
• when joining independent clauses with a coordinating conjunction	I may be young, but I have great ambitions.
• after a subordinate clause that begins a sentence	After I discover a cure for the common cold, I'll receive the Nobel Prize.
• to set off a nonessential adjective clause	My acceptance speech, which will last for hours, will be brilliant.

Use a Semicolon	
• to join independent clauses without a conjunction	It won't be a good speech; it will be a great speech.

Use a Semicolon and a Comma	
• to join independent clauses with a conjunctive adverb	Everyone will adore me; moreover, I will deserve it.

Sentence Structure Pieces and Parts

Kind of Sentence	Structure	Example
Simple sentence	One independent clause	The pilot waves her hat.
Compound sentence	Two or more independent clauses	The pilot waves her hat and the crowd cheers.
Complex sentence	One independent clause and at least one subordinate clause	As she disappears over a hill, the crowd grows quiet.
Compound-complex sentence	Two or more independent clauses and at least one subordinate clause	After an hour passes, the plane reappears, and the crowd rushes to greet it.

Subordinate Clauses Supporting Structures

Kind of Clause	Function	Example
Adjective clause	Modifies a noun or pronoun	The airplane, **which ran entirely on human power,** took off.
Adverb clause	Modifies a verb, adjective, or adverb	It stayed in the air **as long as the pilot worked its pedals.**
Noun clause	Acts as a subject, complement, or object of a preposition	**Whether she would crash** was the main thing on her mind.

CLAUSES

The Bottom Line

Checklist for Clauses and Sentence Structure

Have I . . .

____ made sure that every sentence contains at least one independent clause?

____ put supporting ideas into subordinate clauses?

____ combined some simple sentences to show relationships between ideas?

____ varied sentence structure?

Writing Complete Sentences

Happiness will be yours if you listen to yourself it is very possible that you will achieve greatness in your lifetime.

Theme: Teenagers and Jobs

On the Job

Congratulations! You've just landed a job as a fortune editor at a fortune-cookie factory. Your main responsibility is to make sure that each fortune makes sense and is a complete sentence. As an editor, how would you change the fortune shown above so that it makes sense and fits in the cookie?

If the sentences in your paragraphs are missing punctuation or if they include punctuation in the wrong places, your ideas will run together or be cut short. Be sure to present your ideas in complete sentences so that your readers will understand them.

Write Away: Dream Job

What job would be just perfect for you? Write a paragraph about your dream job. Don't worry if it isn't realistic. Save your paragraph in your 📁 **Working Portfolio.**

Choose the best way to rewrite each underlined word group.

By getting a summer job. You can earn money to spend or save. You can
(1)
also gain valuable work experience and even have fun. Although a job
(2)
may sound boring. It might even give you ideas about future careers.

You may be asking yourself, Where should I begin looking for a job?
Make lists of your talents, skills, and interests. Before you begin your
(3)
search. A list will help you identify the kinds of jobs you might enjoy.

To learn about available jobs, skim the want ads. Also look for Help
(4)
Wanted signs in shops and businesses. A veterinarian may need an
(5)
assistant, a café may need a counterperson. You might even apply for

work at places that haven't advertised for help if they interest you.

1. A. By getting a summer job, you can earn money. To spend or save.
   B. By getting a summer job, and you can earn money to spend or save.
   C. By getting a summer job, you can earn money to spend or save.
   D. Correct as is

2. A. Although a job may sound boring but may turn out to be interesting.
   B. Although a job may sound boring, it could turn out to be interesting and challenging.
   C. Although a job may sound boring, however it may not be.
   D. Correct as is

3. A. Making lists of your talents, skills, and interests before you begin your search.
   B. Make lists of your talents, skills, and interests before begin to search.
   C. Make lists of your talents, skills, and interests before you begin your search.
   D. Correct as is

4. A. To learn about available jobs. Skim the want ads.
   B. To learn about available jobs; skim the want ads.
   C. Skim the want ads. To learn about available jobs.
   D. Correct as is

5. A. A veterinarian may need an assistant, or a café may need a counterperson.
   B. A veterinarian may need an assistant a café may need a counterperson.
   C. A veterinarian may need an assistant, a café may need a counterperson or a short-order cook.
   D. Correct as is

Sentence Fragments

❶ Here's the Idea

▶ **A sentence fragment is a part of a sentence that is punctuated as if it were a complete sentence.**

To figure out whether a word group is a fragment, ask the following questions. If the answer to any of the questions is no, the word group is a sentence fragment.

• Does the word group have a subject?
• Does it have a verb?
• Does it express a complete thought?

The first word group below is a fragment because it doesn't have a subject or express a complete thought.

> **Fragment:** Hired a student to work in the office.

> **Sentence:** The principal hired a student to work in the office.

Subordinate Clauses as Fragments

A subordinate (dependent) clause contains a subject and a verb. By itself, however, a subordinate clause is a fragment because it does not express a complete thought.

> **More and more students have found technology-related jobs.** Although traditional after-school jobs are still popular.
> SUBORDINATE–CLAUSE FRAGMENT

Here's How Fixing Subordinate-Clause Fragments

Here are two ways to fix a subordinate-clause fragment.

• Combine the subordinate clause with the preceding or following sentence.

   More and more students have found technology-related jobs, Although traditional after-school jobs are still popular.

• Write the missing part of the sentence.

   Although traditional after-school jobs are still popular, computers have created new job opportunities for teens.

Sometimes you can correct a subordinate-clause fragment by simply deleting the subordinating conjunction.

~~When~~ we interviewed a group of students about their jobs.

Phrases as Fragments

A phrase is a group of words that functions as a part of speech, such as an adjective or a noun. A phrase by itself is a sentence fragment because it does not have a subject or a verb and does not express a complete thought. The paragraph below shows three kinds of phrase fragments.

STUDENT MODEL

Some students enjoy working for others. However, there are plenty of opportunities for students. To create their own jobs. Maybe you are an outgoing person. With good computer skills. You could teach less-experienced people how to use computers or the Internet. If you like kids, you might want to be a baby sitter. Get experience first by volunteering. At a daycare center. Having worked with children.

INFINITIVE PHRASE

PREPOSITIONAL PHRASES

PARTICIPIAL PHRASE

You can correct a phrase fragment by combining it with the sentence before or after it or by writing the missing subject or verb.

Fixing Phrase Fragments

Type of Phrase	Correction
Infinitive phrase	However, there are plenty of opportunities for students, to create their own jobs.
Prepositional phrase	Maybe you are an outgoing person, with good computer skills.
	Get experience first by volunteering, at a daycare center.
Participial phrase	Having worked with children, you will have an advantage over less-experienced sitters.

SENTENCES

Other Kinds of Fragments

Compound Predicate

Sometimes a fragment occurs when a writer inserts end punctuation between the parts of a compound predicate. Fix this fragment by combining it with the sentence before it.

Fragment: Nicole works at the cash register. **And waits tables.**

Sentence: Nicole works at the cash register **and waits tables.**

Items in a Series

A series of words or phrases cannot stand alone as a sentence. Combine the series with the sentence to which it belongs.

Fragment: Martin has three main responsibilities at the restaurant. **Clearing tables, setting tables, and filling water glasses.**

Sentence: Martin has three main responsibilities at the restaurant: **clearing tables, setting tables, and filling water glasses.**

Because sentence fragments occur naturally in conversation, writers use fragments to make dialogue more realistic.

> **LITERARY MODEL**
>
> "I may have a job, Ma," she said.
>
> "That's nice," Mrs. Wilson said. **"Baby-sitting?"**
>
> **"On the stage,"** Elise said.
>
> —John Cheever, "The Opportunity"

❷ Why It Matters in Writing

You may write fragments when you take notes. If you use your notes to write a formal letter or a report, however, you should turn the fragments into complete sentences.

job notes
photographer's assistant
must have office experience
knowledge of equipment

. . . I am applying for the job of photographer's assistant. I was an office assistant at my mother's travel agency last summer, and I have experience using photo equipment . . .

❸ Practice and Apply

A. CONCEPT CHECK: Sentence Fragments

Rewrite the following paragraphs, eliminating the fragments. You may combine the fragments with complete sentences or add words to them.

The Organizers

Last summer, Lisa, Ruben, and Eva decided. To start their own business. Helping others get organized. Eva wrote advertising copy. And designed a flyer on her computer.

> If you can't find your soccer cleats or haven't seen the top of your desk in weeks. Call the Organizers. We'll help you finish those chores you've been putting off. Cleaning crammed closets, shelving CDs in alphabetical order, and sorting through boxes of junk.

With help from Ruben and Eva. Lisa posted the flyers throughout the neighborhood. The three friends were surprised. By the enthusiastic response to their ad. Having seen the flyer on a telephone pole. One neighbor hired the Organizers to arrange family photos in albums. Because they did such a good job. Using their abilities and interests. They helped people, earned money, and had a lot of fun.

➡ For a SELF-CHECK and more practice, see the EXERCISE BANK, p. 612.

B. WRITING: Adding Missing Parts

Correct each fragment by adding words to make it a complete sentence.

At Work in a Pool

1. Because she has always loved swimming.
2. In the pool.
3. Before Lisa could be a lifeguard.
4. To make sure all the swimmers are safe.
5. The dog paddle, the backstroke, and the crawl.

LESSON 2 Run-On Sentences

❶ Here's the Idea

▶ **A run-on sentence is two or more sentences written as though they were one sentence.**

A run-on is created when sentences are run together with no punctuation between them, or run together with only a comma between them (called a **comma splice**). The easiest way to fix a run-on is to separate the sentences with a period and a capital letter.

A gopher runs errands for others⊙gophers should be energetic.

Here's How Fixing Run-Ons

Here are four more techniques you can use to fix a run-on.

- Add a comma and a conjunction.

  Many professionals are too busy to do errands themselves *so* **they need someone who can help them.**

- If the two sentences are closely related, add a semicolon.

  Some gophers are required to have a driver's license *;* **most gophers ride bicycles.**

- Add a semicolon, a conjunctive adverb, and a comma if needed.

  Gophers may be paid for the gasoline they use *; however,* **they should negotiate the payment before accepting each job.**

- Make one of the clauses subordinate by adding a subordinating conjunction.

  When **Bike-riding gophers ride fast, they can become dangerous to pedestrians.**

When checking for run-ons, don't look only for long sentences. Run-ons can be short.

That's my bike, it has a flat tire.

❷ Why It Matters in Writing

Run-ons are confusing and frustrating. Readers can't tell where one idea ends and the next one begins.

Louisa ran errands for her boss all day now she is exhausted.

❸ Practice and Apply

A. CONCEPT CHECK: Run-On Sentences

Write *R* for each run-on or *S* for each correctly written sentence. Then correct the run-ons using the techniques in this lesson.

Teenage Techies

1. Most students use computers on a daily basis now many students are using their computer skills to earn money.
2. Entrepreneurs are people who start their own businesses, using the Internet, some teenagers are doing exactly this.
3. A 16-year-old in Washington created a Web site for reviews of computer hardware. His site is called *The View*.
4. Another teenager started a business designing Web pages his first customer was an author of novels for preteens.
5. A teen in Ohio created a Web page to sell the beaded jewelry that she makes, many teens have used the Web to find customers for their products.
6. Unlike most adults, many teenagers have been using computers all their lives they have an advantage when it comes to dreaming up computer-related businesses.
7. Twenty years ago, teens might have set up lemonade stands to make money, today they can use computers.
8. Teenagers are also earning money by teaching older people how to use computers.
9. Young children are eager to learn computer skills, many parents do not have the time or knowledge to teach them.
10. For some teens, this situation is a golden opportunity.

➡️ **For a SELF-CHECK and more practice, see the EXERCISE BANK, p. 613.**

B. REVISING: Checking Sentences

Revise this paragraph, correcting run-ons.

Business Basics

If you set up your own business, you need to know how much to charge your customers. You don't want to overcharge you don't want to work for just pennies either. The first thing to do is to find out how much professionals are paid for the same job, you are not yet a professional, you should charge somewhat less than professionals do. After you get a little working experience, you can decide whether your price is right.

Real World Grammar

Summer Internship Letter

When applying for a summer job or internship, you may need to write a letter describing your abilities. You might begin by jotting down notes, in the form of fragments, about what you want to say. As you draft, be careful not to carry the fragments into your letter or create run-ons by combining too many ideas into single sentences. Remember, your letter will make your first impression on the person in charge of hiring. Here is the draft of a letter one student sent with her application. She asked a friend to review the draft.

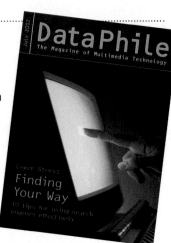

Dear Ms. Epstein:

I am writing in regard to the editorial internship program at DataPhile magazine. I would like to be an intern at DataPhile. Because I am interested in a career that combines writing and technology, I believe that the internship will give me a preview of what such a career might be like. A head start in training and experience.
I am a responsible, well-organized person as well as a hard worker, I learn quickly and have strong communication skills. I have done well in all my courses, especially in English and computers. Enclosed are two teacher recommendations, as requested. I hope you will consider my application. Thank you. For your time. I look forward to hearing from you.

Sentence fragments. Combine with preceding sentences.

Run-on sentence. Separate sentences.

Fix fragment.

CHAPTER 5

Using Grammar in Writing

Avoid sentence fragments and run-on sentences.	After you draft a letter, reread it at least twice. Look for and correct sentence fragments during your first pass. Then do the same for run-on sentences during your second pass.

REVISED LETTER

225 Garland Avenue
Seattle, WA 98197
March 18, 2002

Ms. Gloria Epstein, Editor
DataPhile
1704 Crane Road
Seattle, WA 98199

Dear Ms. Epstein:

I am writing in regard to the editorial internship program at *DataPhile* magazine. I would like to be an intern at *DataPhile* because I am interested in a career that combines writing and technology. I believe that the internship will give me a preview of what such a career might be like and a head start in training and experience.

I am a responsible, well-organized person as well as a hard worker. I learn quickly and have strong communication skills. I have done well in all my courses, especially in English and computers. Enclosed are two teacher recommendations, as requested. I hope you will consider my application. Thank you for your time. I look forward to hearing from you.

Sincerely,

Julia Rowe

Julia Rowe

PRACTICE AND APPLY: Fixing Fragments and Run-ons

A friend is applying for a position as a camp counselor. Read this section of your friend's application letter and correct any run-ons or fragments you find.

> I believe I am an ideal candidate for a counselor-in-training position. At Camp Cedar Lake. First, I like working with young children. And get along well with them. Second, I have interests and talents in drama, music, and dance, I enjoy sharing them with children. I would welcome the opportunity. To work with young campers at Cedar Lake.

A. Fragments and Run-Ons Identify each numbered item as a complete sentence, a fragment, or a run-on. Then revise each incorrect item.

(1) Perhaps you and your friends make beaded bracelets maybe you build wooden toys. **(2)** If you have a craft hobby. You may be able to turn it into a money-making project. You can display your crafts. **(3)** And sell them at craft fairs. **(4)** To find out about the times and locations of fairs. Contact your local craft store. This store should have information. **(5)** About how to rent a sales table at a fair. **(6)** If you doubt there is a market for craftwork, just visit one of these fairs. You'll find crowds browsing and buying all sorts of items. **(7)** Homemade candles, hand-stitched quilted pillows, beaded jewelry, carved animals, and silk-flower arrangements, to name a few. **(8)** Fairs are not the only places to sell your crafts some craft stores and gift shops may agree to sell them for you. **(9)** By visiting stores and showing the owners samples. You may interest them in your work. **(10)** Setting up an agreement to sell your work can be the beginning of a lasting business relationship.

B. Editing and Revising Read the article below. Identify and correct any fragments or run-on sentences.

IDEA DEPARTMENT

A TEEN TURNS FUN INTO CASH

Do you have a great idea? For an invention? You may be able to sell your idea. That's what one teenager did, his inventions are now sold in large chain stores. Modeled on a walkie-talkie. One toy allows swimmers to communicate underwater. Among his other inventions is a pool periscope that people swimming underwater can use to see what is happening in the world above. Because he loves swimming. To produce and market his toys. He started his own company.

Choose the best way to rewrite each underlined word group.

> <u>After eating a meal in a restaurant. Most people leave a tip.</u> <u>Although</u>
>   (1)   (2)
>
> <u>this custom is common.</u> In fact, even the origin of the word *tip* is a
>
> mystery. Tips are usually paid to service workers, such as waiters,
>
> waitresses, taxi drivers, and hairdressers. <u>A tip is often about 20 percent</u>
>   (3)
> <u>of the cost. Of the service.</u>
>
>   Over time, the meaning of tipping has changed. <u>In the past a tip was a</u>
>   (4)
> <u>reward for good service.</u> Now it is an expected payment. <u>Nobody knows</u>
>   (5)
> <u>exactly why tips are given, it seems strange that we continue to follow</u>
>
> <u>this custom.</u> Some social scientists are trying to understand this.

1. A. After eating a meal in a restaurant, and most people leave a tip.
   B. After eating a meal in a restaurant, most people leave a tip.
   C. After eating a meal. In a restaurant, most people leave a tip.
   D. Correct as is

2. A. Although this custom is common. Its origins are unknown.
   B. Although this custom is common, however its origins are unknown.
   C. Although this custom is common, its origins are unknown.
   D. Correct as is

3. A. A tip is often about 20 percent of the cost of the service.
   B. A tip is often about 20 percent of the cost, of the service.
   C. A tip is often about 20 percent. Of the cost of the service.
   D. Correct as is

4. A. In the past a tip was a reward. For good service.
   B. In the past. A tip was a reward for good service.
   C. In the past a tip was a reward and for good service.
   D. Correct as is

5. A. Nobody knows exactly why tips are given it seems strange that we continue to follow this custom.
   B. Nobody knows exactly why tips are given, seems strange that we continue to follow this custom.
   C. Nobody knows exactly why tips are given, so it seems strange that we continue to follow this custom.
   D. Correct as is

Student Help Desk

Fragments and Run-Ons at a Glance

- A **sentence fragment** is a part of a sentence that is punctuated as if it were a complete sentence.

- A **run-on sentence** is two or more sentences written as though they were one sentence.

Putting the Pieces Together

Correcting Fragments

Fragment Type	Example	Quick Fix
Subject is missing.	Repaired Mr. Lotarski's porch.	**The volunteers** repaired Mr. Lotarski's porch.
Verb is missing.	Ten students for the job in the computer lab.	Ten students **have applied** for the job in the computer lab.
Subordinate clause stands alone.	**If you want to learn about a particular field.** Get an internship in that field.	If you want to learn about a particular field, get an internship in that field.
Phrase stands alone.	**To learn about careers in the arts.** You could interview an artist.	To learn about careers in the arts, you could interview an artist.
Series stands alone.	Pilar applied for three after-school jobs. **Web site manager, math tutor, and teacher's aide.**	Pilar applied for three after-school jobs: Web site manager, math tutor, and teacher's aide.

Correcting Run-Ons

Technique	Run-on	Quick Fix
Add a period and a capital letter.	Yoshiko designed the school Web site, she is very creative.	Yoshiko designed the school Web site. **S**he is very creative.
Add a comma and a conjunction.	Several teenagers have started their own computer businesses they are making a profit.	Several teenagers have started their own computer businesses**, and** they are making a profit.
Add a semicolon.	Some students work after school others work on the weekends.	Some students work after school**;** others work on the weekends.
Add a semicolon and a conjunctive adverb.	Alan was not certain he wanted to work in a video store, he applied for the job.	Alan was not certain he wanted to work in a video store**; nevertheless,** he applied for the job.

SENTENCES

The Bottom Line

Checklist for Complete Sentences
Have I . . .

____ included a subject in each sentence?

____ included a verb in each sentence?

____ expressed a complete thought in each sentence?

____ corrected any run-ons?

____ corrected any fragments?

Using Verbs

I care for horses while I grow up

when I ride for six years I offer a job

I work as a cowgirl for two years

Theme: Writers' Lives
What Happened When?

What if you had a set of magnet words with plenty of verbs but no way to show verb forms? It would be hard to say when events happened or even to whom. Compare the version below to the one in the illustration above.

*I **cared** for horses while I **was growing** up. When I **had been riding** for six years, I **was offered** a job. I **have worked** as a cowgirl for two years.*

In this chapter, you will learn to use verb forms in your writing to describe action precisely. Then it's up to you to come up with some good verbs!

Write Away: Let's Talk About You
In a paragraph, tell a few important or interesting facts about your life. Be sure to include information about your past, your present, and your future. Put the paragraph in your  **Working Portfolio.**

Grammar Coach

Choose the best way to rewrite each underlined word or group of words.

Christy Brown's life almost <u>stop</u> before it ever got started. Because he
(1)
<u>was borned</u> with cerebral palsy, he was almost completely paralyzed. Until
(2)
he <u>had been</u> five years old, many people thought he would never be able to
(3)
communicate at all; but Christy's mother <u>has</u> faith that he would.
(4)
Christy's life <u>did change</u> the day he picked up a piece of chalk with the
(5)
toes of his left foot. His mother drew the letter *A* in chalk on the floor and
<u>was asking</u> him to copy it. He tried, but <u>the letter could not be copied by</u>
(6)   (7)
<u>him</u>. After his mother said, "Try again, Chris," he <u>has made up</u> his mind to
(8)
succeed; and with great effort, he did. Now Brown <u>has written</u> four novels,
(9)
a collection of poetry, and the script for *My Left Foot,* a movie based on a
book he wrote about his life. If it <u>was</u> not for Brown's determination, he
(10)
would not have the rewarding life he leads today.

1. A. was stopping
   B. had stopped
   C. stopped
   D. Correct as is

2. A. born
   B. had been born
   C. has born
   D. Correct as is

3. A. was
   B. will be
   C. is
   D. Correct as is

4. A. has had
   B. was having
   C. had
   D. Correct as is

5. A. had changed
   B. have changed
   C. will change
   D. Correct as is

6. A. was asked
   B. asked
   C. did ask
   D. Correct as is

7. A. the letter was not able to be
      copied
   B. he were not able to copy the
      letter
   C. he could not copy the letter
   D. Correct as is

8. A. made up
   B. was making up
   C. makes up
   D. Correct as is

9. A. has wrote
   B. had written
   C. was writing
   D. Correct as is

10. A. is
    B. were
    C. had
    D. Correct as is

VERBS

The Principal Parts of a Verb

❶ Here's the Idea

Verbs take different forms to show time of action and other kinds of information. In the passage below, the use of different verb forms makes it clear when everything occurs.

> **PROFESSIONAL MODEL**
>
> People probably know Maya Angelou best as a poet and as the author of a best-selling autobiography series. But she also has written plays and screenplays, composed music, and performed on stage and screen. Most recently, she directed a feature film, *Down in the Delta*. Currently, she is teaching at Wake Forest University in North Carolina.
>
> **PRESENT ACTION**
>
> **PAST ACTION**

▶ **Every verb has four basic forms called principal parts: the present, the present participle, the past, and the past participle.** The principal parts are used to make all of a verb's tenses and other forms.

The Four Principal Parts of a Verb			
Present	**Present Participle**	**Past**	**Past Participle**
talk	(is) talking	talked	(has) talked
sing	(is) singing	sang	(has) sung

Regular Verbs

The past and past participle of a **regular verb,** like *talk,* are formed by adding *-ed* or *-d* to the present. Most verbs are regular.

talk (present) + ed = talked (past and past participle)

hope (present) + d = hoped (past and past participle)

For some verbs, consonants are doubled in forms other than the present: *hop, hopping, hopped.* For others, an *e* is dropped in the present participle: *hope, hoping.* For more on these spelling rules, see page 651.

Irregular Verbs

The past and past participle of an **irregular verb,** like *sing,* are formed in some way other than by adding *-ed* or *-d* to the present.

Most irregular verbs can be classified into five groups. Learning these groups will help you to remember the verbs.

Common Irregular Verbs

	Present	Past	Past Participle
Group 1 The forms of the present, the past, and the past participle are the same.	burst cost cut hit hurt let put set shut	burst cost cut hit hurt let put set shut	(have) burst (have) cost (have) cut (have) hit (have) hurt (have) let (have) put (have) set (have) shut
Group 2 The forms of the past and the past participle are the same.	bring catch find get lay lead lend lose say send shine sit swing teach	brought caught found got laid led lent lost said sent shone *or* shined sat swung taught	(have) brought (have) caught (have) found (have) got *or* gotten (have) laid (have) led (have) lent (have) lost (have) said (have) sent (have) shone *or* shined (have) sat (have) swung (have) taught
Group 3 The vowel changes from *i* to *a* to *u.*	begin drink ring shrink sink spring swim	began drank rang shrank sank sprang *or* sprung swam	(have) begun (have) drunk (have) rung (have) shrunk (have) sunk (have) sprung (have) swum

VERBS

Common Irregular Verbs

	Present	Past	Past Participle
Group 4 The past participle is formed by adding -*n* or -*en* to the past.	beat	beat	(have) beaten
	bite	bit	(have) bitten *or* bit
	break	broke	(have) broken
	lie	lay	(have) lain
	speak	spoke	(have) spoken
	steal	stole	(have) stolen
	tear	tore	(have) torn
	wear	wore	(have) worn
Group 5 The past participle is formed from the **present**— frequently by adding -*n*, -*en*, or -*ne*.	become	became	(have) become
	blow	blew	(have) blown
	do	did	(have) done
	draw	drew	(have) drawn
	drive	drove	(have) driven
	eat	ate	(have) eaten
	give	gave	(have) given
	go	went	(have) gone
	grow	grew	(have) grown
	know	knew	(have) known
	rise	rose	(have) risen
	run	ran	(have) run
	see	saw	(have) seen
	take	took	(have) taken
	throw	threw	(have) thrown
	write	wrote	(have) written

❷ Why It Matters in Writing

Incorrect verb forms confuse your reader and make a bad impression in situations in which standard English is expected.

STUDENT MODEL

I would like to apply for the part-time job as cashier that I *saw* ~~seen~~ advertised in your window. Your ad *caught* ~~catch~~ my eye because last year I ~~have~~ worked for the whole summer at a pet store just like yours. The owner *said* ~~say~~ I *showed* ~~shown~~ responsibility and a good attitude in my work.

❸ Practice and Apply

A. CONCEPT CHECK: The Principal Parts of a Verb

Write the correct past or past participle of each verb that is shown in parentheses.

Career Beginnings

1. Gwendolyn Brooks (become) a published poet at age 14.
2. But not all writers (begin) their writing careers so early.
3. Before he became a well-known humorist, Mark Twain had (search) for gold as a prospector in California.
4. The poet and historian Carl Sandburg (drive) a milkwagon when he was young.
5. As a baseball captain in college, Sandburg (lead) his team to victory.
6. Isaac Asimov had (teach) biochemistry at Boston University's medical school before he turned to writing full time.
7. Maya Angelou (take) a job as a streetcar driver in San Francisco.
8. The novelist Amy Tan (assemble) pizzas in a restaurant.
9. O. Henry allegedly had (steal) money from the bank he worked in.
10. Even though O. Henry fled the country to escape capture, he was (catch) when he returned to Texas to see his dying wife.

➡ **For a SELF-CHECK and more practice, see the EXERCISE BANK, p. 614.**

B. WRITING: Reporting News

List the principal parts of the following pairs of irregular verbs and then use any of the word pairs to write a paragraph describing an interesting news event.

1. sink–swim
2. bring–take
3. give–get
4. drink–eat
5. lend–lose
6. speak–write

In your 📁 **Working Portfolio,** find the paragraph you wrote for the **Write Away** on page 128. Change three verbs; then make sure you have used the correct principal parts.

Verb Tense

❶ Here's the Idea

▶ **A tense is a verb form that shows the time of an action or condition.**

English verbs have six tenses. These tenses are used to indicate whether an action or condition is in the past, the present, or the future, and to indicate how events are related in time. A verb's tenses are formed from its principal parts.

Simple Tenses

	Singular	Plural
Present + *s* or *es* in third-person singular	I sneeze you sneeze he/she/it sneezes	we sneeze you sneeze they sneeze
Past	I sneezed you sneezed he/she/it sneezed	we sneezed you sneezed they sneezed
Future *will (shall)* + present	I will (shall) sneeze you will sneeze he/she/it will sneeze	we will (shall) sneeze you will sneeze they will sneeze

Perfect Tenses

	Singular	Plural
Present Perfect *have* or *has* + past participle	I have sneezed you have sneezed he/she/it has sneezed	we have sneezed you have sneezed they have sneezed
Past Perfect *had* + past participle	I had sneezed you had sneezed he/she/it had sneezed	we had sneezed you had sneezed they had sneezed
Future Perfect *will (shall) have* + past participle	I will (shall) have sneezed you will have sneezed he/she/it will have sneezed	we will (shall) have sneezed you will have sneezed they will have sneezed

All of the perfect tenses are made from the past participle.

The Far Side by Gary Larson

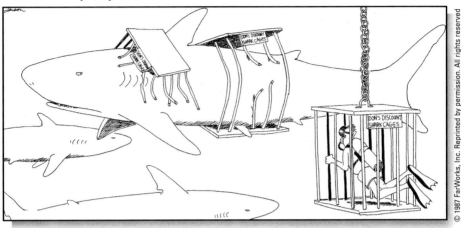

To understand the following examples of how the tenses are used, refer to the cartoon above.

Using the Simple Tenses

The **present tense** shows that an action or condition

• is occurring in the present:

The diver sees a shark wearing the remains of two cages.

• occurs regularly:

He always uses a shark cage when he observes sharks.

• is constantly or generally true:

Sharks are dangerous.

The **past tense** shows that an action or condition occurred in the past:

He bought this cage at Don's Discount Shark Cages.

The **future tense** shows that an action or condition will occur in the future:

Perhaps the shark will add this cage to his collection.

Using the Perfect Tenses

The **present perfect** shows that an action or condition

• was completed at one or more indefinite times in the past:

The diver has used shark cages before.

This time he has brought a new kind along.

• began in the past and continues in the present:

He has waited in this cage for an hour to see a shark.

The **past perfect** shows that an action or condition in the past preceded another past action or condition:

He had looked everywhere for a shark cage before he discovered Don's.

The **future perfect** shows that an action or condition in the future will precede another future action or condition:

Before the day ends, the shark will have eaten three divers.

 The "historical present tense" is sometimes used to make a story more vivid:

Then the driver of the other car starts yelling.

The present is also often used in referring to events in literature:

Julius Caesar ignores the warning to beware the ides of March.

❷ Why It Matters in Writing

Choosing the correct verb tense allows you to be clear about when events occur in time.

STUDENT MODEL

   The most significant experience in my life so far **has been** my trip to an old growth forest in Washington State. I **had** reluctantly **gone** on vacation with my parents, not realizing how much I would enjoy it. We visited a forest that **is** about 10,000 years old. I **will** never **forget** the dark silence and the damp, green smell of ancient cedars, pines, and spruces. The setting **was** like that of a Brothers Grimm fairy tale!

PRESENT PERFECT

PAST PERFECT

PRESENT

FUTURE

PAST

③ Practice and Apply

A. CONCEPT CHECK: Verb Tense

Choose the better tense of the verb in parentheses.

Small-Town Boy Makes Good

1. Even now, four centuries after his death, William Shakespeare (ranks, has ranked) as the greatest writer in English.

2. Over the years, many critics (argued, have argued) that his greatness comes in part from the ordinariness of his life.

3. Perhaps only someone who (has immersed, had immersed) himself completely in the joys and sorrows of normal life could have written with such humanity.

4. Shakespeare (grew, has grown) up in a middle-class family in the small town of Stratford-on-Avon.

5. By the time he was 28, he (became, had become) a popular actor and playwright in London.

6. When the London theaters were closed because of the plague, Shakespeare (writes, wrote) poetry instead of plays.

7. He (has produced, produced) about two plays a year.

8. Not much (is, was) known today about his private life.

9. Although scholars continue to search, it's not likely that they (will find, have found) anything new about Shakespeare.

10. By the 400th anniversary of Shakespeare's death in 2016, many more theatergoers (have become, will have become) admirers of Shakespeare.

➡ **For a SELF-CHECK and more practice, see the EXERCISE BANK, p. 614.**

B. REVISING: Correcting Verb Tense

Revise the following paragraph by correcting the verb tenses.

> **STUDENT MODEL**
>
> The original Globe Theatre, built in 1599, **(1)** <u>will accommodate</u> 3,000 people. This first Globe **(2)** <u>burn</u> down in 1613. By then, performances of some of Shakespeare's greatest plays **(3)** <u>take</u> place on the Globe's stage. Today, visitors **(4)** <u>have enjoyed</u> performances at the new Globe, which opened in 1997. If you visit, you **(5)** <u>will have found</u> that it holds 1,500 people, far fewer than in Shakespeare's day.

Change the verbs in a draft from your 🗂 **Working Portfolio** to another tense.

VERBS

LESSON 3 Progressive and Emphatic Forms

❶ Here's the Idea

▶ **The progressive form of a verb expresses an event in progress.**

She **was reading** a book when the lights went out.

Each of the six tenses has a progressive form, made by using a tense of the verb *be* with the present participle.

The Six Progressive Forms	
Present Progressive	We **are dancing.**
Past Progressive	We **were dancing.**
Future Progressive	We **will be dancing.**
Present Perfect Progressive	We **have been dancing.**
Past Perfect Progressive	We **had been dancing.**
Future Perfect Progressive	We **will have been dancing.**

HOT TIP The present progressive is often used with an adverb of time to indicate future action: **Rosa is leaving next week.**

▶ **The emphatic form gives special force to a verb.** The emphatic form is used only in the present and past tenses. It is commonly used to correct or contradict.

I did finish my homework. I do try to be neat. It does matter.

❷ Why It Matters in Writing

The progressive and emphatic forms allow you to stress verbs in particular ways. Notice their effect in this mother's warning.

LITERARY MODEL

Then she began, patiently, to describe to the girl the difficulties of the theater. Thousands of experienced, beautiful, and talented actresses were out of work. Even those who did work, didn't work often. . . . When Mrs. Wilson had finished, Elise said nothing.

"Well, what are you thinking, dear?"

—John Cheever, "The Opportunity"

PAST EMPHATIC

PRESENT PROGRESSIVE

❸ Practice and Apply

A. CONCEPT CHECK: Progressive and Emphatic Forms

Write a progressive or emphatic form of the verb in parentheses, using the correct tense.

> **Success with Stories**
>
> **1.** American writer John Cheever had some emotional problems, but he (manage) to create many remarkable short stories and novels.
> **2.** While he (attend) prep school, he got expelled for smoking.
> **3.** Although he was not concerned about his formal education, he (care) about becoming a writer.
> **4.** By 1930, he (begin) to publish short stories.
> **5.** Despite his problems, Cheever (succeed) as a writer.
> **6.** His stories include characters who (try) to express individuality in a society that demands conformity.
> **7.** Even though society (tolerate) individuality to a greater extent now, Cheever's writing remains very popular with readers.
> **8.** Booksellers (sell) his books well into the new millennium.
> **9.** Although she began writing at a later age than her father, Cheever's daughter Susan (become) a published writer as well.
> **10.** By the end of 2005, she (write) books for about 25 years.

➜ **For a SELF-CHECK and more practice, see the EXERCISE BANK, p. 615.**

B. EDITING: Different Verb Forms

Substitute progressive or emphatic forms for the underlined verbs.

> **STUDENT MODEL**
>
> Although John Cheever's life may have seemed ordinary, it **(1)** <u>features</u> some interesting ironies. True, he **(2)** <u>got</u> expelled from prep school. However, he wrote about the experience in his first published short story, titled, appropriately enough, "Expelled." Cheever never **(3)** <u>attended</u> college. During the 1950s and the 1970s, however, he **(4)** <u>taught</u> at several prestigious schools, such as Barnard College and the University of Iowa. While teaching writing to convicts at Sing Sing prison in the 1970s, Cheever **(5)** <u>wrote</u> stories about middle-class suburbanites.

A. Verb Tenses and Forms Choose the better verb tense or form.

1. Many critics today (praise, praised) Pablo Neruda as the greatest Latin American poet of the 20th century.
2. Born Neftalí Ricardo Reyes Basoalto in Chile in 1904, he (was writing, has written) poetry by the age of ten.
3. He first published his poems under his pen name, Pablo Neruda, because his father (was not approving, did not approve) of his poetry.
4. By 1946, he (adopts, had adopted) his pen name as his legal name.
5. By the time he was 20, Neruda (has become, had become) famous.
6. Because he couldn't make a living from his poetry, he (went, has gone) to work as a diplomat, living in such countries as Burma, Indonesia, Spain, France, Argentina, and Mexico.
7. Back home in the 1940s, Neruda (served, will have served) in the Chilean senate for two years.
8. He was forced to flee the country, however, after he (did publish, had published) a letter that was critical of another politician.
9. The political climate (is changing, did change) in the 1950s, however, so Neruda returned to Chile and lived a prosperous and productive life as a world-famous poet.
10. In 1971, although he was terminally ill from cancer, Neruda (traveled, had been traveling) to Stockholm to accept the Nobel Prize.

B. Progressive and Emphatic Verb Forms Identify the tense of each underlined verb. Where appropriate, also identify the verb as progressive or emphatic.

> **LITERARY MODEL**
>
> And, lastly, I **(1)** do not think that I **(2)** will forget days spent, a few summers ago, at a beautiful lodge built right into the rocky cliffs of a bay on the Maine coast. We **(3)** met a woman there who **(4)** had lived a purposeful and courageous life and who **(5)** was then dying of cancer. She **(6)** had, characteristically, just written a book and **(7)** taken up painting. She **(8)** had also been of radical viewpoint all her life; one of those people who energetically **(9)** believe that the world *can* be changed for the better and **(10)** spend their lives trying to do just that. And that **(11)** was the way she **(12)** thought of cancer; she absolutely **(13)** refused to award it the stature of tragedy. . . .
>
> —Lorraine Hansberry, "On Summer"

LESSON 4 The Voice of a Verb

1 Here's the Idea

The voice of an action verb indicates whether the subject **performs** or **receives** the action. Voice affects the meaning and tone of the sentence.

Active Voice

▶ **When a verb's subject *performs* the action expressed by the verb, the verb is in the active voice.**

> **Rita Dove writes poetry. She has been writing since childhood.**

Most of the sentences you write will be in the active voice. The active verb forms are the ones shown earlier in this chapter.

Passive Voice

▶ **When a verb's subject *receives* the action expressed by the verb, the verb is in the passive voice.**

> **In 1993, Dove was named poet laureate.**

The passive voice is often used when the person or thing performing the action is indefinite or unknown.

> **The announcement was made in all the major media.**

To form the passive in a particular tense, use the appropriate tense of the verb *be* with the past participle of the main verb.

> **Many people write poetry. Poetry is written by many people.**
> PRESENT➚   PRESENT➚   ➘PAST PARTICIPLE

2 Why It Matters in Writing

The active voice is used more frequently, but sometimes the passive voice will express the exact meaning you need. In the passage below, think about why the author chose the passive.

> **LITERARY MODEL**
>
> God give you a good day, grandfather. This is how I **was taught** as a child to greet my grandfather, or any grown person.
>
> —Rudolfo A. Anaya, "A Celebration of Grandfathers"

Passive voice here focuses attention on the person receiving the teaching.

❸ Practice and Apply

A. CONCEPT CHECK: The Voice of a Verb

Write each verb in parentheses using the correct tense and the correct voice—active or passive.

> **A Child at Manzanar**
> **1.** Jeanne Wakatsuki Houston (live) in Los Angeles; she was seven years old when war broke out between Japan and the United States in December 1941.
> **2.** Because of the war, some Americans (develop) anti-Japanese feelings.
> **3.** Executive Order 9066 (sign) by President Roosevelt.
> **4.** The order (authorize) the removal of all persons of Japanese descent from coastal areas.
> **5.** During 1942, more than 110,000 Japanese Americans living along the West Coast (remove) from their homes.
> **6.** They (send) inland to internment camps.
> **7.** The young Jeanne Wakatsuki (transport) along with members of her family to the internment camp called Manzanar.
> **8.** Earlier, her father (imprison) at a camp in North Dakota.
> **9.** Manzanar (build) in a dry, isolated area in south central California.
> **10.** Each of the camp's wooden barracks (accommodate) about 36 people.

➜ For a SELF-CHECK and more practice, see the EXERCISE BANK, p. 615.

B. REVISING: Being Direct

Revise the following paragraph, changing passive verb forms to active ones where appropriate.

(1) What happened in Manzanar was not even discussed by Jeanne Wakatsuki Houston for 25 years after she was released. **(2)** Her whole life had been affected by the years she spent there. **(3)** But a book about the experience that was written by her and her husband, James D. Houston, helped her deal with the trauma. **(4)** The book was published in 1973. **(5)** It has been hailed by critics and readers alike as a much needed personal account of one of the darker chapters in U.S. history.

Shifts in Tense, Form, and Voice

❶ Here's the Idea

Switch tenses, introduce progressive and emphatic forms, and change active into passive voice only as needed for clarity or style. Improper or unnecessary shifts will make your writing awkward and confusing.

Shifts in Tense and Form

▶ **Combine different verb tenses and forms to show how events are related in time or to emphasize them differently.**

He **arrived** just as he **had promised** he would.
↑ PAST ↑ PAST PERFECT

When the bus **came,** I **had been waiting** for two hours.
↑ PAST ↑ PAST PERFECT PROGRESSIVE

She **hated** lasagna as a child, but now she **thinks** it divine.
↑ PAST ↑ PRESENT

I **have read** your essay, and I **love** it!
↑ PRESENT PERFECT ↑ PRESENT

I **have had** enough, and I **will take** no more.
↑ PRESENT PERFECT ↑ FUTURE

▶ **Stick with one tense when describing actions related to a single period or event or when writing about a series of events.**

> **STUDENT MODEL**
>
> *DRAFT*
> Sammy **clobbered** the ball, and it **sails** over the center-field bleachers. Sammy **drove** in three runs in that game, and the next day he **has knocked** in three more.
>
> *REVISION*
> Sammy **clobbered** the ball, and it **sailed** over the center-field bleachers. Sammy **drove** in three runs in that game, and the next day he **knocked** in three more.

— one event

— two events in a series

HOT TIP

Most of the time, you will use the same tense for both parts of a compound verb or predicate, or in a compound sentence:

Sammy hits the ball and runs. He scores a run, and his team wins.

VERBS

Shifts in Voice

When you change a verb from active to passive, the object of the verb becomes the subject of the sentence. This change alters the focus of the sentence.

Active: Rita Dove won the 1987 Pulitzer Prize in poetry.
  ↑ SUBJECT   ↑ OBJECT

Passive: The 1987 Pulitzer Prize in poetry was won by Rita Dove.   ↑ SUBJECT

You can also change the emphasis of the sentence by changing the verb as well as using the passive voice.

Active: Rita Dove won a Pulitzer Prize in 1987.
  ↑ EMPHASIZES ACTIVE ROLE

Passive: Rita Dove was awarded a Pulitzer Prize in 1987.
  ↑ EMPHASIZES PASSIVE ROLE

▶ **Don't use the passive voice unnecessarily or as a way to avoid indicating who is responsible for an action.**

STUDENT MODEL

DRAFT
Mistakes were made. The assignment was not completed.

| Awkward—performer of action unclear |

REVISION
I made mistakes. I did not complete the assignment.

| Simple and direct—performer of action clear |

❷ Why It Matters in Writing

Shifting voice allows the author of the passage below to keep attention focused on himself regardless of whether he is performing or receiving the action.

LITERARY MODEL

By the time I met Marjorie Hurd four years later, I had learned English, had been placed in a normal, graded class and had even been chosen for the college preparatory track....

—Nicholas Gage, "The Teacher Who Changed My Life"

ACTIVE
PASSIVE

❸ Practice and Apply

A. CONCEPT CHECK: Shifts in Tense, Form, and Voice

Each of the following sentences contains an incorrect or an awkward use of verb tense, form, or voice. Revise each sentence to correct the problem.

A Voice of Her Own

1. Sandra Cisneros grew up for the most part in Chicago, but her father occasionally moves the family to Mexico.
2. As a child, Cisneros watched idealized families on television and wishes they were her own.
3. Because she felt lonely as a child, books were read by Cisneros for comfort.
4. One of her favorite children's books is *The Little House,* because it told of a family in a small but stable home.
5. Although some poetry had been written by Cisneros in high school, she did not start writing seriously until college.
6. By the time Cisneros published her first book, she already spent time teaching high-school dropouts in a Latino neighborhood.
7. Cisneros did not find her own voice for some time; at first she imitates favorite male poets such as Theodore Roethke.
8. Now she recognizes her own female voice and emphasized the importance of her ethnic background.
9. Her unique experience was embraced by Cisneros, and she found her literary voice.
10. Cisneros's loyal readers look forward to her books, which combined elements of fiction and poetry.

➡ **For a SELF-CHECK and more practice, see the EXERCISE BANK, p. 616.**

B. WRITING: Using Verb Tense and Voice Correctly

Use the following time line to write a short biographical sketch about Sandra Cisneros. Use at least three different verb forms.

Born in Chicago	B.A. English Loyola University	M.F.A. Iowa Writers Workshop	*The House on Mango Street*	Before Columbus American Book Award	MacArthur Foundation Fellowship
1954	1976	1978	1984	1985	1995

The Mood of a Verb

❶ Here's the Idea

▶ **The mood of a verb conveys the status of the action or condition it expresses.** Verbs have three moods: indicative, subjunctive, and imperative.

Indicative Use the **indicative mood** to make statements or ask questions. The indicative is the most commonly used mood; all of the verb forms taught earlier in this chapter are indicative.

Subjunctive Use the **subjunctive mood** to express a wish or state a condition that is contrary to fact.

Comparison of Indicative and Subjunctive	
Indicative	**Subjunctive**
Mr. Green **is** my teacher.	I wish Ms. Li **were** my teacher. (wish)
Fran **has** money; I'll ask her for some.	If Ted **had** money, I would ask him for some. (contrary to fact)

Notice that the subjunctive forms in the chart above are identical to past plural forms.

You can also use the subjunctive, in more formal communication, to express a command or request after the word *that*. In this case, the form of the verb is identical to its base form.

She insisted that I sit still and tell the story.

Imperative Use the **imperative mood** to make a request or give a command. This mood has only one tense, the present. Notice that the subject, *you,* is omitted.

Remember to call your sister. Please do it soon.

❷ Why It Matters in Writing

The subjunctive mood allows you to write about things as they might be or might have been rather than simply as they are or were.

LITERARY MODEL

His heart thudded more than if he **had been lying**
behind a bush in the forest waiting for Bilgan the Giant.... **SUBJUNCTIVE**

—Heinrich Böll, "The Balek Scales"

❸ Practice and Apply

A. CONCEPT CHECK: The Mood of a Verb

Identify each underlined verb or verb phrase in the following quotations as indicative, imperative, or subjunctive.

LITERARY MODELS

The Words to Say It
1. Love is not all: it <u>is</u> not meat nor drink
   Nor slumber nor a roof against the rain;
   —Edna St. Vincent Millay, "Sonnet 30"
2. "<u>Put</u> your mother on the phone," I said. "Put *your* mother on the phone," she said, "and I'll ask her how it <u>feels</u> to have a crazy son." "Crazy, huh? . . . <u>Have</u> you already <u>forgotten</u> our plans to have children?" "Well, <u>start</u> without me. I'm definitely not having them if they're yours." —Bill Cosby, *Love and Marriage*
3. I admired the watch at length, and tried it in various of my pockets, and said that, <u>had I known</u>, I would have worn a vest. —David Mamet, "The Watch"
4. I <u>close</u> my eyes, and side by side I <u>see</u> the Charley of my boyhood and the Charley of this afternoon, as clearly as if I <u>were looking</u> at a split TV screen.
   —Eugenia Collier, "Sweet Potato Pie"

➜ For a SELF-CHECK and more practice, see the EXERCISE BANK, p. 617.

B. REVISING: Changing Moods

Rewrite the following sentences as indicated.

1. When I am famous, I will sign autographs for my fans. (Change from indicative to subjunctive.)
2. You shouldn't count on fame in your future. (Change from indicative to imperative.)
3. If I went to Hollywood, I would become a star. (Change from subjunctive to indicative.)
4. If I were you, I'd be more realistic. (Change from subjunctive to imperative.)
5. I want you to give me a chance. (Change from indicative to imperative.)

VERBS

Grammar in Literature

Verbs and Lively Writing

In the passage below, noted writer Maya Angelou shares her memories of working as a streetcar driver in San Francisco. By choosing interesting action verbs and using the active voice, Angelou successfully conveys to readers her elation at getting the job, the excitement of the job itself, and the feelings of freedom and independence she derived from it.

from *I Know Why the Caged Bird Sings*

—Maya Angelou

Mother gave me the money to have my blue serge suit tailored, and I learned to fill out work cards, operate the money changer and punch transfers. The time crowded together and at an End of Days I was swinging on the back of the rackety trolley, smiling sweetly and persuading my charges to "step forward in the car, please."

For one whole semester the streetcars and I shimmied up and scooted down the sheer hills of San Francisco. I lost some of my need for the Black ghetto's shielding-sponge quality, as I clanged and cleared my way down Market Street, with its honky-tonk homes for homeless sailors, past the quiet retreat of Golden Gate Park and along closed undwelled-in-looking dwellings of the Sunset District.

> **VIVID ACTION VERB**
> Conveys the swift passage of time

> **PROGRESSIVE FORMS**
> Stress the flow of ongoing action

> **PRECISE VERBS**
> Bring the scene to life with sensory detail

When good writers revise their sentences, they try to replace overused or vague verbs with ones that are fresh and precise, and they use the active voice whenever possible.

Using Verbs Effectively

Fresh verbs	Attract the reader's interest with unusual, vivid description. **Example:** Mahmoud *deposited* himself at his desk. (instead of *sat*)
Precise verbs	Provide exact, specific information that is easy to picture. **Example:** The dog *trotted* down the sidewalk. (instead of *walked*)
Active voice	Sounds more direct and forceful than the passive voice. **Example:** The opposing guard knocked the ball from Ceretha's hand. (instead of *The ball was knocked from Ceretha's hand.*)

VERBS

PRACTICE AND APPLY: Using Verbs Effectively

The following paragraph needs revision because the writer has chosen several verbs that are dull and imprecise and has used the passive voice inappropriately. Revise the paragraph to make it more lively by replacing the underlined verbs and verb phrases.

My most unusual, although not my favorite, summer job was working as a swimming waitress at a seafood restaurant on Cape Cod in Massachusetts. There were three of us; and our job was to <u>entertain</u> the diners by <u>doing</u> a sort of water ballet in a huge tank, then <u>come out</u> soaking wet and with dripping hair to hurriedly don uniforms and <u>give</u> soggy fish and chips to the customers. If <u>our performances were enjoyed by them</u>, they didn't choose to show it by bestowing lavish tips.

After you have revised the paragraph, discuss with a partner how you think you have made it more effective.

Choose a piece of writing from your 📁 **Working Portfolio** and change some verbs to make the piece more interesting and lively.

Mixed Review

A. Verb Tense, Form, and Voice Read each sentence and write the correct tense, form, and voice of the verb in parentheses.

1. Emily Dickinson's poetry was virtually unknown during her lifetime, although she (write) 1,775 poems by the time she died in 1886.
2. The extent of her genius only became fully known in 1955 when a complete edition of her poems (publish).
3. Dickinson's long anonymity was caused partly by her own shyness, but it also (perpetuate) by the bad judgment of some literary men.
4. By the time a newspaper editor did publish five of her poems, her confidence in the reading public (shake).
5. One literary friend of Dickinson's, Thomas Wentworth Higginson, advised her not to publish her poems because they (be) so unusual.
6. By the time Dickinson was 32 years old, she (decide) not to have any more of her poems published.
7. Even though she had given up trying to publish, she never (give) up writing.
8. While she lived the rest of her life secluded from the world, Dickinson (write) steadily and quietly.
9. After her death, those closest to her were amazed to find so many poems; the poems (tie) in neat packets and hidden in her room.
10. Critics today classify Dickinson as a founder of modern American poetry, and she (stand) among the great American poets.

B. Verb Tense in Different Forms, Voices, and Moods Replace each numbered verb with a verb or a verb phrase whose tense, voice, and mood better express the paragraph's meaning.

> **STUDENT MODEL**
>
> For generations, readers **(1) be** fascinated by Edgar Allan Poe's tales of horror and mystery. If you **(2) get** acquainted with Poe's work, you would see why. Read the opening paragraphs of any story. Soon, you **(3) draw** inside the mind of the main character as if it **(4) be** your own.
>
> In many ways, Poe **(5) lead** a life as mysterious and tragic as one depicted in his stories. Orphaned at age three, he **(6) raise** by foster parents John and Frances Allan. John Allan refused to support Poe's literary ambitions, even though he **(7) provide** Poe with a first-class education earlier in his life. Ultimately Allan **(8) die** without leaving Poe a penny. If Poe **(9) receive** an inheritance from Allan, his life might not have been so desperate and poverty stricken. Poe never succeeded in earning a living from his writing, even though he **(10) become** famous in his lifetime.

Choose the best way to rewrite each underlined word or group of words.

Aside from college and the years he <u>teached</u> in West Africa, Joseph
(1)
Bruchac has lived all his life in a small town in the Adirondacks. Bruchac

is presently <u>lives</u> two lives. In one, he <u>is</u> a writer, a businessman, a father,
(2)   (3)
and a husband; in the other, he is the best-known Native American

storyteller alive today. For his many highly acclaimed story collections,

Bruchac <u>had drawn</u> heavily on his heritage. Moreover, he doesn't just
(4)
write his stories; <u>they are also performed by him</u>. In doing so, he
(5)
<u>does carry on</u> a tradition that <u>begun</u> hundreds of years ago. Bruchac
(6)   (7)
<u>is believing</u> that his first job as a writer and storyteller is to entertain and
(8)
his second is to teach. He <u>taught</u> college students and has also worked to
(9)
help start writing workshops in prisons. Instead of wishing that his life

<u>was</u> different, he believes that "if you follow a sort of natural flow, the
(10)
results are usually much better."

1. A. had taught
   B. taught
   C. will teach
   D. Correct as is

2. A. having lived
   B. being alive
   C. living
   D. Correct as is

3. A. was
   B. were
   C. had been
   D. Correct as is

4. A. has drawn
   B. will draw
   C. was drawing
   D. Correct as is

5. A. he also performs them
   B. he is also performing them
   C. he also performed them
   D. Correct as is

6. A. carried on
   B. carries on
   C. did carry on
   D. Correct as is

7. A. has begun
   B. had begun
   C. began
   D. Correct as is

8. A. has believed
   B. believed
   C. believes
   D. Correct as is

9. A. has taught
   B. had taught
   C. will have taught
   D. Correct as is

10. A. has been
    B. were
    C. is
    D. Correct as is

VERBS

Student Help Desk

Verbs at a Glance

TENSE

	Active VOICE	Passive VOICE
Present	I help.	I am helped.
Past	I helped.	I was helped.
Future	I will help.	I will be helped.
Present Perfect	I have helped.	I have been helped.
Past Perfect	I had helped.	I had been helped.
Future Perfect	I will have helped.	I will have been helped.

MOOD

Indicative	Imperative	Subjunctive
	Help!	If you had helped, the job would be done by now.

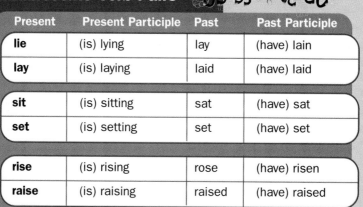

Troublesome Verb Pairs

Present	Present Participle	Past	Past Participle
lie	(is) lying	lay	(have) lain
lay	(is) laying	laid	(have) laid
sit	(is) sitting	sat	(have) sat
set	(is) setting	set	(have) set
rise	(is) rising	rose	(have) risen
raise	(is) raising	raised	(have) raised

Do not take a direct object

Lie: I lie in my bed.
  I lay there yesterday.
Sit: I sit on my chair.
Rise: I rise early.

Do take a direct object

Lay: I lay my book on my bed.
  I laid it there yesterday.
Set: I set my book on my chair.
Raise: I raise my weary eyelids.

Verbs Tenses and Forms

Tense but Not Nervous

Past

Past	I **wrote** a lot of stories as a child.
Past Progressive	I **was** always **dreaming** about something.
Past Perfect	By the age of seven, I **had written** ten stories.

Present

Present	I still **enjoy** the experience of writing.
Present Perfect	Writing **has given** me a way to express my dreams.
Present Progressive	Ideas **are** always **popping** into my head.

Future

Future	One day I **will write** the complete story of my life.
Future Progressive	Probably, I **will be writing** a long time.
Future Perfect	Then I **will have done** something amazing.

Rhymes with Orange

Improve Your Life with Verbs

The Bottom Line

Checklist for Using Verbs

Have I . . .

____ checked forms of irregular verbs?

____ checked to make sure I've used the tenses I need?

____ checked for unnecessary shifts in tenses and other forms?

____ checked for correct use of the passive voice?

Subject-Verb Agreement

Theme: The Movies

What's Up?

In the movies, Superman flies. Dinosaurs spring to life, and starships speed through distant galaxies. How does this happen? Only through special effects.

One kind of special effect is created by combining two separate sequences. The actor playing Superman is first filmed in front of a special screen. The image of the screen is later replaced with the desired background. For the effect to work, the two images must blend together perfectly. In a similar way, a writer must seamlessly match the subject and verb in every sentence.

Write Away: Sentence Loops

Have one person in a small group write the beginning of a sentence on a piece of paper and then pass the paper to another person, who writes the end of that sentence and starts another one. Keep going until each person has had a turn, with the first person finishing the last sentence. Have one group member read the story aloud and save it in his or her  **Working Portfolio.**

Grammar Coach

Diagnostic Test: What Do You Know?

Choose the letter of the best revision for each underlined section.

> Many <u>think of Stephen King as a writer of horror fiction and expects</u> (1) his films to be typical horror films. Rob Reiner <u>has directed two films based on King's books and have said</u> (2) that King's fiction is intelligent and realistic. King's story "The Body," about four young boys, is the basis of Reiner's film *Stand by Me.* The group <u>look for a dead body and confront</u> (3) a gang of thugs. There <u>is</u> (4) scary moments and fighting in the film, but no gory horror-movie effects. *Misery,* King's novel about a writer and a fan, <u>have also been made into a scary movie that has become</u> (5) popular. Neither *Stand by Me* nor *Misery* is a typical horror film.

1. A. thinks of Stephen King as a writer of horror fiction and expects
   B. think of Stephen King as a writer of horror fiction and expect
   C. thinks of Stephen King as a writer of horror fiction and expect
   D. Correct as is

2. A. has directed two films based on King's books and has said
   B. have directed two films based on King's books and have said
   C. have directed two films based on King's books and has said
   D. Correct as is

3. A. looks for a dead body and confront
   B. look for a dead body and confronts
   C. looks for a dead body and confronts
   D. Correct as is

4. A. be
   B. are
   C. am
   D. Correct as is

5. A. has also been made into a scary movie that has become
   B. have also been made into a scary movie that have become
   C. has also been made into a scary movie that have become
   D. Correct as is

SUBJECT-VERB

Subject-Verb Agreement 155

Agreement in Number

① Here's the Idea

▶ **Verbs must agree with their subjects in number.** *Number* refers to whether a word is singular or plural.

Matching Verbs with Subjects

Singular subjects take singular verbs. Plural subjects take plural verbs.

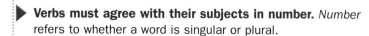

AGREE

A ferocious fistfight looks **real in a film.**

AGREE

The fighters look **as if they were really being punched.**

A stunt person knows **many tricks to avoid being hurt.**

Stunt people know **they must make a scene appear real.**

If a noun ends in s, it is usually plural. However, a verb that ends in s is usually singular.

Agreement with Helping Verbs

In a verb phrase, it is the first helping verb that must agree with the subject.

Some movie stars have been trained **to do stunts safely.**

Often an untrained star has been replaced **by a stunt double.**

② Why It Matters in Writing

When you revise, you might change a subject from singular to plural or vice versa. Watch for errors here. If you change the number of a subject, be sure to change the verb too.

STUDENT MODEL

DRAFT
Stunt people perform action scenes safely and make a film exciting.

REVISION
A stunt person performs action scenes safely and makes a film exciting.

❸ Practice and Apply

A. CONCEPT CHECK: Agreement in Number

For each sentence, write the verb form that agrees with the subject.

Pow! Bam! Crash!

1. A stunt person (undergoes, undergo) training for dangerous scenes.
2. Untrained stunt performers (has, have) had broken bones.
3. Camera angles (helps, help) make a fight seem real.
4. On the set the sheriff (has, have) met an outlaw in an alley.
5. In reality, no punches actually (lands, land) on the actors.
6. The camera (stands, stand) behind one of the actors.
7. The fighter (throws, throw) punches from side to side.
8. The receivers of punches (has, have) learned to throw their head back.
9. Each stunt person also (staggers, stagger) around as if being knocked about.
10. Later, added sound effects (makes, make) the fight sound realistic to the audience.

➡ **For a SELF-CHECK and more practice, see the EXERCISE BANK, p. 617.**

Rewrite each sentence above, changing the number of the subject.

B. PROOFREADING: Making Subjects and Verbs Agree

Find and correct ten agreement errors in these paragraphs.

Fakes Make It Look Real

Audiences has seen many dangerous scenes on the screen. But movie props provides safety for the actors. When a character fall through a glass window, it seem that he or she should be cut to pieces. Actually, the "glass" is made of plastic. The plastic sheet shatter into many pieces without sharp edges. This fake glass is called candy glass. Why? In the old days it were made of hardened sugar syrup.

While one actor plunges through a window, other characters breaks tables over one another's heads. Ouch! Luckily, the tables is constructed of balsa wood. This lightweight material do not cause injury to the actors. Isn't it interesting that it take fake materials to make movies look real!

Phrases Between Subject and Verb

❶ Here's the Idea

▶ **When a phrase comes between the subject and verb, the number of the subject is not changed.** Focus on the subject when deciding whether the verb should be singular or plural.

Prepositional Phrase

The success of Hollywood films is based on the grosses.
    ▲SINGULAR SUBJECT   ▲SINGULAR VERB

Filmgoers at the box office give a financial thumbs up to a film.
    ▲PLURAL SUBJECT   ▲PLURAL VERB

Appositive Phrase

Jurassic Park, a high-grossing film, has made many millions.
    ▲SINGULAR SUBJECT   ▲SINGULAR VERB

Sequels—*The Lost World* and others—generally make less.
    ▲PLURAL SUBJECT   PLURAL VERB ➚

Participial Phrase

Sometimes a movie loved by millions receives a poor review.

Movie lovers, playing critic, turn the movie around.

❷ Why It Matters in Writing

Writers often insert phrases between subjects and verbs in order to put relevant information where it belongs. They must keep track of each subject so that they can make the verb agree.

STUDENT MODEL

    In the popular movie *Jurassic Park,* a rich man creates a theme park filled with dinosaurs. A **professor** from Arizona, an expert in dinosaur remains, visits the park. Unfortunately, the **dinosaurs,** huge and uncontrollable animals, get loose and kill some humans. The park must be destroyed.

> The subject *professor* takes the singular verb *visits.*

> The plural subject *dinosaurs* takes the plural verbs *get* and *kill.*

❸ Practice and Apply

A. CONCEPT CHECK: Phrases Between Subjects and Verbs

For each sentence, write the verb form that agrees with the subject.

Dinosaurs Up Close

1. *Jurassic Park*, a film about a unique theme park, (combines, combine) real science with imaginative theories.
2. In the movie, DNA fragments from a dinosaur (is, are) found in a prehistoric mosquito.
3. Amber, fossilized resin from trees, (has, have) preserved the mosquito and the DNA.
4. The DNA segments, placed in an ostrich egg, eventually (produces, produce) a dinosaur.
5. Soon the theme park, on a supposedly secure island, (contains, contain) several vicious dinosaurs.
6. Bob Bakker, one of today's leading dinosaur specialists, (says, say) the movie's premise is an impossibility.
7. A mosquito with dinosaur DNA (is, are) an impossibility, since the insect would have digested the DNA before being preserved.
8. DNA from prehistoric times (is, are) likely to be contaminated with other organisms' DNA.
9. Chemicals inside a mother animal (is, are) needed to create a baby of the same species.
10. Most plant foods needed by a herbivorous dinosaur (has, have) died out.

➡ **For a SELF-CHECK and more practice, see the EXERCISE BANK, p. 618.**

B. PROOFREADING: Making Subjects and Verbs Agree

Find and correct five agreement errors in this paragraph.

Bringing Dinosaurs to Life

Stan Winston, one of Hollywood's special-effects designers, have brought dinosaurs to life. The *Jurassic Park* creations by his studio seems amazingly realistic. Over a two-year period, small models of a *Tyrannosaurus rex* was transformed into a 9,000-pound, 20-foot sculpture. One model, hooked electronically to the sculpture's joints, were moved about. The movements of the model was reproduced exactly by the life-size "beast."

SUBJECT-VERB

Compound Subjects

❶ Here's the Idea

▶ **A compound subject contains two or more simple subjects. Compound subjects can take either singular or plural verbs.**

Parts Joined by *And*

A compound subject whose parts are joined by *and* requires a plural verb.

Pictures and movement come **together in animated films.**

Some compounds act as a single unit and take singular verbs.

An animator's bread and butter is **cartoons.**

Parts Joined by *Or* or *Nor*

When the parts of a compound subject are joined by *or* or *nor*, the verb should agree with the part closest to it.

> SINGULAR OR PLURAL **+** SINGULAR ➡ SINGULAR VERB

Neither animation cels nor celluloid **film** was used **for that movie.**

> SINGULAR OR PLURAL **+** PLURAL ➡ PLURAL VERB

Neither celluloid film nor animation **cels** were used **for that movie.**

❷ Why It Matters in Writing

In terms of meaning, it often doesn't matter which part of a compound subject comes first. A writer may use whichever order sounds better.

Either the projector or the reels are damaged.

Either the reels or the projector is damaged.

HOT TIP

If a compound subject sounds odd, you can revise the sentence to replace it.

ODD: **Neither the reels nor the projector was replaced.**

BETTER: **No one has replaced the projector or the reels.**

❸ Practice and Apply

A. CONCEPT CHECK: Compound Subjects

For each sentence, write the verb form that agrees with the subject.

Characters in Motion

1. Mickey Mouse and Roger Rabbit (is, are) both products of film animation.
2. In cel animation, an animator and artists called in-betweeners (works, work) together to create a series of drawings.
3. "Extremes" and in-between drawings (makes, make) up an animated scene.
4. Either traditional methods or computer techniques (is, are) used for coloring frames.
5. Neither light pens nor the electronic drawing pad (has, have) been around longer than computers.
6. Animated cartoon figures and human actors (appears, appear) together in *Who Framed Roger Rabbit.*
7. Humans and "toons" (inhabits, inhabit) the same world.
8. Cel animation and computer animation (is, are) not the only animation techniques.
9. Sand-cel animation and finger-painting animation (is, are) two more film animation methods.
10. Hefty box office receipts and high television cartoon ratings (shows, show) the continuing popularity of animation.

➡ **For a SELF-CHECK and more practice, see the EXERCISE BANK, p. 618.**

Rewrite sentences 2, 4, and 5 with the parts of the subjects reversed.

B. WRITING: Interpreting a Cartoon

Describe what's happening in this cartoon, using two sentences that have compound subjects.

By Jack Ziegler

"Action! And this time believe!"

© The New Yorker Collection 1991 Jack Ziegler

SUBJECT-VERB

Indefinite-Pronoun Subjects

LESSON 4

❶ Here's the Idea

▶ When used as subjects, some indefinite pronouns are always singular, some are always plural, and some can be either singular or plural, depending on how they're used.

Indefinite Pronouns	
Singular	another, anybody, anyone, anything, each, either, everybody, everyone, everything, much, neither, nobody, no one, nothing, one, somebody, someone, something
Plural	both, few, many, several
Singular or plural	all, any, more, most, none, some

Singular indefinite pronouns take singular verbs.

Everyone has a favorite film star.

Nobody is without opinions on films.

Plural indefinite pronouns take plural verbs.

Many of the films are nominated for Oscars. Few win, however.

Some indefinite pronouns take singular verbs when they refer to one person or thing. They take plural verbs when they refer to two or more people or things.

REFERS TO

Most of the Oscar show is broadcast from Hollywood.
SINGULAR

REFERS TO

Most of the winners appear at the Oscars.
PLURAL

❷ Why It Matters in Writing

Writers use indefinite pronouns frequently, especially in making generalizations.

> **LITERARY MODEL**
>
> **Everyone** knows the location of any number from 1 to 12 on the clock dial and easily can use such a reference to find an object.
>
> —Isaac Asimov, "Dial Versus Digital"

❸ Practice and Apply

A. CONCEPT CHECK: Indefinite-Pronoun Subjects

For each sentence, write the verb form that agrees with the subject.

> **A Night of Excitement**
> **1.** Many (watches, watch) the Academy Awards show annually.
> **2.** Few (knows, know), however, that the Oscar statuette is named for a Hollywood librarian's uncle.
> **3.** All of the program (is, are) broadcast live on television.
> **4.** Some of the ceremony (consists, consist) of performances.
> **5.** Several of America's most popular actors (has, have) won more than one Oscar.
> **6.** A few, however, (has, have) never won.
> **7.** Nobody ever (agrees, agree) with all the awards.
> **8.** Most of the nominees (prepares, prepare) speeches.
> **9.** Still, many (talks, talk) too long when accepting their awards.
> **10.** Everyone (is, are) not as brief as Barbra Streisand, who said, "Hello, gorgeous!"

➜ **For a SELF-CHECK and more practice, see the EXERCISE BANK, p. 619.**

B. PROOFREADING: Checking Indefinite-Pronoun Agreement

Correct each verb that does not agree with its subject. If a sentence is correct, write *Correct.*

> **A Range of Talent**
> **(1)** Denzel Washington has never realized his ambitions of becoming a doctor or a journalist. **(2)** However, both of these has been played by him on screen. **(3)** Many recalls Washington as a doctor on TV's *St. Elsewhere* and as a reporter in *The Pelican Brief.* **(4)** Some of Washington's best roles has been in historical films. **(5)** Everyone probably remember him as a brave soldier in *Glory.* **(6)** Few have expressed surprise at his Oscar for that role. **(7)** Another of his roles are the title character, an African-American activist, in *Malcolm X.* **(8)** All of the critics has praised Washington's portrayal of the South African activist Steve Biko in *Cry Freedom.* **(9)** Each of these roles have shown Washington's intense dramatic side. **(10)** But none of his fans doubts his talent for light romantic parts, as in *The Preacher's Wife.*

Subject-Verb Agreement **163**

SUBJECT-VERB

Other Problem Subjects

❶ Here's the Idea

Sometimes the number of a subject can be hard to determine. To decide whether a subject takes a singular or a plural verb, you sometimes need to decide whether the subject refers to a unit or to individuals.

Collective Nouns

▶ **A collective noun takes a singular verb if the members of the group act together. A collective noun takes a plural verb if the members of the group act as individuals.**

In *Major League*, **an inferior team** (unit) strives **to improve.**

     🔺 SINGULAR VERB

The team (individuals) have **different ideas about how to improve.** 🔺 PLURAL VERB

Nouns Plural in Form

▶ **Some nouns ending in -s or -ics appear to be plural but are singular in meaning.** Use singular verbs with these subjects.

civics	mumps	physics
mathematics	news	politics

In *The Candidate*, **politics** is **the major theme.**

     🔺 SINGULAR VERB

Some words ending in -ics, such as *ethics*, can be singular or plural, depending on the context.

Ethics does **not** play **much of a role in the movie.**

     🔺 SINGULAR VERB

The candidate's ethics are **questionable.**

     🔺 PLURAL VERB

Titles and Numerical Amounts

▶ **Titles of works of art, literature, film, or music are singular. Words and phrases that refer to weights, measures, numbers, and lengths of time are usually treated as singular.**

Titles and Amounts		
Titles	*Cats* is a long-running musical.	***The Mists of Avalon*** tells about the women of King Arthur's time.
Amounts	**Eight dollars** seems too much to pay for a movie.	**Five cups** is the amount in the largest soft drink.
Time	**Two hours** is the running time of this film.	**Five days** is the limit for borrowing library videos.

Fractions, such as *three-quarters* and *seven-eighths,* can be considered singular or plural, depending on the context.

REFERS TO

Three-quarters of the audience was **asleep.**
                               SINGULAR

REFERS TO

Two-thirds of the viewers were **eager to see another movie.**
                   PLURAL

❷ Why It Matters in Writing

In writing about certain topics, you may need to use tricky subjects, such as titles or nouns that sound plural but are not. If

you are uncertain whether to use plural or singular verbs, try substituting another word or phrase for each problem subject.

Raiders of the Lost Ark is **a very popular movie.**

(The adventure film) is **a very popular movie.**

Twenty million dollars was budgeted **for the film.**

(A large amount of money) was budgeted **for the film.**

❸ Practice and Apply

A. CONCEPT CHECK: Other Problem Subjects

For each sentence, write the verb form that agrees with the subject.

Enduring Classics

1. The big news in Hollywood (is, are) the popularity of films based on classic literature.
2. Jane Austen's novel *Sense and Sensibility* (has, have) been made into a popular movie.
3. In that film, an English family (moves, move) to a new home.
4. A pair of sisters (falls, fall) in love with two very different men.
5. Politics (plays, play) no central role in Austen's novels.
6. In *Emma,* a group of people in an English village (deals, deal) with issues of love and marriage.
7. For many movie fans, two hours in a 19th-century English village (is, are) an engaging experience.
8. The literary audience (has, have) always appreciated films based on Shakespeare's plays.
9. *Romeo and Juliet* (has, have) been the basis of several films.
10. A fine cast (portrays, portray) scenes from Shakespeare's life and works in *Shakespeare in Love.*

➡ **For a SELF-CHECK and more practice, see the EXERCISE BANK, p. 619.**

B. EDITING AND PROOFREADING: Correcting Agreement Errors

Rewrite any sentence that contains an error in subject-verb agreement. Write *Correct* if there is no error.

Mad for Musicals

1. Nine-tenths of us has probably enjoyed a musical film.
2. *The Jazz Singer* is considered the first musical.
3. The most popular dance team in musicals were composed of Ginger Rogers and Fred Astaire.
4. A singing family face Nazism in *The Sound of Music.*
5. "Summer Nights" are sung by John Travolta and Olivia Newton-John in the musical film *Grease.*
6. Thirty-six hours are the time period covered in *A Hard Day's Night,* a musical featuring the Beatles.
7. The band display a zany comedy style.
8. *The Commitments* are a contemporary musical.
9. An Irish rock group are at the center of this movie.
10. The cast of most musicals is usually quite big.

Special Sentence Problems

❶ Here's the Idea

Making a verb agree with its subject can be tricky when the subject is difficult to identify.

Questions

In many questions, subjects follow verbs or come between parts of verb phrases. To find the subject in such a question, rewrite the question as a statement. Use the verb form that agrees with the subject of the statement.

Are **comedians** respected **as much as serious actors?**

Comedians are respected **as much as serious actors.**

Is **comedy harder to perform than drama?**

Comedy is **harder to perform than drama.**

Sentences Beginning with *Here* or *There*

In sentences beginning with *here* or *there,* those words rarely function as subjects. The subjects usually follow the verbs.

There are **many famous comedies in the history of film.**

Here is **a video full of funny scenes.**

Inverted Sentences

In an inverted sentence, the subject follows the verb. Do not confuse a word in an initial phrase with the subject.

Even more touching than the dramatic actors are **the clowns.**

The clowns are **even more touching than the dramatic actors.**

Over the wall scrambles **the runaway thief.**

The runaway thief scrambles **over the wall.**

Predicate Nominatives

In a sentence containing a predicate nominative, the verb must agree with the subject, not with the predicate nominative.

Jan's main passion is the comedies of Robin Williams.

AGREE ↟ PREDICATE NOMINATIVE

The comedies of Robin Williams are Jan's main passion.

PREDICATE NOMINATIVE ↴

AGREE

Relative Pronouns as Subjects

When a relative pronoun (*who, which,* or *that*) is the subject of an adjective clause, its number is determined by the number of the word it refers to.

REFERS TO

An actor who plays both comedy and drama is unusual.

REFERS TO

Actors who play both comedy and drama are unusual.

WATCH OUT Don't be fooled by *don't* and *doesn't.* These words are contractions made up of a helping verb (*do* or *does*) and the word *not.* The helping verb should agree with the subject, as usual.

Comedians don't usually win Oscars.

Sammi doesn't think that makes any sense.

❷ Why It Matters in Writing

When you write, you probably start sentences with *here* and *there* and use predicate nominatives without thinking, just as you do when talking. Check for subject-verb agreement as you revise.

> **STUDENT MODEL**
>
> In *Love and Marriage,* television and film star Bill Cosby tells the story of his courtship. There are some serious moments in the book, but parts of it ~~is~~ *are* sheer comedy. Here ~~are~~ *is* one of the funny parts: when he tries to take out one girl to make another one jealous, both girls catch on.

A. CONCEPT CHECK: Special Sentence Problems

For each sentence, write the correct verb form in parentheses. Then write the subject with which the verb agrees.

> **The Great Stone Face**
> **1.** (Does, Do) Buster Keaton outshine Charlie Chaplin as a film comedian?
> **2.** Revealed in over 40 movies (is, are) Keaton's unique comic character.
> **3.** Keaton's films, which often (includes, include) elements of absurdity, seem modern today.
> **4.** Battles against modern technology (is, are) the subject of many of Keaton's films.
> **5.** (Doesn't, Don't) the greatest chase scene in comedy occur in Keaton's *The General?*
> **6.** Keaton conceived some comedic moments that (is, are) still imitated today.
> **7.** Through all the films (runs, run) Keaton's stone-faced comedy.
> **8.** There (is, are) only one movie that shows Keaton laughing.
> **9.** (Is, Are) "The Great Stone Face" a good nickname for Keaton?
> **10.** Down the faces of Keaton's audiences always (pours, pour) tears of laughter.

➡ **For a SELF-CHECK and more practice, see the EXERCISE BANK, p. 620.**

CHALLENGE

Rewrite each inverted sentence and question as a declarative sentence in which the subject precedes the verb.

B. WRITING: Maintaining Agreement

The photo shows Michael Jordan facing the Monstars in the movie *Space Jam.* Write five sentences describing the scene, using sentence forms discussed in this lesson.

📁 **Working Portfolio**
Return to the group you joined for the **Write Away** on page 154. Take out the sentence loops and work together to check subject-verb agreement. Revise if necessary.

Real World Grammar

Movie Review

A local library is setting up a database of movie reviews and has asked students to contribute to it. Because reviews are written in the present tense, errors in subject-verb agreement can easily creep in. Read Rayla's review of the movie *Glory*. The comments were made by the video librarian, who asked Rayla to correct some errors that might confuse readers.

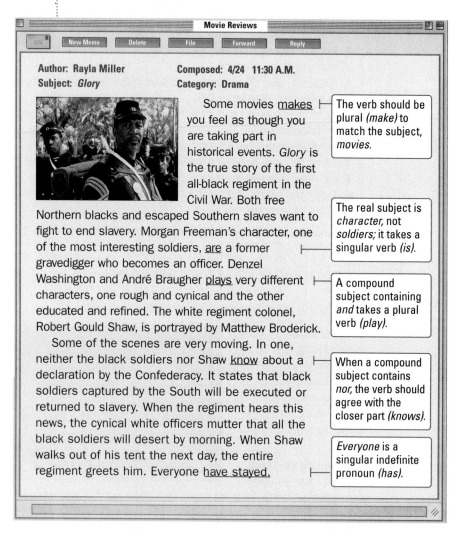

Movie Reviews

New Memo | Delete | File | Forward | Reply

Author: Rayla Miller
Subject: *Glory*

Composed: 4/24 11:30 A.M.
Category: Drama

Some movies <u>makes</u> you feel as though you are taking part in historical events. *Glory* is the true story of the first all-black regiment in the Civil War. Both free Northern blacks and escaped Southern slaves want to fight to end slavery. Morgan Freeman's character, one of the most interesting soldiers, <u>are</u> a former gravedigger who becomes an officer. Denzel Washington and André Braugher <u>plays</u> very different characters, one rough and cynical and the other educated and refined. The white regiment colonel, Robert Gould Shaw, is portrayed by Matthew Broderick.

Some of the scenes are very moving. In one, neither the black soldiers nor Shaw <u>know</u> about a declaration by the Confederacy. It states that black soldiers captured by the South will be executed or returned to slavery. When the regiment hears this news, the cynical white officers mutter that all the black soldiers will desert by morning. When Shaw walks out of his tent the next day, the entire regiment greets him. Everyone <u>have stayed.</u>

> The verb should be plural *(make)* to match the subject, *movies.*

> The real subject is *character,* not *soldiers;* it takes a singular verb *(is).*

> A compound subject containing *and* takes a plural verb *(play).*

> When a compound subject contains *nor,* the verb should agree with the closer part *(knows).*

> *Everyone* is a singular indefinite pronoun *(has).*

Using Grammar in Writing

Agreement in number	Watch out for plural subjects that don't look plural. Examples include plural nouns that don't end in -*s* (*children, mice, deer*) and collective nouns that refer to groups acting as individuals (*the committee take their seats*).
Words between subjects and verbs	When you add a detail by inserting a phrase after the subject of a sentence, make sure the verb agrees with the sentence's real subject.
Compound subjects	When using compound subjects to compare or contrast or to combine sentences, make sure the verbs agree with the subjects.
Indefinite pronouns	When you use an indefinite-pronoun subject to make a generalization, make sure the verb agrees in number with the pronoun.

PRACTICE AND APPLY: Editing and Proofreading

Here is another review of a popular movie. Correct the sentences that contain errors in subject-verb agreement. If a sentence contains no errors, write *Correct*.

STUDENT MODEL

The Fugitive

(1) Good characters, a fast-moving plot, and suspense is all part of *The Fugitive*. **(2)** Dr. Richard Kimble, a convicted murderer, escapes from a prison train. **(3)** He try to prove his innocence and stay ahead of U.S. Marshal Samuel Gerard. **(4)** Kimble sneaks into two hospitals and a federal building. **(5)** A sewer and a St. Patrick's Day parade is places he hides from Gerard. **(6)** Straight over a huge dam plunge Kimble in one scene. **(7)** Is these believable situations? **(8)** It don't really matter, because the story is so exciting. **(9)** Kimble and Gerard are portrayed by the actors Harrison Ford and Tommy Lee Jones. **(10)** The work of these two actors have always been of high quality. **(11)** Does Kimble prove his innocence? **(12)** Doesn't you want to find out for yourself?

Mixed Review

A. Agreement in Number Read the following review of a movie that introduced new animation techniques. Then answer the questions below it.

> **PROFESSIONAL MODEL**
>
> **(1)** *Who Framed Roger Rabbit* is the kind of movie that gets made once in a blue moon.... **(2)** This movie is not only a great entertainment, but a breakthrough in craftsmanship—the first film to convincingly combine real actors and animated cartoon characters in the same space in the same time and make it look real.
>
> **(3)** I've never seen anything like it before. **(4)** Roger Rabbit and his cartoon comrades cast real shadows. **(5)** They shake the hands and grab the coats and rattle the teeth of real actors. **(6)** They change size and dimension and perspective as they move through a scene, and the camera isn't locked down in one place to make it easy, either—**(7)** the camera in this movie moves around like it's in a 1940s thriller, **(8)** and the cartoon characters look three-dimensional and seem to be occupying real space.
>
> —Roger Ebert, review of *Who Framed Roger Rabbit*

1. In sentence 1, find the first verb. Is it singular or plural?
2. In sentence 2, find the two predicate nominatives. Is the verb singular or plural?
3. What are the subject and the verb in sentence 3?
4. In sentence 4, why is the verb *cast* in the plural?
5. What three verbs agree with the subject *They* in sentence 5?
6. Identify the first subject and verb in sentence 6.
7. Identify the first subject and verb in sentence part 7. What phrase appears between the subject and the verb?
8. In sentence part 8, what is the subject of the verbs *look* and *seem*?

B. Additional Agreement Problems Write the verb form that agrees with the subject of each sentence.

1. John Sayles, the director of many independent films, (has, have) written numerous horror movies.
2. The money paid for these scripts (helps, help) finance Sayles's independent films.
3. Sixty thousand dollars (is, are) what Sayles spent on his popular film about college activists, *Return of the Secaucus 7.*
4. Both *Matewan* and *Eight Men Out* (deals, deal) with injustices in American society.
5. Many of the same actors (appears, appear) repeatedly in Sayles's films.

Choose the letter of the best revision for each underlined section.

> Science fiction <u>movies, which remain wildly popular, inspires</u>
> <u>(1)</u>
> speculation about life on other worlds. The idea of extraterrestrial beings
>
> <u>comfort some people and scares</u> others. *E.T. the Extra-Terrestrial,* one of
> <u>(2)</u>
> the most popular movies ever made, <u>introduce a charming creature that</u>
> <u>(3)</u>
> <u>delight</u> audiences. *Aliens* <u>feature a species far different from the lovable</u>
> <u>(4)</u>
> <u>E.T. and frighten</u> some with its vision. Many <u>prefer *Star Wars* and find</u> its
> <u>(5)</u>
> community of humans and nonhumans intriguing. Whether you see aliens
>
> as "cat people" or as robots, you will find a compelling extraterrestrial
>
> vision in science fiction films.

1. A. movies, which remain wildly popular, inspire
   B. movies, which remains wildly popular, inspires
   C. movies, which remains wildly popular, inspire
   D. Correct as is

2. A. comforts some people and scare
   B. comforts some people and scares
   C. comfort some people and scare
   D. Correct as is

3. A. introduces a charming creature that delight
   B. introduces a charming creature that delights
   C. introduce a charming creature that delights
   D. Correct as is

4. A. features a species far different from the lovable E.T. and frightens
   B. features a species far different from the lovable E.T. and frighten
   C. feature a species far different from the lovable E.T. and frightens
   D. Correct as is

5. A. prefers *Star Wars* and find
   B. prefers *Star Wars* and finds
   C. prefer *Star Wars* and finds
   D. Correct as is

SUBJECT-VERB

Student Help Desk

Subject-Verb Agreement at a Glance

Subjects and verbs must always agree in number.

- **A singular** subject takes a singular verb.
- **Plural** subjects take plural verbs.

Phrases Between Subjects and Verbs

If You See	Use This Kind of Verb	Example
Singular subject + phrase + verb	singular	**Nora** on her best days **reads** three scripts.
Plural subject + phrase + verb	plural	**The Nelsons,** partners in movie production, **choose** only the best ones.

Compound Subjects   Double Exposure

If You See	Use This Kind of Verb	Example
and	plural	**Zoe and Zack watch** three movies a week.
or, nor	singular or plural, to agree with the part nearest the verb	**Neither Zoe nor Zack has** time for more. **Neither Zoe nor her friends have** time for more.

Indefinite-Pronoun Subjects

If You See	Use This Kind of Verb	Example
another, anybody, anyone, everyone, everything, neither, nobody, someone	singular	**Everyone** in the cast **arrives** at eight in the morning.
both, few, many, several	plural	**Few** of the costumes **are done.**
all, any, more, most, none, some	singular or plural, depending on whether the pronoun refers to one or more than one	**Most** **wear** their own clothes until the final rehearsal.

The Bottom Line

Checklist for Subject-Verb Agreement

Have I . . .

_____ correctly identified the subjects of all sentences, including questions?

_____ made each verb agree in number with its subject?

_____ recognized that intervening phrases do not affect the number of verbs?

_____ used correct verb forms with compound subjects?

_____ used correct verb forms with indefinite-pronoun subjects?

_____ used correct verb forms with collective-noun subjects?

_____ used correct verb forms with titles and amounts?

_____ made verbs agree with the subjects rather than with predicate nominatives?

_____ used correct verb forms with relative-pronoun subjects?

_____ used *don't* and *doesn't* correctly?

Using Pronouns

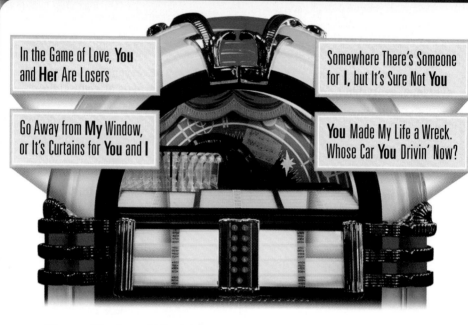

In the Game of Love, **You** and **Her** Are Losers

Somewhere There's Someone for **I**, but It's Sure Not **You**

Go Away from **My** Window, or It's Curtains for **You** and **I**

You Made My Life a Wreck. Whose Car **You** Drivin' Now?

Theme: Music and Musicians

What's Wrong with This Song?

Some country music songs have long and humorous titles like those listed in the jukebox. Many of these songs tell sad stories of heartbreak and betrayal. Unfortunately, whoever wrote the songs above has more than just a broken heart to be sad about—this person doesn't know how to use pronouns correctly! Can you figure out what the pronoun errors are in these song titles?

Using pronouns correctly may not be important for song titles, but you would not want to make these same errors in your own writing. In this chapter you will learn about different pronoun forms and when to use them.

Write Away: Titles for Tunes
Make up two or three song titles of your own. Use pronouns correctly in each title. Put your titles in your **Working Portfolio.**

CD-ROM **Grammar Coach**

Choose the best way to rewrite each underlined word or word group.

When you listen to music, do you think about <u>its</u> origins? People
(1)

typically respond to this question by saying, "<u>My friends and me</u> don't
(2)

think about this. <u>We</u> just like the music." Music has been an important
(3)

part of <u>ours</u> existence since the beginning of humankind. Historians tell
(4)

<u>scholars and we</u> that humans began to sing as soon as <u>them</u> developed
(5)   (6)

language. Like us, people in ancient civilizations used <u>they're</u> voices to
(7)

express feelings. However, most ancient music was not meant to entertain.

Ancient musicians played <u>them</u> mainly during important ceremonies. The
(8)

ancient people <u>whom</u> were most interested in music were the early
(9)

Greeks. They thought music had a positive role in the education of young

people. They also believed that young people <u>who</u> listened to good music
(10)

would become better adults.

1. A. it's
   B. it is
   C. their
   D. Correct as is

2. A. My friends and us
   B. My friends and I
   C. Me and my friends
   D. Correct as is

3. A. Us
   B. Them
   C. You
   D. Correct as is

4. A. our
   B. theirs
   C. their
   D. Correct as is

5. A. scholars and I
   B. scholars and they
   C. scholars and us
   D. Correct as is

6. A. they
   B. their
   C. it
   D. Correct as is

7. A. there
   B. theirs
   C. their
   D. Correct as is

8. A. they
   B. it
   C. its
   D. Correct as is

9. A. whomever
   B. who
   C. whose
   D. Correct as is

10. A. whom
    B. whoever
    C. whomever
    D. Correct as is

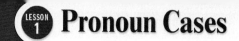

Pronoun Cases

LESSON 1

❶ Here's the Idea

▶ **Personal pronouns take on different forms depending on how they are used in sentences. These forms are called cases.**

There are three pronoun cases: the nominative case, the objective case, and the possessive case. The chart below shows personal pronouns sorted by case, number, and person.

Personal Pronouns

	Nominative	Objective	Possessive
Singular			
First person	I	me	my, mine
Second person	you	you	your, yours
Third person	he, she, it	him, her, it	his, her, hers, its
Plural			
First person	we	us	our, ours
Second person	you	you	your, yours
Third person	they	them	their, theirs

❷ Why It Matters in Writing

The most common errors in writing concern pronouns. Be sure to check your writing for pronoun errors and correct any you find. In this chapter, you will learn the reasons for the corrections shown in the model below.

STUDENT MODEL

>   *I.*
>   **My** friends and ~~me~~ are musicians in a Tejano band. Tejano music comes from the region of Texas that is close to the Texas-Mexico border. **It** is a combination of musical traditions from Spain, Mexico, Germany, and Poland. Different Tejano bands have taken ~~its~~ *their* influences from polkas, waltzes, rock and roll, and other kinds of music. **Our** band has a modern sound, although ~~you~~ *we* sometimes play older styles of Tejano music.

CHAPTER 8

Nominative and Objective Cases

❶ Here's the Idea

Writers often mix up the nominative and the objective cases of pronouns. To figure out which pronoun form to use, you first need to figure out how the pronoun functions in the sentence.

The Nominative Case

▶ **The nominative form of a personal pronoun is used when a pronoun functions as a subject or a predicate nominative.**

We saw Bonnie Raitt in concert. She played the guitar.
　SUBJECT　　　　　　　　　　　　　　　　SUBJECT

Nominative Pronoun Forms			
	First Person	**Second Person**	**Third Person**
Singular	I	you	he, she, it
Plural	we	you	they

A nominative pronoun may be used as part of a compound subject.

Jerry and he went to the concert.
COMPOUND SUBJECT

Use the chart below to help you choose the correct pronoun case in a compound subject.

> **Here's How** Choosing the Correct Case
>
> **Arlo and (I, me) sang a song.**
>
> **1.** Try each part of the compound subject alone in the sentence.
>
> **Arlo sang a song.**
> **I sang a song.** (CORRECT)
> **Me sang a song.** (INCORRECT)
>
> **2.** Choose the correct case for the sentence.
>
> **Arlo and I sang a song.**

When a nominative pronoun is used as a predicate nominative, it is called a **predicate pronoun**. A predicate pronoun immediately follows a linking verb and identifies the subject of the sentence.

　SUBJECT　　PREDICATE PRONOUN
It was they who stood up and cheered.
　　LINKING VERB

PRONOUNS

You may not use these forms in everyday speech, but you should use them in formal writing, such as applications and reports.

The Objective Case

▶ **The objective form of a personal pronoun is used when the pronoun functions as a direct object, an indirect object, or an object of a preposition.**

Rena called her. (DIRECT OBJECT)

Rena lent me the CD. (INDIRECT OBJECT)

Rena gave the poster to us. (OBJECT OF A PREPOSITION)

Objective Pronoun Forms			
	First Person	**Second Person**	**Third Person**
Singular	me	you	him, her, it
Plural	us	you	them

An objective pronoun is used as part of a compound object.

- Direct object **We heard Sam and her in concert.**

- Indirect object **Charlie wrote Sonya and me a song.**

- Object of a preposition **Play your banjo for their class and us.**

To make sure you are using the correct pronoun case in a compound object, look at each part of the object separately.

Here's How **Choosing the Correct Case**

Yuki played a song for Holly and (he, him).

1. Try each part of the compound object alone in the sentence.
Yuki played a song for Holly.
Yuki played a song for he. (INCORRECT)
Yuki played a song for him. (CORRECT)

2. Choose the correct case for the sentence.
Yuki played a song for Holly and him.

Writers often mistakenly use the nominative case after the preposition *between*. Always use the objective case after this preposition.

INCORRECT: **The musician stood between he and I.**

CORRECT: **The musician stood between him and me.**

② Why It Matters in Writing

Many people incorrectly assume that *I* always sounds better than *me*. Remember that *I* is correct only if the pronoun's function calls for the nominative case.

STUDENT MODEL

> My aunt invited my friend Sharon and I to a jazz concert. My
> ^me
>
> aunt and I are big fans of jazz piano. After the concert, Sharon
>
> took a picture of one of the musicians and I.
> ^me

③ Practice and Apply

A. CONCEPT CHECK: Nominative and Objective Cases

For each sentence, write the correct pronoun from those in parentheses. Then identify the pronoun as nominative (N) or objective (O).

Cats on Broadway

1. The composer Andrew Lloyd Webber has given (we, us) many wonderful musicals.
2. It is (he, him) who wrote the long-running musical *Cats*.
3. Lloyd Webber first got the idea for writing this show when (he, him) bought a book of poems by T. S. Eliot in an airport bookstore.
4. Lloyd Webber's mother used to read these poems to (he, him) when he was a child.
5. Eventually, his friend Trevor Nunn and (he, him) turned Eliot's poems into a musical.
6. Choreographers, costume designers, and other creative people worked with (they, them) to develop the show.
7. As the story opens, several cats have gathered in a junkyard where (they, them) take turns singing about themselves.
8. One of the cats is named Grizabella. It is (her, she) who sings the classic song "Memory."
9. Andrew Lloyd Webber is a very successful composer, although some critics have given (he, him) and his shows poor reviews.
10. His fans are loyal to (he, him) and his work. Many have seen *Cats* more than once.

➡ **For a SELF-CHECK and more practice, see the EXERCISE BANK, p. 620.**

B. EDITING: Using Pronoun Cases Correctly

Replace each underlined noun with a nominative or an objective pronoun.

A Young Performer

Concert violinist Midori began playing violin when **(1)** <u>Midori</u> was only a little girl of three. Zubin Mehta, the man who was conductor of the New York Philharmonic orchestra, first heard the young violinist play when **(2)** <u>the young violinist</u> was 11. Her poise and talent impressed **(3)** <u>Zubin Mehta</u>. It was **(4)** <u>Zubin Mehta</u> who gave Midori the opportunity to be a soloist in the Philharmonic's traditional New Year's Eve concert. The audience was amazed at the young girl's talent, and **(5)** <u>the audience members</u> gave **(6)** <u>Midori</u> a standing ovation. Audiences have always been impressed by Midori's maturity and sense of calm on stage. When Midori was 14, concert-goers in Massachusetts heard the Boston Symphony and **(7)** <u>Midori</u>. During the concert, a string on Midori's violin broke twice. **(8)** <u>Midori</u> simply borrowed another violin each time, and **(9)** <u>Midori</u> kept playing. Musical ability seems to run in Midori's family: her mother and **(10)** <u>Midori</u> are both violinists. In fact, Midori's mother was her first violin teacher.

C. WRITING: Sentences with Pronouns

Sidewalk Concert

Imagine that you are part of the scene in the photograph below. You might be one of the musicians, the plant store owner, or a customer. Write five sentences about the photograph using the compound subjects and objects below.

Example: my friends and I

Answer: On Saturdays, my friends and I perform in front of the plant store.

1. the two violinists and me
2. the customers and I
3. my friends and me
4. us and our instruments
5. other musicians and they

The Possessive Case

❶ Here's the Idea

▶ **Personal pronouns that show ownership or relationships are in the possessive case.**

Possessive Pronoun Forms

	First Person	Second Person	Third Person
Singular	my, mine	your, yours	his, her, hers, its
Plural	our, ours	your, yours	their, theirs

Possessive pronouns can be used in two ways.

1. A possessive pronoun can be used in place of a noun. The pronoun can function as a subject or an object.

Where are the earplugs?
Let me borrow yours. Mine are upstairs.
    DIRECT OBJECT ⬆   ⬆ SUBJECT

2. A possessive pronoun can be used as an adjective to modify a noun or a gerund. The pronoun comes before the word it modifies.

Jeb is playing his bongo drums.   **Our complaining doesn't help.**
    NOUN ⬆   ⬆ GERUND

Don't confuse gerunds with present participles. These verbals both end in *-ing*, but a possessive pronoun is used only before a gerund (acting as a noun) and not before a participle.

   ⬐ POSSESSIVE
His playing has improved since last year.
    ⬆ GERUND

We heard him playing in the auditorium.
  OBJECTIVE ⬆   ⬆ PRESENT PARTICIPLE

For more information on gerunds and present participles, see pp. 71–74.

 Some contractions and possessive pronouns sound alike, but they have different spellings and meanings. Be sure to use all of these words correctly.

- **You're** a songwriter. [*you are*]
- **They're** ballads. [*they are*]
- **There's** the CD player. [*there is*]
- **It's** bothering my dog. [*it is*]

- **Your** songs are great.
- **Their** ballads are famous.
- The CD player is **theirs**.
- Listen to **its** howling.

❷ Why It Matters in Writing

It's easy to confuse contractions and possessive pronouns. Be sure to look for and correct these errors in your work.

STUDENT MODEL

George Clinton is the mastermind behind the two greatest funk bands—Parliament and Funkadelic. ~~They're~~ *Their* music is influenced by gospel, doo-wop, and jazz. It's more dance-oriented than rock is.

❸ Practice and Apply

CONCEPT CHECK: The Possessive Case

Write the correct form of the pronoun from those given in parentheses.

The Beatles

1. As a young teenager, John Lennon said to his aunt, "You throw (my, mine) poetry out and you'll regret it when I'm famous."
2. Did Lennon know that someday (he, his) songs would make him a star?
3. In 1956, Lennon met Paul McCartney, and the two musicians worked together to improve (they're, their) playing.
4. With other musicians, Lennon and McCartney formed a band called the Quarrymen, which they named after (their, theirs) high school.
5. Many young people heard (them, their) playing in music clubs.
6. The group changed (it's, its) name to the Beatles in 1960.
7. One British newspaper editorial said this about the Beatles: "If they don't sweep (your, you're) blues away, brother you're a lost cause."
8. In 1964, the Beatles came to the United States, and (them, their) singing made teenagers go crazy.
9. More than one teenage girl waiting outside a theater fainted at the sight of (her, hers) musical idols driving by.
10. In a time like (our, ours), can you think of a music group that makes fans respond this way?

➡ **For a SELF-CHECK and more practice, see the EXERCISE BANK, p. 621.**

LESSON 4 **Using *Who* and *Whom***

❶ Here's the Idea

▶ **The case of the pronoun *who* is determined by the pronoun's function in a sentence.**

Forms of *Who* and *Whoever*	
Nominative	who, whoever
Objective	whom, whomever
Possessive	whose, whoseever

Who and *whom* can be used to ask questions and to introduce subordinate clauses.

Who and *Whom* in Questions

Who is the nominative form. In a question, *who* is used as a subject or as a predicate pronoun.

Who wrote the song "This Land Is Your Land"?
　SUBJECT

The writer was who?
PREDICATE PRONOUN

Whom is the objective form. In a question, *whom* is used as a direct or indirect object of a verb or as the object of a preposition.

Whom did you ask?
　DIRECT OBJECT

From whom did you get the information?
　OBJECT OF PREPOSITION

Here's How Choosing *Who* or *Whom* in a Question

(Who, Whom) are you speaking to?

1. Rewrite the question as a statement.

　You are speaking to (who, whom).

2. Figure out whether the pronoun is used as a subject, an object, a predicate pronoun, or an object of a preposition and choose the correct form. The pronoun in the sentence above is the object of a preposition. The correct form is *whom*.

　You are speaking to whom.

3. Use the correct form in the question.

　Whom are you speaking to?

Who and *Whom* in Subordinate Clauses

Who and *whom* are also used to introduce subordinate clauses. To choose the correct form, you must figure out how the pronoun is used in the clause. *Who* should be used when the pronoun functions as the subject of a subordinate clause.

Pete Seeger is a singer who cares about the environment.

                      SUBJECT   SUBORDINATE CLAUSE

Whom should be used when the pronoun functions as a direct object, an indirect object, or an object of a preposition.

Bob Dylan is one singer whom Pete Seeger influenced.

                  DIRECT OBJECT   SUBORDINATE CLAUSE

Use the chart below to help you figure out whether to use *who* or *whom* in a subordinate clause.

> **Here's How** **Choosing *Who* or *Whom* in a Clause**
>
> **Pete Seeger is a singer (who, whom) I admire.**
>
> **1.** Identify the subordinate clause in the sentence.
> **(who, whom) I admire**
>
> **2.** Figure out how the pronoun is used in the clause. Is it a subject or an object? You may have to rearrange the clause to figure this out.
> **I admire (who, whom).**
>
> The pronoun is a direct object in the clause. The correct form is *whom*.
>
> **I admire whom.**
>
> **3.** Use the correct form in the clause.
> **Pete Seeger is a singer whom I admire.**

---

❷ Why It Matters in Writing

You will be expected to use *who* and *whom* correctly in formal writing, such as application letters, term papers, and reports. Don't assume that *whom* is just a more formal version of *who*. Choose the form that fits the way the pronoun is used.

Peanuts by George Shultz

A. CONCEPT CHECK: Using *Who* and *Whom*

Write the correct form of the pronoun from those given in parentheses.

> **Pete Seeger: American Troubadour**
> **1.** (Who, Whom) is known as "America's tuning fork"?
> **2.** Pete Seeger is a musician (who, whom) many regard as America's greatest folksinger.
> **3.** Seeger is a musician for (who, whom) music has many purposes: to entertain, to bring people together, and to spread ideas.
> **4.** At 16, Seeger heard folk music for the first time when he attended a music festival with his father, (who, whom) was a music historian and scholar.
> **5.** Seeger listened closely to the musicians (who, whom) played the 5-string banjo, and he fell in love with this instrument.
> **6.** As a young man, Seeger traveled thousands of miles around the country, learning new folksongs and playing his banjo for (whoever, whomever) would pay him or give him food.
> **7.** Woody Guthrie and Leadbelly are two other great musicians (who, whom) Seeger admired.
> **8.** For (who, whom) has Seeger played? He has played for audiences in concert halls and auditoriums all over.
> **9.** He plays for (whoever, whomever) is interested in listening.
> **10.** (Who, Whom) will he entertain next?

➜ **For a SELF-CHECK and more practice, see the EXERCISE BANK, p. 622.**

B. REVISING: Correcting *Who* and *Whom* Errors

Rewrite the following paragraph. Correct any errors in the use of *who* and *whom.*

> **New Talent, Ancient Music**
> Do you know whom Anoushka Shankar is? Many people don't yet, but they might know her father. Ravi Shankar is an Indian classical music master and teacher who made Indian sitar music known in the United States. Who did he teach? One of his students was former Beatle George Harrison. Now Anoushka has become a talented sitar player, taught by her father who she gives concerts with. Anoushka, who recorded her first CD when she was 17, began studying Indian music when she was 9. Who does she get her inspiration from? It comes from her father.

PRONOUNS

LESSON 5 Pronoun-Antecedent Agreement

1 Here's the Idea

▶ **A pronoun must agree with its antecedent in number, gender, and person.** An antecedent is the word—a noun or another pronoun—that a pronoun replaces or refers to.

Agreement in Number

Most of the time, making a pronoun agree in number with its antecedent is easy: a plural antecedent takes a plural pronoun, and a singular antecedent takes a singular pronoun.

Here are three trouble spots that confuse writers and readers.

1. A collective noun, such as *team*, *audience*, *herd*, or *family,* may be referred to by either a singular or a plural pronoun. The collective noun's number is determined by its meaning in the sentence.

Use a singular pronoun to refer to a collective noun whose parts act as a single unit.

The orchestra will give its final performance tonight.
(The orchestra is acting as a single unit.)

Use a plural pronoun to refer to a collective noun whose parts act individually.

The orchestra have tuned up their instruments.
(The orchestra members are acting individually.)

2. A plural pronoun is used to refer to nouns or pronouns joined by *and.*

REFERS TO

Marla and Denise played their trumpets together.

3. A pronoun that refers to nouns or pronouns joined by *or* or *nor* should agree with the noun or pronoun nearest to it.

REFERS TO

Neither the conductor nor the musicians have taken their places on stage.
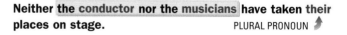 PLURAL PRONOUN

Agreement in Gender

The gender of a pronoun must be the same as the gender of its antecedent. The chart below shows pronouns by gender.

Pronoun Gender		
Feminine	**Masculine**	**Neuter**
she, her, hers	he, him, his	it, its

When the antecedent of a singular pronoun could be either feminine or masculine, you can use the phrase *his or her.*

Each musician played his or her solo.

If using *his or her* sounds awkward, try making both the pronoun and its antecedent plural.

All the musicians played their solos.

Agreement in Person

The person of a pronoun must match the person of its antecedent.

their
All students should bring ~~your~~ favorite CD to class.

The pronouns *one, everyone,* and *everybody* are third person and singular. They are referred to by *he, him, his, she, her,* and *hers.*

Everyone has his or her favorite recordings.

❷ Why It Matters in Writing

Using the correct pronoun when a collective noun is the antecedent will give your readers information about whether the group is behaving as one unit or as individuals.

STUDENT MODEL

The **Bristol High School Jazz Band** finished recording **its** first CD this week. The recording session was the prize for winning the All-County Jazz Band Contest. The **band** were thrilled when **they** learned about the unusual prize.

❸ Practice and Apply

A. CONCEPT CHECK: Pronoun-Antecedent Agreement

Write the correct pronoun from those given in parentheses.

Jazz in the Family

1. The Marsalis family is unusual because five out of eight of (their, its) members are professional musicians.
2. Everyone in this family has (his or her, their) own special talent.
3. Ellis Marsalis, a musician and educator, shared a love of jazz with (his, their) sons.
4. Before Dolores Marsalis married Ellis Marsalis and became the mother of six sons, (she, he) was a jazz singer.
5. Like (their, his) father, Wynton, Branford, Delfeayo, and Jason Marsalis are jazz musicians.
6. Even in high school, these musicians understood that (they, you) had to take music seriously to succeed.
7. Wynton and Branford were taught piano by (his, their) father.
8. Neither Branford nor his brothers chose piano as (his, their) main instrument.
9. The Marsalis brothers learned from (his, their) father that playing music requires education, discipline, and inspiration.
10. New Orleans, a city famous for (their, its) jazz, is the Marsalises' hometown.

➡ **For a SELF-CHECK and more practice, see the EXERCISE BANK, p. 622.**

B. REVISING: Agreement with Collective Nouns

Rewrite each sentence below so that the pronouns agree with their collective noun antecedents. Write *Correct* if there is no error.

All That Jazz

1. Last Saturday night, the jazz band gave their first performance.
2. Before the concert, the band unpacked its instruments.
3. The audience showed its approval by giving the musicians a standing ovation.
4. The jazz group played one more song for their audience.
5. After the concert, the group went its separate ways.

Indefinite Pronouns as Antecedents

LESSON
6

1 Here's the Idea

▶ **An indefinite pronoun may be the antecedent of a personal pronoun.**

Making sure that a personal pronoun agrees in number with an indefinite pronoun can be difficult. This is true because the number of the indefinite pronoun is not always obvious. Refer to the chart below when you are trying to determine the number of an indefinite pronoun.

Indefinite Pronouns			
Singular		**Plural**	**Singular or Plural**
another	everything	both	all
anybody	much	few	any
anyone	neither	many	more
anything	nobody	several	most
each	no one		none
either	nothing		some
everybody	one		
everyone	somebody		
	someone		
	something		

Singular Indefinite Pronouns

Use a singular personal pronoun to refer to a singular indefinite pronoun.

REFERS TO

Each of the instruments has its own special sound.
🔺 SINGULAR INDEFINITE PRONOUN 🔺 SINGULAR PERSONAL PRONOUN

The phrase *his or her* is considered a singular personal pronoun.

Everyone brought his or her clarinet.

One or more nouns may come between a personal pronoun and its indefinite pronoun antecedent. Make sure the personal pronoun agrees with the indefinite pronoun, not with a noun.

INCORRECT: **One of the musicians played their trumpet off key.**
(The personal pronoun agrees with the noun, not the indefinite pronoun.)

CORRECT: **One of the musicians played her trumpet off key.**
(The personal pronoun agrees with the indefinite pronoun.)

Plural Indefinite Pronouns

Use a plural pronoun to refer to a plural indefinite pronoun.

REFERS TO

Both of the pianists played their own compositions.
♦ PLURAL INDEFINITE PRONOUN   ♦ PLURAL PERSONAL PRONOUN

Few of us brought our sheet music.

Singular or Plural Indefinite Pronouns

Some indefinite pronouns can be singular or plural. Use the meaning of the sentence to determine whether a personal pronoun that refers to an indefinite pronoun should be singular or plural.

If the indefinite pronoun refers to a portion of a whole, use a singular personal pronoun.

Some of the music has lost its appeal.

If the indefinite pronoun refers to members of a group, use a plural personal pronoun.

Some of the musicians play their instruments.

Indefinite pronouns that end in *one, body,* or *thing* are always singular.

❷ Why It Matters in Writing

If the personal pronouns and indefinite-pronoun antecedents in your sentences don't agree, your writing will be very confusing for readers.

STUDENT MODEL

    Each of the instruments of the modern

orchestra has ~~their~~ *its* own particular history.

The violin is related to two three-stringed

instruments, the rebec and the Polish fiddle,

played in the 1500s. Both of these had ~~its~~ *their*

limitations.

❸ Practice and Apply

A. CONCEPT CHECK: Indefinite Pronouns as Antecedents

Find and correct the errors in agreement in these sentences.
Write *Correct* if there is no error.

The Electric Guitar

1. Even before guitars became electric, most of the large jazz orchestras included a guitarist among its musicians.

2. Several of the early jazz and blues guitarists, such as Charlie Christian, wanted to make his guitars louder.

3. Early on, some of these musicians used a vibrating metal disc to make its guitars produce more sound.

4. At first, none of the early inventors knew exactly how to make an electric guitar, so he or she experimented with different materials and designs.

5. Each of the inventors contributed their own ideas to the creation of the electric guitar.

6. All of this experimenting served its purpose.

7. By the late 1930s, several of the guitar manufacturers in the United States were producing its first line of electrics.

8. Some of the guitars made by one manufacturer were called Frying Pans because of its shape.

9. Few of the creators of the electric guitar knew how their instrument would change popular music.

10. By the 1950s, anyone who could play electric guitar could start their own rock 'n' roll band.

➜ **For a SELF-CHECK and more practice, see the EXERCISE BANK, p. 623.**

B. EDITING: Agreement with Indefinite Pronouns

Find the five agreement errors in the paragraph below. Rewrite the sentences in which they occur to correct the errors.

Sounds of Bali

A gamelan is the traditional orchestra of the Indonesian island of Bali. Although everyone in the orchestra plays their own instrument, the gamelan sounds like one instrument played by many musicians. This is because each of the gamelans has their own special tuning. A single orchestra is made up of gongs, drums, xylophones, flutes, and stringed instruments. Most of the instruments make its sound through percussion, or striking. Many of the gamelan musicians play his or her instruments with wooden mallets or hammers. Anyone who goes to Bali should attend a gamelan performance during their visit.

Other Pronoun Problems

❶ Here's the Idea

▶ **A pronoun may be used with an appositive, in an appositive, or in a comparison.** You can learn techniques that will help you use pronouns correctly in each of these situations.

Pronouns and Appositives

The pronoun *we* or *us* is sometimes followed by an appositive, a noun that identifies the pronoun.

We pianists will have to rent pianos.
　　　↖APPOSITIVE

The conductor pointed toward us violinists.
　　　　　　　　　　　　↖APPOSITIVE

Use the chart below to figure out whether to use *we* or *us* in front of an appositive.

Here's How **Using Pronouns with Appositives**

The oboe players are having lunch with (we, us) cellists.

1. Drop the appositive from the sentence.

　The oboe players are having lunch with (we, us).

2. Determine whether the pronoun is a subject or an object. In this sentence, the pronoun is the object of the preposition *with*.

3. Write the sentence, using the correct case.

　The oboe players are having lunch with us cellists.

Sometimes a pronoun is used in an appositive. The pronoun helps to identify the noun in front of the appositive.

The sopranos, Eva and I, sang a duet.
　APPOSITIVE ➴

The pronoun's case is determined by the function of the noun it identifies. In the sentence above, the noun *sopranos* is the subject, so the pronoun in the appositive *Eva and I* is a nominative pronoun.

　Use the chart on the next page to help you figure out which case to use when a pronoun is in an appositive.

> **Here's How** **Using Pronouns in Appositives**
>
> **Holly sang for the two tenors, Marcello and (he, him).**
>
> **1.** Rewrite the sentence with the appositive by itself.
>
>   **Holly sang for Marcello and (he, him).**
>
> **2.** Then try each part of the appositive alone with the verb.
>
>   **Holly sang for Marcello. Holly sang for (he, him).**
>
> **3.** Determine whether the pronoun is a subject or an object. In this sentence, the pronoun is the object of the preposition *for.*
>
> **4.** Write the sentence using the correct case.
>
>   **Holly sang for the two tenors, Marcello and him.**

Pronouns in Comparisons

A comparison can be made by using *than* or *as* to begin a clause.

Lily has more CDs than she has.

Carlos plays the saxophone as fast as I play.

When words are left out of such a clause, the clause is said to be **elliptical.**

Lily has more CDs than she.

Fill in the words missing from the elliptical clause to help you choose the correct pronoun case.

You can play as well as (he, him). [can play]

You can play as well as he.

❷ Why It Matters in Writing

If you use pronouns with appositives incorrectly, your writing might be confusing. Readers may not understand your ideas or take them seriously.

THE FAR SIDE   By GARY LARSON

"So, then…Would that be 'us the people' or 'we the people'?"

❸ Practice and Apply

A. CONCEPT CHECK: Other Pronoun Problems

Choose the correct pronoun from those in parentheses.

The Emperor's Daughter and the Unknown Prince

(1) (We, Us) music lovers are big fans of the opera *Turandot,* written by Puccini. The opera is about a clever princess named Turandot who meets a prince even more clever than **(2)** (she, her). Turandot has promised to marry any prince who can answer three riddles. The Prince of Persia and twelve other suitors have failed the test. Those unfortunate men, the twelve suitors and **(3)** (he, him), have been beheaded. An unknown prince believes he can do better than **(4)** (them, they). Turandot feels confident that no one will be smarter than **(5)** (her, she).

In a scene that is particularly entertaining to **(6)** (we, us) audience members, the ghosts of the slain suitors come back to warn the unknown prince. After answering the riddles correctly, the prince tells an unhappy Turandot that if she can guess his name, he will not press her to marry him. Only three people—his father, his servant, and **(7)** (him, he)—know that his name is Calaf. The princess orders her subjects to discover the prince's identity. They are as unsuccessful as **(8)** (she, her). Finally the prince reveals his name. Unexpectedly, Turandot agrees to marry Calaf. The happy couple, Calaf and **(9)** (her, she), declare their love to the crowd in the courtyard. It seems that no one has ever been as happy as **(10)** (they, them).

➡ **For a SELF-CHECK and more practice, see the EXERCISE BANK, p. 623.**

B. WRITING: Pronouns and Appositives

Supply the correct pronouns needed in the following paragraph. Write them on a separate piece of paper.

West Side Story

Last night, ___**(1)**___ drama students gave a performance of *West Side Story.* This musical, set in the 1950s, is an updated version of Shakespeare's *Romeo and Juliet.* Through music and dialogue, the cast, my fellow actors and ___**(2)**___, told the story of two teenagers who fall in love. Like Romeo and Juliet, Tony and Maria are prevented from being together by their friends and families. At one point in the show, the main characters, Tony and ___**(3)**___, sing a beautiful duet. For ___**(4)**___ actors, there are lots of great songs in this show.

Pronoun Reference

① Here's the Idea

If a pronoun's antecedent is missing or unclear, or if there is more than one antecedent, readers will be confused.

Indefinite Reference

Indefinite-reference problems occur when a pronoun's antecedents are not expressed. Writers often make the mistake of using the pronouns *it*, *they*, and *you* without clear reference. You can eliminate indefinite-reference problems by rewriting the sentences in which the pronouns appear.

Indefinite Reference	
Awkward	**Revised**
In the article, it claims that the new Pink Blur CD is terrific.	The article claims that the new Pink Blur CD is terrific.
They state in the article that the songs are fresh and exciting.	The writer states in the article that the songs are fresh and exciting.
On the new CD, you have more slow songs.	The new CD has more slow songs on it.

General Reference

General-reference problems occur when the pronouns *it*, *this*, *that*, *which*, and *such* are used to refer to general ideas rather than to specific noun antecedents. Correct such problems by adding a clear antecedent or by rewriting the sentence without the pronoun.

General Reference	
Awkward	**Revised**
Trudy practices the guitar every day. This has improved her playing.	Trudy practices the guitar every day. Practicing has improved her playing.
Malcolm broke a guitar string, which ended the band's rehearsal.	The band's rehearsal ended because Malcolm broke a guitar string.

Ambiguous Reference

Ambiguous means "having more than one possible meaning." An ambiguous-reference problem occurs whenever more than one word might be a pronoun's antecedent. You can eliminate ambiguous references by revising the sentences.

Ambiguous Reference	
Awkward	**Revised**
Jeb talked to Max while he listened to music.	While Jeb listened to music, he talked to Max. **or** While Max listened to music, Jeb talked to him.
Carol told Rita that she was the next singer to perform.	Rita was the next singer to perform, and Carol told her to get ready.

❷ Why It Matters in Writing

Readers will be confused and frustrated by cases of general, indefinite, or ambiguous reference in your writing. Make your writing as clear as possible by eliminating these problems.

STUDENT MODEL

DRAFT

Bob Marley and Bunny Wailer listened to the records of other reggae music groups before they recorded their music.

REVISION

Before Bob Marley and Bunny Wailer recorded their music, they listened to the records of other reggae music groups.

❸ Practice and Apply

A. CONCEPT CHECK: Pronoun Reference

Rewrite the following sentences to correct indefinite, ambiguous, and general pronoun references.

Reggae Sunsplash
1. In a recent magazine article, it explains that Reggae Sunsplash began as an annual music festival in Jamaica.

2. They say that the popular festival now tours Europe and the United States.

3. The biggest reggae bands in the world play at Sunsplash. That explains why the event has been called "the mother of all reggae festivals."

4. Music is important at the festival, but you also have Jamaican crafts and foods as part of the experience.

5. Bob Marley and the Wailers, Third World, and Toots and the Maytals played at the 1979 festival. This attracted large crowds.

6. When the bands began playing for the fans, they immediately started dancing.

7. One year, the weather during the festival was so wet that a local reporter called it "Reggae Mud-Splash."

8. Bob Marley is reggae's greatest legend, which is why the festival organizers decided to create Bob Marley week.

9. On the Sunsplash Web site, they explain that the Bob Marley Foundation helped organize this tribute.

10. Bob Marley died in 1981, and now his son Ziggy plays with his band at the festival.

➜ For a **SELF-CHECK** and more practice, see the **EXERCISE BANK, p. 624.**

B. REVISING: Pronoun Reference Problems

The four underlined pronouns below have missing or unclear antecedents. Revise the paragraph to eliminate the problems.

Reggae's Next Generation

Bob Marley's son Ziggy Marley formed a reggae band with <u>his</u> sisters and brothers. The Melody Makers sing about history, human struggles, and the problems that all people face. <u>This</u> may explain why the band is popular around the world. On the Melody Makers' Web site, <u>you</u> have information about the four Marley siblings who make up the band: Cedella, Sharon, Stephen, and Ziggy. Many people associate the Melody Makers with <u>their</u> father's music and reputation. Although the Melody Makers are influenced by the music of Bob Marley, they have a sound all their own.

Ziggy Marley

199

Real World Grammar

School Newspaper Article

To be a successful sports reporter on your school newspaper, you need to know the rules of the games you write about. However, no matter how accurate your articles are, readers will be confused if your writing contains pronoun errors. Because sports articles often are about teams (collective nouns) and a number of individuals, it's easy to make these errors. Follow the basic rules of pronoun use to make your articles clear. Here's one high-school sports reporter's rough draft of an article.

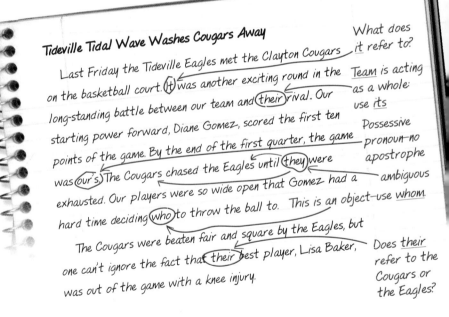

Tideville Tidal Wave Washes Cougars Away

Last Friday the Tideville Eagles met the Clayton Cougars on the basketball court. It was another exciting round in the long-standing battle between our team and their rival. Our starting power forward, Diane Gomez, scored the first ten points of the game. By the end of the first quarter, the game was our's. The Cougars chased the Eagles until they were exhausted. Our players were so wide open that Gomez had a hard time deciding who to throw the ball to.

The Cougars were beaten fair and square by the Eagles, but one can't ignore the fact that their best player, Lisa Baker, was out of the game with a knee injury.

What does it refer to?

Team is acting as a whole: use its

Possessive pronoun—no apostrophe

ambiguous

This is an object—use whom.

Does their refer to the Cougars or the Eagles?

Using Grammar in Writing

After you draft an article, review it to make sure you have used pronouns correctly.

Indefinite reference	• Give every pronoun a specific and stated antecedent.
Pronoun-antecedent agreement	• Make sure pronouns agree with their antecedents in person, number, and gender.
Possessive pronouns	• Avoid confusing contractions with possessive pronouns.
Who and *Whom*	• Use the nominative form *who* as a subject and the objective form *whom* as an object.

Tideville Tidal Wave Washes Cougars Away

By Natalie Young

Last Friday the Tideville Eagles met the Clayton Cougars on the basketball court. The game was another exciting round in the long-standing battle between our team and its rival. Our starting power forward, Diane Gomez, scored the first ten points of the game. By the end of the first quarter, the game was ours. The Cougars were exhausted from chasing the Eagles. Our players were so wide open that Gomez had a hard time deciding whom she should throw the ball to.

The Cougars were beaten fair and square by the Eagles, but one can't ignore the fact that the Cougars' best player, Lisa Baker, was out of the game with a knee injury.

ely

PRACTICE AND APPLY: Revising

You are the editor of your school newspaper. One of your reporters has just handed you the article below. You need to check the article for pronoun errors before you publish it. Use the four pronoun tips to revise the article.

> It is no surprise that our volleyball team will be playing in the state championships. Linda Buffington, the team coach, said the girls have been practicing hard. I asked Coach Buffington whom should get the credit when a team wins a title. After all, not every player is a star, and some players do stand out above the rest. "Its true that every team has it's strengths and weaknesses," said the coach. "Its also true that every team member contributes something important to the team."

A. Using Pronouns Read the passage. Write the correct pronoun from the choices given in parentheses.

People often don't think about **1.** (who, whom) is playing drums in a jazz or rock band. Although drums cannot produce a melody line, they are essential in jazz and popular music. Before the development of jazz, drums were used mainly in marching and classical music. Many of the first jazz drummers didn't have **2.** (his or her, their) own drums. They borrowed **3.** (they're, their) instruments from circus orchestras and marching bands.

Early on, a jazz band hired **4.** (their, its) drummer mainly to impress an audience. Jimmy Crawford and Sonny Greer were two drummers who made **5.** (their, his) mark on jazz in the early 1920s. **6.** (They, Them) and other drummers added loud kettledrums to their sets to make more noise. In the 1930s, some of the jazz drummers in New Orleans and other cities began decorating **7.** (their, his) drum sets with pictures of landscapes or portraits of the bandleader.

Before the 1940s, a jazz drummer's task was simply to keep the beat of the music. Talented drummers like Max Roach changed this. It was **8.** (him, he) who influenced the way jazz drummers play today. Instead of simply keeping rhythm, **9.** (he, him) and other drummers created new playing styles. **10.** (His, Him) playing helped shape the style of jazz known as bebop.

B. Indefinite, General, and Ambiguous References The seven underlined pronouns in the following passage have indefinite, general, or ambiguous references. Rewrite the paragraph to eliminate the reference problems.

In a magazine article about New Orleans, <u>it</u> says that jazz funerals are a cultural tradition in this city. During a jazz funeral, a brass band plays as friends and family walk to the cemetery. In the article, <u>they</u> explain that the band plays sad, serious music and everyone walks slowly at first. However, <u>this</u> changes later on. After <u>you</u> leave the cemetery, the band plays a different kind of music. First the trumpeter plays two notes on his instrument, <u>which</u> means that it's time to play a lively song. The mourners dance behind the band as <u>they</u> hold up colorful umbrellas. Newer brass bands are changing these traditions, but some of <u>them</u> are still followed.

Choose the best way to rewrite each underlined word or word group.

As the opera *H.M.S. Pinafore* opens, the ship's crew welcomes aboard a woman named Little Buttercup. It is <u>her</u> who sells candy and other small
(1)
items to <u>they and other sailors</u>. A sailor named Ralph Rackstraw tells <u>the</u>
(2)
<u>crew and she</u> that he wants to marry the captain's daughter, Josephine.
(3)
Unfortunately, Josephine must marry Sir Joseph, a navy official.

Josephine's father and <u>he</u> have agreed on the marriage. However,
(4)
Josephine is in love with Ralph Rackstraw, even though <u>your</u> position is
(5)
not as powerful as Sir Joseph's. Josephine and Ralph plan <u>they're</u> secret
(6)
wedding. The captain and Sir Joseph become upset when a spy tells <u>him</u>
(7)
about this plan. Sir Joseph asks Josephine, "Have you lost <u>your</u> mind?"
(8)
<u>Who</u> does Josephine finally marry? She marries Ralph, and the captain
(9)
marries someone <u>whom</u> has been very kind to him—Little Buttercup.
(10)

PRONOUNS

1. A. they
   B. she
   C. hers
   D. Correct as is

2. A. other sailors and they
   B. he and other sailors
   C. them and other sailors
   D. Correct as is

3. A. she and the crew
   B. the crew and hers
   C. the crew and her
   D. Correct as is

4. A. him
   B. his
   C. her
   D. Correct as is

5. A. their
   B. his
   C. her
   D. Correct as is

6. A. their
   B. theirs
   C. them
   D. Correct as is

7. A. his
   B. them
   C. they
   D. Correct as is

8. A. yours
   B. you're
   C. my
   D. Correct as is

9. A. Whom
   B. Whomever
   C. Whoever
   D. Correct as is

10. A. whose
    B. who
    C. whoever
    D. Correct as is

Student Help Desk

Pronouns at a Glance

Nominative Case

I	we
you	you
he	they
she	
it	

Use this case when
- the pronoun is a **subject**
- the pronoun is a **predicate nominative**

Objective Case

me	us
you	you
him	them
her	
it	

Use this case when
- the pronoun is the **direct object of a verb**
- the pronoun is the **indirect object of a verb**
- the pronoun is the **object of a preposition**

Possessive Case

my/mine	our/ours
your/yours	your/yours
his	their/theirs
her/hers	
its	

Use this case for
- pronouns that show **ownership or relationship**

Pronoun-Antecedent Agreement   Let's Not Disagree

A pronoun should agree with its antecedent in number, gender, and person.

Agreement in Number

Joan played **her** guitar in the garage. (**singular**)

Dad and Uncle Ralph brought **their** banjos to the picnic. (**plural**)

Agreement in Gender

Beatrice bought **her** drums in Jamaica. (**feminine**)

Mr. Zamorano has a 12-string guitar, which **he** played for us. (**masculine**)

The **trumpet** fell, and now **it** is dented. (**neuter**)

Agreement in Person

I brought **my** kazoo to class today. (**first person**)

You should play **your** tuba in the talent show. (**second person**)

Carly and Lucy sing nicely, although **they** don't like to perform. (**third person**)

Pronoun Problems

In a Pickle with a Pronoun?

Here are some tips for choosing the correct pronoun case in difficult situations:

Problem: A pronoun is part of a compound structure.

Example: Please give the cymbals to Lana and (me, ~~I~~).

Solution
- Drop the other part of the compound.
- Figure out how the pronoun functions in the sentence.

Problem: A pronoun is used in an elliptical clause of comparison.

Example: I play guitar better than (~~him~~, he).

Solution
- Add the missing words to the elliptical clause.

Problem: A pronoun is used with an appositive.

Example: Please give (~~we~~, us) dancers more time to rehearse.

Solution
- Drop the appositive from the sentence.
- Figure out how the pronoun functions in the sentence.

Problem: A pronoun is used in an appositive.

Example: The directors, Yoshi and (~~me~~, I), have a meeting today.

Solution
- Drop the words identified by the appositive.
- Try each part of the appositive separately in the sentence.

The Bottom Line

Checklist for Using Pronouns

Have I . . .

_____ used the nominative case for pronouns functioning as subjects or predicate nominatives?

_____ used the objective case for pronouns functioning as objects?

_____ used the possessive case for pronouns to show ownership?

_____ used *who* and *whom* correctly?

_____ made all pronouns agree with their antecedents in number, gender, and person?

_____ used the correct cases of pronouns in compound structures?

_____ used the correct cases of pronouns in comparisons and appositives?

_____ eliminated any pronoun-reference problems?

Using Modifiers

Theme: Money

Oh, No!

Imagine you were given one wish and only three seconds to say what you wanted. You might name the first thing that came into your head: something to drive! You've been needing a practical, low-mileage car to drive to school or work. You wouldn't mind if it were also sporty. Your wish is granted—with the vehicle shown above.

What went wrong? You forgot to say what *kind* of vehicle. You need to use modifiers, such as adjectives and adverbs, to translate the image in your head into words. That way, when you write, if not in life, you'll get across what you want.

Write Away: Making a Wish
Describe in great detail something you would really like to have, so that another person could make an accurate drawing from what you write. Save your description in your 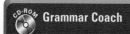 **Working Portfolio.**

Grammar Coach

Choose the best way to rewrite each underlined word or group of words.

Recently the U.S. Treasury did a <u>real good</u> job redesigning the country's
(1)
paper money. The goal was to make currency <u>more harder</u> to counterfeit.
(2)
The $100 bill was the <u>more likely</u> choice for the first redesign. <u>That there</u>
(3)   (4)
bill still has Benjamin Franklin's portrait. However, the portrait is now

<u>bigger</u> and off-center. You <u>can't hardly</u> notice the other changes, which
(5)   (6)
include a watermark, a security thread, and color-shifting ink.

    Now store clerks can spot a fake <u>real easy</u>. The <u>baddest</u> news for
(7)   (8)
counterfeiters is that it would cost them very much to print fake bills with

these security features. American bills are now harder to counterfeit <u>than</u>

<u>the currency of any country</u>. Americans can feel <u>well</u> about the physical
(9)   (10)
safety of their money.

---

1. A. real well
   B. really well
   C. really good
   D. Correct as is

2. A. most harder
   B. harder
   C. hardest
   D. Correct as is

3. A. most likeliest
   B. most likely
   C. likelier
   D. Correct as is

4. A. That
   B. This here
   C. These
   D. Correct as is

5. A. more bigger
   B. more big
   C. biggest
   D. Correct as is

6. A. can hardly
   B. don't hardly
   C. can't scarcely
   D. Correct as is

7. A. really easy
   B. really easily
   C. real easily
   D. Correct as is

8. A. badder
   B. worst
   C. most bad
   D. Correct as is

9. A. than any currency
   B. than the currency of another country
   C. than the currency of any other country
   D. Correct as is

10. A. good
    B. more good
    C. more well
    D. Correct as is

Using Adjectives and Adverbs

1 Here's the Idea

Modifiers are words that describe or give more specific information about—or modify—the meanings of other words. Adjectives and adverbs are common modifiers.

Adjectives

▶ **Adjectives modify nouns and pronouns.** They answer the questions *which one, what kind, how many,* and *how much.*

> **PROFESSIONAL MODEL**
>
> John August Sutter was a short, fat, kindly   **WHAT KIND**
> man whom everyone in California knew for his
> hospitality. He had come to America from
> Switzerland in 1834, and catching the western   **WHICH ONE**
> fever, had traveled across the plains. . . . The
> Mexican governor welcomed his plan to
> develop the country and granted him some land.   **HOW MUCH**
> —"Gold Is Found and a Nation Goes Wild"

Notice that more than one adjective may modify the same noun or pronoun. (For more on punctuating a series of adjectives, see page 224.) Proper adjectives, like *Mexican,* are capitalized.

Other words can often be used as adjectives.

Other Words Used as Adjectives	
Nouns	**stone** wall, **Bob's** cabin
Possessive pronouns	**my** book, **your** song, **his** plan, **their** garden,
Demonstrative pronouns	**this** road, **that** farm, **these** trees, **those** flowers
Participles	**shining** light, **falling** price, **locked** gate, **deserted** look
Indefinite pronouns	**all** signs, **each** direction, **few** options, **many** turns, **much** snow, **several** days, **some** hope
Numbers	**one** time, **10** minutes

Most adjectives come before the words they modify. **Predicate adjectives,** however, follow a linking verb and modify the subject of a clause.

MODIFY

The gold was pure and shiny.
PREDICATE ADJECTIVES

Adverbs

▶ **Adverbs modify verbs, adjectives, and other adverbs.** They answer the questions *when, where, how,* and *to what extent.*

MODIFIES

Prospectors eagerly searched for gold. (MODIFIES VERB)

MODIFIES

The search was often dangerous. (MODIFIES ADJECTIVE)

MODIFIES

Nuggets accumulated very slowly. (MODIFIES ADVERB)

An adverb can be placed before or after a verb it modifies.

MODIFIES   MODIFIES

They slowly examined the rocks and shouted triumphantly.

Place modifiers like *only* close to the words they modify (see page 224). Changing their position changes their meaning.

They only thought about gold. (THEY DID NOTHING ELSE.)

They thought only about gold. (THEY THOUGHT OF NOTHING ELSE.)

❷ Why It Matters in Writing

Adjectives used in groups efficiently add details about a setting. Adverbs can indicate changes over time.

> **LITERARY MODEL**
>
> It was a lovely region, woodsy, balmy, delicious,   ADJECTIVES
> and had once been populous, long years before, but   ADVERBS
> now the people had vanished.
>
> —Mark Twain, "The Californian's Tale"

MODIFIERS

❸ Practice and Apply

A. CONCEPT CHECK: Using Adjectives and Adverbs

For each sentence, find the modifiers (ignoring *a*, *an*, and *the*) and indicate whether they are used as adjectives or adverbs.

California Dreaming

1. In 1848, a mechanic named James Marshall noticed a shiny glint in the sparkling waters of the American River's south fork.
2. His lucky discovery—gold—eventually led to bad luck for his kindly boss, John Sutter.
3. Sutter was generous and openhanded and the proud owner of 49,000 acres of prime gold-mining land.
4. Before he knew it, word of the abundant gold spread across the country to Washington, D.C.
5. There President Polk told Congress that any hard-working miner might find untold wealth in the California territory.
6. Soon afterward, an estimated 100,000 people swarmed Sutter's pristine land.
7. In the first year, about 10,000 miners died because of inadequate shelter, poor food, too few medical supplies, rough crime, and frontier "justice."
8. They trashed Sutter's land, butchered his cattle, and even challenged his land ownership.
9. During the next five years, gold worth more than $285 million was mined in California, but poor Sutter quickly went bankrupt.
10. His was not the only sad story from the California gold rush; still, the gold rush did lay a solid foundation for the state's future economic prosperity.

➡ **For a SELF-CHECK and more practice, see the EXERCISE BANK, p. 625.**

B. WRITING: Describing with Modifiers

The Art of Mining
Two artists who went West with the gold rush painted this picture. Write a descriptive paragraph about the picture, using as many adjectives and adverbs as possible.

Miners in the Sierras (1851-52)
Charles Christian Nahl and Frederick August Wenderoth. National Museum of American Art, Washington DC/Art Resource, NY

Problems with Modifiers

❶ Here's the Idea

Here are several common problems you can have using modifiers.

STUDENT MODEL

My grandfather collects coins, which he calls a **scholar** pursuit. He says it's a good hobby, and he feels **badly** that I don't take a greater interest in it. He's most interested in old coins because they have stories to tell. Most of **them** coins contain real precious metals. Coins minted today in the United States **don't have no** gold or silver in them.

> Should be *scholarly*, an adjective despite its *-ly* ending.

> Should be the adjective *bad*, not the adverb *badly*.

> Should be the adjective *those*, not the pronoun *them*.

> Should be a single negative.

Adverb or Adjective?

It is easy to confuse adjectives and adverbs. For example, you might think that all words that end in *-ly* are adverbs, but some *-ly* words—such as *lovely* and *lonely*—function as adjectives.

MODIFIES   MODIFIES
Collecting lovely coins can be a lonely hobby.

Many words have both adjective and adverb forms. If you're not sure which form of a word to use, look at the word that it modifies. If the modified word is a noun or a pronoun, use the adjective form. If it's a verb, an adjective, or an adverb, use the adverb form.

MODIFIES   MODIFIES
Real coins can be really difficult to identify.

MODIFIES   MODIFIES
The careful collector examines them carefully.

Some words can function as either adjectives or adverbs depending on how they are used.

Kim earns an hourly wage at the clock store. (ADJECTIVE)

The grandfather clock chimes hourly. (ADVERB)

Two pairs of modifiers—*good* and *well, bad* and *badly*—cause writers special problems.

Good = Adjective

MODIFIES

Maria is a good coin collector.

MODIFIES

She feels good when she finds an old coin.

Well = Adjective or Adverb

MODIFIES

She missed a convention because she didn't feel well.

ADJECTIVE

MODIFIES

She handled her disappointment well.

ADVERB

Bad = Adjective

MODIFIES

Once she made a bad investment in coins.

MODIFIES

I felt bad for her.

Badly = Adverb

MODIFIES

That time she was cheated badly.

WATCH OUT

Never write "I feel badly" when referring to a state of mind or health. You are saying that you literally feel (touch things) poorly.

Double Negatives

A negative is a word that negates, or cancels, something. *No, not, none, never,* and contractions and expressions using these words are all negatives. In business and school writing, you should avoid **double negatives,** that is, the use of two negative words in a clause.

Nonstandard: Most coins don't contain no gold.

Standard: Most coins don't contain any gold.

Standard: Most coins contain no gold.

HOT TIP

For this purpose, the words *hardly, barely,* and *scarcely* are considered negatives. Don't combine one of these words with another negative.

You can't hardly use a penny these days.

This, That, These, **and** *Those*

This, that, these, and *those* are demonstrative pronouns that can be used as adjectives. Three rules cover all situations.

1. These words must agree in number with the words they modify.

   This hobby is educational. (SINGULAR)

   These coins are old. (PLURAL)

2. Never use *here* or *there* with one of these words. The adjective already points out which one; it doesn't need any help.

   This ~~here~~ coin is a Lincoln penny from 1909.

3. Never use the pronoun *them* as an adjective in place of *these* or *those*.

   | Nonstandard: | **Them pennies are rare and valuable.** |
   | Standard: | **Those pennies are rare and valuable.** |

② Why It Matters in Writing

When you write dialogue, you may have characters use modifiers in nonstandard ways, just as people use modifiers in everyday speech. You should eliminate nonstandard constructions in more formal writing, however.

STUDENT MODEL

Draft Loan Application

I'm applying for this ~~here~~ loan to pay my tuition. I'm doing
very ~~good~~ *well* in school, even though ~~them~~ *those* classes are hard. I have a
part-time job now that pays practical*ly* all my other expenses. I've
already been promised a good job after graduation. I'm enclosing
a payment plan to show how quick*ly* I'll be able to pay you back.
I can~~'t~~ hardly wait for your decision. Thank you.

MODIFIERS

❸ Practice and Apply

A. CONCEPT CHECK: Problems with Modifiers

For each sentence, choose the correct modifier.

How Many Watermelons Does That Shirt Cost?

1. When there wasn't (any, no) paper or metal money, people used various kinds of objects as currency.
2. They also used barter, which meant trading things they had for things they wanted (bad, badly).
3. Barter didn't work too (good, well).
4. You had to carry around (real, really) big bags of items you were willing to part with.
5. Then you had to find someone who wanted your things and was willing to part with (those, them) things that you wanted.
6. How (like, likely) is that?
7. You probably wouldn't (ever, never) go anywhere.
8. With the invention of coins, people could buy things (easy, easily).
9. They could just say, "I'd like (that, that there) shirt" and hand over some money instead of, say, a watermelon or a chicken.
10. Gold and silver made (good, well) money for many cultures.

➡ For a SELF-CHECK and more practice, see the EXERCISE BANK, p. 626.

B. EDITING AND PROOFREADING: Fixing Problems with Modifiers

Rewrite these sentences, correcting errors in the use of modifiers.

The Invention of Money

(1) The earliest known coins appeared near 9,000 years ago in what is now Turkey. **(2)** The Chinese didn't never use any metal but copper for their early coins. **(3)** The sizes, weights, and values of coins were actual standardized under the Roman Empire. **(4)** Other types of money have worked good for other cultures. **(5)** Cowrie shells served as money for an awfully lot of people from Africa to the Americas. **(6)** These here shells were durable and easy to carry. **(7)** In North America, many tribes used a conveniently kind of shell bead called wampum. **(8)** Women made wampum by breaking clam shells into pieces and careful drilling holes in them. **(9)** They strung them beads as necklaces or made belts of them. **(10)** It wasn't hardly a big step from shells to metals.

Using Comparisons

❶ Here's the Idea

Modifiers can be used to compare two or more things.

Three Degrees of Comparison		
An adjective or adverb **modifies** one word.	Bus A is **long.**	
The **comparative** compares two persons, places, or things.	Bus B is **longer** than Bus A.	
The **superlative** compares three or more persons, places, or things.	Bus C is the **longest** of the three. It is the **longest** bus of all.	

MODIFIERS

Regular Comparisons

Most modifiers are changed in regular ways to show comparisons.

Regular Comparisons			
Rule	**Modifier**	**Comparative**	**Superlative**
To a one-syllable word, add **-er** or **-est.**	cheap kind	cheap**er** kind**er**	cheap**est** kind**est**
For most two-syllable words, add **-er** or **-est.**	simple fancy	simpl**er** fanc**ier**	simpl**est** fanc**iest**
For most words of more than two syllables and words ending in *ly,* use **more** and **most.**	expensive wonderful kindly	**more** expensive **more** wonderful **more** kindly	**most** expensive **most** wonderful **most** kindly

Negative Comparisons To make a negative
comparison, use *less* and *least.*

> **I'm less wasteful than Matt.**
>
> **Jody is the least wasteful of
> all my friends.**

Irregular Comparisons

Some modifiers, like *bad,* have irregular comparative and superlative forms.

It was a bad day when my car broke down.

It was a worse day when I found out I needed a new battery.

The worst news was that the engine block was cracked.

Common Irregular Comparative Forms		
Modifier	**Comparative**	**Superlative**
bad	worse	worst
good	better	best
ill	worse	worst
little	less, lesser	least
many	more	most
much	more	most
well	better	best

When a 2-syllable word sounds awkward with the *-er* and *-est* endings, use *more* and *most* or *less* and *least,* as with longer words. For example: thankful, more thankful, least thankful.

❷ Why It Matters in Writing

Comparative and superlative forms greatly expand your power to describe. To say a building is *tall* paints a vague picture; to say it is *taller* than the Washington Monument makes the image more exact.

> **LITERARY MODEL**
>
> Every place they passed through looked nastier `COMPARATIVE` than the last, partly on account of the dismal light, partly because people had given up bothering to take a pride in their boroughs. And then, just as they were entering a village called Molesworth, the dimmest, drabbest, most `SUPERLATIVES` insignificant huddle of houses they had come to yet, the engine coughed and died on them.
>
> —Joan Aiken, "Searching for Summer"

❸ Practice and Apply

A. CONCEPT CHECK: Using Comparisons

Choose the correct form of comparison for each sentence.

Simplify, Simplify

1. Americans spend money (fast, faster) than any other culture.
2. Since 1950, Americans have used resources (more, most) quickly than the total of everyone who ever lived before then.
3. Many Americans are (prouder, proudest) of their ability to give their children material things.
4. But some people are saying we'd appreciate life more if we spent money (less freely, least freely).
5. They say we'd be (happier, more happy) if we bought less.
6. Spending (carefully, more carefully) than they do now would help people stay out of the rat race.
7. Then they could be (frantic, less frantic) about their jobs and spend more time doing things they enjoy.
8. People who've gotten out of the spending race say they're (calm, calmer) and (serener, more serene) than before.
9. "Buy Nothing Day" is the (newer, newest) holiday.
10. The (better, best) way of all to simplify our lives might be to spend money less freely.

➡ **For a SELF-CHECK and more practice, see the EXERCISE BANK, p. 626.**

B. WRITING: Describing a Graph

Government Spending
The pie graph shows an average state government's budget. Referring to the graph, fill in the blanks in the following sentences with comparative or superlative forms of adjectives, such as *greater* or *greatest*.

Highways
Administration
Health
7%
8%
Other
8%
36%
11%
Public Welfare
30%
Education

Source: *Statistical Abstract of the United States,* 1991

1. A typical state spends a _____ amount on welfare than on education.
2. The government spends a _____ amount on health than on highways.
3. The government spends the _____ amount of all on administration.
4. The _____ amount is spent on highways.

MODIFIERS

LESSON 4 **Problems with Comparisons**

① Here's the Idea

Writers sometimes make the mistake of using a double comparison or an illogical comparison.

Double Comparisons

Don't use both ways of forming comparisons or superlatives at once: *-er* and *more* or *-est* and *most.*

Nonstandard: It's more wiser to save money than to spend it.

Standard: It's wiser to save money than to spend it.

Nonstandard: The most simplest way to shop is with a list.

Standard: The simplest way to shop is with a list.

Illogical Comparisons

Illogical or confusing comparisons can result if you unintentionally compare something to itself or compare two unrelated things.

Illogical: Mariko thinks the quarter is prettier than any coin.
(A quarter *is* a coin, so it can't be prettier than any coin.)

Clear: Mariko thinks the quarter is prettier than any other coin.

Confusing: Isabel likes coins better than her sister.
(Does Isabel like coins more than she likes her sister, or does she like coins more than her sister does?)

Clear: Isabel likes coins more than her sister does.

② Why It Matters in Writing

A double or an illogical comparison can be a sign of trying too hard to emphasize a point.

else

Nick was more concerned about money than anyone. So he

worked ~~more~~ harder on his budget than I.

CHAPTER 9

➌ Practice and Apply

A. CONCEPT CHECK: Problems with Comparisons

Choose the correct form of comparison for each sentence.

Money Can't Buy Happiness
1. The distribution of income is one of the (biggest, most biggest) differences among countries.
2. The United States is richer than (any, any other) country.
3. The average U.S. income is (greater, more greater) than that of most countries.
4. By contrast, the African nation of Chad is one of the world's (poorest, most poorest) countries.
5. At less than $200 a year, its average income is (lower, more lower) than incomes of almost any other country.
6. Some families live even (more cheaply, more cheaplier).
7. Their children begin to work in the fields at about age six; the (older, more older) children move to cities to find work.
8. But they are not necessarily (less happy, less happier) than people with more money.
9. In fact, citizens of the poorer countries may like daily life (more than Americans, more than Americans do).
10. When people grow their own food and make their own clothes, cash is (less importanter, less important) to them.

➡ **For a SELF-CHECK and more practice, see the EXERCISE BANK, p. 627.**

B. REVISING: Eliminating Problem Modifiers

Rewrite the following sentences, revising each double or illogical comparison.

The Income Gap
(1) Income is distributed unevenly within the United States; the rich are getting more richer. **(2)** The most wealthiest 20 percent of Americans receive more than 46 percent of the country's total income. **(3)** Therefore, they have more money to spend than any income group. **(4)** The 20 percent of Americans with the most lowest income receive only about 4 percent of the country's income. **(5)** The income gap has been growing more wider over time.

Grammar in Literature

Modifiers and Lively Writing

In the passage below, O. Henry uses modifiers in several ways to help introduce the characters and start the action. Notice how each adjective and adverb functions to describe or give more specific information about the word it modifies.

O. HENRY
ONE THOUSAND
DOLLARS

"One thousand dollars," repeated Lawyer Tolman, <u>solemnly</u> and <u>severely</u>, "and here is the money."

> **Adverbs** immediately characterize the lawyer's manner and define the mood.

Young Gillian gave a decidedly amused laugh as he fingered the <u>thin</u> package of <u>new fifty-dollar</u> notes.

> **Adjectives** contribute sensory details and key information.

"It's such a confoundedly awkward amount," he explained, <u>genially</u>, to the lawyer. "If it had been ten thousand a fellow might wind up with a lot of fireworks and do himself credit. Even $50 would have been less trouble."

> An **adverb** captures the manner of the second character in the scene and contrasts him to the first.

"You heard the reading of your uncle's will," continued Lawyer Tolman, <u>professionally dry</u> in his tones. "I do not know if you paid much attention to its details. I must remind you of one. You are required to render to us an account of the manner of expenditure...."

> Here as earlier, an **adverb-adjective pair** offers specific information about the action while contributing rhythm and character to the writing style.

"You may depend upon it," said the young man, <u>politely</u>, "in spite of the <u>extra</u> expense it will entail. I may have to engage a secretary, I was <u>never good</u> at accounts."

> Adjectives and adverbs continue to deepen characterization and add details.

Using Modifiers to Create Specific Descriptions

Adverbs	Use adverbs to sketch a character quickly. Notice how the adverb *genially* does for the second character what *solemnly* and *severely* do for the first.
Adjectives	Use adjectives to convey useful information about quantity and quality in an economic way.
Adverb-adjective pairs	Use adverb-adjective pairs to deepen character. Pairs like *decidedly amused, confoundedly awkward*, and *professionally dry* describe and comment on the characters.

PRACTICE AND APPLY: Choosing Modifiers

Replace the underlined modifiers in the following passage with alternatives that would change the nature of the characters.

LITERARY MODEL

Our father was a **(1)** <u>big</u> man, **(2)** <u>outgoing</u> and
(3) <u>immensely</u> active. We thought he was **(4)** <u>immortal</u>, but
then **(5)** <u>most</u> children think that about their father. The
(6) <u>worst</u> thing was that Mother thought he was
(7) <u>immortal</u> too, and when he died, keeling over on the
pavement between the
(8) <u>insurance</u> offices
where he worked, and
the **(9)** <u>company</u> car
into which he was just
about to climb, there
followed a period of
(10) <u>ghastly</u> limbo.
(11) <u>Bereft,</u>
(12) <u>uncertain,</u> **(13)** <u>lost,</u>
none of us knew what
to do **(14)** <u>next</u>. But after the funeral and a little talk with
the family lawyer, Mother **(15)** <u>quietly</u> pulled herself
together and told us.

—Rosamunde Pilcher, "Lalla"

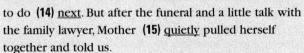

Mixed Review

A. Adjectives and Adverbs Read the following passage. Then answer the questions below it.

(1) Our greatest concern was how we were going to reach the fifty thousand black people of Montgomery, no matter how hard we worked. **(2)** The white press, in an outraged exposé, spread the word for us in a way that would have been impossible with only our own resources.

(3) As it happened, a white woman found one of our leaflets, which her black maid had left in the kitchen. **(4)** The irate woman immediately telephoned the newspapers to let the white community know what the blacks were up to. **(5)** We laughed a lot about this, and Martin later said that we owed them a great debt.

(6) On Sunday morning, from their pulpits, almost every African-American minister in town urged people to honor the boycott.

— Coretta Scott King, *Montgomery Boycott*

1. In what form is the adjective *greatest* in sentence 1?
2. Is the word *hard* in sentence 1 an adjective or adverb? What does it modify?
3. In sentence 2, what word is a participle functioning as an adjective?
4. In sentence 2, what word does the adjective *impossible* modify?
5. What part of speech is *only* in sentence 2, and what does it modify?
6. What part of speech is *our* in sentence 3, and how is it being used?
7. What would be the comparative form of *irate* in sentence 4?
8. What does the word *immediately* modify in sentence 4?
9. What does the word *almost* modify in sentence 6?
10. What part of speech is *every* in sentence 6, and how is it being used?

B. Correcting Problems with Modifiers Read the following paragraph. If an underlined word or phrase is correct, write *Correct*. If there is a problem, write the word or phrase correctly.

What Makes Good Money?

Money **(1)** <u>doesn't have to have no</u> inherent value. It just has to be something people **(2)** <u>readily</u> accept in exchange for their products. The **(3)** <u>bestest</u> money should be durable, compact, divisible, in limited and fairly constant supply, and hard to counterfeit. **(4)** <u>These kind of things</u> wouldn't make good money: bananas, car tires, cows, and sand. Many cultures have used gold because it meets the standards **(5)** <u>better than any money</u>. Gold is one of the **(6)** <u>most longest-lasting</u> things around. But even **(7)** <u>that there</u> metal has its flaws. Gold is **(8)** <u>fair</u> heavy and **(9)** <u>easily</u> to counterfeit with coins **(10)** <u>only made partly</u> of gold.

Choose the best way to rewrite each underlined word or group of words.

It is <u>considerable interesting</u> that the word *money* comes from the
(1)
Latin word *moneta,* which means "she who advises or warns." Moneta was
a name given to Juno, one of the <u>ancient</u> Romans' <u>most greatest</u> deities.
(2)   (3)
She was more powerful <u>than any goddess</u>. Her followers <u>sure</u> did worship
(4)   (5)
her <u>enthusiastically</u>. They established a mint in the Temple of Juno
(6)
Moneta. <u>This here</u> word *moneta* came to mean "mint" and eventually
(7)
"minted coins." The word *dollar* comes from the old German *Taler,* a silver
coin first minted in Germany in 1519. The dollar has held up <u>undeniably</u>
(8)
<u>good</u> as the standard unit of account in the United States for over 200
years. The word *coin* comes from the Latin word *cuneus.* It originally
<u>didn't have no</u> meaning except "corner" or "wedge." Studying <u>these kind</u> of
(9)   (10)
word origins tells us much about how currency systems evolved.

1. A. considerable interestingly
   B. considerably interesting
   C. considerably interestingly
   D. Correct as is

2. A. ancientest
   B. most anciently
   C. too ancient
   D. Correct as is

3. A. most great
   B. greatest
   C. greater
   D. Correct as is

4. A. than anyone
   B. than any other goddess
   C. than another goddess
   D. Correct as is

5. A. surely
   B. more sure
   C. most sure
   D. Correct as is

6. A. more enthusiastic
   B. most enthusiastic
   C. enthusiastic
   D. Correct as is

7. A. That there
   B. Those
   C. This
   D. Correct as is

8. A. undeniably well
   B. undeniable good
   C. undeniable well
   D. Correct as is

9. A. hadn't no
   B. didn't have any
   C. scarcely had no
   D. Correct as is

10. A. this kinds
    B. these kinds
    C. those kind
    D. Correct as is

MODIFIERS

Student Help Desk

Modifiers at a Glance

Adjectives	Modifier	Comparative	Superlative
tell which one, what kind, how many, how much	cool	cooler	coolest
	generous	more generous less generous	most generous least generous
Adverbs			
tell when, where, how, to what extent	generously	more generously less generously	most generously least generously

Adjectives in a Series Smooth Sailing

Use commas between adjectives when their order could be reversed without changing the meaning.

The **elegant, expensive** yacht sailed into view.
The **expensive, elegant** yacht anchored offshore.

Don't use commas to separate modifiers that could not be reversed.

The **miserly yacht** owner forgot to pay the crew.

Don't use commas to separate adjectives that describe color, age, size, or material.

The **old blue** rowboat sprang a leak.
The **new green fiberglass** canoe nearly sank.

Adverbs in Different Positions Safe Harbor

Place adverbs carefully to ensure they refer to the words they modify.

Almost everyone was on time to meet the ship. (Few were late.)
Everyone was **almost** on time to meet the ship. (No one was on time.)

Eliminate confusion in the placement of adverbs.

The captain considers steering **terribly** important. (Confusing)
The captain considers steering to be **terribly** important.

CHAPTER 9

Recognizing Adverbs   Don't Be at Sea

Adverb Types	Adverbs	Example
Many adverbs are formed by adding -ly to adjectives.	angrily, critically, equally, finally, nicely, stubbornly, warmly	The harbor beckons **warmly.**
Some common adverbs do not end in -ly.	afterward, almost, also, even, here, instead, not, then, there, too, yet	We're **not there yet.**
Some nouns can function as adverbs.	home, outdoors, tomorrow, yesterday	We'll sail again **tomorrow.**

The Bottom Line

Checklist for Using Modifiers

Have I . . .

____ chosen adjectives and adverbs that contribute to lively descriptions?

____ used the correct forms of adjectives and adverbs?

____ avoided double negatives?

____ used *this, that, these,* and *those* correctly?

____ formed comparatives and superlatives correctly?

____ avoided illogical and confusing comparisons?

"*This is Fluffy, my pet money.*"

© The New Yorker Collection 1999 Danny Shanahan

Capitalization

dearest granddaughter,

for safekeeping, i have
hidden my valuable
eleanor t jones oil painting
beside the maple river
at the bench.

your loving grandma

Theme: Trash or Treasure?

Which Is It?

Lucy had wondered for years what had happened to the oil
painting that used to hang above her grandmother's fireplace.
Finding this note solved part of the mystery.

Still, Lucy wasn't quite sure where to begin looking. Did *bench*
mean bench, or did it mean BENCH for Bank of East North Central
Highwood? Was the painting called *Beside the Maple River,* or was
it buried beside the Maple River? Because her grandmother had
not capitalized any words, Lucy could not know for sure.

Write Away: Treasured Possessions
Write a paragraph describing one of your favorite possessions.
Choose something that has little value in terms of money but is
important to you. Save your paragraph in your 📁 **Working Portfolio.**

CD-ROM Grammar Coach

For each underlined group of words, choose the letter of the correct revision.

In the shop of <u>mr. Martin Tytell</u>, the writer Ian Frazier found untold
                (1)
treasures. He shared his discovery in <u>"Typewriter Man" in *The Atlantic*</u>
                                                                (2)
monthly magazine. In Tytell's shop, hundreds of manual and electric

typewriters—<u>some with russian, Greek, and Hebrew</u> alphabets—are
               (3)
lovingly preserved. <u>Tytell remarked, "the</u> way these machines continue to
                     (4)
function . . . is a miracle."

Not long ago, typewriters were considered junk, but now they can be

found in museums, antique shows, and collectors' homes both <u>east and</u>

<u>west of the Mississippi river.</u> Some of their value comes from history. In
          (5)
the <u>second World War</u>, for example, <u>the War Production Board</u> was in
        (6)   (7)
charge of typewriters. One shipment of 20,000 typewriters was sunk

during the <u>d-Day invasion of Normandy.</u> For many decades after the war,
              (8)
machines made by <u>Remington, Hermes, Ibm,</u> and countless others kept
                    (9)
communications flowing from <u>8 A.M. to 5 p.m., Monday</u> through Friday.
                               (10)

1. A. Mr.
   B. martin
   C. tytell
   D. Correct as is

2. A. "Typewriter man"
   B. *atlantic*
   C. *Monthly*
   D. Correct as is

3. A. Russian
   B. greek
   C. hebrew
   D. Correct as is

4. A. tytell
   B. Remarked
   C. The
   D. Correct as is

5. A. East and West
   B. mississippi
   C. River
   D. Correct as is

6. A. Second
   B. world
   C. war
   D. Correct as is

7. A. The
   B. war
   C. board
   D. Correct as is

8. A. D-Day
   B. Invasion
   C. normandy
   D. Correct as is

9. A. remington
   B. hermes
   C. IBM
   D. Correct as is

10. A. a.m.
    B. P.M.
    C. monday
    D. Correct as is

People and Cultures

LESSON 1

❶ Here's the Idea

People's names and titles, the names of the languages they speak, and the names of the religions they practice are all proper nouns and should be capitalized.

Names and Initials

▶ **Capitalize people's names and initials.**

Celia Cruz	Eldrick "Tiger" Woods	E. B. White
Frederick W. Douglass	Coretta Scott King	E. M. Forster

Personal Titles and Abbreviations

▶ **Capitalize titles and abbreviations of titles that are used before names or in direct address.**

General Colin Powell   Dr. Brazelton

Secretary of State Madeleine Albright   Mrs. Wilson

Sgt. McDonald interviewed Professor Chandra about the stolen bead collection.

▶ **Capitalize the abbreviations of some titles even when they follow names.**

Edward Jones, Sr.   Deborah Young, C.E.O.   Lewis Kent, Ph.D.

▶ **Capitalize a title of royalty or nobility only when it precedes a person's name.**

King Olaf V   Sir Paul McCartney   Queen Margrethe II

The beaded gown was worn by Princess Catherine.

The dukes and duchesses attended the auction.

CHAPTER 10

Family Relationships

▶ **Capitalize words indicating family relationships only when they are used as parts of names or in direct address.**

Aunt Angela   Cousin Steve   Grandpa Leon

My father bought Uncle Roy's crystal bead collection.

 In general, do not capitalize a title when it follows a person's name or is used without a proper name.

Juanita, my aunt, gave us her handmade quilts.

The Pronoun *I*

▶ **Always capitalize the pronoun *I*.**

My cousin and I were overjoyed.

Ethnic Groups, Languages, and Nationalities

▶ **Capitalize the names of ethnic groups, races, languages, and nationalities, along with the adjectives formed from these names.**

Kurds   Native American   French

Hispanic   African American   Navajo

Religious Terms

▶ **Capitalize the names of religions, denominations or branches of religions, sacred days, sacred writings, and deities.**

Religious Terms	
Religions	Christianity, Buddhism, Islam
Denominations/branches	Baptist, Protestant, Shiite
Sacred days	Ramadan, Christmas, Rosh Hashanah
Sacred writings	Koran, Torah, Bible
Deities	God, Yahweh, Allah

 Do not capitalize the words *god* and *goddess* when they refer to one of a group of gods, as in ancient mythology; but do capitalize the names of such gods.

The Greek god of war was Ares.

CAPITALIZATION

❷ Practice and Apply

A. CONCEPT CHECK: People and Cultures

For each sentence, write the words that should be capitalized.

Beautiful Beaded Bowls

1. Diego j. pérez runs a native american cultural museum.

2. Last June, mr. pérez visited his niece, marta ríos, m.d., in Jalisco, Mexico, and discovered treasures.

3. He and dr. ríos visited huichol indian communities.

4. Although Pérez speaks spanish and english, he needed his niece to interpret the huichol language.

5. The huichols combine christianity with ancient beliefs.

6. Through the influence of roman catholic missionaries, some communities observe christian holidays.

7. Artisans make christmas ornaments to sell; but they also create *rukuri*, beaded gourd bowls, to honor ancient gods.

8. They coat the inside of a gourd with wax and prefer to make designs with czech or japanese seed beads.

9. "The rattlesnake, i believe, represents the fire god," said Pérez, pointing to one design.

10. "Recently, american and european dealers have begun selling the *rukuri*, but i think we must be careful not to exploit the huichol beliefs for profit," concluded mr. Pérez.

➡ **For a SELF-CHECK and more practice, see the EXERCISE BANK, p. 627.**

B. PROOFREADING: Correcting Capitalization

Find and correct 20 capitalization errors in the following passage.

Trinkets or Treasures?

(1) The debate started when grandma Eloise brought out her rare agate bead, which is revered by many himalayan peoples. **(2)** My Grandfather, an Engineer, and his friend, senator Brown, called it a trinket. **(3)** However, james kelly and dr. maggie drews said it had great value. **(4)** Grandma argued that in some asian cultures, beads were offered to appease the Gods. **(5)** Today, roman mosaic face beads and egyptian paste beads are valued highly, and the jewels and beads of empress Catherine II, of Russia, are considered treasures. **(6)** Yet not everyone agrees that the russian beaded flowers made for 18th-century europeans were valuable. **(7)** Nevertheless, i believe that even a seed pendant inscribed with a buddhist prayer is as much a treasure as catherine's jewels.

LESSON 2 — First Words and Titles

❶ Here's the Idea

First words in sentences, most lines of poetry, quotations, and outline entries are capitalized. Greetings and closings in letters and important words in titles are capitalized.

Sentences and Poetry

▶ **Capitalize the first word of every sentence.**

The critics turned up their noses at the new movie.

▶ **Capitalize the first word in every line of traditional poetry whether it begins a new sentence or not.**

> **LITERARY MODEL**
>
> When I see birches bend to left and right
> Across the lines of straighter darker trees,
> I like to think some boy's been swinging them. . . .
>
> —Robert Frost, "Birches"

Contemporary poetry often does not follow this convention.

Quotations

▶ **Capitalize the first word of a direct quotation when the quotation is a complete sentence and is not connected grammatically to the sentence in which it appears.**

Ryan said, "Popular culture is mostly trash."

Ryan had a habit of saying that "popular movies are ridiculous."

▶ **In a divided quotation, do not capitalize the first word of the second part unless it starts a new sentence.**

"It's not true," said Syd, "that pop culture is worthless."
"I agree," said Rosa. "That new movie is terrific."

Parts of a Letter

▶ **In a letter, capitalize the first word of the greeting, the word *Sir* or *Madam*, and the first word of the closing.**

May 24, 2000

Dear Sir:

Thank you for your inquiry. Because of the renewed interest in twentieth-century popular culture, our entire stock of mechanical banks in mint condition has been depleted. I recommend you contact the Mechanical Bank Collectors of America for additional information.

Yours truly,

Jane Wrightwood

Outlines

▶ **Capitalize the first word of each entry in an outline, as well as the letters that introduce major subsections.**

> I. Fine arts
>   A. European
>   1. Artists
>   2. Composers

Titles

▶ **Capitalize the first word, the last word, and all other important words in a title.** Do not capitalize articles, conjunctions, or prepositions of fewer than five letters.

Titles	
Books	*Farewell to Manzanar, The Grapes of Wrath*
Plays and musicals	*Antigone, The Tragedy of Julius Caesar, Lion King*
Short stories	"A Sound of Thunder," "Sweet Potato Pie"
Poems	"Birches," "For the New Year, 1981," "The Sun"
Musical compositions	"I Will Always Love You," "Don't Worry; Be Happy"
Movies	*Jaws, The Sound of Music, The Breakfast Club*
Television shows	*Saturday Night Live, Nightline, All My Children*
Works of art	*Girl with Tear III, American Gothic, The Thinker*
Magazines and newspapers	*News Story, Entertainment Weekly, Ski and Sea, Lewistown Journal*
Games	Word for Word, Brain Battle, Sink or Swim

❷ Practice and Apply

A. CONCEPT CHECK: First Words and Titles

For each sentence, write the words that should be capitalized.

Into the Classics

1. If a friend says, "parting is such sweet sorrow," he or she is quoting from the play *romeo and juliet.*

2. "it's possible," said Mr. Wilcox, "that popular culture can lead us to the classics."

3. For example, watching an episode of *Xena, warrior princess* could inspire someone to read *the Odyssey.*

4. The traditional poet Robert Herrick reminds us of the importance of taking time in these lines from one of his poems:

> Gather ye rosebuds while ye may,
> Old Time is still a-flying;
> and this same flower that smiles today
> tomorrow will be dying.

5. So after seeing a spoof of the painting *american gothic,* check out the original, because "old Time is still a-flying."

➜ **For a SELF-CHECK and more practice, see the EXERCISE BANK, p. 628.**

Write sentences patterned on items 1, 3, and 5, using other titles you know.

B. PROOFREADING: Capitalization Errors

Find and correct 15 capitalization errors in the following letter.

A Classic Look

(1) Dear miss Guided:

(2) in your letter in *The Evening Standard,* you said, "The fine arts are irrelevant and unfamiliar." **(3)** Susan Sontag once wrote, "interpretation makes art manageable, conformable. . . ." **(4)** You can't compare *The war of the worlds* to *The x-Files* or *The Marriage Of Figaro* to *Grease!* **(5)** don't be swayed by the critics. **(6)** "A critic is a man who knows the way," said Kenneth Tynan, "But can't drive the car." **(7)** You can appreciate *Masterpiece theatre* if you try. **(8)** Acquaint yourself with *As you like it* before you rent *Shakespeare In Love.*

(9) Sincerely Yours,

(10) Ann E. Chance

Places and Transportation

LESSON 3

① Here's the Idea

The names of specific places, celestial bodies, landmarks, and vehicles are capitalized.

Geographical Names

▶ **In geographical names, capitalize each word except articles and prepositions.**

Type of Name	Example
Special terms	Southern Hemisphere, North Pole
Continents	Africa, Asia, North America
Bodies of water	Lake Erie, Atlantic Ocean, Nile River
Islands	Galapagos Islands, Philippines, Hawaiian Islands
Mountains	Andes, Mount Everest, Rocky Mountains
Other landforms	English Channel, Painted Desert, Niagara Falls
World regions	Balkans, Southeast Asia, Latin America
Countries/nations	El Salvador, Thailand, England
States	Texas, California, Florida
Counties/townships	Polk County, Ingham Township
Cities/towns	Tulsa, Salt Lake City, Boston
Roads/streets	Pennsylvania Avenue, Rodeo Drive, Central Street

Regions and Directions

▶ **Capitalize the words *north, south, east,* and *west* when they name a particular region of the country or world or are parts of proper nouns.**

The Willises held a garage sale before moving to South Dakota.

Garage sales are popular on the West Coast, where they lived.

Do not capitalize compass directions or adjectives that indicate direction or a general location.

They drove east out of Nevada City, and then turned north.

Bodies of the Universe

▶ **Capitalize the names of planets and other specific objects in the universe.**

    Hale-Bopp Comet   Venus   Milky Way Galaxy

Do not capitalize *sun* and *moon*. Capitalize *earth* only when it refers to our planet or when it is used with other capitalized terms. Never capitalize *earth* when it is preceded by the article *the* or when it refers to land surface, or soil.

    Did water once flow on Mars as it does on Earth?

    The earth has many land forms carved by water.

Buildings, Bridges, and Other Landmarks

▶ **Capitalize the names of specific buildings, bridges, monuments, and other landmarks.**

    Vietnam Memorial   Golden Gate Bridge

    World Trade Center   Space Needle

    Flora found a clock shaped like the Taj Mahal.

Planes, Trains, and Other Vehicles

▶ **Capitalize the names of specific airplanes, trains, ships, cars, and spacecraft.**

Type of Vehicle	Name
Airplanes	*Enola Gay, Spirit of St. Louis*
Trains	*Southwest Chief, City of New Orleans*
Ships	USS *John F. Kennedy, Pinta*
Cars	Malibu, Civic
Spacecraft	*Columbia, Mars Pathfinder*

❷ Practice and Apply

A. CONCEPT CHECK: Places and Transportation

For each sentence, write the words that should be capitalized.

Second Time Around

1. From souvenirs of a trip to the bahamas to a model of the ss *clermont*, secondhand treasures abound.
2. Across the united states, from new England to the west coast, rummagers flock to flea markets.
3. Where else can you find a lamp in the shape of the eiffel tower?
4. Do you need a miniature model t Ford to complete your collection?
5. Are you looking for a velvet painting of mount rushmore for your wall?
6. Try visiting the World's Largest Garage Sale in evanston, illinois, in cook county.
7. Attend the annual rummage sale in north hill, located in the northern blue ridge mountains.
8. Take a stroll from maple street to oak boulevard and try a local garage sale.
9. A model of the Rolls Royce silver spirit may sell for a dollar.
10. A mobile of saturn, neptune, and mercury may have the down-to-earth price of fifty cents!

➡ **For a SELF-CHECK and more practice, see the EXERCISE BANK, p. 628.**

B. WRITING: Postcard from a National Monument

Who Are These People?

Look up Mount Rushmore in a reference book or on the Internet. Learn where it is located, whose faces are on it, and other important information about it. Then write a five-sentence postcard to a friend describing the monument and including the facts you discovered. Use capitalization correctly.

Organizations and Other Subjects

① Here's the Idea

Capitalize the names of organizations, historical events and documents, and months, days, and holidays.

Organizations and Institutions

▶ **Capitalize all important words in the names of businesses, governmental agencies, institutions, and other organizations.**

Adams High School	Ralph's Foreign Car Repair, Inc.
Library of Congress	Guggenheim Museum
Federal Reserve System	Oberlin College

Do not capitalize words such as *school, company, church, college,* and *hospital* when they are not used as parts of proper names.

Abbreviations of Organization Names

▶ **Capitalize acronyms and abbreviations of the names of organizations and institutions.**

UNICEF (United Nations International Children's Emergency Fund)

FTC (Federal Trade Commission)

ADA (American Dental Association)

PTA (Parent Teacher Association)

USC (University of Southern California)

Historical Events, Periods, and Documents

▶ **Capitalize the names of historical events, periods, and documents.**

Historical Events, Periods, and Documents	
Events	Boston Tea Party, Revolutionary War, Gulf War
Periods	Great Depression, Sixties, Information Age
Documents	Mayflower Compact, Americans with Disabilities Act

The period of Reconstruction followed the Civil War.

Time Abbreviations and Calendar Items

▶ **Capitalize the abbreviations B.C., A.D., B.C.E., A.M., and P.M.**
In typeset material, time abbreviations are usually shown in small capital letters.

> The Aztecs founded their capital in A.D. 1325.
> The workshop begins at 8:00 A.M. and ends at 4:30 P.M.

A.D. goes before the date; B.C. goes after.

▶ **Capitalize the names of months, days, and holidays but not the names of seasons.**

October	Wednesday	Labor Day
winter	Monday	Thanksgiving

> Every February we celebrate Chinese New Year with a parade.

Special Events, Awards, and Brand Names

▶ **Capitalize the names of special events and awards.**

World Series	National Medal of Arts
Boston Marathon	Emmy Awards

> Jim Morin won the Pulitzer Prize for Editorial Cartooning.

▶ **Capitalize the brand names of products but not common nouns that follow brand names.**

> Good Stuff spinach   Playpen Toys pacifiers

School Courses

▶ **Capitalize the titles of specific courses and courses that are followed by a number. Do not capitalize the general names of school subjects except languages.**

Business Machines 101	Intermediate Word Processing
algebra	Japanese

Capitalize the names of school years only when they refer to a specific group or event, or when they are used in direct address.

> The Freshman Bake Sale is held every spring.

> Every fall, the juniors hold their toy drive.

> You'd better start preparing, Sophomores.

❷ Practice and Apply

A. CONCEPT CHECK: Organizations and Other Subjects

For each sentence, write the words that should be capitalized.

Toyland
1. Will this year's class trip find seniors visiting the senate and the house of representatives in the spring?
2. Does the senior trip committee need to raise money?
3. Then take a fundraising tip from Mr. Iwo, who teaches social studies at byron high school.
4. Iwo, a member of the marble collectors' society of America, conceived the Toys for Teens sale at the school.
5. Held in november, the sale featured a wide range of toys.
6. Exhibited over a saturday and a sunday from 9:00 a.m. to 6:00 P.M. was a collection of primitive toys that predate the industrial revolution.
7. There were also cast-iron fire engines made by the stanley company after world war II.
8. People could buy die-cast racing cars licensed by NASCAR.
9. In fact, toys ranging from General Toy Company's fashion dolls to nfl action figures were on sale.
10. The successful sale attracted early christmas and hanukkah shoppers as well as avid toy collectors.

➡ **For a SELF-CHECK and more practice, see the EXERCISE BANK, p. 629.**

B. PROOFREADING: Capitalization Errors

Find and correct 21 capitalization errors in the following passage.

Classroom Toys
(1) If they gave an Award for innovative use of toys, the students at worth high school would surely win it. **(2)** Freshman History students have recreated revolutionary war battles with tin soldiers and used Fabusoft software to simulate air campaigns in the persian gulf war. **(3)** In economics 1.1, Juniors have looked at the market for Fuzzy Babies Toys produced by marvo, inc., to study supply and demand concepts. **(4)** Some students have even formed the toy collectors society, which meets on tuesdays at 7:00 p.m. **(5)** If you attend the meetings, you might hear about a soldier doll that looks like General Colin Powell or action figures made by neato.

Real World Grammar

Publicity Poster

If you take part in activities at school or outside of school, you will sometimes need to create a publicity poster. The poster will require names, dates, and other words that should be capitalized. Once you have the basic information down, proofread the poster for errors in capitalization.

Hidden Treasures Flea Market

Sponsored by the Community service Club
of ralph bunche high school

Capitalize names of organizations

Date: Saturday, november 15

Capitalize months

Time: 9:00 a.m. to 4:00 p.m.

Capitalize time abbreviations

Place: East Gym

Find just the right thing to dress up your room or your life!

- Vintage clothing from the '60s, '70s, '80s, and '90s
- Posters, stickers, pins, pennants, bumper stickers
- Books, videos, CDs, and vinyl records
- Toys, games, trading cards, and other collectibles

☆☆☆ SPECIAL FEATURED SECTIONS ☆☆☆

Books
Go tell it on the Mountain and other favorites you won't want to put down

Videos
The Wizard Of Oz and other timeless classics

CDs and Tapes
favorite rap, R & B, rock, blues, jazz, and classical recordings

Capitalize book and movie titles properly.

Don't capitalize titles unless they're used as part of a name

The President of our club is Vicki Sanchez.
Our faculty Sponsor is Mr. Robinson.
All proceeds will go to the Your Place Homeless Shelter.

Using Grammar in Writing

Names of organizations	Watch out for words like *club* and *school;* capitalize these words only when they are part of the name of a group.
Days, months, and time abbreviations	In addition to using capital letters, don't forget to punctuate the abbreviations A.M. and P.M. with periods.
Titles of published works	Remember, short words in a title are not necessarily unimportant words. Words like *Is, It,* and *All* should be capitalized in titles even when they are not the first words.
Personal titles	You may be tempted to capitalize titles like *chairperson* or *sponsor* because they seem important. When they appear apart from a person's name, however, they are ordinary nouns and should not be capitalized.

PRACTICE AND APPLY: Writing

Following are notes taken at a planning meeting for a school play. Create a publicity poster for the play, using the information shown and capitalizing it correctly.

PLAY TITLE: FAHRENHEIT 451
ADAPTED FROM THE NOVEL BY
RAY BRADBURY

SANDRA LOPEZ, A JUNIOR, WILL PLAY
CLARISSE AND TED ROSNER,
A SOPHOMORE, WILL PLAY MONTAG.
MONTAG'S WIFE, MILDRED = PLAYED BY
NAN WONG.
STUDENT DIRECTORS = NATE KEENE
AND LISA FINCH.
FACULTY DIRECTOR = MARTHA LEE

FRI AND SAT, 7
IN THE EVENING
MAY 4 AND 5,
PARTRIDGE AUDITORIUM.
THE WELLSPRING DRAMA
SOCIETY, JEFFERSON HIGH
SCHOOL.

A. Sentence Capitalization One collector of action figures sent the following e-mail message to another. Revise the message to capitalize all the letters in the message that should be capitalized in ordinary writing.

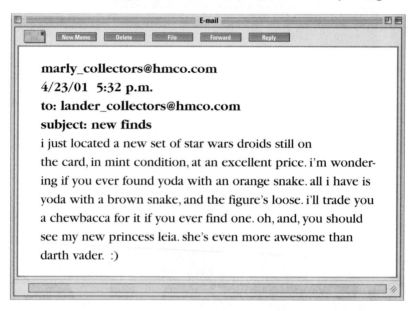

E-mail

New Memo   Delete   File   Forward   Reply

marly_collectors@hmco.com
4/23/01 5:32 p.m.
to: lander_collectors@hmco.com
subject: new finds
i just located a new set of star wars droids still on the card, in mint condition, at an excellent price. i'm wondering if you ever found yoda with an orange snake. all i have is yoda with a brown snake, and the figure's loose. i'll trade you a chewbacca for it if you ever find one. oh, and, you should see my new princess leia. she's even more awesome than darth vader. :)

B. Capitalization of Proper Nouns and Adjectives The following headlines contain some words that should always be capitalized and others that are normally shown in lowercase. Rewrite these headlines as complete sentences using proper capitalization and punctuation.

Example: RECORD CROWDS AT YOSEMITE
Answer: Record crowds visited Yosemite National Park.

1. FIRES RAGE; RED CROSS SAYS 500 DEAD
2. HURRICANE SLAMS CAROLINA COAST
3. 7 DIE AS MOUNT ST. HELENS ERUPTS
4. BLINDING ASH HALTS TRAFFIC ACROSS STATE
5. 52 U.S. HOSTAGES FLOWN TO FREEDOM
6. BRITAIN ANNOUNCES ARGENTINE SURRENDER
7. FLOODS RAGE IN CONNECTICUT; 8 BELIEVED DEAD
8. FOURTH OF JULY PARADE SNARLS CITY TRAFFIC
9. 2 UNIVERSITY PHYSICISTS TAKE NOBEL PRIZE
10. MOVIE DRAWS RECORD NUMBERS TO LEWISTOWN MALL

For each underlined group of words, choose the letter of the correct revision.

After receiving the call from <u>reverend Bates about Mrs. Bates's death,</u>
(1)
Dennis Rocker could almost hear her <u>lovely irish voice</u> saying, "Care for
(2)
my salt shakers <u>when I'm gone." He</u> would treasure them as much as he
(3)
did their long friendship that began with this letter.

<u>dear Mr. Rocker,</u>
(4)
    <u>Lenny Bruce once said, "the liberals</u> can understand everything but the
(5)
people who don't understand them." The same is true of collectors. I'm

glad you enjoyed my story <u>"A Pinch of Salt And Pepper."</u> The picture of my
(6)
ivory shakers of <u>the Leaning tower of Pisa</u> came out well. You'd probably
(7)
also like my shakers shaped like <u>union soldiers from the Civil War</u> and
(8)
<u>the Campbell's soup Kids.</u> Please stop by some <u>Saturday in the Spring</u>
(9)   (10)
<u>after 2:00 P.M.</u> I'd love to show my collection to you.

Sincerely yours,

Ida Mae Bates

1. A. Reverend
   B. mrs.
   C. bates
   D. Correct as is

2. A. Lovely
   B. Irish
   C. Voice
   D. Correct as is

3. A. When
   B. i'm
   C. he
   D. Correct as is

4. A. Dear
   B. mr.
   C. rocker
   D. Correct as is

5. A. lenny
   B. bruce
   C. The
   D. Correct as is

6. A. a
   B. Of
   C. and
   D. Correct as is

7. A. The
   B. leaning
   C. Tower
   D. Correct as is

8. A. Union
   B. Soldiers
   C. civil
   D. Correct as is

9. A. The
   B. campbell's
   C. Soup
   D. Correct as is

10. A. saturday
    B. spring
    C. 2:00 p.m.
    D. Correct as is

Student Help Desk

Capitalization at a Glance

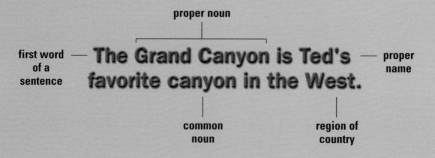

proper noun

first word of a sentence —— **The Grand Canyon is Ted's favorite canyon in the West.** —— proper name

common noun

region of country

Do Capitalize Caps On!

The first word of a sentence:
Building a collection is hard work.

The first word in every line of a traditional poem:
Love is not all: it is not meat nor drink
Nor slumber nor a roof against the rain; . . .

—Edna St. Vincent Millay, "Sonnet XXX" of *Fatal Interview*

The first word of the greeting in a letter:
My dearest,   Darling nephew,

The first word and all important words in titles:
A Raisin in the Sun

Family words when used with names or in place of names:
The world's largest golf ball collection belongs to Mother.
She inherited some of it from Aunt Seretha.

Proper nouns that name people, places, and things:
The *Empire Builder* took them through the Badlands
and the Rocky Mountains.

"If Anderson is C.E.O., and Wyatt is C.F.O., and you're C.O.O., then who am I, and what am I doing here?"

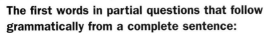

Don't Capitalize   Caps Off!

The first words in partial questions that follow grammatically from a complete sentence:
> Do you collect dolls? model airplanes? stuffed animals? frogs?

The first word in every line of many contemporary poems:
> The song is gone; the dance
> is secret with the dancers in the earth . . .
>
> —Judith Wright, "Bora Ring"

Words after the first word of the greeting in a letter:
> My dearest neighbor,

Articles, coordinating conjunctions, or prepositions shorter than five letters:
> "By the Waters of Babylon"

Family words when used as ordinary nouns:
> Jeb's uncle has an even larger collection.
> He got some of it from his aunt, Maureen.

The common nouns that stand for people, places, or things:
> The train took them through the desolate hills and
> the snowcapped mountains.

©The New Yorker Collection 1994 Eric Teitelbaum

CAPITALIZATION

Punctuation

Theme: In and Around the Ocean

Little Things That Mean a Lot

The fisherman in the picture above uses the same word to express three different thoughts about the shark that is circling his boat. Imagine that you are the fisherman. Then read each thought aloud. How do the punctuation marks make the same word express three different thoughts?

Punctuation marks may look small, but they add a world of meaning to your writing. This chapter offers guidelines for using punctuation to make your ideas clearer and easier for readers to understand.

Write Away: Punctuate It!
Think of a time when something exciting, dangerous, or frightening happened to you. Write a paragraph about this experience, using at least four different punctuation marks, such as periods, question marks, exclamation points, and quotation marks. Put your paragraph in your 🗂 **Working Portfolio.**

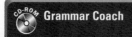 **Grammar Coach**

For each numbered section, choose the letter of the correct answer.

People have long wondered what happened to <u>Atlantis?</u> Have you read
<u>(1)</u>
about the ancient lost <u>continent: some</u> people believe that <u>volcanic</u>
<u>(2)</u>   <u>(3)</u>
<u>eruptions, earthquakes, and tidal waves</u> caused it to sink into the sea. <u>If</u>

<u>this is true the</u> ruins of a magnificent civilization lie on the floor of the
<u>(4)</u>
Atlantic Ocean. <u>Plato, the ancient Greek philosopher wrote</u> that Atlantis
<u>(5)</u>
was destroyed in about 10,000 B.C. He read about Atlantis in ancient

<u>records and wrote</u> about it. His <u>works which are still read,</u> have helped to
<u>(6)</u>   <u>(7)</u>
keep the legend of Atlantis alive. Many people believe in the <u>legend</u>

<u>however,</u> no one has proven that Atlantis actually <u>existed!</u> <u>"Atlantis is an</u>
<u>(8)</u>   <u>(9)</u>
<u>island of the mind, said one historian.</u>
<u>(10)</u>

---

1. A. Atlantis!
   B. Atlantis.
   C. Atlantis,
   D. Correct as is

2. A. continent? Some
   B. continent. some
   C. continent; some
   D. Correct as is

3. A. volcanic, eruptions,
      earthquakes and tidal waves
   B. volcanic eruptions earthquakes
      and tidal waves
   C. volcanic eruptions,
      earthquakes, and, tidal waves
   D. Correct as is

4. A. If this is true: the
   B. If this is true. The
   C. If this is true, the
   D. Correct as is

5. A. Plato, the ancient Greek
      philosopher, wrote
   B. "Plato," the ancient Greek
      philosopher wrote
   C. Plato the ancient Greek
      philosopher wrote,
   D. Correct as is

6. A. records, and wrote
   B. records. And wrote
   C. records, wrote
   D. Correct as is

7. A. works which are still read
   B. works, which are still read,
   C. works, which are still read
   D. Correct as is

8. A. legend; however,
   B. legend—however,
   C. legend: however,
   D. Correct as is

9. A. existed."
   B. existed?
   C. existed.
   D. Correct as is

10. A. Atlantis is an island of the
       mind, "said one historian."
    B. "Atlantis is an island of the
       mind," said one historian.
    C. Atlantis is an island of the
       mind, said one historian.
    D. Correct as is

Periods and Other End Marks

LESSON 1

❶ Here's the Idea

End marks—periods, question marks, and exclamation points—are punctuation marks used at the end of sentences or of complete thoughts. Periods are also used in other ways.

Periods

▶ **Use a period at the end of all declarative sentences and most imperative sentences.**

The waters around Monterey Bay contain sharks. (DECLARATIVE)

Swim with caution. (IMPERATIVE)

When an imperative sentence expresses strong emotion or excitement, use an exclamation point.

Get out of the water!

▶ **Use periods at the end of most indirect questions.**
An **indirect question** indicates that someone has asked a question, but the person's exact words are not shown.

The lifeguard asked whether any sharks had been spotted in the area. (INDIRECT)

Have any sharks been spotted in the area? (DIRECT)

Question Marks

▶ **Use a question mark at the end of an interrogative sentence or after a question that is not a complete sentence.**
INTERROGATIVE SENTENCE

Has the demand for shark fins resulted in overfishing?

INCOMPLETE QUESTION

The truth? Some shark species have been overfished.

Sometimes writers punctuate what looks like a declarative sentence with a question mark to indicate that the sentence should be read as a question.

DECLARATIVE

Marla saw a shark.
The shark was startled.

DECLARATIVE WITH A QUESTION MARK

Marla saw a shark?
The shark was startled?

Exclamation Points

▶ **Use an exclamation point after a strong interjection, at the end of an exclamatory sentence, or after an imperative sentence that expresses strong emotion.**

An **interjection** is a word or group of words that expresses emotion or imitates a sound.

Wow! What sharp teeth he has! Get away!

For information about using end marks with direct quotations, see p. 279.

Other Uses of Periods

▶ **Use a period at the end of most abbreviations or initials.**

If you're not sure how to punctuate an abbreviation, look it up in a current dictionary.

Periods with Abbreviations and Initials	
Personal names	E. B. White Sally K. Ride Kurt Vonnegut, Jr. José Estevez, Sr.
Titles	Mr. Mrs. Ms. Dr. Sen. Gov. Capt.
Parts of business names	Assocs. Bros. Co. Corp. Inc. Ltd.
Addresses	St. Rd. Blvd. Pkwy. Bldg.
Chronology	A.D. B.C.
Time of day	A.M. P.M.
Measurement (U.S.)	12 ft. 5 in.
Time	1 hr. 15 min.

Do not use periods with these abbreviations: metric measurements (cm, ml, kg, g, L), acronyms (NATO, UNICEF, NASA), abbreviations that are pronounced letter by letter (CIA, NBA, EPA, IRS, NAACP), state names in postal addresses (TX, CA, FL), or points on a compass (N, NE, S, SW).

Many abbreviations are not appropriate in formal writing and correspondence. Proofread your formal letters and writing assignments and make sure you've spelled out words you might abbreviate in casual writing.

PUNCTUATION

▶ **Use a period after each number or letter in an outline or a list.**

Outline	List
I. Dangerous sharks	The Most Dangerous Sharks
A. Great white shark	1. Great white shark
1. Size	2. Tiger shark
2. Habitat	3. Bull shark
B. Tiger shark	4. Oceanic whitetip shark

❷ Practice and Apply

A. CONCEPT CHECK: Periods and Other End Marks

On a sheet of paper, write the last word of each sentence in the passage below and add the appropriate end mark.

Man-eating Monsters?

(1) Shark experts are often asked whether sharks are truly man-eating monsters **(2)** Although some species of sharks will attack and eat human beings, sharks are not the crazed killers portrayed in fiction and films **(3)** Phew **(4)** Isn't that a relief **(5)** Are they potentially dangerous **(6)** You bet **(7)** Do they crave people sandwiches **(8)** Don't you believe it **(9)** Most sharks crave fatty food **(10)** In their eyes, humans are just light snacks **(11)** A large sea lion provides more calories for a lot less trouble **(12)** Why, then, do sharks sometimes attack people **(13)** Experts believe that most attacks are cases of mistaken identity **(14)** To a shark, a swimmer's flapping hands and feet may look like plump little fish swimming along **(15)** Watch out

➡ **For a SELF-CHECK and more practice, see the EXERCISE BANK, p. 629.**

B. REVISING: Periods

Rewrite the outline below, adding the seven missing periods.

Shark Facts

I Interesting shark facts

  A Facts about anatomy

    1 Some sharks grow ten inches per year

    2 Whale sharks have about 300 rows of teeth

  B Facts about behavior

Comma Uses

① Here's the Idea

Commas make writing clearer by separating words, ideas, and other elements in sentences.

Commas in a Series

▶ **In a series of three or more items, use a comma after every item except the last one.**

The items in a series may be words, phrases, or clauses.

Rocks, snags, and **shoals** can be hazardous to boats.

The boat **hit a rock, took on water,** and **sank into the sea**.

We do not know **when the boat sank, where it was headed,** or **who was aboard**.

No commas are needed if the items in a series are joined by *and, or,* or *nor.*

The sea was dark **and** deep **and** menacing.

Use a comma after the introductory words *first, second,* and so on when they introduce items in a series.

You'll pass three landmarks on the way to the island: **first,** the lighthouse; **second,** Star Point; and **third,** Lil's Landing.

▶ **Use commas between two or more adjectives that modify the same noun.**

A thick, damp fog blanketed the coastline.

How do you know when to add commas between adjectives?

Here's How — **Adding Commas Between Adjectives**

The captain issued orders in a **low tense** voice.

1. First, switch the order of the adjectives and insert the word *and* between them.

The captain issued orders in a **tense and low** voice.

2. Add a comma if the meaning of the sentence has not changed and if the word *and* sounds natural between the adjectives.

The captain issued orders in a **low, tense** voice.

In general, don't use commas after numbers and adjectives of size, shape, and age.

five small boats   a **big** yellow moon

a **round** nylon cushion   the **old** stone lighthouse

Commas with Introductory Elements

▶ **Use a comma after an introductory word or a mild interjection at the beginning of a sentence.**

No, our crew was unable to call for help.

Eventually, a ship spotted us.

Hey, what's that in the water over there?

▶ **Use a comma after an introductory prepositional phrase that contains one or more additional prepositional phrases.**

In the spring **of 1930,** marine science took a giant step forward.

For the first time **in history,** a scientist explored the ocean's depths.

A single prepositional phrase at the beginning of a sentence may be set off by a comma if it is followed by a natural pause when it is read out loud. Don't use a comma if the phrase is very short or if you would not pause after saying it.

At first they didn't know what they would find.

▶ **Use a comma after a verbal phrase at the beginning of a sentence.**

To make the half-mile dive, scientists and engineers designed a deep-sea vehicle.

▶ **Use a comma after an introductory adverb or an adverb clause at the beginning of a sentence.**

Fortunately, the vehicle worked well.

When scientist William Beebe made the first dive, he was amazed by what he saw.

 Do not use a comma after a phrase or a clause that is the subject of a sentence.

To survive at such depths is difficult.

What he saw amazed him.

Commas with Interrupters

▶ **Use commas to set off a parenthetical expression.**
A parenthetical expression provides explanatory or supplementary
information that is closely related to the sentence.

Beebe did, **of course,** keep a journal.

He took notes, **I believe,** on several previously unknown species.

Common Parenthetical Expressions			
after all	furthermore	I suppose	nevertheless
by the way	however	in fact	of course
for example	I believe	moreover	therefore

▶ **Use commas to set off words of direct address.**
Words of direct address are names, titles, terms of respect, and
phrases used to address an individual directly.

PROFESSIONAL MODEL

"Thank you, **Captain Lowry,** for a job well done."
"It was nothing, **sir."**

Commas with Nonessential Material

▶ **Use commas to set off nonessential clauses and nonessential
participial phrases.** Both of these sentence parts add information
to a sentence, but the information is not essential to the meaning
of the sentence.

Advanced Lifesaving, **which is an excellent course,** prepares
students to be lifeguards. (NONESSENTIAL CLAUSE)
Mrs. Lewis, **worried about her daughter's safety,** paced
nervously on the shore. (NONESSENTIAL PARTICIPIAL PHRASE)

▶ **Use commas to set off nonessential appositives.**
A **nonessential appositive** is a word or a phrase that adds
information about a noun or pronoun.

Scientists transformed the H.M.S. *Challenger,* **a British
warship,** into a floating laboratory.

An **essential appositive** is not set off with commas.

Rachel Carson's book *The Sea Around Us* helped raised public
awareness of ocean pollution.

**For more information on essential and nonessential material,
see pp. 69 and 95.**

➋ Practice and Apply

A. CONCEPT CHECK: Commas

Fourteen commas are missing from the sentences below. Write the word before each missing comma and add the comma.

England's Underwater Rowboat

1. On a warm day in 1620 King James I of England witnessed an amazing test.
2. Cornelis Drebbel a Dutch scientist demonstrated an underwater boat for the king.
3. Drebbel had in fact invented the first successful submarine.
4. To waterproof the wooden vessel Drebbel covered it with greased leather.
5. Because few sources of energy were available Drebbel relied on manpower to propel the vessel.
6. His sub was powered steered and controlled by a crew of oarsmen.
7. The Thames River which runs through the city of London was the test site for Drebbel's invention.
8. Fresh clean air was provided by tubes that floated on the surface of the river.
9. Apparently the sub was submerged by letting water into the hull.
10. Cruising at a depth of 16 feet Drebbel's vessel helped speed the development of the modern submarine.

➜ **For a SELF-CHECK and more practice, see the EXERCISE BANK, p. 630.**

B. PROOFREADING: Correcting Comma Errors

Rewrite the following paragraph, correcting comma errors and inserting commas where they are needed.

A Revolutionary Submarine

Not, surprisingly the *Turtle* was a slow submarine. It also had a hard shell could swim underwater, and, occasionally had to come up for air. Unlike its reptilian namesake, the *Turtle*, packed an explosive punch. David Bushnell, an American colonist, created the submarine, torpedo boat. Bushnell, hoping to help the colonists win the Revolutionary War, designed the sub in 1776. The one-person wooden vehicle was powered by pedals shaped, like an egg, and armed with a keg of gunpowder. Unfortunately the *Turtle's* first target H.M.S. *Eagle*, had a hard shell of its own. Yes the *Turtle* took an early retirement.

LESSON 3 — More Comma Uses

① Here's the Idea

Commas with Quotations

▶ **Use commas to set off the explanatory words (such as *he said* or *she asked*) of a direct quotation.**

Commas, like periods, always go inside closing quotation marks.

STUDENT MODEL

> **Mrs. Lewis called,** "A boat has capsized!"
>
> Her daughter Ida ran down from the house to the dock. "Tell me the location of the accident," **Ida calmly said.**
>
> Mrs. Lewis pointed out at the ocean. "The boat tipped over," **she explained,** "about 100 yards due east of here."
>
> Mrs. Lewis told her daughter that two people were in the boat.

Use a comma to set off explanatory words that come before or after a direct quotation.

Use commas to set off explanatory words in the middle of a direct quotation.

Indirect quotations do not need commas.

Commas in Compound Sentences

▶ **Use a comma before the coordinating conjunction that joins the two independent clauses of a compound sentence.**

Ida Lewis jumped into her rowboat, **and** she headed due east.

Use a comma before the conjunctions *yet* and *for* when they join independent clauses.

Lewis feared the worst, **yet** she hoped for the best.

She was worried about the victims, **for** the water was cold.

Do not use a comma to separate the verb phrases of a compound predicate.

Lewis **jumped into her rowboat and quickly headed due east.**

COMPOUND PREDICATE

Make sure you use both a comma and a conjunction between independent clauses. Using a comma without a conjunction will result in a run-on sentence.

                             and
It was the middle of winter ∧ the water was extremely cold.

For more about run-on sentences, see p. 120.

Commas in Dates, Place Names, and Letters

▶ **In dates, use a comma to separate the day of the month from the year.**

    April 15, 2003   November 1, 1960

Don't use a comma when only the month and the year are given.

    December 1945

When a date is part of a sentence, use a comma after the year.

    On October 1, 1975, a ship was lost at sea.

▶ **Use a comma to separate the name of a city or town and the name of its state, province, or country.**

    Dallas, Texas   Bancroft, Ontario   Mexico City, Mexico

When an address is part of a sentence, use a comma after each item. Do not put a comma between the name of a state and the ZIP code, however.

    Please forward my mail to 4795 Seaside Drive, Manisota, Florida 36006.

▶ **Use a comma after the salutation of a friendly letter and after the closing of a friendly or business letter.**

    Hello Aunt Lucy,   Dearest Charlie,   Dear Mrs. Oliver,

    Love,   Yours truly,   Sincerely,

Commas with Names and Numbers

▶ **Use a comma between a personal name and an abbreviation that follows it, such as *Jr., Sr.,* or *M.D.* Also use a comma between a business name and an abbreviation, such as *Inc.***

    Lara Johnson, M.D.   Paradise Cruises, Inc.

When names and abbreviations are part of a sentence, set off the abbreviations with commas.

    Paradise Cruises, Inc., has hired Lara Johnson, M.D., as its medical director.

Lara Johnson, M.D.
General Practioner

Commas to Avoid Confusion

▶ **Use a comma to separate words or phrases that might be misunderstood when they are read.**

Here are four ways commas can clear up confusion in your sentences.

1. Use a comma before the conjunction *but* or *for* when it may be mistaken for a preposition.

Confusing **The victims were grateful for the young woman** had saved their lives.	**Clear** The victims were **grateful,** for the young woman had saved their lives.

2. Use a comma after an introductory adverb that could be mistaken for a preposition.

Confusing **Inside the boat** was in good condition.	**Clear** **Inside,** the boat was in good condition.

3. Use a comma to separate a short introductory verbal phrase from the noun that follows it.

Confusing **While rocking the boat** almost capsized.	**Clear** **While rocking,** the boat almost capsized.

4. Use a comma to separate repeated words.

Confusing What an "old salt" **is is** an experienced sailor.	**Clear** What an "old salt" **is, is** an experienced sailor.

▶ **Use a comma to indicate the words left out of parallel word groups, or word groups that repeat the same structure.**
In this situation, the comma takes the place of the verb.

The captain was old; the crew, young.

David ordered lobster, and Connie, softshell crabs.

▶ **In numbers of more than three digits, use a comma after every third digit from the right. ZIP codes, phone numbers, years, and house numbers are exceptions to this rule.**

3,000 people   3491 Chestnut Ridge Road (NO COMMA)

❷ Practice and Apply

A. CONCEPT CHECK: More Comma Uses

Write the word before each missing comma and place each comma correctly. Write *Correct* if no commas are needed.

Rhode Island Rescuer

1. It was a lazy day in September 1859. Off Lime Rock Rhode Island the breeze was light; the sea calm.

2. Captain Hosea Lewis leapt out of his rocking chair for he saw an alarming sight.

3. "Have a look out there" he called to his daughter. He added "Those boys bobbing in the water can't swim."

4. Ida Lewis scanned the sea with her eyes and located the problem.

5. Nearby four boys were clinging to their capsized sailboat.

6. Ida hurried to her boat for there was no time to lose.

7. Lewis made her first rescue but it would not be her last.

8. On March 29 1869 she saved two soldiers lost at sea.

9. While touring New England President Grant visited Lewis to thank her.

10. He laughed when he fell on some rocks and got his feet wet. "To see Ida Lewis" he said "I'd gladly get wet up to my armpits."

➜ **For a SELF-CHECK and more practice, see the EXERCISE BANK, p. 630.**

B. PROOFREADING: Mixed Review of Commas

Rewrite the letter below, adding commas where necessary.

Dear Joe

Well it's only noon here but we have already put in a full day. At 5:30 this morning my grandfather yelled "Wake up boy! We're going to the island." The boat race to Mackinac Island ended this morning and there was a lot of excitement around here. *Stars and Stripes*, which finished the 333-mile race in just under 20 hours set a new world's record. What a crowd showed up to cheer the winner! There must have been 1000 people at the harbor.

Drop me a line sometime in care of my grandfather. His name is William Benis M.D. His address is 300 West Bluff Street St. Ignace MI 49781.

Your friend

Bob

LESSON 4

Semicolons and Colons

❶ Here's the Idea

A semicolon separates different elements within a sentence.
A colon indicates that an example or explanation follows.

Semicolons

▶ **Use semicolons to separate items in a series if any of the items contains commas.**

> The divers gathered at dawn**;** put on their tanks**,** masks**,** and wet suits**;** and jumped off the pier into the ocean.

▶ **Use a semicolon between independent clauses joined by a conjunction if either clause contains commas.**

> The deep sea once appeared to be cold**,** murky**,** and lifeless**;** but scientists have discovered strange fish living in this region.

▶ **Use a semicolon to join the independent clauses of a compound sentence if no coordinating conjunction is used.**

Using a semicolon instead of a comma and a conjunction indicates a stronger relationship between the clauses. Don't use a semicolon unless the ideas in the clauses are closely related.

> The storm struck with savage fury**,** but our house was not damaged at all.

> The storm struck with savage fury**;** it demolished most of the coastal town.

▶ **Use a semicolon before a conjunctive adverb or a parenthetical expression that joins the clauses of a compound sentence.**

Use a comma after the adverb or expression.

CONJUNCTIVE ADVERB

> The weather was stormy**;** therefore**,** we postponed our sailing trip.

PARENTHETICAL EXPRESSION

> Storms pose great risks for sailors**;** in fact**,** they can be deadly.

For a list of conjunctive adverbs, see p. 27.

Colons

▶ **Use a colon to introduce a list of items.**

> On a short sailing excursion, you should bring these items**:** a life jacket, a pair of sunglasses, and a tube of sunscreen.

Do not use a colon in the following situations: after a verb, in the middle of a prepositional phrase, or after *because* or *as*.

After a verb

Incorrect: The three longest rivers in the world **are:** the Nile, the Amazon, and the Yangtze.	**Correct:** These are the three longest rivers in the world: the Nile, the Amazon, and the Yangtze.

In the middle of a prepositional phrase

Incorrect: I have swum **in:** the Atlantic Ocean, the Pacific Ocean, and the Mediterranean Sea.	**Correct:** I have swum in the following bodies of water: the Atlantic Ocean, the Pacific Ocean, and the Mediterranean Sea.

After *because* or *as*

Incorrect: The ship was in danger **because:** a terrible storm was approaching.	**Correct:** The ship was in danger because a terrible storm was approaching.

▶ **Use a colon between two independent clauses when the second clause explains or summarizes the first.**

The captain was right: we should have waited out the storm.

▶ **Use a colon to introduce a formal or long quotation.**

Winston Churchill inspired the people of England with these words: "We shall not fail or falter; we shall not weaken or tire."

After a colon, capitalize the first word of a formal statement. If the statement is informal, it should begin with a lowercase letter.

Other Uses of Colons Use a colon in the following situations:

- **After the formal salutation of a business letter**
  Dear Madam:

- **After labels that signal important ideas**
  Beware: These waters contain sharks.

- **Between the hour and minute figures of clock time**
  12:15 P.M.

- **Between chapter and verse when referring to certain religious works, such as the Bible, the Qur'an (Koran), and the Talmud**
  Psalm 23:7

A. CONCEPT CHECK: Semicolon and Colon

Write the word before each missing semicolon or colon in the paragraph below, and insert the appropriate punctuation marks.

Underwater Heat Vents

In 1993 a ship left the shores of Seattle, Washington it headed toward the waters off the coast of Oregon. Geologists had made an interesting discovery a series of seaquakes were occurring on the Juan de Fuca Ridge, an underwater mountain range. Seaquakes occur when areas of the earth's crust shift, collide, and pile up and they are often accompanied by volcanic eruptions. Periodically, sections of the ridge split open, releasing hot lava that heats up the surrounding water.

High ocean temperatures do not usually support life however, some primitive life forms like heat. Scientists aboard the ship were hoping to find at least three forms of life sea-bed microbes, simple plants, and tube worms. All three exist at the bottom of the food chain all three support higher forms of life. The scientists received their reward they found a volcanic chimney growing over a vent. The interior of the chimney reached more than 500 degrees nevertheless, it was crawling with life.

➔ **For a SELF-CHECK and more practice, see the EXERCISE BANK, p. 631.**

B. REVISING: Correcting Semicolon and Colon Use

Rewrite the following paragraph by adding, deleting, or replacing semicolons and colons. Use capitalization correctly.

Godzilla Spotted Near Seattle!

(1) Godzilla has been spotted near Seattle however, there is no need for panic. **(2)** This Godzilla is no lizard it is an undersea volcanic chimney. **(3)** There's a reason why the chimney was named Godzilla It is 15 stories high, almost as tall as the movie monster. **(4)** Other large chimneys dot: the Juan de Fuca Ridge. **(5)** Three of them are named: Beard, Mongo, and Church. **(6)** If you want to visit any of these chimneys, you'll need to buy a few items: a submarine; diving gear; and an underwater robot. **(7)** A team of scientists organized an undersea expedition: to remove a chimney from the sea floor and bring it into a laboratory for study. **(8)** The team included Cindy Van Dover, a biologist, John R. Delaney, a geologist, and Marv Lilley, a geochemist.

Dashes and Parentheses

❶ Here's the Idea

Dashes and parentheses are used to set off information that interrupts the flow of sentences.

Dashes

▶ **Use dashes to show an abrupt break in thought. If the thought continues after the break, use a second dash.**

Your prize will be a cruise to Bermuda—**assuming you win the contest.**

Our room—**supposedly the best on the ship**—was tiny, hot, and noisy.

When writing dialogue, you can use a dash to show interrupted speech.

> **PROFESSIONAL MODEL**
>
> "I'm hiding from a passenger," whispered Tod. "Please don't tell my—"
>
> "Oh, Tod," called Mrs. Wembly, "come and meet my niece."
>
> —Elizabeth Botzow, "At Sea"

▶ **Use dashes to set off a long explanatory statement that interrupts the main thought of a sentence.**

Ocean currents—**the tendency of the oceans' waters to move in a certain direction**—puzzled early navigators.

▶ **Use a dash to set off an introductory list.**

Whales, dolphins, sea lions, exotic fish—all these ocean wonders await you at Seaside Aquarium.

 Do not overuse dashes. Paragraphs filled with dashes are difficult to read and seem carelessly written.

Difficult: The lines at Seaside were long—it was a holiday—and many people had the day off. We were relaxed—we enjoyed our visit—however, the lines tried our patience.

Parentheses

▶ **Use parentheses to set off nonessential explanatory material that is loosely related to the sentence.**

Nonessential material interrupts the flow of the sentence and is helpful but not important to its meaning.

> Although *The Sea Around Us* is somewhat dated **(it was first published in 1951)**, the book is still a fascinating source of information about the sea.

Use the chart below to help you punctuate and capitalize parenthetical information.

When the parenthetical information is . . .	
a complete sentence within another sentence	
The giant waves (they were terrifying!) tossed the ship as if it were a toy.	• It begins with a lowercase letter unless the first word is a proper noun. • It ends without any punctuation or with a question mark or an exclamation point but NOT with a period.
a complete sentence that stands alone	
Amy had never been so seasick in her life. (She still gets queasy at the thought of eating chocolate mousse.)	• It begins with a capital letter. • It ends with a period, exclamation point, or question mark inside the parentheses.
a fragment within another sentence	
The captain (a very nice man) sent a pot of peppermint tea to our room.	• It begins with a lowercase letter. • It ends without any punctuation or with a question mark or an exclamation point but NOT with a period.

PUNCTUATION

▶ **Use parentheses to enclose numbers or letters in a list that is part of a sentence.**

According to the drill instructions, we need to (1) make sure that everyone is wearing a life jacket, (2) prepare the life rafts, and (3) radio the Coast Guard.

▶ **In a research paper, use parentheses to identify the source of any quoted or paraphrased information you use.**

Since ancient times, the sea has been thought of as "a thing of beauty and terror, a giver and taker of life" (Broad, 21).

❷ Practice and Apply

CONCEPT CHECK: Dashes and Parentheses

For each item, write each word that should precede and follow a dash or the words that should be in parentheses. Add the appropriate punctuation.

The Man Behind the Map

1. Government official, inventor, scientist all these titles describe Benjamin Franklin.
2. Although everyone knows that Franklin took a scientific interest in electricity recall his kite experiments, few people know about his interest in the sea.
3. This interest grew out of one of his career positions that of Deputy Postmaster General of the Colonies.
4. Franklin noticed that British mail ships supposedly the fastest in the world took longer to cross the Atlantic than did American ships.
5. Puzzled, he asked Timothy Folger he was an American sea captain why.
6. Folger explained that British captains steered their ships into the Gulf Stream, whereas American ships "run along the side and frequently cross it." Carson, 134
7. The effects of the Gulf Stream were especially noticeable on the westward crossing of the Atlantic the trip from England to the colonies.
8. Sailing against the Gulf Stream one of the strongest currents in all the Atlantic slowed British ships.
9. Franklin hoping to improve mail service had a map of the current drawn up and sent to England.
10. Thus, he became the first person and doubtless the only postmaster to issue an official chart of the Gulf Stream.

➜ **For a SELF-CHECK and more practice, see the EXERCISE BANK, p. 631.**

LESSON 6 Hyphens and Apostrophes

① Here's the Idea

Hyphens

A hyphen connects the following kinds of words, which then function as a single unit.

Words to Hyphenate	
Compound numbers from twenty-one to ninety-nine	thirty-five ships, ninety-two years
Spelled-out fractions	three-fifths of the crew
Certain compound nouns	time-out, brother-in-law
Compound adjectives used before a noun (but not after)	well-known fact (fact that is well known); 27-day ordeal
The prefixes *ex-*, *self-*, *great-*, *half-*, and *all-*; all prefixes used before proper nouns and proper adjectives	ex-captain, self-expression, great-grandmother, half-eaten, pre-Columbian
The suffixes *-elect* and *-style*	president-elect , English-style breakfast

▶ **Use a hyphen if part of a word must be carried down from one line to the next.**

LITERARY MODEL

At last the rain came. It was sudden and **tremen-dous.** For two or three moons the sun had been **gathering** strength till it seemed to breathe a breath of fire on the earth.

—Chinua Achebe, *Things Fall Apart*

Follow these rules to help you decide when and how to hyphenate a word at a line break.

Here's How **Hyphenating at Line Breaks**

- Hyphenate only words with two or more syllables.
- Divide words with hyphens only between syllables.
- Make sure there are two or more letters of the hyphenated word on each line.

Apostrophes

▶ **Use an apostrophe to form the possessive case of a singular or plural noun.**

To form the possessive of a singular noun, add an apostrophe and an s even if the singular noun ends in s.
Ed's journal   a week's salary   Columbus's journey

To form the possessive of a plural noun that ends in s or es, add only an apostrophe after the final s.
five countries' navies   three years' time   the Joneses' boat

To form the possessive of a plural noun that does not end in s, add an apostrophe and an s.
children's swimsuits   people's choice

Some names are difficult to pronounce when an apostrophe and an s are added. In such cases, you may add the apostrophe alone.
Jesus' name   Achilles' heel   Odysseus' journey

If the names of two or more persons are used to show joint ownership, give only the last name the possessive form.
Hyacinth and Maria's party

If the names of two or more persons are used to show separate ownership, give each name the possessive form.
Peter's and Robert's sneakers

▶ **To form the possessive of an indefinite pronoun, add an apostrophe and s.**

one's choices   everybody's favorite   each other's paper

▶ **Use an apostrophe to show where letters or words are missing in contractions.**

you'll (you will)   they're (they are)   can't (cannot)

When writing dialogue that reflects regional dialects or accents, use an apostrophe to indicate missing letters.

Jo smiled and said, "How d'you do, Cap'n! Yer ship's a beaut'."

▶ **Use an apostrophe and s to form the plural of letters, numerals, and words referred to as words.**

ABC's   three A's   two 5's   yes's and no's

▶ **Use an apostrophe to show the missing numbers in a date.**

class of '99 (1999)   blizzard of '04 (2004)

Don't use an apostrophe with plural possessive pronouns (*hers, its, theirs*) or in the plural of decades or temperatures (the Roaring '20s, the 1990s, temperatures in the 60s).

❷ Practice and Apply

A. CONCEPT CHECK: Hyphens and Apostrophes

Rewrite the words that are missing hyphens and apostrophes, adding the missing punctuation.

Mayday! Mayday!

1. Early on October 14, 1980, the teletype in Alaskas Coast Guard Rescue Coordination Center clattered out an ominous message.
2. There was a fire aboard the *Prisendam,* a 427 foot ocean liner.
3. Passengers and crew members lives were in danger.
4. The well equipped liner had a dozen life rafts that could accommodate twenty five people, and six lifeboats that could carry many more.
5. Many of its passengers were experienced voyagers, and the crew had run emergency drills to help ensure everyones safety.
6. However, even well trained passengers may panic during a real emergency, especially during predawn hours, when its difficult to see.
7. In just a few minutes time, the Coast Guards rescue operation was underway.
8. When the first helicopter arrived, about one tenth of the crew and passengers were still aboard the fiery ship.
9. Escape was theirs for the taking: the helicopters rescue basket hovered just above their heads.
10. If not for the fast acting Coast Guard, the *Prisendam* fire of 80 might have been one of the decades worst disasters.

➡ **For a SELF-CHECK and more practice, see the EXERCISE BANK, p. 632.**

B. WRITING: Adding Hyphens

Write the words below, inserting hyphens to show where each word would be divided if it appeared at the end of a line. Some words may be divided in more than one place.

1. marine
2. self-contained
3. laboratory
4. biological
5. estuary
6. monument

Quotation Marks

❶ Here's the Idea

Use quotation marks to set off direct quotations and some titles.

Direct and Indirect Quotations

▶ **Use quotation marks at the beginning and end of a direct quotation.**

The first word of a direct quotation is usually capitalized.

A **direct quotation** is the exact words of a writer or speaker.

> The guide said, "The giant squid is one of the largest creatures in the sea."

Don't use quotation marks to set off an **indirect quotation**.

> The guide said that the giant squid is one of the largest creatures in the sea.

Punctuation and Capitalization with Dialogue

▶ **In dialogue, punctuate a speaker's words with a comma, a question mark, or an exclamation point.**

Put end punctuation marks inside the closing quotation marks.

> "Early sailors believed giant squid were sea monsters," our guide explained.
>
> "Just how big is a giant squid?" asked Tyrell.
>
> "Believe it or not, some may be 75 feet long!" said the guide.

▶ **Place a comma after explanatory words, such as *she said* and *he asked,* that appear at the beginning of a sentence.**

Place a period, question mark, or exclamation point inside the quotation marks at the end of the sentence.

> Tyrell asked, "Just how big is a giant squid?"

For more about how to place punctuation with quotation marks, see p. 279.

▶ **Enclose both parts of a divided quotation in quotation marks.**

Do not capitalize the first word of the second part unless it begins a new sentence.

> "I wonder," said Rebecca, "whether the giant squid is dangerous to humans."
>
> "You wonder?" asked Tyrell. "Look at the size of those tentacles!"

Start a new paragraph and begin the paragraph with a set of quotation marks to show a change in speakers.

> "Don't be afraid," said Rebecca. "Although the giant squid is large, it doesn't usually come into contact with humans."
> "I'm glad to hear that," Tyrell replied, "because that toothed tongue looks nasty."

Use single quotation marks to enclose a quotation within a quotation.

"The guidebook says that Herman Melville called the giant squid 'a vast pulpy mass,'" said Tyrell.

Colons and semicolons at the close of a quotation should be placed outside the quotation marks.

Rebecca said, "I'm staying on land"; however, she soon joined us in the boat.

Punctuation of Excerpts

If a sentence that includes a quotation is a question or an exclamation, place the question mark or exclamation point outside the quotation marks.

Wasn't it Edgar Allan Poe who called the sea a "wilderness of glass"?

When a quoted fragment (a short quoted excerpt that is not a complete sentence) is inserted in a sentence, do not capitalize the first word of the fragment unless it begins a sentence or is a proper noun.

No comma is needed to set the quotation apart from the rest of the sentence.

A 16th-century Swedish cleric described giant squid as "horrible forms with huge eyes."

A direct quotation from an author's work may be several paragraphs in length. Begin each paragraph with quotation marks. Place quotation marks at the end of only the last paragraph.

If you are quoting an excerpt of five or more lines, you can set it off from the rest of the text by indenting the excerpt ten spaces and double-spacing it. Do not use quotation marks if you set off an excerpt in this way.

Titles with Quotation Marks

▶ **Use quotation marks to set off the titles of chapters, magazine articles, short stories, TV episodes, essays, poems, and songs.**

Titles with Quotation Marks	
Chapter titles	"Chapter 10: Rescued!"
Articles	"An Angry Public Backs Champ"
Short stories	"By the Waters of Babylon"
TV episodes	"Two on a Raft"
Essays	"Once More to the Lake"
Poems	"Fifth Grade Autobiography"
Songs	"The Star-Spangled Banner"

For information on setting titles in italics or underlining, see p. 272.

❷ Practice and Apply

A. CONCEPT CHECK: Quotation Marks

Rewrite the sentences below to correct errors in the use and placement of quotation marks, commas, and periods.

Batteries Not Included

1. Are you surprised to learn that, "a great majority of deep-sea fishes have light-generating capabilities?"
2. Richard Ellis explains in his book *Deep Atlantic* that "there are three ways whereby sea animals create living light:" by releasing energy to special organs, by ejecting glowing chemicals, and by hosting bacteria that glow.
3. Having learned how fish emit light, you might very well wonder "what purpose the light serves?"
4. According to Ellis, biologists have long been interested in living light, but there is, "No agreement as to its function or as to why so many different creatures should have developed," this ability.
5. In the chapter Bioluminescence, Ellis explains that the light may serve several purposes.

6. "Lights might be useful" he says "to attract potential mates."
7. "Ellis continues "Light organs around the eyes of some species of lantern fishes probably function as headlights to illuminate prey items immediately before they are consumed".
8. According to Ellis, one scientist even suggested lights may 'serve as a sort of burglar alarm' for fish under attack.
9. By flashing a light, a fish being preyed upon might attract "another predator to prey upon the first, thus protecting the prey".
10. Ellis sums up our lack of understanding by saying 'It is clear that we, like the bearers of the light organs, are in the dark.

➡ **For a SELF-CHECK and more practice, see the EXERCISE BANK, p. 633.**

B. WRITING: Dialogue

Do You See What I See?

Imagine that while walking home from school, you and a friend saw the strange sight pictured below. Write at least 10 lines of the conversation that you and your friend might have about it. Make sure you use quotation marks and other marks of punctuation correctly in the dialogue. If you need help getting started, you can begin with the line below.

"Do you see what I see?" I asked as my jaw dropped.

Ellipses and Italics

1 Here's the Idea

Ellipses

▶ **Use ellipsis points to indicate omission of a word, phrase, line, or paragraph within a quoted passage.**

LITERARY MODELS

A small crowd . . . followed them as they walked the long, dusty, sunlit street.

—James Baldwin, *Go Tell It on the Mountain*

> To show an omission within a sentence, use three dots (. . .) with a space between each dot.

Half a mile from home, at the farther edge of the woods, where the land was highest, a great pine tree stood, the last of its generation. . . . Sylvia knew it well. She had always believed that whoever climbed to the top of it could see the ocean.

—Sarah Orne Jewett, "A White Heron"

> To show an omission at the end of a sentence, use an end mark after the ellipsis points.

Italics

▶ **Use italics or underscoring to set off titles of books, movies, magazines, newspapers, TV series, plays, works of art, epic (long) poems, and long musical compositions.**

Titles to Italicize	
Books	*The Old Man and the Sea*
Movies	*Mr. Roberts*
Magazines	*People, Time*
Newspapers	*The New York Times*
TV series	*Masterpiece Theater*
Plays	*A Raisin in the Sun*
Works of art	Rodin's *The Thinker*
Epic poems	*Aeneid*
Long musical compositions	*The Magic Flute*

For information on punctuating titles with quotation marks, see p. 270.

▶ **Use italics to indicate a word referred to as a word and to set off foreign words or phrases that are not common in English.**

Does anybody know what the word *abyss* means?

A word processing program allows you to italicize words by selecting the italic form of a font. When writing by hand or using a typewriter, underline words that should be italicized.

❷ Practice and Apply

A. CONCEPT CHECK: Italics and Punctuation Errors

Rewrite the sentences, underlining words and titles that should be italicized and adding missing commas and apostrophes.

The Inspiring Sea

1. From ancient epic poetry to the modern musical Titanic many works of art depict the perils of seafaring.
2. William Shakespeare describes the terrible beauty and power of the sea in his play The Tempest.
3. In The Wreck of a Transport Ship artist Joseph Turner captures the terror of sailors lost in a storm at sea.
4. Herman Melvilles epic novel Moby Dick describes a disastrous sea quest.
5. In the novel, Captain Ahab tries to conquer a great white whale; some would use the word nemesis to describe the captains unbeatable opponent.

➡ **For a SELF-CHECK and more practice, see the EXERCISE BANK, p. 633.**

B. PROOFREADING: Ellipses and Italics

Rewrite the paragraph below, adding italics where necessary and replacing the boldface text with ellipsis points.

Movie Review

   To me, the word exciting should **not be thrown around lightly when describing a movie. It should** be used to describe only movies that truly keep me on the edge of my seat. Steven Spielberg's great action film Jaws is just such a movie. **The plot of the movie is simple: a shark attacks swimmers in a resort area, and the chase to capture the killer fish begins.** What makes the film so exciting is that the shark attacks look absolutely real, even though a mechanical shark was used in many scenes.

Real World Grammar

Business Letter

When you're conducting research, you may need to write a business letter to a research institution or other organization to request information on your topic. The letter you write should be clear, courteous, and professional. Once you've completed a final draft of your letter, carefully proofread it to correct punctuation errors. Comma-use errors in particular can make your letter difficult to understand; as a result, you may not get the information you need.

March 1 2003 *add missing comma*

Add your address here.

Frank—watch out for comma errors.

Monterey Bay Aquarium Institute
P.O. Box 628
Moss Landing CA 95039 *comma goes between city and state*
Attention: Research Librarian

use colon for a business letter
Dear Sir or Madam,

I am a sophomore at Washington High School in Newton, Pennsylvania. Currently, I am writing a research report about the dangerous, irreversible effects of global warming on ocean life? I have seen most of the Web site's on this topic, but your site was the most helpful. I read many of the articles posted there; while I was scanning the title of an unpublished article came to my attention: "Global Climate Change and Ocean-Related Processes." Would it be possible to get a copy of this article through your organization.

I would like to receive this article as soon as possible for my paper is due in mid-April. I'll be happy to pay for photocopying, and postage. Thank you for your time. I appreciate your help, I look forward to hearing from you.

add comma between city and state

place comma

not a possessive noun

wrong end mark

place comma

wrong end mark

place comma

delete comma

and — add conjunction to avoid run-on

Sincerely

place comma

Franklin Thomas

274

Imagine that you have written the rough draft of the letter below. Revise the draft to correct punctuation errors. Add your address and the date above the recipient's address. Choose an appropriate closing for the letter.

Student Help Desk: Phrases

(Add your address)
(Add the date)

Ms. LaVonne Reiger
Channel 49
1090 West Woodbury Street
Pines, NY 94100

Dear Ms Reiger

I am writing for information about an organization you profiled on the October 19 edition of your television program titled Our Environment. The name of the organization was Whale Protectors. the person you interviewed from the organization was Dr Karen J Smith.

During the program you offered to send out a free packet— of information about protecting endangered whales—to anyone interested. It just so happens that I am working on a research report on this topic I would like to use your information in my research. My self addressed stamped, envelope is enclosed. Would you please also send me Whale Protectors mailing address if it is'nt included in the packet! Thank you, for your time.

(Add a closing)

PUNCTUATION

A. Punctuation Follow the directions to rewrite each sentence or pair of sentences. Add correct punctuation.

1. The squid and the octopus are similar in many ways, but their body shapes are different. (Use *however* instead of *but*.)
2. The squid has an elongated body that ends in tentacles. The octopus has a large head resting on a ring of tentacles. (Use a semicolon to join the sentences.)
3. Both animals have beaks and well-developed eyes. Both animals have siphons. (Combine, using series commas.)
4. The animals use the siphons to expel water. The water is taken in through the mantle opening. (Combine, using *which*.)
5. Both the squid and the octopus are agile animals. Both the squid and the octopus are flexible animals. (Combine the sentences so that the adjectives are next to each other.)
6. They can be very difficult to catch. (Add a parenthetical expression, such as "in fact.")
7. Scientists have difficulty gathering mature specimens <u>because the adult squid and octopus are good at avoiding capture</u>. (Rewrite so the underlined clause begins the sentence.)
8. The octopus is difficult to catch for another reason. It can live at great depths. (Change punctuation to show that the second sentence explains the first.)
9. Marine scientists use indirect measuring techniques <u>to estimate the size of the squid and octopus populations</u>. (Rewrite so the underlined phrase begins the sentence.)
10. A. de C. Baker wrote, "The world population of squid must be extremely large, for they form the major part of the diet of the sperm and other toothed whales." (Rewrite as a divided quotation.)

B. Proofreading Rewrite the paragraph, adding correct punctuation.

Marine biologists divide the worlds oceans into two regions the benthic and the pelagic. The benthic region is the floor of the sea the pelagic region is the seawater. While many benthic organisms burrow in the seabed other benthic organisms live on the surface of the ocean floor. Pelagic organisms include whales seals turtles fish and plankton. The word plankton comes from the Greek word planktos which means "wandering." The name is appropriate for plankton drift through the water. In his article entitled Plankton Dr George D Ruggieri describes the importance of plankton to sea life. He describes the growth of microscopic plants as "the first and essential link in all the food chains in the sea."

For each numbered item, choose the letter of the correct answer.

Beware. Our wooden boats, docks, and bridges may be under attack.
(1)   (2)
The wood-eating gribble is just waiting to munch on them? Although the
                                           (3)
crustacean is only two millimeters long; it can cause mighty bridges to
                                         (4)
wobble and magnificent ships to sink. Boat-owners ask how this little
monster can cause so much damage? Noted science writer Jack Rudloe
                          (5)   (6)
explains that the gribble has extraordinarily sharp jaws. Its right jaw is
like a small saw; and its left jaw is like a metal file. There is a way to
                 (7)
gribble-proof submerged wood keep it well covered with paint. Any nick or
                               (8)
scratch, that can expose the wood, is an open invitation to gribbles. Rudloe
                      (9)
warns "One little scraped area where the surface is exposed, and they
             (10)
move in and take over."

---

1. A. Beware?
   B. Beware
   C. Beware!
   D. Correct as is

2. A. boats docks, and bridges
   B. boats docks and bridges
   C. boats, docks, and, bridges
   D. Correct as is

3. A. them.
   B. them,
   C. them—
   D. Correct as is

4. A. long.
   B. long,
   C. long:
   D. Correct as is

5. A. damage.
   B. damage,
   C. damage!
   D. Correct as is

6. A. writer, Jack Rudloe, explains
   B. writer, Jack Rudloe explains
   C. writer Jack, Rudloe explains
   D. Correct as is

7. A. saw: and
   B. saw, and
   C. saw; and,
   D. Correct as is

8. A. wood:
   B. wood;
   C. wood,
   D. Correct as is

9. A. scratch that can expose the wood,
   B. scratch that can expose the wood
   C. scratch, that can expose the wood
   D. Correct as is

10. A. Rudloe warns; "One
    B. Rudloe, warns "One
    C. Rudloe warns, "One
    D. Correct as is

Student Help Desk

Punctuation at a Glance

Period ▪

Question Mark **?**

Exclamation Point **!**

Comma **,**

Semicolon **;**

Colon **:**

Dash ▬

(**Parentheses**)

Hyphen ▬

Apostrophe **'**

" Quotation Marks **"**

Ellipses ▪ ▪ ▪

Italics *abc*

Titles & Punctuation   Treating Titles with Care

Use quotation marks to set off titles of	Use italics to set off titles of
• Book chapters	• Books
• Essays	• Epic poems
• Magazine articles	• Long musical compositions
• Poems	• Magazines
• Short stories	• Movies
• Songs	• Newspapers
• TV episodes	• Plays
	• TV series
	• Works of art

Punctuation with Quotation Marks — Inside or Outside?

Periods and commas	Semicolons and colons	Question marks and exclamation points
Rule: Always go inside quotation marks	**Rule:** Always go outside quotation marks	**Rule:** May go inside or outside depending on what they punctuate
Examples "I'm hungry," said Max. Tracy replied, "Me too." *	**Examples** Tracy calls raw fish "an exotic treat"; I prefer my fish cooked. My aunt calls these novels "some of the best literature ever written": *Wuthering Heights, Jane Eyre,* and *Arrowsmith.*	**Examples** **Outside** Did you read the article "Fish for Breakfast"? Stop saying "I'm hungry"! **Inside** "How can you eat that?" Tracy asked. "That looks disgusting!" she cried.

I know it's hard to believe right now, Lawrence, but some day you'll thank me for asking you to punctuate your sentences correctly.

SIPRESS

Q: How come commas and periods stay inside quotation marks?

A: They're too little to stay out by themselves.

The Bottom Line

Checklist for Punctuation

Have I . . .

____ ended every sentence with the appropriate end mark?

____ inserted commas correctly to set off or separate sentence parts?

____ placed semicolons and colons correctly?

____ used dashes and parentheses to set off information?

____ used a dictionary to check hyphenated words?

____ placed apostrophes correctly to create possessive nouns?

____ used quotation marks correctly?

____ italicized words and titles correctly?

PUNCTUATION

Quick-Fix Editing Machine

You've worked hard on your assignment. Don't let misplaced commas, sentence fragments, and missing details lower your grade. Use this Quick-Fix Editing Machine to help you catch grammatical errors and make your writing more precise.

① Sentence Fragments

What's the problem? Part of a sentence has been left out.

Why does it matter? A fragment doesn't convey a complete thought.

What should you do about it? Find out what is missing and add it.

What's the Problem?

Quick Fix

A. A subject is missing.

Fell off my roller skates.

Add a subject.

The wheels fell off my roller skates.

B. A verb is missing.

Having no wheels skating difficult.

Add a verb.

Having no wheels **makes** skating difficult.

C. A helping verb is missing.

The wheels been missing since this morning.

Add a helping verb.

The wheels **have** been missing since this morning.

D. Both a subject and a verb are missing.

On my porch with nothing to do.

Add a subject and a verb to make an independent clause.

I'm sitting on my porch with nothing to do.

E. A subordinate clause is treated as if it were a sentence.

Even though my roller skates were new.

Combine the fragment with an independent clause.

I'm not upset, even though my roller skates were new.

OR

Remove the conjunction.

~~Even though~~ my roller skates were new.

For more help, see Chapter 5, pp. 114–127.

② Run-On Sentences

What's the problem? Two or more sentences have been run together.

Why does it matter? A run-on sentence doesn't show where one idea ends and another begins.

What should you do about it? Find the best way to separate the ideas or to show the proper relationship between them.

What's the Problem?

A. The end mark separating two complete thoughts is missing.

My summer job is fun I work in a pizza parlor.

B. Two complete thoughts are separated only by a comma.

Customers don't always know what they want, I have to make suggestions.

Quick Fix

Add an end mark to divide the run-on into two sentences.

My summer job is fun! I work in a pizza parlor.

Add a conjunction.

Customers don't always know what they want, **so** I have to make suggestions.

OR

Change the comma to a semicolon.

Customers don't always know what they want; I have to make suggestions.

OR

Change the comma to a semicolon and add a conjunctive adverb.

Customers don't always know what they want; **therefore,** I have to make suggestions.

OR

Make one of the independent clauses into a subordinate clause.

Because customers don't always know what they want, I have to make suggestions.

For more help, see Chapter 5, pp. 114–127.

QUICK FIX

3 Subject-Verb Agreement

What's the problem? A verb does not agree with its subject in number.

Why does it matter? Readers may regard your work as careless.

What should you do about it? Identify the subject and use a verb that matches it in number.

What's the Problem?

Quick Fix

A. A verb agrees with the object of a preposition rather than with its subject.

The production of music video **shows are** hard work.

Mentally screen out the prepositional phrase and make the verb agree with the subject.

The **production** ~~of music video shows~~ **is** hard work.

B. A verb agrees with a word in an appositive phrase that comes between the subject and the verb.

Producers, the people in charge of putting together each **show, has** to be creative.

Read the sentence without the phrase and make the verb agree with the subject.

Producers, the people in charge of putting together each show, **have** to be creative.

C. The verb doesn't agree with an indefinite-pronoun subject.

Everyone in the audience **want** to see his or her favorite artists.

Decide whether the pronoun is singular or plural, and make the verb agree with it.

Everyone in the audience **wants** to see his or her favorite artists.

D. A verb in a contraction doesn't agree with its subject.

It don't take long for the viewers to lose interest.

Use a contraction that agrees with the subject.

It doesn't take long for the viewers to lose interest.

For more help, see Chapter 7, pp. 154–175.

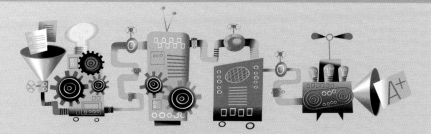

What's the Problem?

Quick Fix

E. A verb doesn't agree with the true subject of a sentence beginning with *here* or *there*.

There is many possible formats for a video.

Mentally turn the sentence around so that the subject comes first, and make the verb agree with it.

There are many possible **formats** for a video.

F. A singular verb is used with a compound subject containing *and*.

The producer and the **bandleader talks** it over.

Use a plural verb.

The producer and the bandleader **talk** it over.

G. A verb doesn't agree with the nearest part of a compound subject containing *or* or *nor*.

Neither **the band members nor the lead singer have arrived** yet.

Make the verb agree with the nearest part.

Neither the band members nor the **lead singer has arrived** yet.

H. A collective noun referring to a single unit is treated as plural (or one referring to individuals is treated as singular).

The **band are** always **getting** in trouble for being late.

If the collective noun refers to a single unit, use a singular verb.

The **band is** always **getting** in trouble for being late.

I. A singular subject ending in *s*, *es*, or *ics* is mistaken for a plural.

Politics have nothing to do with it.

Watch out for these nouns and use singular verbs.

Politics has nothing to do with it.

For more help, see Chapter 7, pp. 154–175.

QUICK FIX

4 Pronoun Reference Problems

What's the problem? A pronoun does not agree in number or gender with its antecedent, or the antecedent is unclear.

Why does it matter? Lack of agreement can cause confusion.

What should you do about it? Find the antecedent and make the pronoun agree with it, or rewrite the sentence to make the antecedent clear.

What's the Problem?

Quick Fix

A. A pronoun doesn't agree with an indefinite-pronoun antecedent.	Decide whether the indefinite pronoun is singular or plural, and make the pronoun agree with it.
Everyone who visits a "cybermall" ends up spending **their** money.	**Everyone** who visits a "cybermall" ends up spending **his or her** money.
B. A pronoun that refers to a compound subject containing *or* or *nor* doesn't agree with the nearest part.	Find the nearest simple subject and make the pronoun agree with it.
Neither **the manager nor the customers** actually leave **his** home.	Neither the manager nor the **customers** actually leave **their** homes.
C. A pronoun doesn't have an antecedent.	Rewrite the sentence to eliminate the pronoun.
On the home page **it** says that service is given with a smile.	**Spendit's home page** says that service is given with a smile.
D. A pronoun's antecedent is vague or indefinite.	Change the pronoun to a specific noun.
The mall guarantees that **they** are always in a good mood.	The mall guarantees that **the clerks** are always in a good mood.
E. A pronoun could refer to more than one noun.	Substitute a noun for the pronoun to make the reference specific.
Roz and Sue are my favorite "cyberclerks"; **she** thinks that a good mood is the only mood there is!	Roz and Sue are my favorite "cyberclerks"; **Roz** thinks that a good mood is the only mood there is!

For more help, see Chapter 8, pp. 176–205.

Incorrect Pronoun Case

What's the problem? A pronoun is in the wrong case.

Why does it matter? Readers may regard your work as sloppy, especially if your writing is supposed to be formal.

What should you do about it? Recognize how the pronoun is being used, and replace it with the correct form.

What's the Problem?

Quick Fix

A. A pronoun that follows a linking verb is not in the nominative case.

The best music student **is her.**

Use the nominative case after a linking verb.

The best music student **is she.**

OR

Reword the sentence.

She is the best music student.

B. A pronoun used as the object of a preposition is not in the objective case.

The teacher asked Danni to play **for** Ben and **I.**

Use the objective case as the object of a preposition.

The teacher asked Danni to play **for** Ben and **me.**

C. The wrong pronoun case is used in a comparison.

Very few people are as patient as **us.**

Mentally complete the comparison and use the appropriate case.

Very few people are as patient as **we [are].**

D. *Who* or *whom* is used incorrectly.

When we want good music, though, it's Danni **who** we listen **to.**

Use *who* if the pronoun is a subject, *whom* if it is an object.

When we want good music, though, it's Danni **whom** we listen **to.**

E. A pronoun followed by an appositive is in the wrong case.

Us kids make a great team.

Mentally screen out the appositive to test for the correct case.

We ~~kids~~ make a great team.

For more help, see Chapter 8, pp. 176–205.

Who and *Whom*

What's the problem? A form of the pronoun *who* or *whoever* is used incorrectly.

Why does it matter? The correct use of *who, whom, whoever,* and *whomever* in formal situations gives the impression that the speaker or writer is careful and knowledgeable.

What should you do about it? Decide how the pronoun functions in the sentence to determine which form to use.

What's the Problem?

Quick Fix

A. *Whom* **is incorrectly used as the subject of a sentence or clause.**

I don't know **whom is giving** me a ride.

Use *who* as the subject of a sentence or clause.

I don't know **who is giving** me a ride.

B. *Who* **is incorrectly used as the object of a preposition.**

Please tell me **who** to go **with.**

Use *whom* as the object of a preposition.

Please tell me **whom** to go **with.**

C. *Who* **is incorrectly used as a direct object.**

Who did you say I **should ask?**

Use *whom* as a direct object.

Whom did you say I **should ask?**

D. *Whomever* **is incorrectly used as the subject of a sentence or clause.**

Whomever wants a ride should tell me now.

Use *whoever* as a subject.

Whoever wants a ride should tell me now.

E. *Whoever* **is incorrectly used as an object.**

You can ride with **whoever** you **like.**

Use *whomever* as an object.

You can ride with **whomever** you **like.**

F. *Who's* **is incorrectly used as the possessive form of *who*.**

Who's car is this anyway?

Use *whose* to show possession.

Whose car is this anyway?

For more help, see Chapter 8, pp. 176–205.

QUICK FIX

⑦ Confusing Comparisons

What's the problem? The wrong form of a modifier is used to make a comparison.

Why does it matter? Incorrectly worded comparisons can be confusing and illogical.

What should you do about it? Use wording that makes the comparison clear.

What's the Problem?

Quick Fix

A. Both -er and more or -est and most are used in making a comparison.

My new schedule is **more crazier** than last year's schedule.

It is the **most hardest** I've ever had.

Eliminate the double comparison.

My new schedule is **crazier** than last year's schedule.

It is the **hardest** I've ever had.

B. The word other or else is missing in a comparison where it is logically needed.

My classes are harder **than anybody's.**

Add the missing word.

My classes are harder **than anybody else's.**

C. A superlative form is used where a comparative form is needed.

I compared my schedule with Rich's to see whose was **worst.**

If you're comparing two things, use the comparative form.

I compared my schedule with Rich's to see whose was **worse.**

D. A comparative form is used where a superlative form is needed.

Of all my classes, geometry is the **harder** by far; it will probably kill me.

If you're comparing more than two things, use the superlative form.

Of all my classes, geometry is the **hardest** by far; it will probably kill me.

For more help, see Chapter 9, pp. 206–225.

8 Verb Forms and Tenses

What's the problem? The wrong form or tense of a verb is used.

Why does it matter? Readers may regard your work as careless or find it confusing.

What should you do about it? Change the verb to the correct form or tense.

What's the Problem?

Quick Fix

What's the Problem?	Quick Fix
A. The wrong form of a verb is used with a helping verb. It was snowing, and a plane full of passengers **had** not yet **took** off.	Use a participle form with the helping verbs *have* and *be*. It was snowing, and a plane full of passengers **had** not yet **taken** off.
B. A helping verb is missing. Irritated passengers **trying** to leave the plane.	Add a helping verb. Irritated passengers **were trying** to leave the plane.
C. An irregular verb is treated as though it were a regular verb. None of the passengers actually **leaved,** however.	Look up the correct form of the irregular verb and use it. None of the passengers actually **left,** however.
D. A past participle is used incorrectly. The passengers **begun** to get restless.	Use the past form of the verb. The passengers **began** to get restless. **OR** Change the verb to the past perfect form by adding a helping verb. The passengers **had begun** to get restless.
E. Different tenses are used in the same sentence without a good reason. The passengers were furious, and most will plan to sue the airline.	Use the same tense throughout the sentence. The passengers were furious, and most **planned** to sue the airline.

For more help, see Chapter 6, pp. 128–153.

Misplaced and Dangling Modifiers

What's the problem? A modifying word or phrase is in the wrong place, or it doesn't modify any other word in the sentence.

Why does it matter? The sentence can be confusing or unintentionally funny.

What should you do about it? Move the modifier closer to the word it modifies, or add a word for it to modify.

What's the Problem?

Quick Fix

What's the Problem?	Quick Fix
A. The adverb *only* or *even* is not placed close to the word it modifies. **Even Tom** was trying to videotape the galloping horses.	Move the adverb to make your meaning clear. Tom was **even trying** to videotape the galloping horses.
B. A prepositional phrase is too far from the word it modifies. However, **in motion** it is very hard to film horses, even with a steady hand.	Move the phrase closer to the word or words it modifies. However, it is very hard to film horses **in motion,** even with a steady hand.
C. A participial phrase is too far from the word it modifies. **Running around the corral,** Tom videotaped his favorite horse.	Move the phrase closer to the word or words it modifies. Tom videotaped his favorite horse **running around the corral.**
D. A verbal phrase does not relate to anything in the sentence. **Having distracted the horse,** the video session went well.	Reword the sentence, adding a word for the phrase to refer to. **Having distracted the horse, the trainer** made sure that the video session went well.

For more help, see Chapter 5, pp. 114–127, and Chapter 9, pp. 206–225.

QUICK FIX

10 Missing or Misplaced Commas

What's the problem? Commas are missing or are used incorrectly.

Why does it matter? Sentences in which commas are used incorrectly can be hard to follow.

What should you do about it? Determine where commas are needed and add or omit them as necessary.

What's the Problem?

Quick Fix

A. A comma is missing before the conjunction in a series.

Bill's family regularly eats tuna, salmon and trout.

Add a comma.

Bill's family regularly eats tuna, salmon, and trout.

B. A comma is placed after a closing quotation mark.

"I don't understand why Bill doesn't eat any of the fish he catches himself", says Sue.

Always put a comma before a closing quotation mark.

"I don't understand why Bill doesn't eat any of the fish he catches himself," says Sue.

C. A comma is missing after an introductory clause.

Although Bill goes fishing often he throws back all the fish he catches.

Find the end of the clause and add a comma.

Although Bill goes fishing often, he throws back all the fish he catches.

D. Commas are missing around a nonessential phrase or clause.

He enjoys fishing in the Cedar River which is close to his house and then buying dinner at a supermarket.

Add commas to set off the nonessential phrase or clause.

He enjoys fishing in the Cedar River, which is close to his house, and then buying dinner at a supermarket.

E. A comma is missing from a compound sentence.

Bill thinks he's being kind to the fish by throwing them back but the fish might not agree.

Add a comma before the conjunction.

Bill thinks he's being kind to the fish by throwing them back, but the fish might not agree.

For more help, see Chapter 11, pp. 246–279.

11 Using Active and Passive Voice

What's the problem? The overuse of the passive voice makes a piece of writing weak.

Why does it matter? The active voice engages readers' attention better than the passive voice.

What should you do about it? Rewrite sentences, using the active voice.

What's the Problem?

Quick Fix

A. The passive voice makes a sentence dull.

Snakes at the bottom of the pit **were sighted** by terrified tourists.

Revise the sentence, using the active voice.

Terrified **tourists sighted** snakes at the bottom of the pit.

B. The passive voice takes the emphasis away from the performer of an action.

The **tourists were warned** by a nervous guide that the snakes could escape from the pit.

Change the voice from passive to active.

A nervous **guide warned** the tourists that the snakes could escape from the pit.

C. The passive voice makes a sentence wordy.

Some of the tourists **were being terrified** by the slithering snakes.

Change the voice from passive to active.

The slithering snakes **were terrifying** some of the tourists.

For more help, see Chapter 16, pp. 369–385.

Note: The passive voice is appropriate when you want to

- emphasize the receiver of an action or the action itself

The snake pit **was closed** shortly after the incident.

- make a statement about an action whose performer need not be specified or is not known

No snakes **have been seen** in the area since then.

12 Improving Weak Sentences

What's the problem? A sentence repeats ideas or contains too many ideas.

Why does it matter? Empty and overloaded sentences are dull and confusing.

What should you do about it? Make sure every sentence has a clearly focused idea.

What's the Problem?

Quick Fix

A. An idea is repeated.

Darren always gets picked for team games because he is an excellent athlete **and he plays sports well.**

Delete the repeated idea.

Darren always gets picked for team games because he is an excellent athlete ~~and he plays sports well.~~

B. Too many loosely related ideas are included in a single sentence.

Darren comes from a competitive family, and everybody in the family loves to play sports, including baseball, basketball, and tennis.

Divide the sentence into two or more sentences, using subordinate clauses to show relationships between ideas.

Darren comes from a competitive family in which everybody loves to play sports. They play baseball, basketball, and tennis.

C. Too much information is crammed into one sentence.

Darren hopes to get a football scholarship eventually, and he wants to go to a fine university—one at which he and other athletes can get a good education while they play football.

Simplify the ideas and divide the sentence into two or more sentences.

Darren hopes to get a football scholarship to a fine university. He wants to get a good education while he plays football.

For more help, see Chapter 16, pp. 369–385.

⑬ Avoiding Wordiness

What's the problem? A sentence contains unnecessary words.

Why does it matter? Readers may be annoyed and confused by wordy sentences.

What should you do about it? Use concise terms and eliminate extra words.

What's the Problem?

Quick Fix

A. A single idea is unnecessarily expressed in two ways.

After turning on the light switch **with my hand,** I sat on the **seat of the** chair.

Delete the unnecessary words.

After turning on the light switch ~~with my hand,~~ I sat on ~~the seat of~~ the chair.

B. A sentence contains words that do not add to its meaning.

Let me explain that I heard a noise and discovered that an owl had flown in through the window.

Delete the unnecessary words.

~~Let me explain that~~ I heard a noise and discovered that an owl had flown in through the window.

C. A simple idea is expressed in too many words.

We figured the owl was seeking shelter **out of the way of** the hailstorm.

Simplify the expression.

We figured the owl was seeking shelter **from** the hailstorm.

D. A clause is used when a phrase would do.

While it was peering at us from an attic rafter, the owl did not seem afraid.

Reduce the clause to a phrase.

Peering at us from an attic rafter, the owl did not seem afraid.

For more help, see Chapter 16, pp. 369–385.

14 Varying Sentence Beginnings

What's the problem? Too many sentences begin in the same way.

Why does it matter? Lack of variety in sentence beginnings makes writing dull and choppy.

What should you do about it? Reword the sentences so that they begin with prepositional phrases, verbal phrases, adverbs, or subordinate clauses.

What's the Problem?

Too many sentences in a paragraph start the same way.

Weather problems are one thing we all have in common. **Weather problems** surprise people on the East Coast and the West Coast and all those in between.

Weather problems can make people tough. **Weather problems** challenge people to come up with creative ways to cope.

Weather problems arise very suddenly. **Weather** can change your plans at a moment's notice.

For more help, see Chapter 16, pp. 369–385.

Quick Fix

Start a sentence with a prepositional phrase.

Weather problems are one thing we all have in common. **From the East Coast to the West Coast,** weather surprises people.

OR

Start a sentence with a verbal phrase.

Dealing with weather problems makes people tough and inventive.

OR

Start a sentence with a subordinate clause.

Because weather problems arise very suddenly, they can change your plans at a moment's notice.

⑮ Varying Sentence Structure

What's the problem? A piece of writing contains too many simple sentences.

Why does it matter? Monotony in sentence structure makes writing dull and lifeless.

What should you do about it? Combine or reword sentences to create different structures.

What's the Problem?

Quick Fix

A. Too many simple sentences are used.

Our student volunteers went to France. They met other students. These students were from all over the world.

Combine the sentences to form a compound sentence.

Our student volunteers went to France, **and** they met other students. ~~These students were~~ from all over the world.

B. Short sentences create a choppy effect.

The officials had other meetings. They were rushed. They promised to address the students' concerns later.

Combine the sentences to form a complex sentence.

Because the hurried officials had other meetings, they promised to address the students' concerns later.

C. Repeated sentence patterns make writing dull.

The students organized a rally. They planned a parade. It attracted many officials.

Combine the sentences to form a compound-complex sentence.

The students organized a rally, **and** they planned a parade **that** attracted many officials.

For more help, see Chapter 16, pp. 369–385, and Chapter 4, pp. 90–113.

QUICK FIX

16 Adding Supporting Details

What's the problem? Unfamiliar terms aren't defined, and claims aren't supported.

Why does it matter? Undefined terms and unsupported claims weaken informative or persuasive writing.

What should you do about it? Add supporting details to clarify and elaborate statements.

What's the Problem?

Quick Fix

A. A key term is not defined.

Because simplicity is attractive, ikebana has become popular.

Define the term.

Because simplicity is attractive, ikebana, **the Japanese art of flower arrangement,** has become popular.

B. No reason is given for an opinion.

Ikebana arrangements are beautiful.

Add a reason.

Ikebana arrangements are beautiful **because they are based on principles of harmony and balance.**

C. No support is given for a fact.

Floral customers are intrigued by ikebana.

Add supporting facts and statistics.

A survey of the Floral Club's 50,000 members revealed that many people are intrigued by ikebana.

D. No supporting examples are given.

Florists are learning more about ikebana.

Add examples.

Florists are learning more about ikebana **by attending workshops and reading the publications of the Ikebana Association.**

For more help, see Chapter 15, pp. 355–367.

17 Avoiding Clichés and Slang

What's the problem? Formal writing contains clichés or slang expressions.

Why does it matter? Clichés convey no new images to readers. Slang is not appropriate in formal writing.

What should you do about it? Reword sentences, replacing the clichés or slang with fresh expressions.

What's the Problem?

Quick Fix

A. A sentence contains a cliché.

Replace the cliché with a description or explanation.

Brenda ran around the hospital lobby **like a chicken with its head cut off.**

Brenda ran around the hospital lobby, **frantically seeking information about her grandmother's condition.**

B. Clichés don't accurately express the intended meaning.

Replace the clichés with more appropriate images or explanations.

Getting to the hospital had been **like fighting World War III.** It was **harder to find than a needle in a haystack.**

Getting to the hospital had been **like competing in a track meet.** It was **harder to find than she expected it would be.**

C. A sentence contains inappropriate slang.

Replace the slang with more appropriate language.

When Brenda didn't find her grandmother's room right away, **she went ballistic.**

When Brenda didn't find her grandmother's room right away, **her frustration turned to anger.**

For more help, see Chapter 17, pp. 387–401.

QUICK FIX

18 Using Precise Words

What's the problem? Nouns, modifiers, and verbs are too general.

Why does it matter? Readers are engaged by writing in which specific words are used to show rather than tell.

What should you do about it? Replace general words with precise words.

What's the Problem?

What's the Problem?	Quick Fix
A. Nouns and pronouns are too general. The **committee** knew that the **event** was the most popular **one** of the school year.	Use specific words. The **dance committee members** knew that the **sophomore mixer** was the most popular **party** of the school year.
B. Adjectives and nouns are too vague. They planned to decorate the gym to resemble an **exotic locale.**	Use more precise adjectives and nouns to paint a picture. They planned to decorate the gym with **crepe-paper palm trees,** a **blue plastic lagoon,** and a **gigantic tin-foil moon.**
C. Adverbs are vague or are omitted when they would clarify the picture. **Slowly** they climbed ladders and hung stars above the tables.	Use descriptive adverbs. **Cautiously,** they climbed ladders and hung stars **high** above the tables.
D. Verbs tell about the action instead of showing it. As the committee **sat** back to admire their work, the balloons they had hidden among the rafters **fell** down.	Use vivid verbs to show the action. As the committee **relaxed** in folding chairs or **reclined** on the gym floor, admiring their work, the balloons they had hidden among the rafters began to come down. At first a few **loosened** and **drifted** toward them; then the whole lot **cascaded** over their weary bodies.

For more help, see Chapter 17, pp. 387–401.

⑲ Using Figurative Language

What's the problem? A piece of writing is lifeless or unimaginative.

Why does it matter? Readers find such writing dull and can't form clear mental pictures of what is described.

What should you do about it? Add figures of speech, but don't weaken their impact by using too many or by combining them illogically.

What's the Problem?

Quick Fix

A. A description is dull and lifeless.

On the girls' basketball team I was known for **my aggressiveness.**

We often won because of our **very tall** center.

Add a simile or metaphor.

On the girls' basketball team I was famous for **playing like a bulldog.**

We often won because our center, **a tree who could shoot,** gave us an edge.

B. Too many figures of speech have been used.

Neeta **ran like the wind** and **shot like a bolt of lightning** before **grinning like a Cheshire cat.**

Replace one of the figures of speech with nonfigurative language.

Neeta **ran like the wind** and **shot quickly and accurately** before **grinning like a Cheshire cat.**

C. Figures of speech have been combined illogically.

We shorter players could always pass to Neeta over the heads of the players on the other team, who scrambled around her **like ants around a giant** and who looked up for the ball **as if they were counting stars.**

Choose a single figure of speech to emphasize.

We shorter players could always pass to Neeta over the heads of the players on the other team, who scrambled around her **like ants around a giant,** looking up for the ball.

For more help, see Chapter 15, pp. 355–367, and Chapter 17, pp. 387–401.

20 Paragraphing

What's the problem? A paragraph contains too many ideas.

Why does it matter? A long paragraph discourages readers from continuing.

What should you do about it? Break the paragraph into smaller paragraphs and delete unnecessary material. Start a new paragraph whenever the speaker, setting, or focus changes.

What's the Problem?

Quick Fix

A. Too many ideas are contained in one paragraph.

Ona's two suns beamed hotly upon Jadok's head as he warmed up in the school's hologym. Sweating hard, Jadok continued preparing for the 1,000-pound discus fling. Jadok had trained for this event while visiting his pal Carl last year.

Start a new paragraph when the main idea changes.

Ona's two suns beamed hotly upon Jadok's head as he warmed up in the school's hologym. Sweating hard, Jadok continued preparing for the 1,000-pound discus fling.

Jadok had trained for this event while visiting his pal Carl last year.

B. Two characters speak in the same paragraph.

Jadok remembered joking, "My brother would laugh! He can fling about ten Earth yards, and he's only eight!" "Yeah, but that's on Ona," said Carl. "He wouldn't be able to fling at all on Earth."

Start a new paragraph when the speaker changes.

Jadok remembered joking, "My brother would laugh! He can fling about ten Earth yards, and he's only eight!"

"Yeah, but that's on Ona," said Carl. "He wouldn't be able to fling at all on Earth."

C. An unnecessary statement clutters a paragraph.

Jadok knew that, because of Earth's gravity, practicing on Earth would be perfect training for his sport. He's smart too. Flinging on Earth was taxing.

Delete the unnecessary information.

Jadok knew that, because of Earth's gravity, practicing on Earth would be perfect training for his sport. ~~He's smart too.~~ Flinging on Earth was taxing.

For more help, see Chapter 14, pp. 337–353.

What's the Problem?

The writing isn't broken into logical paragraphs.

Have you seen images of people walking on the moon? They appear to be moving with more bounce in their steps than we do. Why is this? Simply put, the earth has a greater mass than the moon, so the earth's gravitational pull is stronger than the moon's. That is why it is harder to leap into the air on the earth than it is to leap from the surface of the moon (once you get there!). It is a little-known fact that the force of gravity is not equally strong everywhere on the earth's surface. This can be seen in the level of the ocean above a submerged mountain. The mass of the mountain attracts water toward it, creating a slight rise in the level of the sea around it. The "bump" can be detected in photographs taken from satellites. Gravity, a force that still holds some mystery even for scientists, affects each one of us every day.

For more help, see Chapter 14, pp. 337–353.

Quick Fix

Set off the introduction in its own paragraph.

Have you seen images of people walking on the moon? They appear to be moving with more bounce in their steps than we do. Why is this?

Start a new paragraph to introduce the first main idea.

Simply put, the earth has a greater mass than the moon, so the earth's gravitational pull is stronger than the moon's. That is why it is harder to leap into the air on the earth than it is to leap from the surface of the moon (once you get there!).

Start a new paragraph to introduce another main idea.

It is a little-known fact that the force of gravity is not equally strong everywhere on the earth's surface. This can be seen in the level of the ocean above a submerged mountain. The mass of the mountain attracts water toward it, creating a slight rise in the level of the sea around it. The "bump" can be detected in photographs taken from satellites.

Set off the conclusion in its own paragraph.

Gravity, a force that still holds some mystery even for scientists, affects each one of us every day.

Essential Writing Skills

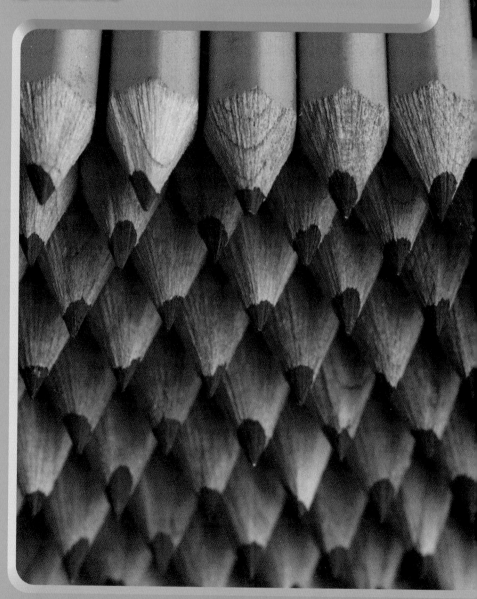

Sharpening Your Skills

Your writing skills are like a stock of sharpened pencils always at the ready. One way to keep them sharp is to practice the fundamentals of writing just as you would practice shooting baskets or playing scales on the piano. That way, when you reach for a word it will be precise, and when you craft a figure of speech it will be fresh.

Power Words
Vocabulary for Precise Writing

Too Little, Too Much

You can describe any creative process with words that refer to extremes. Such words can help you get from an empty page to a million ideas.

The Big Zero

At the very beginning, your page is **empty, blank,** and **vacant.** You have **nothing, naught, nil, nada;** you have **zero, zip, bupkis.** As your math teacher might say, your page contains the **empty set.**

There may seem to be a **space,** a **gap,** a **void,** a **vacuum** in your head; a **lack, shortage,** and **scarcity** of thoughts; a **dearth,** a **deficiency,** an **insufficiency** of ideas; a **paucity** of paragraphs.

Sudden Abundance

Put pencil to paper (or fingers to keyboard) and— what do you know!—words **pour out** in a **plethora** or **plenitude** of paragraphs. They **flow** and **overflow** in a **superfluity** of phrases; **issue forth** insistently; **gush, stream,** and **cascade** onto the page. Suddenly you have too many words!

Time to Cut

It's time to **cut back** by **cutting out.** You need to **remove, pluck out, extract, expunge,** or **excise** the excess; you may have to **suppress** the superfluous and **streamline** the structure. In other words, you have to **edit** (but not **eviscerate**) your essay.

> ▷ **Your Turn** Going for Broke
>
> With a small group of classmates, brainstorm a list of other words that mean "too little" or "too much." Then classify the words by the contexts in which they can be used—for instance, in talking about money, time, luck, or other things of which you can have a dearth or an abundance.

Writing Process

My older brother . . . was at the kitchen table close to tears, surrounded by binder paper and pencils and unopened books on birds, immobilized by the hugeness of the task ahead. Then my father sat down beside him, put his arm around my brother's shoulder, and said, "Bird by bird, buddy. Just take it bird by bird."

—Anne Lamott, *Bird by Bird*

Where to Begin?

The boy in the passage above has been assigned to write a report on birds. If you were given this assignment, how would you begin to tackle it?

When the father said to "take it bird by bird," he meant that his son should figure out the different parts of writing the report and complete them one at a time. This is good advice for any writer. Writing is a process, or series of activities, that includes prewriting, drafting, revising, editing, and publishing. Every writer performs these activities in his or her own way. This chapter contains useful strategies you can apply to all kinds of writing.

Write Away: My Way
Use this chapter to help you complete your next writing assignment. First, answer these questions to help you think about your current writing process: Is there any part of writing assignments that is especially challenging for you? Describe this. Which kinds of assignments are most difficult? Which are most fun? Place your responses to these questions in your 📁 **Working Portfolio.**

Prewriting

When given a writing assignment, do you ask yourself, How will I ever get this done? Where do I begin? Prewriting is the part of the writing process that gets you over this first hurdle. In this part, you begin thinking about your topic, purpose, audience, and form.

❶ Finding a Topic

A writing topic may be assigned to you by your teacher, or you may be free to choose one. When you're not sure what to write about, you can use one of the following techniques to find a topic.

Freewriting

First think of a subject you want to know more about. Then quickly write down whatever comes into your head about it. Don't stop, edit your ideas, or read what you've written until you are finished. Finally, choose your best idea to write about.

Brainstorming

You can brainstorm alone or with others. Try bringing up a topic and letting your brainstorming partners say whatever comes to mind. Don't judge the ideas; just write them down. Later, decide which idea you want to write about.

Creative Questioning

Think up questions (serious or zany) that begin "What if . . ." What if the polar ice caps melted? What if people took vacations on the moon? What if I had amnesia? Choose the question that excites you the most and write about it.

Browsing

Leaf through art and photography books, books of quotations, books of humor, or books of some other kind. Flip through favorite magazines and newspapers. Have a pen and paper ready so that you can jot down ideas as you browse. Use your notes to select a topic.

To decide whether you've found a good topic, ask yourself these questions.

- Does the topic interest me personally?
- Is it clear enough for me to understand and write about?
- Is there enough to say about the topic?

Choose a writing topic that truly interests you. If a topic has been assigned, look for an angle that interests you. For example, if you've been assigned to write about birds, you might choose to deal with new theories about the relationship between birds and dinosaurs.

For more writing ideas, see p. 320.

❷ Purpose, Audience, and Form

Knowing why you are writing and for whom you are writing will help you focus your thoughts about your topic. Use the questions in the chart below to help you define your purpose and your audience.

Defining Your Purpose and Audience	
Purpose: *Why am I writing?*	• Do you want to inform your readers? • Do you want to describe something to them? • Do you want to entertain them? • Do you want to persuade them to believe something?
Audience: *For whom am I writing?*	• Who is going to read your writing? • What do your readers already know about the topic? • What do they need in order to understand your ideas? • How can you capture their interest?

Feel free to combine purposes. You may want to inform and entertain or to describe and persuade.

Often, the first thing you know about a writing assignment is the form you will use. Sometimes, however, you might not think about the form until after you've chosen a topic and considered your purpose and audience. The chart below lists some of the most common writing forms you might decide to use.

Writing Forms		
autobiography	legend	play
book review	memo	poem
editorial	personal letter	research report
how-to essay	persuasive essay	short story

You don't have to settle for an obvious form. Suppose you've decided to write about ancient Egypt and you want to entertain your audience, which happens to be your classmates. What unexpected form might you choose from the chart above?

For more writing forms, see p. 320.

WRITING PROCESS

❸ Exploring and Limiting a Topic

Begin exploring your topic by writing down everything you know or want to know about it. Some techniques for exploring topics and recording information are shown below. If necessary, gather more information about your topic through research. After exploring, you will probably have more information than you can use. Limit your topic by choosing the part of it that is most interesting to you.

Questioning Write down questions about your topic, beginning with *who, what, when, where, why,* and *how.*

> **Who discovered fossils linking birds to dinosaurs? What did the first birds look like? How have birds evolved?**

Web Diagram In a circle, write a word or phrase that states your topic. Write related ideas in other circles, drawing lines between the circles to indicate the relationships between ideas. Continue this process until you run out of ideas.

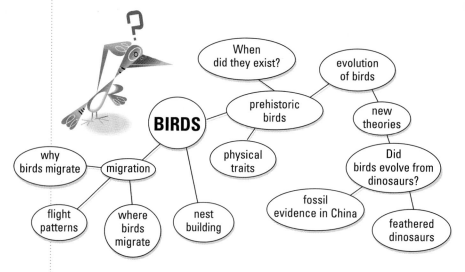

Observation Chart Create a simple chart to record sensory details that relate to your topic.

Environment of the First Birds (About 140 Million Years Ago)

Sight	Hearing	Taste	Touch	Smell
palm trees	dinosaur cries		warm oceans	
flowering plants			mild climate	

Side-by-Side Chart In a chart like the one below, record opposing aspects of an idea or object.

Strengths of First Birds	Weaknesses of First Birds
teeth	poor fliers
clawed wings	many enemies

Limit your topic by circling the idea or ideas that most interest you. If you circle more than one idea, choose the most appealing of the circled ideas. Keep narrowing your choices until you've found the topic that is right for you.

❹ Organizing Information

Will you present information about your topic according to the order in which events occurred? according to similarities and differences? Once you've decided on a way to organize your writing, you can use a graphic device to arrange your information. This will help you get ready to write.

Use a time line to record events in sequential order—the order in which they occurred.

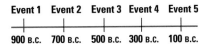

Event 1   Event 2   Event 3   Event 4   Event 5

900 B.C.   700 B.C.   500 B.C.   300 B.C.   100 B.C.

Use a Venn diagram to record similarities and differences between ideas or things.

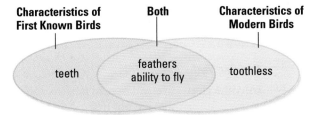

Characteristics of First Known Birds

Both

Characteristics of Modern Birds

teeth

feathers
ability to fly

toothless

Use a flow chart to record the steps in a process.

Step 1 ⊣ Step 2 ⊣ Step 3 ⊣ Step 4

When you use a graphic device to arrange your information, you can quickly see what's missing and develop new questions to research or think about.

LESSON 2 **Drafting**

Drafting means getting your ideas down on paper. How you draft depends on what kind of writing you're doing and what makes you most comfortable. You can create as many drafts as you feel you need.

By Charles Barsotti

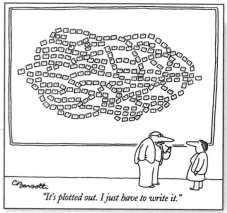

"It's plotted out. I just have to write it."

© The New Yorker Collection 1996 Charles Barsotti

❶ Drafting to Discover

You don't have to know exactly what you want to say when you begin drafting. In creative and personal writing especially, discovery drafting, like freewriting, can be a helpful way to find and explore ideas. Begin by writing what you know about your topic or by writing any ideas you have for telling a story. Don't worry about grammar or organization; just see where your ideas take you.

❷ Drafting from a Plan

When you write in a form that has a particular structure—such as a research report, persuasive essay, or play—you may want to plan what you will write before you begin drafting. You can do this by organizing your notes and creating an outline.

> ***Popular Myths About Birds***
>
> **Introduction**—five widespread notions about birds
> that are not true
>
> I. Hummingbirds' migrating on the backs of geese
>   A. Migration patterns
>   B. Migration timing

Through outlining, you may discover new ideas or ideas that don't fit in. Revise your outline to reflect any changes you make, and begin drafting when you feel your plan is final.

❸ Using Peer Response

The comments and suggestions your classmates make about your writing are called peer response. Feedback from your peers can help you shape and improve your writing. You can ask for peer response at any point in your writing process. Just be clear about the questions you want answered.

Getting and Giving Peer Response

Tips for Writers	Tips for Peer Readers
• Give readers clean copies of your writing. • Ask open-ended questions; they will get you more information than questions that can be answered yes or no. • Give readers enough time to respond thoughtfully. • Encourage readers to be honest in their responses to your writing.	• Respect the writer's feelings. • Begin by telling the writer what you like about the writing. • Answer the writer's questions in a positive way. Don't just point out faults in the writing. • Be specific in your feedback.

You don't have to use all the suggestions you get from your peer readers. Keep their suggestions in mind, however, as you continue to write and revise your work.

Here are some open-ended questions you might ask a classmate or friend about an opinion essay you have written.

• How would you restate the issue I'm writing about?

• What information, if any, is unclear or unneeded?

To find out if you've expressed your ideas clearly, ask a peer reader to summarize the main ideas of your paper in a few words.

For more information about getting peer response, see p. 321.

Revising

When you revise your writing, you try to improve the way you've expressed and organized your ideas. The changes you make during this step may be large or small.

Six Traits of Effective Writing

If possible, set your draft aside for a while before you begin to revise it. The six traits listed below are standards that can guide you in your revision of your draft.

Using the Six Traits	
1. Ideas and content	Make sure your ideas are clear, focused, and supported with relevant details.
2. Organization	Arrange your ideas in a logical order that moves the reader through the text.
3. Voice	Express your ideas in a way that shows your individual style and personality.
4. Word choice	Use language that is precise, powerful, and engaging.
5. Sentence fluency	Improve the rhythm and flow of your sentences by using varied sentence lengths and structures.
6. Conventions	Eliminate errors in grammar, spelling, and punctuation.

The first five traits are covered in this lesson. Conventions are discussed in the next lesson.

Checking Ideas and Content

Use the questions below to check the content of your writing.

> **Here's How Checking Ideas and Content**
>
> - Is my purpose for writing clear?
> - Are my ideas interesting and well-focused?
> - Have I included enough details to explain my ideas and support my opinions?
> - Is all the information I've included important to my purpose?

If you answer no to any of these questions, you need to revise your content.

Checking Organization

Your ideas should be organized in a way that will help your readers understand them. If necessary, revise your organization on the basis of your answers to the questions below.

Here's How **Checking Organization**

- Have I created a clear beginning, middle, and end?
- Is my introduction strong?
- Does each section seem to lead naturally into the next?
- Have I put supporting details where they are needed?
- Is my conclusion strong?

Checking Voice, Word Choice, and Sentence Fluency

A writer's style is the special way he or she puts words together to express ideas. Check the style of your writing by examining your voice, word choice, and sentence fluency.

Voice

Voice is the way you as an individual express yourself in writing. Your voice should be

- honest and natural (Don't try to sound like someone else.)
- appealing to readers
- as interesting as you are

Word Choice

Word choice is the words you choose to use in your writing. The words you use should be

- natural (Don't use a complex word when a simple word will do.)
- precise, strong, and specific
- imaginative and engaging

Sentence Fluency

Sentence fluency is the rhythm and flow of your sentences.
Your sentences should

- be of various lengths and structures
- begin in different ways to avoid repetition
- flow together smoothly

The following model shows these last three traits in action.
Eugenia Collier has a natural and honest voice. She uses
language that is imaginative and appealing, and her sentences
begin in interesting and varied ways. They flow together smoothly.

LITERARY MODEL

    I turn from the window and flop down on
the bed, shoes and all. Perhaps because of
what happened this afternoon or maybe just
because I see Charley so seldom, my thoughts
hover over him like hummingbirds. The
cheerful, impersonal tidiness of this room is a
world away from Charley's walk-up flat in
Harlem and a hundred worlds from the bare,
noisy shanty where he and the rest of us
spent what there was of childhood. I close
my eyes, and side by side I see the Charley of
my boyhood and the Charley of this afternoon,
as clearly as if I were looking at a split TV
screen. Another surge of love, seasoned with
gratitude, wells up in me.

            —Eugenia Collier, "Sweet Potato Pie"

VARIED SENTENCE BEGINNINGS

PRECISE AND IMAGINATIVE WORDS

For more information about style, see pp. 387–401.

Editing and Proofreading

Don't skip the step of checking your writing for errors in grammar, spelling, and punctuation. No matter how good your writing is, readers will be less impressed by it if it's full of careless errors.

❶ Checking Conventions

Conventions are the accepted standards for grammar, spelling, and punctuation in writing. Some of the most common errors writers make are listed below. Be sure to correct these errors in your writing.

- Sentence fragments
- Errors in subject-verb agreement
- Run-on sentences
- Missing or misused punctuation
- Verb tense errors
- Misused or misspelled words
- Incorrect capitalization
- Dangling modifiers

After spending so much time thinking about and shaping your ideas, you may find it difficult to focus on the smaller details in your writing. Use these tips to help you get down to business.

> **Here's How Editing and Proofreading**
>
> 1. Read your work slowly—one sentence at a time.
> 2. Look for the kinds of mistakes you often find in your writing, as well as other kinds of mistakes.
> 3. Look closely at sentences that just don't seem right to you—even if you're not immediately sure why they aren't right.
> 4. Use the Grammar, Usage, and Mechanics chapters of this book to help you correct errors in grammar, capitalization, and punctuation.
> 5. Use a dictionary to check the spellings of unfamiliar words and words that often give you trouble.
> 6. Ask a friend or family member to read your work, looking for errors you missed.

For help in correcting common errors, see the Quick-Fix Editing Machine, pp. 282–292.

❷ Using Proofreading Symbols

The chart below shows some commonly used proofreading symbols. Use them to show the corrections you need to make in your writing.

Proofreading Symbols			
∧	Add a letter or word.	⌒	Close up.
⊙	Add a period.	¶	Begin a new paragraph.
≡	Capitalize a letter.	∧	Add a comma.
ⱡ	Make a capital letter lowercase.	∾	Switch the positions of letters or words.
⌿	Delete letters or words.	#	Add a space.

STUDENT MODEL

    One popular myth‸which sounds like a children's fairy tale,

is

~~states~~ that ⱡummingbirds migrate by riding on the backs of

                                                   e

geese. It's nice to think of our feather⌃d friends being so kind to

one another. Unfortunately, this ni⌒eⱦidea just isn't true. Two

facts about goose and ⱡummingbird migration makes̸ the

impossibility of such cooperation clear: these birds migrate at

different times‸and they migrate to different places.

You'll find it easier to spot errors if you take a break before you begin to edit and proofread.

Publishing and Reflecting

LESSON 5

Publishing your writing means sharing it with others. If your writing is very personal, you may not want to do this. Most of the time, however, you are writing for an audience. Now is the time to let your audience see your work.

❶ Sharing Your Writing

Here are some creative ways to share your writing.

Sharing in Print

• Publish your writing in a school newspaper or literary magazine.

• Submit your writing to a magazine that publishes student writing.

Sharing Electronically

• Post your writing on an electronic bulletin board.

• E-mail your writing to friends and relatives.

• Create a Web site for your writing.

Sharing by Presenting

• Present your work in a dramatic reading or performance.

• Present a persuasive essay as a speech.

 For more publishing options, visit the McDougal Littell Web site: www.mcdougallittell.com

❷ Reflecting on Your Writing

Does your writing process work for you, or do you need to change it? Use the questions below to help you reflect on your writing.

• What did you learn about your topic and the form you used?

• Which part of the process was most difficult? least difficult?

• What would you do differently next time?

As you reflect on a piece of writing, decide whether it belongs in your presentation portfolio. A **presentation portfolio** is a folder that holds your best work—work you are proud to share with others.

Student Help Desk

Writing Process at a Glance

Prewriting   Drafting

Revising, Editing, and Proofreading

Publishing and Reflecting

Writing Topics
The *Write* Idea

- Review a concert, movie, computer program or game, CD, or restaurant.
- Interview someone you think is interesting, and write up the information you obtain.
- Use sensory details to describe your neighborhood, town, or city.
- Compare and contrast two songs, paintings, places, objects, or ideas.
- Compare and contrast yourself with an object, idea, animal, or place.
- Examine the causes and effects of a problem.
- Write a short story about a conflict between two people and how they resolve it.

Writing Forms
Form Finder

advertisement	memo
anecdote	memoir
article	movie script
autobiography	myth
biography	opinion essay
book review	parable
brochure	personal letter
business letter	persuasive essay
cartoon	persuasive speech
catalog	
column	play
commercial	poem
dialogue	press release
editorial	proposal
fable	research report
how-to essay	review
journal entry	short story
lecture	TV script
legend	

Peer Response Techniques

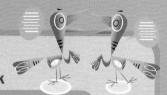

Below are questions you can ask peer readers to get different kinds of feedback about your writing.

Summarizing Ask these questions to figure out if your main idea and goals are clear.

• *What do you think I'm saying? What's my main idea or message?*

Replying Ask these questions to make your writing richer by adding new ideas.

• *What are your ideas about my topic? What do you think about what I have said in my piece?*

Responding to Specific Features Ask these questions to get a quick overview of the strengths and weaknesses of your writing.

• *Are the ideas supported with enough examples? Did I persuade you? Is the organization clear enough for you to follow the ideas?*

Clarifying Ask these questions to find out which parts of your writing are affecting readers the way you want and which parts are confusing.

• *What did you think or feel as you read my words? Would you show me which passage you were reading when you had that response?*

The Bottom Line

Checklist for Writing Process

Have I . . .

_____ presented clear and well-focused ideas?

_____ organized the ideas so that the connections between them are clear and logical?

_____ used words that are precise, powerful, and appropriate to my audience and purpose?

_____ expressed my ideas in a voice that is honest and natural?

_____ written sentences that are varied and interesting and that flow together smoothly?

_____ used correct grammar, spelling, and punctuation?

The Qualities of Sound

You can make your descriptions sing by using precise sound words. Assemble your own vocabulary of words describing what you hear.

Soothing Sounds

How can you describe music you enjoy? To praise a simple tune, say it is **tuneful, lilting,** or **lyrical.** Refer to the **sonorous** strains of the strings, the **mellow** saxophone, the **resonant** bass or cello, the **dulcet** tone of the singer.

Rejoice in the **melodious** harmonies of the Beatles and the **harmonious** outpouring of a gospel choir. Don't you just love to listen to **euphonious** speech and **mellifluous** voices?

Jarring Sounds

There are also adjectives for sounds you dislike. If the sounds are **harsh** and **grating,** you might refer to them as **discordant** or **dissonant;** to their **raucous, strident,** or **shrill** qualities; to the **jarring, jangling, cacophonous** racket. The same words could describe the noise of two cats **squalling** and **squealing, screaming** and **screeching, caterwauling** and **yowling** in the night.

▷ **Your Turn** Hearing the World

Close your eyes and listen. What do you hear? If you didn't know what was making the noises you hear, how would you describe them? Try this experiment at other times during the day, and present your description orally to the class.

CHAPTER 13

sonorous

lyrical

harmonious

discordant

Creating Paragraphs

Assembly Required

The parts of a guitar, when assembled, make an instrument that can produce a variety of musical sounds and melodies. In pieces, however, the guitar cannot make even one musical note. Just as a guitar has to be assembled properly to play music, a paragraph requires proper assembly in order to make sense to the reader.

To function alone or in a composition, a paragraph must possess two key elements: unity (a single focus or unifying theme) and coherence (a logical pattern of organization).

Write Away: Out of the Ordinary

Write a single paragraph in praise of an ordinary object in your house—one that you couldn't live without. Pick something that you can adequately describe in four or five sentences. Save your paragraph in your **Working Portfolio.**

Types of Paragraphs

A **paragraph** is a collection of related sentences dealing with one idea. You can write paragraphs to serve different purposes—to describe, to narrate, to persuade, or to inform. A typical composition requires more than one kind of paragraph to adequately develop its overall theme.

❶ Descriptive Paragraphs

You can use a **descriptive paragraph** to set a scene, to introduce a character, or to create a mood. This kind of paragraph features details that appeal to the five senses—sight, smell, hearing, touch, and taste. In the paragraph below, the writer describes dawn breaking on a farm in the South in 1936.

> **PROFESSIONAL MODEL**
>
> By now it is full glass light, clean, whitening gray, without shadow, and the air is cold, with an odor of pork and damp earth, and the spiring of the roosters has become a commonplace. The whippoorwill has stayed it out long beyond the last ditch, whispering almost visible from among the distinct gray leaves of a near tree; now he is sunk and gone, and the air is brisk with small and skillful birds who whistle, and beat metals with light hammers; and a dog comes casually though somewhat stiffly round the corner of the house, and smoke sprowls up from chimneys: and the light still whitens . . .
>
> —James Agee, *Let Us Now Praise Famous Men*

SIGHT
TOUCH
SMELL

HEARING

❷ Narrative Paragraphs

You can use a **narrative paragraph** to tell a story or relate events as they occurred in time. In both fiction and nonfiction, narrative paragraphs help writers move stories along, present historical events, give accounts of people's lives, explain chains of events, and so on. They answer the questions *who, what, when, where,* and *how.* In the paragraph at the top of the next page, the writer tells about her move from Texas to Ohio.

I brought cassettes of Mexican and Latin American music with us when we drove to Ohio. I'd roll the car window down and turn the volume up, taking a certain delight in sending such sounds like mischievous imps across fields and into trees. Broadcasting my culture, if you will.

—Pat Mora, "The Border: A Glare of Truth"

Tells **who, when, and where.**

Describes **what** happened.

Sums up the event by stating the purpose of the action.

❸ Persuasive Paragraphs

A **persuasive paragraph** presents an argument. Writers use persuasive paragraphs to convince readers that certain opinions, points of view, or courses of action are correct. These paragraphs appeal to emotion or reason or both, supporting the appeal with anecdotes, examples, or facts and statistics. You can use persuasive paragraphs in a variety of types of writing, from personal letters to essays to job applications.

I don't think we should allow snowmobiling in our national parks. The purpose of visiting a national park is to enjoy nature, see animals in their home environment, and get away from the pollution and people in cities. With snowmobiles polluting the air with carbon monoxide and frightening the animals with their engine noise, it seems to me the national parks could not serve their intended purpose.

States opinion.

Appeals to reason by stating parks' purpose and explaining how the use of snowmobiles undercuts the purpose.

PRACTICE A Convincing the Reader

Write a paragraph that would persuade your classmates to take an interest in an activity or a club that you find enjoyable.

❹ Informative/Expository Paragraphs

An **informative,** or **expository, paragraph** presents or explains facts and ideas. Writers use informative paragraphs to define terms, to give directions, to explain processes, and to tell how things work. You can use them in various kinds of writing, from history papers to test answers to game instructions.

PROFESSIONAL MODEL

Historically, clutter is a modern phenomenon, born of the industrial revolution. There was a time when goods were limited; and the rich and fashionable were few in number and objects were precious and hard to come by. Clutter is a 19th-century esthetic; it came with the abundance of products combined with the rise of purchasing power, and the shifts in society that required manifestations of status and style.

> Provides background facts.

> Explains how the subject—clutter—came into being.

—Ada Louise Huxtable, "Modern-Life Battle: Conquering Clutter"

PRACTICE B Writing to Fit Type

Write a descriptive paragraph about the picture shown here. Then write a narrative paragraph in which you tell a story about what is taking place in the picture. How do the details in the two paragraphs differ? How did you approach the writing of each paragraph? Did writing either paragraph help you see the photo with a new perspective?

Creating Unity

Building a paragraph involves presenting a main idea and developing it with supporting ideas and details. When every sentence in the paragraph relates to the main idea, the paragraph has **unity.**

❶ The Main Idea

The **main idea** of a paragraph is a single thought that serves as the paragraph's focus. All the sentences in the paragraph relate to this idea.

Supporting the Main Idea

If you don't support your main idea, readers may not take your idea seriously and may not even understand what you are trying to say. To develop the main idea of a paragraph clearly, you need to include details that support or explain the main idea. **Supporting details** include sensory details, examples, anecdotes, facts and statistics, and quotations.

For more about using supporting details, see pp. 358–363.

STUDENT MODEL

DRAFT

Many types of roller coasters exist in the world. Amusement parks try to offer a variety. Some parks specialize in roller coasters.

> The writer does not provide information to support any of the statements made. In fact, each sentence could be a main idea that begins a new paragraph.

REVISION

Many types of roller coasters exist in the world. The twister, the corkscrew, the stand-up, the double out and back, the mega looper, and the hypercoaster are just a few examples. The thrill elements in these coasters are implied by their names. To meet public demand, each amusement park tries to offer more than one type.

> One main idea is developed with supporting details.

Deleting Stray Ideas and Details

Stray ideas and details—those unrelated to the paragraph's main idea—need to be edited out of the paragraph.

STUDENT MODEL

Most people in my community remember the blizzard of '99 for the huge snowfall we had, but I remember it for the fire at my neighbor's house. I was sitting cozily at home, watching a hockey game on TV. Hockey is one of my favorite sports, and I am on the team at school. Suddenly I heard a loud crack outside and saw a blinding flash, followed by screams. I rushed outdoors and saw my next-door neighbor's yellow house on fire. Just last year there had been another fire on our block. Instantly, I raced back into my house and called 911.

> **MAIN IDEA**

> **UNRELATED DETAILS**

❷ The Topic Sentence

A **topic sentence** is a direct statement of the main idea of a paragraph. Although a topic sentence can appear anywhere in a paragraph, it is often located at or near the beginning.

LITERARY MODEL

On Christmas Eve I saw that my mother had outdone herself in creating a strange menu. She was pulling black veins out of the backs of fleshy prawns. The kitchen was littered with appalling mounds of raw food: A slimy rock cod with bulging fish eyes that pleaded not to be thrown into a pan of hot oil. Tofu, which looked like stacked wedges of rubbery white sponges. A bowl soaking dried fungus back to life. A plate of squid, their backs crisscrossed with knife markings so they resembled bicycle tires.

—Amy Tan, "Fish Cheeks"

> **TOPIC SENTENCE**

> **SUPPORTING DETAILS**

Developing the Topic Sentence

The topic sentence clearly identifies the main idea of a paragraph and sometimes gives the reader a sense of the writer's attitude toward his or her subject. Here are several methods you can use to create a topic sentence:

- Think of the main idea as a problem and state it as clearly as possible in one sentence.

  One problem for the beginning guitar student is deciding what type of guitar to play.

- Write a general statement and revise it by restating the topic in a more specific way.

  GENERAL STATEMENT: Some types of guitars are easier to learn than others.

  SPECIFIC RESTATEMENT: The electric guitar is easier to learn than the acoustic guitar.

- State the main idea in the form of a question.

  What is the best type of guitar for a beginning student?

Using an Implied Topic Sentence

Sometimes a paragraph's main idea is **implied.** The paragraph's sentences relate to an idea that is not directly stated but becomes apparent as the paragraph is read.

LITERARY MODEL

> We had risen before dawn, as on every day. We had received the black coffee, the ration of bread. We were about to set out for the yard as usual. The head of the block arrived, running.
>
> —Elie Wiesel, *Night*

In this model, the implied main idea is that all days were exactly the same until one particular day. This is not stated directly in a sentence like "Every day was alike until this day." Instead, the author gives examples so that the reader draws the conclusion.

PRACTICE Achieving Unity

From your 🗔 **Working Portfolio,** take out the paragraph you wrote for the **Write Away** on page 323. Revise the paragraph as needed so that it has a topic sentence and clearly defined supporting details.

Organization and Coherence

In addition to a main idea and supporting details, a paragraph needs a pattern of organization. A paragraph has **coherence** when it is organized clearly and there is a logical flow from each sentence to the next. Five types of paragraph organization are described below.

❶ Order of Degree

Use **order of degree** to present ideas of unequal importance, familiarity, or complexity or to show a ranking of people, places, things, or events.

> **PROFESSIONAL MODEL**
>
> If a fire starts in your house, the most important thing to remember is this: Don't panic. First, everyone should prepare to leave the house immediately. If you see smoke, get down and crawl toward the nearest door. Before going out the door, feel the door to see if it's hot. The least important thing to do is to try to save your belongings.

TRANSITIONAL WORDS AND PHRASES that help clarify relationships between ideas of unequal importance: *first, second, best, worst, more important, most important, to a lesser degree*

❷ Sequential Order

Use **sequential order** to tell a story or present a series of events. This pattern includes chronological order, in which events are arranged as they occur in time, and step-by-step order, in which the stages of a process or procedure are described.

From disappointment, I gradually ascended the emotional ladder to haughty indignation, and finally to that state of stubbornness where the mind is locked like the jaws of an enraged bulldog.

—Maya Angelou, *I Know Why the Caged Bird Sings*

TRANSITIONAL WORDS AND PHRASES used to show sequential relationships: *after, before, then, next, later, finally, at the beginning, at the same time, first . . . second . . . third . . .* and so on

❸ Cause-and-Effect Order

Use **cause-and-effect order** to show relationships between events and their results. You can use the topic sentence to state a cause and then provide details about its effects, or you can state an effect in the topic sentence and then discuss its causes. Sometimes you may want to present a series of causes and effects in a single paragraph.

Office buildings with poor air circulation are a high-risk environment because cold viruses can't escape. What's worse, low humidity dries the mucous membranes that normally trap and dispose of viral invaders. For the same reason, airplanes are another likely place to pick up cold germs.

—Julia Califano, "15 Ways to Beat a Cold"

TRANSITIONAL WORDS AND PHRASES that show cause and effect: *as a result, because, therefore, since, thus, so, for, if . . . then*

❹ Spatial Order

Use **spatial order** to present details in a way that reflects their positions in space. This pattern allows the reader to picture a scene as it would appear to someone panning it with a camera. You might introduce details as they are arranged from right to left, from near to far, or from top to bottom.

> **LITERARY MODEL**
>
> We explored, finding a wooded lane which led down to a huge inland estuary where it was possible to fish for flounder from the old sea wall. In the other direction, a sandy right-of-way led past the church and over the golf links and the dunes to another beach—a wide and empty shore where the ebb tide took the ocean out half a mile or more.
>
> —Rosamunde Pilcher, "Lalla"

TRANSITIONAL WORDS AND PHRASES that show spatial relationships:
above, below, behind, beneath, beside, by, in front of, in back of, to the right of, near, on top of, inside, over, under, outside, throughout

PRACTICE A Organizing Details in Space

Imagine yourself standing somewhere in the scene pictured below. Write a paragraph describing the scene from your point of view, using spatial order to present the details.

❺ Comparison-Contrast Order

Use **comparison-contrast order** to present the similarities and differences between people, places, things, or events.

STUDENT MODEL

Many people think downhill skiing and cross-country skiing are similar sports. While both require specialized ski gear, athletic fitness, and endurance, each requires different skills. A downhill skier travels at high speed down steep slopes and must respond quickly to sudden turns and obstacles. The skier works with gravity. In contrast, a cross-country skier travels over fairly level trails at a relatively slow speed, striving to maintain a steady pace. The skier works against gravity.

TRANSITIONAL WORDS AND PHRASES that show comparisons and contrasts: *also, like, similarly, in the same way* (to indicate similarities); *in contrast, but, yet, on the other hand, even though, however* (to indicate differences)

The five organizational patterns listed above are also used to organize whole compositions.

PRACTICE B Writing to Compare and Contrast

Write a paragraph in which you compare and contrast the two cars shown below. Begin the paragraph with a topic sentence that clearly states your main idea.

Student Help Desk

Paragraphs at a Glance

| Main Idea | + | Unity (related details) | + | Coherence (organization) | = | Strong Paragraph |

Paragraph Types

What's Your Type ?

Type	Uses
Descriptive	Paints a colorful, exact picture of a person, place, or thing by including details that appeal to the five senses
Narrative	Tells a story or presents a sequence of events with a beginning, middle, and end
Persuasive	Appeals to reason, emotion, or both in an attempt to convince the reader to think or act in a particular way
Informative/ expository	Defines terms, gives directions, or explains how things work by presenting facts or ideas

What's Your Point ?

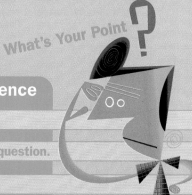

Ways to Write a Topic Sentence

State your topic directly.

State your main idea in the form of a question.

State your main idea as a problem.

Revise a general statement to be more specific.

Achieving Coherence

What's Your Plan?

Pattern of Organization	How It Looks in Writing	Transitional Words and Phrases
Degree	Ideas or things ranked according to importance, familiarity, size, or complexity	first, second, best, worst, more important, most important, to a lesser degree
Sequential	Details arranged in the order they occur from first to last	after, before, then, next, later, finally, at the beginning, at the same time, first . . . second . . . third . . .
Cause-and-effect	Details arranged to show relationships between events and their results	as a result, because, therefore, since, thus, so, for, if . . . then
Spatial	Details arranged according to their locations in space, usually with a reference point provided	above, below, behind, beneath, beside, by, in front of, in back of, to the right of, near, on top of, inside, over, under, outside, throughout
Comparison-contrast	Details arranged to show similarities and differences between ideas or things	also, like, similarly, in the same way, in contrast, but, yet, on the other hand, even though, however

The Bottom Line

Checklist for Creating Paragraphs

Have I . . .

____ presented a main idea or focus?

____ included a topic sentence if one is necessary?

____ used a logical pattern of organization?

____ included enough details to support the main idea?

____ deleted all stray details?

____ used transitional words and phrases to connect ideas?

Power Words
Vocabulary for Precise Writing

Fighting Words

The next time you're looking for a way to describe a fight scene in a movie or on TV, try some of these stouthearted words.

A Long Time Ago, in a Galaxy Far, Far Away

The light saber used in that far-off galaxy is much like weapons from our own past. In addition to the **saber,** there were the **broadsword,** the **backsword,** the **scimitar,** the **rapier,** the **halberd,** the **falchion,** and the **claymore.**

In the Hands of a Master

What action! Obi-Wan **brandishes** his light saber. Darth Maul **flourishes** his double-sided one. They **wield** and **ply** their weapons with abandon; they **lunge, lash out, thrust,** and **have at** each other in an attempt to **dismember, obliterate, pulverize,** and **extirpate** each other—to generally **do each other in.**

The Blade Daunts Not the Pure of Heart

"Daunts not"—doesn't that sound wonderful? To **daunt** is to lessen the courage of. So if you are **dauntless,** you are **fearless, courageous, brave, intrepid, valiant, valorous, resolute, mettlesome,** and **stouthearted.** (You may also be **plucky, spunky, feisty,** or **gutsy.**) And if you are **daunted,** you are **dismayed, discouraged,** or **fazed;** you are **intimidated, menaced,** or **cowed**—or worse!

> ▷ **Your Turn** Drawing Your Sword
>
> Sketch a fight scene for a movie or TV show, and write stage directions for the actors to follow. Use some of the words above—and other words you find—to describe fighting with traditional weapons or bare hands.

Developing Compositions

COMPOSITIONS

What's It All About?

Imagine you get a phone call from the editor of a movie review magazine. "I want you to review a popular movie like *Raiders of the Lost Ark* or *The Phantom Menace*," she says.

"Here's what I need you to do," she continues. "Describe the characters, setting, and plot. Then explain what you liked and didn't like about the movie. Oh, I almost forgot—you've got to fit all this into one paragraph."

How can you possibly include so many ideas in a single paragraph? To be able to cover that much information, you need a longer form—a composition—in which you can fully explain your ideas. This chapter will show you how to develop a composition.

Write Away: One Paragraph at a Time
Think of a movie or television show that you might like to review. Choose one of the elements described above—plot, characters, or setting—and write a paragraph that fully describes it. Save your writing in your ▱ **Working Portfolio.**

Structure of a Composition

❶ From Paragraphs to Compositions

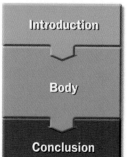

A **composition** is a group of paragraphs dealing with one main idea. A good composition has the same characteristics as a well-written paragraph:

- a main idea
- a variety of details that develop and support the main idea
- a logical flow from each part to the next

A composition has three main sections: the introduction, the body, and the conclusion. In this chapter you will see how to write a basic expository composition that explains an idea. For help with more specific kinds of compositions, such as persuasive essays, go to the Writing Workshops.

❷ Parts of a Composition

Adventure Riders on the Alaska Range

Snowboarding over a cliff, flying off the edge of a mountain in a kayak, biking over remote ice fields—these sound like situations any sane person would try to avoid. Lately, though, more and more people are drawn to these death-defying acts, known as extreme sports. Roman Dial, Carl Tobin, and Paul Adkins are just such people. These three adventure riders endured a grueling seven-week, 775-mile bike trip along the Alaska Range. **They took biking to the extreme by doing it in remote locations and under hazardous conditions.**

> **INTRODUCTION**
>
> This section presents the main idea, grabs the reader's attention, and sets the tone.

> The introduction includes a **thesis statement,** which states the main idea of the composition.

The three men often faced terrain that was dangerous and hostile. Thick alder brush snagged their bikes and snapped in their eyes. Icy rivers contained quicksand and deadly currents. The photographer Bill Hatcher, who joined the group from time to time to record their journey, fell into a deep crack in a glacier and nearly died. He was saved only because his bike broke his fall.

Encounters with animal life added spice to the trip. The trio put up with swarms of bloodthirsty mosquitoes that made sleeping almost impossible. However, the grizzly bears were worse. The bikers crossed paths with nine grizzlies in all. During their fourth week out, one grizzly followed them for about half an hour. The aching bikers were forced to pick up their pace in order to get away from the curious and perhaps hungry bear.

Crossing rivers was the most hazardous part of the journey. The group made several crossings, braving icy water that came as high as their chests. According to Roman Dial, adventure seekers in Alaska all too often drown while crossing rivers because they panic in the fast-moving current. For Carl Tobin, who had a bad knee, fording rivers was especially perilous. Fortunately, Carl doesn't panic easily.

Extreme bikers take an everyday recreation to its ultimate limits—riding in places and over surfaces that don't invite the average cyclist. Clearly, Roman Dial, Carl Tobin, and Paul Adkins are not average, but what are they? Brave? Crazy? Why would anyone take such a trip? Adkins offers this explanation: "You get into a special zone when you ride a bike here. You smile, look around, and say, 'This is it!'"

Adapted from Roman Dial, "A Wild Ride," *National Geographic,* May 1997.

BODY

Each of the paragraphs in the body develops a different aspect of the thesis statement.

In each body paragraph a **topic sentence** states the paragraph's main idea. The other sentences in the paragraph support the topic sentence.

CONCLUSION

This section sums up the ideas presented in the composition.

Thesis and Introduction

LESSON 2

❶ Crafting a Thesis Statement

Just as a topic sentence states the main idea of a paragraph, a **thesis statement** states the main idea of a composition. A thesis statement is usually a single sentence, but it may be two or more sentences. It is almost always located in the introduction.

Thesis Statements	
A successful thesis statement SHOULD	**A thesis statement SHOULD NOT**
• tell the subject of your composition	• be simply a statement of fact: "Mount Everest is popular with mountain climbers."
• show your point of view on the subject	• be stated as an announcement: "In this paper I will show that . . ."
• be a statement that can be supported	• be an opinion that can't be supported with facts: "Mountain climbing is the greatest sport."

The following thesis statements express different ideas about mountain climbing. Each statement is successful because it clearly states a subject and can be supported with facts and reasons.

Example 1: Many climbers have perished on Mount Everest as a result of poor planning, lack of experience, and bad weather.

Example 2: Different climbing routes on a mountain require different kinds of climbing skills.

Example 3: To prepare for a trip up Mount Everest, climbers need money, training, and experienced guides.

Before you write a thesis statement, you need to choose a subject and to conduct some preliminary research on the subject. Then follow the steps below to craft the thesis statement.

> **Here's How Crafting a Thesis Statement**
>
> 1. Study your research notes on your subject.
> 2. Decide what interests you most and use that as your angle of approach to the subject.
> 3. Write one or more sentences that introduce your subject and express your approach to it.

CHAPTER 14

As you draft your composition, you may discover new ideas that hadn't occurred to you before. Adjust your thesis statement so that it continues to reflect your main idea.

PRACTICE A Writing a Thesis Statement

Listed below are four draft thesis statements. Identify each one as strong or weak, giving a reason for your opinion. Rewrite the weak ones.

1. Many states have a maximum highway speed limit of 65 miles per hour.
2. Highway speed limits improve the safety and efficiency of motor vehicles.
3. Speed limits are just one of several ways to keep drivers safe.
4. In this paper, I will explain why highway speed limits should be raised.

❷ Writing an Introduction

The first paragraph of a composition is the **introduction.** This section presents the thesis statement (which may appear anywhere in the introduction) and sets the tone for the composition. Although the introduction comes first, you don't have to write it first. You may draft your introduction at any time, even last.

The introductory paragraph should grab the reader's attention and make him or her want to continue reading. Here are some techniques that will help you capture your audience's attention.

Attention-Grabbing Techniques

- Open with a lively description.
- Begin with an interesting or startling fact.
- Use a quotation.
- Ask a question.
- Address the reader directly.
- State a strong opinion.
- Present a short anecdote.

Three of these techniques for getting the reader's attention are modeled on the next page.

For more examples of attention-grabbing techniques, see p. 352.

Open with a Lively Description

A lively description of an event or a person will immediately capture the attention of your readers.

> **PROFESSIONAL MODEL**
>
> On a cloudy August afternoon, the cry goes up for a fishing party. We dig for worms, rustle through the barn for a net, check the hooks and leaders, grab a few poles, and soon we're off in the old red pickup, headed down to the trout stream through a narrow back road that is closed in winter.
>
> —Christopher Kimball, "A Fisher of Children"

Begin with a Startling Fact

An unusual or startling fact can surprise or shock your readers, making them want to continue reading.

> **PROFESSIONAL MODEL**
>
> Every year in the Danish town of Silkeborg, thousands of visitors file past the face of a murder victim. No one will ever know his name. It is enough to know that 2,000 years ago he was as human as ourselves.
>
> —Maurice Shadbolt, "Who Killed the Bog Men of Denmark? And Why?"

Use a Quotation

A quotation in an introduction can create a sense of informality, add humor, or present a vivid image.

> **PROFESSIONAL MODEL**
>
> "A flute," wrote an early nineteenth-century British critic, "is a musical weed which springs up everywhere."
>
> —Nancy Toff, *The Flute Book*

PRACTICE B Revising an Introduction

Find a composition in your 🗄 **Working Portfolio** and revise its introduction, using an attention-grabbing technique.

Body of a Composition

LESSON 3

❶ Writing the Body

The paragraphs that develop the thesis statement make up the **body** of a composition. The body can range in length from several paragraphs to many pages, depending on the writer's purpose and the amount of detail the writer includes.

In the body of a composition, you carry out the main purpose of the composition. Your purpose might be to explain a process, to support an opinion, to develop a definition, to present an argument, to present research, or to analyze a situation.

What Should Body Paragraphs Do?	
Focus on a single idea	Each paragraph should have a strong topic sentence that develops the idea stated in the thesis statement.
Support the thesis	Just as the body of a paragraph supports the topic sentence, the body of a composition should support the thesis statement.
Reflect a logical pattern of organization	The paragraphs should be clearly organized. Common types of organization include sequential order, cause-and-effect order, and comparison-contrast order.

For more information about topic sentences and patterns of organization, see pp. 328–333.

Use facts, reasons, and statistics—not opinions—to support your thesis statement.

❷ Paragraphing

Have you ever gotten carried away and forgotten to separate your writing into paragraphs? The result is one long string of sentences that may go on for pages. A reader faced with one endless paragraph doesn't know where one idea ends and another begins.

Paragraphing, or separating the body of your composition into paragraphs, makes your writing easier for readers to follow and helps you develop each idea clearly.

For more about paragraphs, see pp. 302–303 and 323–335.

COMPOSITIONS

When to Create Paragraphs

Use the list below to help you decide where to make paragraph breaks in your compositions.

When to Make a Break

Start a new paragraph when you come to

- the end of your introduction
- a new idea or set of facts
- a change of emphasis or mood
- a change of time or setting
- the conclusion of your composition
- a change of speaker (in dialogue)

In the model below, the writer, an airplane pilot in East Africa during the early 1930s, describes a flight from Nairobi to Nungwe. The paragraph break signals a shift in the setting. Without this break, the passage would be difficult to read.

LITERARY MODEL

Ahead of me lies a land that is unknown to the rest of the world and only vaguely known to the African—a strange mixture of grasslands, scrub, desert sand like long waves of the southern ocean. Forest, still water, and age-old mountains, stark and grim like mountains of the moon. Salt lakes, and rivers that have no water. Swamps. Badlands. Land without life. Land teeming with life—all of the dusty past, all of the future.

> In this paragraph the writer describes the landscape of Africa.

The air takes me into its realm. Night envelops me entirely, leaving me out of touch with the earth, leaving me within this small moving world of my own, living in space with the stars.

> When the writer begins to describe her immediate surroundings, she begins a new paragraph.

—Beryl Markham, *West with the Night*

PRACTICE   Analyzing Paragraph Breaks

Cut out an interesting magazine article and paste it on a sheet of paper. Study the paragraph breaks in the article. For each break, write down why you think the writer started a new paragraph.

Conclusion

❶ Writing a Conclusion

A composition doesn't just come to an end; it comes to a conclusion. In the **conclusion** of a composition—usually the final paragraph—you sum up the ideas you have developed and leave the reader with a firm understanding of your position on the subject.

Conclusions

A successful conclusion SHOULD	A conclusion SHOULD NOT
• wrap up the ideas you have developed	• introduce new facts, ideas, or arguments
• follow logically from the rest of your composition	• change the point of view by introducing the pronoun *I*
• leave the reader with something to think about	• simply repeat the introduction

Some types of writing, such as persuasive essays, need specific kinds of conclusions. See the Writing Workshop "Persuasive Essay" for more information.

❷ Techniques for Wrapping Up

Although all good conclusions "wrap things up," they do so in a variety of ways. Here are some techniques you might try.

Techniques for Concluding

- **Review and summarize** the main points you have presented in the body.

- **Restate the central idea** in a new way, reflecting the deeper understanding you have developed in the paper.

- **Make a generalization** about the information you have presented, relating the topic to a larger context.

- **Make a prediction** based on your understanding of the topic.

- **End with a quotation** from someone discussed in the composition.

- **End with a call for action,** urging the reader to do something to solve a problem.

- **End with a question** that leaves the reader with something to think about.

Shown below are two different techniques for concluding the composition "Adventure Riders on the Alaska Range" on pages 338–339. Which technique do you think works best?

End with a Question

Asking a question invites the reader to think about the ideas you have written about.

> **PROFESSIONAL MODEL**
>
> Reading about extreme biking is a great deal easier than living through it. You might wonder what motivated these riders to take the risks they did. Was it excitement? curiosity? pride? a complicated mixture of several motives? What would it take to get you out on that biking trail?

Make a Prediction

Making a prediction leaves the reader with something to think about and can create a feeling of hope or suspense.

> **PROFESSIONAL MODEL**
>
> You'd think that escaping a hungry grizzly bear would be enough adventure for one lifetime, but whatever made these three men bike the Alaska Range probably hasn't been satisfied yet. People who thrive on facing challenges don't usually stop once they've achieved a goal. They might rest for a while, but eventually the bug will bite them again. Right now, Roman Dial is probably wondering if it's possible to bike to the top of Mount Kilimanjaro.

For more examples of conclusions, see p. 352.

PRACTICE Writing an Alternative Conclusion

Write an alternative conclusion for "Adventure Riders on the Alaska Range" or for another published essay. Exchange conclusions with a partner and compare the techniques you used.

Unity

Understanding Unity

Unity in a composition is similar to unity in a paragraph. When a composition displays **unity,** all of its paragraphs support the thesis statement.

Use an outline of the thesis statement and topic sentences in your composition to help you check for unity. By looking at the following outline of "Adventure Riders . . . ," you can see that the topic sentences support and develop the thesis statement.

I. Thesis Statement: They took biking to the extreme by doing it in remote locations and under hazardous conditions.

  A. Topic Sentence: The three men often faced terrain that was dangerous and hostile.

  B. Topic Sentence: Encounters with animal life added spice to the trip.

  C. Topic Sentence: Crossing rivers was the most hazardous part of the journey.

The conclusion of a composition should also relate to and logically support the main idea. Make sure that your conclusion doesn't bring up any new ideas.

Here's How **Checking for Unity**

- Does each body paragraph support the thesis statement?
- Is each topic sentence supported by the other sentences in the paragraph?
- Does the conclusion relate to the main idea?
- Do any sentences or paragraphs interrupt the flow of the composition?

For information about creating unity in paragraphs, see pp. 327–329.

You may not be able to find places in your composition for all of your ideas. Be willing to let go of ideas that don't fit.

PRACTICE Creating Unity

Check for unity in a composition in your 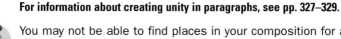 **Working Portfolio.** If necessary, rewrite the paragraphs of your composition to ensure logical progression (order) and support of your ideas.

COMPOSITIONS

Coherence

Like a paragraph, a composition has **coherence** when it is logically organized and when the ideas in it flow smoothly. Use patterns of organization, word chains, and transitional words and phrases to link ideas and achieve coherence in your compositions.

❶ Patterns of Organization

Use patterns of organization to give shape to your compositions. The same patterns you use to achieve coherence in paragraphs can also be used in compositions. Below are four examples.

Comparison-Contrast Order

Present information about subjects by describing their similarities and differences. There are two basic patterns you can use.

Subject by Subject	Feature by Feature
Subject A	Feature 1
Feature 1	Subject A
Feature 2	Subject B
Subject B	Feature 2
Feature 1	Subject A
Feature 2	Subject B

Order of Degree

Arrange ideas according to their importance, usefulness, or familiarity or according to some other quality.

Cause-and-Effect Order

Present information about a problem or an event by discussing its causes or effects. There are two basic patterns.

A Single Cause of Multiple Effects   **A Single Effect with Multiple Causes**

Sequential Order

Present events in the order in which they occur. This works well when you are writing about historical information or when you are describing the steps in a process.

These patterns are only starting points. Sometimes you may need to mix patterns or add a paragraph of background information or description to help your readers better understand your ideas. What's important is to present information in an order that your readers can follow and understand.

For more about patterns of organization, see pp. 330–335.

❷ Word Chains

A **word chain** is a series of words or phrases used to refer to an idea you've already mentioned. Word chains can be used to link ideas within a paragraph and between paragraphs. You can create word chains in the following ways.

- Use **repeated words and phrases** to emphasize images or ideas.
- Use **synonyms and near synonyms** to avoid unwanted repetition.
- Use **pronouns** to avoid unwanted repetition of nouns or noun phrases.

Two types of word chains are highlighted in the model below. One chain connects ideas in both paragraphs. The other connects ideas within the second paragraph. Can you find other word chains in this passage?

> **PROFESSIONAL MODEL**
>
> If you want to know the hardship that Habitat homeowner Meriam Kabonesa has endured, don't look at her face. Look at her hands. Look at her feet. **REPEATED PHRASES**
>
> Like those of most Ugandan women, her hands are calloused from countless hours spent digging **NEAR SYNONYMS** the soil, planting sweet potatoes, peanuts and beans. They're chafed from scrubbing clothes clean with her bare fingers. Her feet are worn from walking long distances while balancing five-gallon containers of water on her head.
>
> —Robin Chenoweth, "Making the Best of Borrowed Time"

Notice in the following model how pronouns link ideas in the two paragraphs by referring to *Mrs. Donovan* in the first paragraph.

LITERARY MODEL

Old **Mrs. Donovan** was a woman who really got around. No matter what was going on in Darrowby—weddings, funerals, house-sales—you'd find the dumpy little figure and walnut face among the spectators, the darting, black-button eyes taking everything in. And always, on the end of its lead, **her** terrier dog.

When I say "old," I'm only guessing, because **she** appeared ageless; **she** seemed to have been around a long time, but **she** could have been anything between fifty-five and seventy-five. **She** certainly had the vitality of a young woman because **she** must have walked vast distances in **her** dedicated quest to keep abreast of events.

—James Herriot, "A Case of Cruelty"

PRONOUNS

❸ Transitional Words and Phrases

Use transitional words and phrases to link ideas in different paragraphs and to indicate how ideas are related. The chart below shows some of the kinds of transitional devices. You are probably using these in your writing already.

Common Transitional Words and Phrases

Time	when, until, first, then, meanwhile, after
Place	below, above, underneath, here, next to
Cause and effect	then, because, as a result, therefore
More information	besides, in addition, furthermore, as well as
Degree	mainly, first, last, primarily, next
Comparison	like, also, too, similarly, in the same way
Contrast	nevertheless, but, on the contrary, unlike

For many more transitional words and phrases, see p. 353.

In the model below, the writer uses time transitions to indicate the sequence of events.

Deep inside the huge limestone cave was a pipe organ made of stalactites and stalagmites. We stood in the middle of the cavern. The giant natural pipe organ was all around us. **When the organist began to play "Shenandoah,"** we heard the beautiful tune ringing from above, from below, and from the most distant corners of the cavern.

After the music died away, the group stood silently for a moment or two, unwilling to break the spell the music had cast. **Then,** slowly and quietly, we began to move on.

> This transition connects events in the second paragraph to events in the first paragraph.

Occasionally you may need more than just a word or phrase to connect paragraphs. Transitional paragraphs are short connecting paragraphs that you can use to remind readers of events described earlier and to prepare readers for the next event.

Here's How **Checking for Coherence**

- Does each idea and paragraph follow logically from the previous one? Do the paragraphs make sense together?
- Are the relationships between ideas and between paragraphs clear?
- Are word chains and transitional devices used where they are needed?

For information about creating coherence in paragraphs, see pp. 330–335.

PRACTICE Revising for Coherence

Find in your **Working Portfolio** the paragraph you wrote for the **Write Away** on page 337. Choose a pattern of organization and rewrite your paragraph, using that pattern. Add transitional words and phrases when necessary.

COMPOSITIONS

Student Help Desk

Compositions at a Glance

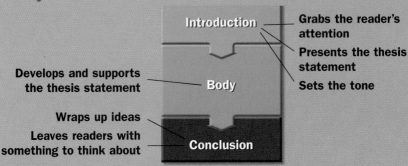

Introduction — Grabs the reader's attention

Presents the thesis statement

Develops and supports the thesis statement — Body

Sets the tone

Wraps up ideas

Leaves readers with something to think about — Conclusion

Introductions Jump Right In!

Ask a question	Why do people take on challenges that seem impossible?
Address readers directly	If you're like most people, you don't want to participate in a sport that could lead to terrible injury or even death.
State a strong opinion	Extreme-sport competitors should be recognized for their athletic ability and not just for their daring.

You can also begin with an interesting or startling fact, a lively description, a quotation, or a short anecdote. (See p. 342.)

Conclusions Out with a Bang

Review and summarize	You don't have to be a born risk taker, then, to become an extreme athlete.
Restate the central idea	Planning ahead and using safety measures are more than just good ideas for extreme athletes. These precautions can mean the difference between life and death.
Make a generalization	Extreme athletes pursue sports that are unusual, surprising, and sometimes downright weird. Clearly, these athletes are creative people.
End with a call to action	Find the extreme sport that fits your personality and go for it!

You can also end with a quotation, a prediction, or a question. (See p. 346.)

More Transitional Expressions

Go with the Flow

Time	finally, next, during, while, last, soon, at the beginning, at the same time, the next day, before, always, simultaneously
Place	behind, in back of, in front of, over, under, around, beneath, down, up, there, on top of, through, in the center, inside, outside
Cause and effect	so, for, thus, consequently, for this reason, accordingly, since, if . . . then, due to, owing to, although, so that
Examples	as, like, such as, in particular, to illustrate, for instance, for example, that is, namely
More information	in addition, besides, furthermore, moreover, also, as well as
Emphasis	indeed, in fact, certainly
Degree	first, second, mainly, best, worst, least important, less important, more important, most important
Comparison	as, than, similarly, likewise, neither . . . nor, either . . . or, in the same way, also, like
Contrast	yet, however, unlike, instead, nevertheless, but, on the other hand, on the contrary, in contrast

The Bottom Line

Checklist for Developing Compositions

Have I . . .

____ grabbed the reader's attention and set the tone for the essay in the introduction?

____ written a thesis statement that clearly describes my subject and my approach to it?

____ created logical paragraph breaks?

____ developed and supported my thesis statement in the body paragraphs?

____ successfully wrapped up my ideas in the conclusion?

____ organized my ideas clearly?

____ used transitional devices and word chains where necessary?

Power Words
Vocabulary for Precise Writing

swift

career

Words in a Hurry

Are you always in a hurry? It doesn't take long to find words you can use to describe speed.

Faster Than a Speeding Bullet

There are adjectives aplenty to describe someone moving fast: **swift, speedy, quick, rapid, hasty, hurried, reckless, moving at breakneck speed** (hmm, wonder where that came from?), and more.

There are some fancier adjectives as well: **fleet, mercurial, precipitate, precipitous.** Someone can move with **dispatch,** with **alacrity,** or with **celerity.** Want some fancy verbs? A speeding car **careers** down a street, **careens** around corners, **hurtles** through an intersection (and is stopped by the police).

So What's the Rush?

A **sluggish** snail moves at a **deliberate, cautious** speed (indeed, as we say, at a **snail's pace**). **Leisurely** and **unhurried,** it slimes its way through the garden. We too can take our time. We **amble** down a path, **inch** our way along an unlit corridor. We **lumber** and **shamble, plod** and **slog** and **trudge, saunter** and **stroll.** No speeding tickets here!

amble

▷ **Your Turn** Fast Charades

With a partner, quickly list verbs that refer to rapid movement on foot. Use a thesaurus to find more, and look up any you don't know. Take turns acting out your words in front of the class. Have your classmates guess the words.

plod

trudge

Elaboration

What's the Danger?

What would you do if you saw this road sign? Look up? Slow down? Turn around? The sign could mean many different things: rocks falling from above, a slippery bridge ahead, or trucks speeding out of a hidden drive. Without more information, you hardly know what to do to avoid the danger.

The addition of relevant information, or **elaboration,** would make the sign clear. As a writer, you need to make all your signals to the reader clear from the start.

Write Away: Please, Remain Calm!
Talk to a partner about a real or an imaginary escape from danger in an ordinary place. Write a paragraph describing the event and save it in your **Working Portfolio.**

The Uses of Elaboration

❶ Why Elaborate?

Look at the one-sentence draft shown below. What questions do you have? You might want to know what kind of trouble the student was in and how the situation turned out. Notice how the writer adds details and explanations in the revision that elaborate the sentence and answer those questions.

STUDENT MODEL

DRAFT

I thought I was in big trouble at school.

REVISION

I thought I was in big trouble at school. Because I couldn't find my calculator, I was about to fail my math final. I rummaged frantically in my backpack. Then I remembered seeing my calculator on the kitchen counter at home. Nervously I sat down to the test. Reaching into my jacket pocket to pull out a pencil, I found my calculator instead!

❷ When to Elaborate

You need to elaborate whenever you answer *no* to any of these questions:

- Have you developed characters, scenes, and actions completely?
- Have you made your descriptions concrete and believable?
- Have you expressed opinions convincingly?
- Have you supported statements with reasons and evidence?
- Have you explained the meaning of unfamiliar terms and ideas?
- Have you illustrated information that is hard to describe in words?

J.B. Handelsman

"It's not enough to write 'Megabucks' on your return, Mr. Clacton. You're supposed to tell us how many."

©The New Yorker Collection 1998
J.B. Handelsman.

❸ Ways to Elaborate

In the passage below, the writer uses several elaboration techniques to explain how an eye scan can replace the identification number typically used for verification by banks.

PROFESSIONAL MODEL

The iris can serve as a human bar code, its unique features captured and translated into a biological personal identification number (PIN). Iris scanning is just one technology in the burgeoning field known as biometrics. The word "biometrics" originally meant the statistical study of biological variation. However, the term now also refers to technologies that analyze human traits for security purposes.

SIMILE

ANALOGY

EXAMPLE

DEFINITION

—Corinna Wu, "Private Eyes"

Following are several of the ways you can elaborate your own writing.

Elaboration Techniques

Techniques	Purposes
Sensory details; specific details; anecdotes	Make descriptions concrete and believable
Similes and metaphors	Compare what you're describing to something your readers already know
Definitions; analogies; examples; anecdotes; facts and statistics	Clarify meaning and explain
Reasons; expert testimony; facts and statistics	Support an opinion or argument
Graphic images; diagrams; charts and graphs	Clarify or illustrate information

PRACTICE Elaborating Sentences

Elaborate the following sentences using any of the techniques described above.

• Tofu (is/is not) my favorite food.

• The woman spoke to her neighbors.

• A boy answered the telephone.

ELABORATION

Elaborating to Describe

LESSON 2

① Sensory Details

In descriptive writing, always choose words that *show* rather than *tell*. For instance, instead of saying that the sky was cloudy, describe the clouds. Use **sensory details**, that is, words that show your reader how the scene is experienced through the senses. Notice how sensory details elaborate the following descriptions.

Version 1: **Tall** clouds **floated** across the sky.

Version 2: **Black** clouds **raced** across the sky.

Version 3: **Peach-colored** clouds **arched** across the sky.

You can go beyond single words, such as verbs and adjectives, to longer expressions that elaborate the whole idea.

Version 4: Peach-colored clouds arched across the sky **above the dingy town.** All was quiet. A **low, black car with smoked windows** slunk **through the dirt streets,** its tires raising **pillars of dust.**

Notice how the writer of the following description uses sense impressions to show exactly how things feel and taste and look.

> **PROFESSIONAL MODEL**
>
> The biscuits are large and shapeless, not cut round, and are pale, not tanned, and are dusty with flour. They taste of flour and soda and damp salt and fill the mouth stickily. They are better with butter, and still better with butter and jam. The butter is pallid, soft, and unsalted, about the texture of cold-cream; it seems to taste delicately of wood and wet cloth; and it tastes 'weak.' The jam is loose, of little berries, full of light raspings of the tongue; it tastes a deep sweet purple tepidly watered, with a very faint sheen of a sourness as of iron.
>
> —James Agee, *Let Us Now Praise Famous Men*

SIGHT

TASTE

TOUCH

To make a description powerful, try to find words to describe smell, taste, and touch, as well as the more common sight and sound.

CHAPTER 15

❷ Similes and Metaphors

One way to elaborate is to create similes and metaphors. Use these tools to express a new idea or to describe something familiar in a new way.

Similes	
Similes compare two things using either *like* or *as*.	Loneliness can strangulate like jungle vines. —Cathy Song, "Lost Sister"
Metaphors	
Metaphors describe one thing in terms of another, without using *like* or *as*.	. . . that body too small to contain the hundred balloons of happiness. —Sandra Cisneros, "Salvador Late or Early"

In the following paragraph, notice the way the writers use a simile and a metaphor to sum up their description of physical details.

> **LITERARY MODEL**
>
> We woke early, shivering and coated with dust that had blown up through the knotholes and in through the slits around the doorway. During the night Mama had unpacked all our clothes and heaped them on our beds for warmth. Now our cubicle looked as if a great laundry bag had exploded and then been sprayed with fine dust. **SIMILE** A skin of sand covered the floor. I looked over **METAPHOR** Mama's shoulder at [my brother] Kiyo, on top of his fat mattress, buried under jeans and overcoats and sweaters. His eyebrows were gray, and he was starting to giggle.
>
> —Jeanne Wakatsuki Houston and James D. Houston,
> *Farewell to Manzanar*

PRACTICE Elaborating Descriptions

Find in your 🗂 **Working Portfolio** the paragraph you wrote for the **Write Away** on page 355. Where could you add more details or fresh comparisons? Revise the paragraph using these elaboration techniques.

Elaborating to Explain

❶ Definitions

Part of elaboration is defining unfamiliar words for your readers. The simplest way to define a word is to explain its meaning in the sentence in which you use it, that is, in context.

> **LITERARY MODEL**
>
> Astronomers also speak of direct motion and retrograde motion, by which they mean counterclockwise and clockwise, respectively.
>
> —Isaac Asimov, "Dial Versus Digital"

DEFINITION

In formal writing and reports, include definitions of all technical terms and words your readers may not know.

❷ Examples and Analogies

Often the best way to explain a general idea is to offer a representative instance, or **specific example**. How well would you understand the following description if it did not include the specific examples to explain the general ideas?

> **PROFESSIONAL MODEL**
>
> On the surface of any moon or planet, there will be external processes, such as impacts from space, and internal processes, such as earthquakes; there will be fast, catastrophic events, such as volcanic explosions, and processes of excruciating slowness, such as the pitting of a surface by tiny airborne sand grains.
>
> —Carl Sagan, *Cosmos*

GENERAL IDEAS
SPECIFIC EXAMPLES

If you have no specific example to offer, an **analogy,** or comparison between similar objects, will do. For example, if you wanted to explain what Carl Sagan means by *pitting,* you could compare it to the pattern made by raindrops on a surface covered with dust.

Sometimes you can use an **anecdote**—or a brief account of an actual event—as an example of a point you're making. If you were giving a humorous speech and wanted to explain what *misery* is, for instance, you might tell the story of the time you got a very bad haircut while you had a terrible cold.

❸ Facts and Statistics

The best explanations may be facts and statistics. For instance, you can explain that lizards grow very large by using the statements below.

Fact	
A statement that can be proved by experience or reference materials	The world's largest lizard is the Komodo monitor.
Statistic	
A fact expressed in numbers	One Komodo monitor measured 10′ 2″ and weighed 365 pounds.

Statistics explain the significance of facts. For example, every year more workers are telecommuting, that is, working from home rather than driving cars to work. Notice how the statistics below elaborate that fact.

> **PROFESSIONAL MODEL**
>
> Telecommuters spare the air about 20 pounds of carbon dioxide, a greenhouse gas, for each gallon of fuel they don't use.... Companies that allow telecommuting just two days a week eliminated 3,475 pounds of carbon dioxide emissions ... per worker a year.
>
> —Kim Erickson, "Home Work: The Green Routine of Telecommuting"

STATISTICS

PRACTICE Collecting Statistics

Collect data from classmates about their favorite foods, hours spent at various activities, and other topics you can describe in numbers. Keep these statistics for use in Lesson 5.

LESSON 4 — Elaborating to Support Opinions

❶ Reasons

When writing a persuasive argument, you can make your opinions more convincing by elaborating them with reasons. Notice how the reasons in the following argument support the writer's conclusion.

STUDENT MODEL

DRAFT

The Hot Doggers' Ski Club needs to get its own Web site. **The Web site would be good for the organization and its members.** Lots of members have personal computers and could log on.

The draft says only that the Web site would be good but does not explain why.

REVISION

The Hot Doggers' Ski Club could **increase its membership and influence** if it had its own Web site. Members could **find out times and places for the outings.** Others could **contribute ideas** without even having to come to meetings.

Use reasons to elaborate an opinion even when that opinion is not controversial. The model below shows how one student thought through the reasons for a popular opinion.

Reason: Builds houses all over the U.S.

Opinion: Habitat for Humanity is a worthy organization.

Reason: Creates housing for poor.

Reason: Has excellent leadership.

Need statistics on this

Reason: Improves neighborhoods.

Look up names and details

By helping people feel good

By making housing better

By cleaning up

Reason: Involves kids in community service.

HOT TIP

If you cannot find facts and statistics to back up your opinion, consider changing your opinion!

❷ Expert Testimony

You can also elaborate persuasive or informative writing with **expert testimony.** An expert is an authority who is educated and experienced in a subject. An expert may be well known but doesn't have to be. The expert's testimony, or educated beliefs and conclusions, serves to support your own opinion.

In the following passage, the writer quotes an expert, in this case a biologist, to support her point about the many species yet to be discovered in the world's rain forests.

PROFESSIONAL MODEL

"Diversity at its utmost," says biologist Terry Erwin   **EXPERT**
of the humble beetle. Scientists have named 350,000
species—one-fifth of all known forms of life. "There   QUOTATION
are millions left to discover in the last biotic frontier,
the rain forest canopy," he says. Erwin fogged one
tree in Peru with biodegradable pesticide and
counted more than 650 beetle species.

                         —Virginia Morell, "The Variety of Life"

PRACTICE   Elaborating Opinions

Choose a topic from the list below, or select one of your own. Write down your opinions about the topic. Use library references, periodicals, experts you know, or the Internet, to compile reasons and expert testimony you could use to support—or to change—your opinions.

Possible topics:

- rain forest preservation
- the greenhouse effect
- beauty pageants
- artificial turf
- helmet laws

Elaborating to Visualize

❶ Images

One of the most effective means of elaborating is with **images,** such as sketches, drawings, photographs, maps, and paintings.

Uses of Images You can use images to demonstrate a process, set a mood, tell a story, or present all kinds of visual information such as color, size, proportion, angles, and physical relationships. Images can add a note of humor to your writing.

Sources of Images Look for images to illustrate your own writing in magazines, newspapers, dictionaries, encyclopedias, multimedia resources, and the Internet. Even better, create your own drawings based on any of these sources, or take your own photographs.

❷ Diagrams

Use **diagrams**—such as time lines, flow charts, and labeled drawings—to elaborate informative writing. The diagram below shows the layout of a regulation basketball court.

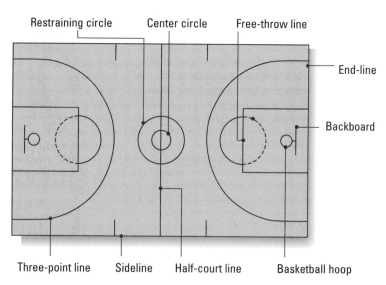

Restraining circle   Center circle   Free-throw line

End-line

Backboard

Three-point line   Sideline   Half-court line   Basketball hoop

❸ Charts and Graphs

Use **charts** like the one below to present facts and statistics visually. This makes numbers easier for readers to grasp.

All-Time Top NBA Scorers: Average Points per Game	
Elgin Baylor	27.4
Wilt Chamberlain	30.1
Michael Jordan	31.5
Karl Malone	26.2
Shaquille O'Neal	27.2
Bob Pettit	26.4
Jerry West	27.0

Graphs are used to illustrate statistics. Their many forms include bar graphs, line graphs, pie graphs, and combinations of these. Notice how the same information that was presented in the chart above is easier to see and compare when presented in a bar graph.

All-Time Top NBA Scorers	
Players	**Average Points per Game**
Michael Jordan	31.5
Wilt Chamberlain	30.1
Elgin Baylor	27.4
Shaquille O'Neal	27.2
Jerry West	27.0
Bob Pettit	26.4
Karl Malone	26.2
Points	25 26 27 28 29 30 31 32

(Source: *The World Almanac and Book of Facts,* 1999)

Try several formats before choosing the best visual format for your particular data. Consider a chart for simple information, a bar graph for comparisons, or a line graph to show trends over time.

PRACTICE ➤ Presenting Information Visually

Analyze the class statistics you gathered in Lesson 3 and find an effective way to present them visually.

Student Help Desk

Elaboration at a Glance

To Describe:
Sensory Details
Metaphors and Similes

To Explain:
Definitions
Examples and Analogies
Facts and Statistics

Elaboration

To Support Opinions:
Reasons
Expert Testimony

To Visualize:
Images
Diagrams
Charts and Graphs

Where to Go for More

Splendid Sources

Almanacs	Current and historical facts and statistics; data about people and populations
Atlases	Geographical information including maps, population distribution, and climate data
Dictionaries	Definitions, pronunciations, and word histories
Encyclopedias	Overviews of topics from A to Z; names, dates, and figures
Newspapers and magazines	Current information and visuals; special interest topics; expert testimony
Internet	News, data, opinions, and introductory information on local, national, and international topics
Biographical dictionaries	Life stories and achievements of people in many fields

Vigorous Visuals

Where is it? Draw a **Map**.

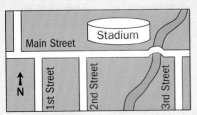

What does it look like? Include a **Photo**.

How is it changing? Draw a **Line Graph**.

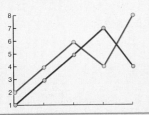

When did it happen?
Give a **Time Line**.

Event 1   Event 2   Event 3   Event 4   Event 5

How does it work?
Show it in a **Flow Chart**.

Step 1 → Step 2 → Step 3 → Step 4

Who gets how much?
Use a **Pie Graph**.

The Bottom Line

Checklist for Elaboration

Have I . . .

____ elaborated descriptions with sensory details?

____ made fresh comparisons using metaphors and similes?

____ clarified meaning with definitions, analogies, and examples?

____ incorporated facts and statistics to explain and support my points?

____ supported my opinions with reasons and expert testimony?

____ used visuals to elaborate written information?

ELABORATION

Power Words
Vocabulary for Precise Writing

Words for Disorder

With the right words, you can describe any mess—from the stuff in the picture on the next page to the messy situations we find ourselves in too often.

What a Mess!

Is your desk **disorderly** and covered with **clutter** or strewn with **litter**? Is it a **hodgepodge**, a **mishmash**, a **jumble**? Is it in total **disarray**?

A Messy Person

If your shirt is half tucked in, you are **untidy**. A bit of ketchup on it? **Sloppy.** Are your hands and face unwashed and your clothes dirty? **Grubby.** Your hair uncombed? **Unkempt** or **disheveled.**

A Messy Life

Are you **confused, upset,** or **agitated**? Is your life **disorganized, unsettled,** or **chaotic**? Is there too much **disorder, upheaval,** or **turmoil** for you to concentrate? Are your days filled with **chaos, commotion, bedlam,** and **pandemonium**?

In a Mess?

Has something gone a little bit wrong? Was it just a **mix-up** or a bit of a **muddle**? Has it left you in a **pickle,** a **fix,** or a **bind**? Are you in a terrible **predicament**? in a **crisis**? Do you find yourself in a **quandary,** or do you have a **dilemma** about what to do?

▷ Your Turn Sketching Trouble

From the terms above, choose one that describes a situation you've been in (for instance, the *pickle* of taking an exam you'd forgotten about or the *pandemonium* after a soccer match). Make a sketch that expresses the feelings you remember.

Revising Sentences

Too Much Stuff

You're reaching inside your backpack for a pencil. You feel a computer disk, headphones, keys, batteries, chewing gum wrappers, your social studies textbook, an extra pair of socks, and something else . . . something disgusting! An old banana! Looks like it's time to clean out your pack by sorting through your stuff, throwing out the junk, and putting similar items together in different pockets.

Revising sentences is similar to cleaning out a backpack. First, you sort through your sentences to find important ideas. Next, you throw out any unnecessary information. Finally, you reorganize your sentences by putting similar ideas together.

Write Away: Favorite Things
What unusual or favorite item do you keep in your backpack or locker? Write a paragraph describing the item and explaining why you keep it. Put your paragraph in your 📁 **Working Portfolio.**

Revising Problem Sentences

❶ Tightening Content

A sentence in which you repeat information, express an opinion without supporting it, or use unnecessary words and expressions may create a problem for your readers. Readers often are confused by such sentences because the ideas in them are not expressed clearly.

Problem Sentences

Draft	Why Revise?	Revision
My neighbor is a professional writer, **and she writes for a living.**	**Repetitive Information** The second part of the sentence expresses the same idea as the first part.	My neighbor is a professional writer.
Students should be required to write for the school newspaper.	**Unsupported Statement** The opinion needs reasons, facts, or examples to support it.	Students should be required to write for the school newspaper because doing so will give them experience in meeting deadlines.
Virginia's picture appeared in the *Bronxville Banner* **because of the fact that** she wrote a prize-winning essay.	**Too Many Words** The expression "because of the fact that" is unnecessary.	Virginia's picture appeared in the *Bronxville Banner* because she wrote a prize-winning essay.

Make sure your sentences include the information needed to express and support your ideas without adding unnecessary information.

Here's How Tightening Content

- Delete repeated information in your sentences.

- Provide reasons, facts, or examples to support your opinions.

- Delete or reduce unnecessary words and phrases.

Unnecessary Phrases	Better
because of the fact that	because, since
on account of the fact that	because, since
what I want to say is that	Delete this expression.

❷ Improving Stringy Sentences

In your draft, you may write a sentence that goes on for too long without showing that the ideas in the sentence are related. Notice how the ideas in the following draft are simply strung together using the conjunction *and.*

DRAFT

Most travel writers write about beautiful places, and readers can imagine visiting those places, and Mark Hertsgaard wrote about places that people had damaged, and he described them in his book *Earth Odyssey,* and he wants readers to know how humans are injuring the planet.

REVISION

Most travel writers write about beautiful places **so that** readers can imagine visiting those places. Mark Hertsgaard wrote about places that people had damaged. He described them in his book *Earth Odyssey* **because** he wants readers to know how humans are injuring the planet.

> The first two ideas and the last two ideas are combined. The third idea stands alone. Transitions show the relationships between combined ideas.

REVISING

Here's How **Revising Stringy Sentences**

1. First, separate the sentence into a list of the ideas it contains.
2. Next, identify the relationships between the ideas.
   - Are they connected by a cause-and-effect relationship?
   - Are they in chronological order?
3. Decide which ideas should be combined and which should stand alone.
4. Choose the transition words you will use to show the relationship between ideas. Common transitions include *if, then, so, when, first, although, finally, however,* and *because.*
5. Rewrite the stringy sentence as two or more shorter sentences.

❸ Reducing Overloaded Sentences

Sometimes you may overload a sentence with too many descriptive words. Instead of helping readers understand an idea, this heap of modifiers actually distracts readers' attention from the idea.

STUDENT MODEL

DRAFT

Straightforward, interesting magazine articles that explain to everyday people how to build new, unusual projects or deal with difficult, embarrassing personal problems have a colorful place in the long history of American journalism.

REVISION

Magazine articles that explain how to build unusual projects or deal with embarrassing personal problems have a long history in American journalism.

Here's How Revising Overloaded Sentences

1. Begin by getting rid of unnecessary modifiers, but keep enough to make your writing clear and interesting.

2. Divide the sentence into the individual ideas it contains.

3. Rewrite the sentence as one or more sentences, using transitions to connect ideas.

HOT TIP

To identify problem sentences, read your writing aloud. If your reading sounds choppy, or if you need several breaths before you finish one sentence, you probably need to revise the sentences.

PRACTICE Revising Problem Sentences

Revise the sentences in the paragraph below, using techniques from this lesson.

Just because of the fact that you are a teenager doesn't mean you can't also be a published writer. Many teenagers are talented writers who write exceptionally well. Today there are more publishing opportunities for teens than ever before, and some magazines are devoted to student work, and others publish only a few pieces per issue, and you should read the latest issue of a magazine, and then you should send your story or poem to the magazine.

Combining Sentences

LESSON 2

A paragraph full of short, repetitive sentences is boring and difficult to read. You can combine short sentences to make your writing smoother, more interesting, and more sophisticated.

❶ Combining Whole Sentences

Use a **coordinating conjunction,** such as *and, or,* or *but,* to combine sentences that contain similar or contrasting ideas.

STUDENT MODEL

DRAFT
Robert Frost was an American poet. Ted *and*
Hughes was a British poet. Both poets wrote
about nature. They understood nature in *but*
different ways. You might enjoy Frost's quiet
images of nature. Perhaps you will prefer Hughes's wild imagery. *or*

Robert Frost

Be sure to use the conjunction that correctly shows the relationship between your ideas.

Coordinating Conjunctions	
To combine similar ideas	and, so, for
To combine contrasting ideas	but, yet
To combine ideas that express choice	or, nor

WATCH OUT

Insert a comma before the coordinating conjunction when you are combining whole sentences.

Use a **subordinating conjunction,** such as *because,* to turn one of two sentences into a subordinate clause. Combine this with the other sentence to create a complex sentence.

STUDENT MODEL

DRAFT
Julia read the book twice. She really liked it. *because*
Rudolph also liked the book. He thought it was too long. *although*

REVISING

Below are some common subordinating conjunctions you can use to create complex sentences.

Subordinating Conjunctions	
Time or sequence	when, after, before, until, while, as long as
Cause and effect	because, since
Condition	although, though, unless, if, whether (or not)

For more subordinating conjunctions, see p. 27.

❷ Combining Sentence Parts

Two sentences may share the same subject or the same verb. Combine the sentences by using a coordinating conjunction to create a compound subject or a compound predicate.

STUDENT MODEL

Creating a Compound Subject
DRAFT

"**Parlor**" is a poem about memories by Rita Dove. "**Fifth Grade Autobiography**" is another memory poem by Rita Dove.

REVISION

"**Parlor**" and "**Fifth Grade Autobiography**" are poems about memories by Rita Dove.

Creating a Compound Predicate
DRAFT

Rita Dove writes about ordinary lives. She describes finding joy in the everyday.

REVISION

Rita Dove writes about ordinary lives and describes finding joy in the everyday.

Rita Dove

 When combining subjects, make sure the verb agrees in number with the new compound subject.

❸ Adding Information with *Who, That,* and *Which*

You can also combine sentences with *who, that,* and *which.* These words are used to introduce subordinate clauses that give additional details about people or things.

Use the word *who* to add details that refer to a person.

STUDENT MODEL

DRAFT

William Moulton Marston was a psychologist and comic-book author. He created the *Wonder Woman* comic in 1941.

REVISION

William Moulton Marston was a psychologist and comic-book author **who** created the *Wonder Woman* comic in 1941.

Use *that* or *which* to add details about a thing.

STUDENT MODEL

DRAFT

Wonder Woman wore a special golden belt. The belt gave her superhuman strength.

REVISION

Wonder Woman wore a special golden belt **that** gave her superhuman strength.

DRAFT

The comic-book series was turned into a TV show in the 1970s. The comic book series is still popular today.

REVISION

The comic-book series, **which** is still popular today, was turned into a TV show in the 1970s.

Using Commas with *Who, That,* and *Which*

The word *which* is used to add nonessential details. Set off these details with commas.

The *Peanuts* comic strip, which originally was called *Li'l Folks,* was created by Charles Schulz.

The word *that* is used to add essential details, so no commas are needed.

This is the comic strip that tells about the lives of Charlie Brown, Snoopy, and their friends.

The word *who* can be used to add essential or nonessential details. Use commas when the details are nonessential.

Lucy, who is often bossy, plays baseball with Charlie Brown.

Snoopy is a beagle who belongs to Charlie Brown.

Peanuts by Charles Schulz

For more on essential and nonessential clauses, see p. 95.

PRACTICE Combining Sentences

Use the word in parentheses to combine the following sentence pairs. Add commas where necessary.

1. *Know Your Own Car* is a useful repair manual. It can teach you how to make basic car repairs. (that)
2. The book lists the tools you need. It gives step-by-step repair procedures. (and)
3. Denise is learning how to do her own car repairs. Her car is always breaking down. (because)
4. She is tired of paying repair bills. They can cost a lot of money. (which)
5. Changing the engine oil is an important maintenance task. Checking the fluids is another important task. (and)
6. Many people don't check the oil level in their cars. A dashboard warning light comes on. (until)
7. Frequently washing a car keeps the paint looking new. Rust cannot be washed away. (but)
8. If you want to learn more about repairing cars, you can take a class in car maintenance. You can also buy a book about car repair. (or)
9. Mr. Goforth teaches a class in basic car maintenance at the high school. He used to work as a car mechanic. (who)
10. Being able to take care of your own car is a great feeling. You still may need a good mechanic to help you with difficult car problems. (although)

Inserting Words and Phrases

Sometimes you may use two sentences to express an idea even though the second sentence adds only a word or phrase of new information. You can express your ideas more clearly by inserting the important details from the second sentence into the first sentence.

❶ Inserting Words

You may be able to reduce one sentence to a single important word and then insert that word into another sentence.

Bob Vila has written several books about tools, home repair, and historical houses. **His books are informative.**

Bob Vila has written several **informative** books about tools, home repair, and historical houses.

Sometimes the form of a word must be changed before it can be added to another sentence. You may need to add one of the following endings to a word: *-y, -ed, -ing, -ly.*

Vila describes home repair projects. **His descriptions are clear.**

Vila **clearly** describes home repair projects.

❷ Inserting Word Groups

You may also be able to combine sentences by inserting a word group from one sentence into another sentence.

A how-to book may give directions for completing home repair projects. **It tells you how you can complete projects on your own.**

A how-to book may give directions for completing home repair projects **on your own.**

You might need to change the ending of a word within a word group before you insert the word group into a sentence. Use the ending *-y, -ed, -ing,* or *-ly.*

Some people rush into a new project. **They neglect to read all the directions first.**

Some people rush into a new project, neglecting to read all the directions first.

❸ Inserting Appositive Phrases

Another way to make your writing more concise is to reduce one sentence to an appositive phrase and then insert the phrase into another sentence. An **appositive phrase** is a group of words that identifies or renames a noun or a pronoun.

Computer manuals are selling like hotcakes. **These manuals are one kind of how-to book.**

Computer manuals, one kind of how-to book, are selling like hotcakes.

Many appositive phrases are set off with commas because they are not essential to the meaning of sentences.

For more on appositives and appositive phrases, see p. 69.

For more on appositives and appositive phrases, see p. 69.

PRACTICE Inserting Words, Word Groups, and Appositive Phrases

Combine the following sentence pairs by inserting a word, a word group, or an appositive phrase. You may need to change word endings.

1. A cookbook is another kind of how-to book. It is a collection of recipes and information about food.
2. Read a recipe several times. You should do this before you begin cooking.
3. Make sure you have all the ingredients. These ingredients are called for in the recipe.
4. Measure all your ingredients with measuring cups and spoons. Your measurements should be accurate.
5. Follow a recipe one step at a time. As you follow the recipe, pay attention to what you are doing.

Revising for Parallelism

❶ Understanding Parallelism

Words and groups of words that have the same function in a sentence and that also have the same form are said to be **parallel**.

The poems are lyrical, imaginative, and brilliant.

The three highlighted words in this sentence are parallel because they have the same **function** (to describe the poems) and the same **form** (adjective).

When words or groups of words that have the same function in a sentence are not parallel, the sentence is awkward. Notice the lack of parallelism in the draft below.

STUDENT MODEL

DRAFT

    When Alice Walker writes poetry, she **locks** herself in her study, **writes** lines and lines and lines, and then **will put** them away for a long time.

> Two verbs in the present tense, one verb in the future tense

REVISION

    When Alice Walker writes poetry, she **locks** herself in her study, **writes** lines and lines and lines, and then **puts** them away for a long time.

Alice Walker

> Three verbs in the present tense

Errors in parallelism are found with clauses and phrases, as well as with individual words.

STUDENT MODEL

DRAFT

    Ray Bradbury says you can live on very little money by **giving up** new clothes, **staying home** from the movies, and **you can eat** inexpensive foods like macaroni and cheese.

> Two phrases and a clause

REVISION

    Ray Bradbury says you can live on very little money by **giving up** new clothes, **staying home** from the movies, and **eating** inexpensive foods like macaroni and cheese.

> Three phrases

DRAFT

Isaac Asimov wrote science fiction, humor, and for adults.

Two nouns and a phrase

REVISION

Isaac Asimov wrote science fiction and humor for adults.

Two nouns

DRAFT

Every writer needs a good idea and to be left alone.

A noun and an infinitive

REVISION

Every writer needs a good idea and time alone.

Two nouns

❷ Creating Parallelism

As you revise, look for sentence parts that lack parallelism and correct them. You can use the following techniques to correct these errors.

Here's How Correcting Parallelism Errors

1. Look for sentence parts that have the same function.
2. Determine whether the sentence parts have the same form.
   - Do they share the same part of speech?
   - If they are verbs, are they in the same tense?
3. Revise the sentence parts so that they are in the correct form.

Reading your sentences aloud will help you find errors in parallelism.

PRACTICE Correcting Parallelism Errors

Find the errors in parallelism in the sentences below. Rewrite each sentence, making sentence parts parallel.

1. Jenny loves playing the saxophone and to read about ancient China.
2. I'll spend tonight sitting by the fire, listening to music, and write letters.
3. Dimitri ran for class president and feels confident about winning the race.

Creating Sentence Variety

❶ Varying Sentence Beginnings

The paragraphs you write may contain interesting information, but readers will be bored if all your sentences have the same structure. The draft below is dull because many of the sentences begin in the same way—with the pronoun *he* or *she.* The revision shows that varying the way sentences begin can make a paragraph much more interesting.

STUDENT MODEL

James Herriot

DRAFT

James Herriot was a veterinarian for 25 years. **He** often told his wife about interesting on-the-job experiences. **His** wife enjoyed his stories. **He** promised to write a book about them. **She** challenged him one day. **She** said that 50-year-old veterinarians don't often become writers. Herriot stormed out of the house immediately. **He** bought some paper. **He** taught himself to type. **He** published his first book when he was 54.

REVISION

For 25 years James Herriot was a veterinarian. **Often,** he told his wife about interesting on-the-job experiences. **Because his wife enjoyed his stories,** he promised to write a book about them. **Challenging him one day,** his wife said that 50-year-old veterinarians don't often become writers. **Immediately,** Herriot stormed out of the house, bought some paper, and taught himself to type. **When Herriot was 54,** he published his first book.

You can vary your sentence beginnings by using single-word modifiers (adjectives, adverbs, and participles), phrases, and subordinate clauses.

Sentence Beginnings

Single-word modifier	**Often,** he told his wife about interesting on-the-job experiences.
Phrase	**For 25 years** James Herriot was a veterinarian.
Subordinate clause	**Because his wife enjoyed his stories,** he promised to write a book about them.

REVISING

❷ Varying Sentence Structure

The draft below seems uninteresting because all the sentences
are simple. The revision is livelier because the sentences have
different lengths and structures. Add variety to your writing by
using simple, compound, and complex sentences.

STUDENT MODEL

DRAFT

    A monologue is a series of jokes or stories.
A talk-show host delivers the monologue at
the beginning of a show. Writing monologues
for a late-night talk show requires an original
sense of humor. It also demands an ability to
work under tight deadlines. A team of writers
must find new ideas every day. The writers
listen to or watch the news and scan many
newspapers. Some news items or headlines
are funny by themselves. Others may be the
sources for clever remarks. Lines may be
rejected. The host, the director, or other staff
writers may do this at any time. In fact, the
final script may be approved only minutes
before showtime.

**SIMPLE
SENTENCES**

REVISION

    A monologue is a series of jokes or stories
that a talk-show host delivers at the beginning
of a show. Writing monologues for a late-night
talk show requires an original sense of humor
and an ability to work under tight deadlines.
To find new ideas every day, a team of writers
listen to or watch the news, and they scan
many newspapers. Some news items or
headlines are funny by themselves; others may
be the sources for clever remarks. Lines may
be rejected by the host, the director, or other
writers at any time. In fact, the final script
may be approved only minutes before
showtime.

**COMPLEX
SENTENCE**

**SIMPLE
SENTENCES**

**COMPOUND
SENTENCES**

The sentence-combining techniques in this chapter can help you create longer and more interesting sentence structures. You can choose from the following four sentence types.

Sentence Types	
Type	**Example**
Simple sentence: one independent clause	Monologue writing is difficult and demanding work with many rewards.
Compound sentence: two or more independent clauses	Monologue writing is difficult and demanding work, but it has many rewards.
Complex sentence: an independent clause and one or more subordinate clauses	Monologue writing is difficult and demanding work that has many rewards.
Compound-complex sentence: two or more independent clauses and one or more subordinate clauses	Monologue writing is difficult and demanding work, but because it has many rewards, writers are eager to go into this field.

For more information on sentence structure, see pp. 101–102.

PRACTICE Varying Sentences

Find in your 📁 **Working Portfolio** the paragraph you wrote for the **Write Away** on page 369. Revise your paragraph to vary the beginnings and structures of your sentences.

Student Help Desk

Revising Sentences at a Glance

A Good Sentence

Should
- express a complete thought
- contain necessary details or support
- use parallel structures

Should NOT
- repeat the same idea
- contain unnecessary details
- include too many ideas or modifiers
- include wordy expressions

Sentences in a Paragraph

Should
- begin in a variety of interesting ways
- include a variety of structures

Correcting Problem Sentences   Do-It-Yourself Sentence Repairs

Problem	Repair
Repeated information	Delete repeated ideas or information.
Unsupported opinion	Add reasons, facts, or examples.
Unnecessary expression	Delete or reduce unnecessary words or phrases.
Stringy sentence	Separate the sentence into two or more shorter sentences.
Overloaded sentence	Get rid of extra modifiers.

Adding Commas   Putting Commas in Their Place

Situation	Do you need commas?
Adding details with *who*	Details may be essential or nonessential. Set off nonessential details with commas.
Adding details with *that*	Details are essential. Commas are not needed.
Adding details with *which*	Details are nonessential. Set off details with commas.
Combining whole sentences	Add a comma before the coordinating conjunction.

Combining Sentences

Use Conjunctions

Whole Sentence
Leon saw the movie twice. He really liked it.
Leon saw the movie twice **because** he really liked it.

Sentence Parts
Kiyo bought popcorn. **Lisa** bought popcorn too.
Kiyo and Lisa bought popcorn.

Use *Who, That,* and *Which*

The movie is about a girl. She dreams of being a racecar driver.
The movie is about a girl **who** dreams of being a racecar driver.

Insert Words and Word Groups

The usher is asking those kids to be quiet. They are **noisy.**
The usher is asking those **noisy** kids to be quiet.

Insert Appositive Phrases

Jennie wrote a review of the movie. She is **a writer for the school newspaper.**
Jennie, **a writer for the school newspaper,** wrote a review of the movie.

The Bottom Line

Checklist for Clear, Concise Sentences

Can I improve my sentences by . . .

____ adding supporting information?

____ taking out unnecessary words or phrases?

____ taking out repeated information?

____ breaking stringy and overloaded sentences into shorter sentences?

____ cutting down on the number of modifiers?

____ combining sentences and sentence parts or inserting words, word groups, or appositive phrases?

____ making sure sentence parts that have the same function are parallel in form?

____ varying the beginnings and structures of sentences?

Power Words
Vocabulary for Precise Writing

Degrees of Affection

If you were to write a song about love, would you have enough words to describe the feeling? Try a handful of those below.

How Do I Love Thee?

How can you know if your love is lasting? Is it **puppy love?** just a temporary **infatuation?** You may be **enamored, enchanted,** and **enthralled,** but are you (and is the object of your affections) capable of **constancy** and **devotion,** of **passion, fervor,** and **ardor**—without falling into **obsession?**

Going Overboard?

Feelings of love can be **deep, profound,** and **heartfelt,** but they can also be overly **sentimental.** Then we use words like **gooey, gushy,** and **mushy; sappy, soppy,** and **sloppy; cloying, maudlin,** and **mawkish.**

Don't Fall for a Cold Fish!

Why are we sometimes interested in those who are **unresponsive, indifferent,** and **unsympathetic; thick-skinned, cold-blooded,** and **hard-hearted?** Do we imagine that we can save these **impassive, callous, dispassionate,** and generally **unfeeling** people from themselves?

▷ **Your Turn** Dear Diary

Examine your feelings about someone who returned your affection. Examine your feelings about someone who did not. Do not turn this assignment in!

Developing Style

Striking a Chord

Which of these CDs would you buy? How would you make up your mind? Since the titles of the CDs are similar, you'd probably base your choice on how you expected the music to sound.

You might expect that the songs in *Smashed Heart* would be loud, with a heavy beat; that Hank Tucker's music would feature a twangy guitar; and that the Ravenswood Symphony's music would be smooth and elegant. In other words, each music would have a different style.

When you write, you are like a musician. You make many choices that shape the style of your work.

Write Away: Sounding Off

Write a letter to a friend, describing your reactions to a movie, concert, or sports event. Tell what made the movie, concert, or event different from others you have seen. Save your letter in your **Working Portfolio.**

Elements of Style

❶ Recognizing Style

When people say that you have style, they mean that you show personality and imagination in what you do. Style in writing is much the same. The word **style** refers to the way something is written, rather than what it is about.

What similarities and differences do you notice in the depictions of people's experiences in the two models below?

LITERARY MODELS

Yossi was murmuring something between his teeth. He must have been praying. I had never realized that Yossi was a believer. I had even always thought the reverse. Tibi was silent, very pale. All the prisoners in the block stood naked between the beds. This must be how one stands at the last judgment.

"They're coming!"

There were three SS officers standing around the notorious Dr. Mengele. . . .

—Elie Wiesel, *Night*

But just then, from somewhere far off, Millicent was sure of it, there came a melodic fluting, quite wild and sweet, and she knew that it must be the song of the heather birds as they went wheeling and gliding against wide blue horizons through vast spaces of air, their wings flashing quick and purple in the bright sun.

Within Millicent another melody soared, strong and exuberant, a triumphant answer to the music of the darting heather birds. . . .

—Sylvia Plath, "Initiation"

- What feelings did each passage evoke in you as you read it?
- How would you compare the lengths of the sentences used by the two writers?
- How are the writers' sentence structures different?
- How do the writers' choices of words differ?
- Which passage seems more straightforward? more poetic?

Your answers to these questions will suggest some of the qualities that characterize each writer's style.

❷ Describing Style

Here are some of the terms used in talking about style.

Elements of Style	
Term	**Explanation**
Standard English	Standard English is language in which the accepted rules of usage, grammar, spelling, and punctuation are observed. In nonstandard English, these rules may be ignored.
Level of language	Formal writing is serious and carefully composed. Informal writing is more relaxed, with the quality of everyday speech. Most writing falls somewhere between the extremes.
Word choice	In a particular passage or work, a writer may prefer to use concrete words or abstract words, specific words or general words, technical words or common words.
Imagery and figurative language	Imagery consists of words that present sensory experiences. Figurative language includes similes, metaphors, and other nonliteral uses of words.
Tone	Tone is an expression of a writer's attitude toward his or her subject. Words like *solemn, humorous, ironic, angry,* and *critical* are used to describe different tones.
Sentence structure	A writer may use sentences of various lengths and structures (simple, compound, complex, and compound-complex) to create particular effects.

PRACTICE Transforming Style

Rewrite the passage below, changing its style. Use whatever different words, expressions, and sentence structures you wish.

LITERARY MODEL

It has taken me a good number of years to come to any measure of respect for summer. I was, being May-born, literally an "infant of the spring" and, during the later childhood years, tended, for some reason or other, to rather worship the cold aloofness of winter.

—Lorraine Hansberry, "On Summer"

STYLE

Levels of Language

❶ Formal and Informal Language

I was at the coolest concert!

I recently attended an exquisite performance!

I just went to an enjoyable concert!

iNFORmaL

FORMaL

The formality of the language you use in a piece of writing depends on your audience, your purpose, and the occasion. Compare the levels of language in the two models below.

PROFESSIONAL MODEL

FORMAL

    A new report by the American Association of University Women shows that a **troubling gender gap in computer use exists in high** schools. Girls make up only a small **percentage of students** who take high-level computer courses that might lead to technology careers. **Yet they are more likely than boys to take data-entry classes, the high-tech equivalent of typing.**

                —*New York Times*, editorial

Contains sophisticated vocabulary

Contains carefully constructed, complete sentences

STUDENT MODEL

INFORMAL

    Not true! I happen to be one of the girls you're talking about and **I oughta know.** Girls like computers as much as boys do. My whole class is practically girls and we're **whizzes.** And I might ask, what's wrong with data entry? At least we're just getting ready for life after school. **Not like some of those gender-gappers I could mention.**

Contains slang and other expressions from everyday speech

May contain fragments and other nonstandard English

You need to use formal language and standard English to make a good impression in schoolwork, interviews, and business letters.

❷ Varieties of Informal Language

There are several types of informal language you may use.

Idioms

Idioms are common expressions that don't mean what their individual words literally mean. Use idioms when you write to friends, give informal talks, or want to create natural-sounding dialogue for characters.

Examples:
Sheila was **green with envy**. Randy **lost his head**.

Dialect

A **dialect** is a kind of English spoken in a particular area or by a particular group of people. You can use dialects in dialogue to give your characters voices that sound real.

Example:
They's rules—you got to be here a year before you can git relief. They say the gov'ment is gonna help. They don't know when.
— John Steinbeck, *The Grapes of Wrath*

Jargon

Jargon is specialized language that is used in a business or profession. Don't use jargon unless you are writing for the group of people who understand it; otherwise, it's puzzling.

Example:
Our primary server will be rebooted today to enable some hardware functionality.

Slang

Slang consists of the playful expressions used in casual speech. Slang is always changing; most slang expressions become outmoded quickly. Slang belongs in very informal writing, such as personal e-mail and letters, or in fictional dialogue.

Examples:
The class was **totally bogus**. I **bombed** the test.

PRACTICE Going Formal

Write five slang expressions and five idioms. Then trade papers with a partner. Translate your partner's expressions into expressions that would be appropriate to use in a composition.

STYLE

Word Choice

❶ Specific Words

In addition to using a particular level of language, a writer may choose to use concrete words or abstract words, specific words or general words. The writer's selection of words makes up his or her **diction**.

Notice how the writer of the movie review below added zest to the description by replacing general words with ones that are more specific.

STUDENT MODEL

DRAFT

The **best scene** in the movie is when a **character holds on** to the train as the train **goes** over a bridge. Just as his fingers **let go**, an **unknown person** saves him. What a scene!

REVISION

The **climax** of the movie comes when the **hero hangs outside** the train, **trembling**, as it **speeds** over a **rickety** bridge. Just as his fingers **slip**, a **bearded stranger** pulls him back.

Specific Words				
Verbs	gobble	slurp	pitch	scrutinize
Adjectives	rubbery	sour	tricky	ancient
Nouns	spaghetti	lemonade	curve ball	text

When you find the right noun or verb, you may not need any modifiers at all. Notice how the writer of the model above replaced "a character" with "the hero."

PRACTICE A ▸ **Getting Specific**

Rewrite the cartoon caption, using a general noun instead of *trudge*. How does the meaning change?

"Care to go for a short trudge?"

© The New Yorker Collection 1986 Henry Martin.

❷ Denotations and Connotations

Words have two kinds of meanings, called denotations and connotations. The **denotation** of a word is its dictionary definition. The **connotation** of a word is the set of associations and feelings the word evokes.

When choosing among words that have almost the same meaning, use their connotations to help you decide which one to use. For example, the following words all have similar denotations.

appreciate, value, prize, esteem, treasure, cherish

Which one would you use to describe an important possession?

Lily prizes her silver-and-gold pen set.

Which one would you use when talking about a person you love?

Lily cherishes her friendship with Jasmine.

Some connotations involve positive or negative value judgments to which you need to pay attention.

Words Expressing Value Judgments		
Negative	**Neutral**	**Positive**
He **hoarded** the gold coins.	He **stored** the gold coins.	He **saved** the gold coins.
The package gave off a **stench.**	The package gave off a **smell.**	The package gave off a **fragrance.**

In many dictionaries you can find explanations of connotations in the lists of synonyms that follow words' definitions. For example, under *smile,* you might find a discussion of the connotations of *grin, simper,* and *smirk.*

PRACTICE B Decoding Connotations

Explain how these three sentences differ in meaning.

Nora **showed** her first-place ribbon to the crowd.
Nora **exhibited** her first-place ribbon to the crowd.
Nora **flaunted** her first-place ribbon before the crowd.

Write two more sets of sentences containing words that have similar denotations but different connotations.

Imagery and Figurative Language

What's the difference between saying that someone dives into a swimming pool and saying that someone dives into his or her homework?

- In the first expression the word *dives* is used in its literal sense of "plunges headfirst."
- In the second expression the word is used figuratively to mean "throws himself (or herself) wholeheartedly."

You can use **figurative language**—which conveys meanings beyond the literal meanings of the words—to add imaginative touches to your writing.

❶ Imagery

Imagery conveys sensory impressions—that is, it helps the reader see, hear, feel, taste, and smell what is being described. Notice how the following description appeals to several senses.

LITERARY MODEL

Scarcely a breath of wind disturbed the stillness   SOUND
of the day, and the long rows of cabbages were
bright green in the sunlight. Large white clouds   SIGHT
drifted slowly across the deep blue sky. Now and
then they obscured the sun and caused a chill   TOUCH
on the backs of the prisoners who had to work
all day long in the cabbage field.

         —Bessie Head, "The Prisoner Who Wore Glasses"

❷ Figures of Speech

Simile, metaphor, and personification are three examples of **figures of speech.** You can use them to create strong, memorable images for the reader.

Simile and Metaphor

A **simile** is a comparison that contains the word *like* or *as*. Fresh similes compare things that a person might not normally think of comparing. Similes are common in poetry, but you can use them in all forms of writing.

I know the stadium will be deserted....The whole place is silent as an empty classroom, like a house suddenly without children.

—W. P. Kinsella, "The Thrill of the Grass"

In a **metaphor** something is treated as though it *were* something else. The comparison is made without the use of *like* or *as*. Use metaphors to create powerful descriptions and to explain things that are hard to put into ordinary language.

There was the feeling, in the house, that he had wept and raged at her, that boulders of reproach had thundered down upon her absence, and yet he had said not one word.

—Nadine Gordimer, "A Chip of Glass Ruby"

"Love is a door we shall open together."

—Carl Sandburg, "Moon Rondeau"

Personification

Personification is a figure of speech in which a writer gives human characteristics to an animal, a thing, or an idea.

Now the fire lay in beds, stood in windows, changed the colors of drapes! ...

The fire rushed back into every closet and felt of the clothes hung there.

—Ray Bradbury, "There Will Come Soft Rains"

PRACTICE Creating Similes and Metaphors

For each figure of speech in the models above, write a new simile or metaphor describing the same thing. Then write similes or metaphors that describe a television, an ear, a diamond, and a football game.

STYLE

Style Gone Mad

When trying to create strong images, you may sometimes find yourself using tired expressions, mixing up metaphors, or piling on words. Here are some tips to help you identify and avoid these mistakes in your writing.

❶ Avoid Clichés Like the Plague

Clichés are expressions that have worn out from overuse. They offer no new insights to the reader. Clichés may come quickly to mind, but resist the temptation to use them when you can write more directly or creatively.

Draft: It rained cats and dogs, flooding the campground.

Revision: Rain fell steadily, flooding the campground.

Revision: Rain pummeled the campground with its watery fists.

HANDS OFF A Cliché Collection

like a drowned rat
as blind as a bat
like a fish out of water
as sick as a dog
like a runaway train
as flat as a pancake
as fresh as a daisy
like a bump on a log
grin and bear it
like a sitting duck
in the nick of time
like a three-ring circus
like a bolt of lightning

THE FAR SIDE   By GARY LARSON

"Boy, he even looks like a drowned rat."

PRACTICE A   Refreshing Clichés

Choose five of the clichés listed above and write fresh expressions that could be used in their place. Think about the qualities that the clichés express, and try to convey those qualities in new words.

❷ Untangle Mixed Metaphors

A **mixed metaphor** compares one thing to several other things at the same time. The result is confusion. The motion-picture producer Samuel Goldwyn was famous for his mixed metaphors as well as for his films. Here is an example.

They always bite the hand that lays the golden egg.

Goldwyn's statement combines two metaphors (both of which are clichés as well):

They bite the hand that feeds them.

They kill the goose that lays the golden egg.

Draft: He was lost in a tidal wave of confusing information.

Revision: He was lost in a maze of confusing information.

Revision: He drowned in a tidal wave of confusing information.

❸ Prune Excessive Language

Sometimes you may go too far. You may use too many words or use big words where little ones will do. You may overload descriptive sentences with adjectives and adverbs.

Draft: The festive celebration was overattended by uninvited guests.

Revision: Too many people came to the party.

PRACTICE B Trimming Extra Words

Rewrite the sentence below, stating in a simple way what the writer has said with too many words.

> **STUDENT MODEL**
>
> In this great, wonderful, splendid nation of ours, with its sturdy, honorable, industrious citizens, there lies the capacity to create an extraordinary wonderland of industry, education, and participatory democracy the likes of which the world has never ever seen before.

STYLE

Developing Your Own Voice

LESSON 6

The personal style of a writer is called the writer's **voice.** A writer develops a distinctive voice gradually, over time, with experience and practice. The more you write and think about your own words, the more you'll discover your own voice in your writing.

① Recognizing a Writer's Voice

Compare these two descriptions of young love. Notice the word choice, tone, sentence structures, and use or absence of figurative language that are characteristic of each voice.

> **LITERARY MODEL**
>
> "It happened that I was greatly in love. I had   **FORMAL DICTION**
> been in love many times, but this was my
> greatest love. . . . At the age of fifteen, she was
> already a remarkable beauty. As a young girl of
> eighteen, she was enchanting: tall, well-formed,   **REFLECTIVE TONE**
> graceful, majestic—most of all, majestic."
>
> —Leo Tolstoy, "After the Ball"

> **LITERARY MODEL**
>
> During my last year of high school, I fell in   **INFORMAL DICTION**
> love so hard with a girl that it made my love
> for Sarah McKinney seem like a stupid
> infatuation with a teacher. Charlene Gibson
> was the Real Thing and she would be Mrs.   **SLANG**
> Charlene Cosby, serving me hot dogs and   **HUMOROUS TONE**
> watching me drive to the hoop and giving me
> the full-court press for the rest of my life.
>
> —Bill Cosby, *Love and Marriage*

PRACTICE A **Comparing Writers' Voices**

Reread the literary and professional models in this chapter and describe the voice of each writer. How do the passages differ in level of language, use of figurative language, word choice, and tone?

CHAPTER 17

❷ Recognizing Your Own Voice

Here are some questions to help you evaluate how well your voice comes through in your writing.

Voice✓Check

Yes	No	
☑	☐	**Are you writing honestly?** Do you believe what you're saying?
☑	☐	**Are you writing naturally?** Do you strain for effects, or do you use simple, well-chosen words?
☑	☐	**Are you avoiding a false tone?** Is your attitude toward the subject sincere?
☑	☐	**Are you using all of your options?** Have you explored imagery and figurative language?
☑	☐	**Are you choosing words carefully?** Have you used the most appropriate nouns, verbs, and adjectives you can think of?
☑	☐	**Are you paying attention to sentence structure?** Do you vary the length and structure of your sentences to achieve particular effects?

PRACTICE B ▸ Evaluating Your Own Voice

Take from your 📁 **Working Portfolio** the letter you wrote for the **Write Away** on page 387. Use the checklist above to evaluate its style. Then revise the letter so that your personal voice comes through more clearly.

STYLE

Student Help Desk

Style at a Glance

- **Level of Language** Make your language fit the situation. Avoid street-corner language at commencement and oratory on the street corner.
- **Word Choice** Use the most precise words you can. If someone collapsed into a seat, don't settle for saying that he or she sat down.
- **Figurative Language** Use imaginative figures of speech.
- **Clarity and Freshness** Take your eraser to clichés and mixed metaphors, or they will sit there like a sore thumb.
- **Voice** Develop an honest and natural personal style.

Idioms — It's a Zoo Around Here

Idiom	Meaning
barking up the wrong tree	making a wrong choice
sitting duck	someone vulnerable to attack
chicken out	to back out because of fear
cry crocodile tears	to be insincere
dog-and-pony show	an elaborate demonstration
eager beaver	a very enthusiastic person
feather in one's cap	an honor

Choosing the Best Word — Survival of the FITTEST

	More Formal	Less Formal
Best	optimum, superlative, unsurpassed	prize, pick, top
Loser	failure, fiasco, washout	bust, dud, flop, lemon, bomb
Tired	exhausted, drained, spent, weary	beat, bushed, done in, rundown, worn-out
Dead	deceased, defunct, extinct, late, lifeless	gone, killed

Figures of Speech   Spinning a Web

Use word webs to help you develop similes, metaphors, and personifications.

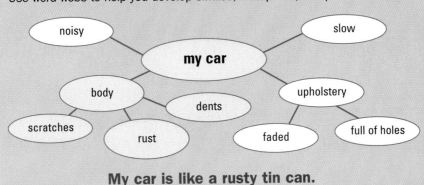

My car is like a rusty tin can.

Dilbert by Scott Adams

The Bottom Line

Checklist for Developing Style

Have I . . .

____ used the right level of language for my purpose?

____ used precise language?

____ considered connotations?

____ used figures of speech?

____ avoided clichés?

____ allowed my own voice to come through?

Writing Workshops

Building with Words

How does an architect begin a new building? With a girder? a picture? a blueprint? a dream? And how do you begin a piece of writing? With a single word? an image? a plan? However you begin, you most likely have an idea of how you want the finished piece to look. That idea is the inspiration from which the composition will grow.

Autobiographical Incident

Learn What It Is

An **autobiographical incident** is a personal account of a significant event in your life. It can reveal an important part of your personality. Writers use these incidents in descriptions of their lives and in essays that reflect turning points in their views on issues.

Basics in a Box

AUTOBIOGRAPHICAL INCIDENT AT A GLANCE

Beginning

Introduces the incident, including the people and the setting

Middle

- Re-creates the incident, using descriptive details
- Makes the significance clear

End

Concludes by reflecting on the outcome and the significance

RUBRIC

Standards for Writing

A successful autobiographical incident should

- focus on a well-defined incident or a series of related incidents
- provide background information for the incident
- use elements such as plot, character, and setting as appropriate
- make the order of events clear
- use description or dialogue as appropriate
- include precise language and specific details
- show why the experience was significant
- maintain a consistent tone and point of view

See How It's Done: *Autobiographical Incident*

Student Model
Elizabeth Kim
New Trier High School

RUBRIC
IN ACTION

My Father the Dragon

As a child, I was curious about many aspects of my life. First, I didn't understand why my parents hadn't raised me in Korea, where all my relatives lived. I only knew that my parents immigrated to the United States after they married. Also, I was always curious about the Chinese zodiac, knowing that I am a rooster. When my father told me that he was a dragon, I thought how well the symbol fit him. Later in my life, I reached an understanding of my parents' hard work and sacrifice to raise a family and of the true meaning of my father's symbol.

One day when I was about 12 years old, my father came home tired and sore from working hard from six o'clock in the morning to six o'clock at night. He works at a small dry cleaners a block away from our house. Its old, shabby appearance seems almost lost and forgotten behind a new row of stores. On this day, I noticed his hand was bandaged. He seemed to be in a lot of pain. I felt confused because I always thought of my father as a strong man showing off his biceps and grinning proudly. When I saw my father in pain with bandaged hands, I was surprised. I used to think of him as a dragon—fierce, strong, and powerful, just like the zodiac. Suddenly that image faded away as I saw my dad with streaks of white in his hair, a frail and overworked body, and injured hands.

I asked him about his hands, and he told me that he had been fixing machines at the store and cut himself badly. He usually tries to fix everything himself. I asked him, "Why do you have to fix machines when you used to teach math in Korea?" I thought about the black-and-white pictures of his class wearing dark uniforms and my father looking handsome in his suit.

❶ The introduction suggests a purpose for retelling the incident.
Another option:
• Start by relating the incident itself.

❷ Gives the background for the incident, including setting and character

❸ Presents specific details to describe the main character

❹ Includes dialogue and specific details to show significance of the event

AUTOBIO.

Then my father told me how he had wanted to come to America because he had heard great things about it. He had dreamed of green lawns, picket fences, and friendly neighbors. He had dreamed about vacuums and different kinds of machines that would make everything easier. Most of all, he had dreamed that his children would grow up in this wonderful country and be happy. He only wanted the best for his children.

<u>Then</u> my eyes fell to look at the bandages on his hands, and I didn't see them as a weakness. I saw a whole new picture. My dad was <u>still</u> a dragon inside. This time, however, he had battle wounds. He had sacrificed his high-status job in Korea for his children and had come to America, knowing little English. He now works hard in a small cleaners. He cares more deeply about supporting and raising his children in a better environment than he cares about his own health or safety. He's determined to work hard so that the future of his children will be better than it would be in Korea.

Every day when he comes home from work, I look at my father proudly. I see a dragon.

5 Includes precise language and details

6 Uses transitional language to make the sequence of emotions clear

7 Shows why the incident is important

8 Indicates the writer's feelings about her father

Do It Yourself

Write an autobiographical incident describing an event in your life that has meaning for you.

Purpose To explore and explain

Audience Classmates, family members, other friends

❶ Prewriting

Examine your memories. Pick an incident from your life that has meaning for you. To jog your memory, look at photo albums and page through old journals and diaries. Ask friends or family members what they remember. Create a "life line" showing high and low points, looking for an event that deeply affected you.

Focus on your purpose and audience. Consider how to tell the incident in a way that will hold the interest of your audience. Select just the parts that illustrate the purpose of your story.

Sketch out ideas. Where did the incident take place? Is there something special about the time or the place it happened? Who are the people involved? How do they look, act, and talk?

❷ Drafting

Begin drafting. Start writing without being overly concerned with wording. Concentrate on the meaning of the incident rather than the details. You can fill in the specifics later.

Organize your ideas. Chronological order is often most appropriate for an autobiographical incident. You can consider using a **flashback**—that is, returning briefly to an earlier time—when it would be effective. Be sure to fill in background information the reader will need.

Elements of an Autobiographical Incident	
Narration	Describes events or actions that occurred
Description	Brings scenes and people to life with detailed language
Dialogue	Shows the events through the characters' own words when possible

Wrap up your account. End with a statement or paragraph that makes the significance of the incident clear.

For friendly feedback from your peers, see p. 411.

For friendly feedback from your peers, see p. 411.

AUTOBIO.

❸ Revising

TARGET SKILL ▶ Showing Action You can describe a person by showing that person in action. Your reader will then be able to form an impression of the person by observing the action. As you revise, review the rubric at the beginning of this chapter.

> I felt confused because I always thought of my father as a strong
> *showing off his biceps and grinning proudly*
> man.

❹ Editing and Proofreading

TARGET SKILL ▶ Parallel Constructions Words and phrases that have the same function in a sentence should also have the same form. Avoid mixing different parts of speech or different kinds of phrases in a parallel list.

> Then my father told me how he had wanted to come to America
> because he had heard great things about it. He dreamed of green
> lawns, picket fences, and neighbors ~~being~~ friendly. He dreamed
> about vacuum~~ing with a machine~~ and different kinds of
> machines that would make everything easier.

For more about parallel constructions, see pp. 379–380.

❺ Sharing and Reflecting

After you have edited and proofread your autobiographical incident, find a way to **share** it with an audience. You might consider reading it aloud to your family or providing copies for your friends. Ask them to give you feedback on your performance.

For Your Working Portfolio As you **reflect** on your writing process, think of what you have learned about yourself and about the topic. Did writing bring back details you had forgotten? Did it cause you to change your mind about the incident? Did your readers' responses affect your process? Attach your answers to your finished work. Save your autobiographical incident in your ▱ **Working Portfolio.**

Real World Autobiographical Incident

Autobiographical narratives are found in the biography section of a bookstore. You might also find one in your own journal or diary. Some places you can find personal narratives include:

- magazines and newspapers
- speeches
- diaries or journals
- the Internet

Book

Fighting Fire

by Caroline Paul

At the top of the stairs, I cannot see my own hand pressed against my air mask. *Hell must be like this,* I think. The nozzle is cool and definite in my hand .... I am first in, where every engine person wants to be, first in, with the nozzle. In front of me is a chasm of black and, somewhere, the seat of the fire.

For a longer excerpt from this book, see MODEL BANK, p. 634.

INTERNET PERSONAL HOME PAGE

BOOK

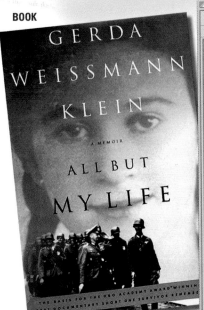

GERDA WEISSMANN KLEIN

A MEMOIR

ALL BUT MY LIFE

THE BASIS FOR THE HBO ACADEMY AWARD WINNING BEST DOCUMENTARY SHORT ONE SURVIVOR REMEMBERS

L-Net

Back Forward Reload Home Images Print Security Stop

Location:

Welcome to my Web page!

I'm Kyle and I live in Connecticut. I've lived here for about three years, but before that I lived in Florida. It was tough, at first, getting used to life up here and making new friends, but now I love it almost as much as my old home. I've got one older brother and two younger sisters. I just started high school, so now I'm in the same school as my brother, which can be strange, but he's OK, I guess.

School Projects
Check out my latest school projects

School Sports
Baseball, basketball, and soccer

Hobbies
I am training my dog at obedience school

AUTOBIO.

Student Help Desk

Autobiographical Incident at a Glance

Beginning	Middle	End
Introduces the incident, including the people and the setting	• Re-creates the incident, using descriptive details • Makes the significance clear	Concludes by reflecting on the outcome and the significance

IDEA Bank

Finding and Developing a Writing Idea

1. Remember specific objects from your past.	• family pet • family photo • childhood toy • most-worn shoes	• baseball glove • swim goggles • post card of vacation spot • tape or CD recording
2. Think about special days.	• Thanksgiving • your birthday • a family member's birthday	• New Year's Eve • school dance or game • last day of school • first day of spring
3. Learn from the pros.	Many successful writers include autobiographical incidents in their writing. Here are a few to check out: • Coretta Scott King, *Montgomery Boycott* and John Steinbeck, *Travels with Charley (Language of Literature,* Grade 10) • Barbara Kingsolver, *High Tide in Tucson* • Dylan Thomas, *A Child's Christmas in Wales* • Carl Sandburg, *Fair and Circus Days*	

Purpose and Audience   Trust Me on This

Consider these questions to focus on purpose and audience:
- Would I like to read this if it were not my own experience?
- What part of my experience would most interest my audience?
- What feelings and information do I want to convey?
- What could I leave out and still have a good story?

Friendly Feedback   Did You Care?

Questions for Your Peer Reader
- What was the most interesting part?
- What details strengthened the writing?
- What would have made it more convincing?
- What could I have left out?

Publishing Options   Here Goes Something!

Print
- Publish your autobiographical incident in a local or school newspaper

Oral Communication
- Read your narrative aloud at a family gathering
- Record it to send to family and friends

Online
- Check out **mcdougallittell.com** for more publishing options

AUTOBIO.

The Bottom Line

Checklist for Autobiographical Incident

Have I . . .
- ____ provided a well-defined incident?
- ____ shown why the incident was important to me?
- ____ given adequate background information?
- ____ made the order of events clear?
- ____ used dialogue and description as appropriate?
- ____ kept my purpose and audience in mind throughout?

Focused Description

Learn What It Is

When you read a passage that describes a person, place, or thing in great detail, you are reading a **focused description.** You can find such descriptions in fiction, biographies, and news reports. Good focused descriptions share the following characteristics.

Basics in a Box

FOCUSED DESCRIPTION AT A GLANCE

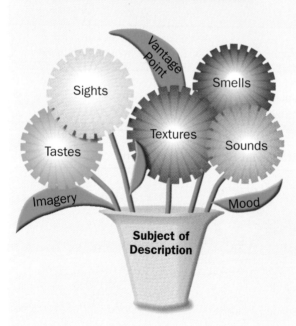

Vantage Point

Sights

Smells

Textures

Sounds

Tastes

Imagery

Mood

Subject of Description

RUBRIC

Standards for Writing

A successful focused description should

- focus on a person, place, or thing
- convey a clear sense of purpose
- include sensory details and precise words to create a vivid picture, establish a mood, or express emotion
- include figurative language or dialogue when appropriate
- follow a consistent method of organization

See How It's Done: *Focused Description*

Student Model
Sophie Tyner
Evanston Township
High School

RUBRIC
IN ACTION

Far Away, Yet Close to My Heart

My lively, funny grandmother, Doosie, lives in Wahroonga, a quiet suburb of Sydney, Australia. She has occupied the same house for over fifty years. This is my favorite place in the world. Whenever I think of the lush gardens by the house, I feel warm and secure.

Walking down Braeside Street in my memory, I reach number ninety-one and turn onto a curving driveway. The crunch of gravel under my sandals sounds like someone walking in autumn leaves. On my left is a mass of brilliantly colored plants and trees that form a jungle-like barrier between Doosie's land and her neighbors'. To my right is a waist-high stone wall separating the land from the road. I have often stood on this crumbling wall to reach the lowest branch of a gigantic gum tree. I pull myself up and climb high into the thick branches, feeling the bark scrape against my sunburnt arms and legs. After feeling the warm breeze blow through my hair, I slowly climb down and drop to the spongy ground.

I run across the sea of grass and catch the scent of the honey-sweet gardenias in Doosie's front garden. Passing the front door, which is hardly used any more, I unstrap my sandals and toss them onto the waiting step. The heat is intense, and to escape I duck beneath a branch draped with ivy. I drink up the coolness of the shade and pause for a moment to watch a pair of tiny lizards disappear behind a rock covered with moss. I continue down the hidden side path, once packed smooth with the footprints of my mother and her four brothers as children. The path leads back to the driveway, curving behind the house. I amble down it once again, hearing my grandmother's chattering voice through the kitchen windows. On either side of the driveway is a sea of bright blue hydrangeas that smell as sweet as freshly pressed apple cider.

❶ The introduction makes clear the focus—the grandmother's house.

❷ The writer has organized her description according to spatial order, beginning at the front of the house.

Other options:

• Tell the story of the house sequentially.

• Describe the parts of the house in order from most to least familiar.

❸ Uses sensory details to appeal to the senses of smell, touch, sight, and hearing

DESCRIPTION

Suddenly, I see a flash of black as Doosie's cat Sooty runs across the hot gravel. I turn and follow her, picking my way through the gnarly bushes. I feel like Alice in Wonderland as I reach the back garden. Doosie rents this land now, but I still enjoy coming here. I remember when I was younger, the garden had flowers so bright your eyes hurt to look at them. The new tenants do not take care of the garden, but it still has its wild beauty. I climb over a rotting tree stump and run down the slight decline.

After glancing at the refreshing blue pools of Doosie's neighbors, I continue into the old tennis court. It is now unused and resembles a tiny field. I can easily imagine my mother with her friends on a hot Australian day playing tennis. Now the grass court is covered with yellow weeds that prickle my bare legs. I gaze at the garden once more and turn to walk back to the house.

Drooping branches tickle my face as I pass underneath the willow. The weather is so warm and dry in Australia that my grandmother rarely uses the drying machine in the laundry house. Instead, Doosie hangs her laundry on a weblike system of rubber-covered ropes wrapped around metal bars. The whole thing resembles an immense umbrella. The sheets flap in the warm breeze and remind me of the sails of yachts gathering in a harbor to start a race. I cross the crunching gravel and enter the cool dimness of Doosie's house. Leaning against the cool brick, I close my eyes and try to ingrain everything in my memory. When I'm at home, the warmth and happiness these memories bring are enough to cheer me up on any occasion.

❹ Creates a distinctive mood by using contrasting details from the past and the present

❺ Uses figurative language to enrich the description

Do It Yourself

Writing Prompt Write a focused description of a place, an event, or an object that has made an impression on you.

Purpose To share an experience with your reader

Audience General readership, classmates, family

❶ Prewriting

Try freewriting to find a subject for your description. Begin writing about the place you're in now, then jump to describing other places you remember. Think of people or even animals you've known well, and write a few sentences about them. Do these people remind you of experiences? Write about a scene you recall.

Once you have a tentative subject in mind, take the following steps:

- **Get in the mood.** Analyze your feelings about the topic and how you want your readers to feel.

- **Recall sensations.** Try to recreate the sights, sounds, smells, textures, and tastes that go with the place or thing you are describing. A cluster chart may help you in getting started. Suppose your subject is a baseball game. Your cluster chart might mention these details: hard seats, green field, running players, loud cheers, cool drinks, and the taste of hot dogs.

❷ Drafting

Begin writing. You may begin your draft at any point in the description. Concentrate at first on getting all your impressions down.

Load your draft with details. Concentrate on precise, sensory language. Try focusing on one small aspect of the scene or object. Use dialogue and figurative language to show your subject to the reader, rather than simply telling about it.

Get organized. The most commonly used forms of organization for descriptions are shown below.

- **Spatial order:** left to right, near to far, top to bottom, and so forth
- **Order of impression:** what you noticed first, second, and so on
- **Order of degree:** least important to most important, least familiar to most familiar, and so on
- **Part-by-part order:** for example, first the place, then the people, and so on

For information about getting feedback from your peers, see p. 419.

❸ Revising

TARGET SKILL ▶ **Elaborating with Sensory Details** Descriptive writing demands details that appeal to the senses. Concrete nouns, strong verbs, and specific adjectives help your readers experience the sights, sounds, smells, and other sensations you describe.

> *is a sea of bright blue hydrangeas*
> On either side of the driveway ~~there is a bunch of nice-smelling~~
> *that smell as sweet as freshly pressed apple cider.*
> ~~blue flowers.~~

❹ Editing and Proofreading

TARGET SKILL ▶ **Correcting Fragments** When sentences are not complete, readers have a hard time following them. Correct your sentence fragments (and add sophistication to your writing) by combining fragments into compound or complex sentences.

> *and*
> I drink up the coolness of the shade, Pause for a moment to
> watch, A pair of tiny lizards disappear behind a rock, Covered
> with moss.

For more about correcting sentence fragments, see pp. 116–119.

❺ Sharing and Reflecting

When you have finished polishing your focused description, **share** it with an audience. Pick a time and place carefully, making sure your audience will be able to pay close attention to your work. Ask class members to listen and respond to your focused description read aloud.

For Your Working Portfolio After sharing your description, **reflect** on what you have learned in writing it. What did you learn about yourself and how you feel about your subject? What did you learn about the writing process? Attach your answers to your finished work. Save your focused description in your 📁 **Working Portfolio.**

Real World Focused Description

Have you ever looked through a nature guide, with its descriptions of different types of plants or animals? If so, you probably saw many short focused descriptions. Or maybe you've written a focused description yourself, perhaps about something amazing you saw on a trip. Check some of the following sources for focused descriptions:

- Magazines and newspapers
- Nature journals
- Travel guides

- Internet
- TV news stories
- Autobiographies

Africa's Wild Dogs

by Richard Conniff

Somewhere deep in Botswana's Okavango Delta, a million miles from nowhere, a dog named Nomad leads his pack on a wild chase through the bush. The sun paints a gaudy orange stripe across the horizon. Night threatens at any moment to rush down and set the lions afoot. **For the complete text of the article, see MODEL BANK, p. 636.**

CLASSIFIED AD

TRAVEL WEB SITE

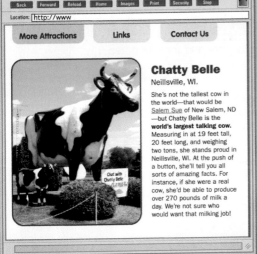

L-Net

Back | Forward | Reload | Home | Images | Print | Security | Stop

Location: http://www

More Attractions | Links | Contact Us

Chatty Belle
Neillsville, WI.

She's not the tallest cow in the world—that would be Salem Sue of New Salem, ND —but Chatty Belle is the **world's largest talking cow.** Measuring in at 19 feet tall, 20 feet long, and weighing two tons, she stands proud in Neillsville, WI. At the push of a button, she'll tell you all sorts of amazing facts. For instance, if she were a real cow, she'd be able to produce over 270 pounds of milk a day. We're not sure who would want that milking job!

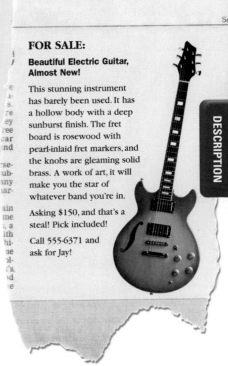

DESCRIPTION

Student Help Desk

Focused Description at a Glance

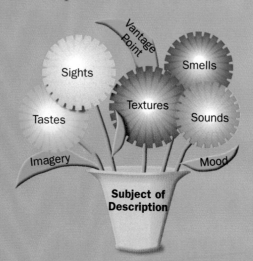

Vantage Point

Sights

Smells

Textures

Tastes

Sounds

Imagery

Mood

Subject of Description

IDEA Bank

Tips for Finding a Subject

Wait and watch.

Sit quietly in a busy place and jot down details of the action.

Put it on a post card.

Think of places you have been. Picture these places as they might appear on a post card.

Go nose to nose with a cat.

Spend time observing an animal and making notes.

Go natural.

Take a walk, a hike, or a bike ride in a natural setting. Observe carefully and make notes.

Read for inspiration.

You'll find wonderful focused descriptions in "Once More to the Lake" by E. B. White (*Language of Literature*, Grade 10).

Using Figurative Language

Play Around with Language

Model simile: The sheets were flapping like sails.

Trigger sentence: The _____ was like a _____.

Model metaphor: The man, a whale in a fishbowl, overflowed the cramped seat.

Trigger sentence: The _____, a _____, tried to _____.

Friendly Feedback

Ask Your Peer Reader

- What mood does my description create?
- Which details most helped you imagine my subject?
- What would you have liked to know that wasn't included?
- Did any part seem unnecessary?

Publishing Options

Make a Name for Yourself

Oral Communication	• Read your description aloud on a radio program. • Use a computer and an authoring tool to combine your description with other media, such as music and pictures, for presentation.
Print	• Send your description to a small magazine or student publication.
Online	• Check out **mcdougallittell.com** for more publishing options.

DESCRIPTION

The Bottom Line

Checklist for Focused Description

Have I . . .

____ conveyed a clear sense of purpose?

____ focused on interesting details?

____ shown the scene or object rather than told about it?

____ used sensory details and precise words?

____ used figurative language and dialogue where appropriate?

Literary Interpretation

Learn What It Is

Have you ever found that reading a story a second time gave you a completely different understanding of it? Sometimes a story's meaning lies beyond the obvious. Writing a **literary interpretation** is a way to find the meaning below the surface of a story or other work of literature. It gives you an opportunity to explore a story's significance to yourself. Here's how to go about it.

Basics in a Box

LITERARY INTERPRETATION AT A GLANCE

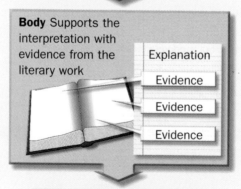

Introduction
Introduces the literary work and includes a thesis statement

Body Supports the interpretation with evidence from the literary work

Explanation

Evidence

Evidence

Evidence

Conclusion
Summarizes the interpretation

RUBRIC

Standards for Writing

A successful literary interpretation should

- identify the author and title and give a brief summary of the work

- give a clearly stated interpretation of the author's message

- present evidence from the text, details and quotations, to support the interpretation

- summarize the interpretation in the conclusion

See How It's Done: *Literary Interpretation*

Student Model
Adam Moses
Oak Park River Forest
High School

RUBRIC
IN ACTION

"By the Waters of Babylon"

Stephen Vincent Benét's "By the Waters of Babylon" could easily be interpreted as a doomsday forecast. Obviously, Benét feels that technology is putting the world on the track to Armageddon. However, Benét believes in humankind's resilience and its ability to look toward the future even when that future looks bleak.

❶ Identifies the author and title

Before the point at which the story begins, the majority of humanity has been destroyed during a war waged with advanced technologies. In the story, John, the main character, visits the site of a destroyed city and realizes not only the enormous loss brought about by the war but also the danger everywhere in trying to have too much too fast.

❷ Gives a brief summary of the story

Benét makes it clear that the technologies were to blame for the catastrophe, but is it correct to say that Benét has a completely dark view of human nature simply because of these technologies? The only reason that humans had these weapons in the first place was their constant quest for more knowledge, which was followed by the development of more technology. Benét is not cursing humans for inventing such weapons; he is merely saying that people sometimes move too quickly in their quest for more knowledge. In the search for more knowledge, humans discovered how to develop weapons of immense power. Much knowledge brings positive consequences; but some new information permits destruction, such as in the development of weapons.

❸ This writer states a common interpretation and disagrees with it.
Other option:
• Ignore other opinions and present your own.

❹ Gives a clearly stated interpretation of the author's message

However, Benét finds plenty of reasons to praise humankind. For example, the very fact that anyone was capable of surviving the Great Burning is a hopeful sign. But more important is that societies were able to form again after the war took place. There was a horrible war. Millions upon millions were killed. Yet, resilient species that we are, humankind

❺ Uses details from the story to support his opinion

INTERPRETING LIT.

was able to come back and start a society going again. Essentially, the worst thing that could possibly happen to us happens in this story—the Great Burning. But how do the survivors react? By starting right back up again! Their "women spin wool on the wheel," and their "priests wear a white robe," just like in the days before the Great Burning. Progress is in effect, and everything can grow again.

❻ Includes quotations from the text to support the interpretation

An additional positive aspect of human nature, Benét stresses, is our ability to learn from our mistakes. John's father advises him against telling the people that the residents of the Place of the Gods were actually humans. John agrees, for he knows what happened in the old days when they "ate knowledge too fast"—there was a Great Burning. If his people were to eat too much knowledge, who knows what might happen? And since one cannot be sure of what might happen, why risk it? Too much knowledge too fast can lead to very bad things. John and his father have learned this from the past and they don't make the same mistake. People can learn from the past and make the appropriate adjustments in their own lives.

❼ Presents details from the story as evidence

Benét doesn't care much for the technology that results in loss of many lives. But otherwise, he has a favorable opinion of humankind. "By the Waters of Babylon" is not just a prediction of worldwide destruction but a belief that humanity will learn from mistakes and recover a civilization lost by unwise choices.

❽ Concludes by restating his interpretation in a summary

Do It Yourself

Writing Prompt   Write an interpretive essay about a story or a poem.

Purpose To explain your reaction to the literary work

Audience Your teacher, your classmates, a literary journal

❶ Prewriting

Choose a piece of literature to explore. Recall a story or a poem about which you had strong feelings. Consider exploring a piece you think you could understand better by looking into it more deeply.

Read the piece several times. Use a **reading log** to write down interesting lines you recall. Write your own interpretation of each of the lines. You might identify and analyze the effect of artistic elements within the text, such as character development, rhyme, imagery, and language.

Jot down main points you want to make about the story, along with details from the story that support each point.

For information about getting feedback from your peers, see p. 427.

❷ Drafting

Begin writing. An easy way to start is by naming the author and the title and giving a brief plot summary. Once you have your basic ideas down, you can add support. Following are some strategies for developing your interpretation.

Strategies for Developing a Literary Interpretation

Describe	Re-create the characters, setting, or mood of the piece by including descriptive details.
Compare and contrast	Compare your initial response to the piece with your thoughts on later readings.
Paraphrase	Explain key passages of the text in your own words.
Use quotations	Include quoted passages that support your interpretation.
Focus on specifics	Trace lines of cause and effect, changes in character, plot developments, and other features of the work that support your opinions.
Summarize	Include a brief summary of your interpretation in the conclusion.

INTERPRETING LIT.

❸ Revising

TARGET SKILL ▶Varying Sentences Many short, choppy sentences make for boring reading. A series of long, complex sentences can be confusing—and also boring. Your literary interpretation will be more appealing to read if you vary your sentences.

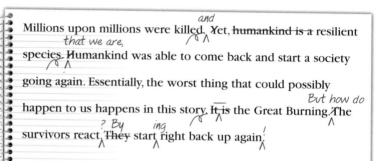

Millions upon millions were killed. Yet, ~~humankind is a~~ resilient *and*
that we are,
species. Humankind was able to come back and start a society

going again. Essentially, the worst thing that could possibly

happen to us happens in this story. ~~It is~~ the Great Burning. The
But how do
survivors react. ~~They~~ start right back up again.
? By *ing*

❹ Editing and Proofreading

TARGET SKILL ▶Punctuating Quotations A solid literary interpretation is strengthened by citations from the literary piece. Use quotation marks around the exact words cited from a work you are referring to.

"Their "women spin wool on the wheel," and their "priests wear a

white robe," just like in the days before the Great Burning.

For more about punctuating quotations, see pp. 268–269.

❺ Sharing and Reflecting

After you have checked your work carefully for content and style, **share** it orally, in print, or electronically with an audience, particularly others who have read the same work. Have classmates evaluate your presentation.

For Your Working Portfolio As you **reflect** on your writing process, think about what you have learned about the literary piece. How will writing this interpretive essay affect how you read another piece of literature? Attach your answer to your finished work. Save your essay in your ▢ **Working Portfolio.**

Real World Literary Interpretation

Interpretation of literature occurs in various settings—from book-club discussion groups, to published reviews in literary journals and newspapers, to films based on literary themes. TV talk shows often have book discussions with famous authors. People who love books can find literary interpretation in many places:

- Newspaper book-review section
- TV interviews
- Literary-discussion Web sites
- Books of literary criticism
- Internet newsgroups
- Book clubs

BOOK CLUB

Book Review

One man's search for light amid the darkness

by Patrick T. Reardon
TRIBUNE STAFF WRITER

HUNTING FOR HOPE: A Father's Journey

"Hunting for Hope" opens in the Rocky Mountains of Colorado, where Scott Russell Sanders and his teenage son, Jesse, are getting on each other's nerves during a camping trip.

Finally, Sanders accuses Jesse of spoiling the day, but his son shoots back: "You're the one who's spoiling it, you and your hang-ups."

For the complete text of the article, see MODEL BANK, p. 638.

WEB BOOK REVIEW

L-Net

Back | Forward | Reload | Home | Images | Print | Security | Stop

Location: http://www

Reviews | Links | Search

Cool Books

Fahrenheit 451
By Ray Bradbury

Ray Bradbury's science fiction classic, which is named for the temperature at which paper burns, takes place in a near-future where free thinking and new ideas are considered subversive and illegal. It's the duty of the firemen not to put out fires, but to create them as they incinerate books wherever they are found. Bradbury's future is similar to the brave new world that Aldous Huxley warned readers about. The story opens with a fireman named Montag, who is proud of his job and who believes

INTERPRETING LIT.

Student Help Desk

Literary Interpretation at a Glance

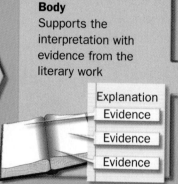

Introduction
Introduces the literary work and includes a thesis statement

Body
Supports the interpretation with evidence from the literary work

Explanation
Evidence
Evidence
Evidence

Conclusion
Summarizes the interpretation

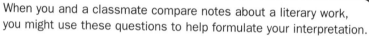

IDEA Bank

Two Heads Can Be Better Than One

When you and a classmate compare notes about a literary work, you might use these questions to help formulate your interpretation.

- Why did I like it?
- Why don't I like it as well as another work?
- What confused me at first?
- What didn't I notice until the second reading?
- What passage did I find most interesting?

Refining Opinions   Create a Lit Meter

With classmates, develop a series of desirable qualities on which to rate the literature read in class. Give a score for each work. Compare scores with classmates. Examples of criteria:

- easy to understand
- hard to understand, but worth the effort
- thought-provoking
- clear organization
- memorable characters
- interesting setting
- effective figurative language

Friendly Feedback Questions for Your Peer Reader

- How would you restate my overall interpretation?
- What main points of evidence did I give for my interpretation?
- What other evidence could I have included?
- What quotations could I have added?
- How does my interpretation of this work compare with yours?

Publishing Options Getting Noticed

Oral Communication
- Share and compare your essay with others in your class.
- Read and discuss your essay with friends in a literary group.
- Create an audiotape or videotape of your essay in the style of a radio or TV book-review program.

Print Options
- Submit your essay to a school literary magazine.

Online Publishing Options
- Check out **mcdougallittell.com** for more publishing options.

The Bottom Line

Checklist for Literary Interpretation

Have I . . .

- ____ given the author and the title at the beginning of the essay?
- ____ provided a thesis statement?
- ____ given a clear statement of my interpretation?
- ____ supported my interpretation with sufficient evidence?
- ____ included quotations where they help to make my points?
- ____ included a summary of my interpretation in the conclusion?

Cause-and-Effect Essay

Learn What It Is

News items on television and in newspapers often tell not only what happened but also why it happened. Like a news story, a **cause-and-effect essay** may describe an event and its causes, consequences, or effects. Writing a good cause-and-effect essay depends upon keeping in mind the logical relationships of the events described.

Basics in a Box

CAUSE-AND-EFFECT ESSAY AT A GLANCE

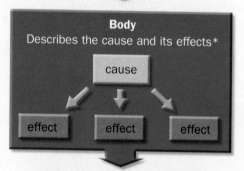

Introduction
Introduces the subject

Body
Describes the cause and its effects*

cause

effect   effect   effect

Conclusion
Summary

*or presents an effect and
then analyzes the causes

RUBRIC

Standards for Writing

A successful cause-and-effect essay should

- clearly identify the cause-and-effect relationship

- provide any necessary background information

- make the relationships between causes and effects clear

- present details in a logical order and include transitions to show relationships

- use language and details appropriate to the intended audience

- summarize the cause-and-effect relationship in the conclusion

CHAPTER 21

See How It's Done: *Cause-and-Effect Essay*

Student Model
Jason Nemo
Evanston Township
High School

RUBRIC
IN ACTION

Moments

I've just run in the state championship 3200-meter relay race with three teammates. We won! In the past I usually chalked up our wins to raw talent, but winning this event in a state meet made me realize how far from raw my talent is. I had actually started working out in seventh or eighth grade. The training that began back then made this victory possible. After the race, I jogged around the track to cool off, and I reflected on the stages of training that led me to this moment.

The summer before I entered high school I joined a track club, where I was able to compete against other clubs for the first time. Our team was good enough to participate in a national meet, so we were able to practice our skills against other track clubs from all over the country. We were often pitted against imposing relay teams of 12- and 13-year-olds who looked like cousins of the Incredible Hulk. Even though we were just training for the upcoming school year, I felt more inadequate than I have ever felt in my running career. The effect of those competitions was that I learned to overcome whatever doubts I had about myself and just run as well as I knew I could.

That fall I ran cross-country for my school. If running two to three miles in a cross-country meet across rugged terrain in pouring rain doesn't build your stamina, I don't know what will. Daily practices throughout the fall and spring paid off when I was named best freshman in the conference in the 400-meter event. It was the first time I had distinguished myself in my sport. Consequently, my pride and confidence increased, and I was ready to push myself to the next level.

❶ This writer begins with the end result, or effect, and then suggests the causes.

Another option:
• Present a cause and then describe its effects.

❷ Provides needed background information

CAUSE-EFFECT

❸ Uses transitions to make the relationships between causes and effects clear

The following summer, I practiced every morning for the fall cross-country season. By steamy August we were pushing six to eight miles a day. It was hard work, but all that cross-country running had prepared me for it. The highlight of my career came in the last meet of the season, on our archrival's track. I won all three races, including the 400-meter, which I won with my fastest time ever. I left the track with three gold medals. As a result, I knew that expectations would be high for next year. That was fine with me. My expectations for myself had been increasing with each new success.

Because of all our success, everyone was expecting us to go all the way. Our hard work and training paid off and we <u>made it to the big show</u>—the state finals. I <u>was a wreck</u> before the race. I had been nervous about races before, though, so I knew that I could overcome it. I stepped onto that <u>big blue track</u>, looking into the huge crowd with my whole season on the line. If I could excel at all the meets before now, I told myself, I could do the same here at the state championship.

My legs felt like lead. When the gun went off the jitters wouldn't go away, and I hardly noticed the race. I finished my leg of the race in less than two minutes, which was a record run for me. Even in my nervous state, I had exceeded my expectations for myself. A couple of minutes later my teammate crossed the finish line. I looked up and saw that we had won. Still exhausted, I hobbled over to my teammates to share the victory.

Thanks to four years of training, facing intimidating opponents, and proving my abilities to myself and others, my team and I had proven ourselves winners. With sweat still pouring off my face, I was already thinking about next year's team.

❹ Presents details in chronological order

❺ Uses language and details appropriate to the audience

❻ Summarizes the cause-and-effect relationship in the conclusion

Do It Yourself

Writing Prompt Write an essay to show the relationship between a cause and its effects or between an effect and its causes.

Purpose To inform

Audience Readers interested in the information, classmates

❶ Prewriting

Pick a topic that interests you. Begin by considering your own experience. Think of an accomplishment you were proud of. What factors led to your success? Move beyond your own life. What event in the news puzzles you? Try to figure out its causes.

For more on finding a topic, see p. 434.

Analyze the topic. Once you have a possible topic, think it through by answering these questions.

- **Is the relationship truly one of cause and effect?** Make sure that events are really linked by a cause-and-effect relationship. Just because B came after A does not mean B was caused by A. Making a cause-and-effect graphic can help. Here's how the author of the student model might have used a graphic to organize his ideas.

| Cause summer track club | ⇒ | Effect more confidence | ⇒ | Cause daily practice | ⇒ | Effect named best freshman |

- **What does your audience know?** Think about who will be reading your essay. What sort of background information will they need?

❷ Drafting

Begin to write. Your first step in drafting your essay should be simply to get your ideas in writing. Once you have completed the first draft, check to see that you have included a statement of the cause-and-effect relationship you are discussing.

Get organized. With your stated relationship clearly in mind, decide how to organize your ideas. Here are two possibilities:

- Describe how one cause leads to many effects.
- Show how several causes lead to a single effect.

Support your statements. Use facts, statistics, quotations, and other supporting details in elaborating your statements.

For information about getting feedback from your peers, see p. 435.

❸ Revising

TARGET SKILL ▶Effective Introductions Capture your reader's attention immediately with an interesting fact, a provocative statement, a lively description, or some other device.

> *I've just run in the state championship 3200-meter relay race with three teammates. We won!*
>
> ∧In the past I usually chalked up our wins to raw talent,
>
> but winning this event made me realize how far from raw
>
> my talent is.

❹ Editing and Proofreading

TARGET SKILL ▶Subject-Verb Agreement When revising, you might switch from a singular subject to a plural subject or vice versa. If you do, don't forget to change your verb and any pronouns to match your subject.

> *Our team was*
> ~~We were~~ good enough to participate in a national
>
> *we were*   *our*
> meet, so ~~I was~~ able to practice ~~my~~ skills against other track
>
> clubs from all over the country.

For more on subject-verb agreement, see pp. 154–175.

❺ Sharing and Reflecting

After you have reviewed and revised your cause-and-effect essay, **share** it with an audience. Ask your peer reviewer to list the causes and effects described in your work.

For Your Working Portfolio After sharing, **reflect** on what you learned in writing your essay. Did you learn more about yourself, the subject, or the writing process? Did you come to understand something new about the relationships among causes and effects? Write down your answers and attach them to your finished work. Save your cause-and-effect essay in your 🗀 **Working Portfolio.**

Real World Cause-and-Effect Writing

Your history textbook describes causes of war and the effects of inventions like the cotton gin. Scientific magazines carry articles on how the extinction of one species will affect the development of another. Advertisements often show their product as the cause of buyers' happiness and success. Cause-and-effect writing is typically found in these places:

- Magazines
- Scientific and medical journals
- TV commercials
- History textbooks
- Newspapers
- Public-service posters

Newspaper Article

NEWSPAPER ARTICLE

Ditch the heavy pack and save your back

If you cram all of your textbooks (and other heavy stuff) into a backpack and carry it from class to class, you could be hurting your back. Here's a look at what could be happening to your body — and what action you could take to ease the pain.

Putting your shoulder into it

When you haul a heavy pack in your hand or on your shoulder, your body tries to maintain its center of gravity by redistributing the weight. Here's what it does:

When you raise your **SHOULDER** to keep your pack from slipping off, your shoulder muscles are immobilized. That prevents your other shoulder from moving correctly.

STRESSED AREA Your **PELVIS** swings out toward the weight-bearing side to balance your body.

PELVIS

Your **HEAD** tilts to maintain a smooth curve of the spine from your lower back to upper neck.

The small and large **MUSCLES** on the opposite side of the raised shoulder stay tense for as long as the weight is carried. These muscles build up waste products (lactic acid), which can cause muscle spasms.

Remember El Niño?

His Sister Has Shown Up, and She's Angry

William K. Stevens

Record snows in Buffalo and Chicago. Record numbers of tornadoes in the country's midsection. All-time low temperatures in Indiana and Maine. Double the normal amount of precipitation, coupled with an extended warm spell, in New York. What accounts for this month's run of extreme weather?

For the complete text of the article, see MODEL BANK, p. 640.

TEXTBOOK CHART

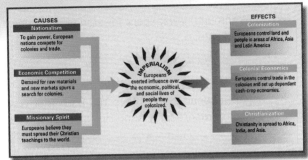

CAUSE-EFFECT

CAUSES		EFFECTS
Nationalism To gain power, European nations compete for colonies and trade.		**Colonization** Europeans control land and people in areas of Africa, Asia and Latin America
Economic Competition Demand for raw materials and new markets spurs a search for colonies.	**IMPERIALISM** Europeans exerted influence over the economic, political, and social lives of people they colonized.	**Colonial Economics** Europeans control trade in the colonies and set up dependant cash-crop economies.
Missionary Spirit Europeans believe they must spread their Christian teachings to the world.		**Christianization** Christianity is spread to Africa, India, and Asia.

Cause-and-Effect Essay **433**

Student Help Desk

Cause-and-Effect Essay at a Glance

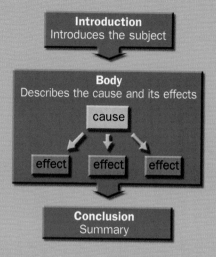

Introduction
Introduces the subject

Body
Describes the cause and its effects

cause

effect   effect   effect

Conclusion
Summary

IDEA Bank Tips for Finding a Topic

Interview

Think of people you know who have done or are doing something interesting. Ask what caused them to do the interesting thing and what effect doing it has had on their life.

Explore Plans

Think of a big decision you may have to make soon. Note the effects each choice might have on your life.

Diagram

Think of a historical or contemporary event that intrigues you, and create a cause-and-effect diagram analyzing it.

Read the Papers

Look through newspapers for stories that describe causes and effects of news events.

Read the Literature

Look for causes and effects in these essays: "The Man in the Water" by Roger Rosenblatt and "Were You Born That Way?" by George Howe Colt based on reporting by Anne Hollister (*Language of Literature*, Grade 10).

Friendly Feedback Ask Your Peer Reader

- What cause-and-effect relationship did I describe?
- What are some of the supporting details I used?
- For which part was the evidence most convincing? least convincing?
- In which parts did you need more information?
- Which parts did you like best?

Publishing Options Tooting Your Horn

Oral Communication	• Deliver your essay as a speech in a history or science class. • Tape-record or videotape your essay and send it to a local radio or TV station.
Print	• Distribute copies of your essay in your community. • Submit your essay to local organizations for publication in their newsletters.
Online	• Check out **mcdougallittell.com** for more publishing options.

The Bottom Line

Checklist for Cause-and-Effect Essay

Have I . . .

____ clearly identified the cause-and-effect relationship in the introduction?

____ provided necessary background information?

____ made the relationships between causes and effects clear?

____ arranged details logically?

____ included transitions to show relationships between effects and causes?

____ used language and details appropriate to the audience?

____ summarized the cause-and-effect relationship in the conclusion?

Persuasive Essay

Learn What It Is

Advertisements, editorials, and petitions are several of the means by which others try to persuade you to act or think in certain ways. From time to time, you yourself need to persuade others. Here's how to go about writing an effective **persuasive essay.**

Basics in a Box

PERSUASIVE ESSAY AT A GLANCE

Tell what the issue is.

State where you stand on the issue.

| Supporting evidence | Supporting evidence | Supporting evidence |

End with a summary or a call to action.

Introduction

Body

Conclusion

RUBRIC

Standards for Writing

A successful persuasive essay should

- clearly state the issue and your position on it in the introduction
- use language appropriate to the audience you're trying to convince
- support your position with facts, statistics, and reasons
- answer possible objections to your position
- provide clear reasoning
- conclude with a summary of your position or a call to action

See How It's Done: *Persuasive Essay*

Student Model
Misha Dworsky
Walt Whitman High School

RUBRIC
IN ACTION

Extracurricular Sports Should Satisfy State Physical Education Requirement

Track, football, soccer, baseball, basketball, and other sports attract dedicated student athletes who often practice every day after school and then participate in weekend games. Should these students be forced to give up an elective class period to take a required physical education class? In order to meet the state's physical education (P.E.) course requirements, that is exactly what Whitman High School asks them to do. I believe that this policy doesn't make any sense. Instead, the [Montgomery County public schools] should exempt student athletes from taking P.E. classes.

❶ Starts by asking a provocative question

❷ Clearly states the topic and the writer's position on it

First of all, participating in an extracurricular sport meets the objectives of the state's course requirements. Those objectives are to promote fitness and improve athletic skill, according to the Whitman course catalog. Involvement in either a varsity or a club sport for one season already makes a student fit and athletically skilled.

<u>A second reason</u> to change the policy is that the physical education requirement forces students to give up an elective class period. High school students can generally choose only eight elective courses from dozens of class offerings. By eliminating the P.E. requirement for student athletes, the county would give students more freedom in selecting their courses.

❸ Gives reasons in a logical order

Another reason to exempt student athletes is that regular P.E. classes would not be so crowded. A large portion of the student body participates in either varsity or club sports. With smaller classes, teachers could provide more supervision during class periods and be more responsive to student feedback. Students in those classes would have a greater chance to improve their athletic skills and confidence.

❹ Supports reasons with facts, examples, and observations

PERSUASION

Finally, exposing students to different sports is one goal of the P.E. requirement, but this objective alone is not important enough to require students to take P.E. class. Students seldom take P.E. class as seriously as they would an extracurricular sport, so students do not always appreciate sports they sample in P.E. class. Also, students have elementary and middle school P.E. classes to try a variety of sports. Most students have already chosen a favorite sport on which to concentrate by the time they reach high school, so it is not worthwhile to make students spend class time experimenting with different sports.

Varsity and club sports require a great deal of time and effort from athletes. The county should recognize that team sports encourage physical activity more effectively than P.E. class and spark more enthusiasm from students. It is more important for student athletes to become well-rounded academically by taking electives than to take P.E. class, since they already understand the value of fitness.

❺ Uses transitions to make the logical connections clear

❻ Answers possible objections to the writer's position

❼ Concludes by clearly restating the writer's position

Do It Yourself

Writing Prompt Decide on an issue you have clear feelings about and write a persuasive essay to gain support for your position.

Purpose To persuade

Audience The community, friends, classmates, family

❶ Prewriting

List possible topics. You may already know exactly what you want to write about. If not, use the following techniques to get your ideas flowing.

- **Search the newspaper.** With a group of classmates, conduct a newspaper search. Look through several issues for news items, editorials, political cartoons, and letters to the editor that grab your interest or spark strong agreement or disagreement.

- **Take an opinion poll.** Interview several students and adults to get their response to this question: What is the most important issue facing us today?

- **Recall arguments.** Think of topics that you have recently argued about or heard others argue about. Would one of these topics be appropriate for presentation to a larger audience?

- **Complete this sentence.** Find as many ways as you can to complete this sentence: This school would be a better place if _____.

Narrow your choices. After you have compiled a list of topics, look it over and pick the one or two topics that interest you most. Then evaluate each choice by asking yourself these questions.

- **Is the topic too big? too small?** If a topic is the subject of great, ongoing controversy, it may be too large to handle in a relatively short essay. However, the topic may have an angle or aspect that you could handle. For example, while censorship in general is too large a topic, censorship of your student newspaper is not.

  A topic can also be too narrow. If you're considering writing about litter on one corner of your block, you probably should look deeper into environmental issues in your community.

- **Is the topic significant?** If most people already share your position—or if few people consider it important—you might want to consider a different topic.

PERSUASION

Consider your audience. The **purpose** of your essay is to make people see things your way. In order to do this, you will need to know who your readers are. Ask yourself these questions.

- What approach will work best with my readers?
- What do they know? What do they need to know?
- Do they agree or disagree with my position, or are they neutral?

Solidify your position. Once you've selected a possible topic, try these methods to discover and strengthen your opinions.

- **Freewrite to explore your topic.** Freewriting about your topic will help you discover what interests you most about it and help you find key points to include in your argument.
- **Examine your ideas.** When you review your freewriting, look for statements that pinpoint your basic position on the issue. Then look for statements that support your position.
- **Think about the other side.** Write down all the arguments that someone might use to support the opposite position. Review your freewriting for statements you could use to counter the opposing arguments.

Gather your evidence. Your feelings alone probably will not sway many readers. To convince your audience, support your opinions with the kinds of details described below.

Supporting Details	
Facts and statistics	Information that can be proved true and numbers that quantify it
Examples	Instances that illustrate your point
Anecdotes	Brief stories that reinforce your ideas
Observations	Reports of events witnessed by you or by people your audience would trust
Expert opinion	Informed opinions expressed by authorities on the subject

❷ Drafting

You may want to begin your essay with a **thesis statement** that clearly shows your position. As you write, you probably will discard some arguments from your notes and develop other arguments to replace them. If you find your opinion changing as you write, be sure to revise your thesis statement. Remember, your arguments should support your thesis.

Choose a pattern of organization. Here are two ways you can structure your essay. In both patterns you present your arguments and answer possible objections to your position.

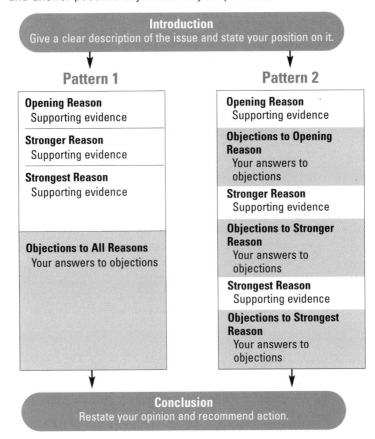

Introduction
Give a clear description of the issue and state your position on it.

Pattern 1

Opening Reason
Supporting evidence

Stronger Reason
Supporting evidence

Strongest Reason
Supporting evidence

Objections to All Reasons
Your answers to objections

Pattern 2

Opening Reason
Supporting evidence

Objections to Opening Reason
Your answers to objections

Stronger Reason
Supporting evidence

Objections to Stronger Reason
Your answers to objections

Strongest Reason
Supporting evidence

Objections to Strongest Reason
Your answers to objections

Conclusion
Restate your opinion and recommend action.

Use logical arguments. To make your argument convincing, make sure your ideas are based on sound logic. Use clear transitions and watch out for logical fallacies—arguments based on faulty reasoning—that you should avoid.

- **Circular reasoning**—trying to prove a statement by repeating it in different words ("A new gym is essential because we need it.")

- **Overgeneralization**—making a statement that is too broad to prove ("Everyone loves to swim.")

- **Either/or fallacy**—claiming that there are only two possible solutions when there are many ("Either we raise new taxes or the roads will become unusable.")

- **Cause-and-effect fallacy**—assuming that because one event follows another, the first event caused the second ("A new mayor was elected in November, and as a result, crime went down in January.")

❸ Revising

> **TARGET SKILL** ►**Supporting Personal Opinion with Facts** Your opinion alone will not sway many readers. Support it with facts.

First of all, participating in an extracurricular sport meets
Those objectives are to promote fitness and improve
athletic skill, according to the Whitman course catalog.
the objectives of the state's course requirements. ∧Involvement

in either a varsity or a club sport, ~~is good for students~~.
for one season already makes a student fit and athletically skilled.

❹ Editing and Proofreading

> **TARGET SKILL** ►**Correcting Run-Ons** When two or more sentences are written as though they were one sentence, the result is confusion for the reader. Change one sentence into a subordinate clause, join the sentences with a semicolon or coordinating conjunction, or make two sentences.

Finally, exposing students to different sports is one goal of
but
the P.E. requirement, ∧this objective alone is not important

enough to require students to take P.E. class.

❺ Sharing and Reflecting

When you have finished revising your persuasive essay, **share** it with an audience. You could read it as part of a debate, present it as a speech, or adapt it as a letter to the editor of your local paper. Ask your classmates for feedback on your presentation.

For Your Working Portfolio After sharing, **reflect** on what you learned in writing the essay. What did you learn about your feelings concerning your subject? What did you learn that can be applied to other writing? Attach your answers to your finished work. Save your persuasive essay in your 📁 **Working Portfolio.**

Real World Persuasive Essay

The persuasive essay is a common form of expression in the real world. Newsgroups on the Internet allow people to post their ideas and opinions on important issues. Advertisements try to persuade you to use a certain product or service. You've probably seen persuasive essays in

- letters to the editor
- magazine articles and advertisements
- junk-mail advertisements

- Internet newsgroups
- newspaper editorials
- public-service posters

BROCHURE

Come to

San Francisco

Editorial Essay

Sectio

Limit use of car phones
Editorial

PIONEER PRESS

Using a cellular phone while driving has been sold as a safety feature for motorists. When you see a hazard, an accident or a motorist in trouble, call the police.

As cellular phones have become more widespread . . . so have the cellular phone calls from the car. And more of those cellular phone calls from the car are business or personal calls, not safety calls. How can drivers on the phone possibly concentrate on the road?

For the complete text, see MODEL BANK, p. 642.

For the complete text, see MODEL BANK, p. 642.

PERSUASION

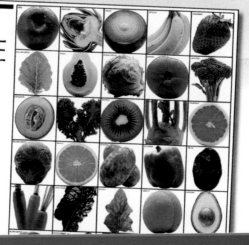

POSTER

Cancer
REDUCE YOUR RISK

These good food choices may help protect you against certain cancers. For more information call the American Cancer Society toll free: 1-800-ACS-2345.

AMERICAN

Student Help Desk

Persuasive Essay at a Glance

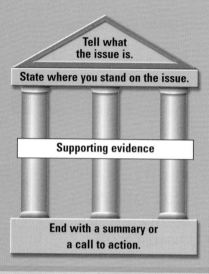

Tell what the issue is.

State where you stand on the issue.

Supporting evidence

End with a summary or a call to action.

IDEA Bank

Tips for Finding a Topic

Scour the Environment

Look around for environmental issues that concern you, from water pollution to trash in city parks.

Search the Media

Look in publications and on the Internet for hot topics about which you have an opinion.

Ransack Your Memory

Consult your journal or your family and friends for subjects about which you have expressed strong opinions in the past.

Read Literature

Reread an opinion piece in a favorite book. You'll find persuasive arguments in "Dial Versus Digital" by Isaac Asimov and "Tolerance" by E. M. Forster (*Language of Literature*, Grade 10).

CHAPTER 22

- What is the issue I'm writing about?
- What did you like best about my essay?
- What is my stand on the issue?
- In what ways could I make my stand clearer?
- What supporting arguments did I leave out?
- What supporting arguments should I have left out?

Publishing Options Getting Your Opinion Across

Oral Communication	• Organize a debate on the issue at a meeting of a group to which you belong. • Using a computer and an authoring tool, create a multimedia presentation from your essay. • Send a tape-recorded reading of your essay to an organization that works for the cause you champion.
Print	• Send your essay as a letter to the editor of your local paper.
Online	• Check out **mcdougallittell.com** for more publishing options.

The Bottom Line

Checklist for Persuasive Essay

Have I . . .

____ clearly stated the issue?

____ clearly stated my position on the issue?

____ geared my argument to my audience?

____ supported my position?

____ answered possible objections?

____ summarized my position in the conclusion?

____ called for action if appropriate?

Problem-Solution Essay

Learn What It Is

Problems are inescapable at home, school, and work. Sometimes a good way to solve a problem is to write an analysis of it to explore solutions. **Problem-solution essays** can be found in magazine articles, editorial pages, and personal letters. Following are tips for writing an effective problem-solution essay.

Basics in a Box

Problem-Solution Essay at a Glance

Body
Present and explain possible solutions

Introduction
Present and analyze the problem

Conclusion
Restate the problem and the solution

RUBRIC

Standards for Writing

A successful problem-solution essay should

- clearly state a problem and explain its significance
- explore all aspects of the problem, including its causes and effects

- offer one or more reasonable solutions and explain how to put them into effect
- use anecdotes, examples, facts, or statistics to support the proposed solution
- use logical arguments to persuade the audience

See How It's Done: *Problem-Solution Essay*

Student Model
Ivan Golden
Niles North High School

RUBRIC
IN ACTION

Test Center Needed

So you're just getting over being sick, and you have to make up that all-important test. You take out your number-two pencil and start. All of a sudden another student comes in for help, so a teacher starts going over yesterday's lessons. You then try to block that out when another teacher walks in and runs off 100 copies. Then, off in the background, you can hear two teachers gabbing about what they want to eat for lunch. Now you can't concentrate, and you're going to fail the test. This is . . . your life.

Many students are being hurt by being forced to take tests in noisy rooms. Last semester, over 3,149 students had to make up tests in room D200 alone. The atmosphere in 200-rooms, where students get tutored and make up tests, is less than ideal for this purpose. This poses a problem: you may be taking a calculus test while only ten feet away from you, well within hearing range, a student is being tutored in geometry. Finally, the constant noise of the copy machine churning out copies also is not conducive to test taking.

We in no way mean to criticize the efforts of the secretaries or teachers; it is not their fault. The problem is that there should be a designated room where students can make up tests or quizzes for any class. This room would be kept absolutely quiet and a test monitor could be stationed in the room to administer tests. Also, this room could be open from 7:30 A.M. until 4:00 P.M., giving students ample time to make up tests.

In the past, we have pointed out the need for a student lounge, but another problem in terms of space has risen. Students need a test make-up center, and we challenge the administration to find a room to set up this much-needed facility.

❶ This writer introduces the problem indirectly through a series of examples.
Another option:
- Address the problem and explain its significance directly.

❷ Offers statistics to show severity of problem

❸ Explores causes of the problem

❹ Offers a reasonable solution and explains how to put it into effect

PROB-SOLUTION

Do It Yourself

❶ Prewriting

Explore possible topics. To decide on an appropriate topic, try one of the following activities.

- **Brainstorm** about problems you have discussed with your classmates or at home with your family.
- **Read newspapers** to find out what people are complaining about in the letters to the editor.
- **Complete this sentence:** One thing that really bothers me is _____ .

For more on finding a topic, see p. 452.

Decide on a topic. To help you decide on your topic, consider these factors for each problem you listed.

Thinking About Your Topic	
Analyze the problem	• What caused it? • What are its effects? • What or whom does it affect? • Is it a serious problem? • Does it interest you?
Brainstorm solutions	• What do you think could resolve the problem? • Are there one or more solutions that could be applied? • Which of these solutions stands out as the best?
Analyze the best solution	• What is needed to put the solution into effect? • Who would carry out the solution? • How will it be paid for if finances are needed?
Explore evidence that supports your solution	• Are there examples, statistics, and facts that support your argument? • What is the logical reasoning behind your argument?

Identify your audience. For each problem, decide who would be interested. Why would the problem interest them? What points in your proposed solution would make sense to them? Once you have a clear picture of your audience, you will be able to write your essay with those readers in mind.

❷ Drafting

Get started. In writing a problem-solution essay, you need to present a logical argument to persuade your audience that your solution is a sound one. To do this, you will need to show logical relationships while avoiding logical fallacies. To give structure to your argument, use a clear pattern of organization, as outlined below.

Structuring Your Argument

Introduction	• Identify the problem.
	• Explain why it is significant.
Body	• Explain the causes and effects of the problem, using examples, statistics, facts, anecdotes, or quotations to support your points.
	• Identify and explain possible solutions, or focus on one solution that seems best.
	• Explain why this solution will work and address concerns your audience may have about the proposed solution.
	• Describe how to achieve the solution.
Conclusion	• Summarize the problem and the benefits of your proposed solution.

Use logical arguments. As you work on your draft, remember that you need to persuade your audience to accept your solution. To encourage and maintain your readers' interest, use logical reasoning in expressing your ideas. Here are some tips for creating sound logical arguments.

Here's How Developing Logical Arguments

- **Express Logical Relationships** Illustrate your points with clear cause-and-effect connections, strong analogies, or significant comparisons and contrasts.

- **Avoid Logical Fallacies** Make sure you are not using circular reasoning, either/or fallacies, or overgeneralizations.

- **Draw Valid Conclusions and Logical Inferences** Don't leap to conclusions. Show a clear connection between the problem and the solution.

- **Watch Your Language** Don't use vague words, such as *all, everyone, always, never,* and *none.*

For more about logical relationships and logical fallacies, see pp. 502–510.

❸ Revising

TARGET SKILL ▶Effective Conclusions An effective conclusion follows logically from the essay's body and leaves the reader with something to think about. It uses forceful language to drive home your point and does not introduce new material.

> In the past, we have pointed out the need for a student lounge, but another problem in terms of space has risen. ~~Even more than we need more variety in the cafeteria meals,~~ students
> *challenge*
> need a test make-up center, and we ~~ask~~ the administration to find a room to set up this much-needed facility.

❹ Editing and Proofreading

TARGET SKILL ▶Avoiding Awkward Shifts in Verb Tense Verb tenses and verb forms—past, present, and future—must be consistent in your writing, or your readers will be confused.

> You take out your number-two pencil and start. All of a
> *comes*
> sudden another student ~~came~~ in for help, so a teacher
> *starts*
> ~~started~~ going over yesterday's lessons. You then try to block
> *walks* *runs*
> that out when another teacher ~~is walking~~ in and ~~running~~ off 100 copies.

For more about shifts in verb tense, see pp. 143–145.

❺ Sharing and Reflecting

Share your finished work with people who are in a position to bring about your solution. Read it aloud in class, using effective verbal and nonverbal strategies, and ask for audience feedback.

For Your Working Portfolio. Later, **reflect** on what you have learned about your writing. Did your problem-solution essay hold up well? Attach your reflections to your finished work. Save your problem-solution essay in your 🗀 **Working Portfolio.**

Real World Problem-Solution Writing

You've probably read articles and editorials that discuss the solutions to problems on everything from getting a good deal on a car to resolving the national debt. You've also seen hundreds of commercials that present a common problem and then offer their product as the solution. Each of these is an example of problem-solution writing. As you read problem-solution writing in places like the following, analyze the strategies the writers use.

- Newspaper and magazine articles and editorials
- Advertisements
- Letters to your representative
- Bills before Congress
- Public-service posters

SUNDAY NEWSPAPER SUPPLEMENT

Magazine Article

Safer Air Bags Are Needed Now

By U S Senator Mike DeWine

. . . In November 1991 Congress, after years of virtual silence on [the issue of air bags], required auto manufacturers to install air bags in all new cars by 1998. Since that time many lives have been saved. An unintended but fatal consequence has occurred, however. Small children and some adults are at risk of serious injury or even death from the deployment of standard air bags. **For the complete text of the article, see MODEL BANK, p. 644.**

CONGRESSIONAL BILL

United States Congress

A BILL

To provide for the defense of the environment, and for other purposes.

Be it enacted by the Senate and House of Representatives of the United States of America in Congress assembled,

SECTION 1. SHORT TITLE.

This Act may be cited as the "Defense of the Environment Act of 1999".

SECTION 2. FINDINGS AND PURPOSE.

(a) Findings. —Congress finds that provisions that reduce protection of the environment have been included in legislation without adequate consideration and an opportunity for Members to vote on the provisions.

(b) Purpose. —The purposes of this Act are to—

(1) require Members of Congress to vote in the House of Representatives and the Senate on provisions included in legislation that reduce protection of the environment; and

451

Student Help Desk

Problem-Solution Essay at a Glance

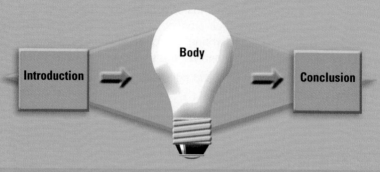

Introduction ➡ Body ➡ Conclusion

IDEA Bank

Tips for Finding a Topic

Look High and Low

Examine your environment and your daily life for problems you can try to solve.

Interview

Ask an official of your school or town what kinds of problems he or she faces and how the problems might be solved.

Look Far and Wide

Examine newspapers, magazines, and the Internet for ideas about problems outside your own community.

Read the Literature

Get inspiration from reading what others have written about problems and solutions. For a real-life account of action on a problem, read *Montgomery Boycott* by Coretta Scott King (*Language of Literature*, Grade 10).

- Why do you think I wrote about this problem?
- Describe the solution I recommended.
- What statements or facts did I use to support my argument?
- What information did you find most convincing? least convincing?
- How can I clarify anything that confused you?

Publishing Options   Getting Your Solutions Across

Oral Communication	• Deliver your essay as a speech to people who can help solve your problem. • Record your essay for broadcast on your school or local radio station. • Use hypertext software to create a multimedia presentation of your essay.
Print	• Send your essay to a local newspaper as a letter to the editor.
Online	• Check out **mcdougallittell.com** for more publishing options.

The Bottom Line

Checklist for a Problem-Solution Essay

Have I . . .

____ stated the problem clearly?

____ explained why it is important?

____ explored all aspects of the problem?

____ offered one or more reasonable solutions?

____ provided support for my proposed solution?

____ used logical arguments?

____ concluded by summing up my proposal?

Poetry

Learn What It Is

Poetry is a form of creative writing that emphasizes language and imagery. Many people mistakenly believe that a poem must describe something beautiful and also must rhyme. In fact, a poem can be about any subject, and rhyme is optional. Poetry can tell a story, make an observation, or describe an experience. Poets show the meaning of an experience or idea through the words they choose.

This workshop focuses on writing poetry, but it also discusses two other creative writing forms: short stories and dramatic scenes.

Basics in a Box

POETRY AT A GLANCE

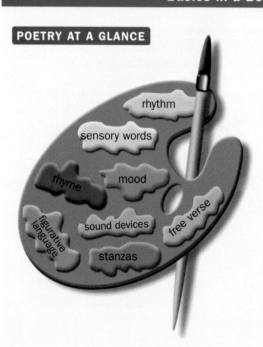

rhythm

sensory words

rhyme

mood

figurative language

sound devices

free verse

stanzas

RUBRIC

Standards for Writing

A successful poem should

- focus on a single experience, idea, or feeling
- use precise, sensory words in a fresh and interesting way
- incorporate figurative language such as similes and metaphors
- include sound devices as appropriate to support the meaning of the poem

See How It's Done: *Poetry*

Student Models

RUBRIC
IN ACTION

Walking

I'm walking across the top of the crusty snow
        without falling through
        without leaving footprints
without leaving any
          indication that I was ever here at all.
        But that's okay.
On the frozen snow that covers the ground
        the walking is easier
         if I take a little care
          in where
            I put my feet.
        —Andrew Love, Alternative Community H.S.

❶ Uses repetition to emphasize solitude

❷ Focuses on a single idea— walking in snow

Stories

❶ Draws readers into the poem with a solid image of a woman looking at old photographs

She sits
Bent over
Her fingers slowly sort through the faded pictures
Telling her old stories again.
Her mind fixes on the black-and-white of
Faraway times
Long-ago feuds
Old friends.

❷ Uses alliteration (the repetition of f sounds) to create rhythm and to shift the focus

She is moving into her childhood world
Like a clock wound slowly backward.
Swimming in the river in July
Eating stolen watermelon
Coming home to find her sweetheart
Waiting on the porch.

❸ Uses a simile to change time in the poem

"Quit running away from me, Mary," he said
And she did.
Soon she will come to the place where all
Life begins and ends,
Shining, radiant, eternal
She will turn to the angels and say,
"Let me tell you a story."
        —Candice Rhodes Mast, Turner Ashby H.S.

❹ Incorporates dialogue

❺ Uses carefully chosen synonyms

POETRY

How to Make a Sweet Potato Pie

First, my child,
you must understand
the history of sweet potatoes.
Like our ancestors, they were
brought to this country
in a cruel manner,
dredged out of the dirt,
leaving many roots behind.
Picked just short of ripeness,
survivors of chilling nights
and hot, parched days,
they did not resist
new surroundings;
instead, they thrived
with a unique style
and character.
They never forgot
where they came from.
Their master's stick
and shovel may have
dug into their sides
a hundred times,
but they never faltered,
never showed fear
or sadness.
No, child! They rose up
in grace and beauty
from their mother,
Earth.

      —Lauren Hart, Towson H.S.

❶ Uses direct address to draw readers into the poem

❷ Uses an unusual and powerful comparison as the focus of the poem

❸ Uses short lines for emphasis

❹ Uses precise words to create strong images

❺ Includes personification

CHAPTER 24

Do It Yourself

Purpose   To write expressively

Audience   Classmates, friends, family members

❶ Prewriting

There are no limits on what your poem can be about. The important thing is to give yourself time to think about ideas.

Reflect. Go to some quiet place where you won't be distracted. Think about memories, events, people, and places that are important to you. Allow yourself to reflect on your ideas.

Freewrite. Write as much as you can about the ideas that come to you as you reflect. If you run out of ideas, read what you've written and circle interesting subjects, images, and details that you'd like to turn into a poem. Continue to write about these.

Focus. Choose an interesting detail or image from your freewriting notes as the focus of your poem. Use a strong image that will give you more ideas as you write.

Consider mood. How do you feel about your topic? Angry? Glad? Sad? Amused? Create the mood of your poem by using words and images that convey your feelings.

❷ Drafting

Write freely about your topic, using strong words to build meaningful images. Choose words for their sound and their ability to express your feelings to readers. Try using the following **sound devices** to add rhythm and unity to your poem.

- **Alliteration**—repeated initial consonant sounds (**f**riendly **f**ace)
- **Assonance**—repeated vowel sounds (s**ou**nd b**ou**nced)
- **Rhyme** (an ocean **haze** dims the summer **days**)

Use figurative language to present ideas in new or unexpected ways.

- **Similes** (His face was like the full moon.)
- **Metaphors** (My love is a bird that cannot fly.)
- **Personification** (Large stones wallowed in the mud.)

Experiment with the form of your poem by grouping lines into stanzas, indenting certain lines, or using a variety of line lengths. Read your lines aloud to help you hear the rhythm of your words.

POETRY

❸ Revising

TARGET SKILL ▶Improving Figurative Language The figurative language you use should be fresh and interesting. Make sure the images you create are sharp and precise. Stay away from clichés—overused expressions and ideas.

> **STUDENT MODEL**
>
> *moving into her childhood world*
> She is ~~going down memory lane~~
> *like a clock wound slowly backwards.*
> ~~and thinking about her childhood,~~
>
> ~~like a backwards clock.~~

❹ Editing and Proofreading

TARGET SKILL ▶Punctuation Punctuation helps readers understand when to pause and how to group ideas. Poets make their own decisions about how to punctuate their poems. In general, use standard rules for punctuating your poetry. Punctuation should make the ideas clear, not confusing.

> **STUDENT MODEL**
>
> Picked just short of ripeness,
> survivors of chilling nights
> and hot parched days,
> they did not resist
> new surroundings;

❺ Sharing and Reflecting

After you have polished and proofread your poem, consider how you might **share** it with an audience. You might hold a poetry reading in which you and your classmates read your poems aloud. Remember to use effective verbal and nonverbal strategies in your reading. Ask your classmates for feedback on your poem and your presentation.

For Your Working Portfolio. After sharing, **reflect** on what you learned from writing your poem. Did the process of writing help you make connections you hadn't thought of before? Did it help you find out anything new about yourself? Attach your answers to your finished work. Save your poem in your 📁 **Working Portfolio.**

Learn What They Are: *Short Stories and Dramatic Scenes*

Short stories and dramatic scenes are two other kinds of creative writing. Use the short-story form when you want to develop and resolve a conflict between characters. You can bring a story to life through a dramatic scene, which tells a story mainly through characters' dialogue.

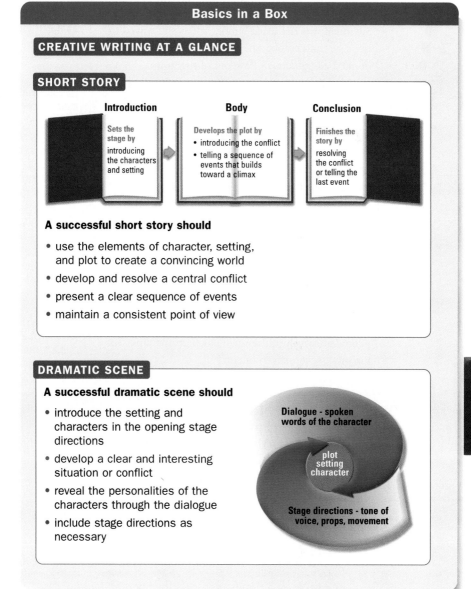

Basics in a Box

CREATIVE WRITING AT A GLANCE

SHORT STORY

Introduction	Body	Conclusion
Sets the stage by introducing the characters and setting	Develops the plot by • introducing the conflict • telling a sequence of events that builds toward a climax	Finishes the story by resolving the conflict or telling the last event

A successful short story should

- use the elements of character, setting, and plot to create a convincing world
- develop and resolve a central conflict
- present a clear sequence of events
- maintain a consistent point of view

DRAMATIC SCENE

A successful dramatic scene should

- introduce the setting and characters in the opening stage directions
- develop a clear and interesting situation or conflict
- reveal the personalities of the characters through the dialogue
- include stage directions as necessary

Dialogue - spoken words of the character

plot
setting
character

Stage directions - tone of voice, props, movement

POETRY

See How They're Done

GUIDELINES
IN ACTION

Prom Night (excerpt)

"You look great! Have a good time! See you later!"
Susannah was her usual bubbly self as she waved to
her sister and grabbed her purse. Outside, a car
honked and Susannah flew out of the house.

"Thanks," answered Janna weakly, as the door
closed. Janna paced the living room floor, thinking of
how she had been planning for this day for months.
She lifted the hem of her long gown, which
seemed to her to have cost a fortune considering the
amount of money she made from her Saturday
clerking job at the library. The little yellow bows on
her medium-heeled shoes still seemed to be just the
right touch. In her hair, a carefully-chosen pearl
barrette held her cascading curls in place.

Dusk slowly gave way to dark, and she watched
each set of car lights as they slipped by the
apartment building. She had purposely not worn her
watch, which would have spoiled the smooth line of
her arm, from tapered sleeve to jeweled ring. She
peered anxiously at the small clock on the table. Six
forty-five, seven, seven fifteen ...

❶ Opens with dialogue

❷ Establishes main character and setting

❸ Suggests a serious, melancholy mood

❹ Presents concrete details

❺ This writer uses a third-person limited point of view.
Another option:
• Write in the first person, the main character's view.

❻ Planning a Short Story

- Choose a **story idea** to write about—something unusual that happened to you or to someone else.
- Think of who the **characters** will be. Who is the main character? What other characters are needed?
- Decide on the **setting**—where and when the story takes place.
- Map out the **plot.** What is the main conflict in the story? How did it happen? How will it be resolved?
- Choose who will tell the story **(point of view).** This might be a character as a first-person or a third-person narrator.
- Create a **mood,** such as sad, scary, serious, or amusing.

CHAPTER 24

Dramatic Scene
Damen Valasquez
Monadnock High School

Blaze (excerpt)

Characters: Johanna *is the captain of the spaceship;*
Jerzy *is the first mate of the ship.*

Setting: *Johanna and Jerzy are seated in front of control panels inside a spaceship. The year is 2305.*

Johanna. *(sternly)* Exactly how long has that blaze of light been in the lower quadrant of our screen?

Jerzy. *(bored)* It's been four hours, 30 minutes, and . . . oh, uh, about 40 seconds. It hasn't changed much. *(He yawns.)*

Johanna. *(pointing to a table behind them)* Read me Staff Sergeant Kofi's report again. The one that gives Captain Dante's first sighting.

Jerzy. *(pulls the journal from a stack and leafs through it)* Let's see . . . here it is. *(reading aloud)* July 23, 2105. A scarlet blaze appeared at X39, Y20 at 0200 hours and stayed in that spot for 48 hours. This blaze was a more brilliant color than any seen in the previous 1,226 missions.

Johanna. Two hundred years ago to the day. Too bad Dante wasn't well enough to come with us this time.

Jerzy. *(laughing)* Just what we need, a 250-year-old retired captain aboard.

*(**Johanna** is looking more intently at the screen and beginning to move controls. She is becoming quite excited, which **Jerzy** hasn't noticed.)*

Johanna. *(quietly, but getting louder)* Jerzy! Jerzy! Come look at this! Quick! What's happening?

❶ Introduces characters and setting in the opening stage directions

❷ Reveals information about the characters through dialogue

❸ Includes stage directions to show body movement

❹ Includes details to give convincing background

❼ Planning a Dramatic Scene

- Think about an interesting **situation or event** to write about.
- Decide who the **characters** are, when and where the story takes place, and what events will happen in your scene.
- Write each **character's words** in a style that fits the character.
- Draft **stage directions** that tell how characters look, sound, speak, and move.
- Convey the **mood** of your scene through the dialogue.

POETRY

Student Help Desk

Poetry at a Glance

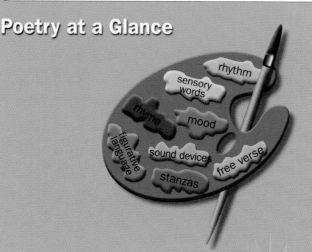

rhythm
sensory words
rhyme
mood
figurative language
sound devices
free verse
stanzas

IDEA Bank

Poetry Possibilities

Borrow a Line

Use a line from another poem as your first line. Choose a line that appeals to you and build on it. You might want to borrow a line from the poem "Grudnow" by Linda Pastan (*Language of Literature*, grade 10).

Five Nouns

Choose five interesting nouns, and write a poem that uses one of the nouns at the end of each line. Mix up the order of the nouns and use them to write five more lines. If you are inspired, keep going.

Find a Form

Find a library book about different poetry forms, such as haiku and sonnet. Write a poem using one of these forms.

Take a Long Look

Go to a museum or an art gallery and look at the exhibits. Once you've found a particularly interesting work of art, sit down in front of it and really study it. Take notes about how it looks, what it reminds you of, and what story it might be telling. Use your notes to write a poem about the piece.

Walk Around the Block

Take a walk in your neighborhood, and focus on the things around you. What can you discover with your five senses? Write a poem about this.

CHAPTER 24

Friendly Feedback

Ask Your Peer Reader

- How would you describe the overall mood of my poem?
- What was the most memorable image in my poem? Why?
- Which images seemed jarring or out of place? Why?

Publishing Options

Tooting Your Horn

Oral Communication	• Organize a class creative writing festival in which student writers of all kinds of creative writing read their work aloud.
Print Options	• Using pens, paints, or a computer drawing program, create posters that illustrate your poems. Hang the posters in your school or in other places such as the public library, the post office, or city hall.
Online	• Check out **mcdougallittell.com** for more publishing options.

POETRY

The Bottom Line

Checklist for Poetry

Have I . . .

_____ focused on a single experience, idea, or feeling?

_____ used precise, sensory words in fresh, interesting ways?

_____ incorporated figurative language such as similes and metaphors?

_____ included sound devices as appropriate to support the meaning of the poem?

Research Report

Learn What It Is

Do you wonder about things around you? Do you have questions about people or events or facts you've read about in history? in science? in art? A **research report** is your opportunity to dig into a subject that interests you and find answers. The following guidelines help you do that.

Basics in a Box

RESEARCH REPORT AT A GLANCE

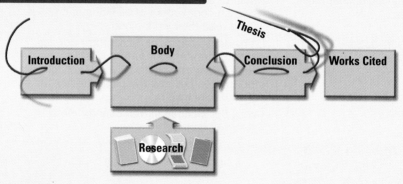

RUBRIC

Standards for Writing

A successful research report should

- include a strong introduction with a clear thesis statement
- use evidence from primary and secondary sources to develop and support ideas
- credit the sources of information

- display a logical pattern of organization, with transitions between ideas
- conclude with a satisfying summary of ideas
- include a correctly formatted Works Cited list at the end

See How It's Done: *Research Report*

Sandra Williams

Ms. Lopez

English II

23 Apr. 1999

Do Animals Possess Language?

Do animals communicate through language? The answer may depend on how language is defined. According to <u>Encyclopaedia Britannica Online</u>, language is "a system of conventional spoken or written symbols by means of which human beings ... communicate." According to this definition, animals do not (and cannot) have language. Yet recent research suggests that some animals do possess language skills, despite the fact that they do not speak.

Is speech a necessary part of language? Professor Philip Lieberman of Brown University writes that speech is "one of the key elements, if not <u>the</u> key element, in fully developed human language and cognition" (150). This would seem to disqualify animals as users of language. On the other hand, Dr. E. Sue Savage-Rumbaugh claims that <u>understanding</u> language is an important element too.

In her research, Savage-Rumbaugh has demonstrated that chimpanzees can be taught to understand human speech. In one study, Savage-Rumbaugh compared the language comprehension of a one-and-a-half-year-old human child named Alia and an eight-year-old ape named Kanzi. Each responded to hundreds of sentences spoken in English (Savage-Rumbaugh et al. 45). While both showed that they understood most of the sentences, Kanzi, the chimp, outscored Alia by 72% to 66% overall (76).

Savage-Rumbaugh has concluded that a chimpanzee can acquire language skills similar to those of a two-year-old child if both the child and the chimp are raised in a "language-rich

---

RUBRIC
IN ACTION

❶ This writer opens with a thought-provoking question.

Other options:
- Present a startling fact.
- Tell an anecdote.
- Begin with the thesis statement.

❷ Includes a clear thesis statement

❸ Cites statistics and supports ideas with quotations from credited sources

REPORT

---

environment." She writes, "Chimpanzees do travel down the language road given the appropriate rearing environment, but they travel more slowly than humans, and not as far" (Savage-Rumbaugh and Lewin 177–78).

Other research provides evidence that animals may be physically able to possess language skills. According to a 1998 <u>Science</u> article, researchers have discovered that a language area of the brain that was once thought to be unique to humans is also present in chimpanzees (Gannon et al. 220).

❹ Uses a transition between paragraphs

Works Cited

Angier, Natalie. "Chimpanzees Doin' What Comes Culturally." <u>New York Times</u> 17 June 1999, natl. ed.: A1+.

Gannon, Patrick J., et al. "Asymmetry of Chimpanzee Planum Temporale: Humanlike Pattern of Wernicke's Brain Language Area Homolog." <u>Science</u> 9 Jan. 1998: 220–22.

Golden, Frederic. "Clever Kanzi." <u>Discover</u> Mar. 1991: 20.

"Language." <u>Encyclopaedia Britannica Online.</u> Vers. 99.1. Encyclopaedia Britannica. 23 Mar. 1999 <http://www.eb.com:180/bol/topic?eu=114866&sctn=1>.

Lieberman, Philip. <u>Eve Spoke</u>: <u>Human Language and Human Evolution.</u> New York: Norton, 1998.

Savage-Rumbaugh, E. Sue, et al. <u>Language Comprehension in Ape and Child</u>. Monographs of the Society for Research in Child Development 58. 3–4. Chicago: U of Chicago, 1993.

Savage-Rumbaugh, E. Sue, and Roger Lewin. <u>Kanzi: The Ape at the Brink of the Human Mind</u>. New York: Wiley, 1994.

❺ **Works Cited**
- Identifies all sources of information credited in the report
- Presents entries in alphabetical order
- Gives complete publication information
- Contains correct punctuation in entries
- Is double-spaced throughout
- Follows a preferred style, such as MLA guidelines

Do It Yourself

Writing Prompt Investigate a topic that interests you, and write a research report about it.

Purpose To share information about your topic

Audience Classmates, your teacher, or anyone else interested in the topic

❶ Developing a Research Plan

To write a research report, you need to consult a wide range of sources to find reliable information.

Finding an Angle on Your Topic

Most likely, you will begin the research process with a very broad topic in mind. You might be interested in Shakespeare or the space shuttle, the influence of Eastern philosophies on Western thought or, as in the paper in this chapter, language and animals. The first step is to briefly explore a variety of sources that touch on your topic, looking for a research direction or **angle** that interests you. You can do this by

- scanning magazines and newspapers
- browsing the Internet using a variety of key terms
- talking over the topic with friends and teachers
- reading introductions, conclusions, and captions in books on your topic (and in books shelved around them in the library or media center)
- exploring videos and other collections in your media center

For more on finding a research topic, see p. 478.

For more on finding a research topic, see p. 478.

Developing Research Questions

In choosing the resources you will use in your research, you will be influenced both by the angle you are pursuing and the amount and kind of information you can find on the topic.

It will help to develop a set of research questions to guide you. For example, the writer of the student report in this chapter was interested in the research of Dr. Savage-Rumbaugh. Her guiding research questions included the following:

- What studies did Dr. Savage-Rumbaugh conduct and what conclusions did she draw?

- Have other researchers found evidence that backs up her findings?
- Do other researchers disagree with her conclusions? If so, what evidence do they point to?
- Can we answer the question of whether animals have language?

You may need to focus and refocus your search as you make discoveries during the research process. Try to stay in touch with the aspect of the topic that grabbed your attention in the first place.

❷ Using and Documenting Sources

Finding and Prioritizing Sources

For a research report, you need to use both primary and secondary sources of information. **Primary sources** provide raw data and original observations. **Secondary sources** provide summaries, reflections, and perspectives on materials from primary sources.

Research Resources

	Characteristic	Examples
Primary sources	Provide direct, firsthand knowledge	Letters, journals, diaries, original manuscripts, questionnaires, interviews
Secondary sources	Provide interpretations, explanations, and comments on material from primary sources	Encyclopedias, textbooks, newspapers, magazines, biographies and other nonfiction books

Evaluating Sources

Not all sources are equally valuable. To **evaluate** your sources so that you can choose the best ones, ask yourself these questions.

- **Is the source up-to-date?** It is best to use the most recent sources, especially when researching rapidly developing fields of science.

- **Is the source reliable?** Is the author a recognized authority on your subject? Is the author from a respected university or other institution?

- **What are the author's viewpoints and biases?** Does the author seem to have a political, ethnic, gender, or other bias? Consider how the author's viewpoints might affect his or her objectivity.

Using a good mix of relevant sources will help you get a range of ideas and will make your report more interesting.

For more help on finding information, see pp. 483–497.

Making Source Cards

For any source you think might be useful, record all the relevant information about it on an index card. You will need this information when you prepare your Works Cited list. Give each card a number that you can use for reference when you take notes. For a library book, it is useful to include the call number.

> **Here's How** **Making Source Cards**
>
> Follow these guidelines when you make source cards.
>
> - **Book** Write the author's or editor's complete name, the title, the name and location of the publisher, and the copyright date.
> - **Magazine or Newspaper Article** Write the author's complete name (unless the article is unsigned), the title of the article, the name and date of the publication, and the page number(s) of the article.
> - **Encyclopedia Article** Write the author's complete name (unless the article is unsigned), the title of the article, and the name and copyright date of the encyclopedia.
> - **World Wide Web Site** Write the author's or editor's complete name (if available), the title of the document, publication information for any print version of it, the date of the electronic publication (if available), the name of any institution or organization responsible for the site, the date when you accessed the site, and the document's electronic address (in angle brackets).

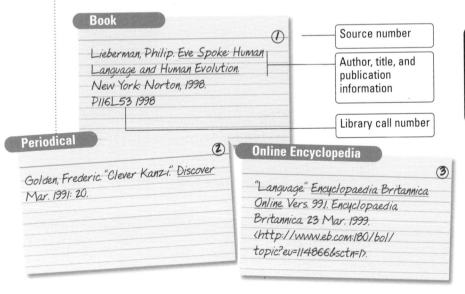

Book

Lieberman, Philip. *Eve Spoke: Human Language and Human Evolution.* New York: Norton, 1998.
P116L53 1998

Source number

Author, title, and publication information

Library call number

Periodical

Golden, Frederic. "Clever Kanzi." *Discover* Mar. 1991: 20.

Online Encyclopedia

"Language." *Encyclopaedia Britannica Online.* Vers. 99.1. Encyclopaedia Britannica. 23 Mar. 1999. <http://www.eb.com:180/bol/topic?eu=114866&sctn=1>.

REPORT

❸ Taking Notes

As you read or view your sources, keep index cards on hand and take notes on material that answers your research questions. You should paraphrase information from your sources, but be sure to include direct quotations that will support your ideas and make your paper more interesting.

> **Here's How** **Taking Notes**
>
> Follow these guidelines as you take notes.
> - **Use a separate index card** for each piece of information.
> - **Write a heading** on each card indicating the subject of the note.
> - **Write the number of the corresponding source card** on each note card.
> - **Put direct quotations in quotation marks.**
> - **Record the number of the page** where you found the material in the source.

Paraphrasing

When you paraphrase, you restate someone else's idea in your own words. If you use any of the author's original words or phrases, put them in quotation marks.

> **PROFESSIONAL MODEL**
>
> By the end of the nine-month test period, both Kanzi and Alia had demonstrated a well-developed ability to comprehend all types (and subtypes) of sentences, with Kanzi scoring just a little ahead.
>
> —E. Sue Savage-Rumbaugh and Roger Lewin, *Kanzi*

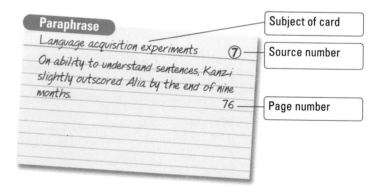

Paraphrase

Language acquisition experiments   ⑦

On ability to understand sentences, Kanzi slightly outscored Alia by the end of nine months.

76

Subject of card
Source number
Page number

Quoting

Whenever you use an author's own words, you must put them in quotation marks. Direct quotations—especially long ones—should be used sparingly. Save them for occasions when the author has

- used strikingly original language
- made an extremely important point
- used unusually concise language

Avoiding Plagiarism

Plagiarism is passing off someone else's work as your own. It is dishonest. You have plagiarized if you borrow, buy, or steal someone else's paper. But you have also plagiarized if you use an author's distinctive words without identifying the author.

STUDENT MODEL

ORIGINAL

Can an ape master anything like human language? Although primatologists have reported such abilities, the high priests of linguistics have scoffed.

PLAGIARIZED VERSION

Can apes master human language? Although researchers have found that they can, the high priests of linguistics have questioned them.

The writer has made changes. She has omitted some words from the original source ("anything like," for example) and replaced others (using *researchers* rather than *primatologists* and *questioned* rather than *scoffed*). But this is not enough. Here is a version that properly cites the source and avoids plagiarism.

STUDENT MODEL

In an article in <u>Discover</u> magazine, Frederic Golden has questioned whether apes can master human language. He has also noted that although some primatologists have reported that apes can acquire language, "the high priests of linguistics have scoffed" at this idea.

> Information is attributed to its author.

> The author's distinctive language is put in quotation marks.

REPORT

➍ Crafting a Good Thesis Statement

Once you have gathered information, you may begin writing. Perhaps the best way to start is to craft a thesis statement. A **thesis statement** contains a central idea that is supported by the research you have collected.

Your thesis statement will typically indicate your point of view, and it should be a statement that can be supported by various kinds of evidence.

Here is a checklist to help you write a good thesis statement for a research report.

> ### Thesis Statement Checklist
> ☑ Will my thesis allow me to write a paper that will fulfill my assignment?
>
> ☑ Is my thesis sharply focused and sufficiently limited?
>
> ☑ Have I stated it concisely, in a sentence my readers will understand?

For more on thesis statements, see pp. 340–341.

➎ Organizing and Outlining

After researching information, taking notes, and writing a good thesis statement, you need to choose an organizational pattern and outline your report.

Choosing an Organizational Pattern

One good way to begin organizing your information is to arrange your note cards according to key ideas. Look for special relationships among the ideas—such as the relationship of causes to effects or main ideas to supporting details. Try arranging the cards in several different ways, experimenting to see which arrangement works best. You may want to use different organizational patterns in different sections of your report.

Next, create an outline using your key ideas as main headings. In the student report on animal language, the writer began with a question and a definition. She then proceeded to make statements and elaborate on them using examples. On the following page is the outline the writer used at the start of her report.

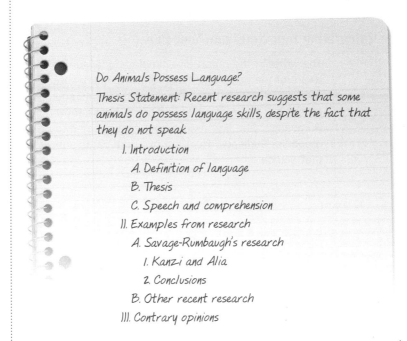

Do Animals Possess Language?

Thesis Statement: Recent research suggests that some animals do possess language skills, despite the fact that they do not speak

    I. Introduction

        A. Definition of language

        B. Thesis

        C. Speech and comprehension

    II. Examples from research

        A. Savage-Rumbaugh's research

            1. Kanzi and Alia

            2. Conclusions

        B. Other recent research

    III. Contrary opinions

Once you have an outline, you can group your index cards into the sections and subsections you have listed. Keep in mind that an outline is intended to guide you, not to limit you. You can always change it as you draft.

Sometimes making an outline seems an unnecessary step, but it usually saves time in the long run. Having an outline will nearly always help you write a better report, and it will help you determine whether any additional information is needed.

For more on organizational patterns, see pp. 343–351.

❻ Drafting

In the drafting stage, gather your note cards and outline and begin writing. You don't have to write the report in sequence from beginning to end. Some writers begin with the section they feel most confident about. You can even begin with your conclusion. Do what feels best to you.

Make sure that you write one or more paragraphs for every major entry in your outline. If you have not worked sequentially through your report, make sure your paragraphs are in order before you begin your revision. Remember to incorporate your own ideas into the report. Your major goal is to support your thesis statement.

Integrating Your Notes into Your Paper

The writer of the report on animals and language first became aware of the unusual abilities of some chimpanzees when she read an Internet article. She did not use this source in her final report, but the information led her to books written by Dr. Savage-Rumbaugh. She first read a book that seemed to be addressed to a popular audience. Here are two note cards she wrote based on that source.

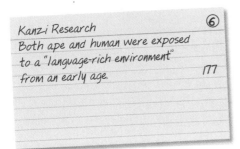

Kanzi Research   ⑥
Both ape and human were exposed
to a "language-rich environment"
from an early age.   177

Kanzi Research   ⑥
Savage-Rumbaugh concludes:
"Chimpanzees do travel down the language road given the appropriate rearing environment, but they travel more
slowly than humans, and not as far."
      177–78

Although the writer liked the succinct and well-phrased statement of Savage-Rumbaugh's conclusion, she felt she should also consult a more technical source for concrete data. She found that information in a monograph written by Savage-Rumbaugh and her colleagues. Here are two note cards from that source.

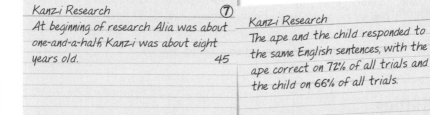

Kanzi Research   ⑦
At beginning of research Alia was about
one-and-a-half, Kanzi was about eight
years old.   45

Kanzi Research   ⑦
The ape and the child responded to
the same English sentences, with the
ape correct on 72% of all trials and
the child on 66% of all trials.   76

Notice how all this information is presented in two paragraphs in the final version of the report, as shown on the following page.

In her research, Savage-Rumbaugh has demonstrated that chimpanzees can be taught to understand human speech. In one study, Savage-Rumbaugh compared the language comprehension of a one-and-a-half-year-old human child named Alia and an eight-year-old ape named Kanzi. Each responded to hundreds of sentences spoken in English (Savage-Rumbaugh et al. 45). While both showed that they understood most of the sentences, Kanzi, the chimp, outscored Alia by 72% to 66% overall (76).

Savage-Rumbaugh has concluded that a chimpanzee can acquire language skills similar to those of a two-year-old child if both the child and the chimp are raised in a "language-rich environment." She writes, "Chimpanzees do travel down the language road given the appropriate rearing environment, but they travel more slowly than humans, and not as far" (Savage-Rumbaugh and Lewin 177-78).

Sharing Your Own Ideas and Interpretations

In researching and writing a report, do more than restate the information you have found. You will have to use facts, examples, and evidence to back up your ideas and make sure that your statements and conclusions are accurate. But be sure to make inferences, analyze and interpret evidence, and draw your own reasonable conclusions.

❼ Documenting Information

Parenthetical documentation is the most common way of giving credit to sources in a research report. In this method, a detailed record of sources appears at the end of the report in a Works Cited list. Brief references in parentheses within the body of the report allow readers to locate complete information about the source in the Works Cited list. You should credit the source of each quotation, paraphrase, and summary that you use.

Here's How Guidelines for Parenthetical Documentation

- **Work by One Author** Give the author's last name and the page number in parentheses: **Chimpanzees even exhibit cultural variations (Angier A1).** If you mention the author's name in the sentence, give only the page number in parentheses: **According to Natalie Angier, chimpanzees even exhibit cultural variations (A1).**

- **Work by More Than One Author** Give the authors' last names and the page number in parentheses: **(Savage-Rumbaugh and Lewin 177)** If a source has more than three authors, give the first author's last name followed by *et al.* and the page number: **(Savage-Rumbaugh et al. 76)**

- **Work with No Author Given** Give the title (or a shortened version of it) and the page number: **(Chicago Manual 126)**

- **One of Two or More Works by the Same Author** Give the author's last name, the title or a shortened version of it, and the page number: **(Lieberman, Eve Spoke 120)**

- **Two or More Works Cited at the Same Place** Use a semicolon to separate the entries: **(Gannon et al. 221; Golden)**

- **Electronic Sources** Give the author's last name, or if no author is named, give the title: **("Language")**

Preparing a Works Cited List

Gather your source cards and then read through your report. Put a check mark on the card for every work you have cited. Put the unused cards aside. (Only works actually referred to in your text should appear on your Works Cited list.) Place the checked cards in alphabetical order according to the authors' last names. For an anonymous source, use the first word of the title (excluding *A*, *An*, or *The*). Then follow these instructions.

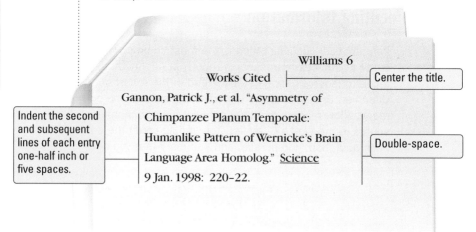

Williams 6

Works Cited ⟶ Center the title.

Gannon, Patrick J., et al. "Asymmetry of

Indent the second and subsequent lines of each entry one-half inch or five spaces. ⟶ Chimpanzee Planum Temporale:

Humanlike Pattern of Wernicke's Brain

Language Area Homolog." Science ⟶ Double-space.

9 Jan. 1998: 220–22.

For more help, see the MLA documentation guidelines on pp. 662–669.

⑧ Revising

TARGET SKILL ▶ **Inserting Quotations** Including a few of the exact words of a source can lend authority and interest to your writing. Begin the quoted section at a point where it fits into your sentence and completes its meaning. Punctuate it correctly.

> **STUDENT MODEL**
>
> **SOURCE**
> "Chimpanzees can acquire language skills spontaneously, through social exposure to a language-rich environment, as human children do. And, again like humans, early exposure is critical" (Savage-Rumbaugh and Lewin 177).
>
> **QUOTATION**
> Savage-Rumbaugh has concluded that a chimpanzee can acquire language skills similar to those of a two-year-old child if both the child and the chimp are raised in a "language-rich environment" (Savage-Rumbaugh and Lewin 177).

⑨ Editing and Proofreading

TARGET SKILL ▶ **Using Parenthetical Documentation** Carefully check the punctuation and spacing in your parenthetical references as well as in your Works Cited list. You can lose points from your grade for mistakes in this area. Remember, when you refer to a source that has several authors, you need include only the first author's name, followed by *et al.* and the page number.

> Each responded to hundreds of sentences spoken in
> *et al.*
> English (Savage-Rumbaugh, ~~Murphy, Sevcik, Brakke,~~ ~~Williams, and Rumbaugh~~ 45).

⑩ Sharing and Reflecting

After you have revised and proofread your report, share it with an interested audience.

For Your Working Portfolio After sharing your report, reflect on what you learned by writing it. Do you have a deeper understanding of your topic? What steps were the hardest? Have you learned ways to make them easier next time? Are there additional things you would like to learn about your topic? Attach your answers to your finished report and save them in your ⬛ **Working Portfolio.**

Student Help Desk

Research Report at a Glance

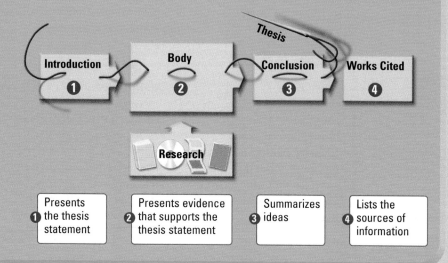

Introduction ❶	Body ❷	Conclusion ❸	Works Cited ❹
❶ Presents the thesis statement	❷ Presents evidence that supports the thesis statement	❸ Summarizes ideas	❹ Lists the sources of information

IDEA Bank

Tips for Finding Topics

Brainstorm List things you would like to know more about. Think up questions about each item. What is life like in a developing country? What do anthropologists do? What's really out in space? Circle questions on your list that hold the most interest for you.

Explore Look through magazines, encyclopedias, and the Internet to find answers or clues toward answers about your topic. Follow leads and examine information that you find interesting.

Look Around You Look at each aspect of your daily life, from your bike to your breakfast food, and ask what is behind it. Who created the games you play or the music you listen to? Who wrote the scripts for your favorite films or TV shows? How are those shows put together? Be curious.

Read Literature Think about authors you have been studying, such as Langston Hughes, Edna St. Vincent Millay, Nadine Gordimer, or Octavio Paz (*Language of Literature,* Grade 10). What would you like to know about them or about the subjects they explore in their writing?

Friendly Feedback

Questions for Your Peer Reader

- What was your favorite part of my report?
- What did you learn about the topic?
- What parts need to be stronger?
- What parts might be cut?
- Was my organizational plan clear? Would a different organizational plan work better?

Publishing Options

Print If you wrote on a topic that might interest a subject-matter teacher, such as your science teacher, share it with her or him and ask if you can publish your results for the class.

Oral Communication Use a computer and an authoring tool to turn your report into an oral or multimedia presentation, either for your English class or some other class. Consider enlivening your presentation with drawings, charts, or photographs.

Online Check out **mcdougallittell.com** for more publishing options.

The Bottom Line

Checklist for a Research Report

Have I . . .

- _____ provided a strong introduction with a clear thesis statement?
- _____ used evidence from primary and secondary sources to develop and support my ideas?
- _____ credited my sources?

- _____ followed documentation guidelines carefully?
- _____ followed an appropriate organizational pattern, using transitions between ideas?
- _____ summarized ideas in a satisfying conclusion?

Communicating in the Information Age

One Message Too Many?

In these days of instant communication and information overload, how do you wade through all the messages and data you receive? Your judgment is the key. Because information is only as good as its source, it is more important than ever that you evaluate wisely all that you see and hear.

Power Words
Vocabulary for Precise Writing

Information, Please!

Some people are information specialists: it is their job to give information. Others are natural fountains of information because of their education, intelligence, or experience. Use the words below to describe them.

Information Dispensers

While a **tour guide** or a **cicerone** gives you information on a trip, a **docent** guides you through a museum. Your school **counselor** gives information about schools and academics, while a **media specialist** helps you gather info in the library. A real expert in one field is a **guru.** If somebody calls you a **rocket scientist,** you must be smart yourself!

Walking Encyclopedias

Most knowledgeable people have a great deal of reading in their background. They are **erudite:** well educated and well read. **Professorial** types are usually **scholars.** The most learned people are **savants.** If they are also wise, they're **sage.** On the other hand, someone who's **savvy** or **shrewd** may have little formal education, but could have a great deal of **street smarts!**

▷ **Your Turn** Web of Workers

Think of all the jobs you can in which a person gives information—such as a telephone operator or a librarian. Create a cluster chart with *Information* in the center. Fill outlying circles with information jobs. Combine your chart with other students' charts to create a complete list.

CHAPTER 26

Finding Information

Finding Your Way

Where do you go when you need information? Do you surf the Web? Scan the library shelves? Speak to an expert? Today, you have more choices than ever when it comes to getting the information you need. In fact, you have so many choices that you might feel a little lost.

Finding information is similar to taking a car trip: you need to plan ahead, know where you're going, and pay attention to the signs around you. Think of this chapter as a road map that can help you find your way when you need to find information.

Write Away: Birthday Research

Using the microfilm or microfiche collection in your school or local library, find the front page of a newspaper from the day and the year you were born. Write a paragraph that describes how you found the front page and what the main news story was on the day you were born. Save your paragraph in your 📁 **Working Portfolio.**

ClassZone at
mcdougallittell.com

FINDING INFO.

The Library and Media Center

Where can you go to find the average price of a used car? information about a career that interests you? the birth date of your favorite actor or musician? You can find out about these and countless other topics at a library. A library is a warehouse of information on almost any subject you can think of.

❶ The Library Collection

The library collection is made up of all the materials and resources a library has to offer. All libraries may not have the same resources, but most have the resources listed below.

Reference materials	Encyclopedias, dictionaries, almanacs, atlases, yearbooks, directories, and chronologies
Stacks	Fiction, nonfiction, poetry, young adult books, children's books
Periodicals and newspapers	Newspapers, magazines, journals, and newsletters (also available on microfiche and microfilm)
Computer resources	Access to the World Wide Web, basic word-processing applications, and online databases
Audiovisual materials	Videotapes, audiotapes, CDs, CD-ROMs
Vertical file	Pamphlets, booklets, catalogs, handbooks, clippings
Special collections	Manuscripts, rare books, public records, correspondence, memorabilia, genealogical information, scrapbooks, maps, journals

Books on the library shelves are sorted into fiction and nonfiction. Fiction books, such as novels, are usually arranged in alphabetical order by the author's last name. Nonfiction books are classified into subject categories and assigned codes, called **call numbers.** The most common classification systems are the **Dewey Decimal** system and the **Library of Congress** system.

For more information on these classification systems, see p. 497.

HOT TIP

Find out whether your library has any special collections that could be useful to you. The librarian may also be able to tell you about helpful collections in nearby libraries.

❷ Finding Materials

The two primary tools for locating materials and information in the library are the library catalog and periodical indexes. A traditional catalog, or card catalog, is a cabinet with many small drawers that hold alphabetically arranged cards. Today, most catalogs are computerized.

Library Catalog The computer catalog lists all the items that the library owns. These include books, periodicals, maps, and audiovisual materials. Each item has its own record, or page, in the catalog. A single record is shown below.

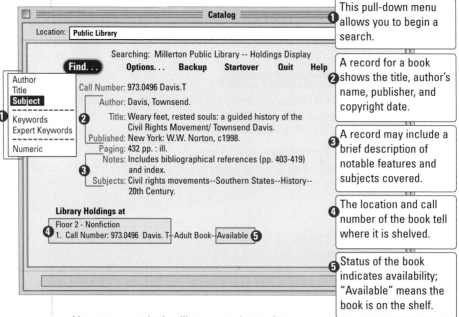

❶ This pull-down menu allows you to begin a search.

❷ A record for a book shows the title, author's name, publisher, and copyright date.

❸ A record may include a brief description of notable features and subjects covered.

❹ The location and call number of the book tell where it is shelved.

❺ Status of the book indicates availability; "Available" means the book is on the shelf.

You can search the library catalog using

- an **author's name**
- the **title**
- the **subject**
- **keywords**
- the **call number**

Catalogs in different libraries may vary in style, but the information they display is very similar. Ask the librarian for help, or use the catalog's *Help* feature if you get stuck.

Periodical Indexes Periodicals are magazines and other publications that are issued at regular intervals. The computer catalog can tell you whether the library receives a particular periodical. However, to find individual articles on a subject, you will need to use a **periodical index.** Such an index lists subjects, authors, and titles of articles from various magazines and journals. It also includes the information you need to locate the articles.

General Indexes

General indexes, such as the *Readers' Guide to Periodical Literature*, will help you find articles in popular magazines. These articles give general information on a subject.

Specialized Indexes

Specialized indexes, such as *Humanities Index* and *General Science Index*, list citations to articles in related subject areas. For example, *Humanities Index* covers subjects related to art and literature. The articles listed in these indexes are written by specialists and give in-depth information.

Newspaper Indexes

Indexes for individual newspapers, such as the *New York Times* and the *Wall Street Journal,* help you to locate newspaper articles.

Many libraries have online indexes, such as *Electric Library* and *InfoTrac,* which you can search using an author's name, a title, a subject, or a keyword.

❸ Special Services

Librarians and **media specialists** are experts in searching for and finding information. They can recommend sources of information, teach you how to use these sources, and tell you about other libraries that may be helpful. Ask a librarian where to begin researching a topic or how to conduct research on the Web.

Many libraries offer telephone reference services. You can call the library reference desk and ask your question.

Some libraries also sponsor lectures, book groups, and other special events.

LESSON 2 — Using Reference Works

The library collection includes many different reference works, which are shelved together in a special section. Most reference works are good sources of reliable information because they have been reviewed by experts. Unlike other books, reference books cannot be checked out of the library.

❶ Print Reference Works

General reference works contain facts and background information on a wide range of subjects. Use more specific reference sources to find in-depth information.

Library Reference Materials

Reference Works	Kinds of Information	How They're Organized
Encyclopedias	**General** Detailed articles on nearly all subjects **Specialized** Collections of articles that focus on a specific field, such as medicine or architecture	Alphabetically by topic
Dictionaries	**General** Word meanings, origins, spellings, and pronunciations **Specialized** Words and terms used in a specific field, such as geology or geography	Alphabetically by word entry
Almanacs and yearbooks	Facts and statistics	By topic, category, or date
Atlases	Collections of maps and geographical data	By region, topic, or historical period
Chronologies	Information on historical, political, and cultural events	By date or time period
Biographical dictionaries	Detailed information on the lives and careers of noteworthy people	Alphabetically by name
Directories	Names, addresses, and phone numbers of people and organizations	Alphabetically by name and sometimes subject

HOT TIP Take a few minutes before using a reference source to figure out how it is organized. Many reference books include a section near the front that explains how to use the book.

FINDING INFO.

❷ Electronic Reference Works

Many types of reference works—including atlases, telephone directories, and dictionaries—are also available in electronic form on CD-ROMs. The CD-ROM encyclopedia is one of the most popular electronic reference works. In addition to text, an electronic encyclopedia offers special features such as sound, video clips, and links to related articles and Web sites.

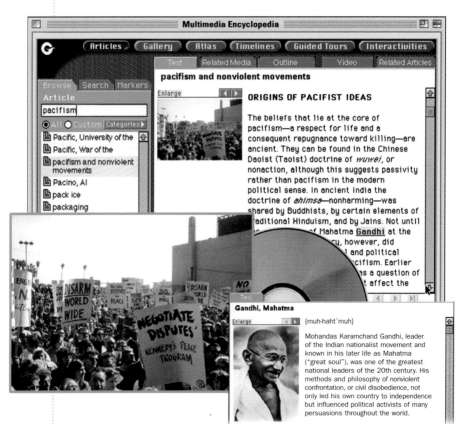

 Just because a reference source is electronic doesn't mean it's up to date. Consult with a librarian to find out if more current sources, either in print or electronic format, are available.

Using the World Wide Web

LESSON 3

If you conduct research on the Web, you need to know how to find helpful sites and how to judge whether sites contain reliable information.

Go to ClassZone at mcdougallittell.com for a complete tutorial on using the Web for research.

❶ How to Search the Web

The World Wide Web is made up of millions of Web sites and Web pages. Fortunately, **search tools** can help you find what you're looking for in this sea of information. Choose a search tool based on the kind of information you need.

Here's How Choosing a Search Tool

1. To find general information about your topic, use a **directory,** which is part of most search tools. A directory is a collection of Web sites organized into categories, such as art, politics, and recreation. Choose a general category and browse through the sites it contains to get background information about your topic.

2. To find specific information, use a **search engine,** such as *AltaVista* or *Infoseek.* A search engine allows you to look for information by using a phrase or term related to your topic. Once you enter a term, the engine finds Web sites that contain that term. This method of searching is called a **keyword search.**

More About Keyword Searches

Wait to conduct a **keyword search** until after you've done some general research on your topic. Use information gathered from this research to create a list of general and specific terms you can use for keyword searches. You can use a cluster diagram to organize your terms.

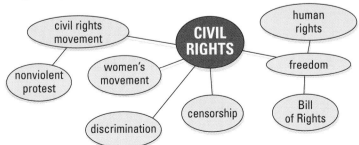

FINDING INFO.

Sometimes a keyword search results in too many sites that are not connected to your topic. You can narrow a search by using a more specific term from your list.

general: civil rights movement **specific:** Martin Luther King, Jr.

On the other hand, if you find your search results are too narrow, use a more general search term. Remember to use the *Help* or *Search Tips* feature of any search engine to guide your search.

Because different search engines scan different sites, use more than one search engine. Ask the librarian or do some research about useful search engines. Then try out several and compare the results.

❷ Understanding Your Search Results

Search engines sift through vast amounts of information and return long lists of Web sites. Follow these tips to interpret your search results.

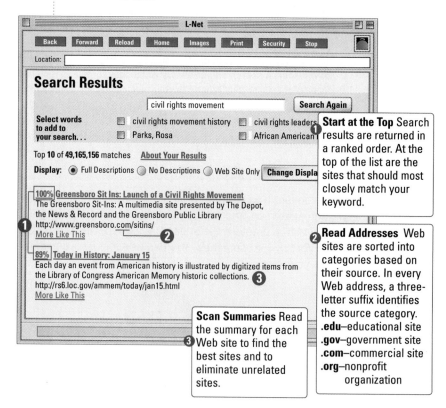

❸ Evaluating the Information You Find

Most traditional reference sources are reviewed by experts to make sure they contain accurate information. Unfortunately, many Web sites are not reviewed. Even when a Web site is related to your topic, you need to determine whether it contains accurate and unbiased information. Use the Web address and the following information to help you do this.

> ### Here's How Evaluating a Web Site
>
> 1. **Who or what is the source of the Web site?** The source may be an individual or an organization. In either case, look for the name and qualifications of the source, and use this information to determine whether the source is a reliable authority. If you can't find source information, or if the source is someone with a general interest in the subject but is not an expert, use a different site.
> 2. **Does the Web site have a bias?** The person or organization that created the Web site may be trying to sell something or convince you to hold a certain point of view. Remember that the information presented on a Web site may be one-sided.
> 3. **Is the information on the Web site accurate and reliable?** Don't rely on the Web alone for your research. Always check the accuracy of Web information using print sources, such as books, newspaper and magazine articles, and reference materials.
> 4. **Is the site up-to-date?** Look for the date of last revision, usually located at the top or the bottom of a Web site.

Although the Web is fun and exciting to use, it isn't always the best or only place to find information. Use a variety of traditional and Web sources when conducting research.

Hi & Lois By Brian & Greg Walker

FINDING INFO.

Reading Graphs and Charts

❶ Reading and Analyzing Graphs and Charts

Graphs, charts, tables, and diagrams present information mainly in pictures instead of in words. These pictures make complex information easier to understand. Here are some common techniques you can use to accurately read and interpret all kinds of graphic aids.

> **Here's How Understanding Graphic Aids**
>
> **Reading**
> 1. Read the title or caption to get the big idea or topic.
> 2. Read the labels to know what kinds of information are included.
> 3. Read keys or legends to understand how colors or symbols are used.
> 4. Read the data to learn what specific information is presented.
>
> **Interpreting**
> 5. Think about the big picture first. What patterns or general impressions do the data suggest?
> 6. Ask questions about what you see. Where are the extremes? What conclusions can you draw from this information? Are there any holes or gaps? Do you see any trends?

❷ Types and Purposes of Graphic Aids

Bar graphs use bars to present data. The lengths of the bars are used to compare the data.

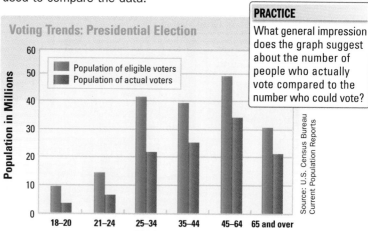

PRACTICE
What general impression does the graph suggest about the number of people who actually vote compared to the number who could vote?

Flow charts are useful in illustrating processes in sequential steps.

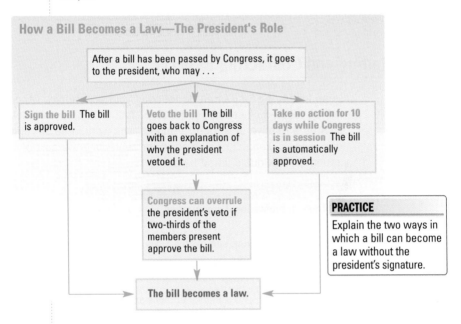

How a Bill Becomes a Law—The President's Role

After a bill has been passed by Congress, it goes to the president, who may . . .

Sign the bill The bill is approved.

Veto the bill The bill goes back to Congress with an explanation of why the president vetoed it.

Take no action for 10 days while Congress is in session The bill is automatically approved.

Congress can overrule the president's veto if two-thirds of the members present approve the bill.

PRACTICE

Explain the two ways in which a bill can become a law without the president's signature.

The bill becomes a law.

Tables present collections of facts arranged in a specific order and show how the facts relate to each other.

Amendments to the U.S. Constitution After the Bill of Rights

PRACTICE

Which amendment provides equal protection of the laws? When was this amendment adopted?

Amendment	Year Proposed by Congress	Year Adopted	What It Does
11	1794	1798	Gives states immunity from certain legal actions
12	1803	1804	Changes the selection of president and vice president through the electoral college
13	1865	1865	Abolishes slavery
14	1866	1868	Defines citizenship and citizen rights; provides due process and equal protection of the laws
15	1869	1870	Extends the right to vote to African Americans
16	1909	1913	Gives Congress power to impose income tax

Experts and Surveys

Talking to a person can be a good way to get information. If the person has expert knowledge in a certain field or has witnessed an important event, he or she may be able to give you information you couldn't find elsewhere.

❶ Finding and Contacting Experts

Some kinds of experts can be found in your community. Others may be located by searching the Web. Talk to people you know, such as a relative or a friend's parent, who work in fields related to your topic. You might also consider contacting the sort of groups or individuals listed below.

- **Trade or professional organization,** such as the American Medical Association
- **Government agency,** such as the Environmental Protection Agency or the Census Bureau
- **Special interest group,** such as the National Audubon Society
- A **professional** who works for or owns a business, company, or corporation related to your topic
- A **teacher or a professor** who teaches a class on your topic
- An **author** of books or magazine articles related to your topic

Your local library has professional **directories** that list phone numbers and addresses for many different groups, businesses, and individuals.

Once you've found the name of an expert, use these guidelines to help you contact and interview the person.

Here's How Contacting an Expert

1. **Choose a method of contact.** You can make contact by letter, e-mail, or telephone. Introduce yourself and describe why you are doing research and what you want to find out.

2. **Set up an appointment.** Once the person has agreed to an interview, set the time and date. Be prepared to offer a time and place convenient to the subject.

3. **Prepare for the interview.** Before the interview date, create a list of clear questions to ask during the interview.

For more information on interviewing, see pp. 528–529.

❷ Planning and Using Surveys

A **survey** is a method of gathering firsthand information from a group of people. Using a survey, you ask many people the same questions and then analyze the answers to find out about trends in opinions and preferences.

In order to get useful results from your survey, you need to ask clear, specific questions. Use different kinds of questions based on the kind of information you want to collect.

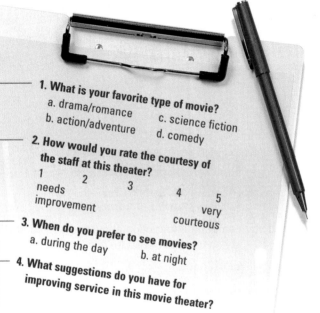

Multiple-choice questions give clear choices and easy-to-categorize answers.

Rating scale questions give data about how people feel about something.

Either/or questions give simple results that are easy to categorize.

Open-ended questions collect individual opinions. More work is required to interpret the results.

1. What is your favorite type of movie?
   a. drama/romance
   b. action/adventure
   c. science fiction
   d. comedy

2. How would you rate the courtesy of the staff at this theater?
   1   2   3   4   5
   needs improvement   very courteous

3. When do you prefer to see movies?
   a. during the day
   b. at night

4. What suggestions do you have for improving service in this movie theater?

You might want to test your survey by asking a few friends to fill it out and make suggestions for revisions.

Interpreting Surveys After you have distributed your survey and collected your data, you need to interpret the responses. Think about what the information tells you about the group of people who answered your survey.

- Do the results indicate a preference or a trend in thinking?
- Are you surprised by any of the results?
- What assumptions can you make, based on the survey results?

Consider representing the information from your survey in a chart or a diagram to help you interpret the results.

Student Help Desk

Finding Information at a Glance

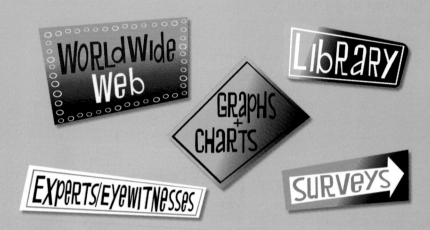

Tips for Evaluating Web Sites

Don't Get Caught in the Web!

Who or what is the source of the site?

If you can't find information about the source of the site, or if the source is not reliable, use a different site.

Does the Web site have a bias?

A site that contains lots of advertising or tries to persuade viewers to believe something is probably only giving one point of view. Look at other sources to find out about other points of view.

Is the information on the Web site accurate and reliable?

Always verify the accuracy of Web site information by checking it against other sources of the same information.

When was the site last updated?

Look for a date on the Web site that tells when the information was last updated. If the information is out of date, find a site that offers more current information.

Classification Systems What's My Number?

Most high-school and public libraries use the Dewey Decimal system to classify materials; many research and college libraries use the Library of Congress system.

Dewey Decimal System

000–099	General Works
100–199	Philosophy
200–299	Religion
300–399	Social Science
400–499	Language
500–599	Science
600–699	Technology
700–799	Fine Arts
800–899	Literature
900–999	History

Library of Congress System

A General Works
B Philosophy, Psychology, Religion
C History
D General History
E–F American History
G Geography, Anthropology, Recreation
H Social Sciences
J Political Science
K Law
L Education
M Music
N Fine Arts
P Language and Literature
Q Science
R Medicine
S Agriculture
T Technology
U Military Science
V Naval Science
Z Bibliography and Library Science

These books have been classified using the Dewey Decimal system. The call numbers indicate that the books are within the fine arts category.

The Bottom Line

Checklist for Finding Information

Have I . . .

____ clearly identified the information I am researching?

____ used periodical indexes and the library catalog to find information sources?

____ used general references to help define and narrow my topic?

____ worked with the reference librarian to find specialized sources of information?

____ used keywords to search the Web?

____ evaluated the reliability of Web sites I've used as information sources?

____ interpreted graphs and charts correctly?

____ talked with experts and used surveys when necessary?

FINDING INFO.

Power Words
Vocabulary for Precise Writing

Words for Distortion

Feeling a bit strange? Select from among these words to help you describe the sensation precisely.

Special FX

Special effects in movies can make things seem so **strange** and **distorted** that they look absolutely **surreal. Dreamlike** shapes and **phantasmal** characters move through a **bizarre** landscape filled with swirling, **kaleidoscopic** colors. **Unearthly** sounds give an **otherworldly** feel to the movie.

Long before such **eerie** movies were made, the American poet Edgar Allan Poe wrote **fantastical** tales and poems full of **outlandish** happenings in **outré** settings and situations that were really **off-the-wall.**

Weird Worlds

If **distortion** and **twisting** of everyday life is your dish, get yourself a pair of special goggles for touring in **virtual reality.** Cut loose in **cyberspace;** take a faster-than-light trip in **hyperspace.** Real life will seem like a **hallucination**—until you take off the goggles.

▷ **Your Turn** An Ocean in the Living Room

Make a sketch of the setting and people in a weird dream or daydream. Notice the subtle or not-so-subtle ways in which the dream has distorted reality. Is there an ocean in the living room? Are you flying? Is your pillow made of mashed potatoes? What distortions do you find?

Evaluating Information

La Chambre d'Ecoute (1958) Rene Magritte. © 2001 C. Herscovici, Brussels./Artists Rights Society (ARS), New York./Christiés Images LTD: 1999

Reality Check

This painting by the Belgian artist René Magritte contains images of two common things: an apple and a room. If shown separately, the images would look perfectly normal. However, when they are combined like this, the apple appears out of proportion, and the scene is illogical.

Like the images in Magritte's painting, pieces of information may make sense in some contexts but not in others. To understand whether information is logical or illogical, you need to examine each statement to make sure it fits comfortably into its context.

Write Away: When Pigs Fly

Think about something you have seen that was unusual or dreamlike or that defied logical explanation. Write a paragraph about what you saw and how you tried to make sense of it. Save the paragraph in your 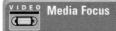 **Working Portfolio.**

VIDEO **Media Focus**

Separating Facts from Opinions

Every day you receive information—from TV and radio broadcasts, school lessons, the Internet, and conversations with friends. To evaluate and make judgments about the information you read or hear, you must be able to recognize the difference between facts and opinions.

❶ Identifying Facts

A **fact** is a statement that can be proved. Two types of facts are observations and definitions.

Types of Facts	
Observation	Kangaroos hop around on their hind legs.
	Many dolphins live off the coast of Florida.
Definition	Kangaroos are marsupial mammals that have short forelimbs and large hind limbs.
	Dolphins are marine mammals that are related to whales but are smaller.

To determine that a statement is a fact, you must be able to prove that it is correct. Here are some ways in which you can test a statement.

- **Make a personal observation.**
- **Refer to your experience.**
- **Ask a recognized expert.**
- **Consult an authoritative written source,** such as a print or online encyclopedia, atlas, almanac, or dictionary.

Make sure that you use reliable sources to back up your own observations and to check your own definitions.

❷ Identifying Opinions

An **opinion** is a statement that tells what a person thinks, believes, or feels about a subject. Unlike a fact, an opinion can't be proved.

Here are some tips you can use to determine whether a statement is an opinion.

- Look for adjectives or adverbs that people use to express judgments—for example, *beautiful* or *ugly, best* or *worst, valuable* or *worthless.*
- Look for words that indicate what a person feels or believes, such as *ought, should, think,* or *believe.*
- If you can't prove a statement by referring to observations, experiences, experts, or authoritative sources, the statement is probably an opinion.

An opinion can be either unsupported or informed. **Unsupported opinions** are not backed up with facts. Sometimes they are exaggerations or overgeneralizations, and sometimes they are statements of personal feelings or beliefs.

> **People should not keep kangaroos as house pets.**

Informed opinions are supported with facts.

> **People should not keep kangaroos as house pets, as they require special care and large open spaces.**

Even though an opinion makes perfect sense and is supported with facts, it's still an opinion.

When evaluating information, keep in mind the difference between fact and opinion. Facts can be proved; opinions can't be proved.

> **Opinion:** Elephants look clumsy.

> **Fact:** With its trunk, an elephant can lift a 600-pound log or can grasp an object as small as a coin.

PRACTICE Fact or Opinion?

Identify each statement as a fact or an opinion. If the statement is a fact, explain how you might prove it.

1. An adult male African elephant weighs about 12,000 pounds.
2. Hunting elephants for their ivory tusks should be banned.
3. The elephant shrew is so called because its nose somewhat resembles an elephant's trunk.
4. An elephant can run at speeds of up to 25 miles per hour.
5. Elephants make odd sounds.

Logical Relationships

In much the same way that a gardener weeds a garden to get rid of unwanted plants, you can use logic to weed out false information. One way to use logic is to analyze the connections between events, ideas, objects, people, and places. A **logical relationship** is a clear and reasonable connection.

❶ Cause and Effect

A **cause** is an event or action that leads directly to another event or action. An **effect** is the direct or logical outcome of an event or action. Words that signal cause-and-effect relationships include *because, therefore, so, as a result,* and *since.*

Being able to understand the connections between causes and effects can be especially helpful to you in history and science classes, where you will often be asked to explain how or why something occurred.

Cause-and-Effect Relationships

Cause	Effect
Rock masses move deep in the earth.	Shock waves are produced that cause tremors on the earth's surface—an earthquake.
Updrafts in thunderstorms carry raindrops to high altitudes, where the water freezes.	The water falls to the earth in the form of ice pellets, or hail.

Try to avoid seeing cause-and-effect relationships where none exist. Beware of the following fallacies.

- When one event follows another, don't assume that the first event is necessarily a cause of the second event. An event that has nothing to do with an event that follows it is called a **false cause.**

  The valley had pleasant weather all spring, so this summer it rains all the time. (The nice weather did not cause the rain.)

- Beware of the **single-cause fallacy,** in which something is said to be the sole cause of an effect when there are actually multiple causes.

  Los Angeles has heavy smog because the area has a lot of traffic. (In fact, there are many other reasons.)

❷ Comparison and Contrast

A **comparison** shows how two or more things—people, places, events, ideas, or objects—are alike. Some words that point to similarities are *also, both, in the same way,* and *likewise.* A **contrast** shows how two or more things differ. Words that indicate differences include *but, however, on the other hand,* and *unlike.* Comparisons and contrasts can help you make judgments and understand relationships.

You can use a Venn diagram to compare and contrast two or more items. The Venn diagram below, for example, clarifies the similarities and differences between tornadoes and hurricanes.

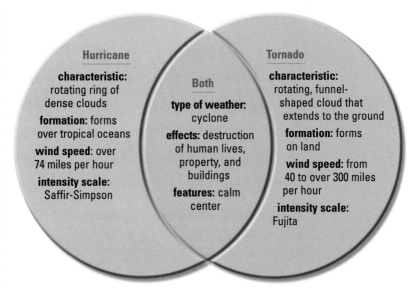

Hurricane

characteristic: rotating ring of dense clouds

formation: forms over tropical oceans

wind speed: over 74 miles per hour

intensity scale: Saffir-Simpson

Both

type of weather: cyclone

effects: destruction of human lives, property, and buildings

features: calm center

Tornado

characteristic: rotating, funnel-shaped cloud that extends to the ground

formation: forms on land

wind speed: from 40 to over 300 miles per hour

intensity scale: Fujita

❸ Analogy

An **analogy** is a type of comparison, often used to explain something unfamiliar by likening it to something familiar. For example, the following analogy compares an item from the 19th century to something used for a similar purpose today. By means of the analogy, the reader can better understand the importance of the item.

In the late 1800s, *The Old Farmer's Almanac* was to farmers what television weather forecasts are to us today.

A weak analogy is vague or stretches a comparison too far. A strong analogy, on the other hand, effectively expresses an essential likeness between two things. Consider the analogies in these passages from two versions of an essay about the greenhouse effect.

STUDENT MODEL

DRAFT

Carbon dioxide in the earth's atmosphere helps regulate our climate. **Like a prism, carbon dioxide absorbs the heat of the sun that is reflected off the earth.** As a result, the atmosphere's temperature is raised.

Weak Analogy
Too vague, offers no explanation of how a prism is similar to carbon dioxide

REVISION

Carbon dioxide in the earth's atmosphere helps regulate our climate. **Like a greenhouse that traps the sun's heat and warms the air so that plants can grow, carbon dioxide absorbs the heat of the sun that is reflected off the earth.** As a result, the atmosphere's temperature is raised.

Strong Analogy
Clearly explains the function of a greenhouse, so the reader more clearly grasps the role of carbon dioxide

For information about false analogy, see p. 508.

PRACTICE Cause-and-Effect Relationships

What cause-and-effect relationship is suggested by this graph? Write a paragraph explaining your answer.

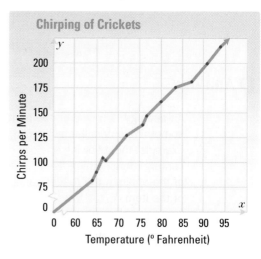

Chirping of Crickets

Interpreting Information

LESSON 3

Sometimes you will come across information that you will have to interpret by making inferences, drawing conclusions, or forming generalizations. These thinking skills are useful when you need to look beyond the obvious in order to make an important decision, solve a problem, or buy a product.

❶ Inferences

An **inference** is a logical guess based on facts and common sense. To make an inference, you "read between the lines" of the given facts, drawing on your own knowledge and experience to figure out what isn't stated directly.

Glaciers are huge moving bodies of ice and, as such, are powerful causes of erosion.

Glaciers must exist in cold parts of the world.

In this example, the reader uses her own knowledge to infer something the author has not stated.

WATCH OUT

People often use the words *infer* and *imply* interchangeably. However, there is a difference. The person making a statement does the implying ("She implied there was a problem"). A person interpreting the statement does the inferring ("From her comment, we inferred there was a problem").

EVALUATING INFO

❷ Conclusions

You draw a **conclusion** when you review a number of facts and details and use your prior knowledge to make a logical statement about a topic. Unlike making inferences, drawing conclusions requires you to read *beyond* the lines. Conclusions are more than just guesses; they are statements based on evidence.

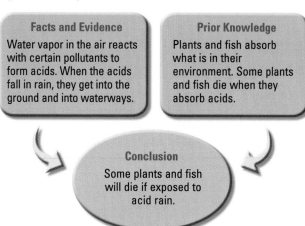

The conclusion above is a **valid conclusion** because it is a statement logically based on the evidence presented. The evidence and prior knowledge have a clear connection (the acids), which is the basis for the conclusion.

An **invalid conclusion** is a statement that is not consistent with known facts and details.

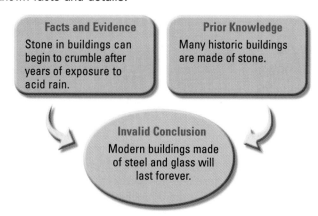

This conclusion is inconsistent with the facts presented, because it introduces an element (buildings made of steel and glass) that is unrelated to the evidence and prior knowledge.

❸ Generalizations

A **generalization** is a general statement based on many specific examples. Generalizations are much broader statements than inferences or conclusions. A sound generalization, like the one in the following diagram, needs to be based on sufficient evidence.

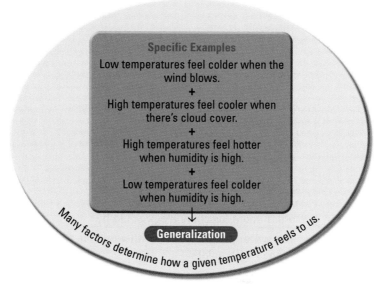

Specific Examples

Low temperatures feel colder when the wind blows.
+
High temperatures feel cooler when there's cloud cover.
+
High temperatures feel hotter when humidity is high.
+
Low temperatures feel colder when humidity is high.
↓
Generalization

Many factors determine how a given temperature feels to us.

For information about overgeneralization, see p. 509.

PRACTICE Making Inferences

Write a few sentences stating the conclusions you can draw from the hurricane probability map shown here. Then write a paragraph about how you came to those conclusions.

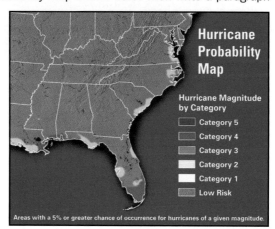

Hurricane Probability Map

Hurricane Magnitude by Category

☐ Category 5
☐ Category 4
☐ Category 3
■ Category 2
■ Category 1
☐ Low Risk

Areas with a 5% or greater chance of occurrence for hurricanes of a given magnitude.

EVALUATING INFO.

Recognizing Logical Fallacies

Sometimes an idea is stated in a way that at first appears to make sense. However, if you examine the statement carefully, you might find that it actually contains a **fallacy,** or an error in logic. There are many types of logical fallacies.

❶ False Analogy

A **false analogy** involves a comparison between things that do not have essential features in common. Whereas a weak analogy (see page 504) is a vague or overextended comparison, a false analogy is an illogical comparison.

> **The writer paints scenes with a pen as the artist paints scenes with colors.**

This analogy is false because the things being compared are not similar. A writer's pen is like an artist's brush, not an artist's colors. A more logical analogy would be

> **The writer paints scenes with words as the artist paints scenes with colors.**

This analogy is valid, since an artist uses colors and a writer uses words to depict scenes.

When examining an analogy, ask yourself these questions:

1. What are the similarities between the things being compared?
2. What are the differences between the things being compared?
3. Is there any one difference that makes the analogy illogical?

Dr. Katz by Blazek and Truxaw

❷ Circular Reasoning

When a person tries to prove a statement by simply repeating it in different words, the person is using **circular reasoning.** This fallacy is also called begging the question. Notice how the "reason" in each of the following sentences repeats the statement it is supposed to justify.

> **Our basketball team, the Cougars, should capture the regional title** because the team deserves to be number one.

> **Mr. Solomita's drama club attracts a large number of students** because many students come to the drama club.

The second part of each sentence offers no supporting evidence; it just restates the claim that was already made in the first part. Now, notice how another writer provides logical reasons.

> **Mr. Solomita's drama club attracts a large number of students** because he's an inspiring teacher and gives students a chance to act in school plays.

Don't think that the word *because* automatically signals a valid reason. Make certain that real support for a statement is provided.

❸ Overgeneralization

An **overgeneralization** is a generalization that is too broad to be valid and can easily be disproved. Overgeneralizations are often signaled by such words as *everyone, no one, always, never, best,* and *worst.*

> **Everyone who lives in the Southern states likes hot weather.**

> **Senator Kim's votes against the Medicare increase and the senior housing bill show that he** always **votes against the elderly.**

In each of these statements, the conclusions have been reached on the basis of too little evidence. Without interviewing everyone in the Southern states, the writer of the first statement cannot prove the statement to be true. In the second statement, only two examples, not the totality of the senator's voting record, are given as evidence.

❹ Either/Or Thinking

A claim that there are only two choices when there are actually more is an **either/or fallacy.** The following letter written by a student concludes with an either/or fallacy.

Dear Editors:

There has been a lot of talk about students' lack of concern for the appearance of our school. You hear about trash in the hallways and graffiti-covered walls. But if the school seemed more worth caring about, students would take better care of it. Most of the school building is very old. The halls are dark because the walls are dingy and the lights don't work. The newest part of our school, the gym, is clean and bright, and for three years now students have kept it that way. **Either** we build a new school, **or** it will be destroyed in three years.

The student focuses on two options, ignoring a variety of ways in which the school's appearance could be improved. For example, the school board could pay to repair the lighting and structure, or students could pitch in and clean up trash in the halls.

PRACTICE Identifying Logical Fallacies

Identify the kind of logical fallacy—either/or fallacy, circular reasoning, overgeneralization, or false analogy—that is illustrated by each of the following statements. Then rewrite the statement so that it's logical.

1. The orchestra was well-rehearsed because it had practiced a lot.
2. No one understands opera.
3. Either you have artistic talent, or you don't.
4. Tuning an instrument is similar to finding the right outfit to wear.
5. Musical talent takes time to develop because it takes years before you have a sense of musicianship.

LESSON 5 Misusing Emotional Appeals

An **emotional appeal** stirs up feelings by means of carefully chosen words and images. Although emotional appeals can be used effectively in editorials, speeches, and essays, some advertisers and politicians use them improperly to deceive people or to manipulate their emotions. Recognizing misuses of emotional appeals can help you see through weak arguments.

❶ Bandwagon Appeal

In old-time political campaigns, politicians traveled from place to place on elaborately decorated parade wagons, urging citizens to "jump on the bandwagon," or join the crowd and vote for them. **Bandwagon appeal** capitalizes on the fun of being part of a crowd and the desire to be socially accepted. It implies that a person should believe or do something because everyone else does.

> **Don't be the last to get the new Rockin' Robots video game.**
>
> **Don't be the only one who doesn't support the Greenville High recycling program.**

❷ Appeals to Pity

Emotional appeals try to touch not only people's minds but, more importantly, their hearts. They are especially effective for charity causes.

> **Each night, 200 children go to bed hungry in St. Sebastian. But you can help. For just one dollar a day, you can take care of one child's needs.**

This statement appeals to an audience's sense of pity for the plight of hungry children. Yet there is no information about how the money is used to feed the children.

EVALUATING INFO

❸ Name-Calling

Name-calling is attacking a person or group in order to discredit an idea with which the person or group is associated. It serves to distract the reader or listener from the real issue.

The narrow-minded senator opposes recycling.

People who support environmental causes are a bunch of tree-huggers.

These statements cast a negative light on the senator and on environmentalists without offering any supporting evidence.

❹ Testimonials

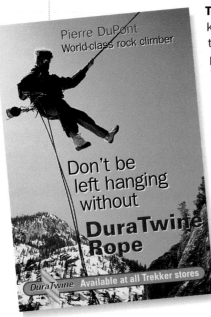

Pierre DuPont
World-class rock climber

Don't be left hanging without **DuraTwine Rope**

DuraTwine Available at all Trekker stores

Testimonials are statements by well-known people or satisfied customers that are used to promote and endorse products, services, people, or ideas. This persuasive technique taps into people's admiration of celebrities and into their needs to identify with others like themselves.

Testimonials can be misleading because they suggest that products or services must be good if people publicly recommend them. Testimonials may be valid, however, if they are supported by facts and evidence.

For more information about persuasive techniques, see pp. 436–445.

❺ Loaded Language

A word's dictionary definition is its **denotation.** The emotions and attitudes suggested by the word are its **connotations. Loaded language** consists of words with strongly positive or negative connotations, intended to influence a reader's or listener's attitude.

Examples of Loaded Language	
Positive	**Negative**
plan	scheme
prosperous	loaded
leisurely	lazy
enthusiast	zealot
honest	blunt
assertive	aggressive

In advertising, words with positive connotations are called **purr words,** and words with negative connotations are called **snarl words.** Purr words, such as *golden, mother, home,* and *success,* create positive thoughts and favorable or sentimental impressions of a product or service. Snarl words, such as *ugly, unsightly, wrinkles,* and *dirt,* create a negative reaction to the situation that a product claims to remedy.

Weasel words are qualifiers—such as *almost, nearly, virtually,* and *close to*—that are unclear and purposely used to mislead. Writers of advertising slogans and political rhetoric are frequently accused of using these words.

Sudso leaves dishes virtually spotless.

Since *virtually* means "almost but not quite," Sudso probably leaves some spots on dishes, though the ad implies it does not.

When used properly, emotional language can add depth to writing that's meant to persuade. The misuse of loaded language, however, can cloud factual information, disguise poor reasoning, or unfairly manipulate people's emotions in order to shape their opinions.

PRACTICE Identifying Emotional Appeals

Find all of the misused emotional appeals in this ad and identify each as an example of name-calling, bandwagon appeal, loaded language, or testimonial.

50 MILLION satisfied customers CAN'T BE WRONG!

Get rid of unsightly wrinkles. Have the youthful complexion of a supermodel

with

CLASSIQUE CREAM

"I wouldn't be caught in front of the camera without Classique!"
—Alisa Jackson, TV Star

Student Help Desk

Evaluating Information at a Glance

Recognize logical relationships.

Make valid generalizations.

Draw valid conclusions.

Make valid inferences.

Identify facts and opinions.

Reliable Information and Good Decisions

Recognize logical fallacies.

Recognize emotional appeals.

Types of Logical Relationships   Applied Science

Relationship	Statement	Why It's Logical
Cause and effect	Rocks in rivers become smooth as a result of water currents swirling around them.	One event causes another.
Comparison and contrast	Both ice and steam are forms of water; but ice is the solid form, and steam is the gaseous form.	Two things are alike in one way and different in another.
Analogy	A geyser ejects water into the air the way a whale spews water from its blowhole.	A valid comparison is made between an unfamiliar concept and a more familiar concept.

Types of Logical Fallacies

Dead-End Experiments

Fallacy	Example
Either/or thinking does not leave room for other alternatives.	**Either all animal testing should be stopped at once, or manufacturers should not be allowed to develop any new commercial products.**
Circular reasoning just goes around in circles.	**Testing products on animals is inhumane because conducting animal experiments to test new products is cruel.**
An **overgeneralization** is based on only a limited sample.	**Nobody supports the testing of new products on animals.**
A **false analogy** is based on an assumption that two things have a similarity that, in fact, they don't.	**Scientists who conduct animal experiments are like violent criminals on a crime spree.**

The Bottom Line

Checklist for Evaluating Information

Have I . . .

____ correctly identified facts and opinions?

____ figured out logical connections between ideas?

____ made valid inferences, conclusions, and generalizations?

____ recognized errors in reasoning?

____ recognized the misuse of appeals to emotion?

Power Words
Vocabulary for Precise Writing

loquacious *talkative* *gabby* *blather* *garrulous*

Wordy or Wordless

Here are bushels of words you can use to describe the situation when someone talks your ear off—or doesn't say a word.

Too Much Talk!

When you have a lot to say, you're feeling **talkative.** You'll probably get **gabby** or **chatty** on the phone. If you go on too long, someone might call you **voluble** or **loquacious** or **garrulous,** even **verbose** or—good grief—**logorrheic!** And all you wanted was to be smoothly **eloquent** by using lots of well-chosen words.

What's That Racket?

It can get pretty noisy when everyone **chatters** and **prattles** at once. You may wonder how people can **blather** and **run off at the mouth** like that. Quit **nattering** and **jabbering,** you might say, and try quietly **rapping** and **confabbing** among yourselves.

Golden Silence

Those who don't contribute to the din may be **speechless** or **wordless** for good reason: perhaps they are naturally **reticent, reserved,** or **tightlipped.** They may be **taciturn, close-mouthed,** and **incommunicative** because they are keeping a secret, staying **mute** because they've been told **mum's the word.**

mum's the word

▷ **Your Turn** Eloquent Insults

Use the words in this lesson and other words you find to make up names for characters on TV or in movies who talk too much or too little. Try using devices like rhyming and alliteration: Chatty Patty and Taciturn Ted.

Oral Communication

Are You Ready?

Communication is often something you take for granted—until you have to give a speech. Then, suddenly, you need to know everything that will make a roomful of people listen to you.

Yet communication skills are not just something you need when you face a large audience. Success in school, on the job, in sports, and in relationships depends heavily on your ability to listen and speak. And although talking casually with a friend is quite different from speaking formally to a large group of people, both activities rely on effective communication.

Write Away: Speaking Up

Write a paragraph or two on how you feel about speaking in front of a large group. What, if anything, about the experience makes you nervous? What might help you feel better? Save your paragraph in your ▭ **Working Portfolio.**

ORAL COMM.

LESSON 1 Effective Communication

❶ Communication Flow

Oral communication involves three elements: a **speaker,** a **message,** and an **audience.** The communication can be either one way or two way.

In a **one-way communication,** the speaker delivers a message to an audience. The audience usually doesn't respond to the message out loud, except perhaps by asking questions or applauding. Most forms of entertainment are one-way communications, as are news programs, announcements, and formal speeches.

"Tickets for this exciting concert go on sale today. Don't miss it!"

Speaker
Radio DJ

MESSAGE →

Audience
Chris

In a **two-way communication,** the speaker delivers a message to an audience, who responds with feedback.

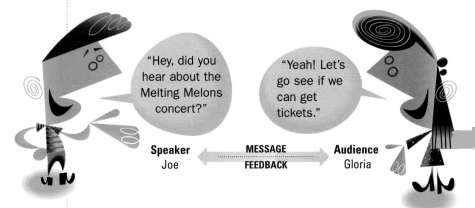

"Hey, did you hear about the Melting Melons concert?"

"Yeah! Let's go see if we can get tickets."

Speaker
Joe

← **MESSAGE** →
FEEDBACK

Audience
Gloria

For oral communication to be effective, the **purpose** of the message has to fit the **occasion** that prompts it and fit the **audience** that receives it. Yet, even when both these criteria are met, there still may be communication barriers that can hinder the message.

❷ Communication Barriers

Static on the radio, noise from a siren, people whispering behind you, a room that is too hot, too cold, or too crowded—these are just some of the annoying **external barriers** that can cause communication to break down. There are also more subtle **internal barriers** coming from the speaker and the audience that can distort or block a message, as shown below.

Speaker

Audience

Barriers could be caused by

- Distracting appearance (hair, clothes, jewelry)

- Irritating mannerisms (fidgeting, frequently saying "um" or "you know")

- Unclear or inappropriate message (may be too technical for audience or too informal for occasion)

- Obvious bias toward or lack of knowledge about the subject

- Speaking too fast or too slow

Barriers could be caused by

- Daydreaming

- Personal worries or concerns

- Physical discomfort (headache, fatigue, illness)

- Prejudice or lack of knowledge about or interest in the subject

PRACTICE Breaking Down Barriers

Think of a recent situation in which you found it difficult to communicate with someone. Write a paragraph describing what communication barriers were present and how each could have been corrected or eliminated.

LESSON 2 **Active Listening**

Listening is such a natural activity that we rarely think of it as a skill to be learned. But listening is more than just hearing. You may hear someone talking, but if the message doesn't interest you, you won't listen to it. However, if you need or want to know the message, you will probably listen actively to it.

❶ Establishing Listening Purpose

Active listening is a complex process of receiving, interpreting, evaluating, and responding to a message. Whenever you prepare to listen, determine your purpose for listening and use the strategies outlined below to get as much as you can from the message.

Active Listening

Purpose	Strategies
Informational: listening for facts, explanations, instructions, directions, and news	• Take notes covering major points and ideas. • Ask questions to clarify.
Critical: examining and judging a message; useful for analyzing information, persuasive messages, political speeches, and arguments	• Separate facts from opinions. • Listen for evidence supporting a claim. • Look for the motivation behind the message.
Creative: using your imagination to interpret and create mental pictures of stories, poems, and other artistic expressions, and to work on problem-solving projects with others	• Visualize images and events as you listen. • Brainstorm solutions to problems. • Keep your mind open to new ideas.
Empathic: listening to and understanding another person's feelings; important for relationships with family, friends, and co-workers	• Imagine the other person's feelings. • Don't feel you have to solve another person's problems. • Respond by showing you care.

Many communication problems can be avoided if you keep in mind your responsibility as an active listener: Pay attention and think about what you hear.

CHAPTER 28

❷ Examining Verbal and Nonverbal Cues

In active listening you not only examine a message for its content, you also look at accompanying verbal and nonverbal cues. These cues can tip you off to the real meaning behind the words. For instance, if someone says, "Sure, that makes sense," you interpret the verbal and nonverbal cues in order to know whether the statement is serious or sarcastic. By being aware of these cues, you will get a more complete and accurate message.

A **verbal cue** is any of the sound qualities of the speaker's voice. In a political speech, for instance, you may hear the speaker's voice become loud at times and soft at others. Some words may be spoken with a lot of feeling behind them, others in a lighthearted manner. Below is a list of verbal cues and the voice qualities each represents.

- **Volume:** loudness or softness of the voice
- **Stress:** emphasis on a word or phrase
- **Pitch:** highness or lowness of the voice
- **Tone:** emotional quality of the voice
- **Articulation:** clarity of pronunciation
- **Rate:** speed of speaking
- **Pausing:** use of silence between words

A **nonverbal cue** is a message expressed without words; nonverbal cues are also known as body language. You might be surprised at how effective a nonverbal cue is in stressing a point or getting an audience's attention. Study the kinds of nonverbal cues described below.

Eye contact: Looking at individual audience members helps make a personal connection and projects confidence and sincerity.

Facial expressions: Smiling, frowning, raising eyebrows, and other facial movements reveal the speaker's feelings about his or her topic.

Gestures and movements: Pointing, waving arms, shrugging shoulders, pacing, and other expressive movements can show emphasis.

Posture: Standing with shoulders back and head up shows confidence and self-respect.

ORAL COMM.

Oral Communication **521**

❸ Analyzing Word Choice

Word choice, or diction, is a speaker's particular selection of words. While word choice is important in communicating exactly what the speaker means, it can also be used to manipulate an audience. In the examples below, notice how the word choice in the claim masks a less attractive reality.

Identifying Misleading Word Choices

Technique	Example
Vague terms	**Claim:** "Our computer offers a <u>complete</u> system for one <u>low</u> price." **Reality:** It has the basics, but no extras or upgrades.
Technical terms	**Claim:** "In creating these unique hiking boots, we've added the <u>micropolyfibre</u> sole." **Reality:** This material is in all types of boots.
Hyperbole, or exaggeration	**Claim:** "That actor gave the <u>worst</u> portrayal <u>ever</u> seen on stage or screen." **Reality:** He gave one bad performance.
Loaded language, or emotionally charged words	**Claim:** "It is your <u>patriotic duty</u> to serve on this committee." **Reality:** Your participation could help your town.

❹ Evaluating a Message

When you **evaluate** a message, you judge it for accuracy, reliability, usefulness, or relevance. Evaluating requires you to listen "between the lines" and judge what's true and valuable in a message. Here are some guidelines for use in evaluating a message.

Consider what you and the speaker know about a subject. The more you know, the better able you'll be to judge. Even if you don't know much about a topic, you can still evaluate whether the speaker has offered enough evidence as support.

Be aware of bias—both your own and the speaker's. Don't let your preconceived notions interfere with your judgment. At the same time, be alert for signs that the speaker's message may be one-sided.

Ask questions. If something is confusing or if you did not understand the message the first time, ask the speaker for clarification.

Keep an open mind. Listen to the complete message before making a final judgment.

Preparing a Speech

If you're like most people, the thought of giving a speech in front of an audience terrifies you. Don't worry, though. Thorough preparation can build your confidence and equip you for anything.

❶ Planning

Planning a speech is similar to planning a written paper. The key to a good speech lies in matching the purpose to the audience and the occasion.

Suppose you want to organize volunteers to clean up debris in a vacant lot near your school. Your English teacher has allowed you 15 minutes to ask the class for volunteers. Follow these steps in planning what you'll say.

Planning a Speech

- **Focus content to fit the occasion.** Plan to speak for 10 minutes and allow 5 minutes for questions. Narrow your topic to the basics your classmates will need to know to become interested in the project.

- **Identify purpose and audience.** For this speech, your purpose is to inform and persuade. Consider your audience members' knowledge about the topic and their level of interest in volunteering. Think of a "hook," an attention-grabbing fact, statement, or question that will capture their interest.

- **Research.** Use local resources and references to find out the exact nature of the problem and possible ways to remedy it. You will need to provide enough information to convince your audience members that there is a real need for action and their participation in it.

- **Organize and outline.** Write a thesis statement summarizing your speech's main idea. Then, write an outline that organizes your material in a logical order. Prepare an introduction, a body, and a conclusion for your speech.

 HOT TIP

Be sure to footnote all your sources of information: someone may ask you where you got your facts.

ORAL COMM.

❷ Writing

The main difference between writing a speech and writing a paper is in the language and sentence length. In a speech, the language must be clear and simple and the sentences short and direct. The following excerpt from a student speech shows the techniques you will need to use.

> Last week, Mr. Jackson, the janitor, captured a rat in the girl's locker room. He said it probably came from that vacant lot two blocks from the school. . . . I have called the City Council's office, and a spokesperson said there is no money in the budget for cleaning up that lot anytime soon. So it's up to us. **We have to clean up that area to keep our school and our neighborhood safe from vermin and possible injury.**
>
> I'm looking for a few good volunteers for April 16, National Youth Service Day. What better time to do our part to improve our neighborhood? . . .
>
> So far, here's the plan for the cleanup. . . .
>
> By volunteering, you not only help improve our community, but you can claim a part of our neighborhood as your own. . . .

Attention grabber

Clear, simple language

Thesis statement

Short, direct sentences

Appeal to audience

❸ Rehearsing

Rehearsing your speech will help you spot problems, such as awkward phrasing and irritating mannerisms. Practice in front of a mirror or ask friends and relatives to be your audience and give you feedback.

Here's How Rehearsing a Speech

- Read your speech out loud several times, timing each reading.
- Vary the pitch and rhythm of your voice to emphasize certain points.
- Practice using eye contact and gestures to reinforce ideas.
- Practice using visual aids to ensure they fit smoothly with your speech.
- Mark your speech for places to pause, speak louder, use a visual aid, and so on.

Delivering a Speech

LESSON 4

1 Choosing a Method of Delivery

You can choose from four methods of delivery to find one that fits your occasion and your personal style.

Manuscript Method

Write the speech in its entirety and read the manuscript to the audience.

Pros	Cons
• No information is omitted.	• Delivery may not sound natural.
• Wording is always the same.	• Maintaining eye contact with audience is difficult.
• Speech fits time allotted.	• Speech cannot be adapted to audience reaction.

Memorization Method

Write the speech in manuscript form, memorize it, and recite it to the audience word for word.

Pros	Cons
• Speaker relates directly to audience.	• Remembering whole speech is difficult.
• Eye contact is easy to maintain.	• Memorization is time-consuming.

Extemporaneous Method

Write the key concepts as entries in an outline or on note cards, which you'll use as prompts. Determine the wording of the speech as you deliver it to the audience.

Pros	Cons
• Delivery is fresh and natural.	• Some dependence on memory is required.
• Speaker can adapt material on the spot.	• Thorough knowledge of subject matter is required.

Impromptu Method

Speak "off the top of your head," without using a prepared draft, outline, or notes.

Pros	Cons
• Delivery is spontaneous.	• Speech may lack organization.
• Speaker can directly respond to audience's reactions.	• Complete knowledge of subject is required.

❷ Delivery

The success of your speech often depends as much on the verbal and nonverbal aspects of your delivery as on the content. Look again at the verbal and nonverbal cues listed on page 521, then study the following guidelines.

Using Verbal Cues

DO	DON'T
• speak at a moderate rate	• talk too slow or too fast, which you may tend to do when you're nervous
• speak at an average volume and pitch	• talk too softly or in a high-pitched voice
• pronounce words clearly	• mumble or say "um" and "like, you know"
• use pauses and vary tone	• halt abruptly or speak in a monotone

Using Nonverbal Cues

DO	DON'T
• be neat in appearance and use good posture	• slouch or appear stiff and ill at ease
• scan the audience and pick three people with whom you can make eye contact	• hang your head or too frequently shift your eyes
• use gestures and facial expressions only when you emphasize a point	• gesture constantly, roll your eyes, or fidget with your clothing and hair

Stage Fright Just about everybody gets the jitters before speaking in public. Before your speech, try to relax by taking slow, deep breaths. Then, move around: walk, do knee bends, stretch your arms, touch your toes. Relaxing your body helps to slow down racing thoughts and soothe frayed nerves.

LESSON 5 — Evaluating Speeches

❶ Judging Content and Delivery

When you evaluate someone else's speech, you not only help the speaker, you also help yourself learn more about effective public speaking and sharpen your critical listening skills. Use the questions in the chart below as a guide to evaluating someone's speech.

Evaluation Guide	
Judging Content	• Did the introduction capture the audience's attention?
	• Did the topic fit the occasion?
	• Was the speech appropriate to the audience's level of knowledge and interest?
	• Was the speech logically organized and easy to follow?
	• Was there enough evidence to support the thesis?
	• Did the conclusion reinforce the thesis?
Judging Delivery	• Did the speaker make eye contact with the audience?
	• Was the speaker's voice loud enough? Was there enough variation in pitch and rhythm?
	• Did gestures and facial expressions reinforce ideas, or did they distract from the message?
	• Were visual aids helpful and presented well?

❷ Giving Verbal Feedback

When you comment or provide criticism on a speech, try following these suggestions.

Be specific. Tell the speaker exactly what you liked and why: "Your opening story about the rat in the locker room made me want to hear more."

Discuss only the most important points. Be specific, but don't dwell on minor details. Instead, focus on the main points.

Point out both positives and negatives. Balance what you see as a strength ("Your argument was convincing") with what you see as a weakness ("But I got confused by all the cleanup details").

Offer concrete ways to improve. Suggestions can be helpful if they are specific: "Next time, don't wave your hands so much; it's distracting."

ORAL COMM.

Oral Communication **527**

Interviewing

An interview is a type of formal conversation that serves a purpose: to find out information. To conduct a successful interview, follow these guidelines and strategies.

❶ Preparing for the Interview

Good preparation will give your interview structure and direction and will help you feel confident during the interview.

Checklist

- Choose someone knowledgeable and request an interview.

- Arrange a time and place to meet. Ask permission to use a tape recorder.

- Research the subject so you'll be informed for the interview.

- Prepare a list of 10 to 12 questions arranged in a logical order.

- Arrive on time and bring what you need.

☑ Contact: Allan Watson, local coordinator of Youth Service America

☑ Where and when: his house (1500 Greenleaf) on Sunday at 3:00 P.M. OK to tape interview.

☑ Internet search: www.SERVEnet.org and www.americaspromise.org

☑ Questions:
How do you organize a volunteer project?
How do you get teens to volunteer?
What other support is available?

☑ Ride bike to his house; bring tape recorder (get new tape & batteries), pen, paper, & research.

If you interview someone over the phone, you won't be able to record the conversation unless you have special equipment as well as permission from the person to tape the conversation.

❷ Conducting the Interview

When you conduct an interview, you are the one who steers the conversation. But don't forget to listen to each answer completely and show interest in the subject. On the next page are some important guidelines for conducting an interview.

Strategy: Conducting an Interview

1. Begin with a neutral question that will relax both you and the interviewee: "How did you first get involved in volunteer work?"

2. Phrase questions to encourage a detailed response instead of simply *yes* or *no:* "What kind of help did the city give you?" instead of "Did the city help?"

3. If the interviewee strays from the subject, gently get him or her back on track: "That's interesting, but back to the issue of . . ."

4. Repeat or summarize important points to make sure you've understood them: "So you're saying that . . ."

5. Ask follow-up questions to clarify a response: "What do you mean by that?" or "Could you give an example?"

6. Take notes on important points and strong feelings brought out in the interview, even if you are taping it. You may want to follow up on these later.

7. Make sure you have the correct spelling of all names (especially the interviewee's) and similar information.

8. Ask permission to follow up on questions later.

 At the end of the interview, ask if there is anything the interviewee would like to add. That way, he or she can elaborate on a point made earlier or bring up information you may not have asked about.

❸ Follow-up

Take the time to go over the interview while it is still fresh in your mind and take the following steps.

- Review your notes and transcribe the tape recording.
- Call the interviewee to clarify confusing information or to ask further questions.
- Write a thank-you note.
- Send a copy of your completed piece to the interviewee.

ORAL COMM.

LESSON 7 — Group Communication

How many times have you worked with a group to complete a project, come up with a plan of action, solve a problem, or achieve some other stated goal? Both in school and once you have a job, you will probably spend some time in formal or semiformal group settings. Here are some guidelines and strategies to help you make the most of group communication.

❶ Roles in Groups

Groups function better when their members take on specific roles, such as facilitator (or leader), note taker, and participant. This distribution of responsibility provides a structure for discussions and helps in dealing with problems.

Participants
- Contribute ideas or information
- Respond constructively to other members
- Reach agreement or vote on final decision

Facilitator
- Guides discussion
- Keeps group on task
- Summarizes or restates discussion throughout or at end

Note Taker
- Takes notes on discussion
- Reports on past suggestions and decisions
- Organizes and writes up notes

❷ Group Etiquette

Reaching agreement, or consensus, within a group requires every member's cooperation and effort. The group will be more productive and will accomplish its goals more easily if everyone follows these simple rules of conduct.

> **Here's How** **Participating in Groups**
>
> - Come prepared by being informed and ready to work.
> - Be an active listener and be willing to accept and build on a good idea, even if it conflicts with what you think.
> - Respect different viewpoints.
> - Don't interrupt or talk while someone else is talking.
> - Encourage participation by other members.
> - Support your opinions with reasons and/or evidence.
> - Keep the goal in mind and avoid getting sidetracked by digressions or conflicts.

Conflict Resolution Conflicts are inevitable in a group discussion—they're even part of the process. The group's aim should be to resolve conflicts, not to avoid or stifle them. Next time you're in a group locked in conflict, try these strategies.

1. **Listen attentively to each side.** Instead of taking sides, members should first listen open-mindedly to both sides.
2. **Find out reasons for each opinion.** When the reasons for each opposing position are revealed, you may find common ground on which to build a compromise.
3. **Focus on issues, not personalities.** While it's perfectly appropriate to disagree with a person's opinion, it's not fair to attack someone personally.
4. **Agree to disagree.** If you can't agree on something, take a five-minute break from discussing it, and then take it up again later. A solution may present itself.
5. **Look for a reasonable solution.** Work toward a solution that will meet the needs of both parties. If compromise isn't acceptable, look for an alternative solution that is more agreeable.

Student Help Desk

Oral Communication at a Glance

For oral communication to be effective, the **purpose** of a message has to match the **occasion** that prompts it and the **audience** that receives it.

One-way communication:　　Speaker　→ Message → Audience

Two-way communication:　　Speaker　← Message / Feedback → Audience

Effective Listening　Good Reception

- Be attentive to the speaker.
- Don't let external or internal distractions interfere.
- Take notes, if necessary.
- Pay attention to verbal and nonverbal cues.
- Analyze word choice to detect misleading or faulty reasoning.
- Keep an open mind.
- Ask questions.

Group Participation　Playing in Unison

- Come prepared to participate.
- Respect different viewpoints.
- Don't interrupt.
- Work to resolve conflicts.
- Always work toward the goal.

Choosing the Appropriate Delivery

A Method to the Madness

Manuscript Method

Use for formal occasions (graduation speeches, political addresses) and to present technical or complicated information (academic lectures).

Memorization Method

Use for short speeches, as when introducing another speaker or accepting an award.

Extemporaneous Method

Use for informal situations and persuasive messages, or whenever you want a more personal connection with the audience.

Impromptu Method

Use for panel discussions, question-and-answer forums, and spur-of-the-moment requests to speak.

The Bottom Line

Checklist for Giving a Formal Speech

Have I . . .

____ focused my speech to fit the occasion and audience?

____ researched the subject thoroughly to support my ideas or proposals?

____ begun my speech with an attention-grabbing statement or question?

____ clearly stated the thesis?

____ organized my ideas logically?

____ rehearsed the speech so that my delivery is smooth and shows confidence?

____ relaxed before delivering my speech?

ORAL COMM.

Power Words
Vocabulary for Precise Writing

People in Groups

Some groups form spontaneously and last only a few minutes; others are formed deliberately to last much longer. You can choose from among a swarm of words to describe each group of people in your writing.

Sudden Swarms

When you arrive at the stadium for a concert, you may find yourself in a **throng,** a **horde** of people heading toward the gates. There may be a **crush** or a **swarm** around the refreshment stand and a **press** surrounding the ticket office. If people push, the **mass** of people could become a **mob** described as **rabble.**

The **multitude** thins out behind the stage, where a small **bevy** of admirers surrounds the star and a **flock** of reporters waits patiently in hopes of an interview.

Deliberate Assemblies

Organizations don't depend on chance but plan their **gatherings** deliberately. People in the same profession often hold **conventions.** Churches, mosques, and synagogues have **congregations. Councils, caucuses, congresses,** and **Congress** do the business of governing. When academics want to get together, they hold a **panel discussion** or **symposium.** When they disagree, even academics form competing **coteries** or **cliques.**

▷ **Your Turn** Groups in the News

Check the news to find descriptions of different groups and organizations. Add names of groups to which you belong.

With a small group of classmates, make a continuum of words, from those with the most spontaneous meaning to those with the most permanent.

Analyzing News in the Media

What's the Scoop?

Every day you probably watch television, leaf through a magazine, listen to the radio, or surf the World Wide Web. Whenever you do this, you are acting as a media consumer, taking in facts and news about the world you live in. Without realizing it, you are forming opinions and beliefs based on this information. But how do you know the information is accurate? How do you know you've heard enough to make an informed opinion?

By looking at the ways news and information are packaged, you can better understand how the news media affect your thinking.

Write Away: Getting the Scoop
Write a list of all the news and information programs you watch on television. Then list the newspapers, magazines, and Web sites you browse for news. Save the list in your ⬜ **Working Portfolio.**

ANALYZING MEDIA

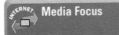
Media Focus

Media as News Source

What does *media* really refer to? Television, newspapers, magazines, radio, and the World Wide Web—each is a medium that carries information, entertainment, and advertisements to a mass audience. Together they are called **media.**

❶ Types of News

What is *the news*? The news is information on events, people, and places in your community, region, nation, and world. This massive amount of information includes facts, figures, and explanations. The news can be categorized by type, as shown in the chart below.

Types of News	
Type	**Description**
Hard news	Fact-based accounts of current events
Soft news	Human-interest stories and other accounts that are less current or urgent than hard news
News features	Stories that elaborate on news reports
Commentary and opinion	Essays and perspectives by experts, professionals, and media personalities

❷ Types of News Media

Each medium packages news to fit its own unique format, which, in turn, shapes the information you receive. For instance, television can tell a news story through real-life sound and video, while newspapers and magazines must rely on print alone. These distinct formats can create different impressions of the same story.

How often the news is broadcast or published also affects the stories reported. A monthly magazine would need to find a fresh perspective on a news story that had been reported weeks earlier on a nightly newscast. The amount of space available for a story also determines how much information you will receive. A story told in 30 seconds on the evening news won't reveal as much as one given 20 minutes on a television newsmagazine.

Television

What types of TV news programs do you watch? News programs on television come in a wide variety. Can you tell the difference between a tabloid program and a serious news show?

Television News

Type of Program	Type of News	Content
Newscasts *Today,* CNN news, network and local newscasts	Hard news, soft news, commentary	Brief summaries of current news topics with a local, national, or international focus
TV Newsmagazines *Dateline NBC,* *60 Minutes,* *20/20*	Soft news and news features	More in-depth stories that have a human-interest angle and that sometimes relate to current news topics
Documentaries National Geographic Society specials, *Nature* and history programs on PBS	Soft news, news features, commentary	In-depth reporting on a wide variety of subjects, from current to historical; often instructional in nature
Tabloid TV shows *Hard Copy,* *Entertainment Tonight*	Soft news and news features	Summaries of current sensationalistic stories and celebrity gossip

WATCH OUT An infomercial looks like a television program but is really a long commercial. Its purpose is to sell something, rather than to give objective information or commentary.

ANALYZING MEDIA

Print

Print media include newspapers, magazines, books, brochures, posters, billboards, and flyers. News covered in newspapers and magazines is focused on either a broad or narrow range of subjects. General-interest magazines cover a broad range of subjects, including politics, sports, arts, lifestyles, and celebrities. Special-interest magazines, however, cover news related only to their specific subject areas.

Print News

Type of Print Media	Profile
Newspapers local newspaper, *USA Today*	Printed daily or weekly; feature all types of news; may focus on local, regional, or national news
Magazines *Newsweek, Sports Illustrated, TV Guide*	Printed weekly or monthly; feature all types of news; often expand upon and analyze news from preceding weeks
Tabloids *National Enquirer, Star*	Printed weekly or monthly; feature sensationalistic stories and celebrity gossip

World Wide Web

With their ability to publish news reports at any time, news sources on the World Wide Web can often provide breaking news before the television and print media. Below is a chart on the types of Web sites that provide news and information.

News on the World Wide Web

Type of Web Site	Profile
Online wire services	Up-to-the-minute news on current events; feed stories to journalists in other media
Online newspapers and magazines	Online versions of newspapers or magazines that also have printed versions; sometimes updated hourly
E-zines	Magazines that publish on the Web only; may cover a variety of topics
Corporate, government, organization, and university sites	News and information relevant to an organization or business, and its specific topics or products
Personal home pages	Information specific to the interests and opinions of the Web site's publisher

Deconstructing Content

It is the job of the journalist to gather, write, and edit news stories. A news story's written text or script is its **content**. While developing the news story, the journalist makes a variety of decisions about how to construct the content, such as what information to include and how to organize it.

When you examine and evaluate the parts that make up the whole of a news story, what you're doing is called **deconstruction**.

❶ Standards for News Reporting

The ideal of journalism is to present news that is objective, accurate, and thorough.

- **Objective** Takes a balanced point of view on the issues; is not biased; does not reflect a specific attitude or opinion

- **Accurate** Presents factual information that can be verified

- **Thorough** Presents all sides of an issue; includes background information; tells *who, what, when, where, why,* and *how*

In practice, however, these ideals are not always met. Those who work on a story—the writer, the editor, and the photographer who takes the accompanying pictures—have their own perspectives that may get into the story, despite their efforts to keep their biases out.

❷ Factors That Affect Reporting

Who Chooses the News?

To deconstruct a news report, you first need to know who decided the information is news. The decision makers include news directors, producers, editors, journalists, and owners of media companies. Traditionally, the decision makers have been known as **gatekeepers** because they control the flow of information.

The gatekeeper's goals, attitudes, and values can play a factor in determining what the gatekeeper believes is newsworthy. For instance, a TV news director who supports recycling is likely to view stories about recycling as worth reporting, whereas another news director might dismiss such stories altogether.

How the News Is Chosen

When choosing which information they will present as news, journalists typically look for items that meet several of the following criteria:

- **Timeliness** Current events have priority over previous events.
- **Consequences** The more people the information could affect, the more likely it is to be newsworthy.
- **Proximity** Events and news that affect a particular city, region, or country are of most interest to the people who live there.
- **Human Interest** Interesting or funny stories appeal to many people.
- **Uniqueness** Very uncommon events or circumstances are often considered newsworthy.

How the News Is Reported

A journalist's job is to answer *who, what, when, where, why,* and *how* in any type of news report. During this process, the journalist also chooses the angle of the story, the sources for the story, and the amount of information to be included in the story.

Angles and Slants A journalist usually looks for a "peg" to hang a story on. Even an objective report must have an **angle,** or a point of view from which it is written. Sometimes the journalist may intentionally or unintentionally **slant** the content of a story, that is, give it an angle that is biased. Consider these two headlines that describe the same house fire.

Focuses on facts of family loss; human-interest angle

Focuses on opinion of firefighters' response; negative slant

Balanced Versus Biased Reporting Objectivity in news reporting can be measured by how balanced or biased the story is. **Balanced reporting** means that all sides of an issue are represented equally and fairly. **Biased** reporting means that one side is favored over another or that the subject is unfairly represented. Biased reporting may show an overly negative view of a subject, or it may encourage racial or gender stereotypes or prejudices.

> **Here's How** **Recognizing a Balanced News Story**
>
> A balanced news story
>
> - represents people and subjects in a neutral light
> - treats all sides of an issue equally
> - does not include "leading" or inappropriate questions; for example, "Will you seek counseling after this terrible tragedy?"
> - does not show stereotypes or prejudice toward people of a particular race, gender, age, religion, or other group
> - does not leave out important background information that is needed to establish a context or perspective

Sometimes biased reporting is apparent in the journalist's choice of sources. **Sources** refer to the people interviewed for the news report and to any written materials and documents the journalist used for background information. From each source, the journalist gets a different point of view.

For a news story on a new medicinal drug, for instance, if the journalist's only source is a representative from the company that made the drug, the report may be biased. But if the journalist also includes the perspective of someone neutral, such as a scientist who objectively studies the effects of drugs, the report may be more balanced.

ANALYZING MEDIA

Deconstructing Design

LESSON 3

While the writer and editor are crafting the story, a crew of producers, designers, and technicians is developing the **design,** or visual presentation, of the news piece. In the same way that content is developed from an angle or is slanted to present a particular point of view, design is also used to shape the story.

❶ Design in Television and Film

The design format of a television program or documentary refers to the graphics, video, and audio that are used. These can be manipulated and packaged for a desired effect in several ways:

- choice of camera angles and shots
- addition of music and special effects
- editing of images and sound

Camera Angles and Shots Camera angles and shots refer to how the camera looks at or presents an image. For instance, the camera angle can be close-up, tilted, or distant. Each angle is carefully planned to draw your attention to something in particular.

Camera Angles	
Angle	**Effect**
Close-up—view taken at close range, usually of the face and shoulders when the subject is a person	Establishes intimacy between viewer and image
Long shot—view that takes in the whole scene	Allows viewer to see "big picture" and establishes setting
Reaction shot—view of someone responding to action or words in the preceding shot	Allows viewer to see how the subject feels and can create empathy in the viewer

Close-up makes audience feel familiar with subject.

Long shot gives more information about the subject and setting.

Music, Sound, Lighting, and Special Effects Music, sound, lighting, and special effects all add to the impact and meaning of a scene. Lighting and sound can be deliberately manipulated to set the mood of the scene. Music is often used to cue the viewer that the story or scene is happy, sad, frightening, or fun. Special effects can be used to alter or exaggerate the image shown, as in the photo below. These techniques serve to highlight certain aspects of the subject.

Editing The news stories reported on television are edited to tell the story a certain way. During the editing process, shots are joined together by a common setting or purpose and organized to create a scene. The editor carefully plans the sequence of shots, placing close-ups followed by long shots, for example. As you watch news programs, be aware of how one image follows another. What does the sequence of shots tell you about the subject?

❷ Design in Print and on the Web

If you surf the Web—roam from site to site—or flip through a magazine or newspaper, you will come across a variety of design styles. Web pages are designed like magazine and newspaper pages. Both have a combination of text, photographs, and graphics. Some articles are featured on the front or home pages and are highlighted with accompanying photos.

What does the design of a page—whether it is in print or on the Web—tell you about its content? How does it attract your attention?

For an example of a page from a news organization's Web site, see p. 547.

Layout, Graphics, and Photographs When you look at the front page of a newspaper or the home page of a Web site, what do you see first? A large photo? A headline? An altered photo? Whatever it is that catches your eye was probably planned by the designer or editor to attract your attention. The two-page magazine spread below shows how photos and layout grab a reader's attention and highlight aspects of the article's content.

Large, bold headline with the word BACK in yellow is placed over a ghost image of the story's subject as he looked in the past, reminding reader of the subject's past experience in space.

Story's subject looms in the center of a two-page spread and clearly shows that he is the focus of the article.

Article's introduction takes up only one-quarter of the spread.

Multimedia Features **Multimedia** refers to a presentation that combines several types of media to convey a message. Video and sound clips, as well as interactive opportunities (which allow you to participate in some way), can be used to make the information more appealing, informative, and accessible. Multimedia features engage the viewer and often provide access to information not otherwise available. For example, some Web sites allow you to explore newly discovered shipwrecks on the bottom of the ocean, listen to interviews with newsmakers, and interact in forums with authors, celebrities, and sports figures.

Comparing Media

❶ Pros and Cons of Each Medium

Every medium has its own strengths and weaknesses. The design of each medium forces the content to conform to its particular characteristics. The medium, therefore, shapes the message. Photos and video clips are more likely to draw an immediate emotional response from the viewer. A report in a newspaper, by contrast, allows the reader more distance from the subject. You can determine the source that will give you the best information based on your needs for a particular project or your own interests and abilities.

Weighing the Pros and Cons

Medium	Pros	Cons
Television	Information is up-to-the-minute. Images communicate what words cannot.	News reports are brief summaries. Commercial interruptions are common. Viewer is passive with no control over order of information.
Print	Stories provide in-depth reporting. Reader can choose items of interest at own pace.	Viewer is limited to reading and has no access to video or sound clips, which may give a different understanding of subject.
Web	Information is up-to-the-minute. Stories can provide in-depth coverage. User can view items of interest at own pace. Interactive opportunities often available.	Computer is required to gain access. Not all computers allow access to multimedia or interactive features. Some sites are not up-to-date. Sources may not be trustworthy.

❷ Comparing News Treatments

By comparing how different media treat the same news story, you can better understand how the design of each medium affects the content. In the examples on the next two pages, notice the difference in the amount of information you immediately receive about the subject—the Oklahoma City bombing incident. When you first encounter these images, which one draws your attention first? Why?

Television Newscast Television programs have many opportunities to show dramatic video footage of news events. Nightly news programs also rely heavily on close-up camera shots of the news anchorperson. This way viewers become familiar with the anchorperson and may develop loyalty to the program because of him or her.

Background shows contrast of damaged and undamaged portions of the building to illustrate impact of tragedy.

Live video footage, with news anchor on the scene, indicates importance of story and creates "you are there" feeling.

Newspaper Below is the front page of the *New York Times* the day after the Oklahoma City bombing. The *New York Times* devoted its entire front page to articles on the story.

Three-line headline indicates story is important. Most top headlines are only one line.

Photos are given the same amount of space as text to convey the massive destruction.

Only a few column inches in the lower left-hand corner are used to guide readers to other news of the day on the inside pages.

Photo of an injured baby draws the viewer's sympathy and immediately tells the viewer there were innocent victims.

Web Site This Web site page contains no actual information on the Oklahoma City bombing. Instead, there are links to pages with information. Everything on this page is designed to attract your interest and draw you in.

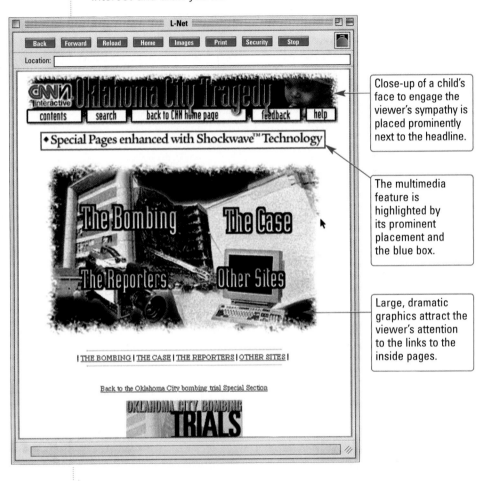

Close-up of a child's face to engage the viewer's sympathy is placed prominently next to the headline.

The multimedia feature is highlighted by its prominent placement and the blue box.

Large, dramatic graphics attract the viewer's attention to the links to the inside pages.

PRACTICE Staying Tuned

Finally—an assignment that tells you to watch TV! In your **Working Portfolio,** find your **Write Away** list from page 535. Choose one of the television news programs listed and watch it this week. Write down your responses to the following questions: What news story was reported first? How much time was spent on it? Did it contain video or photos of scenes or people's faces? What did the story make you think about the subject? What do you think was the story's intended angle?

Student Help Desk

Analyzing News Media at a Glance

Types of News Media

Television	Print	Web
News programs	Newspapers	Online wire services, newspapers, magazines
Newsmagazines	Magazines	E-zines
Documentaries	Tabloids	Corporate, government, organization, and university sites
Tabloid TV shows		

Recognizing Bias — Hanging in the Balance

Content	Analysis
Angle	Gives a point of view to the story
Slant	Creates bias in the story
Balanced reporting	Explains both sides of a story or issue equally
Biased reporting	Skews the information to favor one side over another

Analyzing Design — Lights, Camera, Action!

TV/Film Technique	Purpose
Camera angles	Indicate perspective
Music, sound, lighting	Set the mood
Special effects	Alter, heighten, or exaggerate aspects of the subject

Print/Web Techniques	Purpose
Layout	Indicates important aspects of the story
Photos, graphics	Draw your attention to a particular news item
Interactive features	Engage you in the topic

Audience Participation

Here are five questions to help you evaluate news stories and information on any given topic.

1. Who created this message, and why is it being sent?
2. What techniques are being used to attract your attention?
3. What lifestyles, values, and points of view are represented in the message?
4. How might someone else's understanding of this message differ from yours?
5. What is omitted from this message?

"This concludes the conscious part of your day. Good night."

© 1999 Michael Maslin

The Bottom Line

Checklist for Analyzing News in the Media

Have I . . .

___ looked at several media to get a range of perspectives?

___ examined the accuracy, objectivity, and thoroughness of the news reporting?

___ considered the lifestyles, values, and points of view presented?

___ analyzed the use of images and layout?

___ compared the treatment of a news story by different media?

ANALYZING MEDIA

Power Words
Vocabulary for Precise Writing

air
chronicle
dispatches
news flash
document
expose

Telling the Story

From news shows to personal Web pages, media products are full of stories. You can choose from among numerous words to describe the kind of storytelling you see.

From Newscast to News Flash

News reports and broadcast news programs **document** current events, and sometimes they **chronicle** the history leading up to those events. They **recount** the facts, **air** interviews with the participants, and **narrate** the steps in a sequence.

Good news writers don't repeat **rumor** or **hearsay,** but they get their information, or **intelligence,** from **dispatches** from the field. They issue **bulletins** and **communiqués** to the public. When a story is important enough to stop the presses or break into regular programming, it's a **news flash.** When a scandal is revealed, it's an **exposé.**

From Fiction to Confession

Fiction on the page—or in a film—moves at a different pace from the news and depends on inner sources of inspiration. Its creators **depict, portray,** or **delineate** their characters, **render** the settings with exact details to make them seem real, and **fabricate** elaborate plots to maintain the suspense.

These days **personal narratives** may contain **confessions** or **revelations.** They may **exhume,** or **disinter,** old secrets, **unveiling** information best left in the dark.

▷ **Your Turn** Broadcast Stories

Work in a small group to describe and evaluate the storytelling that you can observe on television. One group can discuss news programs, another dramas, another news magazines, and so on. Compare notes on the storytelling techniques you observe.

Creating Media Products

● Record   12:52:00

Calling the Shots

What if you had to make a documentary of a day in your life? How would you begin the project? What would you include? Would you use humor to tell the story? Would you include interviews with your friends and music that you like?

When you create a media product, such as a video documentary or a Web site, it needs to be based on detailed planning and careful development of verbal, visual, and audio elements.

Write Away: Adventure in Media
Make a list of topics you think could be explored in a documentary. What subjects really interest you? What visual, sound, and design techniques could you use to help convey your message? Save your list in your 🗁 **Working Portfolio.**

MEDIA PRODUCTS

VIDEO
Media Literacy

Choosing Your Medium

Sometimes words are not enough to express your ideas. In some cases, you may want to use video, narration, photographs, music, or illustrations as well. Visual and electronic media can bring new dimensions to your projects, allowing you to express ideas and themes in new ways.

❶ Media Options

In creating media products, you will need to consider the various forms of presentation that can be used. Choosing a medium is similar to choosing a style in writing. You want to use a form that is appropriate to your message. Here are several options and their most appropriate uses.

When to Choose a Specific Media Product	
Product	**Best Use**
Video	• To explain complex information, particularly in cases where visual images would be helpful
	• To capture and share a real-world event
	• To easily duplicate and present information that does not have to be frequently updated
Web site	• To communicate with a broad audience, including people outside your local area
	• To present information that needs continual updates
	• To interact with others who have similar interests
Multimedia presentation	• To give a dynamic presentation before a large group
	• To present instructional information (e.g., science and geography topics) that needs movement and sound
	• To present customized information for different audiences

❷ Making Your Choice

In planning your media project, you will need to choose a form of presentation that best suits your message, purpose, and audience. Here are some questions that will help lead you to the most appropriate choice.

• Does your message have any interesting visual possibilities?

- Would music enhance the delivery of the message?
- Do you want to be able to interact with your audience?
- Does your topic need to be constantly updated to stay fresh?

Try to imagine how your topic would be presented in each of the various forms. For instance, if you wanted to encourage your classmates to support a paper recycling program at your school, you could create a colorful print ad or flier, or a video. For the video, you might imagine scenes of students walking through the halls, carrying stacks of books and papers. You might also imagine music set to video images showing the efforts of people using a successful recycling program.

Who's Your Audience?

Before choosing the media product, you will also need to clearly define the audience you wish to reach. Is your audience the students at your school? business owners in your community? people who live in your area or in other parts of the country who share the same interest in the topic you wish to present? Each of these audiences would require a different approach, and perhaps a different type of media product.

For instance, if you're trying to teach preschool children about household hazards, you might create an illustrated book or an animated video to explain the concepts in a format children would enjoy. But if you were to present a report on the same topic to a group of adults, you might prepare a multimedia presentation using photos of real-life situations.

PRACTICE You Ought to Be in Pictures

Pick one of the following topics, and write a short paragraph on the type of media product you would use to present it. Also describe who your audience would be and what you would want to tell and show in your presentation.

- How to play basketball (or another sport)
- What it's like to volunteer for a local charity
- Adventures while traveling in another state or country
- Achievements of your drama (or another) club

MEDIA PRODUCTS

LESSON 2 **Creating a Video**

A video allows you to incorporate verbal, audio, and visual elements in presenting information. You can use video to create documentaries, news programs, campaign promotions, and instructional pieces.

❶ Preproduction

Preproduction involves planning and preparing for the production of your video. Here are the tasks you will need to do.

Preparing for Video Production	
Task	**Description**
Write a treatment	Prepare a brief summary of your video, and describe the action that will occur in it.
Write a script	Write down the complete text of verbal, audio, and visual details, including narration, dialogue, and titles.
Prepare a storyboard	Create a storyboard showing the sequence of scenes and the types of shots required.
Determine roles	Choose participants, and coordinate the tasks of those who will narrate, interview sources, act in scenes, and serve as part of the technical crew (camera, lighting, sound).
Do a site survey	Visit locations where you can videotape your scenes. Imagine where the action will take place and where the equipment and props will go. Get permission, if needed.
Organize equipment	List and then gather all the equipment you will need, such as cameras, microphones, lights, and props.

A **storyboard** is a series of simple sketches or descriptions of scenes in the video, including the dialogue or narration that goes with the scenes. The storyboard will help keep you organized. Here is a sample storyboard.

Narrator: "Every morning Jeff leaves home at the same time . . ."

"listens to the same radio station . . ."

"and travels the same road."

Once you have completed your script and storyboard, you need to rehearse any dialogue or narration in the script. For scenes that involve acting, you also need to **block** the scene, or coordinate the placement and movement of the actors, props, and cameras.

❷ Production

In the production stage, you will videotape, or "shoot," the actual scenes. With your storyboard, you've already determined the settings and camera shots for your scenes, the person or people in them, and the dialogue that will occur. Now you will bring your storyboard to life.

While you are "on the set" and shooting the scenes, you will need to perform the tasks listed below.

- **Direct the participants** by telling them where to sit, stand, or move; how to say their lines; and how to present themselves.
- **Select and adjust camera angles and shots.** Try shooting a scene from different angles for different effects.
- **Make sure microphones are in place and sound equipment is working.** Camcorders have built-in microphones that automatically record while the camera is running.
- **Make sure lighting is appropriate.** Indoor and outdoor scenes require different lighting, for instance.
- **Make sure the props are set up as needed.**

Shoot titles, credits, and graphics as you go, instead of adding them later.

Use a tripod to keep the camera steady during the shoot.

Videotape each scene at least twice. This way, if one of the elements, such as sound or lighting, is of poor quality in the first shoot, you will have the second as a backup and won't have to reshoot the scene.

❸ Postproduction

In the postproduction stage, you edit your video to obtain a polished product. Editing involves the following tasks:

- Placing scenes in a logical sequence
- Adding sound effects, music, and special effects
- Ensuring sound and image are matched up properly
- Adding graphics, titles, and credits not included during production

During the editing phase, you will need to keep in mind three important concepts.

- **Pace** As you are cutting and shaping scenes, keep in mind that a series of short, quick cuts creates a fast pace in a story, whereas long cuts slow a story down.

- **Continuity** Be sure that each shot blends seamlessly into the next. Abrupt cuts—called jump cuts—are visually jarring. Also be sure that props, people, and other visual elements are the same from one shot to the next.

- **Purpose** Each shot should advance the story. Choose only relevant sound bites from interviews, or use cutaways—inserted shots that show related action, objects, or people—to avoid long interview scenes.

❹ Evaluation and Revision

To evaluate how effective your video will be, hold a sneak preview or screening with a small audience of peers. After the screening, have them fill out questionnaires, or hold a discussion. Here are some questions to ask.

- Was the story or message clear?
- Were any scenes too short or too long?
- Were the camera techniques effective or distracting?
- Was the sound quality good?
- Did the narration help clarify the message?

Use the feedback to revise and improve your video. You may need to do additional editing or add music, narration, or captions.

Creating a Multimedia Presentation

At some point in school or at work, you may be asked to present a report or a proposal to a group of people. **Multimedia presentations** allow you to present information in an interesting way through the use of multiple media—text, graphics, sound, and video—that are linked together. The media components are designed and developed with a special program, or authoring tool, such as *HyperStudio, PowerPoint,* or *Harvard Graphics.*

❶ Planning the Presentation

Detailed planning makes development of your presentation go smoothly. During the planning stage, you decide on the information and tools you will use when you actually create the presentation.

Here's How Planning the Presentation

1. Brainstorm the topic, content, and main points of your presentation.
2. Research background material on your topic as you would for a writing assignment. Check books, newspapers, and magazines; talk to experts; check out other media sources.
3. Decide on the authoring tool you will use to design and develop the presentation.
4. Create a flow chart to organize your information, and a storyboard to show where visual and audio elements will complement the text.

A flow chart shows how the screens in your presentation will connect to each other. The structure of your flow chart depends upon the authoring tool you use and the complexity of your topic. Shown below is a tree-structure flow chart for a presentation on hazardous household products.

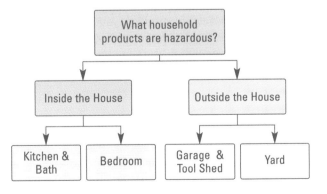

❷ Designing the Presentation

In the design stage, you determine the appearance of the screens in your presentation by creating a storyboard and screen templates.

A storyboard provides you with a visual method for organizing materials. In creating a storyboard for a multimedia presentation, you draw rough sketches of what you would like your screens to look like. Each frame of your storyboard contains a sketch of the placement of the text and visual images you want to include on that screen.

A **screen template** is a slide that displays your information on the projection screen. The purpose of the template is to give your screens a uniform design. You can use a template provided by the authoring tool, or you can create your own. Here is a template for a screen for the presentation on hazardous household products.

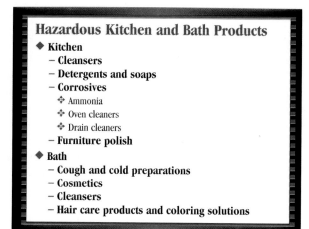

Hazardous Kitchen and Bath Products
- ◆ **Kitchen**
  - – **Cleansers**
  - – **Detergents and soaps**
  - – **Corrosives**
    - ❖ Ammonia
    - ❖ Oven cleaners
    - ❖ Drain cleaners
  - – **Furniture polish**
- ◆ **Bath**
  - – **Cough and cold preparations**
  - – **Cosmetics**
  - – **Cleansers**
  - – **Hair care products and coloring solutions**

❸ Developing the Presentation

In the development stage, you create your media components and combine them into one package, using the authoring tool and the screen templates you have created. The chart on the next page shows a broad outline of the process.

Creating the Media Components

1. Write brief informational paragraphs and lists to go on the screens.

2. Produce graphics and images—such as charts, diagrams, maps, time lines, photos, and drawings—to present information that is better shown in pictures than described in words.

3. Add sound elements, such as music, voice recordings, and sound effects. These can be used to emphasize a particular point.

4. Use video clips to provide real-life or simulated action related to your topic.

You can download audio clips, visual images, and video clips from the Internet. But make sure these are copyright-free, or you will need to get permission to use them.

❹ Evaluation and Revision

Before you formally present your work, have a group of friends or peers view your presentation and provide feedback. In a discussion or on a questionnaire, ask the following questions.

• Did you find the presentation interesting?

• In what ways could it be more exciting?

• Were the visual images and audio elements helpful or distracting?

• Was the presentation appropriate to the topic?

Use the feedback to revise and improve those areas that were confusing, uninformative, or uninteresting.

❺ Giving the Presentation

To deliver your presentation, you will use a computer that is hooked up to a TV monitor or to a projector that will project your screens onto a large classroom screen.

Be sure you know how to use the equipment before giving your presentation. Rehearse your presentation several times, until you are comfortable using the equipment.

MEDIA PRODUCTS

Creating a Web Site

Creating a site on the World Wide Web is much easier now than it once was because there are programs available to ease you through the development phase. Since the success of your Web site will depend on its content and design, you need to plan these carefully.

❶ Planning the Site

A Web site consists of multiple Web pages that contain text, visuals, audio elements, and interactive opportunities. The chart below lists steps for planning a Web site.

> **Here's How** **Planning Your Content and Design**
>
> 1. Choose your topic, purpose, and target audience.
> 2. Research information and media components to include.
> 3. Decide which information you will include as text and which as visuals and audio.
> 4. Determine how many pages your site will include, the design elements and techniques you will use, and the layout of pages.
> 5. Create a flow chart to show how the pages will be linked, and a storyboard to show how each page will look.

The home page, or first page of a site, introduces the topic and tells what other pages are available. The flow chart below shows how pages are linked with the home page for the Drama Club site shown on the following page.

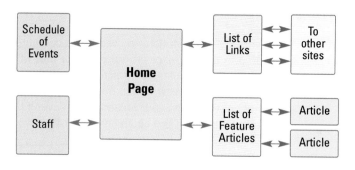

CHAPTER 30

② Developing the Web Site

Once you've planned the site, you can fully develop the Web pages by using a program or hypertext mark-up language (HTML). Here's what you'll need to do.

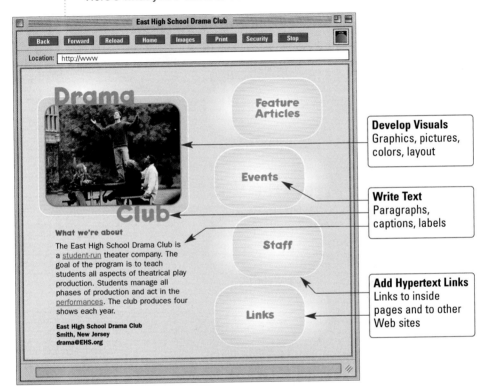

Develop Visuals
Graphics, pictures, colors, layout

Write Text
Paragraphs, captions, labels

Add Hypertext Links
Links to inside pages and to other Web sites

③ Evaluation and Revision

Ask a group of peers to visit your Web site and give you feedback on the questions below.

• Does the home page effectively introduce the subject?

• Is the site easy to navigate?

• Do the links work?

• Is the site visually interesting?

Student Help Desk

Creating Media Products at a Glance

1. DECIDE
- Choose and refine topic
- Brainstorm content
- Do research
- Choose type of product

2. DESIGN
- Outline content
- Create flow chart
- Create storyboard

3. DEVELOP
- Write text or script
- Create media components

4. EVALUATE
- Ask peers or experts for feedback
- Examine feedback
- Revise

Creating a Video   In the Director's Chair

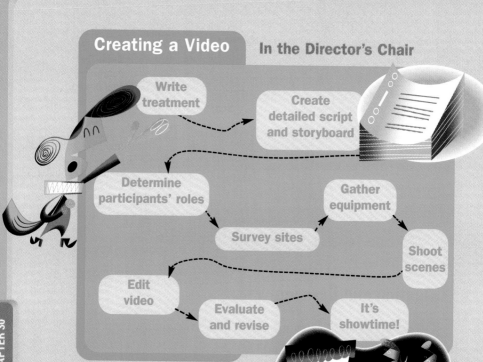

Write treatment

Create detailed script and storyboard

Determine participants' roles

Gather equipment

Survey sites

Shoot scenes

Edit video

Evaluate and revise

It's showtime!

Creating a Web Site   Elements.com

Visual Information
- pictures
- graphics
- colors and layout

Verbal Information
- paragraphs
- captions
- labels

Hypertext Links
Links to supporting documents and other Web sites

Web Site

What to Do with the Finished Product

- Enter contests for that type of product.
- Send it out for review by experts in the field.
- Use it as a work sample when applying for a job or internship.
- Establish your Web site on the World Wide Web.
- Submit your video to a local TV station.

The Bottom Line

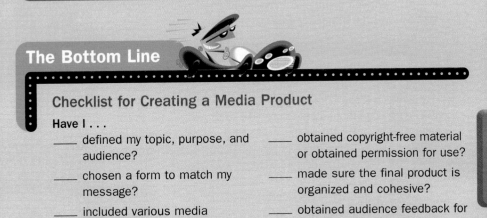

Checklist for Creating a Media Product

Have I . . .

____ defined my topic, purpose, and audience?

____ chosen a form to match my message?

____ included various media components?

____ obtained copyright-free material or obtained permission for use?

____ made sure the final product is organized and cohesive?

____ obtained audience feedback for final revisions?

MEDIA PRODUCTS

Power Words
Vocabulary for Precise Writing

discombobulated

lexicographer

Word Smart

Why would you want to be a walking thesaurus? Perhaps you'd like to be ready in a word emergency. Use these words to describe your vocabulary expertise—or the lack of it.

Are You Clueless in Wordland?

When someone asks you for a word in a crossword puzzle, do you pretend to be **insouciant,** or blithely indifferent? Inside are you **confused, uncertain,** and **perplexed,** or—as the more informal terms have it— **discombobulated** or **flummoxed?**

Don't let ignorance **frustrate** or **disconcert** you. Don't be **inconvenienced** or **discommoded** by a lack of word knowledge. Instead, you can become **fluent, lucid, expressive,** and **eloquent** by consulting the lexicon, or dictionary.

Or Did You Write the Book?

Perhaps you already know more words than most. If you have compiled a dictionary or word book yourself, you are a **lexicographer.** If you are fluent in several languages, you can call yourself a **linguist.** With enough confidence, you might even **coin** your own words, or **neologisms.**

lucid

perplexed

linguist

fluen

eloquen

insoucian

coin

▷ Your Turn Name That Tuna!

Make a game of creating new words using portions of old ones. For example, you could call a fish that walks on water a **ichthyhydroambulater.** With a small group of classmates, each write a made-up mystery word on a folded piece of paper and pass it to your left. Try to decode the word you receive.

Expanding Your Vocabulary

Which Button Should I Push?

The plane is going into a nosedive, and the pilot is unconscious. You have to figure out which of the many controls will make the plane go up again, but you don't recognize the labels: *aileron, elevator, gyrostabilizer.*

Then you take a second look at *elevator.* An elevator on an airplane? Impossible, you think, but might the two kinds of elevators have similar functions? You push the button, and the nose of the plane rises, clearing the top of a mountain by inches.

There's no reason to crash and burn just because you come across a term you don't know. In this chapter, you will learn strategies that will help you build vocabulary as you read and use words with more precision in your writing.

Write Away: Explain Your Terms
Write a paragraph explaining a word or phrase that you know but that some of your classmates might not be familiar with. You might choose a term from a sport, hobby, or artistic medium. Add the paragraph to your 🗀 **Working Portfolio.**

VOCABULARY

Developing Your Word Power

Building Your Vocabulary

Building a strong vocabulary does not necessarily mean memorizing unfamiliar words after looking them up one at a time in a dictionary. Good writers and readers acquire strong vocabularies slowly in the process of reading, writing and communicating.

Building Passive Vocabulary Words that you recognize when you read but might not be able to use in a sentence are considered your **passive vocabulary.** You can add to your passive vocabulary by looking up words, but more often you "pick them up" by reading.

Building Active Vocabulary Words that you recall and use accurately in writing and speaking make up your **active vocabulary.** Most active vocabulary comes from passive vocabulary that you become aware of and begin to use.

A Strategic Approach

The three strategies described below will help you build your passive vocabulary and convert passive into active vocabulary.

Strategies for Building Your Vocabulary	
Using context clues	Words you don't know are usually accompanied by words you do know. By examining the surrounding text, or the context, of a word, you can often figure out what the unfamiliar word means.
Analyzing word structure	In addition to looking around a word for clues, you can look at the word itself. Different parts of a word will give you clues to its meaning.
Exploring shades of meaning	To use words effectively, you need to know the different meanings a word can have and the differences among words with similar meanings.

Fox Trot by Bill Amend

CHAPTER 31

Using Context

❶ Context Clues

The **context** surrounding an unfamiliar term may provide all the information you need to understand that term. In the passage below, for example, the meanings of *employ, aghast,* and *confirmed* can be understood from context clues.

> **LITERARY MODEL**
>
> So far, I had not **opened my eyes**. . . . I longed, yet dared not to **employ** my vision. I **dreaded** the first glance at objects around me. It was not that I **feared** to look upon things horrible, but that I grew **aghast** lest there should be *nothing* to see. At length, with a wild desperation at heart, I quickly unclosed my eyes. **My worst thoughts**, then, were **confirmed. The blackness of eternal night encompassed me.**
>
> —Edgar Allan Poe, "The Pit and the Pendulum"

The phrase "employ my vision" is a restatement of "opened my eyes."

Being "aghast" must be similar to feeling dread or fear.

The narrator's worst thoughts are "confirmed" when they are shown to be true.

❷ Specific Context Clues

Familiarizing yourself with the most common kinds of specific context clues will help you to spot them when you read.

Specific Context Clues		
Type of Clue	**Key Words/Phrases**	**Example**
Definition or restatement of the meaning of the word	or, which is, that is, in other words, also known as, also called	His first *conjecture*, or guess, was correct.
Example following an unfamiliar word	such as, like, as if, for example, especially, including	She loved *macabre* stories, such as those by Poe or Stephen King.
Comparison with a more familiar word or concept	as, like, also, similar to, in the same way, likewise	Despite his physical suffering, his mind was as *lucid* as any rational person's.

VOCABULARY

Specific Context Clues		
Type of Clue	**Key Words/Phrases**	**Example**
Contrast with a familiar word or experience	unlike, but, however, although, on the other hand, on the contrary	Unlike her clumsy partner, she was an *agile* dancer.
Cause-and-effect relationship in which one term is familiar	because, since, when, consequently, as a result, therefore	Because they hadn't eaten in days, the rats were *ravenous*.

PRACTICE A Specific Context Clues

Write a definition for each of the italicized words in the right-hand column of the chart above and use each word in a sentence.

❸ General Context Clues

Sometimes the meaning of a word must be inferred from the context of an entire passage.

LITERARY MODEL

The story eventually got to the little village in the heart of the Ibo country that Nnaemeka and his young wife were a most happy couple. But his father was one of the few people in the village who knew nothing about this. He always displayed so much temper whenever his son's name was mentioned that everyone avoided it in his presence. By a tremendous effort of will he had succeeded in pushing his son to the back of his mind. The strain had nearly killed him, but he had **persevered** and won.

—Chinua Achebe, "Marriage Is a Private Affair"

HOT TIP

You will usually understand more if you concentrate on the meaning of a passage as a whole rather than on the definition of each individual word.

PRACTICE B General Context Clues

Write a definition for the word *persevered* based only on the context of the paragraph above. Then explain how you arrived at your definition.

Analyzing Word Structure

Analyzing the structure of an unfamiliar word is another way to determine its meaning. All English words are made up of one or more of the following parts: base words, word roots, prefixes, and suffixes.

❶ Base Words

A **base word** is a complete word to which a prefix, a suffix, or another base word is added to form a new word.

Realism is a literary style.

Real	ism
BASE WORD	SUFFIX

I plan to retrofit my computer with a video card.

retro	fit
PREFIX	BASE WORD

If you can identify the base word in an unfamiliar term, then you can often figure out its meaning.

❷ Word Roots

The **root** of a word contains its basic meaning. Unlike a base word, a root cannot stand alone. One root is often the basis of a **word family**—several words that share a related meaning.

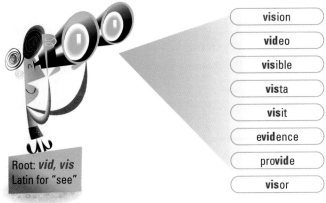

vision
video
visible
vista
visit
evidence
provide
visor

Root: *vid, vis*
Latin for "see"

HOT TIP

Word roots often name concrete things or physical actions. For example, the English words *comprehend* and *apprehend* come from the Latin verb *prehendere,* which means "to grasp."

VOCABULARY

❸ Prefixes and Suffixes

A **prefix** is added to the beginning of a word to form a new word.

> **pre** ("coming before") + **fix** (from *figere,* "to fasten") = **prefix**

A **suffix** is added to the end of a word to form a new word and tends to determine a word's part of speech.

> **read** (verb) + **able** = **readable** (adjective)
>
> **home** (noun) + **ward** = **homeward** (adverb)

If you know the meaning of a prefix or suffix and the base word or root, you can often recognize an unfamiliar word or even create a new word. Many words have both prefixes and suffixes. Changing either one changes the meaning of the word.

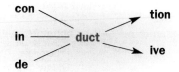

Words can also have more than one suffix and/or prefix. For example, the word *reconstructionist* is made up of two prefixes (*re-* and *con-*), the root *struct* (from Latin *struere,* "to build"), and two suffixes (*-ion* and *-ist*).

❹ Word Analysis

If you break down an unfamiliar word into parts, you may recognize each of its elements, even though the word itself is unfamiliar. If you don't recognize a particular element, try thinking of other words with similar elements.

Charles Dickens was sometimes called the Inimitable.

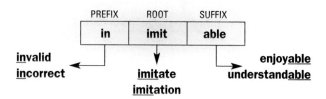

> **PRACTICE** Analyzing Unfamiliar Terms
>
> Using the charts on pages 577–578, analyze the following words and explain what you think they might mean: *antipathy, autocratic, dehydrate, hydrophobic.*

Exploring Shades of Meaning

❶ Correctly Identifying Words

Before using a word, you need to make sure you have identified it correctly. Many words are easily confused because they are **homophones**—they sound alike but have different meanings. For example, *compliment* (an expression of praise) and *complement* (something that completes another thing) are homophones.

> **She gave me a nice compliment on my clothes.**
>
> **That hat is the perfect complement to your outfit.**

Other words are **homonyms**—they look alike but are in fact separate words. For example, *entrance* (a place to enter) and *entrance* (to put into a trance) are homonyms.

> **Does this stadium have any entrances?**
>
> **The snake charmer entrances the snake.**

Notice that in the sentences above, the context makes clear which word is meant.

For more commonly confused words, see pp. 656–661.

❷ Multiple Meanings

Many words have more than one meaning. For example, here are the first three meanings listed in one dictionary for the noun *animal.*

animal	
A multicellular organism that differs from plants	Dogs, humans, and fleas are members of the **animal** kingdom.
A nonhuman organism	In my house live five people and an assortment of **animals.**
A person who behaves in a bestial manner	The kids who use the lunchroom before we do are **animals.**

Using a word precisely means not only knowing which meaning you intend but also making that meaning clear to the reader by providing sufficient context.

VOCABULARY

❸ Synonyms and Antonyms

In addition to the different meanings one word can have, you need to know different words that have similar meanings, or **synonyms.**

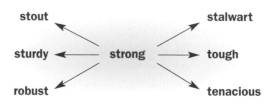

stout	stalwart
sturdy ←	strong	→ tough
robust	tenacious

Knowing several ways to express a concept can make it easier to choose the exact term you need, vary your terminology, explain your terms, and craft your style.

Knowing **antonyms**—words with opposite meanings—can also help you use terms precisely. The words *soft, fragile,* and *weak,* for example, are each antonyms of a different meaning of *tough.*

❹ Denotation and Connotation

What synonyms have in common is a particular **denotation,** or dictionary definition. The differences between synonyms are often a matter of **connotation,** or flavor. This old saying illustrates different connotations for three synonyms:

Horses **sweat,** men **perspire,** and women **glow.**

When choosing between words with similar meanings, consider the flavor a particular choice will add and how it will fit in with the rest of the text.

For more about denotation and connotation, see p. 393.

For more about denotation and connotation, see p. 393.

PRACTICE Being Consistent with Connotation

Use each of the following synonyms for *eat*—*scarf down, dine upon, ingest*—in a sentence that puts it in an appropriate context.

Tools for Developing Word Power

❶ Using a Dictionary

Adopting a strategic approach to developing your word power does not mean avoiding using a dictionary. Dictionaries are powerful reference tools that contain the most reliable information available about words and how they are used. But you will be able to use a dictionary much more effectively if you have thought about a word's context, structure, and shades of meaning.

❷ ❸ ❹

❶ **vin•dic•tive** (vĭn-dĭk′tĭv) *adj.* **1.** Disposed to seek revenge; revengeful. **2.** Marked by or resulting from a desire to hurt; spiteful. ❺ [From Latin *vindicta*, vengeance, from *vindex, vindic-*, surety, avenger. ❻ See VINDICATE.] ❼ —**vin•dic′tive•ly** *adv.* — **vin•dic′tive•ness** *n.*

❽ *SYNONYMS:* vindictive, vengeful, revengeful. These adjectives mean desiring or proceeding from a desire for revenge. *Vindictive* suggests gratuitous or unmotivated rancor and a disposition to retaliate for wrongs, real or imagined: ❾ *"He seemed to take a vindictive pleasure in punishing the least shortcomings"* (Mark Twain). *"Like many men whose self-love is wounded . . . he felt vindictive"* (George Meredith). *Vengeful* and *revengeful* imply the impulse to inflict or the infliction of suffering or punishment as retribution for evil or an injury: *"the vengeful massacre of Toulon"* (Joseph Conrad). *"I had a keen, revengeful sense of the insult"* (Nathaniel Hawthorne).

—The American Heritage®Dictionary of the English Language, Third Edition

❶ **Entry word**

❷ **Pronunciation**

❸ **Part of speech**

❹ **Definitions** denotations

❺ **Etymology** word origins

❻ **Cross-reference** to a related word

❼ **Derived words**

❽ **Synonyms** and their shades of meaning

❾ **Literary examples** of vocabulary in use

PRACTICE A Using a Dictionary

Look up in a dictionary the italicized words in the chart of specific context clues on pages 567–568. For each word, write down two pieces of information that help you better understand its meaning.

❷ Using a Thesaurus

A **thesaurus** is a dictionary of synonyms. Most thesauruses list synonyms and antonyms after each basic meaning of the entry word.

Some thesauruses also group entries by category in a separate section called a **category index.** The main entry of a word will often contain one or more cross-references to this index, where logically associated terms can be found.

❷

❶ **poor** *adjective*

❸ **1.** Having little or no money or wealth: **❹** beggarly, destitute, down-and-out, impecunious, impoverished, indigent, necessitous, needy, penniless, penurious, poverty-stricken. **❺** *Informal:* broke, strapped. **❺** *Idioms:* hard up, on one's uppers. **❻** *See* RICH. **2.** Below a standard of quality : bad, bum, unsatisfactory. *Idioms:* below par, not up to scratch (*or* snuff). *See* GOOD. **3.** Of decidedly inferior quality : base, cheap, lousy, miserable, paltry, rotten, shodden, sleazy, trashy. *Informal:* cheesy. **❺** *Slang:* crummy, schlocky. *See* GOOD. **4.** Conspicuously deficient in quantity, fullness, or extent : exiguous, meager, puny, scant, scanty, skimpy, spare, sparse, stingy, thin. *Slang:* measly. *See* BIG, EXCESS. **5.** Arousing or deserving pity: pathetic, piteous, pitiable, pitiful, rueful, ruthful. *See* PITY

❶ Entry word
❷ Part of speech
❸ First meaning
❹ List of synonyms
❺ Levels of usage
❻ Category index reference

—Roget's II: The New Thesaurus, Third Edition

Beware of substituting synonyms for words without considering connotations and other shades of meaning.

PRACTICE B Using a Thesaurus

Look up the following words in a thesaurus: *color* (verb), *care* (noun), *rude* (adjective), *view* (noun). For every word, list each meaning given and write down one of the synonyms corresponding to that meaning.

❸ Keeping a Personal Word Bank

One of the best ways to prepare yourself to use new words effectively in writing is to write. List the words. Use them in sentences. Include anything that helps you remember, understand, and get a feel for the word. Add drawings or other visual aids, like diagrams, if you find them helpful.

You may want to have a special notebook, or "word bank," just for the purpose of keeping track of your expanding vocabulary.

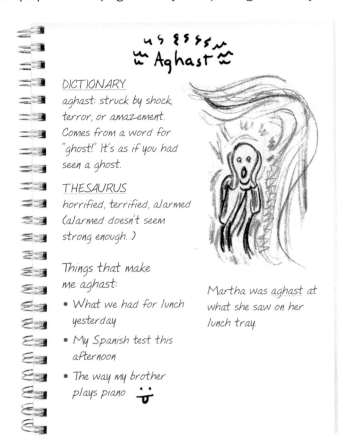

ᵁˢ ᵉˢˢˢ
☁ Aghast ☁

DICTIONARY
aghast: struck by shock, terror, or amazement. Comes from a word for "ghost!" It's as if you had seen a ghost.

THESAURUS
horrified, terrified, alarmed (alarmed doesn't seem strong enough.)

Things that make me aghast:
• What we had for lunch yesterday
• My Spanish test this afternoon
• The way my brother plays piano ☺

Martha was <u>aghast</u> at what she saw on her lunch tray.

In your 📁 **Working Portfolio,** find the paragraph you wrote for the **Write Away** on page 565. Use a dictionary and a thesaurus to replace some of the words you used with ones that are more precise or interesting.

Student Help Desk

Vocabulary at a Glance

CONTEXT

The Text Around a Word

The **denunciation** of the bandmaster by the football coach must stop. Coach should be praising his colleague in public, not condemning him.

STRUCTURE

The Parts of a Word

de	nunci	ation

root *nuntiare,* to announce
+ prefix *de-,* (do opposite of)
+ suffix *–ation,* (action)
=   denunciation

SHADES OF MEANING

Multiple Meanings
1. Open condemnation
2. Formal accusation

Synonyms
  condemnation
  defamation

Antonym praise

Word Context   Powerful Friends

Context   **Kinds of Clues**

The bandmaster's **aberrations** are becoming intolerable. For example, just the other day, he had ——o **example**
the band march in their underwear. He is like a ——o **comparison**
goose that flies north for the winter. I, however,
always behave the way I am supposed to. I think the ——o **contrast**
bandmaster's behavior is the result of his desire to ——o **cause and effect**
shock and confuse people. Whatever the reason, his
departures from the normal have to stop. ——o **restatement**

Word Structure   Powerfully Built

Word: Disestablishmentarian

dis	establish	ment	arian
Prefix	**Base Word**	**Suffix**	**Suffix**
opposite of	from *stabilis,* "firm"	result of action	believer in

Definition: An opponent of an established order.

Shades of Meaning Power Options

Walk

ambulate trudge pace promenade

ramble saunter stroll meander

amble tread plod rove shuffle

stride strut step tramp traverse

Useful Greek Roots

Root	Meaning	Examples
auto	self, alone	autobiography, autograph, automobile
crac, crat	rule, govern	aristocrat, bureaucracy, theocracy
dem	people	democracy, demography, epidemic
hydr	water	dehydrate, hydroelectric, hydrogen
ortho	straight, correct	orthopedist, orthodontist, orthodox
path	feeling, suffer	antipathy, pathetic, pathology
phil	love	philharmonic, philosophy, philanthropy
phob	fear	claustrophobia, phobic, xenophobia
tele	far, distant	telecommunications, telephone

Useful Latin Roots

Root	Meaning	Examples
cred	believe	creed, credit, discredit, incredible
dict	speak, tell	contradict, dictionary, verdict
duc, duct	lead	aqueduct, conduct, educate, induce
mot, mob	move	mobile, motility, motion, promote
quer, quest	ask, seek	query, question, quest, request
pend, pens	hang	appendix, pendulum, suspense
rupt	break	abrupt, bankrupt, erupt, interrupt
spect	see	inspect, respect, suspect, spectator

Some Common Prefixes

Prefix	Meaning	Examples
anti-	against	antibiotic, antisocial, antiwar
cent-	hundred	cent, centigrade, century
de-	opposite of	degrade, deceive, derail
il-, im-, in-	not	illegal, immature, inaccurate
inter-	between	intercede, international, interpret
mal-	bad	maladjusted, malice, maltreatment
micro-	small	microchip, microcosm, microscope
mis-	bad, wrong	misconduct, misfortune, misspell
re-	again, back	reappear, redo, repay, return
sym-, syn-	together	sympathy, symbol, synonym
trans-	across	transatlantic, transfer, translate

Some Common Suffixes

Suffix	Meaning	Examples
Nouns		
-ant, -ist, -ician	doer	occupant, geologist, politician
-ance, -ence,	state or quality of	avoidance, independence
-ation	action or process	strangulation, filtration
Adjectives		
-ful, -ous	full of	thoughtful, spacious, joyous
-al, -ic, -ish	relating to	natural, heroic, stylish
-ant, -ive, -some	inclined to	defiant, active, tiresome
-less	without	careless, fearless, worthless
-ate	state or quality of	desolate, desperate, fortunate
Adverbs		
-ly	in what manner	greedily, happily, slowly, quickly
-ward	toward	backward, homeward, upward
Verbs		
-ate, -fy	to make	activate, fascinate, simplify
-en	to become	frighten, lengthen

Mother Goose & Grimm by Mike Peters

The Bottom Line

Checklist for Expanding Vocabulary

Have I . . .

_____ tried to understand new words by considering them in context?

_____ tried to make sense of new words by analyzing their structure?

_____ refined my knowledge of new words by considering different shades of meaning?

_____ used the dictionary to supplement rather than replace my word-comprehension strategies?

_____ taken advantage of all the kinds of information available in a dictionary or thesaurus?

_____ kept a list of important new words that I can add to and refer to later?

Power Words
Vocabulary for Precise Writing

Multiple-Choice Words

The one choice you don't have on a multiple-choice test is whether to take the test in the first place. Use words like those below to talk about your test-taking blues.

A Lack of Alternatives

If you have no choice about taking a test, the test is **obligatory, mandatory,** and pretty much **inescapable. Compulsory** examinations are required to qualify you for advancement in school or certification in everything from driving a car to practicing veterinary medicine.

The big question is do you have the **requisite** knowledge? Have you learned the **indispensable** facts and picked up the **necessary** skills? If not, you may face an information **crisis,** a testing **exigency.**

A Bewildering Array of Choices

What if you get to the test and don't know which alternatives to choose? Is the material suddenly **obscure, recondite,** and **arcane**? Are you being asked about **abstruse** or **esoteric** points? Is the whole thing **enigmatic, puzzling, mysterious,** and **cryptic?** You can of course **opt** for "all of the above." But a better option might be to use your head and make an **educated guess.**

> ▷ **Your Turn** Getting the Odds on Your Side
>
> With a small group of classmates, calculate the odds of guessing correctly on a multiple-choice item with four alternatives and one with five alternatives. In each case, how many alternatives do you have to eliminate to raise your odds to 50–50?

Preparing for Tests

Panic Attack

Be-be-be-beep! The alarm goes off, and it's already 8 A.M. You have only 5 minutes to get to school. A big test awaits you and you're not prepared. You could have studied if you'd known about the test, but somehow, you didn't even know about the class! You leap out of bed, pull on some clothes, and race to school for the test of your nightmares.

Have you ever had that dream or felt that way in real life? One way to ward off that experience is to use study and test preparation strategies like the ones you'll find in this chapter.

Write Away: It Was a Nightmare

Discuss with classmates experiences you've had in which you felt unprepared or dreams you've had in which you were unable to do what was expected of you. Write a paragraph, a story, or a poem describing the experience and keep it in your 🗂 **Working Portfolio.**

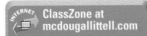
ClassZone at
mcdougallittell.com

PREP. FOR TESTS

Studying in the Content Areas

You can make the best use of your study time if you use some basic content-area reading strategies. Use the tips in this lesson as you prepare for math, social studies, and science tests.

❶ Active Reading Strategies

Does your mind sometimes wander when you read your textbooks? Use these basic strategies to stay actively involved with the material.

Active Reading Strategies	
Previewing	Skim and scan the page while looking at key words, major heads, topic sentences, visuals, and captions.
Questioning	Ask and answer questions as you read. Jot down any questions you can't answer.
Using context clues	Use the words you know to help you infer the meaning of words you don't know.
Rereading	Reread paragraphs and sections that are especially important or parts that aren't clear the first time.
Taking notes	Jot down main ideas, related details, and key terms.
Using graphic organizers	Use a graphic organizer—such as a chart, Venn diagram, or time line—to organize your notes.

❷ Reading and Studying Mathematics

A key to understanding math is studying the examples provided each time a new concept is introduced.

❶ Preview. Find the two basic parts of the example: the problem and the solution.

Example 1 Connection: Algebra

Find the geometric mean of 2 and 18.

Solution

Let x = the geometric mean of 2 and 18. Write and solve a proportion.

$$\frac{2}{x} = \frac{x}{18}$$

$$36 = x^2$$

The geometric mean is always positive.

$$\sqrt{36} = x$$

$$6 = x$$

The geometric mean of 2 and 18 is 6.

❷ Read and reread. Read the problem to understand what is being asked and what information is provided.

❸ Note the sequence. Study the steps to see how each step leads to the next.

❹ Try it yourself.

❸ Reading and Studying History

When reading history texts, you want to understand the big picture so you can answer essay questions. You also want to focus on key facts and dates that might be part of an objective test.

Here's How Studying for History Tests

1. **Preview.** Scan the page. Note the titles, subtitles, and visual elements to see what the page is about. Note any key terms that might be in bold-faced print.

2. **Look for and summarize main ideas.** Read any summaries that are provided. After each subtopic, take the time to summarize the key ideas. You might want to include these in your notes.

3. **Make connections.** As you read, think about the cause-and-effect relationships that may be stated or just suggested. Note the sequence of events. Make a time line to keep track of what happened when.

4. **Interpret maps, graphs, and charts.** Key information is often presented in graphic aids. Use the keys to help you interpret what is being shown.

5. **Draw conclusions.** Think about what happened and why. Think beyond the text and use logical thinking to draw your own conclusions.

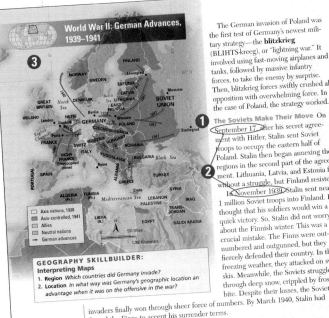

❶ Preview. Note titles, subtitles and visual elements.

❷ Make connections.

❸ Interpret maps.

The German invasion of Poland was the first test of Germany's newest military strategy—the **blitzkrieg** (BLIHTS-kreeg), or "lightning war." It involved using fast-moving airplanes and tanks, followed by massive infantry forces, to take the enemy by surprise. Then, blitzkrieg forces swiftly crushed all opposition with overwhelming force. In the case of Poland, the strategy worked.

The Soviets Make Their Move On September 17, after his secret agreement with Hitler, Stalin sent Soviet troops to occupy the eastern half of Poland. Stalin then began annexing the regions in the second part of the agreement. Lithuania, Latvia, and Estonia fell without a struggle, but Finland resisted.

In November 1939, Stalin sent nearly 1 million Soviet troops into Finland. He thought that his soldiers would win a quick victory. So, Stalin did not worry about the Finnish winter. This was a crucial mistake. The Finns were outnumbered and outgunned, but they fiercely defended their country. In the freezing weather, they attacked on swift skis. Meanwhile, the Soviets struggled through deep snow, crippled by frostbite. Despite their losses, the Soviet invaders finally won through sheer force of numbers. By March 1940, Stalin had forced the Finns to accept his surrender terms.

The Phony War For almost seven months after the fall of Poland, there was a strange calm in the land fighting in Europe. After their declaration of war, the French and British had mobilized their armies. They stationed their troops along the Maginot (MAZH-uh-NOH) Line, a system of fortifications along France's border with Germany.

GEOGRAPHY SKILLBUILDER:
Interpreting Maps
1. **Region** Which countries did Germany invade?
2. **Location** In what way was Germany's geographic location an advantage when it was on the offensive in the war?

THINK THROUGH HISTORY
A. Analyzing Motives What would you say were the political reasons behind Stalin's actions in Europe at the beginning of World War II?
A. Possible Answer Stalin aimed at expanding the Soviet Union's territory and power, while keeping his country out of the war. He seemed ready to make an agreement

❹ Reading and Studying Science

Reading science texts requires skills similar to those used when reading history texts. You need to focus on key terms and facts that support the basic concepts in the chapter. Scientific writing often poses a hypothesis and then provides research and data that prove or disprove that hypothesis.

Here's How **Reading Science Texts**

1. **Preview.** Scan the page. Note the titles, subtitles, and visual elements to see what the page is about. Note any key terms that might be in dark print.

2. **Examine main ideas and conclusions.** Often the main idea is stated in the beginning of a section. The conclusion, usually stated at the end, is often a restatement of that main idea.

3. **Look for cause-effect relationships.** Scientific study depends on defining which causes produce which effects and then drawing valid conclusions from this evidence. Think about cause-effect relationships as you read.

4. **Use context clues.** Key terms are often defined as restatement context clues. Examples of a concept can also provide clues to unfamiliar terms.

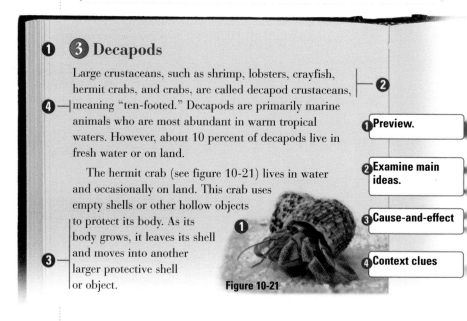

❶ ❸ Decapods

Large crustaceans, such as shrimp, lobsters, crayfish, hermit crabs, and crabs, are called decapod crustaceans, ❷ ❹ meaning "ten-footed." Decapods are primarily marine animals who are most abundant in warm tropical waters. However, about 10 percent of decapods live in fresh water or on land.

The hermit crab (see figure 10-21) lives in water and occasionally on land. This crab uses empty shells or other hollow objects to protect its body. As its ❶ body grows, it leaves its shell and moves into another ❸ larger protective shell or object.

Figure 10-21

❶ **Preview.**

❷ **Examine main ideas.**

❸ **Cause-and-effect**

❹ **Context clues**

HOT TIP

Match your reading rate and style to the material. For new or difficult material, slow down and reread sections that don't make sense to you. Take notes and try to restate important concepts in your own words.

Taking Classroom Tests

❶ Study and Review Strategies

When you need to prepare for a big test, what do you do? Outline, study with friends, reread the chapters? To choose the best study strategies for your learning style, think about how you learn best.

Learning Styles and Study Strategies

Learning Style	General Description	Study Strategies
Visual	Learns best from seeing material	• Read and reread. • Create flash cards. • Study outlines.
Oral	Learns best from talking about and hearing material	• Study with a group. • Work with a partner on oral quizzes. • Recite material out loud.
Kinesthetic	Learns best from writing, acting out, or other method involving movement	• Photocopy text and underline key points. • Rewrite notes. • Outline and summarize.

Listen carefully for information about what will be covered on a test, what kinds of questions will be included, and how important the test will be for your final grade.

Review your class notes. Whatever your teacher has stressed in class will probably be on the test.

❷ Strategies for Objective Questions

Quizzes and some tests are made up largely of objective questions. Such questions are short and have a single correct answer. They assess your ability to recall facts and ideas and, sometimes, to use your reasoning skills as well.

 Tips for Success

- Read the directions and questions carefully before answering.
- Notice how you are instructed to supply your answers (for instance, write the letters of the answers, fill in ovals on an answer sheet, circle the answers, or write the answers).
- Don't just pick the first alternative that might be right. Pick the best answer.

True-False Questions

True-false questions test your ability to recognize what you've learned when that material is presented as a statement of fact.

> **Directions:** Indicate whether each statement is true or false.
> **1.** Plants depend only on water to live.

Answer: False

 Tips for Success

- Remember that for a statement to be true, every part of the statement must be true. Any exception makes it false.

- Look for words such as *all, always, never, only,* and *every.* These words often signal a false statement. In the example, *only* makes the statement false because plants need more than just water to survive.

- Look for qualifying words such as *may, most, few, probably, usually, typically,* and *sometimes,* which often signal a true statement.

Multiple-Choice Questions

Multiple-choice questions test your ability to choose the correct answer from several alternatives. In a well-written test, each wrong answer represents an error in thinking that you might make if you are careless or don't know the material.

> **Directions:** Write the letter of the correct answer.
> **1.** The organized crime figure Al Capone was convicted of
>   **A.** bribery.
>   **B.** smuggling.
>   **C.** tax evasion.
>   **D.** manufacturing alcoholic beverages.

Answer: **C**

 Tips for Success

- Read the beginning of the sentence and try to complete the sentence before you read the alternatives.

- Consider all the alternative answers before making a choice. Eliminate any answers that you know are wrong. Then choose the best of what remains.

- Notice key words in the question. In this example, the word *convicted* makes all the difference. Capone may have been *accused* of some of the other crimes.

- *Always, never,* and *only* often signal incorrect answers.

Matching Questions

Matching questions test your ability to recognize the relationship between the items in two columns and to pair items accordingly.

> **Directions:** Match each item in the left column with one item from the right column.
>
> | | |
> |---|---|
> | **1.** strings | **A.** oboe |
> | **2.** percussion | **B.** cello |
> | **3.** woodwinds | **C.** trombone |
> | **4.** brass | **D.** drum |
> | | **E.** piano |

Answers: **1B, 2D, 3A, 4C**

 Tips for Success

- Read the directions to find out whether you may use an item more than once.

- Notice whether there are extra items in either column. In this example, the second column has more alternatives than the first, and you are not instructed to match an item more than once, so you'll have one left over.

- Match the items you are sure of first.

- Check off items as you match them.

- Note that if you change one answer, you may have to change others as well.

Fill-in-the-Blank Questions

Fill-in-the-blank questions ask you to supply a missing word or words.

> **Directions:** Supply the missing word or phrase.
>
> **1.** The _____ of the Constitution gives citizens the right of free speech.

Answer: First Amendment

 Tips for Success

- Your answer must fit grammatically into the sentence.

- Your answer should be the best possible answer. In this example, for instance, Bill of Rights would also fit in the blank, but it is a less specific answer.

Answering Essay Questions

LESSON 3

Essay questions test your ability to think logically, write persuasively, and communicate your ideas in an organized fashion. They also test your recall of facts and details, since you need to support your statements and opinions.

❶ Deconstruct the Prompt

 Tips for Success

- Read the question carefully. Underline important content words. Look for and circle words that signal how to organize your answer.
- If you have a choice of questions, take a moment to decide which one you can answer best.

Directions: Write an essay to answer the following question.

1. Discuss the impact of the Internet on society.

Key content words are *Internet* and *society*. The word *discuss* signals that you need to provide a detailed examination from several points of view.

Key Terms in Essay Prompts

Term	Strategy
Discuss	Examine in detail and consider the big picture.
Compare/contrast	Explore similarities and differences.
Explain	Make a problem, relationship, concept, process, or term clear and understandable.
Analyze	Break something down into its parts; explain how its parts are related and how each contributes to the whole.
Persuade	Clearly state your position and use logical arguments to convince the reader that it is correct.
Prove	State a fact; support the fact (and disprove its alternatives) by citing evidence and building logical arguments.
Summarize	Present a condensed version of an event or a process.
Define	List the distinguishing characteristics of a subject or describe it exactly.
Synthesize	Logically derive a theory or a general idea from diverse facts.
Interpret	Give your opinion of the meaning of something and support it with reasons and details.

CHAPTER 32

❷ Plan and Write Your Essay

 Tips for Success
- Plan your answer by using notes, an outline, or a graphic organizer.
- Leave time to read over your answer and correct mechanical errors.

STUDENT MODEL

Prompt: (Discuss) the impact of the <u>Internet</u> on <u>society</u>.

Internet = Rapidly developing communication network linking people in
all countries
    started in universities
    now has uses in education, commerce, government, personal
       communication as well
social impact
    education: explosion in research
    children: too much exposure? how to limit?
       everyone: e-mail replacing regular mail? returning to written word?
general impact
    rapid communication
    information overload
    problems in validating information found on Web sites

Here's How **Writing an Essay**

1. **Plan** carefully. You won't be able to revise.
2. **Write** quickly, but keep your handwriting legible.
3. **Support** your main points with details and examples.
4. **Reread** your essay to make sure the connections are logical and you haven't omitted any key ideas. Cross out and insert words neatly.
5. **Proofread** to correct grammar and spelling mistakes.

❸ Evaluate Your Work

As you reread your essay, recall the six traits of effective writing—ideas and content, organization, voice, word choice, sentence fluency, and conventions. Similar guidelines will be used to evaluate your response. These standards are called a **rubric.**

For more about the six traits, see p. 314–318. For a sample rubric, see p. 597.

Standardized Tests: Language

❶ Preparing for Standardized Tests

Here are some of the tests for which you may have to prepare.

Common Standardized Tests	
Test	**Description**
Scholarship Assessment Test (College Board)	College entrance exam that uses objective questions to measure verbal and math skills
PSAT	Preliminary SAT, with math, verbal, and writing skills sections, administered in 10th or 11th grade and used to select National Merit Scholarship finalists
SAT II	Achievement tests in particular subjects (Many colleges require students to take three of these tests.)
American College Testing (ACT)	College entrance exam that uses objective questions to measure achievement in English, math, reading, and science
P-ACT	Practice ACT to help familiarize students with the ACT and predict future scores
Stanford 9 (SAT 9)	Achievement test administered in grades K–12 that uses multiple-choice and open-ended questions in reading, math, language, and science
State tests	Tests given in specific states that assess content knowledge and writing skills

You can prepare for these tests by doing all of the following:

- Use review books and computer programs tailored to the exam. Find these in bookstores, school libraries, and on the Internet. Many are also available on CD-ROM.
- Send away for pamphlets and sample tests from the testing institution and visit the testing institution's Web site.
- Enroll in a school or a private test preparation class.
- Study with a tutor or with friends.

Take all the practice tests you can get your hands on. Getting to know the question formats and directions is one of the most important things you can do to prepare.

 The SAT takes off points for wrong answers; the ACT does not. Therefore, if you are unsure about an answer, it pays to guess on the ACT but not on the SAT.

❷ Usage and Mechanics

Many standardized tests have questions testing grammar, usage, and mechanics.

Directions: Choose the best way to write each underlined phrase.

1. <u>Traveled nine hours,</u> the guests were ready for refreshments.

   A. Nine hours after traveling,
   B. Having traveled nine hours,
   C. After traveled nine hours,
   D. No change

Answer: **B** *Explanation:* The complete participial phrase describes the guests. Alternative A would fit grammatically into the sentence but changes the meaning of the sentence. C and D are both grammatically incorrect.

❸ Sentence Completion

Sentence completion questions, which frequently appear in standardized tests, test the ability to identify the word or phrase that fits most logically into a blank (or blanks) in the sentence.

Directions: Choose the words that best complete the meaning of the sentence.

1. Chinese explorers reached the coast of Africa long _____ European explorers reached the coast of North America; historians have concluded, therefore, that the Chinese could have reached North America _____ than Columbus.

   A. since . . . sooner
   B. after . . . earlier
   C. before . . . later
   D. before . . . earlier

Answer: **D** *Explanation:* Answer A does not fit grammatically into the sentence; B and C do not make logical sense in the context.

Look for the logical relationship between parts of a sentence. Common types of relationships include contrast, similarity, paraphrase, and cause and effect.

❹ Reading Comprehension

Reading comprehension sections test the ability to understand and answer questions about material you are reading for the first time.

Tips for Success

- Preview the questions.
- Skim the passage and read it once quickly.
- Underline key words and phrases, circle dates, and write marginal notes on your second reading.

Directions: After reading the passage, select the best answer to each question.

(1) In ancient Rome an hour meant one-twelfth of the daylight or darkness on a particular day. Thus, the actual length of an hour varied from season to season and from one day to the next. Nonetheless, Romans created a water **(5)** clock to keep track of the shifting hours. In its simplest form, this timing device was like a bowl with a hole near the bottom that emptied in a fixed amount of time. The clock could be used to time specific events, such as the periods allowed for each advocate's arguments in a legal proceeding.

1. The Roman water clock as described in the passage is comparable to
   A. a digital watch.
   B. a dial watch.
   C. an atomic clock.
   D. an hourglass.

2. The word *proceeding* in line 9 most nearly means
   A. law.
   B. debate.
   C. judge.
   D. verdict.

Answers: **1D** *Explanation:* The water flows out of the bowl as sand flows out of the top of an hourglass.
2B *Explanation:* Debate is the only choice that refers to an event.

Standardized Tests: **Vocabulary**

❶ Synonyms and Antonyms

Synonym questions require you to find the word that is nearly the same in meaning as a given word. Antonym questions require you to find the word that is nearly the opposite in meaning.

Directions: Choose the synonym for the underlined word.

1. Hesitant

   A. hasty   **C.** diligent
   B. unsure **D.** innocence

Answer: **B**

Directions: Choose the antonym for the underlined word.

2. Malevolent

   A. violent   **C.** malicious
   B. masculine **D.** benevolent

Answer: **D**

⭐ Tips for Success

- Make sure you know whether you're being asked for a synonym or an antonym.
- Watch for antonyms among the answer choices in a synonym question (and vice versa) and eliminate them. (In the second sample question, *malicious* is a synonym for *malevolent.*)
- Eliminate any answers that are not the same part of speech as the given word. (In the first sample question, because *hesitant* is an adjective, you can eliminate *innocence,* a noun.)
- Don't fall for trick answers such as words that sound like the original word or have some other association with it. (Don't choose *masculine* because *malevolent* starts with *male.*)

PRACTICE A · Synonyms

Write the synonym for each bold-faced word.

1. vague	clarify	obscure	incorrectly
2. desolate	crowded	dissolved	forlorn
3. superfluous	excessive	excellent	necessary
4. antagonist	competing	rival	annoying
5. compensate	pay	agree	cheat companion

❷ Analogies

An **analogy** compares two things. An analogy test item asks you to find a second pair of words that are related in the same way as a first pair of words.

> **Directions:** Select the pair of words that expresses a relationship most like that expressed in the original pair.
>
> **1.** TERRIER : DOG : :
>
> **A.** rat : fish
> **B.** kitten : cat
> **C.** trout : fish
> **D.** fish : trout
> **E.** poodle : collie

Answer: **C**

⭐ Tips for Success

- Read the set of word pairs like this: "Terrier is to dog as *what* is to *what?*"
- Determine the relationship between the pair of words and create a sentence that expresses the relationship: A terrier is a specific kind of dog.
- Mentally plug the answer choices into your sentence. (For instance, A rat is a kind of fish.) Does the sentence work?
- If two pairs fit the sentence, choose the pair that is most like the original pair. (For example, a kitten *is* a kind of cat, but not in the same way that a terrier is a kind of dog. A kitten is a baby cat.)
- Don't fall for analogies in the wrong order. (For instance, TERRIER : DOG : : trout : fish, *not* fish : trout.)
- Don't fall for alternatives that are only superficially related. (For instance, don't select poodle : collie just because they are dogs.)
- Look for alternatives that are the same parts of speech as the original pair.

The more precisely you state the relationship, the better your results will be. For example, if you are given HAND : CLOCK, your sentences might be as follows:

> **vague:** A clock has a hand.

> **better:** A hand is part of a clock.

Watch out for words that have more than one meaning and therefore could make possible more than one relationship.

Some analogies are unique; many others belong to one of the categories shown below.

Common Relationships in Analogies

Relationship	Example
Synonyms	FURY : ANGER : : bliss : happiness
Antonyms	HOPE : DESPAIR : : trust : doubt
Part to whole	PETAL : BLOSSOM : : finger : hand
Cause to effect	RAIN : FLOOD : : drought : dust
Tool to user	BRUSH : PAINTER : : pen : writer
Product to source	PAINTING : PAINTER : : poem : poet
Action to object	CASH : CHECK : : pay : bill
Connotative differences	HOVEL : MANSION : : jalopy : limousine

PRACTICE B Recognizing Analogies

Write the pair of words that expresses a relationship most like that expressed in the original pair.

1. FRESH : NOVEL : :
   A. new : old
   B. taste : texture
   C. story : book
   D. bulky : massive
   E. tedious : exciting

2. RIGID : FLEXIBLE : :
   A. push : yield
   B. tame : feral
   C. rigor : severity
   D. ferocious : bellicose
   E. certain : inevitable

3. MICROSCOPE : PROTOZOA : :
   A. computer : data
   B. speedometer : car
   C. television : actors
   D. microwave : food
   E. telescope : stars

4. TIMIDITY : HESITATE : :
   A. mendacity : conform
   B. courage : proceed
   C. temerity : caution
   D. laziness : failure
   E. caution : hesitation

5. DENSE : FOREST : :
   A. cavernous : yawn
   B. submerged : cave
   C. copious : praise
   D. thick : crowd
   E. victorious : team

6. SHAPE : CONCAVE : :
   A. sight : blind
   B. form : function
   C. taste : bitter
   D. style : choice
   E. function : use

Student Help Desk

Test Taking at a Glance

Before the Test

- Know the material that will be covered.
- Know the format the test will take.
- Use appropriate review strategies.

During the Test

- Read the directions and questions carefully.
- Circle important words and analyze the prompts.
- Plan your time.
- Check your answers.

Reading in Content Areas Mastering the Text

Math	• Study the examples. • Read and reread the problem. • Think about the sequence of the solution steps.
History	• Scan the titles, subtitles, and visual elements to see what the page is about. • Look for and summarize main ideas. • Interpret maps, graphs, and charts. • Think beyond the test and draw conclusions.
Science	• Scan the titles, subtitles, and visual elements to see what the page is about. • Examine main ideas and conclusions. • Look for cause-and-effect relationships. • Use context clues.

Classroom Tests A Stellar Performance

Last-Minute Tips for Objective Questions

True or false	First, try to prove the statement false.
Multiple-choice	Eliminate alternatives one by one.
Matching	Watch out for misleading extra answers.
Short answer	Include key terms in your answer.
Fill-in-the-blank	Reread the sentence with the chosen words in it.

Rubric for Essay Questions

Flight Check

☑ **Topic**

Did you address the topic called for in the prompt?

☑ **Purpose**

Did you directly respond to the question?

☑ **Content**

Is your content strong?

☑ **Organization**

Do your ideas flow logically? Did you use an appropriate organizational structure?

☑ **Elaboration**

Did you develop and expand on your ideas?

☑ **Support**

Did you use reasons and examples to support your claims?

☑ **Tone**

Did you write in an objective and impartial voice?

Short Answer

The Bottom Line

Checklist for Preparing for Tests

Have I . . .

____ learned what material will be covered on the test?

____ become familiar with the test format?

____ used appropriate study techniques?

____ used active reading techniques to analyze the questions?

____ carefully planned the use of my time?

____ left time to check my answers?

Student Resources

Exercise Bank

1 The Parts of Speech

1. Nouns (links to exercise on p. 8)

➡ **1.** *life:* common, singular; *safari:* common, singular; *perspective:* common, singular; *humans:* common, plural; *animals:* common, plural

2. *camps:* common, plural; *Kenya's:* proper, singular; *parks:* common, plural; *fences:* common, plural

Write the nouns in these sentences, identifying each as common or proper and as singular or plural.

1. Elephants are the largest land-dwelling animals in existence.
2. Only some varieties of whales are greater in size.
3. During the 19th century an African elephant named Jumbo became something of a celebrity.
4. After 17 years in the London Zoo, Jumbo was bought by P. T. Barnum and exhibited in his circus in America.
5. Wild elephants can still be seen in parts of Africa and Asia, although hunters have killed many for their tusks.

2. Personal Pronouns (links to exercise on p. 10)

➡ **1.** his, Malcolm; their, Malcolm and his family **2.** They, Malcolm and his family; her, grandmother

Write each pronoun and identify its antecedent.

1. With his powerful body and huge teeth, an adult male gorilla can appear threatening.
2. In fact, though, the creature is milder than he looks.
3. Gorillas sometimes pound their chests in a display of aggression.
4. They use the display to scare away humans and other gorillas.
5. At other times, they use it to maintain order in the group.
6. When a female gives birth to an infant, she cares for it intensively.
7. An infant is helpless for the first three months of its life.
8. The baby rides on its mother's back and sleeps in her nest at night.
9. Gorillas build their sleeping nests on the ground or in trees.
10. If you travel deep into the Ugandan forest, keep your eyes and ears open for signs of gorilla life.

3. Other Kinds of Pronouns (links to exercise A on p. 13)

➡ **1.** *they:* personal; *few:* indefinite **2.** *which:* relative

Write each pronoun and indicate what kind it is.

1. Everyone has seen chimpanzees clowning in human clothes.
2. That is how many of us imagine chimpanzees.
3. Ask yourself how much you know about chimpanzees' behavior.
4. Did you know chimps usually walk on all fours but can carry themselves upright if they choose?
5. Chimps eat fruits, berries, leaves, and seeds that they gather.
6. Some of their diet consists of small animals, which they stalk and kill.
7. They need not be taught everything by humans; chimps themselves are good at using tools.
8. A chimp can feed itself ants and termites by pushing a stick into the insects' nest and pulling some of them out.
9. Who would think chimps could talk to us?
10. Chimps, who are highly intelligent, can learn sign language and communicate with humans.

4. Verbs (links to exercise on p. 16)

➡ **1.** *want:* action **2.** *seems:* linking

Write each verb or verb phrase and identify it as linking or action. Circle the auxiliary verbs.

1. Squids are mollusks that live in oceans and coastal waters.
2. The smallest squid measures less than an inch in length.
3. The giant squid, however, can be more than 60 feet long!
4. A squid's head is short and compact; its body is long and tubular.
5. Eight arms and two tentacles surround the squid's mouth.
6. Rows of suckers run along the ends of the tentacles.
7. Although some squids drift in the current, others swim rapidly.
8. Some squids are even luminescent; they have special organs that can produce light.
9. Squids are eaten by sperm whales, fish, and people.
10. Enormous giant squids may have been responsible for some sea-monster sightings.

5. Adjectives (links to exercise A on p. 18)

➡️ **1.** *An, enjoyable: way*; *a, new: country*; *a: horse* **2.** *a, unique, horseback: ride*

Write each adjective in these sentences, along with the word it modifies.

1. Wolves have remarkable coats, which are thick and luxurious.
2. The short, dense fur of the inner layer of the coat is light in color.
3. The outer layer of the coat is made of long hairs, which repel moisture and keep the inner fur dry.
4. The long hairs are referred to as guard hairs; the inside layer of the coat is called the underfur.
5. Long, thick guard hairs grow across the broad shoulders.
6. Short fur grows on the muzzle and down the powerful legs.
7. In cold climates, thick fur protects wolves from bitter temperatures.
8. To keep warm, a wolf curls into a tight ball with the nose under the furry tail.
9. The fur has special properties that keep the warm breath of the wolf from forming hard ice on the fur.
10. A wolf can enjoy a comfortable sleep when the mercury is very low.

6. Adverbs (links to exercise A on p. 22)

➡️ **1.** Quite, often, anywhere **2.** crazily

Write each adverb in these sentences.

1. The platypus is a very strange mammal.
2. Almost all mammals give birth to live babies.
3. The platypus, however, actually reproduces by laying eggs.
4. The platypus's feet are completely webbed, like those of a duck.
5. Its broad, flat tail rather resembles that of a beaver.
6. The claws on its feet help it to dig burrows quickly.
7. Platypuses generally live on the banks of streams.
8. Their diet consists almost exclusively of worms, small shellfish, and other animals that live at the bottom of streams.
9. Once people hunted the platypus for its fur.
10. Now such hunting is illegal.

7. Prepositions (links to exercise A on p. 25)

➡️ **1.** (for) students **2.** (in) other countries

Write the prepositional phrases in these sentences. Circle the prepositions.

1. With its peculiar shape and features, the camel does not look like a triumph of nature.

2. Because of its odd features, the camel is well suited to its desert habitat.
3. Among camels' unusual physical attributes, the best known may well be their humps.
4. These humps—the Arabian camel has one of them, and the Bactrian camel has two—store food in the form of fat.
5. By means of its huge feet, which spread flat when it walks, the camel avoids sinking in loose desert sand.
6. The camel's eyes are protected from sand by long, curly lashes, while hair inside its ears keeps them sand free too.
7. In addition to its value to desert travelers as a beast of burden, the camel is a source of milk and meat.
8. The camel's hair is soft and warm, and Arabs weave it into cloth for clothing, blankets, and tents.
9. Camels can be difficult on account of their bad disposition.
10. In spite of these drawbacks, camels remain the most useful domestic animals for people of the desert.

8. Conjunctions (links to exercise A on p. 28)

➡ 1. or 2. because

Write the conjunctions and conjunctive adverbs in the following sentences.

1. Penguins look clumsy on land, but they are graceful swimmers.
2. These birds live either on the continent of Antarctica or on landmasses that border the cold seas of the Southern Hemisphere.
3. Although the penguin's stubby wings are totally unsuited for flying, they function as paddles when the penguin swims.
4. Penguins have thick layers of fat under their skin and short, dense feathers; consequently, they can thrive in cold climates.
5. Penguins are fish eaters and spend much of their lives in the water, although they lay their eggs on land.
6. Female emperor penguins lay single eggs on the Antarctic ice; otherwise, they have no role in hatching the eggs.
7. The male penguins keep the eggs warm until they hatch, and the males feed the newly hatched babies.
8. The females then return to care for the young so that the males can hunt for food.
9. When the males return with food, both they and the females form a circle around the tightly grouped young to keep them warm.
10. Young penguins that neither starve nor fall to predators become self-sufficient in six months.

2 The Sentence and Its Parts

1. Simple Subjects and Predicates (links to exercise A on p. 39)

➜ **1.** Maria Fernanda Cordoso, runs **2.** She, owns

Write the simple subject and simple predicate of each sentence.

1. A professor once tested an elephant's memory.
2. He marked two wooden boxes with different symbols.
3. The box with a square on it contained food.
4. The box with a circle was empty.
5. He then gave the boxes to an elephant.
6. The elephant eventually learned the symbol for food.
7. Months later, the test was repeated with the same elephant.
8. Again and again, the animal chose the correct box.
9. The elephant must have remembered the symbol for food.
10. Otherwise, it would not have chosen the correct box every time.

2. Complete Subjects and Predicates (links to exercise A on p. 41)

➜ **1.** Crazy tests of endurance / swept the nation during the 1920s. **2.** "Shipwreck" Kelly / sat atop an Atlantic City flagpole for 49 days.

Write each sentence, drawing a line between the complete subject and the complete predicate.

1. Pop culture in the late 1950s and early 1960s reflected Americans' fear of the atom bomb.
2. Antibomb slogans appeared on bumper stickers.
3. Bob Dylan bitterly criticized leaders in his song "Masters of War."
4. Stanley Kubrick won rave reviews for his antibomb comedy *Dr. Strangelove*.
5. TV's *The Twilight Zone* featured cautionary tales about nuclear war.
6. One famous episode shows the aftermath of a nuclear attack.
7. A lonely survivor seeks companionship in the company of books.
8. Another episode depicts a desperate search for food and water.
9. President Kennedy had warned Americans about the need for community bomb shelters.
10. War between the United States and the Soviet Union seemed imminent.

3. Compound Sentence Parts (links to exercise A on p. 43)

➡ **1.** people; walk, jog **2.** Dave Kunst; took, ran

Write the sentences below, underlining each simple subject once and each verb twice.

1. Charles Lindbergh was born in Michigan but spent his childhood in Minnesota.
2. Airplanes and aviation fascinated him from an early age.
3. He became a pilot and flew a mail route between Chicago and St. Louis.
4. In 1926 he heard about a contest and entered it.
5. He could win $25,000 and make aviation history by successfully completing a solo trans-Atlantic flight.

4. Kinds of Sentences (links to exercise A on p. 45)

➡ **1.** interrogative **2.** declarative

Identify each sentence as declarative, imperative, interrogative, or exclamatory.

(1) Have you ever eaten in that diner? **(2)** The servers call out orders in "hash house Greek." **(3)** Hash house Greek is old-time restaurant slang. **(4)** Order beef stew there sometime. **(5)** They call it bossy in a bowl. **(6)** I am not kidding! **(7)** What do they call milk? **(8)** They call it moo juice. **(9)** Try the nervous pudding for dessert. **(10)** Nervous pudding is gelatin, of course!

5. Subjects in Unusual Positions (links to exercise A on p. 48)

➡ **1.** you, can get **2.** (You), come

Write the simple subjects and simple predicates in these sentences. Be sure to include all parts of verb phrases.

1. How did starch make football history?
2. Here are the facts.
3. There was a starch company in Decatur, Illinois, in 1920.
4. Among its employees was George Halas.
5. Would he organize and coach a football team for the A. E. Staley Manufacturing Company?
6. Believe it.
7. From Chicago came an offer.
8. Move the Decatur Staleys to that city.
9. What did Halas and the team do?
10. Into the pages of football history marched Halas and his Chicago Bears.

6. Subject Complements (links to exercise A on p. 50)

➡ **1.** *fashionable:* predicate adjective **2.** *Harlem:* predicate nominative

Write each subject complement and identify it as a predicate adjective or a predicate nominative.

1. Gum was a chewy treat even in ancient times.
2. The discovery in Sweden of a 9,000-year-old wad of chewed tree sap is proof.
3. Would 9,000-year-old gum taste stale?
4. Gum remains popular almost everywhere in the world.
5. In the Czech Republic, *žvýkačka* is the word for gum.
6. The word appears quite appropriate.
7. "Cud chewing" is the word's literal meaning.
8. In Turkey, gum is big business.
9. To the citizens of Singapore, gum factories might seem scandalous.
10. Gum is illegal there!

7. Objects of Verbs (links to exercise A on pp. 52–53)

➡ **1.** *Francis A. Johnson:* indirect object; *credit:* direct object
  2. *world:* indirect object; *patience:* direct object

Each sentence below contains at least one object. Write each object, identifying it as a direct object, an indirect object, or an objective complement. Identify each objective complement as a noun or an adjective.

1. Throw a few thousand of your friends a party.
2. Make your party memorable.
3. For a snack, serve everyone a burrito from California's La Costeña and Burrito Real restaurant.
4. The editors of *The Guinness Book of Records* consider at least one of the restaurant's burritos quite extraordinary.
5. In fact, they named the restaurant's 4,456-pound burrito the largest in the world.
6. Don't forget dessert.
7. Offer your guests a special treat.
8. Order them a cake from EarthGrains in Alabama.
9. This bakery once created a 128,000-pound cake that many considered a delicacy.
10. Of course, a cake like that might give you the world's largest stomachache!

3 Using Phrases

1. Prepositional Phrases (links to exercise A on p. 68)

➡ **1.** *in any bird record book*: adverb phrase; *belongs*
2. *of approximately two inches*: adjective phrase; *length*

Write each prepositional phrase and tell whether it is an adverb phrase or an adjective phrase. Also identify the word or words that the prepositional phrase modifies.

1. You'll surely find bats at the baseball park.
2. However, you wouldn't expect the kind with wings.
3. Yet that's exactly what the New York Mets encountered at their 1998 Florida training camp.
4. The stadium had become home to more than 30,000 bats.
5. As a protected species, the bats couldn't be harmed.
6. Yet both players and fans didn't want the bats inside the stadium.
7. One night, park management put screening around the park.
8. When the bats returned from hunting, they found the park closed.
9. Far from their home, the bats needed new lodging.
10. Local builders provided new accommodations when they erected a bat house near the stadium.

2. Appositives and Appositive Phrases (links to exercise A on p. 70)

➡ **1.** The Wright brothers, Wilbur and Orville, owned a bicycle shop in Dayton, Ohio, in the late 1800s. **3.** The book was written by the German engineer Otto Lilienthal.

Add the appositive or appositive phrase in parentheses to each sentence. If the appositive is nonessential, set it off with commas.

1. Our solar system is located in the Milky Way. (a huge spiral galaxy)
2. At the center of the solar system is the sun. (our local star)
3. Circling it are the planet and eight other planets. (Mercury)
4. Our planet is special in several ways. (the third from the sun)
5. We depend on the presence of the gas in its atmosphere. (oxygen)

3. Verbals: Participles (links to exercise A on p. 72)

➡ **1.** *Appreciated for their color and grace*: past participle **2.** *Often bursting with color*: present participle

Write the participle or the participial phrase from each sentence. Indicate whether the participle is a present participle or a past participle.

1. Imagine a spring without the delightful sounds of singing birds.
2. Honored in 1999 as one of the most influential people of the 1900s, Rachel Carson warned of such a spring.
3. Worried about the overuse of chemical pesticides, such as DDT, this environmentalist wrote about their effects in *Silent Spring*.
4. Sprayed on farm fields and forestland, DDT killed useful as well as harmful insects.
5. Lasting a long time, it was absorbed by plants.
6. Animals eating the plants also absorbed the DDT.
7. It soon became apparent that animals exposed to DDT were in danger.
8. The alarm sounded by *Silent Spring* was finally heard.
9. Responding to it, governments restricted the use of DDT.
10. As a result, we can still enjoy chirping birds.

4. Verbals: Gerunds (links to exercise A on p. 74)

➡ **1.** *communicating with others*: object of a preposition
   2. *Honking during migration:* subject

Write the gerund or gerund phrase that appears in each sentence. Indicate whether it is a subject, a direct object, an indirect object, a predicate nominative, or an object of a preposition.

1. Ancient Greek mythology offers a story about one of the first disasters in the history of flying.
2. Daedalus, the designer of the labyrinth, probably never dreamed of becoming a prisoner in it.
3. Yet after displeasing King Minos of Crete, he and his son, Icarus, were imprisoned there.
4. Now his challenge was escaping the confines of the labyrinth.
5. Soon Daedalus began to consider making two pairs of feather-and-wax wings.
6. The wings made leaving the labyrinth and Crete possible.
7. They put on the wings and gave flying a try.
8. Soaring too high, however, led to Icarus' death.

9. When he got too close to the sun, he began to notice the melting of the wax in his wings.
10. Instead of gaining freedom, he plummeted to his death.

5. Verbals: Infinitives (links to exercise A on p. 76)

→ **1.** *to form a honeybee colony:* adverb **2.** *to lay eggs:* noun

Write each infinitive or infinitive phrase and tell whether it functions as a noun, an adjective, or an adverb.

1. You have probably heard some of the words to live by known as proverbs.
2. In some proverbs our winged friends, birds, are used to make a point.
3. For example, maybe you have been told not to count your chickens before they hatch.
4. This proverb reminds you not to assume you have something before you actually get it.
5. Have you been asked to remember that the early bird catches the worm?
6. To reach a goal, you need to start working right away.
7. According to one proverb, you are likely to find that birds of a feather flock together.
8. To be comfortable, people often associate with others who have the same interests.
9. As another proverb has it, chickens come home to roost.
10. Therefore, you are likely to experience the consequences of earlier actions.

6. Placement of Phrases (links to exercise A on p. 79)

→ **1.** For many inventors, combining a car and an airplane into one vehicle was a long-time dream. **2.** Ford and other automobile manufacturers produced prototypes of flying cars called "flying flivvers."

Rewrite these sentences to eliminate misplaced and dangling modifiers. If a sentence has no errors in modifier placement, write *Correct.*

1. By running fast down a hill, a hang glider can be launched.
2. The pilot by a harness is attached to the glider.
3. After being launched like a large bird with wings extended, a glider pilot rides the air currents.
4. Using the control bar, the glider's speed can be adjusted.
5. The pilot also uses the control bar to steer the glider.

4 Clauses and Sentence Structure

1. Kinds of Clauses (links to exercise A on p. 94)

➡ **1.** None
   2. which became popular in the early 1900s

Write the subordinate clause in each sentence below.

1. Some of the world's most important inventions were developed before history was written.
2. These include basic tools, such as the lever, that people use to move and lift objects.
3. The wheel, which many consider humanity's most important invention, has made many other inventions possible.
4. Another development that was important was the ability to make fire.
5. Although you may not think of pottery as an invention, the ability to make containers is considered essential for civilization.
6. More recent inventions help us to travel faster, communicate better, and live longer than people did before.
7. Automobiles make it possible for people to travel to places where they could never otherwise have gone.
8. Antibiotics help us fight illnesses that were formerly incurable.
9. Inventions that range from the pen and pencil to the telephone and computer help people exchange messages.
10. Thomas Edison, who invented the electric light bulb and the phonograph, made people's lives easier and more pleasant.

2. Adjective and Adverb Clauses (links to exercise A on p. 97)

➡ **1.** Long before the Wright brothers flew the first airplane, was testing
   2. who was a French physicist, Louis Sébastien Lenormand

Write the adjective and adverb clauses in the following sentences. After each clause, write the word or words that it modifies.

1. Several devices, which are among the world's most important, are known as simple machines.
2. You may not think of these as machines at all, but they are the foundations of all machines that have ever been invented.
3. The simplest is the inclined plane, a sloping surface that helps us move heavy objects up and down.
4. If a road going up a mountain is an example of an inclined plane, a road winding around a mountain exemplifies another simple machine, the screw.

5. An everyday example of a wedge, which is really two inclined planes that meet at an edge, is an ax or a knife.
6. With a lever, one can easily lift a heavy load, as a small child can lift an adult on a seesaw.
7. When you open a kitchen drawer, you may find an example of a lever—a bottle opener.
8. Anyone who has rolled a suitcase on wheels knows the importance of the wheel and axle, another simple machine.
9. The sixth simple machine is the pulley, which reduces the effort needed to lift or pull a heavy load.
10. When you use any complex machine, from a pair of scissors to a ski lift, you are using some combination of these six simple machines.

3. Noun Clauses (links to exercise A on p. 99)

➡ 1. *who invented the first eyeglasses*: direct object
2. *whoever wore them*: indirect object

Write the noun clause in each sentence. Indicate whether the clause functions as a subject, a direct object, an indirect object, a predicate nominative, or an object of a preposition.

1. Remarkable inventions throughout the ages have helped human beings expand what they know of the universe.
2. That is why we are able to keep learning more and more about the world around us.
3. Few people know which individuals invented the space shuttle, but NASA was credited with the invention in 1977.
4. Whoever worked on the space shuttle was no greater an inventor than Roger Bacon, an Englishman who may have invented the magnifying glass around 1250.
5. That the two-lens microscope was invented as long ago as 1590 may come as a surprise to you.
6. The name Fahrenheit is probably familiar to whoever has read a thermometer.
7. The reason is that Gabriel Daniel Fahrenheit invented the mercury thermometer in 1714 and developed the temperature scale that most of us use in the United States.
8. Any book on space travel will tell whoever reads it that Robert H. Goddard invented the liquid-fueled rocket engine in 1926.
9. Whoever is interested in oceanography has heard of Jacques Yves Cousteau, coinventor of the Aqua-Lung.
10. What more we learn about the universe will depend on inventors like these.

4. Sentence Structure (links to exercise A on p. 103)

➡ **3.** compound **4.** complex

Identify each sentence as simple, compound, complex, or compound-complex.

1. Some inventions entertain us.

2. Radio and television have entertained us for many years, and now VCRs and CD players entertain us as well.

3. The piano was invented by Bartolomeo Cristofori in Italy around the year 1709.

4. In the 1890s several inventors developed the moving-picture projector, without which we would have no movies today.

5. Vladimir K. Zworykin is sometimes credited with the invention of television, but there were others, including Philo T. Farnsworth and John Baird, who contributed to the invention.

6. If you can't imagine life without video games, you should thank the U.S. inventor Nolan Bushnell, who invented the video game Pong.

7. Pong is a simulation of table tennis.

8. It features two "racquets" that hit a ball back and forth while sound effects simulate the ball's hitting the racquets.

9. Credit for some modern inventions is given to corporations rather than individuals.

10. Sony, a Japanese corporation, was the inventor of the videotape cassette; and RCA, a U.S. corporation, is credited with the invention of the compact disc.

5 Writing Complete Sentences

1. Sentence Fragments (links to exercise A on p. 119)

➡ Last summer, Lisa, Ruben, and Eva decided to start their own business. They earned money by helping others get organized.

Rewrite the following paragraph, eliminating the fragments.

According to experts, an Asian breed of gray wolf may be the ancestor of all domestic dogs. Regardless of their breed. Although some scientists think that dogs began evolving from wolves more than 100,000 years ago. The fossils of modern dogs are not nearly that old. Found in southwestern Asia. The oldest fossils are only 11,000 to 12,000 years old. Most domesticated dogs have changed a great deal. And no longer resemble primitive dogs very much. However, in some remote areas wild dogs still have characteristics of primitive dogs. As an example of a modern dog that resembles a primitive dog. Take a look at the dingo, which is a wild dog of Australia. The dingo has these primitive characteristics. A short ginger-colored coat, pointy ears, and a foxlike snout. Dogs can thank their wolf ancestors. For many of their inherited behavioral traits too. For example, by "hanging out" together. Dogs are exhibiting wolf-pack behavior. Dogs that enjoy chasing cats are using their hunting skills. Even though their food most likely comes from the supermarket.

2. Run-On Sentences (links to exercise A on p. 121)

➡ **2.** Entrepreneurs are people who start their own businesses; Using the Internet, some teenagers are doing exactly this. **6.** Unlike most adults, many teenagers have been using computers all their lives, so they have an advantage when it comes to dreaming up computer-related businesses.

Write R for each run-on and S for each correctly written sentence. Then correct the run-ons using techniques from the lesson.

1. A shooting star is not really a star it is a meteor.
2. A meteor is a glowing trail this trail is produced by a meteoroid's passing through the earth's atmosphere.
3. Meteoroids are chunks of metal or rock racing through space sometimes they enter the earth's atmosphere.
4. Friction causes them to heat up in our atmosphere the heat is responsible for the bright streaks that we call meteors.
5. Usually meteoroids burn up in the atmosphere, sometimes they hit the earth, they are known as meteorites.
6. If you don't know these terms, don't worry as recently as the 19th century, people didn't even believe there were meteorites.
7. In 1998 a meteoroid streaked into the earth's atmosphere and exploded over a back yard near Portales, New Mexico.
8. It left behind a black meteorite that was as large as a basketball and weighed 37 pounds.
9. This was a rare occurrence most meteoroids do not fall in populated areas.
10. In fact, few people ever see newly fallen meteorites they usually land in the ocean or unpopulated areas.

6 Using Verbs

1. The Principal Parts of a Verb (links to exercise A on p. 133)

➡ **1.** became **2.** began

Indicate which principal part of a verb each underlined word is.

1. Many people are still <u>reading</u> the detective fiction of Agatha Christie.
2. Over the years, fans have <u>purchased</u> more than 100 million copies of her works.
3. But many readers have not <u>learned</u> about the huge success of Christie's stories on stage and screen.
4. Her most successful play, *The Mousetrap,* <u>ran</u> for more than 21 continuous years at one London theater, <u>setting</u> a world record.
5. Successful adaptations of her fiction into films <u>include</u> *Murder on the Orient Express* and *Death on the Nile.*
6. Christie <u>led</u> a relatively quiet life.
7. As a child, she had <u>received</u> her education at home from her mother.
8. She <u>began</u> to write detective stories while she was <u>working</u> as a nurse during World War I.
9. In 1930 she <u>married</u> an archaeologist.
10. She <u>traveled</u> with him on expeditions to Iraq and Syria for several months every year.

2. Verb Tense (links to exercise A on p. 137)

➡ **1.** ranks **2.** have argued

Choose the better tense of the verb in parentheses.

1. Many readers (will recognize, had recognized) O. Henry as the author of many cleverly plotted short stories.
2. This writer, whose real name was William Sydney Porter, (live, lived) in New York City the last eight years of his life.
3. Before that, he (has spent, had spent) a large part of his short life in Texas.
4. After working on a Texas ranch, he (moved, had moved) in with a family friend in Austin.
5. O. Henry (married, has married) in 1887 and later settled in a small house at 409 East Fifth Street in Austin.
6. The house (has been restored, had been restored) recently and is now the O. Henry Museum.

7. The museum contains a lot of O. Henry's personal belongings that the curators (collect, have collected) over the years.
8. About 15,000 fans (visit, visited) the O. Henry Museum every year.
9. During his life O. Henry (writes, wrote) about Texas in a collection of stories called *The Heart of the West.*
10. Once you have finished reading that book, you (will read, will have read) some of the best stories about Texas ever written.

3. Progressive and Emphatic Forms (links to exercise A on p. 139)

➡ **1.** did manage **2.** was attending

Write the progressive or emphatic form of the verb in parentheses, using the correct tense.

1. The African-American writer Gwendolyn Brooks (compose) poetry almost all her life.
2. By the time she finally published her first book of poetry at the age of 28, she (write) for some time.
3. Her second volume of poetry, *Annie Allen,* was based on ideas she had gathered while she (grow) up in Chicago.
4. Although Brooks is primarily a poet, she (write) a novel, *Maud Martha*, in 1953.
5. By 1960 critics (praise) the poems collected in *The Bean Eaters* as her best verse.
6. Brooks continued to publish poetry throughout the '60s, '70s, and '80s, but she (have) other accomplishments.
7. She (serve) as poet laureate of Illinois when she was named poetry consultant to the Library of Congress in 1985.
8. Though she was 73 years old, she (accept) a professorship of English at Chicago State University in 1990.
9. Brooks (inspire) young poets all her life, and many consider her a personal hero.
10. Her fans hope that Brooks (create) poetry well into the 21st century.

4. The Voice of a Verb (links to exercise A on p. 142)

➡ **2.** developed **3.** was signed

Write each verb in parentheses using the correct tense and the correct voice—active or passive.

1. Readers and critics alike (enjoy) Kurt Vonnegut's satirical fiction for five decades.
2. Vonnegut (study) biochemistry at Cornell University.

3. Vonnegut (join) the U.S. Army in World War II.
4. Vonnegut (capture) by the Germans during the war.
5. His captors (assign) him to a work group in Dresden, Germany.
6. Dresden (firebomb) by Allied planes near the end of the war.
7. Vonnegut and his fellow prisoners (hide) in an underground meat locker.
8. Everything but the cellars (destroy) by the bombs.
9. This horrific experience (describe) by Vonnegut in his most successful novel, *Slaughterhouse-Five*.
10. Numerous plays, works of nonfiction, and short stories (write) by Vonnegut.

5. Shifts in Tense, Form, and Voice (links to exercise A on p. 145)

➡ 1. Sandra Cisneros grew up for the most part in Chicago, but her father occasionally moved the family to Mexico.
3. Because she felt lonely as a child, Cisneros read books for comfort.

Some of the following sentences contain awkward uses of verb tenses or voices. Revise those sentences to correct the problems. If a sentence contains no such problems, write *Correct*.

1. Although Langston Hughes was born in Joplin, Missouri, he lives most of his life in Harlem in New York City.
2. For many years literary historians have identified Hughes with the Harlem Renaissance, a black arts movement of the 1920s, because he contributed his energy and talent to it.
3. The poet Arna Bontemps recognized Hughes's achievements and was calling Hughes and his contemporary Countee Cullen the "twin stars of the black Awakening in literature."
4. Hughes's long literary career began with his poem "The Negro Speaks of Rivers," which he has written the summer after his high school graduation.
5. Even though a number of his poems had appeared in black periodicals, Hughes did not receive national attention until his "discovery" by the popular white poet Vachel Lindsay.
6. Hughes was working as a busboy in a hotel restaurant when he had slipped three of his poems beside Lindsay's plate.
7. Lindsay was impressed with Hughes's poems, and he helps to bring Hughes to the notice of a wider public.
8. The publicity gave Hughes the attention he will need, as well as finances to finish college.

9. By the end of the 1920s, Hughes had graduated from college and published his first two books of poetry.
10. Ironically, Hughes's reputation as a poet ultimately surpassed Lindsay's, and Hughes is remembered in the future as one of the great American poets of the 20th century.

6. The Mood of a Verb (links to exercise A on p. 147)

➜ **1.** indicative **2.** imperative, indicative, indicative, imperative

Identify each verb or verb phrase in the following sentences as indicative, imperative, or subjunctive. Then rewrite five of the sentences, changing the mood of a verb.

1. "We passed that farmhouse an hour ago."
2. "Look at the map and locate the intersection of Route 40 and Jolly Lane."
3. "There is no Jolly Lane on the map."
4. "Give me the map!"
5. "If I were you, I'd ask for directions."
6. "If there were a gas station, I would."
7. "Look, another farmhouse—pull in there!"
8. "I wish we had never left home."
9. "Well, ask at the farmhouse where a gas station is."
10. "No, I insist that we look for a gas station ourselves."

⑦ Subject-Verb Agreement

1. Agreement in Number (links to exercise A on p. 157)

➜ **1.** undergoes **2.** have

For each sentence, write the correct form of the verb in parentheses.

1. A stunt person's essential equipment (includes, include) a calculator, paper, and a pencil.
2. Good stunt persons (has, have) also used dummies.
3. A stunt dummy (has, have) the same weight and height as the stunt person.
4. Before the person (performs, perform) a stunt, the dummy does it.
5. Perhaps a character (plans, plan) to jump from a helicopter.
6. First, crew members (pushes, push) the dummy out of the helicopter.
7. If the dummy (hits, hit) the safety air bag on target, the person will do the stunt next.

8. Dar Robinson (is, are) considered the best stuntman who ever worked.
9. Stunt people usually (earns, earn) about $500 per day.
10. Robinson (was, were) once paid $250,000 for a single stunt!

2. Phrases Between Subject and Verb (links to exercise A on p. 159)

➡ **2.** are **3.** has

For each sentence, write the verb form that agrees with the subject.

1. Special effects in a movie (is, are) referred to as FX.
2. A film about blizzards (uses, use) salt, plastic, or shredded paper for snow.
3. An icicle, a larger formation, (is, are) made from plastic.
4. A wind machine placed in different positions (blows, blow) snow into actors' faces or into drifts.
5. Computers in the studio (creates, create) snow and ice FX too.
6. *Twister,* a disaster movie, (combines, combine) computer imagery with footage of real tornadoes.
7. No actor in this film ever (goes, go) near an actual storm.
8. A film such as *The Hunt for Red October* (suggests, suggest) an underwater submarine by combining models, a smoke machine, and creative lighting effects.
9. The actors in *Hard Rain* probably (was, were) wishing for a similar setup.
10. This film, about a flood, (features, feature) no scene without some form of moving water.

3. Compound Subjects (links to exercise A on p. 161)

➡ **1.** are **2.** work

For each sentence, write the verb form that agrees with the subject.

1. Lon Chaney and Boris Karloff (is, are) known for playing some of the most frightening monsters ever seen on film.
2. Neither computer graphics nor any modern effects (appears, appear) in the movies these actors made in the 1920s and 1930s.
3. Both *The Hunchback of Notre Dame* and *The Phantom of the Opera* (features, feature) the silent-movie star Lon Chaney.
4. Chaney's own makeup techniques and materials (remains, remain) a well-kept secret even today.
5. A 70-pound "hump" and an eggshell pasted over an eye (was, were) used to create a realistic hunchback.

4. Indefinite-Pronoun Subjects (links to exercise A on p. 163)

➡ **2.** know **4.** consists

For each sentence, write the verb form that agrees with the subject.

1. Nobody (predicts, predict) all the Oscar winners correctly.
2. Every year, several of the awards (is, are) surprises.
3. Many (feels, feel) that no movie should win too many awards.
4. Some (thinks, think) the awards should be better distributed.
5. But some (doesn't, don't) mind if a good film wins a lot of awards.
6. Anyone who wins a big award (expects, expect) to receive applause.
7. Most (seems, seem) happy when a charming film wins.
8. Few (has, have) challenged *Forrest Gump*'s best-film award or Tom Hanks's best-actor award for his work in that movie.
9. But many (questions, question) the giving of major awards to violent films.
10. Some (wonders, wonder) whether violence should be rewarded.

5. Other Problem Subjects (links to exercise A on p. 166)

➡ **1.** is **2.** has

For each sentence, write the verb form that agrees with the subject.

1. Mathematics (comes, come) in handy when you research facts about movies.
2. Four and a half million dollars (is, are) what Macaulay Culkin earned for *Home Alone 2: Lost in New York.*
3. Charlie Chaplin's *City Lights* (has, have) a single scene that was reshot 342 times.
4. Two hundred four (is, are) the number of films in which the fictional character Sherlock Holmes has appeared.
5. The cast of extras in *Gandhi* (numbers, number) 300,000.
6. The film audience in China (chooses, choose) from over 152,000 different movie theaters.
7. *Jaws* (was, were) the first movie to earn over $100 million.
8. According to some sources, 180 million dollars (is, are) what the film *Waterworld* cost.
9. Eighty years (was, were) the age of the oldest Oscar winner ever, Jessica Tandy.
10. Eighty-five hours (is, are) the running time of the U.S. film *The Cure for Insomnia!*

6. Special Sentence Problems (links to exercise A on p. 169)

➡️ **1.** Does, Buster Keaton **2.** is, character

Write the correct verb form in parentheses. Then write the subject with which the verb agrees.

1. There (is, are) few comic actors as popular as Robin Williams.
2. Williams is the actor who (is, are) known for playing an extraterrestrial on TV's *Mork and Mindy.*
3. Williams (is, are) a hilarious housekeeper in *Mrs. Doubtfire.*
4. Into a family's home (comes, come) Williams dressed as a 50-year-old woman.
5. On display in *Patch Adams* (is, are) many of Williams's comic talents.
6. (Isn't, Aren't) a funny nose and a clown suit enough to cheer up hospital patients?
7. Dramatic roles (is, are) another aspect of Williams's career.
8. (Doesn't, Don't) Williams portray a sensitive high school teacher in *Dead Poets Society?*
9. He plays an eccentric psychologist who (helps, help) a brilliant young man in *Good Will Hunting.*
10. There (is, are) many fans who enjoy watching Williams be himself.

8 Using Pronouns

2. Nominative and Objective Cases (links to exercise A on p. 181)

➡️ **2.** he, N **3.** he, N

Write the correct form of the pronoun in parentheses. Identify the form as nominative (N) or objective (O).

1. Although some historians believe that a King Arthur of Britain actually existed, they know little about (he, him).
2. We know a number of stories about Arthur through the writings of Sir Thomas Malory; it was (him, he) who wrote *Le Morte d'Arthur* around the year 1469.
3. Later authors—such as Mark Twain, T. H. White, and John Steinbeck—also wrote about the legendary king. Malory's original work gave (they, them) many ideas.
4. In Mark Twain's hilarious novel *A Connecticut Yankee in King Arthur's Court,* the main character and (us, we) travel back in time to the days of King Arthur.

5. In the first part of *The Once and Future King,* T. H. White wrote about Arthur's childhood and the magician Merlin's education of (him, he) and his foster brother Kay.

6. The book tells about a contest that Arthur and Kay enter. The competition between (he, him) and Kay, which also involves other knights, is to pull a sword out of a stone.

7. Whoever does it will be the future king of England. "Who will it be, Kay?" Arthur asks. "Will it be you or (I, me)?"

8. Arthur says, "It looks like the winner will be (I, me)!"

9. In *The Acts of King Arthur and His Noble Knights,* John Steinbeck wrote about the knights of the Round Table and the battles between (they, them) and other knights.

10. The book also tells how King Arthur met the beautiful Princess Guinevere and fell in love with (her, she).

3. The Possessive Case (links to exercise A on p. 184)

➡ **3.** their **4.** their

For each sentence, choose the correct word in parentheses.

1. *The Guinness Book of Records* is a well-known compilation of statistics and record-breaking events, but many people do not know the story of (it's, its) origin.

2. Sir Hugh Beaver of Ireland got the idea for the book when friends couldn't forget (him, his) arguing whether the golden plover was Europe's fastest game bird.

3. The argument may sound trivial; however, three years later, (their, theirs) dispute flared again, and still no one had the answer.

4. Beaver thought other people must have similar disagreements, so he decided to produce a book that would make settling (our, ours) disputes possible.

5. The first edition, published in 1955, shot to the top of the British bestseller list; many people bought (there's, theirs) as soon as it appeared in bookstores.

6. (Mine, my) is always nearby.

7. (Your, Yours) appears well used too.

8. Was (your, you're) copy a gift?

9. According to the book, the fastest birds on land are ostriches. (Their, They're) running speed can reach 37 miles per hour.

10. (Our, Ours) fruitless searching for answers to such odd questions is over, thanks to Sir Hugh Beaver.

4. Using *Who* and *Whom* (links to exercise A on p. 187)

➡ **1.** Who **2.** whom

Choose the correct pronoun in parentheses.

1. The *Ramayana* is an epic poem of India, supposedly written by the poet Valmiki, (who, whom) lived during the 200s B.C.
2. By (who, whom) was it translated from the original Sanskrit?
3. The author of the Hindi version was (who, whom)?
4. In the *Ramayana,* Rama is the son of a king, by (who, whom) he is made to leave the country.
5. Sita is the beautiful woman (who, whom) Rama marries.
6. The main conflict of the story is between Rama and Ravana, an evil king (who, whom) kidnaps Sita.
7. (Who, Whom) do you think wins this battle?
8. (Who, Whom) helps Rama rescue his wife?
9. It is said that Valmiki made the *Ramayana* delightful for (whoever, whomever) hears it.
10. The *Ramayana* remains immensely popular today, and (whoever, whomever) reads it discovers an exciting traditional tale of India.

5. Pronoun-Antecedent Agreement (links to exercise A on p. 190)

➡ **1.** its **2.** his or her

Write the correct pronoun given in parentheses.

1. Whether you read the full-length story or an abbreviated version of *Gulliver's Travels,* you are sure to find (it, them) fascinating.
2. Jonathan Swift wrote the book as a satire, but the groups he satirized may not have realized he was making fun of (it, them).
3. The book tells of Gulliver's wild adventures and describes (it, them) in highly entertaining ways.
4. During Gulliver's first adventure, he finds himself in a land called Lilliput, where he discovers, to (his, your) surprise, that the inhabitants are only six inches tall.
5. In the description of these miniature people and their emperor, Swift makes fun of (him, them) and all other people who take themselves too seriously.
6. On his second voyage Gulliver ends up in a land where every person is a giant. There, a young girl adopts him as (his, her) pet.
7. Neither Gulliver nor the fantastic characters he meets seem aware of (its, their) unusual lives.
8. At one time, Gulliver finds himself in a city where the residents spend most of (your, their) time making up ridiculous scientific theories.

9. Gulliver also visits other imaginary lands; these extraordinary places have (its, their) purposes in Swift's clever satire.

10. A talking horse and other odd characters play (his, their) part in Gulliver's final adventure.

6. Indefinite Pronouns as Antecedents (links to exercise A on p. 193)

➡ **1.** . . . their musicians. **2.** . . . their guitars louder.

Find and correct the errors in agreement in these sentences. Write *Correct* if a sentence contains no error.

1. Many of America's cities have summer festivals, but few have more than Chicago.
2. It seems clear that everyone can find a summer festival that appeals to them in the "Second City," where the possibilities include the blues festival and the gospel festival.
3. Both of these festivals draw its share of music lovers.
4. Everyone who performs brings their own talent to the festival.
5. Few of the concertgoers can keep his or her feet still when the music gets going.
6. Perhaps the most famous festival is Taste of Chicago, where many have their own favorite food booths.
7. Each of the restaurants has their own specialty.
8. All of the food is selected for their appeal to the public.
9. Most of the restaurants provide samples of their most famous foods.
10. Some of the restaurants make half their annual food sales at Taste of Chicago.

7. Other Pronoun Problems (links to exercise A on p. 196)

➡ **1.** We **2.** she

Choose the correct pronoun in parentheses.

1. At an early age Rupert started taking piano lessons from his mother, and soon he played as well as (she, her).
2. (Us, We) cousins enjoyed listening to Rupert learn new pieces, and he rarely needed encouragement to play for us.
3. When Rupert's mother came home from work in the evening, the two of them, Rupert and (her, she), would sometimes practice duets together.
4. Though he had a lot of fun playing with his mother, Rupert soon decided that he wanted a teacher who had more experience than (she, her).

5. Rupert's mother had great respect for her former piano teachers, Samantha and Jabi Bean; and since she had less time than (them, they) to teach Rupert, she was glad to have him learn from them instead.

6. When Rupert went to the Beans' house for the first time, he was delighted to discover that they were as enthusiastic about playing the piano as (he, him).

7. Rupert enjoyed meeting the other students, but he was intimidated because he had not been playing as long as (them, they).

8. After two months of taking lessons from the Beans, Rupert was overjoyed to learn that he was going to be included in a recital, and he invited (we, us) relatives to attend.

9. The night of the recital, Rupert found out that he would be playing first. Judit, one of the other students, told him, "When you've taken lessons as long as (me, I), you'll be able to choose when you play."

10. Rupert's mother made sure that his most avid fans, his father and (she, her), had good seats for his premiere, and they cheered wildly when he finished his piece.

8. Pronoun Reference (links to exercise A on pp. 198–199)

➜ **1.** A recent magazine article explains that Reggae Sunsplash began as an annual music festival in Jamaica. **2.** The article says that the popular festival now tours Europe and the United States.

Rewrite the following sentences to correct instances of indefinite, ambiguous, and general pronoun reference.

1. An old reference book may be out-of-date, but you have fascinating firsthand information about what life was like at the time of its publication.

2. For example, in *The Wonder Book of Knowledge,* published in 1927, they refer to "the new science of radio."

3. The book provides a history of adding machines, but they did not know about computers then.

4. In the article on an up-to-date farm, a photograph depicting "a modern grain binder" shows a machine on a farm, which is being pulled by a team of horses.

5. In the section on airships, it says, "This record breaking machine developed a speed of over 250 miles per hour," under a picture of a navy racing plane.

6. The book describes a new device that could reproduce music and other sounds on a record, which it calls a "talking machine."

7. Photographs of what was then a modern fire engine or a modern motion-picture camera are interesting because they look like quaint antiques.
8. Some of the sections of the book do not focus on technology, but rather on natural processes and historical events; therefore, they are not in the least outdated.
9. For instance, in one section you learn how bees make honey, and another describes the building of the Panama Canal.
10. *The Wonder Book of Knowledge* is interesting to look at, which can help you realize that today's reference materials will probably be viewed by future generations as quaint and old-fashioned.

9 Using Modifiers

1. Using Adjectives and Adverbs (links to exercise A on p. 210)

➡ 1. *named:* adjective; *shiny:* adjective; *sparkling:* adjective; *American River's:* adjective; *south:* adjective 2. *His:* adjective; *lucky:* adjective; *eventually:* adverb; *bad:* adjective; *his:* adjective; *kindly:* adjective

Write the modifiers (except *a, an,* and *the*) in these sentences, identifying each as an adjective or an adverb.

1. A hundred years ago, the forerunners of today's personal checks were issued not just by banks but by mines, railroads, and other commercial enterprises.
2. Most checks were both beautiful and functional.
3. They featured finely wrought engravings of gold mines, spouting geysers, and redwood forests.
4. An endorsed check was as good as cold cash in the stores and saloons of the Old West.
5. Some people today collect these checks for their historical interest, their artistic quality, or their expected increase in value.
6. Some like to map the travels of the checks around the western territories by the endorsements on their backs.
7. Other collectors specialize in checks from specific states, mines, banks, or ghost towns.
8. Wells Fargo is one bank that issued many checks in the 1800s.
9. The in-house historian of the bank collects early checks printed by the Women's Cooperative Printing Union of San Francisco.
10. That co-op, founded in 1868 by the activist Agnes B. Peterson, employed women workers when other companies did not.

2. Problems with Modifiers (links to exercise A on p. 214)

➜ **1.** any **2.** badly

For each sentence, choose the correct modifier.

1. Everyone knows how (convenient, conveniently) vending machines are for buying snacks.
2. You can use (these, them) machines to buy anything from an apple to the junkiest junk food.
3. But did you know how long (these, them) machines have been around?
4. The first recorded vending machine worked (good, well) nearly 2,000 years ago.
5. (That, That there) machine dispensed holy water when a coin dropped into it struck a lever.
6. Vending machines have been improved (great, greatly) since then.
7. Now you can hardly (ever, never) tell the difference between their performance and that of humans.
8. (Those, Them) machines can recognize the right coin by testing its size, weight, and electric and magnetic properties.
9. Some even cook, though how (good, well) they cook is debatable.
10. Some vending machines, known as ATMs, (even, evenly) dispense money.

3. Using Comparisons (links to exercise A on p. 217)

➜ **1.** faster **4.** less freely

Choose the correct form of comparison for each sentence.

1. One of the (large, largest) archaeological digs to date is in North America, at Oak Island, Nova Scotia.
2. The island, named for its red oak trees, is one of the (small, smallest) islands in Nova Scotia's Mahone Bay.
3. The hope of finding treasure draws (great, greatest) numbers of people, seeking untold riches.
4. (Many, Most) pirates, such as William Kidd and Blackbeard, are rumored to have buried treasure on Oak Island.
5. The (better, best) historical records, however, fail to support the claim that Oak Island is the site of buried treasure.
6. Between 1795 and 1987, fifteen expeditions went to Oak Island, each with (great, greater) hopes than the group before.
7. The (few, fewer) pieces of evidence that have been found are three links of a gold chain, a quill pen, and a scrap of parchment.
8. Skeptics say that there is (little, less) hope of finding the famous riches on Oak Island.

9. This does not discourage those who are prepared to enter into one of the (most costly, costly) treasure hunts of all time.
10. The excavation of Oak Island continues, with each expedition digging (deep, deeper) than the last.

4. Problems with Comparisons (links to exercise A on p. 219)

➡ **1.** biggest **2.** any other

Choose the correct form of comparison for each sentence.

1. It used to be that the (biggest, most biggest) money to be made in entertainment was in movies.
2. Today, television is more profitable than (any, any other) kind of entertainment.
3. That's due partly to the (greater, more greater) number of TV networks today and the advent of cable.
4. Another reason is that TV shows, especially situation comedies, are much (cheaper, more cheaper) to make than movies.
5. Half-hour sitcoms are also (easier, more easier) to syndicate than hourlong shows.
6. Syndication is (more lucrative, most lucrative) than one-time use.
7. The sitcom *Seinfeld* has earned more money than (any, any other) entertainment product in history.
8. Syndicated even before its prime-time run was over, it outearned the (highest-earning, most highest-earning) movie of all time.
9. The Carsey-Werner TV production company is worth more than (any, any other) movie production company.
10. With total earnings of well over $1 billion, it's even (richer, more richer) than Steven Spielberg's company, DreamWorks SKG.

10 Capitalization

1. People and Cultures (links to exercise A on p. 230)

➡ **1.** J. Pérez, Native American **2.** Mr. Pérez, Marta Ríos, M.D.

For each sentence, write the words that should be capitalized.

(1) Ophelia Johnson, ph.d., and dr. Frederick Johnson, jr., are my aunt and uncle. **(2)** Recently i noticed that aunt ophelia and uncle fred have developed a passion for beads. **(3)** Their interest in beads began when my cousin Jeff, a methodist seminary student, went to Ireland to learn gaelic. **(4)** My aunt and uncle visited cousin Jeff there and then went to England. **(5)** In England they learned about african beads and saw a british collection amassed by a. j. arkell. **(6)** A museum guide explained that Arkell began collecting beads when he was stationed in several sudanese districts in Africa. **(7)** In the 1930s muslims from Africa would go on the haj, a sacred pilgrimage to Mecca. **(8)** In Mecca they traded beads with indian and other islamic peoples. **(9)** Years later, professor Arkell became a curator at a museum of egyptian antiquities. **(10)** My aunt and uncle returned from England with mauritanian powder-glass beads and tuareg necklaces.

2. First Words and Titles (links to exercise A on p. 233)

➡ **1.** Parting, *Romeo, Juliet* **2.** It's

For each sentence, write the words that should be capitalized.

1. Have you read *The Cat in the hat* and *The pilgrim's progress?*
2. Do you prefer a poster for *Star wars* to the painting *Starry night?*
3. If you don't know *The Rite of spring* but you know the theme music of *the Simpsons,* you probably need to learn more about the arts.
4. In 1930 Arnold Bennett wrote, "good taste is better than bad taste, but bad taste is better than no taste."
5. so who's to judge what is good or bad?
6. Is it the book reviewer for the *Post* or a critic for *TV guide?*
7. It helps to outline the sources of opinion:
   I. experts
      A. critics
      B. scholars
8. Another resource is *the dictionary of Cultural Literacy.*
9. In the introduction, the authors write, "to become part of cultural literacy, an item must have lasting significance."
10. Examples of entries on a single page are ones for the opera *carmen,* the movie *casablanca,* and the song "casey jones."

3. Places and Transportation (links to exercise A on p. 236)

➡ **1.** Bahamas, SS *Clermont* **2.** United States, New, West Coast

For each sentence, write the words that should be capitalized.

(1) I vow I'm going to start a west coast group to help children of bargain hunters. **(2)** My parents own a novelty store on west aspen street, just north of the coyote river. **(3)** Every summer my family heads north toward vancouver, british columbia, or east to the great plains on buying trips. **(4)** One year we even took a cruise around the mediterranean sea and went shopping in europe. **(5)** Mom and Dad bought models of the rock of Gibraltar and the parthenon. **(6)** In palermo, sicily, they even found a door knocker in the shape of mount etna. **(7)** During a storm in the strait of messina, I was sure that our ship, the *atlantis searcher,* would sink from the weight of all our souvenirs. **(8)** My dream vacation is to visit cape canaveral on the eastern side of florida, watch a space-shuttle launch, and not buy anything! **(9)** But I know that wherever we vacationed, even on the space station *mir,* my parents could probably find treasures to bring home. **(10)** If we colonized a planet such as mars, my folks would probably spend their time bargaining to buy rocks at the right price.

4. Organizations and Other Subjects (links to exercise A on p. 239)

➡ **1.** Senate, House, Representatives **2.** Senior Trip Committee

For each sentence, write the words that should be capitalized.

(1) The Massachusetts institute of technology (mit) is serious about toys. **(2)** Mit's media laboratory is researching the role that computers will play in designing toys of the future. **(3)** Can you imagine enrolling in Technology and toys 101? **(4)** The freshman class of a.d. 2010 might sign up for it and other computer-science courses as well. **(5)** Some may enroll with the hope of receiving the national inventor of the year award for a cutting-edge toy. **(6)** At first, Bandai company's Tamagotchi and the giga pets of Tiger Electronics, inc., seemed innovative. **(7)** However, virtual pets have had to compete with electronic games on the internet. **(8)** At the end of the next millennium, will high-tech toys inspire the nostalgia that cracker jack novelties do today? **(9)** Will mattel's barbie software be as collectible as dolls from world war I? **(10)** Will the Smithsonian institution have a wing for nintendo games and computer chips?

⑪ Punctuation

1. Periods and Other End Marks (links to exercise A on p. 250)

➡ **1.** monsters. **3.** Phew!

Write the last word of each sentence, adding the correct end mark.

1. Is it safe to surf in shark territory
2. Ask Eric Larsen
3. He was riding the waves off Monterey when he felt a blinding pain
4. Larsen wondered what could possibly be wrong
5. Suddenly, he felt himself being dragged beneath the waves

6. Oh, no! A shark had seized him
7. Larsen frantically beat the predator with his fists
8. Miraculously, the shark surrendered and swam away
9. Larsen was badly bitten but lived to tell his tale
10. What is the moral of his story Never surf with sharks

2. Comma Uses (links to exercise A on p. 254)

➡ **1.** 1620, **2.** Drebbel, scientist,

Write the word before each missing comma, adding the comma.
Write *Correct* if no commas are needed in a sentence.

1. In 1954 the actors Kirk Douglas Peter Lorre and James Mason took an imaginary trip beneath the waves.
2. They starred in *20,000 Leagues Under the Sea,* an underwater fantasy movie.
3. Based on a novel by Jules Verne the movie was a huge hit.
4. At the center of the tale is mad vengeful Captain Nemo.
5. Professor Aronnax a naturalist from the Paris Museum of Natural History takes a wild ride in Nemo's submarine the *Nautilus.*
6. During their long trip in the depths of the sea the men have many adventures.
7. First they sink a warship; second they battle a giant squid.
8. Finally the men explore the seafloor.
9. Thrilled by the sight of ancient grottoes Aronnax cries out in wonder.
10. Although the tale was factually inaccurate it helped generate public interest in the sea.

3. More Comma Uses (links to exercise A on p. 258)

➡ **1.** Rock, Island, sea, **2.** chair,

Write the word before each missing comma, adding the comma.
Write *Correct* if no commas are needed in a sentence.

1. Danny Ferrington grew up in Enterprise Louisiana during the 1950s.
2. His father was a cabinetmaker; his mother a homemaker.
3. As a child Ferrington liked music and enjoyed working with wood.
4. His mother recalling his passion for woodworking said "We knew he had a gift."
5. Ferrington attended college but he did not receive a degree.
6. Worried Ferrington settled for a low-paying job in a guitar repair shop.

7. At the Old Time Pickin' Parlour which paid him only $2 an hour Ferrington learned to make guitars.

8. Today he is famous for his handmade guitars are among the best.

9. Musicians searching for unique guitars flock to his Los Angeles California shop.

10. "Each of his guitars" says Linda Ronstadt "is a unique creation."

4. Semicolons and Colons (links to exercise A on p. 261)

➡ **1.** Washington; **2.** discovery:

Write the word before each missing semicolon or colon, adding the the correct punctuation mark.

1. In February of 1945, three powerful leaders met in Yalta, a seaside resort in Soviet Russia and they discussed the future of the postwar world.

2. Attending the conference were Franklin D. Roosevelt, president of the United States Winston Churchill, prime minister of Great Britain and Joseph Stalin, premier of the Soviet Union.

3. World War II was not yet over nevertheless, the "Big Three" were confident that Germany would soon surrender.

4. The Big Three were concerned about Germany they didn't want this nation to start a third world war.

5. The Allied leaders planned to divide postwar Germany into four zones one controlled by the United States, one by Great Britain, one by Russia, and one by France.

6. The war with Japan was also on the agenda unlike Germany, Japan was not on the brink of surrender.

7. The Soviet Union was at war with Germany it had not, however, declared war on Japan.

8. Roosevelt wanted the Soviet Union to join the war against Japan in return, Stalin wanted the United States to support its recovery of former territories.

9. Roosevelt and Stalin struck a bargain Russia would declare war on Japan if the United States would support the Soviet Union's plans.

10. The Yalta agreements were presented as proof of Allied unity but Roosevelt and Churchill did not, in reality, trust Stalin.

5. Dashes and Parentheses (links to exercise A on p. 264)

➡ **1.** scientist—all **2.** (recall his kite experiments)

Insert dashes, parentheses, or commas wherever necessary.

1. Ricky, Lucy, Fred, Ethel these were once the most famous names on American TV.

2. *I Love Lucy* the show in which these characters appeared was a 1950s megahit.
3. By the end of the show's first season it premiered late in 1951, about 11 million TV sets were tuned to *I Love Lucy* every Monday night.
4. If you consider the total number of TVs in U.S. households at that time about 15 million sets you will understand just how much Americans really did love Lucy.
5. Comedian Lucille Ball she was such a riot played the role of Lucy Ricardo.
6. Desi Arnaz Ball's Cuban-born real-life husband played Ricky Ricardo.
7. Ball and Arnaz supposedly one of the happiest couples in Hollywood shocked their fans when they later divorced.
8. Ball went on to star in three shows of her own: a *The Lucy Show,* b *Here's Lucy,* and c *Life with Lucy.*
9. She also starred in *Wildcat* a Broadway show and the movie *Mame.*
10. In 1989 Lucille Ball star of stage, film, and TV died at the age of 77.

6. Hyphens and Apostrophes (links to exercise A on p. 267)

➡ **1.** Alaska's **2.** 427-foot

Rewrite the words that need hyphens or apostrophes, adding the missing punctuation.

1. Although about three quarters of the earths surface is covered by oceans and seas, peoples knowledge of the worlds waters is limited.
2. Water is not peoples natural habitat.
3. The human body has its needs, and they cant be ignored.
4. With todays diving gear, however, the underwater world can be yours to enjoy.
5. First and foremost, youll need breathing apparatus and oxygen tanks.
6. In addition, a wet suit will help you retain your bodys natural heat.
7. Its cold underwater: while it may be in the 80s on land, the temperature below may be a bone chilling 40 degrees.
8. Protect your eyes with a pair of high quality goggles.
9. If you dont have an underwater camera, you may want to borrow a friends.
10. Finally, for your own well being, dive with other people, and be aware of your partners locations at all times.

7. Quotation Marks (links to exercise A on pp. 270–271)

➜ **1.** Are you surprised to learn that "a great majority of deep-sea fishes have light-generating capabilities"?

Rewrite this paragraph, adding quotation marks, other punctuation, and paragraph divisions where appropriate.

My sister loves poetry; I don't. So when I had to write a poem for my English class, I knocked on her door and screamed Help She opened her bedroom door and said Is the house on fire No I answered just my brain. I have to write a poem, and I don't know what to say. Is it supposed to rhyme she asked My English teacher always says Poems don't have to rhyme I explained Just then, her phone rang. It was Gary, her boyfriend. Listening to my sister argue with him, I came up with a great idea for a poem. When she hung up, I announced that my poem was almost finished. You're almost done my sister cried in amazement Let me see that Sure I replied, handing over the poem. About all you did was copy down what I said to Gary she said angrily. I guess she didn't like my little poem, The Big Breakup Now I love poetry; my sister doesn't.

8. Italics (links to exercise A on p. 273)

➜ **1.** From ancient epic poetry to the modern musical *Titanic,* many works of art depict the perils of seafaring.

Write and underline the words that should be italicized in these sentences. If a sentence needs no italics, write *Correct.*

1. When someone says the word sports, my brother's eyes light up.
2. Jeb pores over the sports section of the Los Angeles Times daily.
3. I often use the word obsession to describe my brother's fascination with sports.
4. After school, he thumbs through his collection of Sports Illustrated magazines.
5. On summer evenings, you can find him looking up sports statistics in his Complete Baseball Record Book.
6. Come September, he studies a book called Football Pro.
7. When the snow falls, he rents Space Jam at the video store and reads his basketball books.
8. His bedroom walls are plastered with posters of sports stars, and over his bed hangs a copy of the painting Baseball at Night.
9. Each week, he studies TV Guide and circles the time of every televised sporting event.
10. The only time I get to watch my favorite TV series, Biography, is when it happens to be about the life of some sports star.

Model Bank

Autobiographical Incident

Fighting Fire (excerpt)
by Caroline Paul

When the alarm comes in for Masonic and Grove, it is late afternoon. There is nothing faster than the speed with which firefighters dash to the rig when a full box [alarm] comes in....The pole holes open with a crash like thunder, and bodies speed down the filament as if from heaven. Doors swing wide and other bodies plunge past; they grab coats, fire helmets, flashlights as they go....

Station 91 is half a minute away from Grove and Masonic. When we pull up, black smoke is already spewing from an open doorway. A man is doubled over and gasping. Later I will learn that he is an off-duty firefighter who tried to rush in but was kept back by the intense heat and smoke. Near the doorway people are screaming and pointing, and one woman is being restrained from running back in....

❶ Provides background information

At the top of the stairs, I cannot see my own hand pressed against my air mask. *Hell must be like this,* I think. The nozzle is cool and definite in my hand....I am first in, where every engine person wants to be, first in, with the nozzle. In front of me is a chasm of black and, somewhere, the seat of the fire.

My officer is saying something to me. I hear only a muffled yelling as he tries to tell me something from behind his air mask. "What? What?" I say, but it comes out an elongated, flattened sound that falls away into the dark. He presses his mask close to me, striking my helmet. This time I hear him a little better, and then he is gone, back down the stairs.

❷ Makes the order of events clear

All this has taken seconds. *Gone? Where could he go? Is this a test?* Later I will find out that he forgot his flashlight and went down to get it. What he thinks a flashlight will do in such unpenetrably thick blackness is beyond me. Nevertheless, there is only one thing to do:

I step forward into the smoke. I don't understand why I have been left here alone, but I know that if I do not move forward, that will somehow indicate that I am afraid. Perhaps they are waiting, clipboard and stopwatch in hand, for a panicked retreat.

❸ Shows why the experience is important

I crouch and slide into the absolute black. . . . The utter dark is so thick that, thus separated, I feel that I, too, have disappeared. The nozzle in my hand and the hose that leads out behind it are the only proof that I have not. And it is hot. It is a cloying, leaden heat that makes me feel that the very walls are moving inward. I know the numbers: 300 degrees one foot above the floor, 500 degrees five feet above the floor, 1200 degrees at the ceiling. I drop lower. . . .

Then I feel a hand on my coat, pulling. Someone is behind me. The hand, all-knowing and seemingly all-seeing (or, more likely, adjusted to non-seeing), guides me to the left and we crawl down what must (it must!) be a hallway. The heat heightens. Shafts of lightning streak out in front of us.

❹ Focuses on a clear incident

Heavy unvented fire does not look like carved flame and color. Instead, the thick blanket of smoke allows only gradations of light, slivers of non-black that dart and disappear like hallucinations. The person behind me is yelling now, and I spray the nozzle above us, in wide circles and then at the streaks of light. This simultaneously cools us down and ensures that the fire does not sneak above us then attack from behind, trapping us. . . .

The heat is worse now, and we lie down, bellies on the floor, air bottles like shells on our backs, hot water hitting the ears, the neck, soaking our pants, our gloves. The thick protective leather on our hands inhibits touch, the air masks narrow our sense of smell to the rubber lining and our own sweat, our mouths taste only the sour fumes of our excitement. Finally, the black smoke muffles sound and sight. Every sense is dulled, yet never do we feel so alive as when suddenly we turn and there, in a wide grin of light, is the fire full force.

❺ Includes specific details

Focused Description

Africa's Wild Dogs
by Richard Conniff
from *National Geographic*
May 1999

RUBRIC
IN ACTION

Somewhere deep in Botswana's Okavango Delta, a million miles from nowhere, a dog named Nomad leads his pack on a wild chase through the bush. The sun paints a gaudy orange stripe across the horizon. Night threatens at any moment to rush down and set the lions afoot. Our Land Rover bucks and jumps through a dense thicket of mopani trees, struggling to keep up, then breaks out onto a floodplain through the . . . windshield-high sage. Giraffes and tsessebes scatter ahead of us, kicking up panicky clouds of dust. Nomad is the orphan child of a male named Chance and a [female] named Fate, and maybe more sensible men would take the hint and give up, go home, get dinner.

❶ Identifies the place

❷ Uses sensory details and precise language

The driver, a wildlife biologist named John "Tico" McNutt, spots a herd of impalas, fast food for the wild dogs we are following. But there are no dogs in sight. He listens to his earphones for the signal from Nomad's radio collar, and then the Land Rover dives back into the bush. "Uh-oh," McNutt says as he muscles the wheel one way and then the other. "Uh-oh." He circles a tree once to get his bearings, then lurches off in the direction that makes his earphones ping strong as a heart monitor. Thorny acacia branches <u>howl down the sides</u> of the truck and <u>leap in</u> at the open windows. A rotten log explodes under our tires, showering us with debris. "Captain, we've been hit!" McNutt reports and guns the engine.

❸ Uses figurative language to make the descriptions vivid

And then we see the dogs out ahead of us, long-legged and light-footed, barely skimming the ground. They stand more than two feet tall at the shoulder, mottled all over with patches of brown, yellow, black, and white. Their ears are round as satellite dishes, and their mouths are slightly open. Everything about them as they glide through the mopanies seems effortless.

❹ Gives precise visual details

Then they vanish, dappled shadows moving among the dappled shadows of dusk.

They're commonly called African wild dogs, an unfortunate name suggesting house pets gone bad. In fact, *Lycaon pictus,* the lone species in its genus, is utterly wild and only distantly related to our domestic dog or any other canid. Wild dogs most closely resemble wolves in their social behavior, though they seem more gentle. They are like wolves, too, in that humans have vilified and persecuted them into extinction over most of their range.

5 This writer gives background information to help readers.

Wild dogs once roamed throughout sub-Saharan Africa in every habitat except jungle or desert. A traveler in the 1960s sighted them even in the snows of Mount Kilimanjaro. But they hang on now in just a few isolated pockets, with a total population estimated at fewer than 5,000 animals. They are nearly as endangered as the black rhino, but less celebrated.

Literary Interpretation

One Man's Search for Light Amid the Darkness
by Patrick T. Reardon
from *Chicago Tribune* (Jan. 29, 1999)
book review of *Hunting for Hope: A Father's Journey*
by Scott Russell Sanders

RUBRIC
IN ACTION

Hunting for Hope opens in the Rocky Mountains of Colorado, where Scott Russell Sanders and his teenage son, Jesse, are getting on each other's nerves during a camping trip.

❶ Identifies the title and author and gives brief background information including quotations from the text

Finally, Sanders accuses Jesse of spoiling the day, but his son shoots back: "You're the one who's spoiling it, you and your hang-ups." A little later, Jesse elaborates: "You hate everything that's fun. You hate television and movies and video games. . . . You hate malls and fashions and cars. . . . You make me feel the planet's dying and people are to blame and nothing can be done about it."

The outburst jars Sanders, an essayist, novelist and children's book author who is on the creative writing faculty at Indiana University in Bloomington. And it sets him to thinking about what gives him hope in a world that, he acknowledges, he sees being plundered by humankind. The result, *Hunting for Hope,* is his effort to explain the light he sees amid the darkness.

❷ Provides more background information

Yet, for much of the book, one can only sympathize with Jesse.

The fact is: Sanders is a nag, a pain, a burr under the saddle. This is not exactly a criticism. The points he makes about the need to protect the environment and the shallowness of much modern entertainment and the obligation to be honest, loving and true are certainly valid. But there's a strong take-your-medicine quality to it all. For Sanders, hope resides in a small grab bag of human experiences, attitudes and relationships—in wildness, the senses, family, fidelity, skill, simplicity and beauty. Yet, even as he waxes eloquently about the richness of a hopeful life, he can't help but find fault.

❸ Gives a clearly stated evaluation of the book

And, then, in the section on beauty, something happens.

Sanders tells about the moment just before the start of his daughter's wedding when he looks at her and her bridesmaids. "I realize they are gorgeous not because they carry bouquets or wear silk dresses, but because the festival of marriage has slowed time down until any fool can see their glory."

It's at this moment that Sanders' lecturing tone falls away, and, instead of being weighed down by guilt, the reader gets a glimpse of the wonder of life—of Sanders' awe at the overwhelming pulchritude of existence. This awe is what has been behind all his nagging; this is what he has been struggling for nearly 150 pages to get to. This, and one more thing—perhaps the riskiest, scariest thing that an academic or an intellectual can do in this modern, skeptical world.

❹ Continues the evaluation by noting a change in the work

He says he believes in God.

"I believe," Sanders writes, "that Creation is not finished, but rather is a fabulous experiment whose outcome not even the Creator foresees.... Our part in the cosmic story is to gaze back, with comprehension and joy, at the whole of Creation."

There is a mystical quality to this that is profoundly at odds with much of modern life. But, as a starting point for hope, it's not bad.

❺ Concludes with an overall statement about the value of the work

Cause-and-Effect Essay

Remember El Niño? His Sister Has Shown Up, and She's Angry
by William K. Stevens
from *New York Times*
January 27, 1999

RUBRIC
IN ACTION

Record snows in Buffalo and Chicago. Record numbers of tornadoes in the country's midsection. All-time low temperatures in Indiana and Maine. Double the normal amount of precipitation, coupled with an extended warm spell, in New York. What accounts for this month's run of extreme weather?

❶ Introduces the subject with thought-provoking facts and a question

One big factor, experts say, is probably La Niña: an abnormally cold pool of water stretching across the equatorial Pacific that <u>causes</u> far-flung changes in the atmosphere's behavior.

❷ Identifies the cause-effect relationship clearly

La Niña may not be as familiar as its opposite number, El Niño, which warms the Pacific instead of cooling it. It does not appear as often, and its impact is somewhat less predictable and clear-cut. But this winter, Government scientists say, its interaction with routine climate behavior has <u>produced</u> an unusual run of weather in North America.

"It's La Niña plus the normal chaotic variability of the atmosphere," said Dr. Gerry Bell, a researcher at the Climate Prediction Center of the National Weather Service in Camp Springs, Maryland. While no single weather event can be directly attributed to La Niña (or to El Niño, for that matter), it has been "a big player" in this winter's events, Dr. Bell said.

❸ Provides necessary background information

The El Niño-La Niña cycle is wholly natural. But some scientists believe that extreme weather generally is increasing as a result of an observed rise in the average global surface temperature of 1 degree Fahrenheit over the last century. A warmer atmosphere stimulates more precipitation, for instance. Whether the warming is also modifying the El Niño-La Niña cycle in some way is an open question. . . .

La Niña's <u>effects</u> on the atmosphere now, as it impinges on North America, seem clear. Its <u>main impact</u> has been to alter the path of the jet stream, the high-altitude river of air that runs from west to east and marks the boundary between cold air masses from the north and warm ones from the tropics. It is along this boundary, where warm and cold air clash, that most winter storms develop.

La Niña's main signature in North America is an exaggerated pattern of jet stream flow in which the jet, leaving the North Pacific region, frequently curves northward around a vast high-pressure system near Alaska, then plunges down into Montana and the Northern Plains and then into the central part of the country before curving northeastward again. On the northern and western sides of the downward bulge is cold winter air from Canada; on the southern and eastern sides, warm tropical air from the South. These circulation patterns typically span the entire country. The weather any locality gets depends on where it is situated in relation to them.

> ❹ Makes the cause-effect relationship clear through specific examples

The clash of the two big air masses is what led to this month's tornadoes—more than 100 so far, almost double the previous record for January, 52. Thirty-one twisters touched down in Tennessee, Arkansas and Mississippi on January 17, followed by an outbreak of 55 more across the South on January 21 and 22. . . .

The other major <u>effects of</u> La Niña, Dr. Bell said, have been mostly in the tropics. For instance, there have been good rains in Indonesia, just the opposite of El Niño's drought last year. But La Niña, he said, has also "completely shut down" rainfall in the eastern tropical Pacific.

> ❺ Continues to list effects

Persuasive Essay

Limit Use of Car Phones
from *Pioneer Press*
May 6, 1999

RUBRIC
IN ACTION

Using a cellular phone while driving has been sold as a safety feature for motorists. When you see a hazard, an accident or a motorist in trouble, call the police.

❶ Introduces subject and addresses audience

As cellular phones have become more widespread ... so have the cellular phone calls from the car. And more of those cellular phone calls from the car are business or personal calls, not safety calls. How can drivers on the phone possibly concentrate on the road?

Common sense says they can't. And recent studies indicate that is the case.

❷ States the issue and the writer's position

A study published in the *New England Journal of Medicine* ... says that the risk of getting in an accident increases by four times when a driver is using a cellular phone. It adds that talking on the phone can be just as distracting as dialing or answering a call.

A report by the National Highway Transportation Safety Administration, which evaluated studies on cellular phone use in cars, concludes cellular phones can create distractions that increase a driver's risk on the highway. It also suggests crashes may increase with increasing numbers of cellular phone users.

❸ Offers results of studies to support position

[Illinois] State Rep. Robert Bugielski, D-19th, sponsored a bill limiting cellular phone use in cars to hands-free models only. Only a few legislators supported the bill, and he decided not to put it for a vote. But 11 other states are considering such measures and last month a suburb of Cleveland, Ohio, voted to limit cellular phone use while driving.

❹ Gives brief history of past efforts to address the issue

Bugielski's bill is a good idea. It should be supported and passed. Also, Illinois should require information on cellular phone use be collected by state police on accident reports. Oklahoma and Minnesota do so now.

❺ Makes a plea for action

The industry says more information is needed before regulating cellular phones. And the federal government also stops short of calling for banning cellular phone use in cars, saying more data are needed.

⑥ States opposing view

But saying a complete ban on cellular phones in cars is not warranted is hardly a reason to do absolutely nothing. How many crashes would suffice for the critics? Waiting for studies is an accident waiting to happen.

⑦ Conclude with a question directed at audience

Problem-Solution Essay

Safer Air Bags Are Needed Now
by U.S. Senator Mike DeWine (R-Ohio)
from *Chicago Tribune*
June 1, 1999

RUBRIC
IN ACTION

... In November 1991 Congress, after years of virtual silence on [the issue of air bags], required auto manufacturers to install air bags in all new cars by 1998. Since that time many lives have been saved. An unintended but fatal consequence has occurred, however. Small children and some adults are at risk of serious injury or even death from the deployment of standard air bags. NHTSA [National Highway Traffic Safety Administration] reported that since 1990, 108 children and 45 adults have been killed by the deployment of air bags.

❶ Gives history of the subject and presents the problem

In less time than it takes to blink an eye, an air bag inflates to protect a driver from crushing his chest against a steering wheel or a passenger from being propelled into a windshield. When children and some adults sit too close to air bags, they are at risk of being hurt or killed by the explosive bag.

❷ Explains the problem in detail

In response to this problem, NHTSA last year issued a regulation that allows consumers to obtain an air bag "on-off" switch from auto dealers and repair shops if consumers can show that air bag deployment poses a health and safety risk.

❸ Describes an attempt at a solution

The "on-off" regulation is understandable but should not be seen as the last word on this subject. Another solution is a move toward what's being called a "smart restraint system." ...

For less money than a decent stereo—an estimated $125 per vehicle—consumers could have access to what promises to be the safest air bag for children and adults. These devices have a sensing mechanism that can tell whether a person is wearing a seat belt or not, whether the person is small or large by the weight on the seat, or whether the passenger is in a child carrier by the configuration. The sensor then relays the information so that the air bag can be configured in shape and size to deploy safely.

❹ The writer presents what he feels is a stronger solution, describing it in detail as sensible and effective.

Currently arguments over the methodology and testing techniques threaten to cause unconscionable delays. This is unacceptable.... Government safety officials at NHTSA can and should work with air-bag developers, auto manufacturers and advocacy groups to ... arrive at a final testing standard based on sound science.

❺ Ends with a call to action

Writing for History

PROMPT: Why were the Assyrians' attacks on enemy cities successful?

The Assyrians were successful in their attacks on enemy cities because they planned their attacks in stages and used engineers, archers and foot soldiers.

❶ Strong introduction summarizes the answer.

When deep water blocked their way, the Assyrian engineers built a bridge out of floating structures, or pontoons, to get across. First, they made the pontoons by tying inflated animal skins together. Then they connected these pontoons to the shore with wooden beams. Finally, they made a raised dirt roadway at both ends of the bridge so the army could cross.

❷ Paragraph describes first stage in sequential order; includes facts and terms.

When the army got to the city, soldiers dug beneath the city's walls to weaken them. Then, with a lot of courage and careful coordination, the foot soldiers approached just close enough to the city walls to be able to fire their arrows. When their commander signaled, they strung their bows and released a shower of arrows. Meanwhile, another group of troops hammered the city's gates with huge battering rams tipped with iron.

❸ Paragraph describes the next stage; includes details; shows multiple events using time words.

When the city gates finally shattered, the Assyrian army charged through. Once inside the city, the soldiers showed no mercy. They killed or enslaved their victims, beheading many of them to collect a bounty on severed heads.

❹ Paragraph describes last stage; names actions (effects) and reasons (causes).

These efficient methods of warfare gave the Assyrians great power. Their empire was at its peak around 650 B.C.

❺ Strong conclusion summarizes effects of methods.

Writing for Science

PROMPT: Describe how a typical solar-powered home is heated.

Solar-powered homes get their heat from water that is pumped through solar panels on the roof. The panels heat the water with the sun's radiation. Then air heated by the water is circulated through the house.

In the basement of a solar-powered home is a large storage tank of water. Water is pumped from the tank to solar panels on the roof that collect the sun's radiation. The panels are made of black copper plates with thin copper pipes running underneath them. The copper plates have black plastic sheets covering them to allow the sun's heat in, but keep it from escaping.

After the water is heated in the thin copper pipes, it enters a larger pipe and is sent back down to the storage tank. When heat is needed, the hot water is pumped from the tank and through a coil of pipe in the furnace called a heat exchanger. A fan blows cool air on these hot pipes. The water in the pipes loses some of its heat to the air and is returned to the storage tank, which is still being heated by water from the solar panels. Meanwhile, the fan blows the now heated air into ducts that carry it throughout the house.

In addition to this main system, solar-powered houses have windows positioned to get the most direct sunlight. Drapes are used to hold in the heat in the winter and to keep it out in the summer.

The water storage tanks are big enough to hold enough hot water to last for three to five cloudy days during the warmer months. In the winter, however, most solar homes have to use a supplementary heating system, such as gas or oil, which is the standard in non-solar homes.

❶ Introduction briefly summarizes process.

❷ Paragraph provides physical description of equipment.

❸ Paragraph shows step-by-step process and uses specific terms.

❹ Conclusion offers advantages and drawbacks to this system.

Résumé

Leah Nash
2620 Courtland Oval
Pasadena, CA 90124

(917) 555-1212

e-mail: Gnash@hmco.com

Employment Objective

After-school and summer job in a retail environment

Work Experience

- Summer 1998 Cashier in family-owned stationery store
- Summer 1997 Baby sitter; junior camp counselor; volunteer at animal shelter

Education

- Mather High School, Class of 2002; Honor Roll
- Tokeneke Middle School, Class of 1998

Activities and Accomplishments

- First Place in State Math Competition
- Short story included in annual collection of student writing
- Presidential Council on Physical Fitness Award
- Flute player, Mather Mongoose Marching Band
- Editorial Assistant, 1998 Mather yearbook
- Girls' lacrosse team

References

- Helping Paw Animal Shelter, 401 Michael Street, Pasadena, CA
- Phone numbers of families I've baby-sat for, available upon request

❶ Includes name, address, phone number, and e-mail address, if available

❷ States employment objective

❸ Gives work experience in descending chronological order
Other option: List relevant experience.

❹ Lists educational background and academic honors

❺ Lists activities and accomplishments to further present herself

❻ Offers references

Business Letter

37 Conley Street
Boulder, CO 62846
June 16, 2000

Mr. Conrad Fisk
Curlicue Publishing
250 Montgomery Avenue
Philadelphia, PA 24895

Dear Mr. Fisk:

Two months ago I sent a card in to your company requesting a subscription to your magazine *Special Girl*. On the card it said to allow two to three weeks for the first issue. After sending in another card and calling your subscriptions office twice, I still have not received anything.

Friends of mine have ordered subscriptions to your magazine and received them with no problem, so I'm assuming there has been some sort of miscommunication along the line. I hope that sending this letter directly to you will result in the speedy correction of this delay.

Thank you very much for your help. I look forward to reading my weekly issues of *Special Girl* for years to come!

Sincerely,

Ann Risen

Ann Risen

❶ Heading includes sender's address and date.

❷ Inside address directs letter to a specific person.

❸ Greeting

❹ Body opens with complaint, giving some background leading to the problem.

❺ Writer expresses patience and an expectation of action.

❻ Closes with thanks

Personal Letters

Thank-You Letter

June 19, 2002

Dear Mr. McGuiness,

Thank you very much for taking the extra time to help me out with math after school these last few weeks. As you know, I needed the help badly. Thanks to you, my math final was a breeze!

You'll say that I deserve most of the credit because I did the work. It was your help, though, on your own time that made the difference. I'll always appreciate it.

Sincerely,

Chris Turner

❶ Date

❷ Opens with thanks and mentions the good deed

❸ Closes by reiterating the importance of the teacher's help

Letter of Condolence

October 14, 2002

Dear Mrs. Travers,

We heard from the principal that your son passed away this week. I wanted to write and offer my condolences.

I never knew your son, but you're the best teacher I've ever had, so I know you must have raised him well. He was lucky to have a mom like you.

I know a lot of the other students feel the same way. We're all looking forward to when you're ready to come back.

Yours truly,

Simon Booker

❶ Date

❷ Mentions the deceased and offers condolences

❸ Offers support by expressing personal feelings for the recipient

Guidelines for Spelling

Forming Plural Nouns

To form the plural of most nouns, just add -s.

prizes   **dreams**   **circles**   **stations**

For most singular nouns ending in *o,* add -s.

solos   **halos**   **studios**   **photos**   **pianos**

For a few nouns ending in *o,* add -es.

heroes   **tomatoes**   **potatoes**   **echoes**

When the singular noun ends in *s, sh, ch, x,* or *z,* add -es.

waitresses   **brushes**   **ditches**   **axes**   **buzzes**

When a singular noun ends in *y* with a consonant before it, change the *y* to *i* and add -es.

army—armies   **candy—candies**   **baby—babies**
diary—diaries   **ferry—ferries**   **conspiracy—conspiracies**

When a vowel *(a, e, i, o, u)* comes before the *y,* just add -s.

boys—boys   **way—ways**   **array—arrays**
alloy—alloys   **weekday—weekdays**   **jockey—jockeys**

For most nouns ending in *f* or *fe,* change the *f* to *v* and add -es or -s. Since there is no rule, you must memorize such words.

life—lives   **calf—calves**   **knife—knives**
thief—thieves   **shelf—shelves**   **loaf—loaves**

For some nouns ending in *f,* add -s to make the plural.

roofs   **chiefs**   **reefs**   **beliefs**

Some nouns have the same form for both singular and plural.

deer   **sheep**   **moose**   **salmon**   **trout**

For some nouns, the plural is formed in a special way.

man—men   **goose—geese**   **ox—oxen**
woman—women   **mouse—mice**   **child—children**

For a compound noun written as one word, form the plural by changing the last word in the compound to its plural form.

stepchild—stepchildren   **firefly—fireflies**

If a compound noun is written as a hyphenated word or as two separate words, change the most important word to the plural form.

brother-in-law—brothers-in-law   **life jacket—life jackets**

Forming Possessives

If a noun is singular, add 's.

mother—my mother's car   **Ross—Ross's desk**

Exception: The **s** after the apostrophe is dropped after *Jesus'*, *Moses'*, and certain names in classical mythology (*Zeus'*). These possessive forms, therefore, can be pronounced easily.

If a noun is plural and ends with **s**, just add an apostrophe.

parents—my parents' car   **the Santinis—the Santinis' house**

If a noun is plural but does not end in **s**, add 's.

people—the people's choice   women—the women's coats

Spelling Rules

Words Ending in a Silent *e*

Before adding a suffix beginning with a vowel or **y** to a word ending in a silent **e**, drop the **e** (with some exceptions).

amaze + -ing = amazing   **love + -able = lovable**
create + -ed = created   **nerve + -ous = nervous**

Exceptions: *change + -able = changeable; courage + -ous = courageous*

When adding a suffix beginning with a consonant to a word ending in a silent **e**, keep the **e** (with some exceptions).

late + -ly = lately   **spite + -ful = spiteful**
noise + -less = noiseless   **state + -ment = statement**

Exceptions include *truly, argument, ninth, wholly,* and *awful.*

When a suffix beginning with **a** or **o** is added to a word with a final silent **e**, the final **e** is usually retained if it is preceded by a soft **c** or a soft **g**.

bridge + -able = bridgeable   **peace + -able = peaceable**
outrage + -ous = outrageous   **advantage + -ous = advantageous**

When a suffix beginning with a vowel is added to words ending in **ee** or **oe**, the final silent **e** is retained.

agree + -ing = agreeing   **free + -ing = freeing**
hoe + -ing = hoeing   **see + -ing = seeing**

Words Ending in *y*

Before adding a suffix to a word that ends in **y** preceded by a consonant, change the **y** to *i.*

easy + -est = easiest	crazy + -est = craziest
silly + -ness = silliness	marry + -age = marriage

Exceptions include *dryness, shyness,* and *slyness.*

However, when you add **-*ing,*** the **y** does not change.

empty + -ed = emptied but empty + -ing = emptying

When adding a suffix to a word that ends in **y** and is preceded by a vowel, the **y** usually does not change.

play + -er = player	employ + -ed = employed
coy + -ness = coyness	pay + -able = payable

Exceptions include *daily* and *gaily.*

Words Ending in a Consonant

In one-syllable words that end in one consonant preceded by one vowel, double the final consonant before adding a suffix beginning with a vowel, such as **-*ed*** or **-*ing.*** These are sometimes called 1+1+1 words.

dip + -ed = dipped	set + -ing = setting
slim + -est = slimmest	fit + -er = fitter

The rule does not apply to words of one syllable that end in a consonant preceded by two vowels.

feel + -ing = feeling	peel + -ed = peeled
reap + -ed = reaped	loot + -ed = looted

In words of more than one syllable, double the final consonant (**1**) when the word ends with one consonant preceded by one vowel and (**2**) when the word is accented on the last syllable.

be•gin´ per•mit´ re•fer´

In the following examples, note that in the new words formed with suffixes, the accent remains on the same syllable.

be•gin´ + -ing = be•gin´ ning = beginning
per•mit´ + -ed = per•mit´ ted = permitted

In the following examples, the accent does not remain on the same syllable; thus, the final consonant is not doubled.

re•fer´ + -ence = ref´ er•ence = reference
con•fer´ + -ence = con´ fer•ence = conference

Prefixes and Suffixes

When adding a prefix to a word, do not change the spelling of the base word. When a prefix creates a double letter, keep both letters.

dis- + approve = disapprove   re- + build = rebuild
ir- + regular = irregular   mis- + spell = misspell
anti- + trust = antitrust   il- + logical = illogical

When adding *-ly* to a word ending in *l,* keep both *l*'s. When adding *-ness* to a word ending in *n,* keep both *n*'s.

careful + -ly = carefully   sudden + -ness = suddenness
final + -ly = finally   thin + -ness = thinness

Special Spelling Problems

Only one English word ends in *-sede:* supersede. Three words end in *-ceed: exceed, proceed,* and *succeed.* All other verbs ending in the sound of *seed* (sēd) are spelled with *-cede.*

concede   precede   recede   secede

In words with *ie* and *ei,* when the sound is long e (ē), the word is spelled *ie* except after *c* (with some exceptions).

i before *e*	thief	relieve	piece	field	grieve	pier
except after *c*	conceit	perceive	ceiling	receive	receipt
Exceptions:	either	neither	weird	leisure	seize

Commonly Misspelled Words

abbreviate
accidentally
achievement
amateur
analyze
anonymous
answer
apologize
appearance
appreciate
appropriate
argument
associate
awkward
beginning
believe
bicycle
brief
bulletin
bureau
business
calendar
campaign
candidate
certain
changeable
characteristic
column
committee
courageous
courteous
criticize
curiosity
decision
definitely
dependent
description
desirable
despair
desperate

development
dictionary
different
disappear
disappoint
discipline
dissatisfied
efficient
eighth
eligible
eliminate
embarrass
enthusiastic
especially
exaggerate
exceed
existence
experience
familiar
fascinating
February
financial
foreign
fourth
fragile
generally
government
grammar
guarantee
guard
height
humorous
immediately
independent
indispensable
irritable
judgment
knowledge
laboratory
license

lightning
literature
loneliness
marriage
mathematics
minimum
mischievous
mortgage
necessary
nickel
ninety
noticeable
nuclear
nuisance
obstacle
occasionally
occurrence
opinion
opportunity
outrageous
parallel
particularly
permanent
permissible
persuade
pleasant
pneumonia
possess
possibility
prejudice
privilege
probably
psychology
pursue
realize
receipt
receive
recognize
recommend
reference

rehearse
repetition
restaurant
rhythm
ridiculous
sandwich
schedule
scissors
seize
separate
sergeant
similar
sincerely
sophomore
souvenir
specifically
strategy
success
surprise
syllable
sympathy
symptom
temperature
thorough
throughout
tomorrow
traffic
tragedy
transferred
truly
Tuesday
twelfth
undoubtedly
unnecessary
usable
vacuum
vicinity
village
weird
yield

Commonly Confused Words

Good writers master words that are easy to misuse and misspell. Study the following words, noting how their meanings differ.

accept, except : *Accept* means "to agree to something" or "to receive something willingly." *Except* usually means "not including."
Did the teacher *accept* your report?
Everyone smiled for the photographer *except* Jody.

adapt, adopt : *Adapt* means "to make apt or suitable; to adjust." *Adopt* means "to opt or choose as one's own; to accept."
The writer *adapted* the play for the screen.
After years of living in Japan, she had *adopted* its culture.

advice, advise : *Advice* is a noun that means "counsel given to someone." *Advise* is a verb that means "to give counsel."
Jim should take some of his own *advice*.
The mechanic *advised* me to get new brakes for my car.

affect, effect : *Affect* means "to move or influence" or "to wear or to pretend to have." *Effect* as a verb means "to bring about." As a noun, *effect* means "the result of an action."
The news from South Africa *affected* him deeply.
The band's singer *affects* a British accent.
The students tried to *effect* a change in school policy.
What *effect* did the acidic soil produce in the plants?

all ready, already : *All ready* means "all are ready" or "completely prepared." *Already* means "previously."
The students were *all ready* for the field trip.
We had *already* pitched our tent before it started raining.

all right : *All right* is the correct spelling. *Alright* is nonstandard and should not be used.

all together, altogether : *Altogether* means "completely." *All together* means "as a group."
The news story is *altogether* false.
Let's sing a song *all together*.

a lot : *A lot* may be used in informal writing. *Alot* is incorrect.

among, between	are prepositions. *Between* refers to two people or things. The object of *between* is never singular. *Among* refers to a group of three or more. **Texas lies *between* Louisiana and New Mexico.** **What are the differences *among* the four candidates?**
anywhere, nowhere, somewhere, anyway	*Anywhere, nowhere, somewhere,* and *anyway* are all correct. *Anywheres, nowheres, somewheres,* and *anyways* are incorrect. **I don't see geometry mentioned *anywhere.*** ***Somewhere* in this book is a map of ancient Sumer.** ***Anyway,* this street map is out of date.**
borrow, lend	*Borrow* means "to receive something on loan." *Lend* means "to give out temporarily." **Please *lend* me your book.** **He *borrowed* five dollars from his sister.**
bring, take	*Bring* refers to movement toward or with. *Take* refers to movement away from. **I'll *bring* you a glass of water.** **Would you please *take* these apples to Pam and John?**
can, may	*Can* means "to be able; to have the power to do something." *May* means "to have permission to do something." *May* can also mean "possibly will." **We *may* not use pesticides on our community garden.** **Pesticides *may* not be necessary, anyway.** **Vegetables *can* grow nicely without pesticides.**
capital, capitol, the Capitol	*Capital* means "excellent," "most serious," or "most important." It also means "seat of government." *Capitol* is a "building in which a state legislature meets." The *Capitol* is "the building in Washington, D.C., in which the U.S. Congress meets." **Proper nouns begin with *capital* letters.** **Is Madison the *capital* of Wisconsin?** **Protesters rallied at the state *capitol.*** **A subway connects the Senate and the House in *the Capitol.***
choose, chose	*Choose* is a verb that means "to decide or prefer." *Chose* is the past tense form of *choose.* **He had to *choose* between art and band.** **She *chose* to write for the school newspaper.**

desert, dessert	*Desert* (des´ ert) means "a dry, sandy, barren region." *Desert* (de sert´) means "to abandon." *Dessert* (des sert´) is a sweet, such as cake. **The Sahara in North Africa is the world's largest** *desert.* **The night guard did not** *desert* **his post.** **Alison's favorite** *dessert* **is chocolate cake.**
differ from, differ with	*Differ from* means "to be dissimilar." *Differ with* means "to disagree with." **The racing bike** *differs* **greatly from the mountain bike.** **I** *differ with* **her as to the meaning of Hamlet's speech.**
different from	is used to compare dissimilar items. *Different than* is nonstandard. **The hot sauce is much** *different from* **the yogurt sauce.**
farther, further	*Farther* refers to distance. *Further* refers to something additional. **We traveled two hundred miles** *farther* **that afternoon.** **This idea needs** *further* **discussion.**
fewer, less	*Fewer* refers to numbers of things that can be counted. *Less* refers to amount, degree, or value. *Fewer* **than ten students camped out.** **We made** *less* **money this year on the walkathon than last year.**
good, well	*Good* is always an adjective. *Well* is usually an adverb that modifies an action verb. *Well* can also be an adjective meaning "in good health." **Dana felt** *good* **when she finished painting her room.** **Angela ran** *well* **in yesterday's race.** **I felt** *well* **when I left my house.**
imply, infer	*Imply* means "to suggest something in an indirect way." *Infer* means "to come to a conclusion based on something that has been read or heard." **Josh** *implied* **that he would be taking the bus.** **From what you said, I** *inferred* **that the book would be difficult.**
its, it's	*Its* is a possessive pronoun. *It's* is a contraction for *it is* or *it has.* **Sanibel Island is known for** *its* **beautiful beaches.** *It's* **great weather for a picnic.**

kind of, sort of	Neither of these two expressions should be followed by the word *a*.
	What *kind of* **horse is Scout?**
	What *sorts of* **animals live in swamps?**
	The use of these two expressions as adverbs, as in "It's kind of hot today," is informal.
lay, lie	*Lay* is a verb that means "to place." It takes a direct object. *Lie* is a verb that means "to be in a certain place." *Lie,* or its past form *lay,* never takes a direct object.
	The carpenter will *lay* **the planks on the bench.**
	My cat likes to *lie* **under the bed.**
lead, led	*Lead* can be a noun that means "a heavy metal" or a verb that means "to show the way." *Led* is the past tense form of the verb.
	Lead **is used in nuclear reactors.**
	Raul always *leads* **his team onto the field.**
	She *led* **the class as president of the student council.**
learn, teach	*Learn* means "to gain knowledge." *Teach* means "to instruct."
	Enrique is *learning* **about black holes in space.**
	Marva *teaches* **astronomy at a college in the city.**
leave, let	*Leave* means "to go away from." *Leave* can be transitive or intransitive. *Let* is usually used with another verb. It means "to allow to."
	Don't *leave* **the refrigerator open.**
	She *leaves* **for Scotland tomorrow.**
	Cyclops wouldn't *let* **Odysseus' men** *leave* **the cave.**
like	as a conjunction before a clause is incorrect. Use *as* or *as if*.
	Ramon talked *as if* **he had a cold.**
loan, lone	*Loan* refers to "something given for temporary use." *Lone* refers to "the condition of being by oneself, alone."
	I gave that shirt to Max as a gift, not a *loan.*
	The *lone* **plant in our yard turned out to be a weed.**
lose, loose	*Lose* means "to mislay or suffer the loss of something." *Loose* means "free" or "not fastened."
	That tire will *lose* **air unless you patch it.**
	My little brother has three *loose* **teeth.**

majority	means more than half of a group of things or people that can be counted. It is incorrect to use *majority* in referring to time or distance, as in "The majority of our time there was wasted." **Most of our time there was wasted.** **The *majority* of the students study a foreign language.**
most, almost	*Most* can be a pronoun, an adjective, or an adverb, but it should never be used in place of *almost,* an adverb that means "nearly." ***Most* of the students enjoy writing in their journals.** (pronoun) ***Most* mammals give birth to live young.** (adjective) **You missed the *most* exciting part of the trip.** (adverb) ***Almost* every mammal gives live birth.** (adverb)
of	is incorrectly used in a phrase such as *could of.* Examples of correct wordings are *could have, should have,* and *must have.* **I *must have* missed the phone call.** **If you had played, we *would have* won.**
principal, principle	*Principal* means "of chief or central importance" and refers to the head of a school. *Principle* is a "basic truth, standard, or rule of behavior." **Lack of customers is the *principal* reason for closing the store.** **The *principal* of our school awarded the trophy.** **One of my *principles* is to be honest with others.**
quiet, quite	*Quiet* refers to "freedom from noise or disturbance." *Quite* means "truly" or "almost completely." **Observers must be *quiet* during the recording session.** **We were *quite* worried about the results of the test.**
raise, rise	*Raise* means "to lift" or "to make something go up." It takes a direct object. *Rise* means "to go upward." It does not take a direct object. **The maintenance workers *raise* the flag each morning.** **The city's population is expected to *rise* steadily.**
real, really	*Real* is an adjective meaning "actual; true." Really is an adverb meaning "in reality; in fact." ***Real* skill comes from concentration and practice.** **She doesn't *really* know all the facts.**

seldom	should not be followed by *ever*, as in "We seldom ever run more than a mile." *Seldom, rarely, very seldom,* and *hardly ever* are correct. **I** *seldom* **hear traditional jazz.**
set, sit	*Set* means "to place" and takes a direct object. *Sit* means "to occupy a seat or a place" and does not take a direct object. **He** *set* **the box down outside the shed.** **We** *sit* **in the last row of the upper balcony.**
stationary, stationery	*Stationary* means "fixed or unmoving." *Stationery* means "paper for writing letters." **The wheel pivots, but the seat is** *stationary.* **Rex wrote on special** *stationery* **imprinted with his name.**
than, then	*Than* is used to introduce the second part of a comparison. *Then* means "next in order." **Ramon is stronger** *than* **Mark.** **Cut the grass and** *then* **trim the hedges.**
their, there, they're	*Their* means "belonging to them." *There* means "in that place." *They're* is the contraction for *they are.* **All the campers returned to** *their* **cabins.** **I keep my card collection** *there* **in those folders.** **Lisa and Beth run daily;** *they're* **on the track team.**
way	refers to distance; *ways* is nonstandard and should not be used in writing. **The subway was a long** *way* **from the stadium.**
whose, who's	*Whose* is the possessive form of *who. Who's* is a contraction for *who is* or *who has.* *Whose* **parents will drive us to the movies?** *Who's* **going to the recycling center?**
your, you're	*Your* is the possessive form of *you. You're* is a contraction for *you are.* **What was** *your* **record in the fifty-yard dash?** *You're* **one of the winners of the essay contest.**

MLA Citation Guidelines

Forms for Working Bibliography and Works Cited Entries

The following are some basic forms for bibliographic entries. Use these forms on the bibliography cards that make up your working bibliography and in the list of works cited that appears at the end of your paper.

Whole Books

The following models can also be used for citing reports and pamphlets.

A. One author
Liptak, Karen. Coming-of-Age: Traditions and Rituals Around the World. Brookfield: Millbrook, 1994.

B. Two authors
Dolan, Edward F., and Margaret M. Scariano. Illiteracy in America. New York: Watts, 1995.

C. Three authors
Rand, Donna, Toni Parker, and Sheila Foster. Black Books Galore!: Guide to Great African American Children's Books. New York: Wiley, 1998.

D. Four or more authors
The abbreviation *et al.* means "and others." Use *et al.* instead of listing all the authors.

Quirk, Randolph, et al. A Comprehensive Grammar of the English Language. London: Longman, 1985.

E. No author given
Science Explained: The World of Science in Everyday Life. New York: Holt, 1993.

F. An editor, but no single author
Radelet, Michael L., ed. Facing the Death Penalty: Essays on a Cruel and Unusual Punishment. Philadelphia: Temple UP, 1989.

G. Two or three editors
Langley, Winston E., and Vivian C. Fox, eds. Women's Rights in the United States: A Documentary History. Westport: Greenwood, 1994.

H. Four or more editors

The abbreviation *et al.* means "and others." Use *et al.* instead of listing all the editors.

Brain, Joseph D., et al., eds. <u>Variations in Susceptibility to Inhaled Pollutants: Identification, Mechanisms, and Policy Implications</u>. Baltimore: Johns Hopkins UP, 1988.

I. An author and a translator

Rabinovici, Schoschana. <u>Thanks to My Mother</u>. Trans. James Skofield. New York: Dial, 1998.

J. An author, a translator, and an editor

LaFontaine, Jean de. <u>Selected Fables</u>. Trans. Christopher Wood. Ed. Maya Slater. New York: Oxford UP, 1995.

K. An edition other than the first

Metcalf, Robert L., and Robert A. Metcalf. <u>Destructive and Useful Insects: Their Habits and Control</u>. 5th ed. New York: McGraw, 1993.

L. A book or a monograph that is part of a series

Simon, Rita James. <u>The Jury System in America: A Critical Overview</u>. Sage Criminal Justice System Annuals 4. Beverly Hills: Sage, 1975.

M. A multivolume work

If you have used only one volume of a multivolume work, cite only that volume.

Tierney, Helen, ed. <u>Women's Studies Encyclopedia</u>. Rev. ed. Vol. 2. Westport: Greenwood, 1999. 3 vols.

If you have used more than one volume of a multivolume work, cite the entire work.

Tierney, Helen, ed. <u>Women's Studies Encyclopedia</u>. Rev. ed. 3 vols. Westport: Greenwood, 1999.

N. A volume with its own title that is part of a multivolume work with a different title

Cremin, Lawrence A. <u>The National Experience, 1783–1876</u>. New York: Harper, 1980. Vol. 2 of <u>American Education</u>. 3 vols. 1970–88.

O.   A republished book or a literary work available in several editions

Give the date of the original publication after the title. Then give complete publication information, including the date, for the edition that you have used.

Hemingway, Ernest. <u>The Sun Also Rises</u>. 1926. New York: Scribner, 1954.

P.   A government publication

Give the name of the government (country or state). Then give the department if applicable, followed by the agency if applicable. Next give the title, followed by the author if known. Then give the publication information. The publisher of U.S. government documents is usually the Government Printing Office, or GPO.

United States. Dept. of Labor. Bureau of Labor Statistics. <u>Perspectives on Working Women: A Databook</u>. By Howard Hayghe and Beverly L. Johnson. Washington: GPO, 1980.

- - -. Dept. of Health and Human Services. U.S. Public Health Service. Centers for Disease Control and Prevention. <u>The ABCs of Safe and Healthy Child Care: A Handbook for Child Care Providers</u>. Washington: GPO, 1996.

Parts of Books

A.   A poem, a short story, an essay, or a chapter in a collection of works by one author

Hawthorne, Nathaniel. "Young Goodman Brown." <u>The Portable Hawthorne</u>. Ed. Malcolm Cowley. Rev. ed. New York: Viking, 1969. 53–68.

B.   A poem, a short story, an essay, or a chapter in a collection of works by several authors

Faulkner, William. "Race and Fear." <u>Voices in Black and White</u>. Ed. Katharine Whittemore and Gerald Marzorati. New York: Franklin, 1993. 83–94.

C.   A novel or a play in an anthology

Cather, Willa. <u>My Mortal Enemy</u>. <u>The Norton Anthology of American Literature</u>. Ed. Nina Baym. 4th ed. Vol. 2. New York: Norton, 1994. 975–1025.

D. **An introduction, a preface, a foreword, or an afterword written by the author(s) of a work**

Bloom, Harold. Introduction. <u>Modern Crime and Suspense Writers</u>. Ed. Harold Bloom. New York: Chelsea, 1995. xi–xii.

E. **An introduction, a preface, a foreword, or an afterword written by someone other than the author(s) of a work**

Primack, Marshall P. Foreword. <u>Phobia: The Crippling Fears</u>. By Arthur Henley. Secaucus: Stuart, 1987. 1–4.

F. **Cross-references**

If you have used more than one work from a collection, you may give a complete entry for the collection. Then, in the separate entries for the works, you can refer to the entry for the whole collection by using the editor's last name or, if you have listed more than one work by that editor, the editor's last name and a shortened version of the title.

French, Warren G., ed. <u>A Companion to</u> The Grapes of Wrath. New York: Viking, 1963.

- - -. "What Did John Steinbeck Know About the 'Okies'?" French, <u>Companion</u> 51–53.

Steinbeck, John. <u>Their Blood Is Strong</u>. 1938. French, <u>Companion</u> 53–92.

G. **A reprinted article or essay (one previously published elsewhere)**

If a work that appears in a collection first appeared in another place, give complete information for the original publication, followed by *Rpt. in* and complete information for the collection.

Searle, John. "What Is a Speech Act?" <u>Philosophy in America</u>. Ed. Max Black. London: Allen, 1965. 221–39. Rpt. in <u>Readings in the Philosophy of Language</u>. Ed. Jay F. Rosenberg and Charles Travis. Englewood Cliffs: Prentice, 1971. 614–28.

Magazines, Journals, Newspapers, and Encyclopedias

A. **An article in a magazine, a journal, or a newspaper**

Allen, Jodie. "Working Out Welfare." <u>Time</u> 29 July 1996: 53–54.

"Dumping by the Coast Guard." Editorial. <u>New York Times</u> 6 Sept. 1998, late ed., sec. 4: 10.

Eisenberg, David M., et al. "Unconventional Medicine in the United States: Prevalence, Costs, and Patterns of Use." <u>New England Journal of Medicine</u> 328.4 (1993): 246–52.

B. An article in an encyclopedia or other alphabetically organized reference work
Give the title of the article, the name of the reference work, and the year of the edition.

"Storytelling," The World Book Encyclopedia. 1999 ed.

C. A review

Schwarz, Benjamin. "Was the Great War Necessary?" Rev. of The Pity of War, by Niall Ferguson. Atlantic Monthly May 1999: 118–28.

Miscellaneous Print and Nonprint Sources

A. An interview you have conducted or a letter you have received
Jackson, Jesse. Personal interview [or, Letter to the author]. 15 July 1992.

B. A film

Star Wars. Screenplay by George Lucas. Dir. George Lucas. Perf. Mark Hamill, Harrison Ford, Carrie Fisher, and Alec Guinness. 20th Century Fox, 1977.

C. A work of art (painting, photograph, sculpture)

Ward, John Quincy Adams. The Freedman. The Art Institute of Chicago, Chicago.

D. A television or a radio program
Give the episode name (if applicable) and the series or the program name. Include any information that you have about the program's writer and director. Then give the network, the local station, the city, and the date of the airing of the program.

"A Desert Blooming." Writ. Marshall Riggan. Living Wild. Dir. Harry L. Gorden. PBS. WTTW, Chicago. 29 Apr. 1984.

E. A musical composition
Chopin, Frédéric. Waltz in A-flat major, op. 42.

F. A recording (compact disc, LP, or audiocassette)
If the recording is not a compact disc, include *LP* or *audiocassette* before the manufacturer's name.

Marsalis, Wynton. "Fuchsia." Think of One. Columbia, 1983.

G. A lecture, a speech, or an address

Give the name of the speaker followed by the name of the speech, if available, or the kind of speech (*Lecture, Introduction, Address*). Then give the event, the place, and the date.

King, Martin Luther, Jr. Speech. Lincoln Memorial, Washington, D.C., 28 Aug. 1963.

Electronic Publications

The number of electronic information sources is great and increasing rapidly, so please refer to the most current edition of the MLA Handbook for Writers of Research Papers *if you need more guidance. You can also refer to "MLA Style" on the Modern Language Association Web site <http://www.mla.org/>.*

Portable databases (CD-ROMs, DVDs, laser discs, diskettes, and videocassettes)

These products contain fixed information (information that cannot be changed unless a new version is produced and released). Citing them in a research paper is similar to citing printed sources. You should include the following information:

- Name of the author, if applicable
- Title of the part of the work used (underlined or in quotation marks)
- Title of the product or the database (underlined)
- Publication medium (CD-ROM, DVD, laser disc, diskette, or videocassette)
- Edition, release, or version, if applicable
- City of publication
- Name of publisher
- Year of publication

If you cannot find some of this information, cite what is available.

"Steinbeck's Dust Bowl Saga." Our Times Multimedia Encyclopedia of the 20th Century. CD-ROM. 1996 ed. Redwood City: Vicarious, 1995.

Eyes on the Prize: America's Civil Rights Years, 1954–1965. Prod. Blackside. 6 videocassettes. PBS Video, 1986.

Beowulf. Great Literature. CD-ROM. 1992 ed. Parsippany: Bureau Development, 1992.

"Jump at the Sun: Zora Neale Hurston and the Harlem Renaissance." <u>American Stories</u>. Videodisc. Evanston: McDougal, 1998.

Online Sources

Sources on the World Wide Web are numerous and include scholarly projects, reference databases, articles in periodicals, and professional and personal sites. Not all sites are equally reliable, and therefore material cited from the World Wide Web should be evaluated carefully. Entries for online sources in the Works Cited list should contain as much of the information listed below as available.

- Name of the author, editor, compiler or translator, followed by an abbreviation, such as *ed., comp.,* or *trans.,* if appropriate
- Title of the material accessed. Use quotation marks for poems, short stories, articles, or similar short works. Underline the title of a book.
- Publication information for any print version of the source
- Title (underlined) of the scholarly project, database, periodical, or professional or personal site. For a professional or personal site with no title, add a description such as *Home page* (neither underlined nor in quotes).
- Name of the editor of the scholarly project or database, if available
- For a journal, the volume number, issue number, or other identifying number
- Date of the electronic publication, of the latest update, or of a posting
- For a work from a subscription service, list the name of the service and—if a library is the subscriber—the name of the library, its city, and the state abbreviation.
- The number range or total number of pages, paragraphs, or other sections, if they are numbered
- Name of any institution or organization that sponsors or is associated with the Web site
- Date the source was accessed
- Electronic address, or URL, of the source. For a subscription service, use the URL of the service's main page (if known) or the keyword assigned by the service.

Scholarly project
Documenting the American South. Aug. 1999. Academic Affairs
    Lib., U of North Carolina at Chapel Hill. 11 Aug. 1999
    <http://metalab.unc.edu/docsouth/>.

Professional site
American Council of Learned Societies Home Page. 13 Aug. 1999
    <http://www.acls.org/jshome.htm>.

Personal site
Fitzgerald, Evan. A Students' Guide to Butterflies. 5 July 1999.
    The Butterfly Farm S.A. 11 Aug. 1999
    <http://www.butterflyfarm.co.cr/farmer/bfly1.htm>.

Book
Poe, Edgar Allan. Tales. New York: Wiley, 1845. "A Digitized Library
    of Southern Literature: Beginnings to 1920." Documenting the
    American South. 16 Sept. 1998. Academic Affairs Lib., U of
    North Carolina at Chapel Hill. 13 Aug. 1999
    <http://metalab.unc.edu/docsouth/poe/poe.html>.

Article in reference database
"Dickinson, Emily." Encyclopaedia Britannica Online. Vers. 99.1.
    11 Aug. 1999 <http://www.eb.com:180/bol/
    topic?eu=30830&sctn=1#s–top>.

Article in journal
Tanter, Marcy, and Diana Wagner. "New Dickinson Letter Clarifies
    Hale Correspondence." Emily Dickinson Journal 7.1 (1998):
    110–117. 29 July 1999 <http://MUSE.JHU.EDU/
    demo/emily_dickinson_journal/7.1wagner.html>.

Article in magazine
Swerdlow, Joel L. "The Power of Writing." National Geographic
    Aug. 1999. 28 July 1999
    <http://www.nationalgeographic.com/ngm/9908/fngm/
    index.html>.

Work from a subscription service
"Cinco de Mayo." Compton's Encyclopedia Online. Vers. 3.0.
    1998. America Online. 29 July 1999. Keyword: Compton's.

Weiss, Peter. "Competing Students' Science Skills Sparkle."
    Science News 30 Jan. 1999: 71. InfoTrac SearchBank,
    General Reference database. Online. The Gale Group.
    Evanston Public Lib., Evanston. 16 Aug. 1999
    <http://www.searchbank.com/searchbank/evanston_main>.

Glossary for Writers

Allegory	a story in which the major events and characters have hidden or symbolic meanings. A quarrel between friends, for example, might represent a conflict between their native cultures.
Alliteration	the repetition of beginning sounds of words in poetry or prose; for example, the "c" sound in "creeping cat"
Allusion	a reference to a historical or literary person, place, event, or aspect of culture
Analogy	a comparison used to explain an idea or support an argument. For example, an analogy for how a government works might be a family.
Analysis	a way of thinking that involves taking apart, examining, and explaining a subject or an idea
Anecdote	a brief story told as an example to illustrate a point
Argument	speaking or writing that expresses a position or states an opinion with supporting evidence. An argument often takes into account other points of view.
Audience	one's readers or listeners
Autobiography	a biography (life story) told by the person whose life it is
Bias	a preference to lean toward one side in an argument; to be unbiased is to be neutral
Bibliography	a list of sources (articles, books, encyclopedias) in a paper or report used to document research or to recommend further study
Body	the main part of a composition, in which its ideas are developed
Brainstorming	a way of generating ideas that involves quickly listing ideas as they occur without stopping to judge them
Cause and Effect	a strategy of analysis that examines the reasons for actions or events, and the consequences or results of those actions

Characterization	the way people (characters) are portrayed by an author
Chronological	organized according to time sequence
Clarity	the quality of being clear and easy to understand
Classification	a way of organizing information by grouping or categorizing items according to some system or principle
Cliché	an overused expression, such as "quiet as a mouse"
Clustering	a brainstorming technique that involves creating an idea or topic map made up of circled groupings of related details
Coherence	connectedness; a sense that parts hold together. A paragraph has coherence when its sentences flow logically from one to the next. A composition has coherence when its paragraphs are connected logically and linked by transitional words and phrases.
Collaboration	the act of working with other people on projects or to problem solve
Colloquial	characteristic of conversational style in speech or writing; linguistically informal, the way people ordinarily speak in conversation
Comparison and Contrast	a pattern of organization in which two or more things are related on the basis of similarities and differences
Conclusion	a judgment or a decision that is reached based on evidence, experience, and logical reasoning; also, the final section of a composition that summarizes an argument or main idea with added insight, and points the reader toward action or further reflection
Connotation	the meaning of a word that carries ideas and feelings, as opposed to the word's strictly literal definition (denotation)
Context	the setting or situation in which something happens; the parts of a statement that occur just before and just after a specific word and help determine its meaning

Controversy	a disagreement, often one that has attracted public interest
Counter-argument	a refutation; an argument made to oppose (counter) another argument
Critical Thinking	what a writer *does* with information; thinking that goes substantially beyond the facts to organize, analyze, evaluate, or draw conclusions about them
Criticism	discourse (usually an essay) that analyzes something (usually a literary or artistic work) in order to evaluate how it does or does not succeed in communicating its meaning
Cubing	a method for discovering ideas about a topic by using six strategies of investigation (in any order): describing, comparing, associating, analyzing, applying, and arguing for or against
Deconstruction	the process of taking apart for the purpose of analysis
Deductive Reasoning	the process of deriving a specific conclusion by reasoning from a general premise
Denotation	the meaning of a word that is strictly literal, as found in the dictionary, as opposed to the ideas and feelings the word carries (connotation)
Descriptive Writing	an account, usually giving a dominant impression and emphasizing sensory detail, of what it is like to experience some object, scene, or person
Dialect	a form of a language (usually regional) that has a distinctive pronunciation, vocabulary, and word order
Dialogue	spoken conversation of fictional characters or actual persons; the conversation in novels, stories, plays, poems, or essays
Documentation	the identification of documents or other sources used to support the information reported in an essay or other discourse; usually cited in footnotes or in parentheses
Editorial	an article in a publication or a commentary on radio or television expressing an opinion about a public issue

Elaboration the support or development of a main idea with facts, statistics, sensory details, incidents, examples, quotations, or visual representations

Evaluation writing that purposefully judges the worth, quality, or success of something

Expository Writing writing that explains an idea or teaches a process; also called informative writing

Expressive characterized by expression; refers to descriptive discourse full of meaning or feeling, often used by writers in personal writing to explore ideas

Fiction made-up or imaginary happenings as opposed to statements of fact or nonfiction. Short stories and novels are fiction, even though they may be based on real events; essays, scientific articles, biographies, news stories are nonfiction.

Figurative Language language that displays the imaginative and poetic use of words; writing that contains figures of speech such as simile, metaphor, and personification

Formal Language language in which rules of grammar and vocabulary standards are carefully observed; used in textbooks, reports, and other formal communications

Freewriting a way of exploring ideas, thoughts, or feelings that involves writing freely—without stopping or otherwise limiting the flow of ideas—for a specific length of time

Gender Neutral refers to language that includes both men and women when making reference to a role or a group that comprises people of both sexes. "A medic uses his or her skills to save lives" and "Medics use their skills to save lives" are two gender-neutral ways of expressing the same idea.

Generalization a statement expressing a principle or drawing a conclusion based on examples or instances

Gleaning a method of picking up ideas to write about by observing events, by scanning newspapers, magazines, and books, and by talking to others

Graphic Device a visual way of organizing information. Graphic devices include charts, graphs, outlines, clusters, and diagrams.

Idea Tree	a graphic device in which main ideas are written on "branches" and related details are noted on "twigs"
Imagery	figurative language and descriptions used to produce mental images
Inductive Reasoning	a method of thinking or organizing a discourse so that a series of instances or pieces of evidence lead to a conclusion or generalization
Inference	a logical assumption that is made based on observed facts and one's own knowledge and experience
Informative Writing	writing that explains an idea or teaches a process; also called expository writing
Interpretation	an explanation of the meaning of any text, set of facts, object, gesture, or event. To interpret something is to try to make sense of it.
Introduction	the opening section of a composition, which presents the main idea, grabs the reader's attention, and sets the tone
Invisible writing	writing done with a dimmed computer screen or with an empty ballpoint pen on two sheets of paper with carbon paper between them
Irony	a figure of speech in which the intended meaning is the opposite of the stated meaning—saying one thing and meaning another
Jargon	the special language and terminology used by people in the same profession or with specialized interests
Journal	a record of thoughts and impressions, mainly for personal use
Learning Log	a kind of journal used for recording and reflecting on what one has learned and for noting problems and questions
Literary Analysis	critical thinking and writing about literature that presents a personal perspective
Looping	a repetitive process for discovering ideas on a topic through freewriting, stopping to find promising ideas, then producing another freewriting on that subject, and repeating the loop several times

Media : various forms of mass communication, such as newspapers, magazines, radio, television, and the Internet; the editorial voice and influence of all of these

Memoir : an account of true events told by a narrator who witnessed or participated in the events; usually focuses on the personalities and actions of persons other than the writer

Metaphor : a figure of speech that makes a comparison without using the word *like* or *as.* "All the world's a stage" is a metaphor.

Monologue : a speech by one person without interruption by other voices. A dramatic monologue reveals the personality and experience of a person through a long speech.

Mood : the feeling about a scene or a subject created for a reader by a writer's selection of words and details. The mood of a piece of writing may be suspenseful, mysterious, peaceful, fearful, and so on.

Narrative Writing : writing that tells a story—either made up or true. Some common types of narrative writing are biographies, short stories, and novels.

Onomatopoeia : the use of words (usually in poetry) to suggest sounds; examples are "the clinking of knives and forks," and "the trilling of a flute."

Order of Degree : a pattern of organization in which ideas, people, places, or things are presented in rank order on the basis of quantity or extent. An example is listing items in order from most important to least important.

Paraphrase : a restatement of an original passage in one's own words that stays true to the original ideas, tone, and general length

Parenthetical Documentation : the placement of citations or other documentation in parentheses within the text

Peer Response : suggestions and comments provided by peers or classmates on a piece of writing

Personal Writing : writing that focuses on expressing the writer's own thoughts, experiences, and feelings

Personification	a figure of speech in which objects, events, abstract ideas, or animals are given human characteristics
Persuasive Writing	writing that is intended to convince the reader of a particular point of view or course of action
Plagiarism	the act of dishonestly presenting someone else's words or ideas as one's own
Point of View	the angle from which a story is told, such as first-, second-, or third-person point of view
Portfolio	a container (usually a folder) for notes on work in progress, drafts and revisions, finished pieces, and peer responses
Précis	a short summary or abstract of an essay, story, or speech, capturing only the essential elements
Proofreading	the act of checking work to discover typographical and other errors; usually the last stage of the revising or editing process
Propaganda	discourse aimed at persuading an audience, often containing distortions of truth; usually refers to manipulative political discourse
Prose	the usual language of speech and writing, lacking the special properties of meter and form that define poetry; any language that is not poetry
Satire	a literary form that ridicules or mocks the social practices or values of a society, a group, or an important individual
Sensory Details	words that express attributes of the five senses—the way something looks, sounds, smells, tastes, or feels
Sequential Order	a pattern of organization in which information is presented in the order in which it occurs, as in telling a story chronologically or describing the sequence of steps in a process
Simile	a figure of speech that uses the word *like* or *as* to make a comparison. "Trees like pencil strokes" is a simile.
Spatial Order	a pattern of organization in which details are arranged in the order that they appear in space, such as from left to right

Style	the distinctive features of a literary or artistic work that collectively characterize a particular individual, group, period, or school
Summary	a brief restatement of the main idea of a passage
Symbol	something (word, object, or action) that stands for or suggests something else. For example, a flag can stand for or symbolize a nation; a withered plant may suggest or symbolize a failing relationship.
Synthesis	the combining of separate elements to form a coherent whole
Theme	the underlying idea or central concern of a work of art or literature
Thesis Statement	a statement in one or two sentences of the main idea or purpose of a piece of writing
Tone	the writer's attitude or manner of expression—detached, ironic, serious, angry, and so on
Topic Sentence	a sentence that expresses the main idea of a paragraph
Transition	a connecting word or phrase that clarifies relationships between details, sentences, or paragraphs
Tree Diagram	a graphic way of showing the relationships among ideas; particularly useful in generating ideas; also known as an idea tree or spider map
Trite Phrase	a phrase used so much that it loses meaning and suggests a lack of imagination on the part of the user
Unity	a consistent focus on a single writing purpose. A paragraph has unity if all its sentences support the same main idea or purpose; a composition has unity if all its paragraphs support the thesis statement.
Venn Diagram	a way of visually representing the relationship between two items that are distinct but that have common or overlapping elements
Voice	the "sound" of a writer's work determined by stylistic choices such as sentence structure, diction, and tone

Index

RESOURCES

indenting, 270
punctuation of, 269–270
Excessive language, 397
Exclamation points, 249
with exclamatory sentences, 44, 249
with imperative sentences, 44, 248
with interjections, 29, 249
with parenthetical information, 263
with quotation marks, 268, 269, 279
Exclamatory sentences, exclamation
points for, 44, 249
Expert opinion
for elaboration, 357, 363
as information source, 494
in persuasive essay, 440
Explanation, elaboration for, 360–361
Expletives, 46
Expository writing. *See*
Informative/expository writing;
Research report
Extemporaneous method of delivering a
speech, 525, 533
Eye contact
in delivering a speech, 526
as nonverbal cue, 521
E-zines, 538

F

Facial expression
in delivering a speech, 526
as nonverbal cue, 521
Facilitator of a group, 530
Facts
in drawing conclusions, 506
for elaboration, 357, 361
identifying, 500
in informative/expository paragraphs,
326
in introduction of a composition, 342
opinions distinguished from, 500–501
in persuasive writing, 325, 436, 440
in problem-solution essay, 448
types of, 500
Fallacies. *See* Logical Fallacies
False analogy, 508, 515
Family relationships, capitalization of,
229, 244, 245
Feedback. *See also* Peer response
in oral communication, 518, 532
to speeches, 527
Figurative language, 301
for effective language, 400
in focused description, 419
in poetry, 458
as style element, 389, 394–395
Figures of speech. *See also* Hyperbole;
Metaphors; Similes
personification, 395, 457

for style, 394–395
webs of words for developing, 401
Fill-in-the-blank test questions, 587
Film. *See* Movies
first, comma after, 251
First-person pronouns
personal, 9
reflexive and intensive, 11
First words, capitalization of, 231–233,
245
Flashbacks, for autobiographical incident,
407
Flow charts, 493
for multimedia presentations, 557
for organizing information, 311
for Web site design, 560
Focused description, writing workshop for,
412–419
for
commas with, 255, 257
as coordinating conjunction, 26
Foreign words or phrases, italics for, 273
Form
defining for writing, 309
examples of, 309, 321
Formal language
abbreviations in, 249
informal language compared with, 390
as style element, 389
Fractions
hyphens in spelled-out, 265
as singular or plural, 165
Fragments. *See* Sentence fragments
Freewriting
for focused description, 415
for persuasive essay, 440
for poetry, 457
in topic selection, 308
Future perfect progressive tense, 138
Future perfect tense, 134
using, 136
Future progressive tense, 138
Future tense
as simple tense, 134
using, 135

G

Game titles, capitalization of, 232
Gatekeepers, 539
Gender, pronoun-antecedent agreement in,
189, 204
Generalizations, 507. *See also*
Overgeneralization
General pronoun reference, 197
General Science Index, 486
General Ideas. *See* Prewriting
Geographical names, capitalization of,
234

Gerund phrases, 73
    for description, 85
    diagramming, 82
Gerunds, 73–74
    possessive pronouns modifying, 183
    present participles distinguished from, 73, 183
Gestures
    in delivering a speech, 526
    as nonverbal cue, 521
god, 229
goddess, 229
good, 212
Graphic organizers cluster chart, 415
    Venn diagrams, 311, 503
Graphics
    charts, 357, 365, 492–493, 560, 567.
    diagrams, 357, 364, 492
    for elaboration, 364–365, 367
    graphs, 357, 365, 492–493
    images, 357, 364, 544
    in print or Web site design, 544
    reading and analyzing, 492–493
    tables, 492, 493
    types of, 492–493
Graphs
    for elaboration, 357, 365
    reading and analyzing, 492–493
Greek word roots, 577
Greeting of a letter, capitalization of, 231–232, 244, 245
Group communication, 530–531
    conflict resolution in, 531
    etiquette in groups, 530, 532
    roles in groups, 530

H
....
hardly, 212
Hard news, 536
have, as auxiliary verb, 15
Helping verbs. *See* Auxiliary (helping) verbs
here
    subject position in sentences beginning with, 46
    subject-verb agreement in sentences beginning with, 167
    and this, that, these, and those, 213
his or *her,* as singular, 189
Historical documents, capitalization of, 237
Historical events, capitalization of, 237
Historical periods, capitalization of, 237
Historical present tense, 136
History, reading and studying, 583, 596
Holidays, capitalization of, 238
House numbers, 257
Humanities Index, 486
Hyperbole, 522
Hyphenated words, 7, 265

Hyphens, 265–267
    in hyphenated words, 265
    for line breaks, 265

I, J, K
....
I, capitalization of, 229
Ideas
    for autobiographical incident, 410
    checking during revising, 314
    for focused description, 418
    in informative/expository paragraphs, 326
    for literary interpretation, 423
Idioms, 391, 400
Illogical comparisons, 218
Imagery
    action verbs for creating, 16
    in poetry, 454
    as style element, 389, 394
Images
    for elaboration, 357, 364
    in print or Web site design, 544
    sources of, 364
Imperative mood, 146
Imperative sentences, 44
    exclamation points for, 44, 248
    periods for, 248
    subject position in, 47
Implied main idea, 329
imply, 505
Impromptu method of delivering a speech, 525, 533
Incomplete questions, question marks with, 248
Indefinite article, 17
Indefinite pronoun reference, 197
Indefinite pronouns, 12
    as adjectives, 208
    apostrophes for forming possessives of, 266
    pronoun-antecedent agreement with, 191–193
    singular and plural, 12, 162, 191–192
    subject-verb agreement with, 162–163, 175
Independent clauses, 92
    colons between, 260
    comma and conjunction separating, 112, 255
    in complex sentences, 102
    in compound-complex sentences, 102, 106–107
    in compound sentences, 101
    conjunctive adverbs expressing relationships between, 27
    semicolons separating, 259
    in simple sentences, 101, 104
    subordinating conjunctions joining, 26

informal, 389, 390, 391
as style element, 389, 390–391
Libraries, 484–486
classification systems, 484, 497
finding materials in, 485
the library collection, 484
reference works in, 484, 487
special services, 486
Library catalog, 485
Library of Congress system, 484, 497
lie, lay, 152
Lighting
in television and film, 543
in video, 555
Line breaks, hyphens for, 265
Linking verbs, 14–15
Listening
active, 520–522, 532
creative, 520
critical, 520
empathic, 520
Lists
colons for introducing, 259
dashes to set off introductory, 262
parentheses for numbers or letters, 264
periods after each number in, 250
Literary criticism. *See* Literary
interpretation, writing workshop on
Literary interpretation, writing workshop
on, 420–427
Loaded language
analyzing in oral communication, 522
as appeal to emotion, 512–513
Logical fallacies, 508–510
cause-and-effect, 441
circular reasoning, 441, 449, 509, 515
either-or-thinking, 441, 449, 510, 515
false analogy, 508, 515
overgeneralization, 441, 449, 509, 515
in persuasive essay, 441
in problem-solution essay, 449
types of, 515
Logical reasoning
in persuasive essay, 436, 441
in persuasive paragraphs, 325
in problem-solution essay, 448–449
Logical relationships, 503–504. *See also*
Analogies
cause-and-effect, 502, 514, 568, 595
comparison, 503, 504, 567
contrast, 503, 514, 568
in problem-solution essay, 449
types of, 514
Long shots, 542

M

Magazine index, 486
Magazines

capitalization of titles, 232
citation form for, 665–666
italics for titles, 272
in library collection, 484
as news medium, 538
on-line versions, 538
for publishing your writing, 319
source cards for, 469
as source for elaboration, 366
Main clauses. *See* Independent clauses
Main idea, 327–328
implied, 329
in introduction of a composition, 338
the topic sentence identifying, 330,
339
Manuscript method of delivering a
speech, 525, 533
Matching test questions, 587
Mathematics, reading and studying, 582,
596
Meaning
in context, 571
definitions, 357, 360, 500, 567
denotation and connotation, 393, 572
multiple, 571
shades of, 566, 571–572, 577
synonyms and antonyms, 572
Measurement, periods used with
abbreviations, 249
Media, the. *See also* Internet; Movies;
Print media; Television
analyzing news in, 535–549
balanced reporting in, 541
choosing your medium, 552–553
citation forms for, 666–667
comparing, 545–547
creating media products, 551–563
deconstructing content, 539–541
deconstructing design, 542–544, 548
evaluating news stories, 549
factors affecting reporting, 539–541
how news is chosen, 540
how news is reported, 540–541
as news source, 536–538
standards for reporting, 539
types of, 537–538, 548
types of news, 536
who chooses the news, 539
Media center, 484–486
Memorization method of delivering a
speech, 525, 533
Message
evaluation of, 522
in oral communication, 517, 532
Metaphors
action verbs for creating, 16
for elaboration, 357, 359
in focused description, 419
mixing, 397

in poetry, 457
for style, 394–395
Metric measurements, periods not used
with abbreviations, 249
Misplaced modifiers, 78, 88
Mixed metaphors, 397
MLA citation guidelines, 662–669
Modifiers, 206–225, 291. *See also*
Adjectives; Adverbs
comparisons, 195, 215–219
dangling, 78, 85
misplaced, 78, 88, 291
in overloaded sentences, 372
prepositional phrases as, 23, 66
problems with, 211–214
for sentence variety, 381
and simple subjects and predicates, 38
for specificity, 31
Months, capitalization of, 238
Mood (of a verb), 146–147
imperative, 146
indicative, 146
subjunctive, 146
Mood (of a written work)
in poetry, 457
sentence types for varying, 44
Mountains, capitalization of, 234
Movies
capitalization of titles, 232
design in, 542–543
italics for titles, 272
lighting, 543
Multimedia presentations
choosing a medium, 552
creating, 557–559
designing, 558
developing, 558–559
evaluating and revising, 559
planning, 557
running, 559
storyboard, 554, 558
video, 554–556
in Web site design, 544
Multiple-choice test questions, 586
Music
capitalization of titles, 232
italics for titles of long compositions,
272
in television and film, 543

N

Name calling, 512
Names
businesses, 249, 256
capitalization of, 228, 237
organizations, 237, 241
personal, 228, 256
places, 234–236, 256

Narrative writing
in autobiographical incident, 407
paragraphs in, 324–325
Nationalities, capitalization of, 229
Nations, capitalization of, 234
Negative comparisons, 215
never
in double negatives, 212
in overgeneralizations, 509
as vague, 449
News
analyzing media news, 535–549
balanced reporting of, 541
bias in news reporting, 541, 558
comparing the media, 545–547
deconstructing content, 539–541
deconstructing design, 542–544, 548
evaluating, 549
factors affecting reporting, 539–541
how news is chosen, 540
how news is reported, 540–541
the media as source, 536–538
standards for reporting, 539
types of, 536
types of news media, 537–538, 548
who chooses the news, 539
Newscasts, 537
News features, 536
Newsmagazines (television), 537
Newspapers
capitalization of titles, 232
citation forms for, 665–666
indexes of, 486
italics for titles, 272
as news medium, 538, 546
on-line versions, 538
for publishing your writing, 319
source cards for, 469
as source for elaboration, 366
no, 212
Nominative case, for personal pronouns,
178, 179–180, 204
none
in double negatives, 212
as vague, 449
Nonessential (nonrestrictive) adjective
clauses, 95, 112
Nonessential (nonrestrictive) appositives,
69, 253, 375–376, 384
Nonverbal cues
in delivering a speech, 526
examining, 521
no one, in overgeneralizations, 509
north, 234
not, 212
Note taking
in group communication, 530
for research reports, 470–471, 472
Noun clauses, 98–100

revising, 477
sharing and reflecting on, 477
sources for, 468–469
thesis statement for, 472
topics for, 467, 478
your own ideas and interpretations in, 475
Response to literature. *See* Literary interpretation, writing workshop on
Restrictive (essential) adjective clauses, 95
Restrictive (essential) appositives, 69, 253, 375–376, 384
Revising, 314–316
of autobiographical incident, 408
of cause-and-effect essay, 432
combining sentences, 373–376, 385
of focused description, 416
inserting words and phrases, 377–378
of literary interpretation, 424
for parallelism, 379–380
of persuasive essay, 442
of poetry, 458
problem sentences, 370–372, 384
of problem-solution essay, 450
research reports, 477
sentences, 369–385
subject-verb agreement when changing number, 156
for variety in sentences, 109, 381–383
of a video, 556
of a Web site, 561
Rhyme, in poetry, 454, 457
rise, raise, 152
Road names, capitalization of, 234
Roots of words, 569, 577
Run-on sentences, 120–121
checking during editing, 317
comma splices, 120
correcting, 127, 283
from omitting comma and conjunction between clauses, 255

S

Sacred days, capitalization of, 229
Sacred writings, capitalization of, 229
Salutation of a letter, comma after, 256
SAT 1 (Standardized Aptitude Test), 590
scarcely, 212
School courses, capitalization of, 238
School years, capitalization of, 238
Science, reading and studying, 583, 596
Screen templates, 558
Search engines, 489–490
Searching the Web, 489–490
Seasons, capitalization of, 238
second, comma after, 251
Secondary sources, 468

Second-person pronouns
personal, 9
reflexive and intensive, 11
Semicolons, 259–261
in clauses, 112
in compound sentences, 101, 259
between independent clauses, 259
with quotation marks, 269, 279
for run-on sentences, 120
in series, 259
Sensory details
in descriptive paragraphs, 324
for elaboration, 357, 358
in focused description, 415, 416
Sentence combining, 373–378
conjunctions for, 27
by inserting an appositive, 378, 385
by inserting a phrase, 377–378, 385
by inserting a word, 377, 385
parts of sentences, 374, 385
with relative pronouns, 375–376, 385
whole sentences, 373–374, 385
Sentence completion test questions, 591
Sentence fragments, 116–119
checking during editing, 317
compound verbs as, 118
correcting, 126, 282
items in a series as, 118
phrases as, 117
subject or predicate missing, 38
subordinate clauses as, 92, 93, 116–117
Sentences, 36–63, 294–297. *See also* Sentence structure
basic parts of, 38, 62
capitalization of first word of, 231, 244
combining, 27, 373–378, 385
complete, 114–127
declarative, 44, 248
diagramming, 54–57, 80–83, 104–107
exclamatory, 44, 249
fluency, 315–316
fragments, 38, 92, 93, 116–119, 126, 317
imperative, 44, 47, 248
inverted, 46, 167
overloaded, 294, 372, 384
parallelism in, 379–380
problem, 370–372, 384
revising, 369–385
run-on, 120–121, 127, 255, 317
stringy, 371, 384
tightening content in, 295, 370
topic sentence, 328–329, 334, 339, 347
types of, 44–45
variety in, 45, 381–383, 424

T

Tables, reading and analyzing, 492, 493
Tabloids, 538
Tabloid television shows, 537
Technical terms, 522
Television
    capitalization of titles of shows, 232
    design in, 542–543
    italics for titles of shows, 272
    lighting, 543
    as news medium, 537, 545
    quotation marks for titles of shows,
      270
Temperatures, apostrophes not used in,
    267
Tenses of verbs, 134–137
    checking during editing, 317
    future, 134–136
    past, 130, 134, 135, 136
    perfect, 134, 136
    present, 130, 134, 135, 136
    shifts in, 143
    simple, 134, 135
    verb phrases for expressing, 15
Testimonials, 512
Tests, 581–597
    active reading strategies, 582
    classroom tests, 585–587, 596
    content areas, 582–584, 596
    essay questions, 588–589, 597
    history, 583, 596
    mathematics, 582, 596
    objective questions, 585–587
    science, 584, 596
    standardized language tests, 590–592
    standardized vocabulary tests,
      593–595
    study and review strategies, 585
than, in comparisons, 195
that
    for combining sentences, 375
    without comma, 375, 384
    as demonstrative pronoun, 11
    for introducing adjective clauses, 95
    rules for adjectival use of, 213
them, and *this, that, these,* and *those,* 213
there
    subject position in sentences
      beginning with, 46
    subject-verb agreement in sentences
      beginning with, 167
    with *this, that, these,* and *those,* 213
Thesaurus, for vocabulary development,
    574
these
    as demonstrative pronoun, 11
    rules for adjectival use of, 213
Thesis statement, 341–342

the body of a composition developing,
    339
    in introduction of a composition, 338,
      340
    of persuasive essay, 440
    of research report, 472
    of a speech, 523
    for unity in a composition, 347
Third-person pronouns
    personal, 9
    reflexive and intensive, 11
this
    as demonstrative pronoun, 11
    rules for adjectival use of, 213
those
    as demonstrative pronoun, 11
    rules for adjectival use of, 213
Time abbreviations
    capitalization of, 238, 241
    periods with, 249
Timelines, for organizing information, 311
Time order. *See* Chronological order
Titles (of works)
    capitalization of, 232–233, 241, 244,
      245
    italics for, 272, 278
    quotation marks for, 270, 278
    subject-verb agreement with, 165
Titles (personal)
    capitalization of, 228, 241
    periods with abbreviations of, 249
to, in infinitives and prepositional
      phrases, 75
Tone
    sentence types for varying, 44, 47
    as style element, 389
Topics
    for cause-and-effect essay, 431
    exploring and limiting, 310–311
    finding, 308–309
    for persuasive essay, 439–440, 444
    of problem-solution essay, 448, 452
    for research reports, 467, 478
Topic sentences, 328–329
    in body of a composition, 339
    developing, 329
    implied, 329
    for unity in a composition, 347
    ways to write, 334
Towns
    capitalization of, 234
    comma separating from state,
      province, or country, 256
Townships, capitalization of, 234
Train names, capitalization of, 235
Transitional words and phrases
    for cause-and-effect order, 331
    for coherence in compositions,
      350–351, 353

Acknowledgments

For Literature and Text

Andrews McMeel Publishing: Excerpt from the movie review "Who Framed Roger Rabbit" in *Roger Ebert's Movie Home Companion 1990 Edition* by Roger Ebert. Copyright © 1990 by Roger Ebert. Reprinted with permission of Andrews McMeel Publishing. All rights reserved.

The Apprentice Writer: "How To Make a Sweet Potato Pie" by Lauren Hart, *The Apprentice Writer*, vol. 15, 1997. Copyright © 1997 by *The Apprentice Writer*. Published by Susquehanna University. Reprinted by permission of *The Apprentice Writer*, Susquehanna University, Selinsgrove, Pennsylvania.

Elizabeth Barnett, Literary Executor: Excerpt from "Sonnet XXX" of *Fatal Interview*, from *Collected Poems* by Edna St. Vincent Millay (HarperCollins). Copyright © 1931, 1958 by Edna St. Vincent Millay and Norma Millay Ellis. Reprinted by permission of Elizabeth Barnett, Literary Executor.

Beacon Press: Excerpt from "The Sun" from *New and Selected Poems* by Mary Oliver. Copyright © 1992 by Mary Oliver. Reprinted by permission of Beacon Press, Boston.

Carcanet Press: Excerpt from "Bora Ring," from *Collected Poems, 1942-1985* by Judith Wright. Copyright © 1994 by Judith Wright. Reprinted by permission of Carcanet Press Limited.

Chicago Tribune: "One Man's Search for Light Amid the Darkness" by Patrick T. Reardon, a review of *Hunting for Hope: A Father's Journey* by Scott Russell Sanders, in the *Chicago Tribune*, January 29, 1999. Copyright © 1999 by the Chicago Tribune Company. Reprinted by permission of the Chicago Tribune Company.

Don Congdon Associates: Excerpt from "There Will Come Soft Rains" by Ray Bradbury. First published in *Collier's*, May 6, 1950. Copyright © 1950 by Crowell-Collier Publishing Company, renewed 1977 by Ray Bradbury. Reprinted by permission of Don Congdon Associates, Inc.

U.S. Senator Mike DeWine: Excerpt from "Safer Air Bags are Needed Now" by U.S. Senator Mike DeWine, *Chicago Tribune*, June 1, 1999. Copyright © 1999 by Senator Mike DeWine. Reprinted by permission of Senator Mike DeWine.

Sandra Dijkstra Literary Agency: Excerpt from "Fish Cheeks" by Amy Tan. First appeared in *Seventeen Magazine*. Copyright © 1987 by Amy Tan. Used by permission of Amy Tan and the Sandra Dijkstra Literary Agency.

Discover Magazine: Excerpt from "Celestial Mechanics" by Fred Guterl, *Discover Magazine*, May 1997. Copyright © 1997 by *Discover*. Reprinted by permission of *Discover Magazine*.

Misha Dworsky: Adaptation of "Extracurricular Sports Should Satisfy State Physical Education Requirement" by Misha Dworsky, *Black & White*, November 20, 1998, a publication of Walt Whitman High School, Bethesda, Maryland. Copyright © 1998 by Misha Dworsky. Used by permission of Misha Dworsky.

Nicholas Gage: Excerpt from "The Teacher Who Changed My Life" by Nicholas Gage, *Parade*, December 17, 1989. Reprinted from *A Place for Us* by Nicholas Gage. Copyright © 1989 by Nicholas Gage. Reprinted by permission of the author.

Ivan Golden: "Test Center Needed" by Ivan Golden, from the student newspaper *North Star*, May 9, 1997. Copyright © 1997 by *North Star*. Used by permission of Ivan Golden.

Gruner & Jahr USA Publishing: Excerpt from "25 Ways to Beat a Cold" by Julia Califano, *Family Circle*, January 7, 1997. Copyright © 1997 by Gruner & Jahr USA Publishing. Reprinted by permission of Gruner & Jahr USA Publishing.

Hanging Loose Press: "Walking" by Andrew Love. Reprinted from *Bullseye: Stories and Poems by Outstanding High School Writers*, edited by Mark Pawlak, et al. Copyright © 1995 by Hanging Loose Press.

Harper's Magazine: Excerpt from "The Leap" by Louise Erdrich, *Harper's Magazine*, March 1990. Copyright © 1990 by *Harper's Magazine*. Reproduced from the March 1990 issue by special permission of *Harper's Magazine*. All rights reserved.

Henry Holt & Company: Excerpt from "Birches" by Robert Frost, from *The Poetry of Robert Frost,* edited by Edward Connery Lathem. Copyright © 1944 by Robert Frost. Copyright 1916, © 1969 by Henry Holt & Company. Reprinted by permission of Henry Holt & Company, Inc.

Candice Rhodes Mast: "Stories" by Candice Rhodes, *Virginia Writing,* February 1995. Copyright © 1995 by Candice Rhodes Mast. Used by permission of the author.

National Geographic Society: Excerpt from "The Variety of Life" by Virginia Morell, *National Geographic,* February 1999. Copyright © 1999 by the National Geographic Society. Reprinted by permission of the National Geographic Society. All rights reserved.

Excerpt from "Africa's Wild Dogs" by Richard Conniff, *National Geographic,* May 1999. Copyright © 1999 by the National Geographic Society. Reprinted by permission of the National Geographic Society. All rights reserved.

The New York Times: Excerpt from "Girls and Computers," an editorial in *The New York Times,* October 19, 1998. Copyright © 1998 by *The New York Times.* Reprinted by permission.

Excerpt from "Remember El Niño? His Sister Has Shown Up, and She's Angry" by William K. Stevens, *The New York Times,* January 27, 1999. Copyright © 1999 by *The New York Times.* Reprinted by permission.

Newsweek: Excerpt from "It's Time to Open the Doors of Our Prisons" by Rufus King, *Newsweek,* April 19, 1999. Copyright © 1999 by Newsweek, Inc. Reprinted by permission. All rights reserved.

Pioneer Press: Excerpt from "Limit Use of Car Phones," *Evanston Review,* May 6, 1999. Copyright © 1999 by Pioneer Press. Used by permission of Pioneer Press.

St. Martin's Press: Excerpt from *Fighting Fire* by Caroline Paul. Copyright © 1998 by St. Martin's Press. Reprinted by permission of St. Martin's Press, LLC.

Illustrations by Daniel Guidera

1, 6, 7, 8, 11, 14, 20, 24, 29, 34, 35, 38, 40, 47, 51, 54, 57, 62, 63, 83, 88, 96, 112, 117, 118, 120, 126, 127, 131, 138, 152, 160, 174, 175, 179, 181, 185, 188, 192, 197, 205, 209, 215, 224, 228, 231, 238, 241, 244, 245, 246, 249, 268, 278, 307, 308 *top, bottom,* 310, 312, 315, 317, 321, 328, 333, 334, 341, 345, 352, 358, 361, 363, 366, 371, 372, 377, 383, 384, 390, 391 *top, bottom,* 396, 400, 418, 419, 475, 483 *background,* 486, 496 *top, bottom,* 505, 511, 514, 515, 518 *top left, top right, bottom right, bottom left,* 523, 526 *top left, bottom right,* 532 *top, bottom,* 536, 539, 548, 554, 556, 562 *top right, bottom right, left,* 567, 568, 569, 576, 577, 596.

Art Credits

CHAPTER 1   2–3 © Copyright 1999 PhotoDisc, Inc.; **4** *background* © James Balog/Tony Stone Images; *foreground* Tabletop by Sharon Hoogstraten; **6** © Manoj Shah/Tony Stone Images; **9** *Calvin and Hobbes* © 1986 Watterson. Dist. by Universal Press Syndicate. Reprinted with permission. All rights reserved; **19** *left* © George Hunter/Tony Stone Images; *right* © SuperStock; **22** © Jon Eisberg/FPG International/PNI; **27** © Robert Frerck/Tony Stone Images; **30** Photo by Sharon Hoogstraten; **35** © The New Yorker Collection 1998 Roz Chast from cartoonbank.com. All rights reserved.

CHAPTER 2   36 © Zig Leszczynski/Animals Animals; **43** *bottom right* © Copyright 1999 PhotoDisc, Inc.; **44** © 1997 Cindy Karp/Black Star; **46** AP/Wide World Photos; **53** Copyright 1999 by Kirby, Smith, Wilkins, www.roadsideamerica.com.

CHAPTER 3   64 *background* © Copyright MCMLXXXVIII Chris Sorensen. All rights reserved; *foreground* Photofest; **68** © Cicero Dias Viegas/The Image Bank/PNI; **72** © Luiz C. Marigo/Peter Arnold, Inc.; **75** © John R. MacGregor/Peter Arnold, Inc.; **76** © Werner H. Muller/Peter Arnold, Inc.; **84** *Springtime* (1885), Lionel Percy Smythe. Watercolor, $20\frac{3}{4}$" x $15\frac{1}{4}$", private collection. Photo by Christopher Newall; **86** © 1975 Tom McHugh, The National Audubon Society Collection/Photo Researchers, Inc.; **89** © Tribune Media Services, Inc. All rights reserved. Reprinted with permission.

CHAPTER 4   90 Photo by Sharon Hoogstraten; **93** *Peanuts* reprinted by permission of United Feature Syndicate, Inc.; 100 AP Photo/University of Florida, Ray Carson; **107** *Frank & Ernest* reprinted by permission of Newspaper Enterprise Association, Inc.; **108** *background* Photo by Sharon Hoogstraten; *foreground, Yellow Vase* (1990), Roy

Lichtenstein. Copyright © 1990 Estate of Roy Lichtenstein/Gemini G.E.L.

CHAPTER 5   **114** Photo by Sharon Hoogstraten; **119** © Bob Daemmrich/Stock, Boston/PNI; **122, 124** © Copyright 1999 PhotoDisc, Inc.

CHAPTER 6   **128** *background* Tabletop by Sharon Hoogstraten; *foreground* © C. Bruce Forster/AllStock/PNI; **135** © 1987 FarWorks, Inc. All rights reserved. Reprinted by permission; **140** AP/Wide World Photos; **153** © 1999 King Features Syndicate, Inc. World rights reserved. Reprinted with special permission of King Features Syndicate.

CHAPTER 7   **154** © 1980 Warner/MPTV; **159** © Universal Studios/Photofest; **161** © The New Yorker Collection 1991 Jack Ziegler from cartoonbank.com. All rights reserved; **163** © Hollywood Pictures/Photofest; **165** © Paramount/Photofest; **169** © 1996 Warner Bros./Photofest; **170** © Tri-Star/Photofest.

CHAPTER 8   **176** © Bill Lisenby/Corbis; **182** © Phyllis Picardi/Stock South/PNI; **186** *Peanuts* reprinted by permission of United Feature Syndicate, Inc.; **195** © 1982 FarWorks, Inc. All rights reserved. Reprinted by permission; **199** AP/Wide World Photos; **201** Photograph © Jim Whitmer; **202** Photograph © 1993 Bob Sacha.

CHAPTER 9   **206** © Steve Shapiro/Black Star/PNI; **210** *Miners in the Sierras* (1851–1852), Charles Christian Nahl and Frederick August Wenderoth. Oil on canvas. National Museum of American Art, Smithsonian Institution, Washington, D.C./Art Resource, NY; **212–213** Photo by Sharon Hoogstraten; **215** Corbis/Bob Rowan; **221** Courtesy Cluett, Peabody & Co., Inc.; **225** © The New Yorker Collection 1999 Danny Shanahan from cartoonbank.com. All rights reserved.

CHAPTER 10   **226** *background* © J. Harrison/Stock Boston/PNI; *foreground* Photo by Sharon Hoogstraten; **229** Photo by Sharon Hoogstraten; **235** Corbis/Kevin Fleming; **236** © Paul Damien/Tony Stone Images; **245** © The New Yorker Collection 1994 Eric Teitelbaum from cartoonbank.com. All rights reserved.

CHAPTER 11   **250** Corbis/Karl Weatherly; **258** © Copyright 1999 PhotoDisc, Inc.; **264** Corbis/Bettmann; **267** © Rosanne Olson/AllStock/PNI; **271, 275** © Copyright 1999 PhotoDisc, Inc.; **279** © 1999 David Sipress from cartoonbank.com. All rights reserved.

CHAPTER 12   **304–305, 306** *background, foreground* © Copyright 1999 PhotoDisc, Inc.; **312** *top* © The New Yorker Collection 1996 Charles Barsotti from cartoonbank.com. All rights reserved.

CHAPTER 13   **322** *background* © Jason Langer/Image Bank; *foreground* © 1992 Dick Luria/FPG International; **323** *background* Photo by Sharon Hoogstraten; *foreground* © Jim Corwin/AllStock/PNI; **326** © Copyright 1999 PhotoDisc, Inc.; **332** © Jeff Greenberg/PhotoEdit.

CHAPTER 14   **336** *left, right* © Copyright 1999 PhotoDisc, Inc.; **337** © 1999 Annie Leibovitz, Contact Press Images; **346** © Ales Fevzer/Corbis.

CHAPTER 15   **354** *background, foreground* © Copyright 1999 PhotoDisc, Inc.; **355** *background* Donald Johnston © Tony Stone Images; *foreground* © Patti McConville/The Image Bank; **356** © *The New Yorker Collection 1998* J. B. Handelsman from cartoonbank.com. All rights reserved; **364** AP/Wide World Photos; **367** © Image Club.

CHAPTER 16   **368** © Copyright 1999 PhotoDisc, Inc.; **369** *background* Photo by Sharon Hoogstraten; *foreground* © Copyright 1999 PhotoDisc, Inc.; **373** © Corbis; **374** AP/Wide World Photos; **375** *Wonder Woman* is a trademark of DC Comics © 1999. Used with permission; **376** *Peanuts* reprinted by permission of United Feature Syndicate, Inc.; **379** © 1999 Lawrence Barns/Black Star; 381 AP/Wide World Photos.

CHAPTER 17   **386** *background, foreground* © Copyright 1999 PhotoDisc, Inc.; **387** Photo by Sharon Hoogstraten; **392** © The New Yorker Collection 1986 Henry Martin from cartoonbank.com. All rights reserved; **396** © 1986 FarWorks, Inc. All rights reserved. Reprinted by permission; **401** © 1999 United Feature Syndicate, Inc.

CHAPTER 18   **402–403** © Tony Stone Images; **409** *top right* Photograph © Rex Rystedt; *bottom right* © Copyright 1999 PhotoDisc, Inc.; *bottom left* Jacket-design from *All but My Life* by Gerda Weissmann Klein. Copyright © 1957 and copyright renewed © 1995 by Gerda Weissmann Klein. Reprinted by permission of Hill and Wang, a division of Farrar, Straus and Giroux, LLC.

CHAPTER 19 **417** *top* © Chris Johns/National Geographic; *bottom right* © Copyright 1999 PhotoDisc, Inc.; *bottom left* Copyright 1999 by Kirby, Smith, Wilkins, www.roadsideamerica.com.

CHAPTER 20 **425** *top* © Kaluzny/Thatcher/Tony Stone Images; *bottom* Illustration by Arthur Kotarba © 1998 McDougal Littell Inc.

CHAPTER 21 **433** *top* Chuck Burton/AP/Wide World Photos; *bottom left* "Test Your Backpack" © 1997 by Consumers Union of U.S., Inc. Yonkers, NY 10703-1057, a nonprofit organization. Reprinted with permission from the September/October 1997 issue of *Zillions, Consumer Reports* for kids, for educational purposes only.

CHAPTER 22 **443** *left* © John Lamb/Tony Stone Images; *right* © Peter Cade/Tony Stone Images; *bottom* Reprinted by the permission of the American Cancer Society, Inc.; *bottom left* San Francisco Golden Gate Bridge © Bruce Hands/Tony Stone Images

CHAPTER 23 **451** *top* Reprinted with permission from *Parade,* copyright © 1999. Photograph by Eric O'Connell. Article written by Bernard Gavzer; *bottom left* © Don Spiro/Tony Stone Images

CHAPTER 25 **469** © Copyright 1999 PhotoDisc, Inc.

CHAPTER 26 **480–481** © Copyright 1999 PhotoDisc, Inc.; **482** Corbis/Roger Ressmeyer; **483** *foreground,* **484** © Copyright 1999 PhotoDisc, Inc.; **488** The 1999 Grolier Multimedia Encyclopedia (R) Copyright © 1998 by Grolier Interactive Inc. All rights reserved; *bottom right* © Corbis-Bettmann; *bottom left* Copyright © Archive Photos/American Stock; 491 © 1999 King Features Syndicate, Inc. World rights reserved. Reprinted with special permission of King Features Syndicate.

CHAPTER 27 **498** © Copyright 1999 PhotoDisc, Inc.; **499** *La Chambre d'Ecoute* (1958), Rene Magritte, © 2001 C. Herscovici, Brussels/Artists Rights Society (ARS), New York/Christie's Images Ltd, 1999; **501** © Martin Harvey/The Wildlife Collection; **508** Copyright 1998, *Los Angeles Times.* Reprinted by permission; **512** Starfoto/Mauritius/H. Armstrong Robberts; **513** © Copyright 1999 PhotoDisc, Inc.

CHAPTER 28 **516** *background* © Copyright 1999 PhotoDisc, Inc.; *foreground* © Stockbyte; **517** © Carlos Humberto T.D.C./Contact Press Images/PNI; **519** *left* © Scott Robinson/Tony Stone Images; *right* © Bruce Ayres/Tony Stone Images; **521** © Copyright 1999 PhotoDisc, Inc.; **525** *top* © Copyright 1999 PhotoDisc, Inc.; *bottom* © 1997 Charles Gupton/The Stock Market; **530** © Robert E. Daemmrich/Tony Stone Images

CHAPTER 29 **534** Corbis/Morton Beebe, S.F.; **535** © Arthur Grace/Stock, Boston/PNI; **541** © Dennis Brack/Black Star/PNI; **542** *left, right* © Michael Newman/PhotoEdit/PNI; **543** © Chris Speedie/Tony Stone Images; **544** © 1998 Time Inc. Reprinted by permission. Color photo of John Glenn © Shelly Katz/Gamma Liaison. Black & white photo of John Glenn AP/Wide World Photos; **546** *top* © Copyright 1999 PhotoDisc, Inc.; *top inset* NBC News Archives; *bottom* Copyright © 1995 by The New York Times. Reprinted by permission; **547** © 1999 Cable News Network. All rights reserved. Used by permission of CNN; **549** © 1999 Michael Maslin from cartoonbank.com. All rights reserved.

CHAPTER 30 **550** © Copyright 1999 PhotoDisc, Inc.; **551** © A. Ramey/PhotoEdit; **553** J. R. Eyerman/*Life* Magazine © Time Inc.; **554** *background* Photo by Sharon Hoogstraten; **555** © David Young Wolff/PhotoEdit; **561** *inset* © Copyright 1999 PhotoDisc, Inc.; **562** *top* © David Young Wolff/PhotoEdit.

CHAPTER 31 **564, 565** © Copyright 1999 PhotoDisc, Inc.; **566** *FoxTrot* © 1992 Bill Amend. Reprinted with permission of Universal Press Syndicate. All rights reserved; **572** © Copyright 1999 PhotoDisc, Inc.; **579** © Tribune Media Services, Inc. All rights reserved. Reprinted with permission.

CHAPTER 32 **580** © Copyright 1999 PhotoDisc, Inc.; **581** © Juan Silva/The Image Bank/PNI; **584** © Phototake/PNI; **592** © Owen Franken/Stock, Boston/PNI; **597** *Peanuts* reprinted by permission of United Feature Syndicate, Inc.

McDougal Littell Inc. has made every effort to locate the copyright holders of all copyrighted material in this book and to make full acknowledgment for its use.